CIM
TUTORIAL TEXT

**Professional
Postgraduate
Diploma**

Case study
Strategic Marketing in Practice and Analysis and Decision

by Juanita Cockton
and Angela Hatton

In this September 2004 Tutorial Text

This text contains:
- Revision and self-testing material
- A teaching case covering a variety of skills
- Interactive action programmes to build skills
- Analysis of cases representing recent exams and a variety of industry contexts

**BPP Professional Education
September 2004**

First edition 1999
Sixth edition September 2004

ISBN 0 7517 1617 0 (Previous edition 0 7517 1255 8)

British Library Cataloguing-in-Publication Data
A catalogue record for this book
is available from the British Library

Published by

BPP Professional Education
Aldine House, Aldine Place
London W12 8AW

www.bpp.com

Printed in Great Britain by W M Print
45-47 Frederick Street
Walsall, West Midlands
WS2 9NE

All our rights reserved. No part of this publication may be reproduced, stored in a retrieval system or transmitted, in any form or by any means, electronic, mechanical, photocopying, recording or otherwise, without the prior written permission of BPP Professional Education.

We are grateful to the Chartered Institute of Marketing for permission to reproduce in this text the syllabus, tutor's guidance notes, past cases, examination questions and extracts from the examiner's reports.

We are grateful to Dr Ashok Ranchhold, the examiner, for his contribution to this tutorial text.

©
BPP Professional Education
2004

		Page
Preface		(v)
How to use this tutorial text		(vi)
Syllabus overview (old syllabus)		(vii)
Syllabus overview (new syllabus)		(viii)
Senior Examiner's view of the paper		(x)

Part A: Introducing Case Study

1	Why a Case Study?	3
2	The tools and planning skills needed: a healthcheck	14

Part B: The sample case: Biocatalysts

3	The process case: the 10 steps	59
4	Step 1: Overview of Biocatalysts	109
5	Step 2: The interview - Internal analysis	125
6	Step 3: External analysis	149
7	Step 4: Prioritisation and critical success factors	167
8	Step 5: Establishing strategic direction. Corporate/business decisions	174
9	Step 6: Marketing management and business implications	193
10	Step 7: Marketing strategy and marketing mix plans	205
11	Step 8: Contemporary issues and management plans	233
12	Step 9: Control	239
13	Step 10: Managing your materials and preparing for the exam	250
14	Biocatalysts Ltd: The examination	258

Part C: Practice cases

Reiss

15	Tackling a practice case: Reiss	279
16	Reiss Analysis: Steps 2 – 4	345
17	Reiss: Decision making Steps 5 –10	381
18	The Reiss exam	399

Centrica

19	A final practice case: Centrica	413

Part D: Exam notes

20	Exam preparation	517

Order form

Review form & Free prize draw

Introduction

Preface

The exam

The Postgraduate Diploma awarded by the Chartered Institute of Marketing is a management qualification which puts a major emphasis on the practical understanding of marketing activities. At the same time, the Institute's examinations recognise that the marketing professional works in a fast changing organisational, economic and social environment. *Strategic Marketing Management: Analysis and Decision* is one of the two compulsory CIM Diploma papers. It is compulsory as the marketing professional is expected to be a **manager**. Knowledge and skills in analysis and decision, together with an appreciation of the role of marketing in the corporate structure, are essential ingredients of managerial competence in this field.

This BPP Tutorial Text (September 2004 edition)

A transition text

2004/5 is a year of transition between the old Diploma in Marketing and the new Professional Postgraduate Diploma in Marketing.

For this paper the changes are more cosmetic than substantial in terms of case study process or the rationale and intent of the subject. Therefore the teaching cases and examples provided are equally relevant whichever programme you are enrolled on. Differences relate to the actual exam 'rules' and materials which can be taken to the exam or appended to your script.

Step 1   Ensure you know which exam is relevant to you.

Postgraduate Diploma in Marketing	Professional Postgraduate Diploma in Marketing
Analysis and Decision ■ The case is issued four weeks in advance. ■ A totally open book exam – so you may take in notes and materials for use in the exam *but* you cannot add anything to your script. Everything submitted must be written into your exam booklet.	**Strategic Marketing in Practice** ■ Case is issued four weeks in advance. ■ More of a closed book exam. You may take the case study annotated into the exam room and six pages of A4 analysis which can be added to your script.

You will see the main aims are very similar between the two papers.

The secret of exam success is effective study material which is focused and relevant to the exam *you* will be sitting. This is the philosophy underpinning this *Tutorial Text*, which has been especially written for candidates sitting this case study examination. It is divided into five parts.

This *Tutorial Text* starts in Part A with a description of the case study and a health-check to cover your knowledge of planning and control. We apply a detailed 10 step process to a 'teaching case', *Biocatalysts*, selected as it is good example of the processes you have to go through. We cover Enzymes UK, and then Reiss and Centrica, as a service sector company.

Help us to help you

Your feedback will help us improve this *Tutorial Text*, so please complete and return the Review Form at the end of this *Tutorial Text*; you will be entered automatically in a free prize draw.

A final word

This *Tutorial Text* offers a professional solution to your needs in preparing for this challenging exam.

BPP Professional Education
September 2004

> Other elements in the BPP study package for CIM exams are listed on the Order Form at the back of this *Tutorial Text*.
>
> For information about all the products and services offered by the BPP Holdings plc group, visit our website. The address is: *www.bpp.com*

How to use this tutorial text

1 What is the CIM case study?

There is no formal syllabus for the CIM's case study examination. Instead the examination is based on a case study normally comprising 40 to 70 pages of narrative, charts and tables and issued to examinees by post about **four weeks in advance of the examination**. The issue of the case study some four weeks in advance allows time for considerable analysis and discussion.

The case study is a **practical** test of the candidates' knowledge of marketing (gained in Certificate and Diploma, or equivalent, studies) and their ability to apply it. Normally candidates will also have some practical experience in marketing to bring to bear. At the same time, some **background knowledge** is necessary. Those who are coming to the case study 'cold' will find the theoretical revision a useful complement to their practical experience. This is provided in Part A of this *Tutorial Text*.

Whilst case study methods vary according to the institution and lecturer concerned, a particular model embodying a comprehensive approach is detailed in this *Tutorial Text*.

2 Discussing the case study

Students are strongly advised to conduct in-depth discussion with colleagues on the case study analysis and its issues. This is often accomplished at colleges by the forming of **syndicate groups** of four to six people and the holding of frequent **plenary sessions** where all candidates gather together. In this way, a syndicate member not only hears the view of his or her syndicate, but also those of other syndicates. In this way a much more balanced, integrated and secure approach can be developed. Of course, whilst classroom discussion may be the best for obtaining this sort of feedback, you may benefit from using the Internet if you cannot attend class. How about conducting a discussion with another person using instant messenger?

Having said this, **candidates should not copy out group answers** word for word: these will be failed. Candidates must offer their own **individual** work on the day of the examination.

3 Practice

In Part B, we explore a practice case, *Biocatalysts*, for teaching purposes. We do another run through with *Reiss* (December 2003) and, for a service sector perspective, *Centrica* (June 2004).

One of the key success factors in case study examination (apart from being thoroughly prepared) is to be well organised in the exam room itself, freeing the mind to think more calmly and clearly about the exam questions.

A note on pronouns

On occasions in this *Tutorial Text*, 'he' is used for 'he or she', 'him' for 'him or her' and so forth. Whilst we try to avoid this practice, it is sometimes necessary for reasons of style. No prejudice or stereotyping according to sex is intended or assumed.

Syllabus overview (old syllabus)

Analysis & Decision (old Diploma)

This Analysis and Decision paper tests a potential candidate's ability to demonstrate knowledge from different areas of marketing in order to develop appropriate strategies plans and innovative solutions for organisations. As each case is different, candidates should possess the capability to draw upon some of the key topic areas from across the CIM syllabus that will need to be refreshed in order to tackle case studies effectively especially at diploma level.

Strategic thinking ability, coherence of argument, absorption of detail and clear justification of any solutions offered will be measured outcomes of the effective understanding of the case studies.

Aims and objectives

Objectives of the Analysis and Decision module are outlined below and students will be expected:

- To utilise the practical and marketing skills which are pre-requisites for analysis of the case and engage students in justifying their strategic recommendations.
- To analyse the case within given constraints and understand possible barriers to implementation.
- To apply the marketing processes within a wide variety of market sectors.
- To develop the ability to cross reference knowledge from other Diploma subjects.
- To develop creative and innovative applications of knowledge of strategic marketing.
- To be able to apply relevant marketing planning models and display critical analytical and decision-making skills within the Case Study examination.
- To comprehend and resolve a wide variety of marketing problems and provide realistic and innovative solutions.

Learning outcomes

Students will be able to:

- Demonstrate an in-depth understanding of the strategic marketing planning process and to develop a creative and innovative strategic marketing plan.
- Critically evaluate case studies using a wide variety of marketing techniques, concepts and models and an understanding of contemporary marketing issues.
- Understand and apply competitive positioning strategies within a given case study.
- Critically evaluate various options available within given constraints and justify any decisions taken.
- Demonstrate the ability to analyse numerical data and management information and utilise it to make decisions about key underlying issues within the Case Study.
- Synthesise various strands of knowledge from the different Diploma subjects effectively in the context of the Case Study examination.
- Apply both practical and academic marketing knowledge within a given Case Study.
- Comprehend and resolve a wide variety of marketing problems.
- Develop appropriate control aspects and contingency plans.

Syllabus overview (new syllabus)

Strategic Marketing in Practice (new Professional Postgraduate Diploma)

Aims and objectives

Marketing has to be firmly rooted in both theory and practice. Practice informs theory and vice versa. Strategic Marketing in Practice is designed to allow participants to put strategic marketing into practice. As the final subject in this qualification, it not only builds on the knowledge and skills developed in all the preceding modules, but also looks for an overall competence in marketing that encompasses all the various subject areas covered in the lower qualification levels. As marketing is constantly evolving, continuously informed by both academic and business research, one of the aims of this module is to explore the latest trends and innovations relevant to marketers who are operating at a strategic level within organisations. One of the other aims is to understand marketing as an activity, which is important in all contexts (profit, not-for-profit, societal, global). It is expected that participants will be able to add value to both their marketing experience and marketing knowledge. Therefore there is no specific syllabus for this subject.

Learning outcomes

Participants will be able to:

- Identify and critically evaluate marketing issues within various environments, utilising a wide range of marketing techniques, concepts and models.

- Assess the relevance of, and opportunities presented by, contemporary marketing issues within any given scenario including innovations in marketing.

- Identify and critically evaluate various options available within given constraints and apply competitive positioning strategies, justifying any decisions taken.

- Formulate and present a creative, customer-focused and innovative competitive strategy for any given context, incorporate relevant investment decisions, appropriate control aspects and contingency plans.

- Demonstrate an understanding of the direction and management of marketing activities as part of the implementation of strategic direction, taking into account business intelligence requirements, marketing processes, resources, markets and the company vision.

- Promote and facilitate the adoption and maintenance of a strong market and customer orientation with measurable marketing metrics.

- Synthesise various strands of knowledge and skills from the different syllabus modules effectively in developing an effective solution for any given context.

Knowledge and skill requirements

The essential skills assessed as part of this subject are:

- Analysis, interpretation, evaluation and synthesis of information, including the ability to draw conclusions.
- Identification, exploration and evaluation of strategic options.
- Selection and justification of an appropriate option using decision criteria.
- Establishing the activities, resources and schedule needed to implement the chosen strategy.
- Working with others to implement and control the strategy.

Participants will be expected to demonstrate their awareness of current issues and an ability to make recommendations for a given context. From time to time CIM will publish a list of trends and innovations to guide tutors and participants in their preparation for assessment. Participants will be expected to read widely in the area of strategic marketing as part of their studies at this level.

Introduction

Senior Examiner's view of the paper

1 Overview of the area

The case paper is the culmination of all the marketing subjects covered at all levels, but especially the Diploma and the Advanced Diploma. For this reason, there is no specific syllabus for this paper. The new syllabuses now give a clear strategic focus. This type of expertise will be needed to tackle the Case Study paper. It is also clear that it will not be possible to tackle the Case Study without a clear grasp of the fundamentals of marketing communications and international marketing. In this sense, for all students, the Case Study is a culmination of the application of all the marketing knowledge they have gained over several years.

The title of the paper 'Analysis and Decision' implies that the candidates are competent enough to analyse problems within a marketing context and subsequently take appropriate decisions to implement marketing strategies for an organisation. In order to achieve competence in this area, prospective candidates will need to be conversant with all aspects of marketing, as strategic marketing problems do not come in neat packages. A comprehensive grasp of the basic subjects at the lower levels together with the key subjects of the Diploma is needed.

2 The changing focus of the paper

- Marketing as a subject area is undergoing major changes. These changes are taking place as a result of dramatic shifts in technology, demographics, globalisation, systems of production, logistics and ecological issues. In future, therefore, the paper will be designed to reflect more of these contemporary issues in addition to the knowledge base mentioned above.

- The case studies will also be designed to develop strategic marketing issues which can be operationalised and implemented within realistic constraints. It is often forgotten that marketing is not just about positioning and growth, but also about **effectiveness** within **given constraints** within most organisations. These constraints mean that strategies have to be sensibly evaluated and chosen, with hard decisions being made. When particular strategies are chosen, it is clear that the constraints could be many and varied. Constraints, for instance could be financial, organisational (both employee and culture related), marketing (image, size of markets, branding, distribution systems, networks) and, if the organisation is a division of a large entity, headquarter-imposed constraints.

Globalisation

- The rapid changes in technology are far reaching as they are changing the normal paradigms of marketing. The four P's cannot be discussed with certainty. The nature and direction of marketing strategies, necessarily have to take into account the massive computing power available and the advent of business on the Internet. Many multi-nationals have operated globally for decades, but technology is changing the patterns of production and consumption.

- For instance, global brands are available anywhere and production facilities may be located in a myriad of different countries. For smaller companies, the Internet holds the promises and pitfalls of operating in a global arena.

- The introduction of the Euro means that Pan-European marketing strategies have to be thought through in a different manner. The changing nature and the growth of south Asian markets has an enormous impact on the marketing strategies of organisations. The nature and strength of the American market is often forgotten in many marketing cases. The case studies will reflect these changes and will embrace many different sectors of industry.

Organisational issues

- When developing marketing strategies it is important that the culture and nature of the organisation is taken into account. Marketing strategies often succeed and fail as a result of inappropriate personnel, inappropriate structures or climates within organisations. Organisations are therefore always striving to create the appropriate structures and develop appropriate cultures to meet the demands of the market place.
- The customer is king and marketing strategists have to place the level of market orientation at the centre of their thinking.

Sustainability

- Marketing literature has for long been concerned with growth and market share. It is important that issues surrounding the constraints imposed by the environment are taken into account. The world is facing an enormous challenge in terms of the availability of resources and the needs of the population. In some respects a challenge posed to marketing strategists is the need to consider constraints and responsibility.

Financial issues

- Financial issues will also play a key role in developing strategies.
- A good knowledge of basic financial statements such as profit and loss accounts, balance sheets and cashflow statements is required.

Knowledge of contemporary marketing issues

- Each case is different and will therefore test some knowledge of contemporary issues. Students need to be encouraged to read journal articles pertaining to the case study.

Application of previous knowledge

- The need to apply models for analysis will continue. However, a more critical approach in applying these techniques will be needed. The paper will reflect the need for both academic and practical knowledge as a true marketer needs to have experience of both areas for developing sensible strategies.

Issues of implementation and control

- An awareness of the clear decision-making and implementation strategies will be tested. As will be strategic positioning, innovation and branding in the context of implementation and control

Introduction

3 Links with other papers

The paper is the culmination of all the knowledge gained at all CIM levels. The foundations laid by the marketing syllabuses underpin this paper. The fundamental underpinning knowledge needed is the ability to undertake strategic analysis. In tutoring and preparing students for this paper, tutors need to be aware of the linkages with other areas and they need to be able to draw from a variety of literature sources in order to enhance and improve their analytic and decision-making skills. In each case there is an emphasis on understanding international issues as well as communications issues.

The examiners are looking for candidates to demonstrate analytical ability, interpretive skills, insight, innovation and creativity in answering questions. They are also looking for candidates to take clear and sensible decisions within the context of the case study. A critical awareness of the specific issues involved, relevant theoretical underpinning, attention to detail, coherence and justification of strategies adopted will also be assessed.

To perform well on the paper, candidates will have to exhibit the following.

- A need to concentrate on the strategic aspects of marketing underpinned by the necessary detail
- The ability to identify 'gaps' in the case study and to outline the assumptions made
- The ability to critically apply relevant models for case analysis
- The ability to draw and synthesise from any of the diploma subject areas as relevant
- Concentration on the question set rather than the pre-prepared answer
- The ability to answer in the report format with comprehensive sentences rather than providing simplistic lists
- The judicious use of diagrams for illustrative purposes
- The ability to draw disparate links together and give coherent answers
- The use of interesting an useful articles from journals in their answers
- Innovation and creativity in answering the questions
- Demonstration of practical applications of marketing knowledge
- Sensible use of time and an ability to plan the answer within the set time
- A good understanding of the cases study set
- The ability to draw up a comprehensive and convincing marketing plan with accompany costs and schedules
- The ability to suggest appropriate control mechanisms and contingency plans

Part A

Introducing Case Study

Why a Case Study? 1

Chapter Topic List	
1	What the Case Study is and how it differs from other CIM papers
2	The value of Case Study in the work place
3	The challenges of a Case Study approach, the problems people face and how to overcome them
4	How to get the most from this Tutorial Text
5	CIM's expectations
6	The characteristics of an excellent case candidate and the secret of winning examiner support

1 What the Case Study is and how it differs from other CIM papers

1.1 The final paper for the CIM qualification is the case study. No-one is exempt and both syllabuses are without doubt very demanding examinations. The Case Study paper requires that you **integrate** all your previous studies and it provides a realistic assessment of whether you have acquired the knowledge and skills to tackle a practical marketing challenge in a commercially credible way.

1.2 The case study is distinctly different from other CIM exams, both in terms of its assessment and its syllabus.

1.3 The Examiner can call upon any aspect of the eleven CIM subjects. CIM expects you to be conversant with the breadth and depth of these other papers either through previous studies or on the basis of the exemptions you have been awarded.

Part A: Introducing case study

Valuable information

1.4 You should **not** attempt to tackle this case study paper until you have studied the other three Diploma papers.

1.5 Case studies represent **real organisations** and describe the marketing challenges they face. Often, cases are also set in real time and so you may well be faced with a very topical issue. In the sample case we are using in the first part of this manual, **Biocatalysts**, the issue was GM products and biotechnology. At the time of the case, GM crop trials were headline news. You will be given management and marketing data in the form of a narrative with various appendices. This may well include financial data.

1.6 You are sent a copy of the exam case study four weeks prior to the exam date. You then have time to complete your analysis of the case data and to think through your strategic recommendations.

1.7 In the exam room, you will be faced with specific questions and some additional data and, having taken account of this, you will be expected to present and justify your decisions.

1.8 You are able to take some pre-prepared work into the exam with you. There are **two approaches** to this, depending on the syllabus you are studying and arrangements at your college.

(a) Strategic Marketing in Practice students are allowed to take in a limited number of pre-prepared appendices which you can attach to your exam script and refer to in your answers. You can also annotate your copy of the case study.

(b) Those studying on the Old Diploma Analysis & Decision syllabus are allowed to take unlimited notes for reference into the exam room, but in this case all work submitted must be written up in the exam room.

We will say more about these options and how to prepare for them later in this manual, but the basic approach, case technique and requirements for exam success remain the same.

1.9 There are few short cuts when it comes to tackling a case study and it is a time-consuming exercise, but you will find the process extends your knowledge and improves skills which have immediate relevance to your work.

2 The value of Case Study in the work place

2.1 Case Study is a very **practical** examination. A knowledge of marketing theory on its own will not be sufficient to gain you an exam pass. You have to be able to apply that theory in the context of a real business issue and situation. This means that you must:

(a) Know the framework for developing both strategic marketing and operational marketing plans

(b) Be able to apply the various tools of analysis, recognising and acknowledging the limitations of these where appropriate

(c) Be able to make decisions, in a way which reflects customer needs and be able to justify those decisions

(d) Be able to explain broader implications to the business

(e) Have the skills to present your views and ideas in a convincing way

2.2 Even experienced marketers often pay little more than lip service to the marketing planning process. Faced with the pressure of an impending examination, many candidates are amazed at the depth and quality of strategic thinking possible, even with the limited information supplied in a case. This experience can be a useful **benchmark for marketing planning in your own business**.

2.3 Some students get concerned about not being expert in the sector of the featured case study. It can seem daunting if you have B2C experience and are suddenly faced with a B2B challenge, like Biocatalysts. This may seem unrealistic and less representative of life in the business world. However, in our experience as consultants, it is a very real reflection of the situations we face. Our expertise is marketing, and the disciplines and concepts of marketing travel well between sectors. If anything, **lack of detailed industry or product knowledge makes it easier to avoid the myopia so often characteristic of those who are product focused**.

2.4 Besides the chance to practise analysis and decision-making skills, the case study also provides the opportunity further to develop **team-work skills**. Unless you are studying independently, you will probably be tackling the case as part of a formal syndicate or study group. This is an excellent idea as it provides a time efficient way of tackling analysis as well as providing a forum for brainstorming and creative thinking. However, to make a syndicate work, you need to have and use team working skills and be disciplined in how you communicate with other members. Again, these are practical skills highly valued in the workplace.

3 The challenges of a Case Study approach, the problems people face and how to overcome them

3.1 Case study brings with it its own set of problems and challenges which you need to be aware of before beginning your studies.

3.2 In practice, relatively few candidates fail examinations because of lack of knowledge. **Much more common is a lack of exam technique**. This results in any one of a number of common problems including failing to **manage time** or answer the question set. Similarly, with the Case Study exam, it is often a failure of technique not knowledge which causes exam failure. Exam technique is rather different for a case exam, but none the less requires practice and the development of a wide range of skills already alluded to, from analysis to persuasive communication, skills which you would expect to find in a **competent, practising marketing manager**.

3.3 Exam technique for the case study starts when the exam case is **issued**. Finding enough time for preparation and using that time effectively is all part of case technique. The seeds of success or failure are sown during this important preparation time, so **preparation is key**.

Valuable information

3.4 The exams may seem like a long way off, but it is never too early to start planning for them. Check out the date of your Case Study exam. This will be on the first or second Friday of December or June, but the **exact date should be available on the CIM website**. Calculate back four weeks from this date. This is the latest date the case should be issued to you. By this date, you want to have broadly completed any work on other examination subjects, so

Part A: Introducing case study

you have the maximum time available for the case study. You will need to find about 40 hours preparation time during these weeks. Where will it come from?

- Avoid planning too many events for those pre-exam weekends
- Talk to your employer about taking some study leave
- Book holiday time for study if necessary

3.5 **Using your preparation time well** is the next case challenge. **Sharing the workload** by being part of a study group is to be advised whenever possible. There is no doubt that cracking a case study alone is hard and lonely work, but, whether working alone or as part of a group, you need a timetable and plan of action. In this Tutorial Text, we are going to work through a sample case in detail, showing you what must be done and providing you with a recommended framework, but you will need the self-discipline to apply that to the exam case.

3.6 Some candidates fail to meet the challenge of analysis. They do too little or too much. Both are recipes for failure. Watch out for indications of which trap you are most likely to fall into.

The Too Little Analysis Candidate	The Too Much Analysis Candidate

The Reader. Confuses reading the case with analysis of it. Does not see the importance of analysing appendices and cross referencing findings.	**The Analysis Addict**. Suffers from the complaint we know as **Analysis Paralysis**. The symptoms are fear of decision-making and finding comfort in the safe activity of analysis.
The Too Little Analysis Candidate	The Too Much Analysis Candidate

The Juggler. Typically puts off tackling the analysis till the week before the exam. With so many other things to do, it is easy to not take this paper seriously. Sadly what might seem straightforward and obvious at the first read often proves much more complex after detailed analysis.	**The Detail Fanatic**. It is easy to get hung upon calculations to the third decimal place, or be brought to a halt by inconsistencies in a case. There will be inconsistencies and discrepancies but successful candidates do not let this distract them. They keep focused on the bigger picture, and where necessary, they make assumptions and move on.

1 ♦ Why a Case Study?

3.7 Adequate analysis will ensure you have a sound grasp of the case issues and have the facts and figures needed to support your recommendations and convince the examiner of their commercial credibility.

3.8 Moving on from analysis to decision-making is another exam challenge for case students. Analysis **can be comforting**; you are busy doing something and there is almost always something else that could be done. Case tutors tend to despair when, despite all our warnings, a student phones the week of the exam and says 'you know the figures in table 3...'. This candidate has been paralysed by analysis and is unlikely to do very well in the exam. They have failed to move on. **Decisions and recommendations need to be made**.

(a) The examiner does **not** want to be told to 'choose a profitable segment.' What he/she does want is to be told how to go about choosing a profitable segment, specific advice on the criteria to be applied and the decision framework to be used. If **enough data exists, the examiner wants you to apply the criteria and come up with the recommendation of which segment to target**.

(b) Advice which is a generality will not gain marks. 'Set a quantified objective' will not do. You need to set detailed objectives which are underpinned by quantitative measures.

> 'I recommend that an ambitious growth objective is set, with profit reaching £10 million by 2006 (a £4 million increase). I believe this is achievable because:
>
> (i) The key competitor is tied up in merger talks.
> (ii) The overall market is forecast to grow by 20% pa.
> (iii) Our new service level package will provide us a strong competitive advantage'

It is this clarity of advice and strong justification which the examiner will be looking for. You can see how a grasp of the facts and figures can help you.

3.9 Before the examination day, you will need to have a broad picture of the strategic options open to the business and which options you would support in what circumstances. **At this stage you must not over prepare**. This is the final pre-exam trap. The candidate who wants to pre-write a strategic marketing plan with the i's dotted and the t's crossed, feels perfectly prepared, but in fact has committed a cardinal marketing and exam sin – the product oriented answer.

> Essentially he/she is saying to the examiner 'here is the answer I want to give you, irrespective of your needs and:
>
> (a) The extra information you have given me
> (b) The detail of the question you have set
> (c) The importance you want me to attach to this part of the exam as indicated by the marks you have allocated for this question

Irrespective of all these clues which allow well prepared candidates to 'customise' their answers, our over prepared student has a **'one size answer'** which has to fit all questions – another recipe for failure.

3.10 The focus and level for this paper can also cause problems. It is a **strategic** level focus, where the emphasis is on helping the organisation to determine:

(a) Which products and markets to serve
(b) The competitive strategy likely to be most effective in winning business from these markets

Part A: Introducing case study

(c) Which segments of the selected markets to target
(d) How best to deploy the marketing mix to gain a competitive advantage within these segments
(e) The implications for the organisation and management
(f) Contemporary issues

It is easy to end up working with the detail and not the big picture. The colour for staff uniforms or the design for the new logo are only important when the strategy has been agreed and your job in the case is to convince the examiner about the **strategic level. This will not be achieved with ad hoc tactical ideas, no matter how creative they are.**

3.11 The Case Study exam is **not** simply an exercise in writing out pre-prepared work. It is a tough, thinking paper, where you will need to have your wits about you to adapt and rethink in line with the specifics of the exam paper. The secret of success lies in a well managed decision file or clearly thought through prepared appendices.

3.12 **Questions for this paper must be answered in the order set**. Consider mark allocation to ensure you manage your time effectively. Remember that **how** you communicate our answer is critical and that there are two aspects to this.

(a) **Presentation**, report formats and clear lay out play a key role and make an important first impression.

(b) The **style and tone** of your work needs to be appropriate to the case role you have been allocated and your arguments need to be persuasive.

3.13 As you work through this *Tutorial Text*, we will help you improve your exam technique and case skills, but it is helpful if you have an honest evaluation of your likely strengths and weaknesses in terms of case exam skills and techniques. Once you have identified your weaknesses, you will be able to take positive steps to tackle them.

3.14 Take time now to identify your strengths and weaknesses against the following.

	Strengths	Weaknesses
Prioritising case and managing the four weeks prior to the exam		
Handling the analysis: ■ Quantifying data ■ Qualitative data		
Focusing at strategic not tactical level		
Moving on to decision-making		
Making clear decisions		
Organising your case or materials		
Presentation and communication		
Managing time in the exam		
Being flexible in the light of additional information		
Using data to justify decisions		

4 How to get the most from this Tutorial text

4.1 Objectives of this Tutorial Text

(a) Provide you with a simple to follow case process

(b) Ensure you are familiar with the examiner's expectations in terms of level, tone and focus

(c) Demonstrate a sample case analysed in a step by step process

(d) Give you the opportunity to practise case technique in the context of past cases prior to the exam to help you build skills and confidence

(e) Alert you to the most common mistakes made by unsuccessful case students

(f) Help you review your knowledge and develop the skills needed to apply these tools and frameworks to deliver a coherent and integrated set of plans from the strategic to the operational

(g) Encourage you to review your presentation and communication skills so that your work has maximum impact

4.2 What this *Tutorial Text* will not do is teach you the tools and frameworks of the other CIM subjects – we assume you have studied these, but in the next chapter we will help you audit that knowledge and identify any gaps.

4.3 This Tutorial Text has been developed in three sections,

(a) Introducing Case Study
(b) A sample case
(c) Two further practice cases

4.4 It is tempting to try and speed up the process by missing out sections, in particular the practice cases in section C. We strongly advise you **not** to do this. You cannot pass a case exam simply by reading about the process; you **must** give yourself some hands on practice.

4.5 To get the most out of this Tutorial Text, you should use it as a guide through your preparation. We will provide you with signposts to help you assess your progress and will identify places where you might do additional work and practice. It is, however, important to recognise you are learning about the case process. Every case study is different and, like you, we will not know about the sector or industry of the case until the exam month.

4.6 In Section A, we will show you a generic process for tackling a case study. In Section B, we will apply that process to a past CIM Case. In section C, you will have two more recent CIM exams on which to build your own skills in applying the process.

Part A: Introducing case study

Time

4.7 Remember when planning your case study preparation that the exam case will be issued four weeks in advance, so you need to have completed your work through this study manual by then. We recommend you allow:

	Minimum	Maximum	
Part A of this Tutorial Text	2 hours	4 hours	Introduction to the subject
Part B	20 hours	40 hours	Guided tour of the case process
Part C	40 per case	60 per case	Individual practice cases: time varies according to the depth you work these
Exam Case preparation	40 hours	60 hours	

5 CIM's expectations

5.1 You will perhaps have already gathered that the case study is treated as something of a jewel in the crown. This final paper is the **last hurdle** to your official recognition as a professionally qualified marketer and it is seen as being the acid test of your commercial credibility.

5.2 In fact **commercial credibility** has, for a number of years, been one of the **key measures the examiners have used in assessing case candidates.**

(a) Does the proposed strategy make sense – can it be substantiated from the analysis?
(b) Is the proposal convincing?

5.3 Remember that, for the CIM examiner, the case study is simply a vehicle for assessing your commercial competence. Every six months the scenario changes but the **characteristics CIM are looking for in a successful candidate remain the same.**

(a) Does the candidate **appreciate the context** of the case scenario? Is the strategy realistic in terms of the available resources and are constraints such as time frames recognised?

(b) Is there evidence of an appreciation of the **broader business implications** of proposals in terms of the impact on profitability, the resources and budgets needed for implementation and the effect of any proposed changes on people within the organisation?

(c) Are **plans supported by specific strategies** to ensure implementation and do they incorporate proposals for **measuring performance** and progress.

Action Programme 1

If you have the opportunity, take time to review a marketing plan you have worked on or which has been developed within your organisation. How would you implement it based on the comments above?

1 ♦ Why a Case Study?

5.4 **CIM expect you to spend up to 60 hours preparing for a case examination.** You have plenty of time to present well-thought out and sensible arguments. If you worked for the company in question, would your script be taken seriously?

Action Programme 2

In the *Sunday Times Business News* there is usually a featured company – their situation described and a number of experts asked their views. This is essentially a case study in action. Make a point of looking at these and in particular assess the experts. Who impresses you and why? Which of them would you be prepared to pay as a consultant?

What advice could you give to the business?

5.5 It is easy to get so involved in the case scenario that you forget that the real challenge is to **pass the exam**. You must make certain that you make the right impression. Irrespective of the quality of your strategy your paper tells the examiner a lot about you.

What it says about you	Symptom
Failure to finish the questions	A poor resource manager the exam task was clear and the resource available predicted
Poor presentation	A careless, unprofessional approach
Lack of quantification in the form of objectives, budgets etc	A fear of financial aspects
Unconvincing arguments	A poor communicator
Too much attention to the detail	A lack of strategic overview

5.6 The examiners are looking only for evidence of the characteristics you would expect in a competent marketing professional. We will be considering these required skills in detail in Chapter 2. Before you move on you might like to spend five minutes thinking through what you would expect these to be.

6 The characteristics of an excellent case candidate and the secret of winning examiner support

6.1 The excellent candidate is well prepared. Case study is a long process and careful preparation helps ensure precious study time is used both efficiently and effectively.

6.2 The best candidates are well organised. They have an action plan which they keep to and where possible they involve other people in the process.

6.3 Their analysis is thorough and is used as a basis for strategy and decision-making, not as an end in its own right.

6.4 The successful candidate presents a script that wins examiner support.

Part A: Introducing case study

Presentation

Well written in report format with clear structure. Lots of white space, diagrams and use of colour help to present information quickly and effectively.

✗   ✓

The Wall of Words	Successful scripts
Examiners do not want to be confronted by whole pages of written narrative, unbroken and unstructured – the horror of a wall of words	**Structure** Clear headings and sub headings make structure clear **White space & colour**

Perspective is incorporated to ensure the audience is convinced you have thought about the commercial realities

A major above the line communication strategy for a small regional player	✗
Acknowledgement of the profit pressure and likely demands of the shareholders	✓
Product development suggested for the firm with limited time or money	✗
Product development for the cash-rich player with a dated portfolio	✓

Persuasion is incorporated to ensure the audience is convinced.

✗   ✓

I recommend we adopt a differentiated strategy and target European customers first.	In this highly competitive sector a differentiated strategy rolled out across Europe would give us the opportunity to: ■ Win a premium price ■ Reflect the very real buyer behaviour – differences evidenced by our research ■ Learn from each successive launch

6.5 The best candidates know the case well enough to be able to respond flexibly in the exam room changing emphasis, and even strategy, in light of the questions and extra information.

1 ♦ Why a Case Study?

Chapter Roundup

- This chapter has tried to provide the context for your case study preparations.

    You should now be aware of the characteristics of a good candidate and understand how CIM has positioned the case study examination.

- You should be able to explain to others the value of the case process and identify a list of skills which both the successful case candidate and the experienced marketing practitioner need to demonstrate.

Quick Quiz

1. Case study differs from other CIM exams in two significant ways. What are they? (see paras 1.3 and 1.6)
2. How long before the exam day can you expect to receive your case study? (1.6)
3. Case study is a very practical examination. Identify how the examiners might test whether you have the ability to apply the theory in the context of a case study. (2.1)
4. What do we mean if we described a case candidate as suffering from Analysis paralysis? (3.6)
5. Why do students sometimes find it difficult to move on from analysis to decisions? (3.8)
6. How would you describe to someone the focus and level which characterise how CIM has positioned this paper? (3.10)
7. What are the two levels of communication which are critical to the successful case candidate? (3.12)
8. Where will you get a knowledge of the planning tools essential for this paper? (4.2)
9. Identify four ways in which an examiner might assess the commercial credibility of a case candidate. (5.3)
10. How much should you be prepared to invoice the case client for at the end of the examination? (5.4)
11. Identify four ways in which your approach to the exam paper gives the examiner an insight into your performance as a manager. (5.5)
12. What characteristics would you look for in a successful marketer? (5.6)
13. Three P's are important in a successful script. What are they? (6.4)
14. Why is flexibility an important characteristic for the case student and the practising manager? (6.5)

The Tools and Planning Skills Needed: a Healthcheck

Chapter Topic List	
1	Key skills
2	Knowledge check
3	Contemporary issues
4	Brand strategy and management
5	E-commerce and Internet strategies
6	Collaborative partnerships
7	Customer relationship management
8	Supply chain management
9	Ethical, social and environmental responsibilities
10	Integrating the Diploma subjects
11	Case study: technique and pitfalls
12	Exam technique

Introduction

- ☑ A thorough knowledge of the planning and control, communications and international diploma subjects is essential for Analysis and Decision. Analysis and Decision provides you with the opportunity to demonstrate your ability to apply this knowledge by using your marketing management skills to solve the problems of a real case.

- ☑ If you take the opportunity to do at least one practice case study, as well as preparing you for the examination, it has the added benefit of allowing you to improve existing marketing management skills and develop new skills that should help you improve your performance at work (or for a new job).

1 Key skills

1.1 You have already considered the key skills a marketing manager should have. Our list includes:

Characteristics	Evidence
1 Structured	Uses P&C frameworks and presents in clear report format
2 Knowledgeable	Working command of the marketer's tools, the confidence to adapt them and an appreciation of their limitations
3 Financially aware	Confident to use and include numbers, and a clear appreciation that marketing decisions will impact on profitability
4 Analytical	Decisions made on the basis of analysis not hunch
5 Creative	Able to look at problems in a different way, innovative ideas and approaches encouraged
6 Decisive	Criteria for decisions laid out but clear decisions then made – no procrastination: in today's fast moving markets, speed is often of the essence
7 An Implementer	Anyone can write plans, but it takes real skill to implement them from internal marketing plans to contingency plans and timetables. The examiners will be looking for evidence that you can go from paper to action
8 A Resource Manager	Budgets and appreciation of costs is key here. Control measures demonstrate your understanding of the value of resources… and remember the evidence of time management

2 Knowledge check

Check your knowledge and assess your knowledge gaps

2.1 Now is a good time to remind yourself of the other diploma subjects and establish your strengths and weaknesses in each of these subjects in preparation for the case study. Amongst other skills, the case study will provide you with the opportunity to develop your analytical and decision-making skills. It is not the intention to check comprehensively your knowledge of the diploma subjects in this chapter, but rather to prompt and remind you of some of the theory. Remember, the practice case studies are a test of your knowledge as well as your skills.

2.2 Check the subject syllabus for more detail if you are not familiar with the current CIM syllabuses.

2.3 The key aims and objectives of each of these subjects will be covered briefly as a reminder of what the subject involved, followed by knowledge checks. Answers to these knowledge checks can be found at the end of the chapter.

Part A: Introducing case study

Tutor Tip

Test yourself on the knowledge check questions, without referring to notes or books. If you have not studied the subjects for some time, it may be difficult at first.

As you work your way through this text, identify and address any knowledge gaps. Keep 'Notes to Self' as a way of ensuring that anything you are unfamiliar with, or need to revise, is dealt with. You do not want to be doing this with the exam case study.

Issues of planning and control

2.4 What you need to know

- The theoretical concepts, techniques and models that underpin the marketing planning process.
- Practical skills associated with the management of the planning process
- How to justify strategic decisions and recommendations
- Understand the barriers that exist to effective implementation of strategy
- How to tailor marketing plans and processes to allow for the specific sector and situational factors that apply to any given organisation
- The techniques that underpin innovation and creativity in organisations

Action Programme 1

Knowledge check of planning and control issues

1. What is the purpose of analysis, and what is the desired outcome?
2. What are the key components of an internal and external corporate or business audit?
3. Name four models the marketer can use during the analysis process. Briefly explain their purpose.
4. What is the role of the vision and mission statements? Distinguish between them.
5. What is planning gap analysis?
6. What are strategic options/business strategies and how might they be evaluated?
7. What competitive positions might a business adopt? What are their implications?
8. Note common methods of consumer and business to business segmentation.
9. What is the Decision Making Unit (DMU) and why is it important to marketers?
10. How can marketing research help in the analysis, planning and control processes?
11. What does the term 'Balanced Scorecard' mean?
12. What are the key components of a marketing information system (MkIS)?

Check your answers with ours at the end of the chapter.

Issues for integrated marketing communications

2.5 What you need to know

- Have a sound understanding of the formulation and implementation of integrated marketing communications plans and associated activities
- How to manage marketing communications within a variety of different contexts
- How to recognise, appreciate and contribute fully to the totality of an organisation's systems of communications with both internal and external audiences
- The processes, issues and vocabulary associated with integrated marketing communications in order that they can make an effective contribution to their working environment

Action Programme 2

Knowledge check of integrated marketing communications issues

1. What contexts affect marketing communications?
2. What factors affect customers' purchase decision making?
3. What is the decision making process (DMP)?
4. What types of perceived risk are involved in purchase decisions and how can marketers reduce perceived risk?
5. What internal factors affect communications with an organisation's external audiences?
6. What internal factors influence corporate image and reputation?
7. What models are there for establishing communication objectives?
8. A brand is made up of many parts, both tangible and intangible. What are the components of a brand?
9. How can a brand help to build loyalty?
10. Briefly define the meaning of push, pull and profile communication strategies.
11. How can marketers change attitudes?
12. What does 'share of voice' (SOV) mean?

Check your answers with ours at the end of the chapter.

Part A: Introducing case study

Issues for international marketing

2.6 What you need to know

- International marketing theory and key concepts
- Vocabulary associated with international/global marketing strategy in different types of economies, organisations and market situations
- The complexities of international and global marketing in a mix of economies
- Processes, context and influences associated with international and global marketing strategies in a range of economies
- The implications for implementation, monitoring and control of the international marketing planning process

Action Programme 3

Knowledge check of international marketing issues

1. Name three World Institutions that have helped to promote world trade.
2. What are market agreements and what types of agreements are there?
3. What is an economic trading bloc and name three?
4. What do NIC and LDC stand for?
5. What are the currents and cross currents referred to by Porter?
6. What are tariffs?
7. What are Harmonised Tariff System (HTS)?
8. What does high context and low context culture mean?
9. What is critical dissonance, often found in international marketing?
10. What is the process of internationalisation?
11. What direct methods of entry are available to exporters?
12. What are the four dimensions Hofstede uses to describe different national cultural characteristics?

Check your answers with ours at the end of the chapter.

Issues for managing marketing performance

2.7 What you need to know

- Key issues involved in effective implementation of plans
- Key stakeholders and how to win support in a variety of contexts
- Strategies for managing change effectively
- How to improve knowledge management in an organisation
- How to improve performance in a range of contexts

Action Programme 4

Knowledge check of managing marketing performance

1. Compare and contrast the problems you might encounter managing knowledge in a power culture and a role culture.
2. What are the three key functions of Adair's action centred leadership?
3. Name three styles of leadership and an advantage and disadvantage of each. What are the most reliable sources of leadership power?
4. What five key factors need to be taken into account when designing a team and what are the key issues of managing teams through stages of development?
5. What are typical symptoms of poor motivation and causes of poor motivation? Name and briefly explain three theories of motivation.
6. What two key factors affect an organisation's ability to develop good standards of customer service? How do these and other factors contribute to customer expectations being formed?
7. What is the customer's chain of experience?
8. What broad markets/stakeholders do relationship marketing strategies target?
9. What are the stages people might go through during periods of change?
10. Why would you segment your internal market during management of change and what might these segments be?
11. What are the key factors in effective management of change?
12. Quantitative measures are a very narrow way of measuring organisation performance, what other models of measurement might be more appropriate?

Check your answers with ours at the end of the chapter.

Part A: Introducing case study

How did you get on?

2.8 Make sure you take the time to review your answers thoroughly and honestly. The run up to a case exam is the wrong time to discover knowledge gaps. None of us knows it all, so don't be surprised if you have identified content you need to brush up on.

2.9 **Make a list of topics for review or revision.** Tick off one or two a week until you are confident with your underpinning knowledge.

Notes to Self

Topics for Review	Deadline date
1	
2	
3	
4	
5	
6	
7	
8	
9	
10	

3 Contemporary issues

3.1 Business practice and academic theory continually evolves to reflect our changing environment. The way we solved problems yesterday will not be the same way we solve problems today or tomorrow. Different business models, environmental conditions, competitive behaviour etc. means we need to respond with new ideas and solutions.

What they are

3.2 The case study syllabus is **strategic** marketing planning and control, marketing communications and international marketing strategy. We can therefore always expect these core elements to be reflected in one way or another in the case study and the examination. What the changes are the latest **developments** in these areas. **Contemporary issues** are the latest thinking on how businesses operate – how they manage people, produce goods, develop strategies and so on. We do not intend to take an exhaustive look at contemporary issues, as they are many and varied, and are continually evolving.

3.3 The contemporary issues we will look at briefly here are:

- Brand strategy and management
- Customer relationship management
- Collaborative partnerships
- Supply chain management
- E-commerce and internet strategies
- Ethical, social and environmental responsibilities

How you identify contemporary issues in the case

3.4 The contemporary issues are usually fairly easily identified and flagged in the case studies. For example, with Biocatalysts we look at **partnerships** with stakeholders, **customer relationship management** and **environmental** issues which we identify with clear headings and text and/or models.

3.5 Contemporary issues have never been difficult to identify. Ignoring them, however is possible, particularly if a tick box approach to developing plans is adopted.

How you use contemporary issues in the case

3.6 Sometimes there is a specific question on a contemporary issue raised in the case study but often not. This does not mean that the issues should be ignored, far from it, the expectation is that you understand these often strategic issues and incorporate into your plans and solutions as and where appropriate.

3.7 For example if we had developed an Internet strategy and it did not come up as a question then you would look for opportunities to include elements of your internet strategy in the appropriate and relevant answers to questions.

4 Brand strategy and management

4.1 The brand plays a more significant role that ever before. Its value to the organisation as a source of competitive advantage and means of securing customer loyalty has been recognised and the nature of brand management has changed as a result.

Brands and their strategic role

4.2 Managing brands at a tactical level was always straightforward. It did not require co-ordination across the organisation or consideration of integrating business activities.

4.3 The role of the brand has become much more strategic in the last decade. This has been driven by brands appearing on balance sheets as assets. Suddenly organisations realised the financial value of brands. To build and maintain financial value requires a strategic approach. This in turn requires long-term commitment to the brand, investment and innovation. It also requires effort to co-ordinate and integrate all business activities in order to represent the desired meaning and values of the brand.

What is a brand?

4.4 A brand is more than just a physical product or service, it can help build relationships with customers. This is particularly important in markets where the organisation has no face to face contact with customers eg fmcg. A brand is also more than just the component parts that make up a product, it has additional values attributed to it **by customers**.

4.5 A brand adds value to the product. Added value often has more potential to differentiate one product from another than the **core** and **expected** functional **benefits** sought by customers.

Part A: Introducing case study

Where is value added?

Total brand concept ~ adding value

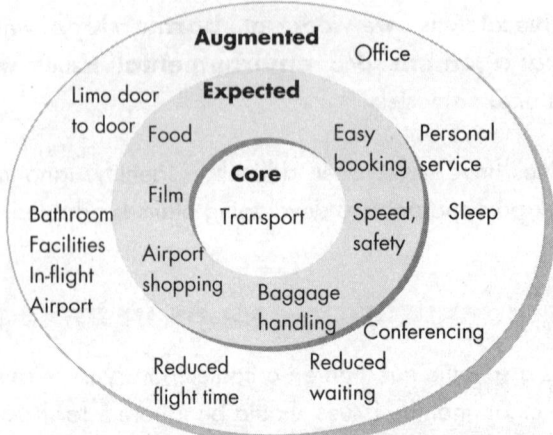

Brands and corporate image/reputation

4.6 Image and reputation come from a number of sources, how the business performs in its markets can help build a positive image and reputation (or not). Customers' views and perceptions and competitor actions will also affect image and reputation.

4.7 A key factor in building a positive image and reputation will be the effectiveness of the organisation's communication activities. Fundamental to this will be the brand and what it has come to represent. The brand can be the company name (and increasingly is) or product names.

4.8 The communications effort, amongst other things, should be concerned with promoting positive associations with the brand that are meaningful and valued by customers. Sony is a good example of a brand that is perceived as trustworthy, high quality and performance and reliable. This reduces the customer's need to take time deciding between brands. The Sony brand is trusted and reduces risk.

Brands, corporate culture and customer service

4.9 Corporate culture can affect perceptions of the brand either positively or negatively. An organisation that receives bad publicity for the way it treats its staff may damage its image in the eyes of its publics. An organisation that values its staff and is perceived as a good place to work **may** add value to the brand. This also extends to its role in the local community, society and environmental responsibility.

4.10 Customer service, increasingly a source of competitive advantage, is one of the most difficulty elements of the marketing mix to manage. Variability in service affects customers' perceptions of the value of the brand.

4.11 To ensure consistent and desired customer service levels, the right people need to be recruited, employees need to feel valued and receive the appropriate customer service training if the desired levels of service are to be achieved and maintained.

Brands, positioning and the marketing mix

4.12 The marketing department does not have control over all of the marketing mix; the whole organisation is involved. The marketing department should, however have significant influence over the marketing mix, particularly if the brand is to perform effectively and provide a source of competitive advantage.

4.13 The entire marketing mix must represent and reflect the brand values. Any inconsistencies confuse customers and damages the brand's reputation and performance. The marketing task is to ensure that, in the first place it understands the brand values as perceived by customers and, secondly, manages the mix to build positive brand values effectively position the mix in the market.

4.14 We have seen reference to brand building, image and strategies in many of the case studies. Many case studies, as you will learn, make specific reference to brand models and concepts.

Kevin Keller (2003) believes there are four key steps of brand building.

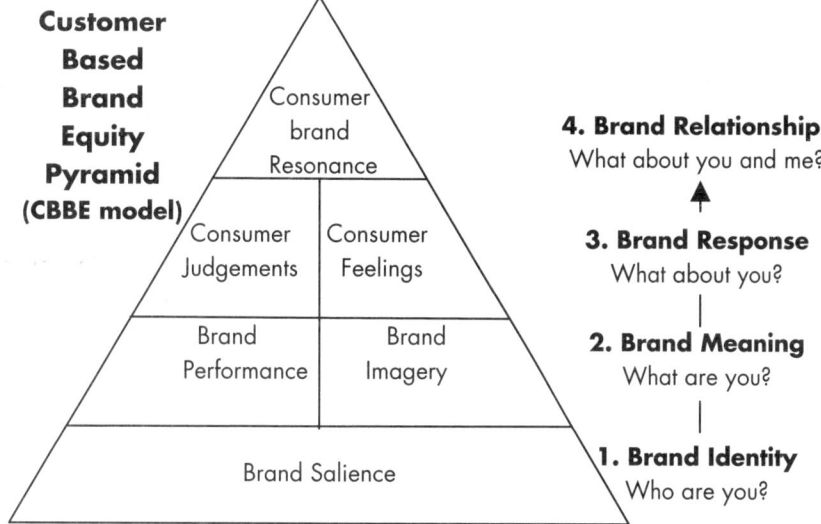

Part A: Introducing case study

4.15 In identifying where value is added Keller provides another model to assess the brand value chain.

Brand Value Chain (Keller 2001)

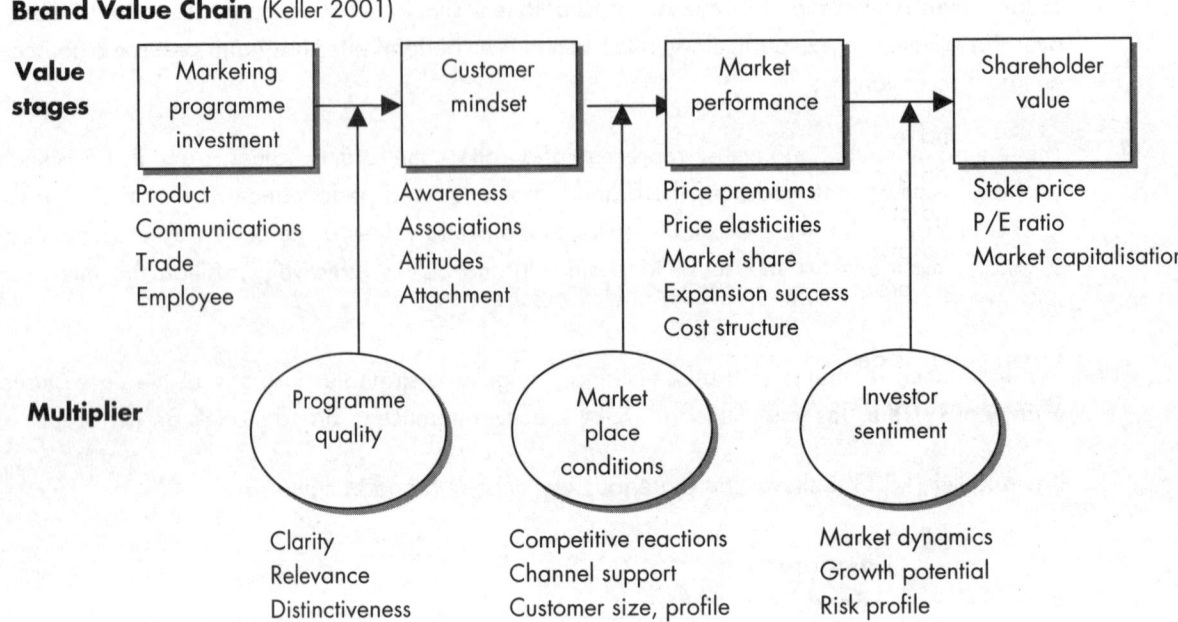

Criteria for choosing brand elements

4.16 Keller identifies six brand elements that are essential in building a brand. These are:

1. Memorability
2. Meaningfulness
3. Likeability
4. Transferability
5. Adaptability
6. Protectability

These elements provide an excellent checklist of what we need to take into account when identifying values, names, symbols, slogans etc. We can then develop our brand and ensure it meets these requirements.

Sub dimensions of brand building blocks (Keller 2001)

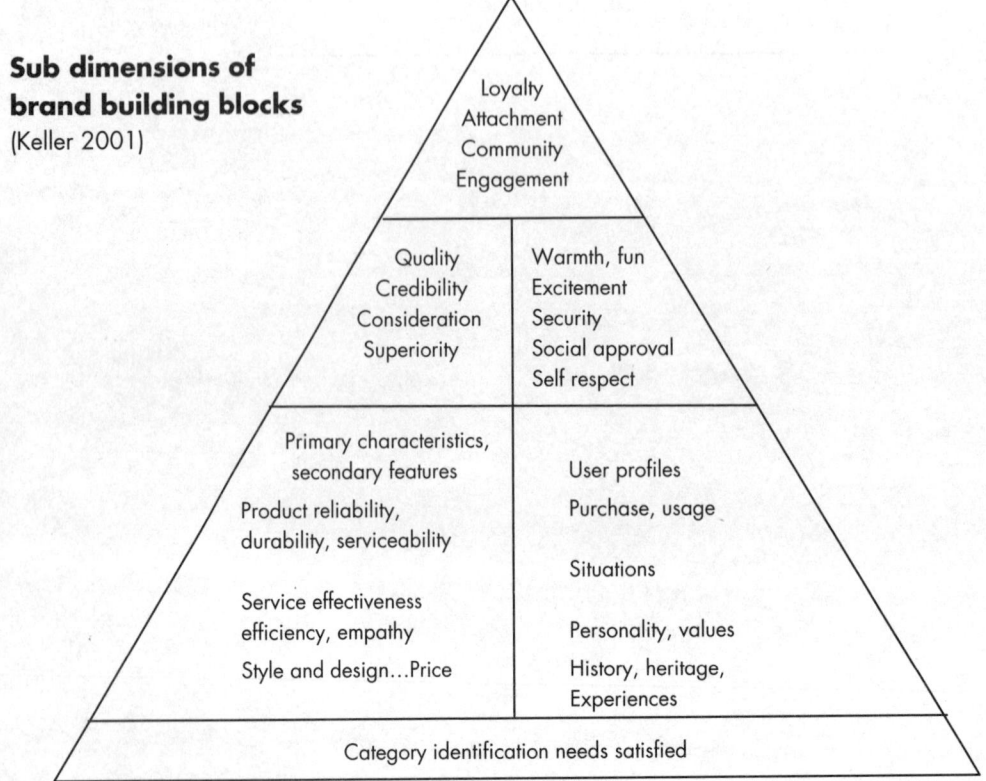

Brand equity

4.17 The equity of a brand lies in the name, symbol, slogan, the meaning of the brand and, ultimately its perceived value to the customer. The resources and effort, invested in the product and/or service delivered to the customer, all contribute to brand equity. Representative of this investment is:

- Brand loyalty
- Brand quality
- Brand association
- Brand awareness
- Brand properties (patents, trademarks etc.)

4.18 Brand equity is derived from the value it represents to both customers and the organisation.

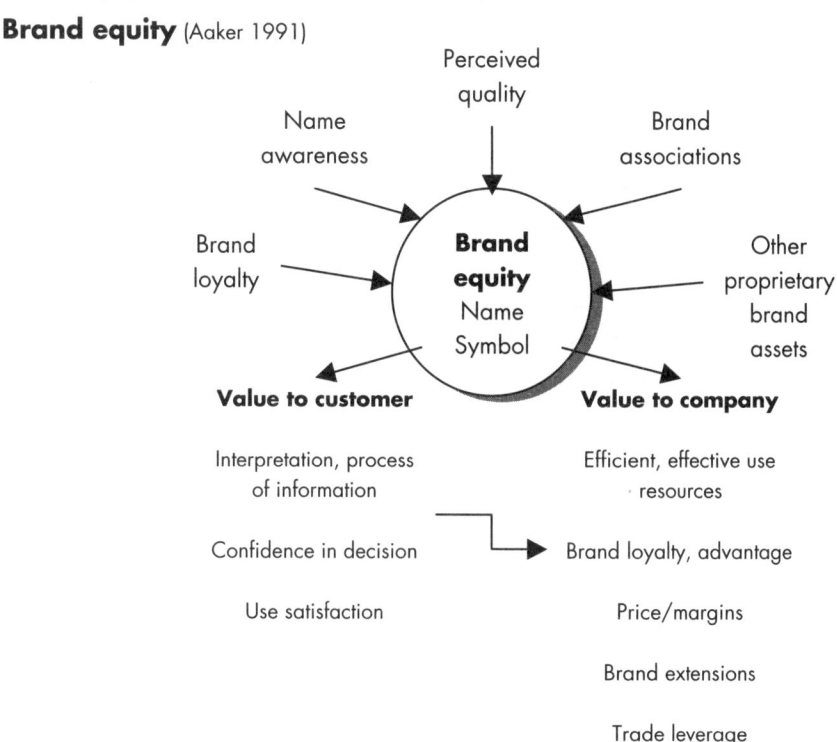

Brand equity (Aaker 1991)

Inputs to Brand equity (Name, Symbol):
- Name awareness
- Perceived quality
- Brand associations
- Brand loyalty
- Other proprietary brand assets

Value to customer
- Interpretation, process of information
- Confidence in decision
- Use satisfaction

Value to company
- Efficient, effective use resources
- Brand loyalty, advantage
- Price/margins
- Brand extensions
- Trade leverage

Brand quality

4.19 Quality is relative to the customer's perception of quality, what it means to the customer. A lot of effort and resources can be invested in improving quality, to be competitive, and still fail to maintain the existing customer base and/or attract new customers.

4.20 If quality is defined by managers, without reference to customers, it will not deliver the desired results. Customers' definition of quality is relative to their needs, uses and motives for buying. This criteria is often a mix of both tangible functional benefits, which can be objectively measured, and of intangible emotional benefits which are far more difficult to measure objectively. Even the rational evaluation is susceptible to subjective evaluation.

4.21 Quality is derived from a number of sources

- Component quality (the ingredients of the product)
- Process quality (the way in which the product or service is made or delivered)
- Service quality (how the product or service is delivery through personal service)

Part A: Introducing case study

4.22 Perceptions of quality can be influenced by a number of factors, some of which are a result of deliberate strategies by the organisation and some of which are not. Those that are not can be both positive and negative eg good or bad press coverage or accidents. Brand associations also influence to perceptions of quality.

Brand association

4.23 Brand association comes from the connections people make between names, symbols and slogans. McDonald's are associated with golden arches, Cadbury's chocolate with the colour purple, the 'Orange' mobile phone company with the colour orange and so on. The brand image is a set of associations derived from a number of sources.

4.24 The value of the brand is represented in these associations and provides meaning to the values attributed to the brand. Associations can contribute to the success of the brand by:

- Speeding up evaluation through easy retrieval processing and of information
- Provoking positive attitudes towards the brand
- Broadening definitions of the brand's know how and ability
- Aiding and enlightening interpretation of name, symbol and slogan
- Providing a context for positioning (with whom does the brand mix)

4.25 Associations are not confined to the activities of the organisation such as the marketing mix but also of the circle within which the brand moves. High tech, celebrity status, adventurous, all say something about the brand to the customers. Aaker provides a model for brand associations as follows.

Brand Associations (Aaker 1991)

```
              Product
   Country /  attributes
   geographic          Intangibles
                              Customer
                              benefits
   Competitors   Brand
                 Name
                 Symbol       Relative
                              price
   Product
   class
                              Use /
   Life style /                application
   personality
            Celebrity   User /
            / person    customer
```

Building the brand

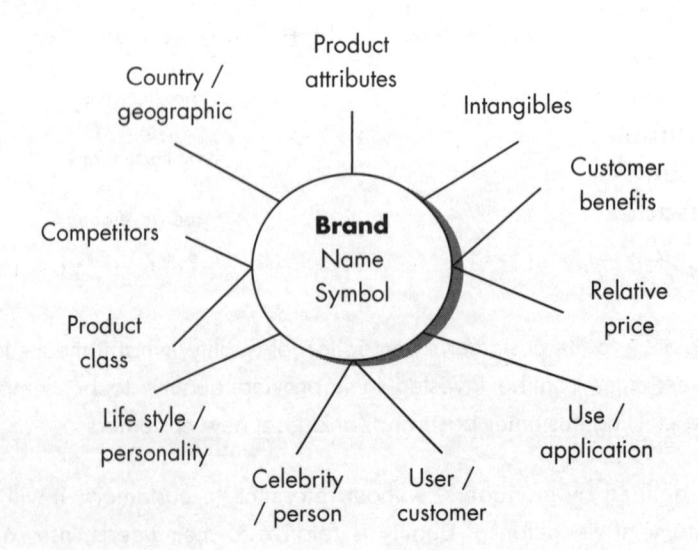

4.26 Building the brand requires **vision**. Where is the brand going, what is its future? A long-term vision should be established and then strategies and plans designed to build the brand to achieve the vision. This will take time and there will be distinct stages and tasks during the building of the brand, with possibly, a different emphasis at each stage.

Brand awareness

4.27 In building the brand, developing credibility and raising visibility are important tasks. Brand awareness objectives will depend on the industry, the company's position in that industry and its markets. '**Top of mind**' awareness requires establishing the brand as one people know without reference to an industry or a prompt. '**Brand recall**' awareness requires a context prompt (eg industry, product category). **Brand recognition** awareness requires the brand being named, among others, and people will recognise the brand name. Each objective has implications for investment and resources. Top of mind will require heavy investment and effort and may not be worth the return. The objective must be realistic and practical.

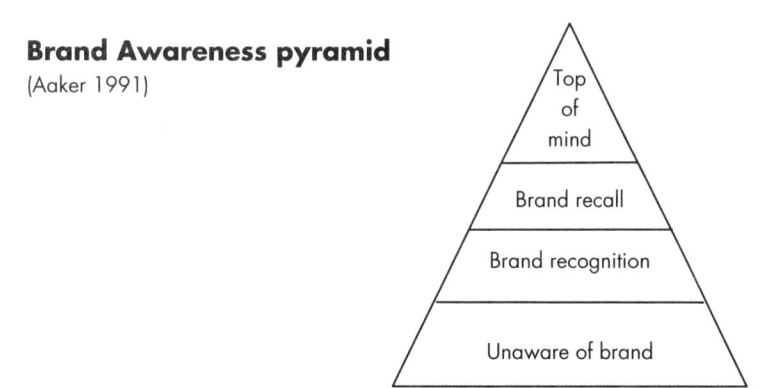

Brand Awareness pyramid
(Aaker 1991)

- Top of mind
- Brand recall
- Brand recognition
- Unaware of brand

5 E-commerce and Internet strategies

Role of the Internet in business

5.1 Businesses should establish what the role of the Internet is to be. The Internet has four broad functions:

- **Communications** – dynamic two-way interactions
- **Information** – gathering, sharing, retrieval, transmission
- **Distribution** – physical direct and intermediary
- **Transactions** – ordering, negotiating, invoicing, paying

The Internet offers an organisation many benefits, particularly as diffusion globally increases.

5.2 Benefits of the Internet

(a) *Now (potential)*

- Speed – transactions, communications, innovation, products received
- Quantity
- Quality – improved consistency, better control, easier standardisation
- Cost efficient (operations, packaging, promotions)
- Operation efficient
- Communication – interaction – two way – engaging customers
- Flexibility
- Information – searching, distributing and sharing, retrieval
- Stakeholder partnerships and collaboration
- Entry barriers
- Market penetration (depending on markets)
- Innovation
- Trial options

Part A: Introducing case study

(b) *In the future* (All of the above will improve but as the diffusion of technology spreads, the size of memories improve and speed increases also)

- Increased visibility
- Market development
- Global niches

These benefits will only be realised if valid strategies are developed and implemented. One of the issues marketers need to keep in mind is customers' attitudes to the internet.

(c) *Resistance to the internet*

- Security
- Impersonal, remote, faceless
- Credibility of on line companies
- Predominance of features not benefits
- Relationship with personnel – intermediary or company

Customer behaviour

5.3 One area that can easily be overlooked as attention is focused on building Websites and Internet architecture is that of customer behaviour. The increasing ease of the internet as a search tool is likely to change buyer behaviour from a tendency to be reactive to promotion/sales to being proactive and searching for information and engaging with sellers who can provide what is wanted.

5.4 As customers become more familiar and comfortable with the internet they will begin to play an increasing role in driving the development and character of the internet. Companies who ignore changes in behaviour and identifying real benefits of the internet from a customer's perspective do so at their peril.

Developing internet strategies – a clear strategy?

5.5 There is a subtle difference between (a) taking a leap into the unknown with the clear objective of learning all you can and (b) translating this into a strategy for future development, and following the latest craze. The first (a) accepts the unknown but has a vision, if hazy, for the future and ensures there are systems and processes in place to facilitate **learning** and incorporate continuous improvement. The latter will waste a lot of resources on tactical activities that might deliver very short-term gains and fail to learn or improve in readiness for the future.

5.6 Unfortunately there are too many companies who fall into the latter category and are dazzled by the features of the internet. They have yet to interpret the benefits of the internet from the customer's perspective and as a strategic goal. However, some companies are now addressing internet strategies which will change the dynamics of competition and customer service.

5.7 The key to success, in the early days of implementing internet strategies, is ensuring that designed into the strategy are mechanisms to ensure learning takes place and is transferred across the organisation and into new strategies. This requires **continuous improvement links** that are designed to build on each learning experience and improve practice before moving on to the next stage.

5.8 Organisations need to establish their own needs and the needs of other stakeholders and then they can design their strategy.

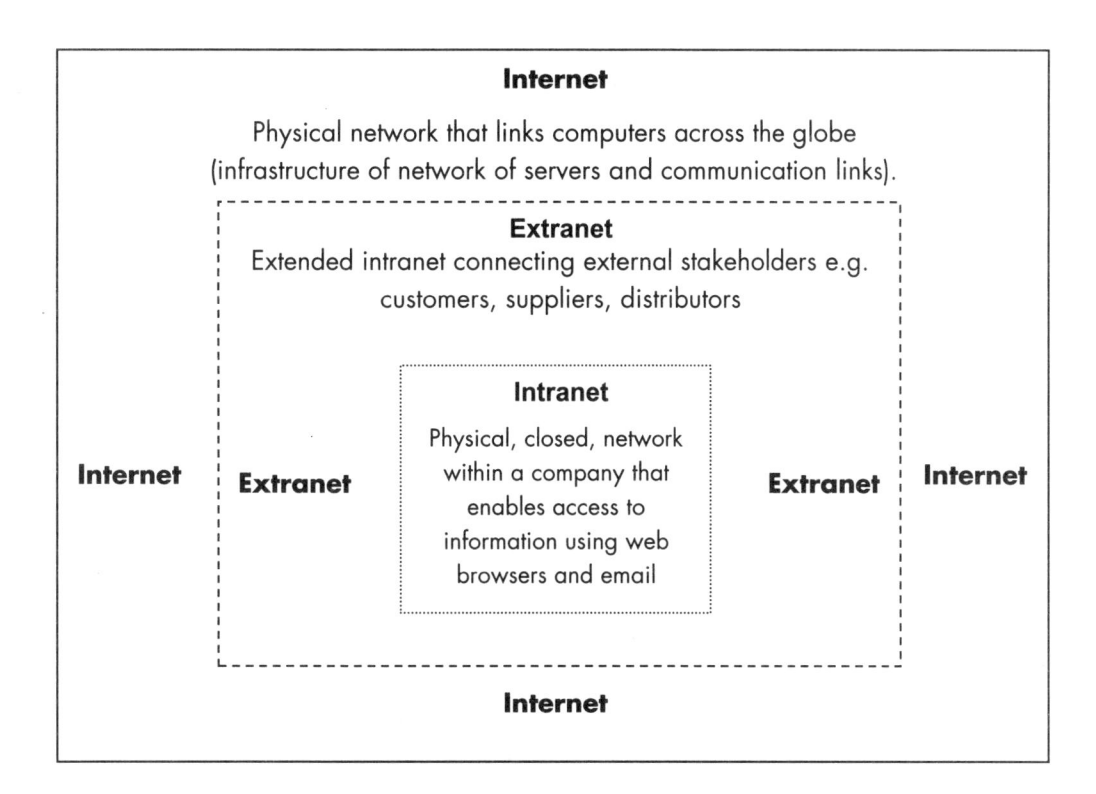

```
┌─────────────────────────────────────────────────────────────┐
│                          Internet                           │
│         Physical network that links computers across the globe │
│         (infrastructure of network of servers and communication links). │
│     ┌ ─ ─ ─ ─ ─ ─ ─ ─ ─ ─ ─ ─ ─ ─ ─ ─ ─ ─ ─ ─ ─ ─ ─ ┐     │
│     │                    Extranet                      │     │
│     │    Extended intranet connecting external stakeholders e.g. │
│     │         customers, suppliers, distributors        │     │
│     │         ┌ · · · · · · · · · · · · · · ┐          │     │
│     │         │          Intranet             │          │     │
│     │         │  Physical, closed, network   │          │     │
│  Internet │ Extranet │ within a company that │ Extranet │ Internet │
│     │         │   enables access to          │          │     │
│     │         │  information using web       │          │     │
│     │         │   browsers and email         │          │     │
│     │         └ · · · · · · · · · · · · · · ┘          │     │
│     │                                                   │     │
│     └ ─ ─ ─ ─ ─ ─ ─ ─ ─ ─ ─ ─ ─ ─ ─ ─ ─ ─ ─ ─ ─ ─ ─ ┘     │
│                          Internet                           │
└─────────────────────────────────────────────────────────────┘
```

Internet distribution strategies

5.9 Internet distribution strategy dependent on a number of factors

- Customer groups served – their needs, preferences
- The role and power of current intermediaries
- Size of business and ability to adopt/embrace company wide technology (structure, operations)
- Culture of the business – innovative, low risk avoidance
- Products/services provided (digital, non digital, value per unit, volumes, level of incorporated technology

5.10 **Internet as a direct distribution channel**. The internet provides an ideal channel for **digital** product categories (software, text, image, sound). Examples of industries/businesses that can benefit include:

- Publishing
- Information services
- Technology companies – computers, software, entertainment games
- Multi media – films, music etc.
- Financial services

5.11 **Internet as an indirect distribution channel – intermediaries**. Many products and services cannot be distributed down the line and therefore intermediaries are still needed. The role of the internet in these circumstances can be:

- Communications and information channel
- Transaction channel

Part A: Introducing case study

- Extranet link with intermediaries who distribute goods
- Co-ordinating/monitoring physical logistics

5.12 Role of traditional intermediaries. Examples of traditional intermediaries:

```
                    Intermediary
   ┌────────┐       FSAs              ┌────────┐
   │ Seller │                         │ Buyer  │
   └────────┘       Retailers         └────────┘
                (eg video and music stores)
```

Are they extending the chain or adding value? Many intermediaries may eventually disappear if they do not redefine the value they add. As with any intermediary strategy, a business must have clear objectives of what it expects from its intermediaries. Internet distribution strategies require their role to be re-defined.

5.13 Emergence of new intermediaries. New intermediaries are emerging as a result of the need for new services and expertise including Infomediaries and Cybermediaries. These intermediaries currently have distinct services to offer. They pose a threat to some distribution channels because of the experience and skill they have of the internet. They could buy in the necessary skills and re-define their roles.

5.14 Internet channel management

(a) Many of the same issues in channel management are still applicable. There is still a need to:

- **Set objectives** (volumes, margins, contribution to relationships)
- **Strategy** (market penetration, development, competitive position)
- **Communications** and motivating the channel
- **Tactics** (promotional support, negotiations, order/payment, information)
- **Customer service** service dimensions that customers value and prioritise.
- **Control** (ie Agree and set performance standards and targets)

(b) **Some differences still exist however**

- Immediacy and two-way process. **Push strategies** into channels will have to be more sophisticated.
- Integrated and electronically linked channels require greater freedom in sharing and using information.

(c) **Factors to consider**

- Importance of **compatible** technology, processes and operations. In an electronically connected world compatible is fundamental.
- Importance of honest and open communications and flow of information

5.15 Internet communication strategy

(a) Again many of same **processes and frameworks** can be used.

- Need for objectives
- Strategy – push, pull and profile

- Positioning and messages – consistent with brand values and targets
- Targets – identifying who talking to
- Promotional techniques – can use on line brochures
- Controls – measuring effectiveness

(b) **Some differences**

- Targets are still limited and often poorly defined – assumptions made about who is on line
- On-line communications is interactive and can engage target audiences in a way traditional communications cannot.
- It is dynamic, can be instantly updated, moving and changing in direct response to demands of customer
- Different measures for on line activities
- Role of the database management. Requires a sophisticated process for managing. Current poor practice will expose companies as sloppy.
- Far greater risk of information overload on the internet

(c) **Factors to consider**:

- How are (or can) brand values interpreted? Will the internet affect perceptions in anyway and if so how?
- Ensuring it is a two way process – capturing customer information
- Matching experience with expectations – ensuring communications is clear, unambiguous, helpful avoid 'click help' syndrome
- Because it is dynamic it must engage, interact
- Do not use as an alternative to all other forms of communication – in particular if a telephone call will do the job better make the call.

Case studies and the Internet

5.16 The Internet and e-strategy are no longer new, but each case study will have an organisation with a particular problem and e-strategies may form part of the solution. In particular markets must ensure organisations to implement e-strategies from a customer perspective not a technology perspective.

6 Collaborative partnerships

6.1 Recent years have seen an increase in collaborative partnerships, for example competitors collaborating on research and development and market development. Reasons for collaborating include reducing risk and cost, and increasing revenue.

Collaborating with the customer/consumer

6.2 Prahalad and Ramaswamy (*Harvard Business Review* Jan-Feb 2000) comment that the changes in our business environment have resulted in the breaking down of clearly defined roles in corporate relationships, deregulation, globalisation, technological convergence and the

Part A: Introducing case study

evolution of the internet. This therefore require a new approach to the way businesses operate, and that we now need to co-opt customer competence. They make the following observations.

> 'Consider the relationship between Ford and its main suppliers. Far from being passive providers of materials and parts, Ford's suppliers have become close collaborators in the development of new vehicles. At the same time, however, they compete for value by negotiating the prices for the parts and the materials they supply.
>
> The story's the same for distributors. For example, Wal-Mart does more than just distribute Procter & Gamble's goods. It shares daily sales information and works with P & G in product warehousing and replenishment to ensure that consumers can always find the goods they want at low prices. In some categories Wal-Mart competes head to head with P&G.
>
> The talk now is of companies competing as a family. They talk about alliances, networks and collaboration among companies. But managers and researchers have largely ignored the consumer, the agent that is most dramatically transforming the industrial system as we know it.'

6.3 Customers in many business to business markets have been involved in product and service development with companies for decades. The organisation's stakeholders, including B2B customers, can now participate in the organisations innovative processes using technology such as 3-D CAD online. This allows organisations to set up global innovation teams that go beyond direct employees.

6.4 The involvement of consumers in the development process is now possible thanks to the Internet. They can comment, make suggestions, share ideas with each other and with companies. They become co-creators of value, and so they are a source of organisational competence. Even in business to business markets, while they might have played a significant role in co-creation, many companies may not have recognised or formally identified this as a source of competence or even of competitive advantage.

6.5 This source of competence and competitive advantage is only a reality if it has firstly been identified and recognised by the organisation and secondly harnessed to the organisation's advantage. We need to collaborate with people to ensure we maximise the positive outcomes of our creative and innovative process.

6.6 Key collaborators in the creativity and innovation process include the following.

Collaborator	Comment
Actual customers	The ultimate consumers of whatever an organisation produces; will decide whether or not what is on offer meets their needs
Employees	The people who are responsible for developing, designing and delivering what customers want. They have unique insights into the process of getting products and services through the value adding process to the customer.
Employers	We should not exclude those who own and run the organisation. In small to medium sized businesses they are often the entrepreneurs who originally developed an idea that was marketable, they tend to be creative and innovative.
Intermediaries	If we are reliant on our channels to get to our customers our distribution chain is critical to our success. They may be the only contact with our customers and therefore have knowledge that informs creative and innovation ideas.

Collaborator	Comment
Suppliers	Part of the value adding supply chain. Their knowledge of supplies and developments in the supply chain can enable them to provide useful insights and ideas from a different perspective
Potential customers or non users	There may be a reason why these people do not buy or use the product or service other than they do not need it. It maybe that the product or service in its current form does not solve their problem, meet their need. These people can provide unique insights into new and quite different ideas.
Innovation incubators	Or innovation/idea companies such as IDEO, Idealab etc.
Academics	People who research and think about environment and business provoke and challenge old ways of thinking and doing and present ideas on new ways of thinking and doing.
Industry experts and analysts	Could be the captains of industry who challenge traditional business practices and evangelise their ideas or experts in a particular technology or craft.
Authors, journalists	These people, as well as coming up with their own ideas, will be well read and, as part of their job, collectors of ideas and thoughts from a wide variety of sources. They can make connections between diverse ideas and thoughts, industries and organisations that can lead to creativity and innovation.
Anthropologists	Who study societies and customs, make connections between different civilisations. Some companies have started to recruit anthropologists and they literally go out and mingle with the crowds. They observe behaviour, what people are doing, with what, where, how etc. and come back to the organisation with their observations. Anthropologists, in the telecommunications industry, recognised the growing importance of text messaging long before organisations believed this would become the main form of communicating between the young.
Inventors	You may know some! A neighbour, someone in the local community or be able to access inventors through writings in journals etc.

6.7 Collaboration requires a strategy and management and good communications skills. Some of the marketing communications processes can help in managing collaborative partnerships as can customer relationship management strategies.

7 Customer relationship management

7.1 Building customer relationships in business to business markets has been long understood and practised. The difference now is that there is a focus on the **formality** and **process** for building relationships with customers. Objectives are set and strategies developed to ensure the efforts succeed. Building relationships in consumer markets can be more complex, particularly where the organisation never comes into direct contact with consumers. The relationship here is built with the brand. Reasons for building relationships in business to business markets are usually the result of a need one or more of the **Five Relationship Needs**:

	Comment
Need for trust	If the product or service involved saving, maintaining or improving life, for example, the caring professions
Need for security	If secrecy, privacy or sensitivity were issues the customer had to believe their interests would be protected, for example financial services
Need for time	If projects had long time scales e.g. 5, 10 even 15 years businesses had to be patient, think and act in the time scales typical of the industry, for example, the military
Need for co-operation	Products required the input of customers in development, working partnerships with customers are a feature of business operations
Need to reduce risk	If large sums of money were involved the investment had to be worthwhile, solve problems and prove beneficial, for example aerospace

Source: *Five Relationship Needs*, J. Cockton 1998

7.2 In markets where demand exceeds supply, there is little or no incentive to focus on building relationships. As markets became increasingly competitive and customers have a choice, businesses have to find ways to improve customer retention and the concept of 'relationship marketing' held the answers.

Relationship marketing

7.3 Relationship marketing is about building long term customer relationships with profitable customers. Another term is customer relationship management (CRM). In some organisations that means changing behaviour from short term transactions to long term relationships.

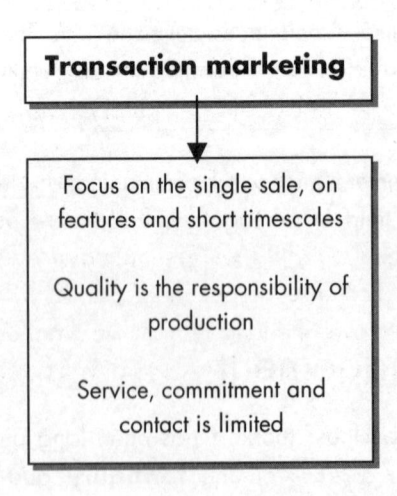

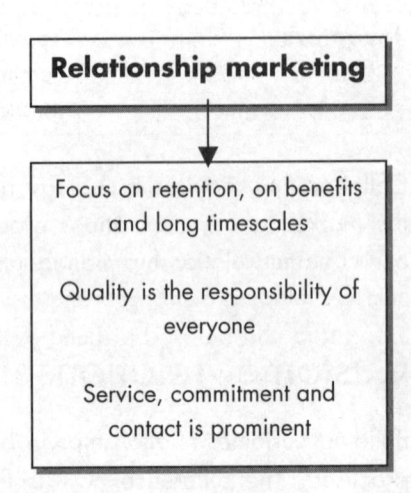

Transaction marketing

- Focus on the single sale, on features and short timescales
- Quality is the responsibility of production
- Service, commitment and contact is limited

Relationship marketing

- Focus on retention, on benefits and long timescales
- Quality is the responsibility of everyone
- Service, commitment and contact is prominent

7.4 Relationship marketing requires that within marketing strategy development there is a focus on:

- **Genuinely valuing people** both internally and externally and this is evident in working practices
- **Quality** as central to all operations and evident in the belief that it is the responsibility of each and every person in the business
- A prevailing culture that facilitates **continuous improvement** evident in the organisation's responsiveness to change and the employees willingness to do so
- **Marketing orientation** as a feature of the culture and evident in professional marketing practices and activities focused on customer benefits and retention
- **Customer service** designed and developed with the product

It involves the bringing together of quality, customer service and continuous improvement, managed through marketing activities.

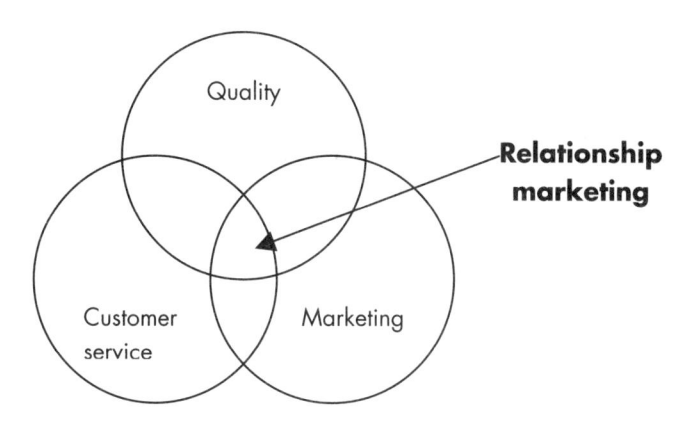

Christopher, Payne, Ballentyne

7.5 The principles of managing the three Ps of customer service and broader integration and coordination of the marketing mix ensure the customer receives value. The objective of relationship marketing is to build the loyalty of **valuable customers**, not **all or any customers** and therefore use the limited resources of the organisation effectively.

7.6 Relationship-building requires a sustained effort over time and one of the most effective tools an organisation has to do this is communication. If we take the difficulty of building relationships with consumers, communications and promotional activities will be the major method for doing this. Developing a strong brand that customers recognise, respect and connect with establishes a bond and can be used to build customer loyalty over the long term. If we want customers to be loyal we need strategies that move them from occasional customers to devoted advocates of the brand.

Part A: Introducing case study

The loyalty ladder

7.7 Through customer service **and communications** the aim is to move customers up the loyalty ladder.

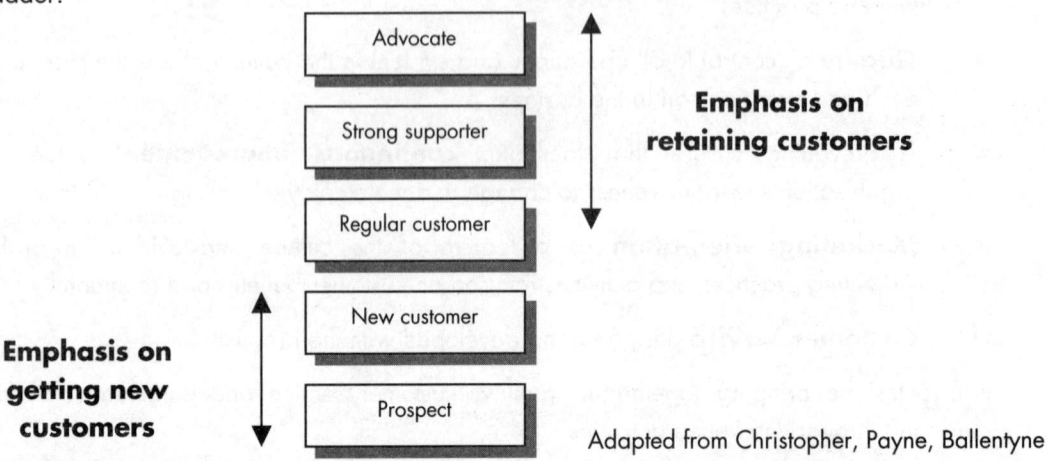

```
                    Advocate
                                    ↕  Emphasis on
                  Strong supporter     retaining customers

                  Regular customer

                    New customer
   Emphasis on   ↕
   getting new       Prospect
   customers
```

Adapted from Christopher, Payne, Ballentyne

7.8 Advocates of the organisation and/or brand are both valuable and loyal customers. They will actively and willingly refer others to the organisation, promoting, through word of mouth, the organisation and what it offers. The power of word of mouth communications has already been discussed and the advantages it offers should not be underestimated. It has credibility, far and above that of other promotional activities. Advocates bring new customers to the organisation reducing the effort and expense usually associated with acquiring customers.

7.9 Relationship marketing requires us to recognise and develop strategies with all key stakeholders. These strategies will be interlinked and key to all will be communications.

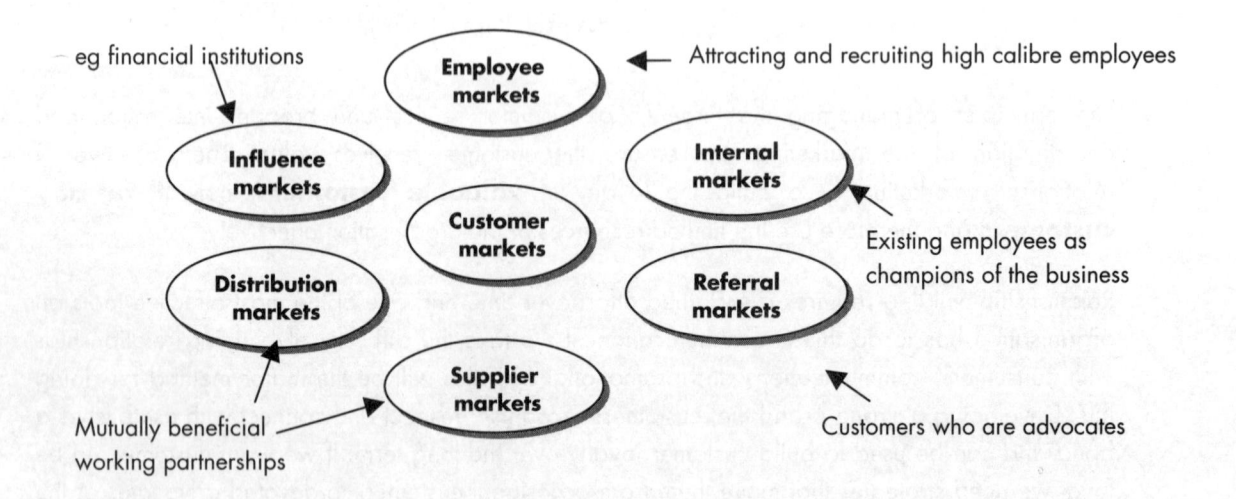

- eg financial institutions → **Influence markets**
- **Employee markets** ← Attracting and recruiting high calibre employees
- **Internal markets** ← Existing employees as champions of the business
- **Customer markets**
- **Referral markets** ← Customers who are advocates
- **Distribution markets**
- **Supplier markets** — Mutually beneficial working partnerships

Adapted from Christopher, Payne, Ballentyne

7.10 Key contacts between employees within the organisation and the stakeholders of the organisation are identified, and strategies developed to communicate and build long term relationships. These relationship strategies will focus on stakeholder needs and motives, so that communication tools and messages will be tailored to the stakeholder group. The great advantage of relationship strategies is the emphasis on collaboration and partnerships and encouraging two way communications.

7.11 Relationship strategies are designed to manage the different phases of a **customer's life cycle** and communications used to manage the transitions in the relationship. Needs change over time as does the relationship and these phases and transitions need to be understood and strategies designed to reflect the changing needs and the transitions.

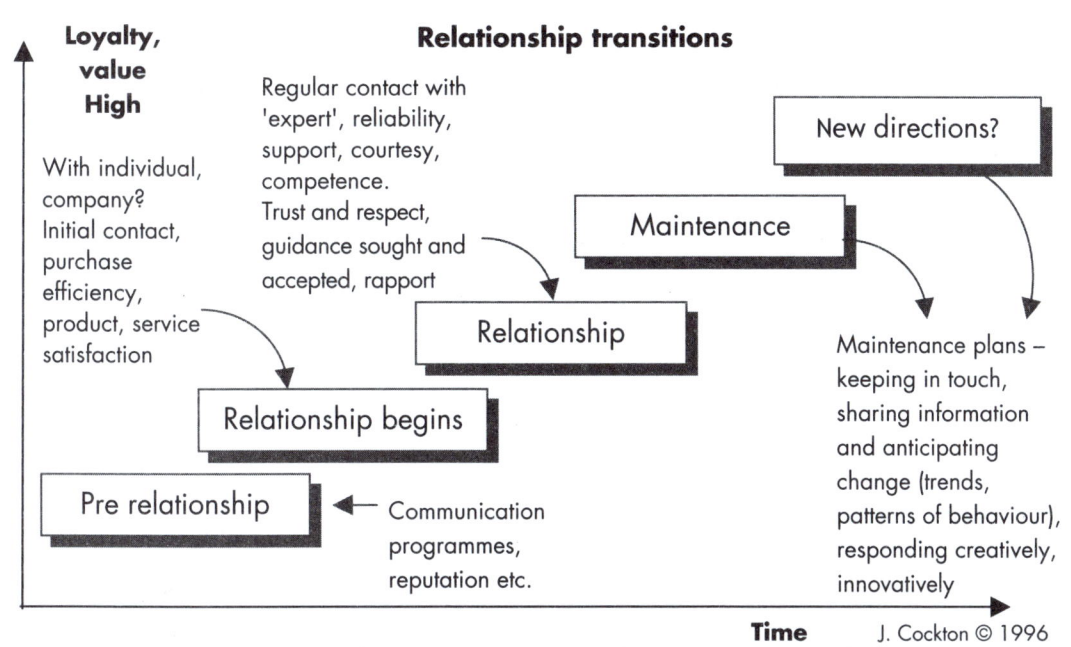

Relationship transitions

Loyalty, value High
- With individual, company? Initial contact, purchase efficiency, product, service satisfaction
- Pre relationship
- Communication programmes, reputation etc.
- Relationship begins
- Regular contact with 'expert', reliability, support, courtesy, competence. Trust and respect, guidance sought and accepted, rapport
- Relationship
- Maintenance
- New directions?
- Maintenance plans – keeping in touch, sharing information and anticipating change (trends, patterns of behaviour), responding creatively, innovatively

Time   J. Cockton © 1996

There are many examples of customers being lost during organisational change or a customer's transition. This happens because no thought is given to communicating with customers during these developments.

8 Supply chain management

8.1 Supply chain management has become increasing important for a number of reasons including:

- Distribution of goods and services becoming more complex
- Distribution of goods and services becoming more expensive
- Increasing need for speed and timeliness in movement of goods
- The need to build competitive advantage through the value chain

8.2 Supply chain management is a comprehensive activity that involves the movement of materials from source of supply through to the finished product being delivered to the customer. Material management concerns the procurement of supplies, movement of materials and components and assembly of products or services into the business and during production. Physical distribution concerns the movement of finished products to customers. It includes all financial aspects and costs involved and information requirements and flow. Logistics management embraces all movements of goods, including storage and inventory management, to achieve the most efficient and effective outcomes for both the business and the customer. Central to supply chain management is identifying added value opportunities and developing appropriate solutions.

8.3 Companies in the grocery trade have benefited from supply chain management in terms of significant savings (Wal-Mart reduced inventories by 90% saving the company hundreds of millions of dollars) and in terms of customer satisfaction (GE's Trading Process Network allows all parts of the business around the world involved in buying to find and purchase products from approved suppliers electronically at far greater speed and more efficiently than before.

Part A: Introducing case study

8.4 Supply chain management is essential in industries where companies need to operate JIT inventory systems.

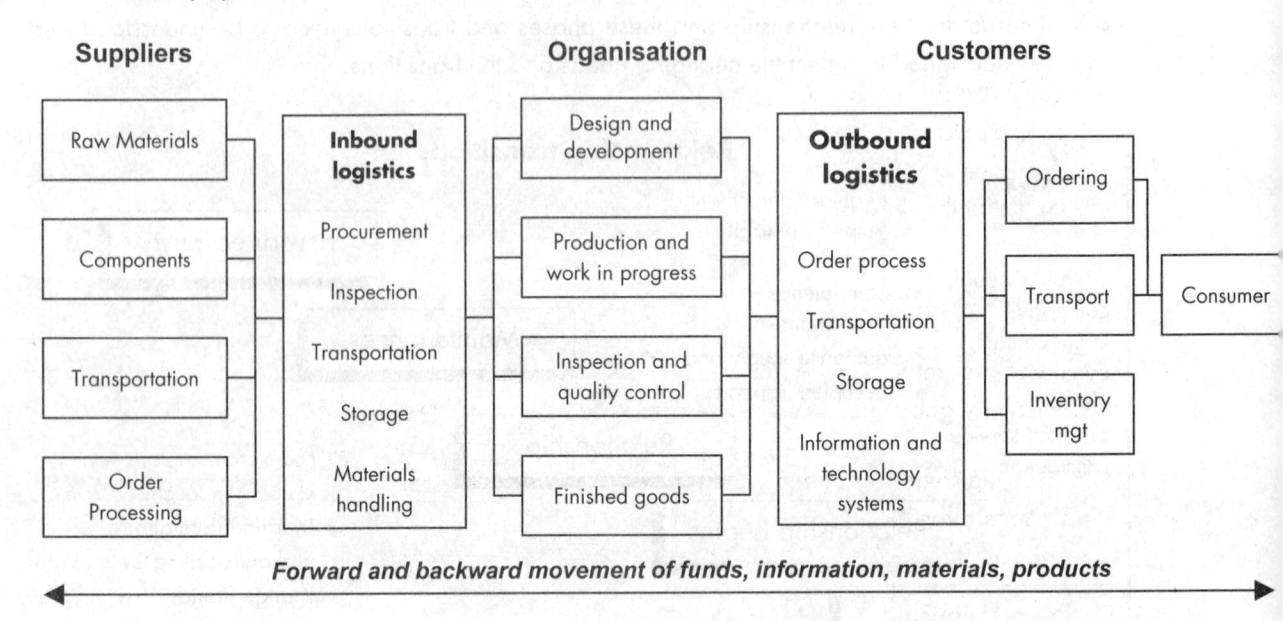

Suppliers		Organisation		Customers
Raw Materials	**Inbound logistics**	Design and development	**Outbound logistics**	Ordering
Components	Procurement	Production and work in progress	Order process	Transport → Consumer
Transportation	Inspection / Transportation / Storage	Inspection and quality control	Transportation / Storage	Inventory mgt
Order Processing	Materials handling	Finished goods	Information and technology systems	

Forward and backward movement of funds, information, materials, products

8.5 Another driving force behind supply chain management is the trend of **strategic alliances**. Decisions to form an alliance with one company or more are usually the result of the need to improve profits and reduce costs and risk. Alliances based on research and development, technological expertise, access to distribution outlets etc. can all potentially improve competitive and business performance. Once the decision has been made management should be developing a strategy to make the alliance work including attention to organisation cultural and operation differences. It will also be important to manage the supply chain as this will now become more complex and the potential for more to go wrong increases, damaging any gains the alliance was designed achieve. For the same reasons **outsourced** activities also requires Supply Chain Management.

The role of the Internet and supply chain management

8.6 The Internet is putting new demands on companies that make supply chain management an even more important issue. 24 hour service, 7 days a week and the customer's need for information and progress reports mean companies must be able to offer service at all times and provide information, almost instantly, on the current situation of any order. To be able to do this companies have no choice but to manage the supply chain through electronic links.

8.7 The internet can also provide benefits in adding value for customers by improving opportunities to customise. Electronic links that integrate supply through to demand mean that customisation becomes easier and more cost effective. Comprehensive information on what a customer wants and comprehensive information on what a supplier can provide can quickly (and relatively cheaply) be collected and accessed. This does require sharing and exchanging information.

(a) Well designed and effective Intranets and Extranets linking employees internally, particularly in global businesses, and linking suppliers and distributors with employees can ensure that information on customer orders and responses to queries can be accessed and dealt with immediately.

(b) Tesco have a system called Tesco Information Exchange (TIE) based on extranet technology. This system links Tesco to a number of suppliers so suppliers can access information on sales of their products and promotional activities in store.

8.8 Supply Chain Management requires sophisticated technology such as Telematics and Electronic Data Interchange (EDI). For example retailers use Efficient Consumer Response (ECR) to improve stock flow. ECR requires sharing Electronic Point of Sale (EPOS) information to ensure that the retail supply chain responses efficiently.

Reverse distribution systems / reverse supply chains

8.9 Goods are returned to producers for a variety of reasons. Incorrect goods received and particularly goods past their sell by date require systems for returning goods.

8.10 A growing trend in **reverse distribution systems** is the result of environmental objectives. As concern for the environment grows and the power of global environmental pressure groups increases, there is an increasing need for businesses to be able to facilitate disposal and recycling of goods. This has moved on from bottle banks and recycling plastics goods and now includes recycling cars, fridges and industrial goods. This requires being able to manage the process of retrieving products from the market once used and either disposing of them or recycling them. Again sophisticated Supply Chain Management processes will make this task easier and keep the costs down making it more acceptable and attractive to businesses.

8.11 Environmental regulations may force companies to develop reverse supply chains, for example the ISO 14000 standard assesses a company's environmental performance at two levels, the organisation (management and operations) and the product (quality, standards, packaging etc.). In 2003 EU legislation will require tire manufacturers operating in Europe to arrange for recycling of one used tire for every new tire they sell.

8.12 Some companies are seeing the benefits, reduced operating costs by reusing products or components and taking the initiative. Kodak remanufactures its single use cameras after the film has been developed. Over the past decade the company has recycled more than 310 million cameras in more than 20 countries.

8.13 Tracking product life cycles becomes an important part of proactively managing reverse distribution. The chain needs to be analysed for options, costs and benefits of the following.

- Product acquisition – retrieving the used product – quality (is it reusable), quantity (are they manageable), timing (not being overwhelmed by returns)

- Reverse logistics – collection, transported to facilities for inspection, sorting, disposable – depends on bulk, volumes etc.

- Inspection and disposition – testing, sorting and grading of products is labour intensive and time consuming. Quality standards, sensors, bar codes all improve this process

- Reconditioning – depends on product condition on return and processes needed as to whether or not to recondition or reuse parts

- Distribution and sales – is there a demand for recycled products? Requires communications – education, persuasion to end users and distribution channels

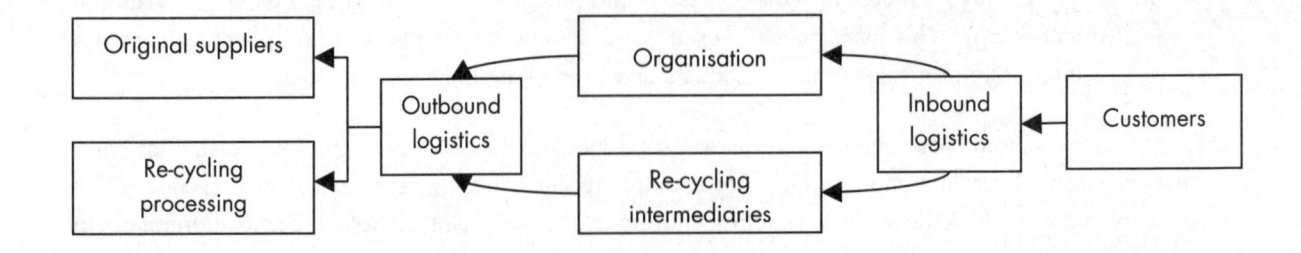

```
Original suppliers  →  Outbound logistics  →  Organisation  →  Inbound logistics  ←  Customers
Re-cycling processing              Re-cycling intermediaries
```

The role of marketing and supply chain management

8.14 Improvements in technology and the use of the internet in supply chain management can result in organisations becoming obsessed with the technology and how clever it is and fail to remember supply chain management involves the customer. The marketing manager's task is to ensure supply chain management is customer focused. Key aspects to ensure customer focus include:

- Identifying key issues in the supply chain of importance to customers
- Customer access to information (accurate, relevant and timely)
- Proactive sharing of information (do not wait until the customer asks if all is not going according to plan)
- Sourcing materials ('the best' from the customers' point of view not just the business)
- Journeys (ensuring transportation and routing of journeys is also in the best interests of the customer not just the business)
- Anticipating customer supply needs – particularly in business to business markets

8.15 Many processes are implemented to improve business performance through increased efficiency and reduced costs. It is important that processes affecting customers in any way are evaluated for their impact on the customer and how 'user friendly' they are. This is no less important with supply chain management and the use of the Internet.

8.16 While many involved in the management of the supply chain will be focused on efficiency (improving processes for speed, cost reduction etc.) it is marketing that should be focused on effectiveness. This requires attention to where value can be added and how. For example JIT inventory management may be attractive in business to business markets where significant savings can be made but in consumer markets availability often means providing a product or service when the customer wants it – now – and that may require holding stocks.

8.17 In business to business markets supply chain management provides real opportunities to offer valued added services for business customers. Companies who have invested in the technology can offer the service of managing the supply chain for business customers.

8.18 Supply chain management should not just be managed as a business objective but also as a customer satisfaction objective.

9 Ethical, social and environmental responsibilities

9.1 A central theme of marketing orientation must be **ethical behaviour** and social responsibility. Marketing is not about selling goods and services at any cost, it is about conducting business in a way that is irreproachable. While some might think this is uneconomic or impractical, it does not take a very demanding review of history and current conditions to recognise that cutting corners, ignoring ethical codes of conduct and focusing on short term bottom line will eventual damage something. That something could be people, our natural environment or our society. Organisations have a significant impact on society and cannot ignore their responsibilities. An intelligent approach is one that takes the long term view and a broad perspective.

9.2 Evidence of our collective lack of social responsibility is all around us. Packaging, the materials used and our disposal of it, failing to recycle materials and goods and lack of provision of facilities to encourage and enable people to recycle are all part of the problem. Our 'disposable' as opposed to 'repairable' attitudes to all goods are just a few examples.

9.3 It does take a concerted effort by all of us, not just a dedicated few, if we are to be socially responsibility. **Collectively** people need to believe in our social responsibilities, adopting green or environmental principles and practices. **Collaboratively** organisations need to provide the enablers that allow people to be socially responsible. It is all very well insisting we recycle waste, but unless there are relatively easy methods for us to do this we are unlikely to engage in action and rarely get beyond engaging in the debate.

9.4 A marketing orientation can encourage ethical practices internally and externally. Ethical behaviour does not just confine itself to social and environmental responsibilities. Unfortunately it is not a simple question of defining ethical codes of conduct and making sure everyone abides by them. How we conduct business also raises questions about what is acceptable behaviour. Bribery or 'softeners' are not uncommon in business practice in different parts of the world and in fact expected as part of business and seen as acceptable. On such occasions organisations are faced with the challenge of whether or not their code of ethical conduct is reasonable in the context of the culture the business might be operating in.

Summary of contemporary issues

- We have briefly covered here just some of the contemporary issues that have emerged in case studies. It is very important that you pick up on the contemporary issues in the exam case study you work on and ensure these issues are reflected throughout your plans and solutions.

- It is of course a common problem in organisations to 'do what we have always done'. Marketers need to encourage organisations to embrace new ideas and thinking on how to solve problems and sustain competitive advantage.

> **Tutor Tip**
>
> *Remember to visit the CIM website's Cutting Edge pages for the latest on contemporary marketing.*

Part A: Introducing case study

10 Integrating the diploma subjects

10.1 The aims and objectives of Analysis and Decision are to convert theory and knowledge into practice. Throughout this Tutorial Text and the practice case studies you will have the opportunity to test your knowledge further and to practise your marketing skills. At each stage of the analysis and decision process, you will be encouraged to use models and techniques on the case study to help you establish the current situation and develop credible solutions.

Introduction to the case study

10.2 The case paper has always been a compulsory paper and is intended to assess not just knowledge and understanding of marketing planning, but that candidates have the ability to tackle real issues in a commercially credible way.

10.3 Your practical experience will be immensely important in this exercise. If you **treat the case study** as though it was **another project at work** and your **exam preparation** as though you were getting ready for a **presentation to senior management**, then you will have an idea of the level, depth and degree of detail which is needed.

10.4 The case study is a vehicle for the examiners to assess your marketing management competence. It is critical to your success in this paper that you remember that the **problems of the case are not the central focus for the examiner**. Your skills, the processes you go through, and the tools and techniques you use are what are being assessed.

10.5 The emphasis of the case study syllabus is on strategy not tactics. It is easy to get side tracked producing lots of tactical detail which detracts from the strategic issues. The examination is called Analysis and Decision – both dimensions are tested.

A typical case study

10.6 CIM supplies the examination case in the form of an A4 booklet, printed on both sides of the page. You should make a working copy of the exam case for use in preparation.

10.7 For those students working towards an exam where an appendix can be taken into the exam, this advice is critical. You will only be allowed to take the original case study into the exam with you and this may be notated. You will want to leave it to the end of your preparation to add the most useful notes to your case study – so **work on a copy**.

10.8 Typically, the CIM diploma case will be 40 to 70 pages long. It will consist of 5 to 10 pages of text followed by appendices. The case study data is likely to include some or all of the following.

- Background and historical data on the company featured
- Corporate and group organisation
- Marketing and sales operations
- Strengths, weaknesses, opportunities and threats (indicative only)
- Market size, segments, competitors, trends
- Environmental factors
- Marketing mix
- Marketing research
- Consolidated accounts (profit and loss, balance sheet)

10.9 As is usual in most management case studies, the CIM case will:

- Include information which is not particularly useful
- Exclude data which you might feel is essential

10.10 This is to test your **ability to discern information needs** and also to design a marketing research plan and/or improvements to the marketing information system. You are likely to find some anomalies and contradictions in the case study, obliging you to make assumptions. Do not be distracted by these. This is usual and has never caused problems. In reality often it is difficult to obtain information, check its validity or comparability.

10.11 On the inside front cover of the case you will find **important notes** for candidates, followed by a page **candidate's brief**, which you must of course read thoroughly and have in mind when interpreting the subsequent data in the case itself.

11 Case study: technique and pitfalls

Practising case study technique

11.1 Nowhere is a lack of technique more likely to result in exam failure than when tackling case studies. The aim of a **practice case** is to give you the opportunity to:

(a) See the **whole process** of case study from beginning to end

(b) **Analyse the process** to **identify strengths and weaknesses** in your approach

(c) Consolidate your knowledge and understanding of other diploma syllabuses and practical marketing skills

Pitfalls to avoid

11.2 Avoid 'Analysis Paralysis'

In Chapter 1, we warned of the dangers of too much or too little analysis. We now want you to think about some other potential pitfalls.

11.3 Avoid 'wobbly' decisions

Remember the paper is strategic and the expectations are that managers can be focused on both the broader picture and implementation. Plans must be **integrated** and **consistent** to ensure that objectives and **recommendations do not conflict** with each other.

11.4 Avoid being a 'type'

(a) **The jumper** – knows the best solutions instantly and feels that developing and evaluating alternative solutions before making a choice menial and unnecessary. 'It's obvious' is the catch-phrase (delivered with thinly disguised scorn for those people who cannot see the obvious). Impatient and keen to finish the job in half the time.

(b) **The sitter** – finds it difficult to come to a decision and sits on the fence equivocating brilliantly on both sides. There is a tendency to forget that the subject they are being examined in is analysis and **decision.**

(c) **The Xerox** – with no strong views of his/her own and no real inclination to hard work, this person copies other people's ideas – unfortunately often those of the **jumper**. The

Xerox is caught out by the exam question, that puts a slightly different slant on the matter and blindly copies out his/her pre-prepared answer regardless.

(d) **The tree** – never sees the wood. Tends to receive the case and plunge into analysis of all tables etc with calculator smoking. Works hard and is extremely difficult to beat in discussion since he/she can bring more and more data to bear on the question, endlessly splitting hairs, crossing t's and dotting i's.

(e) **Blinkers** – sees things only from his/her narrow experience. Tends to have one textbook approach for each situation and will not listen to the views of others or any evidence that indicates a contrary view.

Recognise any traits? We all have our weaknesses: being able to recognise them is a great strength and can help you avoid some of the pitfalls of working the case study.

12 Exam technique

Additional information

12.1 Additional information is presented to students in the examination room. This is usually in the form of a memo or letter and usually gives information about either developments in the market place eg competitive information, or may inform you of a decision by management.

12.2 Sometimes the information decides a course of action for you, in which case you must be prepared to develop appropriate plans to deliver what has been decided. On other occasions the additional information leaves you to decide what course of action to take in light of the information.

Questions

12.3 Typically there have been three or four questions of unequal marks, requiring you to calculate how much time to allocate to each question. You must answer all questions and in sequence. In the past questions have included:

- Strategic marketing plans
- Promotional plans
- Recommendations on implementing a marketing orientation
- Segmentation
- Brand values and positioning
- International strategy development
- E-strategy development

Case study examination rules

12.4 Space will be at a premium, the desks are usually very small and wobbly!

12.5 Time allocation

This table shows how many minutes to allocate to each question in a three hour exam based on the number of marks per question. The time allocated marks **includes** planning and checking time. You will not be spending all this time writing.

Marks	Minutes
5	9
10	18
15	27
20	36
25	45
30	54
35	63
40	72
45	81
50	90
55	99
60	108
65	117
70	126
75	135
80	144
85	153
90	162
95	171
100	180

Going forward

12.6 In this *Tutorial Text* we are going to show you a number of case studies.

(a) Firstly, **Biocatalysts**, where we will take you step by step through the process of analysing case material and developing decisions. Biocatalysts is a particularly good teaching case as it **remains current** and stretches the **marketers who think they can throw money at problems**. The case will be used to introduce principal concepts and demonstrate key aspects of analysis. Remember the analysis given in examples is not exhaustive and is not the only way to conduct analysis.

(b) The remaining cases will bring you up to date with the latest case studies, provide further examples, give you the opportunity to practise further and allow you to see the variety of industries, companies and problems you will encounter. These cases also provide a reminder that in some industries short, medium and long term can be a matter of months while in others it can be years and that some companies have immediate short term problems while others face the challenge of a longer term vision for the future.

Part A: Introducing case study

12.7 There are a number of ways you can use the material in this *Tutorial Text*. The **least** effective is to simply turn the pages – reading other people's analysis will not give you the experience and practice you need when it comes to the exam.

You can work all the cases completely, using our analysis or comments as prompts and feedback: to do this thoroughly will take time and effort, but your reward will be increasing confidence and valuable marketing skills.

Between these two extremes are many variations. You can use Biocatalysts as a guided tour for you to see what is expected and then work the next case in depth.

Think about the time you have available and then use the material in the most appropriate way for you.

Action Programme review

1 *Knowledge check answers for planning and control issues*

1.1 The purpose of analysis is to establish the effectiveness of business performance in the environment in which it operates and the business's position in the market. This includes establishing internal strengths and weaknesses of the business and external opportunities and threats offered by market conditions, competition and customer behaviour.

1.2 The internal audit identifies the strengths and weaknesses of business activities. The components of the internal audit include evaluating the effectiveness of the business's structure, culture, financial performance, people (and management), business operations (processes and technology used), strategic purpose and planning and its market position. The external audit identifies the opportunities and threats in the business environment. The components of the external audit includes evaluating macro factors (PEST) and micro factors (competition, customers, suppliers, distribution etc).

1.3 Examples of models the marketer can use during the analysis process include:

- Product life cycle (PLC) – used to establish the stage of the product (eg introduction, growth, maturity, decline) and to provide indicators of investment needs and how the marketer should manage the product (eg heavy competition likely during maturity so differentiation important)

- Boston matrix (BCG) – used to evaluate products (and SBUs) for their cash generation and cash requirements. Helps the marketer make decisions about investing, harvesting

- Multifactor matrices – GE matrix used to evaluate business strengths and market attractiveness

- Porter's Five Forces – provides a framework for identifying the forces that affect the competitive structure of an industry and potential sources of profitability. The marketer is encouraged to consider new entrants into the market and barriers to entry, suppliers and supplier power, buyers and buyer power, potential or actual substitute products and possible unsatisfied needs.

1.4 The vision and mission statements are important communication statements that inform stakeholders of future intentions and the purpose of the business. The mission clarifies the purpose of the business by communicating what the business does, who for and how. The vision signals future aspirations, for example a future desired position in the market.

1.5 Planning gap analysis establishes the gap between the forecast of what the business can achieve if it carries on with its current strategies and performance in the predicted market conditions, and its desired corporate goals. The gap is the financial shortfall between forecast and target that will need to be filled by new and/or different strategies and performance.

1.6 The Ansoff matrix is a very useful model for identifying strategic options/business strategies. These are the broad product market opportunities identified during analysis. The GE matrix is one of the models that might be used to evaluate which options to select.

1.7 The best known theory on competitive position is Porter's generic competitive strategies. The positions are:

Cost leadership advantage: aims to achieve overall cost leadership being low cost provider requires:

- Cost and efficient objectives
- Tight cost and overhead control
- Pursuit of high value customers only
- Cost minimisation in all areas
- Achieving critical mass
- Achieving economies of scale

Implications

Usually requires high relative market share certainly requires volume
Possibly favourable access to raw materials
Investment up front and heavy investment in latest technology
Continued re-investment to maintain low cost leadership position

Differentiation advantage: aims to create unique offering (something perceived as different from rest) and requires:

- Design or brand image
- Technology
- Features
- Customer service
- Dealer network
- Combination of these to differentiate

Implications

Can preclude high market share if differentiation built on exclusivity
Balance between high costs of providing differentiation and profits
Need for professional marketing skills and ability to attract skilled people
Product engineering and capability in R and D, creativity/innovation
Needs corporate reputation for quality or technological expertise
Needs strong co-operation from channels
Needs strong co-ordination of R & D, marketing
Qualitative measurements

Focus advantage: aims to focus on needs of a particular buyer group, area of product line or geographic market and to do so more efficiently/effectively than competition. Requires:

- Cost leadership
- Differentiation, or
- Both the above

Implications

Vulnerability of niche approach
Doubts regarding profit potential
Implications as covered in cost and differentiation

1.8 Segmentation methods available to the marketer include:

Geographic: postcode, city, town, village, rural, coastal, county, region, country, continent, climate

Demographic: age, sex, family life cycle, family size, religion, income, occupation, ethnic origin, socio economic group

Behavioural: benefits sought, purchase behaviour, purchase occasion, usage

Psychographic: personality, attitude, lifestyle

Geodemographic: combines geographic and demographic **plus** overlay of psychographic **and** patterns of purchasing behaviour

Business to business: SIC codes, process or product, geographic, size of company, operating variables, circumstances, purchase methods; increasingly DMUs and behavioural factors are used

1.9 The Decision Making Unit (DMU) is the unit made of those people involved in the decision to buy. It is a model that has become most helpful in organisation buying (although also relevant in some consumer markets). It is important to marketers because it is a useful framework for ensuring that all members of the buying process are identified and their needs addressed.

1.10 Marketing research can help throughout the analysis, planning and control process.

Marketing research can help during **analysis** by gathering information that establishes the current situation. The business can establish its current position against competitors, customer perceptions and the likely impact of market forces.

Marketing research can help the **planning process** by ensuring decisions are informed. Decisions can be made on customer groups to serve, positioning and the development and design of the marketing mix to ensure efficient and effective use of resources.

Marketing research can help the **control process** in measuring business and marketing effectiveness and performance. This can be done using questionnaires, focus groups etc to ask customers, distribution channels and other stakeholders for their assessment of the business and its marketing mix.

1.11 The balanced scorecard refers to the linking of objective-setting to measuring performance and is a balance of both quantitative and qualitative measures. Customer feedback and input is an important part of measuring effectiveness as well as measuring business operations at a broader level. Measuring the effectiveness of the organisation in terms of its learning, innovation and continuous improvement is also important.

1.12 The key components of a marketing information systems are:

Marketing Information System MkIS

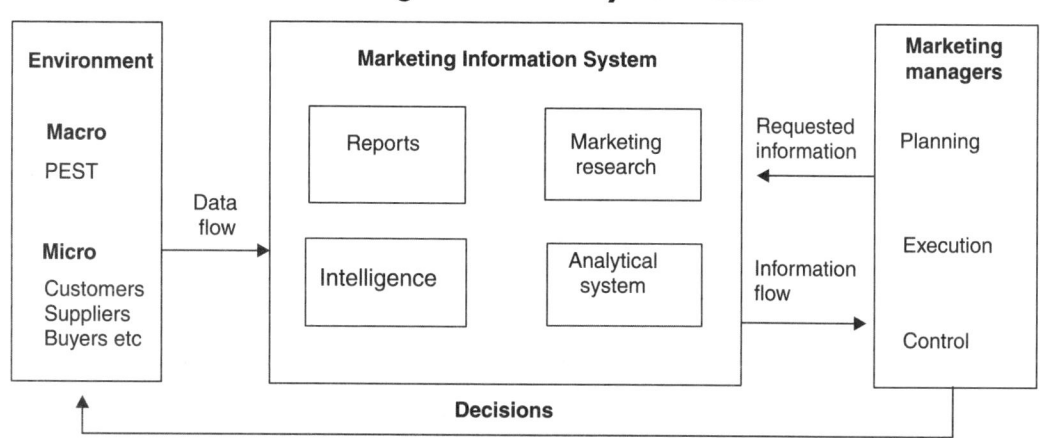

```
Environment          Marketing Information System         Marketing
                                                          managers
Macro
PEST              Reports         Marketing          Requested      Planning
                                  research          information
         Data flow →                              ←
Micro
Customers         Intelligence    Analytical       Information      Execution
Suppliers                         system           flow        →
Buyers etc
                                                                    Control
                            Decisions
```

2 Knowledge check answers for integrated communications issues

2.1 The external contexts that affect marketing communications include legislative, economic, societal, corporate responsibility, technology (information and communications).

2.2 Factors that affect customers' purchase decision making include segmentation factors (eg geographic, demographic, behavioural, psychographic), involvement with purchase (high or low involvement), decision making process, wants, needs and motives, attitudes and beliefs.

2.3 The decision making process (DMP) refers to the process consumers go through when deciding to buy. This process most typically, but not always, is:

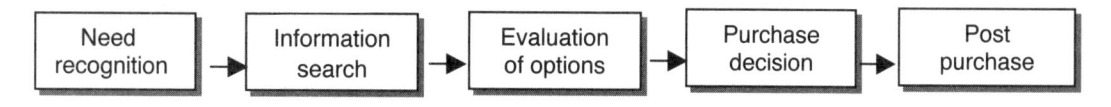

Need recognition → Information search → Evaluation of options → Purchase decision → Post purchase

2.4 Perceived risk involved in purchase decisions include performance, financial, physical, social, ego and time. Marketers can try to reduce perceived risk by providing information, building brand loyalty, guarantees, endorsements, money back/exchange and samples.

2.5 Internal factors that affect communications with an organisation's external audiences include corporate vision, mission and strategy, culture and ethics, management and leadership style, employee attitudes and behaviour.

2.6 Internal factors that influence corporate image and reputation include corporate personality (culture, attitudes, values and beliefs) and corporate identity (cues and signals that are real indicators evident in product, place, communications and behaviour).

Part A: Introducing case study

2.7 Some of the better known models for establishing communication objectives include:

STAGE	AIDA	ADOPTION	DAGMAR
			Unaware
COGNITIVE		Awareness	Awareness
	Attention		[Comprehension]
	Interest	Interest	
			Conviction
AFFECTIVE	Desire	Evaluation	
		Trial	
CONATIVE	Action	Adoption	Action

2.8 A brand is made up of tangible attributes: product components eg reliability, durability and measurable business and marketing mix, and performance e.g. accessibility of place, timeliness of messages. It is also made up of intangible attributes: the emotional values customers associate with the brand such as perceptions of reputation and trust, friendly and helpful staff. Brands are affected by corporate culture and behaviour, people's attitudes and behaviour as well as marketing mix performance.

2.9 Every purchase is a risk for the customer and they are looking for clues of what they can expect. A successful brand is a very effective way of reassuring customers of quality and reliability and of reducing risk. Providing the organisation continues to deliver what the customer wants and achieve high satisfaction levels, the brand can be very effective in building loyalty.

2.10 A push strategy is designed to encourage the organisation's channels or outlets to take products. A pull strategy is designed to attract customers into the organisation's channels or outlets. A profile strategy deals with the overall image and positioning of the company.

2.11 Marketers can change attitudes by changing beliefs, changing order of importance, changing attributes of product or service, changing associations, changing attitudes to comparable products.

2.12 Share of voice (SOV) refers to the total advertising spend in the market by all advertisers.

3 *Knowledge check answers for international marketing issues*

3.1 World Institutions that have helped to promote world trade are the World Trade Organisation, WTO; International Monetary Fund, IMF: World Bank, IBRD: United Nations Conference on Trade & Development, UNCTAD; Group of 8, G8; OECD.

3.2 A market agreement is a trading agreement between countries on the exchange goods and broader business operations. The types of agreements are free trade area, customs union, common market, economic union and political union.

3.3 An economic trading bloc is a group of countries that come together to form a trading area offering favourable conditions to member countries. Examples include APEC (Australia, Brunei, Canada, Chile, China, HK, Indonesia, Japan, South Korea, Malaysia, Mexico, New Zealand, Papua New Guinea, Philippines, Singapore, Taiwan, Thailand, US), Southern Common Market MerCoSur (Argentina, Brazil, Paraguay, Uruguay) as well as NAFTA, EU and ASEAN.

3.4 NIC stands for Newly Industrialised Country; LDC for Less Developed Country. They are examples of economic stages of development. Other terms include Advanced Industrialised Countries, Newly Emerging Economies, Big Emerging Economies.

3.5 Currents are primary macro forces affecting competition; cross currents are evolving trends driving international competition to behave differently.

3.6 Tariffs are rules, duties, rate schedules, regulations of trade. Examples include customs duties (% value of goods), preferential tariff (in certain circumstances eg historical preference arrangements), specific duty (amount per weight, volume etc), countervailing (additional duties levied to offset subsidies granted in exporting country) variable import levies (levies on imported goods costing less than domestic}, temporary surcharges) anti dumping regulations.

3.7 Harmonised tariff system (HTS) has been developed by importers and exporters to determine the correct classification number for product/service that will cross borders. With HT Schedule B export classification number is same as import number.

3.8 Extent to which language and communication is diffuse/implicit – high context [culture depends heavily on external environment, situation, non verbal behaviour in creating and interpreting communications] specific/explicit – low context [environment less important, non verbal behaviour often ignored, directness/bluntness valued, ambiguity disliked]). Example of a country with a high context culture is Japan and of a country with a low context culture is Switzerland.

3.9 Criticality dissonance refers to respondents transforming/disguising responses for fear of how responses will be used.

3.10 The process of internationalisation is when an organisation moves from indirect exporting to a global business, from being uninterested in exporting through to formulating long term strategies for international markets. An organisation might move through various stages including domestic marketing, experimental involvement, active involvement and finally to committed involvement.

3.11 Direct methods of entry include agents, distributors, licensing, franchise, JVs, SBAs, wholly owned subsidiaries.

3.12 Hofstede's four dimensions used to describe different national cultural characteristics are:

- Power distance – the extent of equality between management and subordinates
- Uncertainty avoidance – attitudes to risk and change
- Masculinity – traditional definition of sex roles
- Individualism – extent of recognition of the individual or the group

Part A: Introducing case study

4 Knowledge check answers for managing marketing performance

4.1 Power culture

- Information gathering processes are unlikely to be formalised and the informality may result in lack of connections between separate pieces of information being made
- There is unlikely to be formalised analysis of information allowing interpretation and objective evaluation
- There may be selectivity and filtering of information by those closest to the central figure if this information does not fit with desired ambitions regardless of outcomes

Role Culture

- Bureaucratic processes and systems would result in a lack of selectivity in information gathering
- Information gathered would tend to be over complicated and may involve many unnecessary procedures
- Information gathering would be a slow process and may result in information being out of date before its significance is recognised.

4.2
- Building the team
- Achieving the task
- Developing the individual

4.3
- *Autocratic*

  Advantage: decisive, get things done quickly

  Disadvantage: Employees lack motivation, commitment

- *Democratic*

  Advantage: Employees involved so motivated, committed

  Disadvantage: can slow down decision making, and action taking

- *Lassez faire*

  Advantage: Employees take responsibility for decisions, fully involved

  Disadvantage: Manager can lose control, can become chaotic

Most reliable sources of leadership power

- Respect and trust
- Teams

4.4 Key factors in designing a team

- Assessing team knowledge and skills – audit
- Deciding on structure of team – balance of functional (technical) skills and team role skills
- Ensuring team size is appropriate to the task and managing and controlling the team
- Functional roles
- Team roles

Key issues of managing teams through stages

Getting the team to performing stage as soon as possible.

- Forming – design introductions and activities that allow people to get to know each other quickly – focus on positive aspects
- Storming – allow differences to emerge, encourage people to deal openly with conflicts – focus on strengths people bring to the team
- Norming – formalisation of tasks and procedures/processes for carrying out work– focus on skills that are needed
- Performing – clarify objectives and tasks, planning and implementation – focus on performance and recognition for achievement of objectives and contribution to team effectiveness

4.5 *Symptoms of poor motivation*

- Absenteeism, possibly symptoms of stress
- Reduction in productivity and a refusal or reluctance to do anything except the minimum that has to be done
- Behaviour reflecting non co-operation, withdrawal, aggression or defensiveness
- Increasing complaints about work loads, routines and conditions and opposition to any new ideas, changes etc.
- Poor time keeping and a general sense of "it can wait"
- Increasing staff turnover

Causes of poor motivation include:

- Poor management – eg criticism, threats, lack of interest in employees
- Poor working conditions
- Poor pay – inequality in pay structures or bonuses
- Poor communications – lack of information, one way
- Poor training and development – people poorly equipped to carrying out their tasks and responsibilities
- Unreasonable targets and lack of explanation of expected standards

Three theories of motivation

Maslow's hierarchy of needs

A description of human needs that should be satisfied if people are to be happy and work productively. These needs are arranged in order of importance with the most basic needs physiological, security and safety being the most important and social, esteem and self fulfilment less important until basic needs are met. The hierarchy indicates that basic needs must be satisfied before other needs higher up the hierarchy become important and can be satisfied. If circumstances change and basic needs are under threat eg. changes in the work place or redundancy, the higher needs become less important again and lower needs become important and are defended.

Hertzberg's hygiene factors and motivators

- Hygiene factors are lower order needs which do not motivate but can cause dissatisfaction if they are missing or wrong eg salary, status, working conditions, working relationships, supervision, job security
- Motivators are higher order needs that do motivate but can only do so (or it is difficult for them to do so) if lower order needs are missing eg achievement, recognition, job interest, responsibility, advancement

McClelland's three motivation needs

- Need for achievement – being able to take responsibility for design and development that results in successful outcomes
- Need for power – to have control and influence over events and people
- Need for affiliation – to have relationships and belong

Vroom's theory of motivation

Expectancy theory – people are motivated by what they value and different people value different things. The reward must be easily understood and be perceived as of value to the person receiving the reward, so for example one person might be motivated by promotion, another by recognition for achievement. People will interpret the route to achieving the reward differently and therefore will put in the effort and performance they believe appropriate to achieving the reward.

McGregor's theory X and theory Y

- Theory X assumptions – people are lazy, untrustworthy and dislike work or responsibilities. They therefore require high levels of supervision and control and will be uninterested in the organisation or its activities.
- Theory Y assumptions – people are willing to work and interested in work and personal development and growth. They are prepared to take responsibility, are self disciplined and creative. They require minimal levels of supervision and control and should be encouraged to use their creativity in improving the organisation's performance

4.6
- Organisation culture – its values, beliefs and attitudes to people
- People – their attitudes to customers and what represents good customer service

You may also have included eg training, management skills, which are relevant and important, but customer service cannot be developed without the right culture and people.

What contributes to customer expectations being formed?

- The organisation's own activities which include promotional activities, product/service performance and reputation
- Other influences such as press coverage, customer's own experience and background (of the industry, other companies, products etc.)

4.7 The customer's chain of experience or moments of truth is the process the customer goes through when buying from an organisation. It involves the people and processes the customer comes in contact with and the nature of that contact. This process can be a poor or good experience.

4.8 Seven markets:
- Customers
- Referral markets
- Employees (internal)
- Distribution channels
- Suppliers
- Prospective employees
- Influence eg institutions such as financial, trade, education

4.9
- Shock and denial – difficulty in coming to terms with changes and refusal to accept what is happening
- There can be a danger of hopelessness and a feeling of being out of control
- Acceptance – providing they are supported
- Experimentation – to allow understanding and to build confidence
- Commitment – engaging in work routines again and focusing on goals

4.10 Internal markets need to be understood if resistance to change and perceptions of threats are to be minimised. Change can only be successful if the people responsible for managing and implementing change accept the change.

To understand these internal markets we need to understand how people perceive the intended changes and what affect it will have on them. Different people will be affected in different ways and if we know how they are affected we can set up support systems and training programmes that will help them come to terms with the change and take on their new tasks and responsibilities.

4.11
- Clear objective of the purpose of change
- Planning for change
- Communications – internal marketing
- Segmenting internal market
- Involving people – project and design teams
- Training and development
- Support systems

4.12 **Balanced scorecard –** Traditional measures have tended to focus on finances and volumes and draw on historical data to enable measurement to take place. The balanced scorecard goes beyond purely financial measures and attempts to evaluate, anticipate and inform the measurement process on current and future drivers of performance.

The balanced scorecard takes a far broader and more comprehensive approach to measurement and informing strategic development and embraces strategic as well as tactical performance.

- Customer – satisfaction, loyalty, value, complaints, repeat purchases
- Financial performance – Profitability, ROCE etc.
- Culture (innovation and learning) – NPD success, idea generation/transference into success
- People and management – staff morale, staff contribution to new ideas, staff turnover, absence,

It requires effective information systems, essential for measurement. The balanced scorecard objectives are derived from a top-down process driven by the mission, vision, corporate objectives and strategies, which are translated into tangible objectives and measures. The measures represent a balance between external measures for shareholders and customers, and internal measures of critical business processes, innovation, learning and growth. The measures are balanced between the outcome measures (past performance) and measures that drive future performance. The scorecard is balanced between objective easily-quantified outcome measures and subjective, somewhat-judgemental performance drivers of the outcome measures.

Part B

The Sample Case: Biocatalysts

The Process Case: the Ten Steps

Chapter Topic List	
1	The case study process
2	What we are trying to achieve? The output of the case process
3	Working the maxi case
4	Introducing the ten-step case process
5	Teamwork and the importance of your own work
6	Introducing the Biocatalysts case

1 The case study process

1.1 In the previous chapter, you checked your underpinning knowledge from the other diploma papers. This provides you with critical foundations on which you can build your case skills.

1.2 However, **knowledge** of planning and control is not enough to ensure a pass in this paper. You must **understand** the **process and techniques of case study** and have the practical **skills** to apply those recognised frameworks to the case scenario in a commercially credible way.

1.3 It is important that you recognise there are two aspects to the case or planning process:

(a) The stages that make up the process

(b) The outcomes of those stages recorded as decisions and actions in the planning document and supported by analysis

1.4 The stages you will go through will be familiar.

- Where are we now? analysis and auditing
- Where do we want to be? corporate decisions
- How are we going to get there? marketing decisions
- How do we ensure we arrive? control decisions

Part B: The sample case: Biocatalysts

> **Tutor Tip**
>
> *Planning to pass*
>
> Students reading this Tutorial Text will already have made the decision that they want to pass, and have taken a step in planning to do so. This is an important decision and while it may seem obvious, it is surprising how many students fail to acknowledge that passing the case study requires personal planning and considerable effort. The CIM diploma is not handed out to marketers who cannot demonstrate their marketing knowledge and skills.
>
> We have already identified for you the type of student that puts in lots of effort, working non stop up to the exam, developing detailed and fully written out plans in anticipation of the questions on the exam paper. These students are planning to fail.
>
> The diligent student must remember not to plan to fail.

2 What are we trying to achieve? The output of the case process

2.1 Professionally qualified and trained marketing managers can make a significant difference to an organisation, given a chance! In today's competitive environment, few organisations have the luxury of not needing marketing. Marketing is not just a matter of survival, and the challenge for marketers is to ensure their organisations are successful.

2.2 To do this requires using to the organisation's advantage the analytical and decision making skills we have been discussing.

2.3 Too often business success is measured by the bottom line: 'how much profit did we make this quarter'. It is short sighted, often short-term, and usually tactical. Sooner or later the lack of strategic perspective and customer focus will result in the organisation failing.

2.4 The desired outcome for business is success and this can be measured as profitability (in the broader sense if a non profit making organisation shareholder aspirations).

2.5 Success can be short-term survival, medium-term market development and/or long-term achievement of the vision. It should also be measured as:

- High customer satisfaction, value and loyalty
- High employee morale, productivity and loyalty
- Excellent and strong working partnerships with other stakeholders
- A strong and powerful brand
- A strong and distinct competitive position in the market
- Continued sustainable growth

2.6 The desired outcome of the case study process is the same but with an important additional goal, that of passing the exam.

2.7 Your goal is therefore to ensure you add value by **providing insights** into the current situation through your analysis and, through **effective decision making**, develop **credible** plans that will ensure organisation success. As has already been mentioned, exam technique is as important as your analysis and decision skills. The exam is your opportunity to demonstrate to the examiner your ability to communicate convincingly and persuasively.

2.8 To ensure you adopt a professional approach to working the case study process the following steps are recommended.

3 Working the maxi case

3.1 Tackling the case study requires a systematic and methodical approach. The amount of data you will be presented with provides you with ample opportunity to get lost. The skill you are required to demonstrate is that you can **sort**, **organise** and **analyse** this data, **disregarding** data that cannot help in the planning process and converting the rest into marketing intelligence that is useful for decision making purposes. (In other words, what good marketing professionals should be doing for their organisations.) One of the factors that separates successful managers and companies from the mediocre is their ability to gather, analyse and use information to inform decision making.

3.2 The case is first analysed to determine the **current situation**. Decisions that will solve problems and ensure success can then be made. Each stage of the planning process is covered by working the case study.

(a) **Where are we now?** Analysis tools and models are used to help establish current business performance and market conditions.

(b) **Where do we want to be?** Corporate decisions: tools and models are used to help determine future direction.

(c) **How can we get there?** Marketing decisions: further planning techniques and frameworks help to formulate marketing plans.

(d) **How can we ensure we arrive?** Control models and techniques are used to establish standards and measure and evaluate performance.

3.3 One of the difficulties experienced by many students, and by many marketing managers in their jobs, is that of knowing where to start and how to proceed. The following framework has proved to be a successful way of working the case study and ensuring a methodical and systematic approach that delivers results.

3.4 It is worth remembering that in reality a company does not stop what it is doing to start an audit. There is often a logical sequence of events but **many activities can and would be carried out simultaneously**. However, for simplicity, we will be describing the auditing process step by step.

3.5 We will give guidelines on how long each stage may take. These are guidelines only as everyone works at a different pace and each case study is different, but the guidelines will help give you some idea of the time you should allocate.

Part B: The sample case: Biocatalysts

4 Introducing the ten-step process

Ten-step process

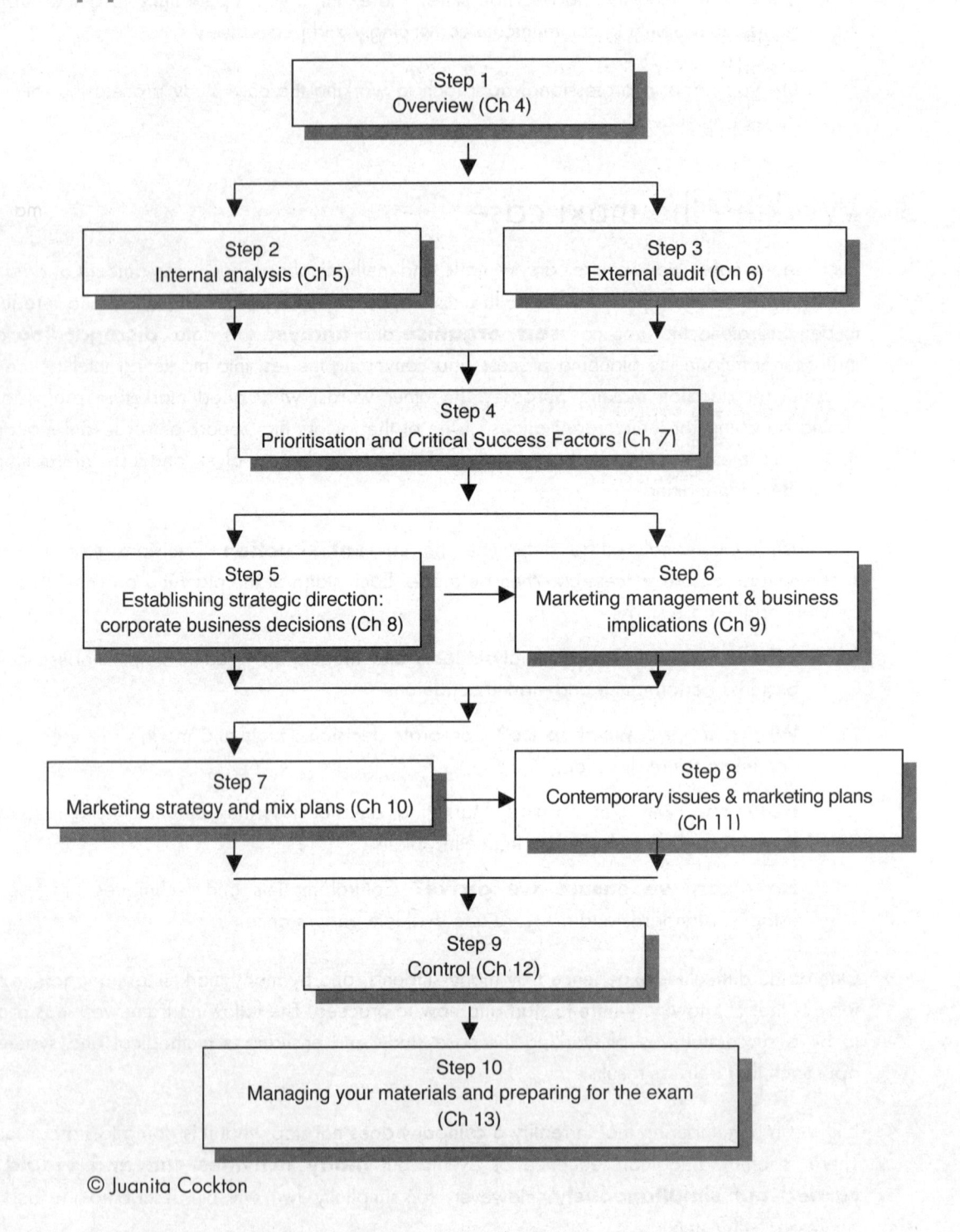

```
Step 1
Overview (Ch 4)
   │
   ├──────────────┬──────────────┐
   ▼                             ▼
Step 2                        Step 3
Internal analysis (Ch 5)      External audit (Ch 6)
   │                             │
   └──────────────┬──────────────┘
                  ▼
              Step 4
   Prioritisation and Critical Success Factors (Ch 7)
                  │
        ┌─────────┴─────────┐
        ▼                   ▼
     Step 5              Step 6
Establishing strategic    Marketing management & business
direction: corporate      implications (Ch 9)
business decisions (Ch 8)
        │                   │
        └─────────┬─────────┘
        ┌─────────┴─────────┐
        ▼                   ▼
     Step 7              Step 8
Marketing strategy and   Contemporary issues & marketing plans
mix plans (Ch 10)        (Ch 11)
        │                   │
        └─────────┬─────────┘
                  ▼
              Step 9
           Control (Ch 12)
                  │
                  ▼
              Step 10
   Managing your materials and preparing for the exam
                  (Ch 13)
```

© Juanita Cockton

Step 1. Overview

4.1 When you are ready to start work on the practice case study, wait until you have a quiet hour or two and **read it through once and put aside.** When you have more time, read through again and this time begin making notes.

(a) **Consider your focus: who are you, (position, responsibility) and what have you been asked to do?** You are getting into **role** and tackling the case study from the perspective of either an employee of the company or an external consultant to the company. This initial acknowledgement of your task is important. From time to time, when perhaps you are in one of those phases when you are overwhelmed by the case, you can return to your initial thoughts to focus you on the important issues.

(b) **Begin your marketing research shopping list** – start identifying information gaps. **Identifying information needs from the start is important**. You will add to this list throughout your working of the case study, but sometimes the obvious gaps you notice at the beginning can be forgotten as you start thinking of your information gaps in terms of the strategies you are developing.

(c) **Establish an overview of the industry you are operating in.** You may not work in this industry, and need to get a sense of what is going on. Experience shows that those who do work in the industry that the case study is set in are often more disadvantaged than those who do not because of the wealth of information they have. These people have to be very disciplined at staying within the case study and not allowing their knowledge to distract them from the scenario set.

(d) **Establish, broadly, the challenges facing the organisation.** At this stage you are not trying to identify every problem and challenge but rather impressions of what this organisation is doing. You will sort out the available information into themes or functional areas like sales information or competitor data.

> Step 1 will take you approximately 3 – 6 hours.

Step 2. Analysis: internal audit

4.2 Now the real work starts.

(a) From this point on, your analysis will be in **depth** and needs to produce results of value.

(b) The intention is to establish the **organisation's strengths and weaknesses**.

(i) The case material and appendices are analysed to determine, where possible, what the organisation is doing well and where it is under performing.

(ii) A structured approach ensures we do not miss anything out that could impact on current and future performance.

(iii) We will need to do this in detail for the marketing activity and then for the whole business. This requires the marketer to put on the hats of others in the organisation to review the financial, HR or operational dimensions of the business.

Step 3. Analysis: external audit

4.3 This step requires analysis of both the micro and macro external environments.

(a) **Micro**: The market, its dynamics, customers and competitors

(b) **Macro**: Analysis of the external environment provides insights into the macro factors affecting the business (eg PEST). We may have information on market conditions such as value of markets, stage of growth, maturity or decline or be left with no more than assumptions and impressions.

Part B: The sample case: Biocatalysts

> Steps 2 and 3 will take you approximately 23 – 33 hours. (It is difficult to break up the hours between the steps sometimes because of a lot of the information on the organisation is required for two or more steps. You may break some of this work down by sharing analysis with others if you are working in syndicate groups.

Step 4. Critical Success Factors (CSFs)

4.4 The danger of the analysis process is that you end up with long lists of strengths, weaknesses, opportunities and threats which, while useful, will not focus management on what needs to be done. Before moving on to decisions, the final stage of analysis is to **prioritise our findings**. There are models and techniques to help do this.

The conclusion of analysis will be to prioritise the factors that are critical to the organisation's success and implementation of plans. Each CSF will have key issues associated with it. Terminology varies between companies. You may have your own terminology.

> Step 4, a review of your analysis, prioritising and reaching conclusions, will take you approximately 1 – 2 hours. In case study, this step is particularly important as the case questions are often drawn from these critical success factors.

Step 5. Corporate/business decisions

4.5 We now move into the decision stage. From this point on, you are generating alternative solutions/ideas in **outline only**. You will not be developing fully written out plans.

(a) The future desired, and/or necessary, direction of the organisation is determined and expressed through a **vision** (if applicable) and the **mission statements**. **Corporate objectives** are set if none exist or clarified, and the planning gap established. These will have to be quantified.

(b) **Strategic options**, identified during analysis, are reviewed and criteria to evaluate them are developed. **Selected strategies must be able** to fill the identified gap.

(c) The strategic role of the **brand** and **competitive positioning** will need to be agreed.

> Step 5 will take you approximately 4 – 5 hours.

Step 6. Marketing management & implications

4.6 Often an important aspect of developing and implementing a new strategic direction is the organisation's **current business operations**. The plans may require a **change in, for example, organisational culture or structure.** There may be implications for managing the brand strategically or improving international management.

Management and leadership style, and the management of marketing teams, influence the way in which an organisation delivers value and satisfaction to stakeholders. They are part of the challenge of improving overall organisation performance.

Your internal analysis will have established what changes need to take place if the business is to succeed, for example adopting a marketing orientation, and at this stage you need to consider the issues.

> Step 6 will take you approximately 2 – 3 hours.

Step 7. Marketing strategy & marketing mix plans

4.7 When decisions on strategic direction have been finalised, and product market opportunities and competitive positioning have been agreed, decisions on **marketing objectives and strategy** can be agreed and developed. These decisions include **translating the business objective** into a **marketing objective**, segmenting markets identified, and selecting those segments the organisation should target, the positioning statement and targeting strategy. This work needs to be done for every selected business strategy.

Outline marketing mix plans (the 7Ps) are developed to implement marketing strategies. These plans must be consistent with the organisation's overall competitive positioning and help to differentiate the business in a meaningful way.

Marketing research needs are identified and an outline plan prepared. Again this is needed for each selected segment.

> Step 7 will take you approximately 6 – 8 hours.

Step 8. Contemporary issues and management plans

4.8 Each case study has its own specific issues, for example customer relationship management, supply chain management, brand building and so on. Most decisions, whether strategic or operational, will have an impact on the wider business and its management. Training in customer relationship management is an example. In Step 8, we identify what these issues are, then we develop outline plans or solutions to address them.

Step 9. Implementation and control

4.9 Plans are only of value if they are implemented, and thoughts about not only who must do what but how you will sell the strategy to senior manager colleagues and teams will earn you credit with the examiners.

Control is an important factor in successful marketing planning. It ensures we use our resources effectively and that plans will be delivered on time. Budgets, timetable of activities, targets and measurement all need to be considered and agreed.

> Step 9 will take you approximately 1 – 3 hours.

Step 10. Managing your material and preparing for exam

4.10 Review plan for consistency. Have the business, financial and human resource implications been considered and included? Is the plan consistent and integrated?

For your analysis and solutions to be sound, consistent and credible, you need to organise yourself to manage large amounts of paperwork. We provide tips on how you can organise your case materials and yourself. This will become your checklist to help you manage your case material.

> Step 10 will take you approximately 1 – 2 hours.

Part B: The sample case: Biocatalysts

> **Action Programme 1**
>
> Look ahead to when you are taking the exam. During the four weeks leading up to the exam, where are you going to find those 40 – 60 hours? Do a timetable and identify who you need to negotiate time with (employer, partner, friends etc). Log that time and protect it; it will be essential to passing. As you work through the practice cases, note how long each step takes and amend your time planner as appropriate.

5 Team work and the importance of your own work

5.1 All those sitting the case study are required to work the case study individually and 'own' the analysis and decision. There are of course tempting short cuts 'a quick read through will do it', someone else's analysis etc and these are usually a short cut to failure.

5.2 There are a number of problems in working the case study alone, all of which can be overcome. It is important to acknowledge these early on and have strategies for overcoming them. For example, a lack of confidence that you are interpreting material correctly or a personal weakness in some area – for marketers the favourite is financial! – are problems that can be resolved, and any good marketing professional will review and utilise appropriate resources available.

5.3 Some students of case study work in groups, either in colleges or companies.

   (a) There are obvious advantages of group work, particularly that of dealing with the quantity of work that will be generated. More importantly, if you have the advantage of working in a team, make sure you recognise and play to each others' strengths. In particular try not to duplicate effort. Work can be broken down between team members to make the most of the limited time available. Good communications, participation and support are vital ingredients for effective teams.

   (b) However you cannot abdicate responsibility for the analysis. You need to review work generated by others, understand it and agree with it. You cannot simply **use** it, as you will not be able to adapt your thinking in the light of extra information in the exam room.

5.4 Whilst it is perfectly acceptable to share analysis in this way, you cannot work together after you move onto decision making. The examiner does **not** want group answers, each student repeating the same mission and strategy.

5.5 If you do not have the advantage of a case study group, you can still 'recruit' help in the form of, for example, a marketing manager who develops marketing plans, a financial manager who understands ratios. Do not expect these people to do the job for you. The intention is to gain their support in helping you understand and interpret, or develop a new skill that will enable you to analyse the case material and arrive at credible solutions.

5.6 Particularly during the practice case, there will never be a better opportunity for you to experiment and learn by applying the theory in a practice case scenario.

6 Introducing the Biocatalysts case

Action Programme 2

To finish this chapter, we would like you to familiarise yourself with a typical CIM case – Biocatalysts.

You will need to find half an hour and some peace and quiet. You need to read through the narrative to get a feel for the case. This can be quite a quick read through, rather as you would a magazine article. **Do not** at this stage try and do anything with the material you are certainly not about to make any decisions at this stage. Treat it like a story. What is the setting, the business context? Who are the key players and what is happening?

Only read to page 16, the end of the narrative.

Tutor Tip

To make it easier for your to refer to the case material as we work though the next section, you may find it helpful to copy or remove the case pages so you have a separate case document to work on.

The Chartered Institute of marketing

Case Study
December 1999

Strategic Marketing Management: Analysis & Decision

Biocatalysts Ltd.

Part B: The sample case: Biocatalysts

Case Study – June 1999

Strategic Marketing Management: Analysis & Decision

Important Notes

The examiners will be marking your scripts on the basis of questions put to you in the examination room. Candidates are advised to pay particular attention to the *mark allocation on the examination paper and budget their time accordingly.*

Your role is outlined in the candidate's brief and you will be required to recommend clear courses of action.

You WILL NOT be awarded marks merely for analysis. This should have been undertaken before the examination day in preparation for meeting the specific tasks which will be specified in the examination paper.

Candidates are advised not to waste valuable time collecting unnecessary data. Although cases are based upon real world situations, facts have been deliberately altered or omitted. No useful purpose will therefore be served by contacting companies in this industry and candidates *are strictly instructed not to do so* as it would simply cause unnecessary confusion.

As in real life, anomalies will be found in this case situation. Please simply state your assumptions where necessary when answering questions. The CIM is not in a position to answer queries on case data. Candidates are tested on their overall understanding of the case and its key issues, not on minor details. There are no catch questions or hidden agendas. In addition, for this particular case, the CIM is not prepared to answer any scientific queries.

Additional information will be introduced in the examination paper itself which candidates must take into account when answering the questions set.

Acquaint yourself thoroughly with the Case Study and be prepared to follow closely the instructions given to you on the examination day. To answer examination questions effectively, candidates must adopt report format.

The copying of pre-prepared 'group' answers written by consultants/tutors is strictly forbidden and will be penalised by failure. The questions will demand analysis in the examination itself and individually composed answers are required in order to pass.

Candidate's Brief

You are Joseph Mendes, a Marketing Consultant of some repute, who has been appointed by Biocatalysts Ltd. to undertake the development of a marketing report, prior to undertaking a strategic exercise. Joseph's previous work ranged across many industry sectors, but he had not undertaken any work in the biotechnology sector. He is keen to understand the sector and the company profile before he develops any plans. As part of his internal and external research he has prepared the following report. At the end of this report are appendices relating to the main body of the text. Joseph has prepared this report for the Managing Director, Stewart North, ready for the next Board Meeting.

Important Notice

This case material is based on an actual organisation and existing market conditions. However, the information provided and some real data has been disguised to preserve commercial confidentiality.

Candidates are strictly instructed not to contact Biocatalysts Ltd. or other companies in the industry. Additional information will be provided at the time of the examination. Further copies may be obtained from The Chartered Institute of Marketing, Moor Hall, Cookham, Maidenhead, Berkshire, SL6 9QH, UK.

© The Chartered Institute of Marketing

> **Page 2 of Biocatalysts**

Report by Joseph Mendes
Private and Confidential

Biocatalysts Ltd.

Background Information

Biocatalysts Ltd. is an independent speciality enzyme company operating in the low-volume high-value end of the industrial enzyme market. Biocatalysts Ltd. started trading in 1986 as a wholly owned subsidiary of Grand Metropolitan. It occupies a large factory unit in Wales. Following a management buyout from Shell Ventures in 1991 it is now a totally independent company.

The company is one of the UK's leading developers and producers of speciality enzymes (natural proteins which act as catalysts). It produces enzymes in one of two ways. For the food and textile industries it produces speciality enzyme complexes complete with additional chemicals which are sold for moderate margins; for the diagnostic and pharmaceutical industries it has developed its own unique enzymes which it manufactures and sells at higher margins. The development costs of these higher margin manufactured enzymes are paid for by the profit and from Government/European grants which the company has so far been successful in obtaining.

Biocatalysts' customers use enzymes to improve the efficiency and convenience of processes in a wide range of industries, including flavour production, brewing, fruit processing, baking and textiles (enzyme fading of denim jeans). In addition, some of the higher value enzymes currently available and under development are used in diagnostic kits, used for testing for abnormalities in humans and pharmaceutical manufacturing. This broad spread of markets and wide geographical sales gives the company a balanced portfolio with steady, profitable income streams.

Enzyme Technology

Enzymes are nature's biological catalysts. They accelerate rates of reaction, helping the conversion of substances into other types of chemicals more useful for industrial processes. In the commercial arena, enzymes have two broad kinds of use: process aids and active ingredients. Enzymes have been used by mankind for at least 4,000 years in the form of natural microbial fermentations for making beer, wine, cheese and many other products. However, the recognition of enzymes as entities only began 170 years ago. In Germany, in 1830, a paper was first published which discussed the isolation of an enzyme which could convert starch to sugar. The substance is now known as amylase. By 1860, many other enzymes were recognised and isolated. Among these were pepsin, polyphenol oxidase, peroxidase and invertase.

Refined enzymes were first commercialised by a Danish chemist, Christian Hansen, who produced the first isolated preparation of rennet from dried calf stomach. It was primarily used for cheesemaking and the original company Danisco is currently a major supplier of enzymes for the dairy industry. In 1900, a Japanese scientist, Takamine, developed a fermentation for the industrial production of a fungal amylase for making soy sauce and other oriental seasonings. The Takamine laboratories are now part of CPC International. The early 1900s saw the development of a heat stable bacterial amylase in textile production, used for 'desizing', a process used to remove starch from fibres after completion of the weaving process. The use of this enzyme stopped the use of dilute acid in water which often damaged the textiles. Otto Rohm, a German chemist, developed the use of digestive enzymes for leather curing. Before this, dog and pigeon excrement was used for curing leather. The Rohm company is now a significant player in the enzyme business (see Appendix 1.).

After the Second World War, enzyme technology received a boost from developments which were taking place in the antibiotic field. The method of growing cultures in liquid media was adopted by the enzyme industry, increasing yields and lowering costs.

In essence, enzymes can be described as the catalysts of the living world. For example, enzymes are responsible for nearly all the metabolic processes taking place in the human body. These processes have been harnessed by industry so that a small amount of enzyme can enable a large scale chemical reaction to take place under very mild conditions. This increases the cost effectiveness of the production of a number of food and other products (see Appendix 2.). The enzymes are highly specific in their catalytic power and their ability to transform chemicals.

Part B: The sample case: Biocatalysts

Page 4 of Biocatalysts

World Market

The estimated sales of value of the sales of industrial enzymes was estimated to be in excess of $1 billion in 1994 – Figure 1. (about $1.3 billion in 1997). Sales growth is increasing in the more speciality applications sectors ('other' in pie chart) and tending to level out in the commodity sectors (Figure 2.). Technical research, however, continues to develop large volume enzymes for existing applications such as paper and pulp, textiles and in the longer term, waste treatment and environmental maintenance. Industry analysts (Enzymology, 1998), see the market for enzymes expanding from $1.7 billion to $2 billion by 2005. The Russian market is as yet undeveloped, owing to economic pressures, but could be large. The Chinese market is quite large, especially for food enzymes, but again this market is relatively 'closed' and full scale Western style processes have yet to be adopted.

Distribution of Enzyme Sales (1994)

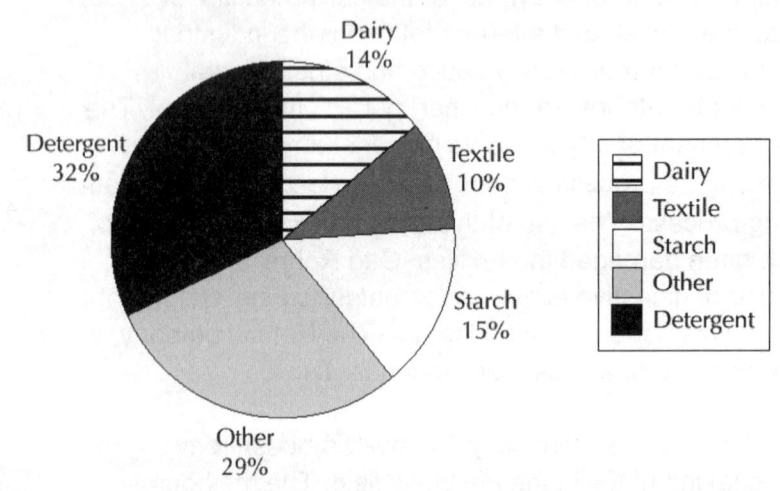

- Dairy 14%
- Textile 10%
- Starch 15%
- Other 29%
- Detergent 32%

Figure 1.

Forecast Distribution of Enzyme Sales (2005)

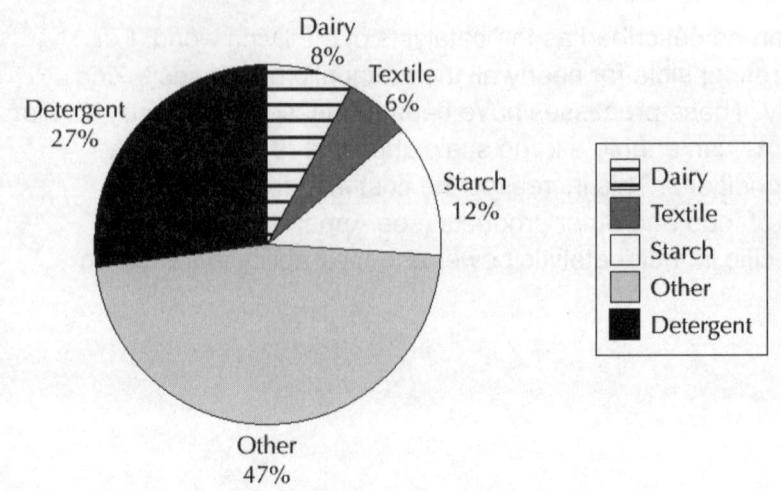

- Dairy 8%
- Textile 6%
- Starch 12%
- Other 47%
- Detergent 27%

Figure 2.

Page 5 of Biocatalysts

There are now approximately 12 major global producers, with increasingly distinct separate product ranges between them. This number of key producers helps to reduce total domination by any one of them. At the same time, it shows a trend towards a reduction in customer choice of producer for a particular enzyme type. Approximately another 60 companies produce substantial amounts of a smaller range, and there are around 400 companies producing industrial quantities of a very limited range of enzyme types. Essentially all these companies are selling into a global market. For many companies that are producing enzymes in 15-40m^3 fermenters, difficult decisions have to be made regarding economies of scale. For them it is a classic case of 'being stuck in the middle'. They will either have to expand their facilities (costly) to compete with the market leaders or specialise in niche markets where they may not have the requisite expertise (see Figure 3.).

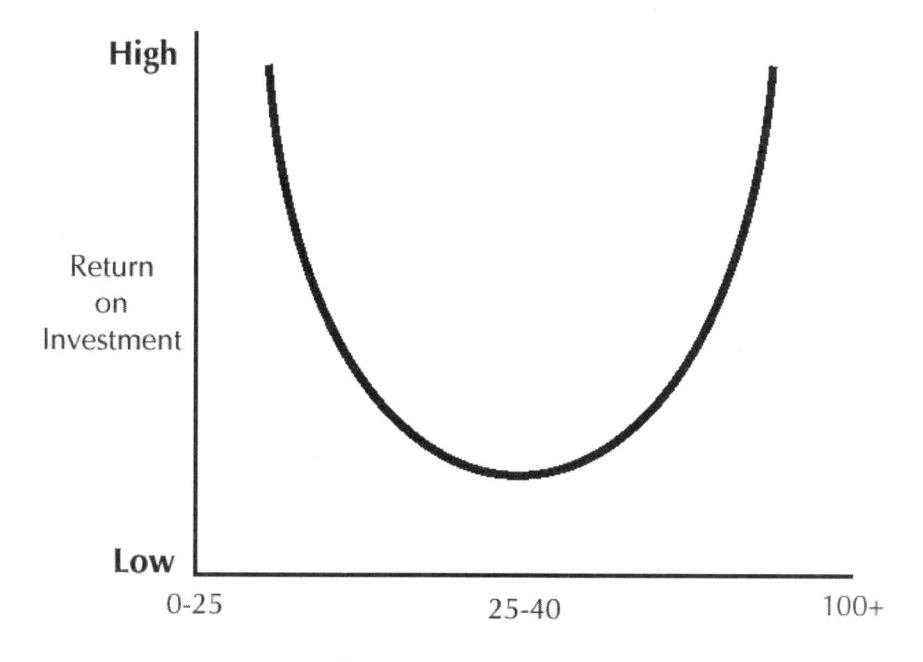

Figure 3.

M^3 Enzyme Production Capacity

The estimates show that nearly 60 per cent of the total world supply of enzymes is prepared in Europe, mainly within the European Community. Another 15 per cent is produced in North America, primarily 'in-house' for large scale application by large scale processors of natural materials, such as alcohol and sugar syrup. Numerous Japanese companies produce many, but not all, types of commercial enzyme, contributing another 12 to 15 per cent of the world production. The Russian and the Chinese markets probably use a wide variety of enzyme types for indigenous use, but are not yet active commercially. It is likely that their active entry into the market will expand the global market by a considerable degree.

Part B: The sample case: Biocatalysts

Page 6 of Biocatalysts

Enzyme Types and Sources

Proteinases are a very important enzyme type because of their enormous use in the dairy (coagulants) and detergent industries, and collectively they account for approximately 40 per cent of all enzyme sales. Carbohydrases which are used in baking, brewing, distilling, starch and textiles, form the second largest group. The conventional approach to the division of world sales of enzymes is to assess them by their sectoral applications (detergent, dairy, textiles, starch, and 'other') as shown in Figure 1. It is useful to examine the 'other' section as it helps to determine the possible composition of the future markets. Currently the 12 main sectors under the 'other' market are alcohol, animal feed, baking, chemical biotransformations, diagnostics, fats and oils, flavour, fruit and wine, leather, protein (other than for milk coagulation, flavour and detergents), pulp and paper and water. These are the sectors that Biocatalysts Ltd. mainly operates in. Growth in these areas is expected to be very rapid and the division of sales in the year 2005 will be very different from that portrayed in Figure 1. This 'other' sector is likely collectively to be the largest section of the enzyme market, accounting for over 47% of the sales. This sector is expected to exceed $500 million worth of sales by 2005, accounting for approximately 70% of the growth of all industrial enzymes.

Out of the original 30 common enzyme types used in 1983, the number used has doubled, owing to accelerated Research and Development in both universities and biotechnology companies. The advent of Genetic Engineering Techniques, (see Appendix 3. for an explanation) has created many opportunities for specific enzymes to be manufactured.

Enzyme Types

Microbial Enzymes

Most enzymes used in industrial processing are produced by the fermentation of micro-organisms (approximately 90%). Currently, the identity of the source microbe is very important in the assessment of permitted use for food processing in most countries. The use of genetically modified organisms in the production of enzymes means that these have to be approved by food agencies, as 'novel' foods are supposedly created. These then have to be tested differently for approval. All information has to be open and transparent. In many cases too, a new enzyme preparation is likely to have a different compositional spectrum from the one produced in the traditional manner, with differing side activities. It could be that critical components of the customer's process were not identified when GMOs (Genetically Modified Organisms) were used. In some cases some side activities may well be absent, even if critical. Therefore in any new development, the customer has to be kept aware of the changes. For instance, previously all insulin (for diabetics) originated from pigs, with an enzyme used to convert the insulin to human insulin. A by-product from this process was sold cheaply for leather curing. As a result of the use of biotechnology, 50% of human insulin is now produced directly by fermentation and does not contain the by-product enzyme. This has meant that the by-product, used in the leather industry, has now become the *main product,* increasing the costs of leather curing. The advent of the new technology has created considerable problems in that industry sector. Nonetheless, producers are using sophisticated purification and recovery techniques to build up stocks of enzymes. These stock levels can pose problems, depending on supply/demand situations. Production changes usually take 6 weeks to implement and different applications may need differing purity standards. For many bulk produced enzymes, such as the ones used in detergents, dairy, starch and textiles, the systems produce enzymes continuously and the prices are effectively half those of about ten years ago.

Plant Enzymes

These include proteases such as papain, bromelain and ficin, enzymes of cereals and soya beans and the more specialised enzymes from citrus fruits. Increased supplies of plant enzyme are very dependent on growth cycles, climate, new long-term suppliers and world political and agricultural policies. This area is particularly ripe for the use of GMOs. The shortage of papain in recent years has been a good example of these particular issues affecting this market.

Animal Enzymes

These include pancreatic, lipases and proteinases, pepsins, pregastric esterases and rennets. These can be produced as ultra-refined entities or in bulk. The supply and demand of these enzymes depends on food and agricultural policies which control the numbers of livestock available for slaughter. Owing to viral and other problems such as BSE[1], there is a need for potential purchasers to take considerable safety measures. Consumers too are becoming more aware of the end products they consume. Owing to this, companies are increasingly purchasing enzymes that have been produced microbially or through genetic engineering processes. There is also an increasing demand for producing kosher certified enzymes for food production (see Appendix 4.).

---

1 BSE stands for Bovine Spongiform Encephalopathy, passed on to humans through ingestion of beef products which contain the disease. Humans suffer Creutzfeldt-Jakob Disease (CJD), leading to brain deterioration and death. Currently in the UK no-one is sure of the extent or prevalence of this disease in the general population. It is possible that the disease is prevalent in many other developed countries.

Part B: The sample case: Biocatalysts

Page 8 of Biocatalysts

Factors Customers Need to Consider when Purchasing Enzymes for Industrial Processes

For companies purchasing enzymes, it is important that they get a clear indication of how specific the chemical reactions are, the optimum level of acidity or alkalinity (pH) at which the enzymes perform, and the temperature range of performance. Activators and inhibitors are also of vital importance, as certain food processes need enzymes to be 'switched off' at the end of a particular process. Currently research is directed at producing molecules which can do this safely in food production, as it can be difficult to 'switch off' enzymes easily (enzymes often catalyse reactions, and continue to be effective until another chemical which stops the reactivity is introduced). Customers need to have similar analytical techniques to those used by the suppliers, so that the strength of an enzyme is clearly understood by both parties. The other key factors which purchasers take into consideration are availability with consistency in quality and activity in a particular enzyme type, together with a track record for safety. A supplier who is prepared to disseminate information actively on new and current developments is not only educating the customer (and potential customers), but possibly offering new and better processing methods. Finally price is always an issue and suppliers are required to establish enzyme purity and activity levels which are consistent with the price set.

Bulk enzymes are being produced more and more from GMOs (Genetically Modified Organisms) mainly by two European companies and one US company, Gist Brocades, Novo Nordisk and Genencor. Japan is weak in bulk enzyme production but strong in speciality enzymes, particularly for medical diagnostics. Its exports of bulk enzymes to Europe and the USA are consequently relatively low, but beginning to grow. In the UK, Biocatalysts Ltd., Rhone-Poulenc, Biozyme and Genzyme (the last two, diagnostics only) are the manufacturers of speciality enzymes. The research leading to this method of production has cost millions of dollars, with much of the development work taking place in the 1980s. The costs of developing GMO production for new enzymes range from tens to hundreds of thousands of dollars. Many, but not all speciality enzymes will be produced increasingly by GMOs, and will be cheaper and purer.

Non-GMO trade is expected to continue for some time. There are certain food manufacturers who will not use GMO produced enzymes, owing to the 'bad' publicity received in general by GMOs (see Appendices 3. and 4.). 'Other' processes justify the need for the 'side' (extra) activities of bulk enzymes, made traditionally for efficient performance. GMO produced enzymes do not contain side activities which are usually vital for the optimum performance of enzymes within the food industry. Companies like Biocatalysts Ltd. are in the market to purchase these enzymes, from which they can reprocess some of the enzymes they need.

> **Page 9 of Biocatalysts**

Biocatalysts' Place in the Enzyme Industry

Biocatalysts Ltd. is rather special in that it offers a full technical service to present and potential customers, including giving clients access to a database of non-competing enzymes available commercially. As part of this service, Biocatalysts Ltd. offers valid cost comparisons between products whose performance is measured on different scales, as there is no internationally accepted scale. Enzymes, for instance, can be produced in different strengths, offering different levels of activity.

The pricing ranges reflect these differences; however, consumers may only be aware of prices and not strength and efficacy. In this sense, Biocatalysts Ltd. attempts to provide a high level of technical support to its customers. Biocatalysts Ltd. sells its products (see Appendix 9.) into the following markets:

Food

Many parts of the food industry use enzymes, mainly as processing aids. Examples include baking, brewing, protein modification, fruit processing and flavour production. Most bulk enzymes, as produced by the big manufacturers, are usable in many food processes but are not optimum for each particular process. Biocatalysts Ltd. specialises in producing optimum performing products for the food industry, which outperform (in function and price) the competing bulk enzymes. Examples of this are specific enzymes for apple and pear juice extraction, as opposed to using just one enzyme for both types of fruit.

Textiles

Most stone washed denim jeans are now enzyme washed. This is almost a commodity business, where a small percentage of a large market can be readily picked up by supplying special blends of enzymes and chemicals that produce specific types of styles of faded jeans. As faded jeans are going out of fashion, this is not seen as a long-term business, but this sector generates very useful short-term margins.

Part B: The sample case: Biocatalysts

Page 10 of Biocatalysts

Diagnostics

All babies born in developed countries are tested for a genetic disorder, PKU (phenylketonurea). A test involving the Biocatalysts enzyme Phenylalanine Dehydrogenase can be undertaken in minutes, replacing a slow labour-intensive method of detecting phenylalanine in the blood. Twenty-four million tests are done every year. Biocatalysts Ltd. is the only producer of this enzyme. Quanatase and ICN have received FDA (Food and Drug Administration) approval in the USA for this system. This means that the growth will now be very rapid over the next few years. The margins are good in this area. Customers are often tied into this market as, once a kit has been approved, they are very loath to change any of the components.

Market Breakdown of Sales for 1997 for Biocatalysts Ltd.

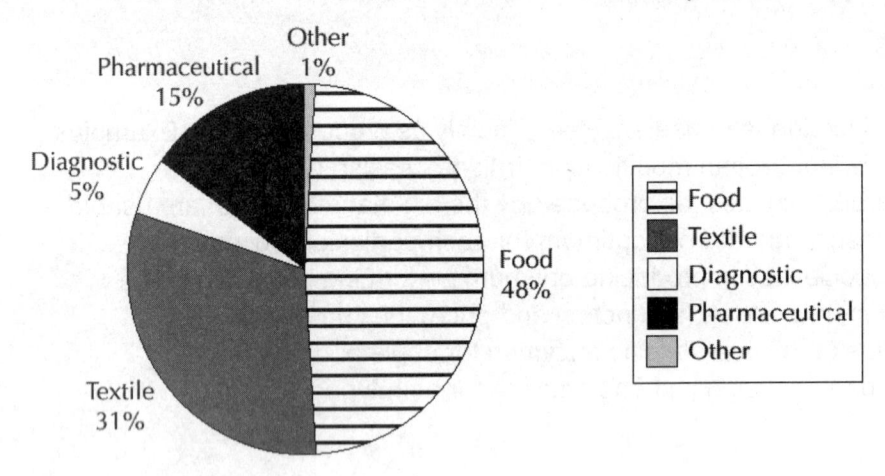

- Food 48%
- Textile 31%
- Pharmaceutical 15%
- Diagnostic 5%
- Other 1%

Figure 4.

Biocatalysts Ltd. Geographical Sales for 1997

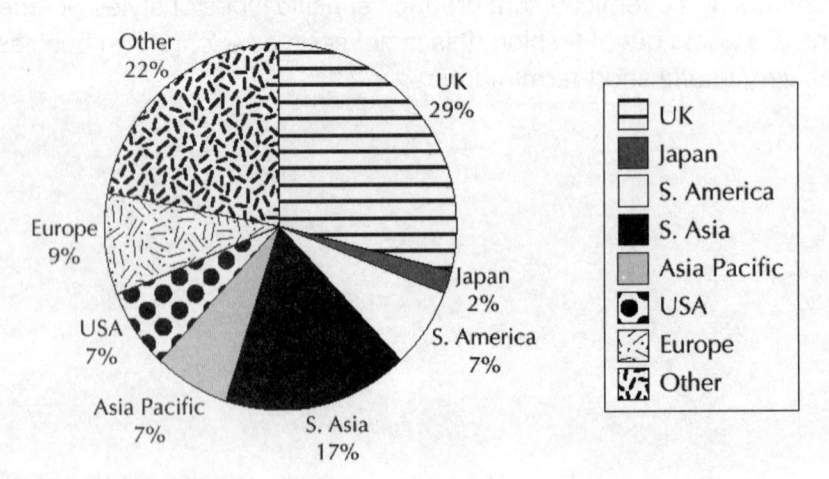

- UK 29%
- Other 22%
- S. Asia 17%
- Europe 9%
- USA 7%
- Asia Pacific 7%
- S. America 7%
- Japan 2%

Figure 5.

Figures 4. and 5. show the market and geographical breakdown of the main areas of sales for Biocatalysts Ltd.

> **Page 11 of Biocatalysts**

Customer Focus

Biocatalysts Ltd is unique amongst the world's enzyme companies. Its willingness to supply custom-tailored products for its clients means that the whole company focus is directed towards customers, attempting to provide total customer satisfaction. This customer focus has resulted in Biocatalysts Ltd. growing at more than twice the industry average over the past ten years. The company has many exclusive agreements with blue-chip companies around the world, who value the product and technical services that Biocatalysts Ltd. provides. Small- and medium-sized companies are also offered a competing range of services. Biocatalysts Ltd. does not make or sell high-volume commodity enzymes, such as those used in the detergent or starch processing industries. They operate in selected parts of the enzyme market where their technical support and willingness to work with customers on a one-to-one basis is highly valued. These enzyme sectors usually require, not single enzyme entities, but enzyme complexes, where the ratios of each of the components are crucial to the efficacy of the whole enzyme product and the customer's process. Biocatalysts Ltd. does not believe in the customers 'making do' with compromise enzyme products, just because that is the way they came off the fermenter. In order to be more customer focused, the fermentation for the manufacture of Biocatalysts is sub-contracted out. This allows for more flexibility and a focus on investment on enzyme technology, not in capital intensive massive stainless steel vats for large batches of production.

Research and Development

Much of the Research and Development programme is focused on the development of new enzymes and enzyme complexes, mainly identified by the customers. New application ideas and opportunities for the current range of blended enzymes are identified from contacts with clients. The development of these is mainly handled by technical sales staff (see Appendix 5.). Sales of current products (or variants of current products) for these new applications, accounts for much of the short-term growth in sales. Biocatalysts Ltd. has many allegiances with leading UK universities, where most of the basic research into new enzymes is carried out (see Figure 6.). This allows the company to focus its in-house scientists on the needs of its customers and keeping fully up-to-date with the latest developments in bio-research.

Part B: The sample case: Biocatalysts

Page 12 of Biocatalysts

R&D Cycle/Sales Cycle

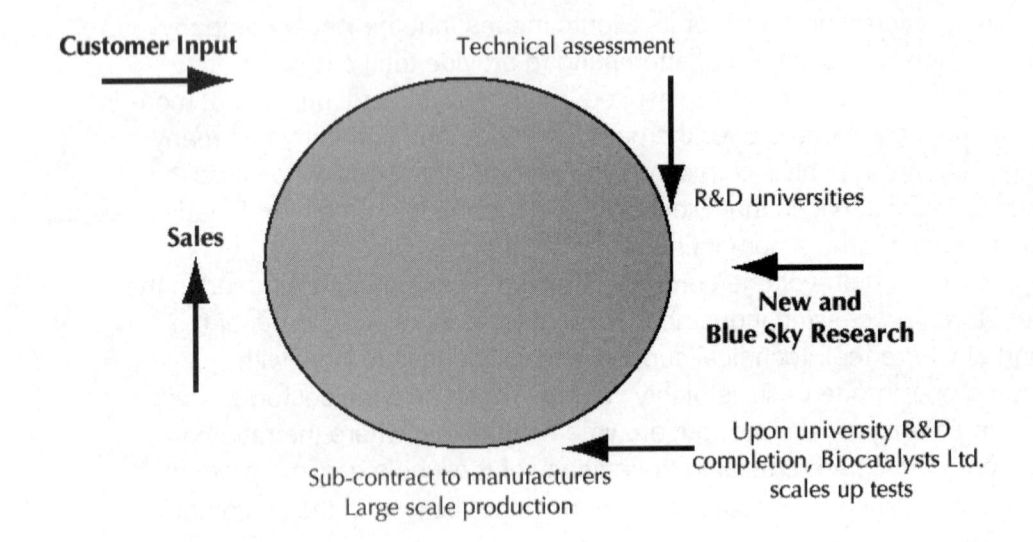

- Customer Input
- Technical assessment
- R&D universities
- New and Blue Sky Research
- Upon university R&D completion, Biocatalysts Ltd. scales up tests
- Sub-contract to manufacturers Large scale production
- Sales

Production

The production plant and laboratory take up around 8,000 square feet of a modern factory unit. The plant includes equipment for liquid and powder blending, fermentation (small scale) and filtration and pilot chromatographic purification and drying. Large scale fermentation is contracted out. The intention of the company is to continue sub-contracting fermentation as there is general over-capacity in the marketplace and to continue investing in downstream processing equipment. Additional investment of around £1 million would be needed to carry out all fermentation in-house, covering all the volume forecasts for the next five years.

The laboratory has all the necessary technical equipment, which is fully depreciated and can still function for at least a further five years. Quality control tests are carried out in-house on all incoming materials and finished products. The company has received the ISO 9000[2] accreditation. The factory is not fully utilised and it is estimated that sales could double with small additions to the existing plant and by employing one or two more production personnel. Batch sizes are flexible and most stock is kept as raw materials or work in progress to maximise flexibility.

---

2   ISO 9000 stands for Quality Accreditation of processes and products on a worldwide basis.

> **Page 13 of Biocatalysts**

Marketing

The sales and marketing for the company is carried out by 5 people (see organisation chart in Appendix 5.), including the Managing Director. This team looks at the possibilities for new product development and sets out the long-term strategy for the company. The three active sales staff are either home or office based and they spend 80 per cent of their time on sales. The products are sold all around the world and 70 per cent of the products are exported. Most of the exports are generated by agents or distributors who often carry a range of imported products in their portfolio. Biocatalysts Ltd. has a presence in 35 countries. The sales team in the UK supports the agents in the other countries. Agents are used extensively by Biocatalysts Ltd. as their products can be classified as mainly being business to business. The use of agents is not without its problems, as in many cases the range of products offered by Biocatalysts Ltd. may form just a small amount of a particular agent's product portfolio. Unlike selling other products, the agents in the enzyme business need constant updating. The biggest issue facing the company therefore is the quality of the agents and the way they undertake sales. For example, Biocatalysts Ltd. has an enzyme for olive oil processing, so that yields can be increased. In Italy, there are numerous family farms with small olive oil processors. In this instance the agent needs to know something about that sector and also needs to 'educate' the farmers. In order to improve the sales focus, the company is now looking to recruit an agent who actually sells olive oil processing equipment to the farmers. Biocatalysts Ltd. produces a newsletter every six months. This is sent to all its distributors and customers and helps to update them on the current Research and Development activities of the company and any further developments in their current products.

As price is often an issue with many buyers, it is important to Biocatalysts Ltd. that it has the following factors in place:

a. The right agent, i.e. an agent who understands the different sectors well.

b. An agent who is working efficiently and effectively.

c. That the agent is selling the 'right' product.

> **Page 14 of Biocatalysts**

The last issue of selling the 'right' product is very important, as enzymes come in differing strengths, and often customers may choose one brand over another simply on price, without realising the efficacy of the product(s). The agents are on a 5 per cent commission. Agents are a useful way of expanding the market, but Biocatalysts Ltd. is aware that there is no substitute for having its own sales marketing staff in the marketplace. However, the sales need to take off considerably before the company can justify recruiting another marketer. Most agents are difficult to control and the company relies a lot on their market research and knowledge of country specific issues. Agents mainly carry a range of products which they sell into different markets. Their motivation is often financial and they are therefore more willing to sell products which may offer greater returns. In many cases, they may not be adept at gauging incipient markets in enzymes. Currently therefore the quality of the agents is clearly an issue. Each year the company pays for all its agents to come for a few days' training sessions at the company headquarters. However, not all the agents attend these sessions. The training is particularly important as the markets have narrowed and niche markets require a greater degree of customer focus.

Marketing Issues

Targeting

It is important that Biocatalysts Ltd. develops a marketing strategy for the new products it introduces into the marketplace. One particular strategy could be the way in which innovators are targeted and then followed through with the early adopters. This strategy requires a sustained and expensive marketing effort. The other way in which markets could be opened up would be to bring in a big end-user from the outset, so that application trials could be carried out on an exclusive basis. This would probably mean lower margins, but guaranteed sales and income. More generally exhibitions and mailshots play an important part in the company's targeting strategy. The exhibitions also provide a forum for discussion for the agents. Targeting users is important if marketing effort is not to be dissipated. In order to target effectively, a considerable amount of market research needs to be undertaken for each country. This is costly and difficult, as the statistics and secondary information for many countries can be quite poor.

Web Site

Many biotechnology based companies offer excellent web sites which are both educational and interactive. Currently Biocatalysts Ltd. does not have a web site (but it does have an email address) and is looking to develop a fully interactive site, which can be used for both the agents as well as potential and existing customers. An added benefit would also be good links with its suppliers and the university R&D teams, providing them with updates on product availability, trialling results and scale-up problems or successes. However, the development of such a site will need resourcing and ongoing commitment with regular updating.

Pricing

Enzymes usually form a small part of most customers' product costs. The reliability of the product and service from the supplier is usually more important to customers than finding the cheapest source. In addition, alternative enzyme supplies cannot be identified from paper cost studies. The only way to find out whether an enzyme works and if it is cost-effective is to undertake a trial production run. If potential cost savings are small, many food manufacturers will be unwilling to do the test runs. Pricing therefore can be complex and needs to be customised according to the needs of the customers' product and process costs.

The Future

Food is arguably the most important product of consumption for the average person. Food is vital for sustaining life. At the same time it can be, certainly in well-developed economies and the wealthier sections of communities in most countries, a significant symbol of culture and refinement. The marketing of GMOs presents a new challenge in marketing communications. Currently many companies producing GMOs advertise discreetly. However, many companies, such as Monsanto, have created a very powerful web site devoted to the subject. There are many arguments about risks and benefits to the consumer and the need for open debate, whereas many pressure groups such as Friends of the Earth question the ethics of the production of GMOs in general. The whole debate is now out in the open and many newspaper articles are devoted to the subject. Given the sensitive nature of food and the adverse publicity generated by the BSE crisis, it is important to consider in a rational manner the main communication and advertising strategies that GMO producers could possibly adopt. In this respect Biocatalysts Ltd. has been open in its discussions on the subject (see Appendix 3.). In some instances, GMOs are likely to have positive benefits for the consumer, especially in the production of rennet or porcine based enzymes which would then be granted 'kosher' status as they are not animal derived (see Appendix 4.). This would then provide Biocatalysts Ltd. with a positive positioning strategy in niche markets. Most companies in this sector are likely to be considering effective ways of developing their communications strategies, so that the customers and downline consumers have a clear and rational picture of the issues involved.

Page 16 of Biocatalysts

Summary

Biocatalysts Ltd. has a range of different business markets with a 'near commodity' business in textiles, which needs little or no R&D. The 'New Technology' business is mainly in the food market and represents 50 per cent of the sales (see Figure 4.). The diagnostics (hi-tech) side of the business accounts for 10 per cent of the sales, but the margins are above average, as high development costs have to be met. The company is growing at 20 per cent per annum at a conservative estimate (see Appendix 6.). Biocatalysts Ltd. is generally quite well prepared for the advent of the Euro (see Appendix 7.). It is clear that there is considerable market potential within the enzyme industry; however, the advent of new genetic engineering techniques and the growth of new applications create their own marketing problems. Biocatalysts Ltd. has to consider how well it can grow into being an important, but respected, niche player in the marketplace.

> 3 ♦ The process case: the ten steps

Page 17 of Biocatalysts

Appendix 1.

Some Competitor Profiles

As described in the text, the enzyme business is quite complex and fragmented; nonetheless it is useful to consider some of the other companies in the business.

Some Suppliers of Enzymes for Biocatalysts Ltd.

Supplier	Country	Supplier	Country
Alko	Finland	Grinsted Products	Denmark
Amano Int.	Japan (UK)	Kyowa Hakko Europe	Germany
Biocatalysts Ltd.	UK	Larbus S. A.	Spain
Biopole	France	Meito Sangyo	Japan
Biocon (part of ICI Quest)	Ireland	Miles Laboratories	USA
Biozyme	UK	**Novo Nordisk**	**Denmark**
Boehringer	Germany	Oriental Yeast	Japan
Boll	France	Recordati	Italy
Calbiochem	USA	Rohm	Germany
Cultor	Finland	Rhone-Poulenc-ABM Brewing	France
Dafa S. A.	France	SAF-ISIS	France
E. Merck	Germany	Sigma Chemicals	USA
Fluka	Switzerland	Solvay Enzymes GmbH	Germany
Genencor International	**USA (Finland)**	Stern Enzymes GmbH	Germany
Genzyme	USA (UK)	Toyo Jozo	Japan
Girona S. A.	Spain	Viobin Corporation	USA
Gist Brocades	**The Netherlands**	Worthington	USA

Despite many companies producing enzymes, the market as a whole is dominated by three major suppliers: Novo Nordisk (50% of the world enzyme sales) with Gist Brocades and Genencor International having substantial market shares (together around 25%).

Japanese Companies

The Japanese companies tend to be complex with the enzyme business 'hidden' amongst the general shareholding. Also it is worth remembering that a lot of Japanese enzyme production is food related and is produced by 'surface' fermentation, giving poorer yields than their European counterparts.

Part B: The sample case: Biocatalysts

Page 18 of Biocatalysts

Nagase & Co. Ltd.

Figures for 1997	US Dollars
Net Sales (Total Trading Transactions)	4,608,766
Dyestuffs	414,301
Chemicals	1,714,671
Plastics	1,590,662
Electronic systems and materials	745,078
Healthcare and others	144,054
Net income	45,839
Net income per share	0.30
At Year End:	
Total assets	2,664,674
Shareholders' equity	958,217

Nagase has a subsidiary which is called Nagase Biochemical Sales Co. Ltd.

Amano Pharmaceuticals Co. Ltd.

With subsidiaries in Europe (Amano Enzymes Europe Ltd., Milton Keynes, UK) and the USA (Amano Enzyme USA Co. Ltd., Lombard, Illinois).

The company calls itself the 'World No. 1 Speciality Enzyme Producer Founded in 1899'. The company also produces Kosher certified enzymes.

Employees: 420, Products: 400, Patents: 50, Turnover: $92m.

Amano Sales Breakdown

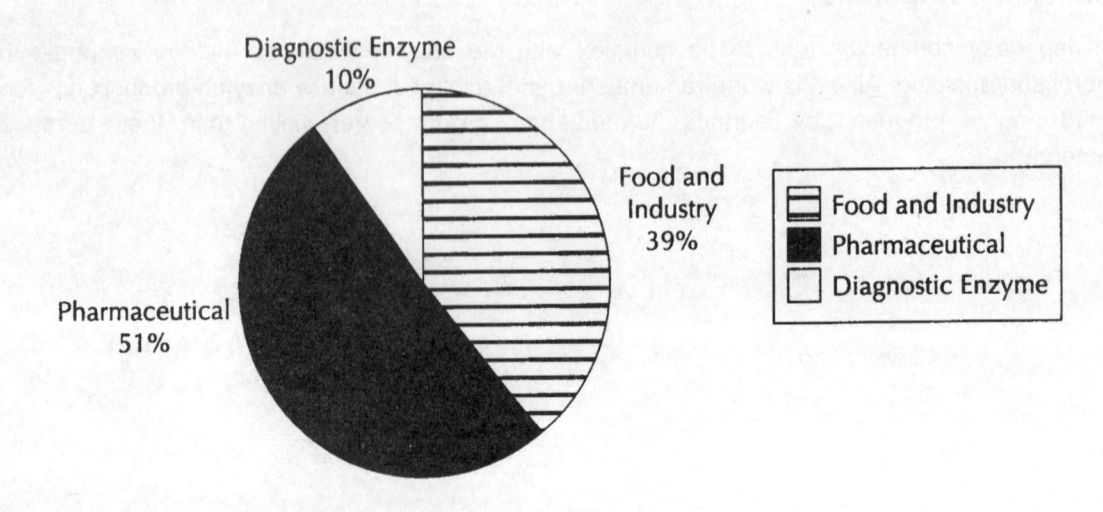

- Pharmaceutical 51%
- Food and Industry 39%
- Diagnostic Enzyme 10%

> Page 19 of Biocatalysts

Pharmaceutical Enzyme Area

Business Unit	Products
Digestive Enzymes	Regular type (Amylase, Protease, Lipase, Cellulase), Speciality type (Lactase, α-Galactosidase).
Anti-inflammation	Microbial protease (Crystalline protease).
Chiral Synthesis	Lipase, Esterase.
Others	OTC Medicines.

Food Industry Enzyme Area

Amano is focused on the production of speciality enzymes, with worldwide acceptance for food processing.

Business Unit	Application
Baking	Bread, Crackers.
Protein Hydrolysis	Flavour, Functionality, Dietary needs,
Fats/Oils	Hypo-allergenicity.
Starch Processing	Flavour, Functionality.
Brewing	Glucose, Maltose, Maltotriose, Isomaltose
	Oligosaccharides, Cyclodextrin.
	Japanese Sake Wine, Beer, Spirits.

The diagnostic area is growing and Amano are actively seeking new enzymes to improve the effective detection of diseases.

Tests	Items
Substrate determination	Glucose, Cholesterol, Triglyceride, Bilirubin, Free fatty acids, Others. (Used for health checks and individuals with cholesterol problems).

Key European and US Based Companies

Rohm

Produces high quality enzymes for baking and other food uses.

Danisco

Established since 1872. Food ingredients, sweeteners. Sales DKK 25 billion.

Part B: The sample case: Biocatalysts

> **Page 20 of Biocatalysts**

Novo Nordisk

Novo Nordisk's two core business areas are healthcare and enzymes. Novo Nordisk has about half of the world market for industrial enzymes. The enzyme business employs 3,000 people worldwide.

Key Strengths

A large company with a good R&D facility; internationally based with regional and local business development centres. The regional centres are based as follows:

Europe, Middle East and Africa	Paris, France
North America	Franklinton, NC, USA
Latin America	Curitiba, Brazil
Asia Pacific	Hong Kong, China

These RBDCs ensure that markets receive customer service matched to their own specific regional characteristics. They give Novo Nordisk the flexibility to adapt to local conditions and needs.

Financial Statement for the First Nine Months of 1998 (Unaudited)

	1998	1997	% Change
Net turnover	2,053	1,938	6
Operating income	422	346	22
Net financials	16	15	6
Income before tax	438	361	21
Tax	153	131	17
Net income	285	230	24
Employees at end of period	14,770	13,916	6
Earnings per share of DKK 10	3.82	3.09	24

Report on Enzyme Business (EB) Alone

EB sales rose by 1% in the first nine months of 1998. The modest sales increase is due in particular to a decrease in sales of technical enzymes. The market for industrial enzymes continues to be negatively affected by two factors. Firstly the situation in Asia has hit sales of industrial enzymes harder than previously expected and, as a result, sales in the region, including the textile area, are approximately 13% lower than in the same period last year. Around half of the decrease is due to weaker currency exchange rates in the region. Secondly, the value of the market for enzymes for the textile industry has decreased significantly as a result of a considerable decline in the number of blue jeans sales towards darker garments. Sales to the textile industry are thus 38% lower than last year. Exclusive of sales to Asia and to the textile industry, enzyme sales in the first nine months of 1998 increased 7% compared with the same period last year.

Page 21 of Biocatalysts

Against this background, the world market for industrial enzymes in 1998 is now expected to remain at the same level as in 1997. This also applies to Novo Nordisk's sales of industrial enzymes. It is anticipated that the financial impact of the reduced sales expectations will be countered by outgoing productivity improvements and cost-cutting measures in EB.

Biozyme

Established in 1971. The company is based in the UK and the USA.

Genzyme

This company is one of the oldest in biotechnology and was formed in 1981. The company is based in Cambridge, Massachusetts. It is mainly a healthcare company with much of the enzyme production developed for tissue repairs, therapeutics, surgical use and diagnostic tests. For the first nine months of 1998 its turnover was around $490 million. The revenues reflected higher sales of Ceredase and Cerezyme enzymes.

Gist Brocades

This company has worldwide operations, but the headquarters are in the Netherlands. The company is the world's largest antibiotics manufacturer within the pharmaceuticals sector. In the food market it offers baking, cheese and yoghurt making, brewing and fruit juice processing. Flavours and flavouring are another growth area. The company also produces enzymes for the animal feed industry, so that pigs and poultry can digest their foods better. Gist Brocades is very active in the growth markets of Asia and Latin America. The company is very active on the patent front. It employs 7,000 people in 70 locations, in more than 25 countries. Three quarters of all employees are based outside the Netherlands.

Genencor International

The company is based in the USA. It is the world's largest company dedicated exclusively to industrial biotechnology; through its new genetic engineering techniques, it develops and markets enzymes and biocatalysts. The company has hundreds of successful products, with more than 1,200 worldwide patents. The company has a $60 million facility in Stanford, California. Genencor International revolutionised industrial biotechnology with the world's first industrial-scale recombinant enzyme, and the world's first protein engineered industrial enzyme. These innovations introduced state-of-the-art genetic engineering techniques into the industry.

Appendix 2.

Major Industrial Enzyme Types and their Applications

Enzyme	Application
α-Amylase	Corn syrup, baking, textile sizing, paper sizing, fuel alcohol, detergents, lens cleaners.
β-Amylase (Malt)	Beer, fuel alcohol, starch, production of maltose.
D-amino oxidase	Purification of L-amino acids.
Glucoamylase	Corn syrup, fuel alcohol.
Catalase	Egg desugaring, fruit and vegetable conservation.
Cellulase	Wine, beer, fruit juice.
Glucose isomerase	High-fructose corn syrup.
Glucose oxidase	Egg desugaring, oxygen scavenging, fruit conservation.
Invertase	Invert sugar.
Lactase	Dairy.
Lipase	Cheese.
Amyglycosidase	Starch, conversion of dextrin to glucose.
Proteinase	Protein (milk), production of peptone (soya bean), pre-treatment of soy sauce.
Papain, Proteases	Protein in beer, removal of turbidity, tenderising meat, cheese and flavour production.
Rennin (chymosin), Rennet	Casein, production of cheese.
Pectinase	Pectin, production of fruit juice, wine, beer, coffee.
Triacylglycerol lipase	Lipid, hydrolysis of lipid, flavour modification, cheese ripening, fat degradation.
Penicillin acylase	Semisynthetic Penicillin based antibiotics.
Pregrastric esterase	Cheese, butter flavour.
Protease	Detergents, lens cleaners.
Trypsin	Leather tanning.
β-Fructofuranosidase	Sucrose, production of inverted sugar.
β-Galactosidase	Lactose, decomposition of lactose.
α-Galactosidase	Raffinose, decomposition of raffinose.
Anthocyanase	Anthocyan, decolouration of anthocyan.
AMP deaminase	Adenylic acid, production of L-amino acid.
Aminoacylase	D, L-Acyl amino acid, production of L-amino acid.
Lysozyme	Egg white, against chlostridia in cheesemaking.
Lactase	Yeast, production of lactic acid, decomposition of whey.
Invertase	Sucrose, dethickening in chocolate.

Many industrial enzymes have multiple applications, as it makes good business sense to extend the utility of a product to as many applications as possible. This helps to increase sales and reduces the risk of having only a few customers. For example, alpha-amylase (α-amylase) is used in corn syrup manufacture, baking, textile sizing, fuel alcohol production, and an alkaline type, alpha-amylase, is used in detergents and lens cleaners.

Microbial Enzymes Legally used in Food Processing in the USA

Amyloglucosidase from *Rhizopuis juveus*	Degradation of gelatinised starch into constituent sugars, in the production of distilled spirits and vinegar.
Carbohydrase from *Aspergillus ginger*	a. Removal of visceral mass (bellies) in clam processing. b. Aid in the removal of shell in shrimp processing.
Carbohydrase from *Rhizopus, oryzae*	Production of dextrose from starch.
Catalase from *Micrococcus lysodeiktus*	Destruction and removal of hydrogen peroxides in the manufacture of cheese.
Esterase (lipase) from Mucor miehei	Flavour enhancer in cheeses, fats and oils and milk products.
α-Galactosidase from *Mortierella vinaceae* (free enzyme and mycelia) (var. raffinoseutilizer)	Production of sucrose from sugar beets, by addition as mycelia pellets to the molasses to increase the yield of sucrose, followed by the removal of the spent mycellial pellets by filtration.
Microbial Milk-clotting Enzymes from *Endothia parasitica bacillus cereus Mucor pusillus (var. Lindt) Mucor miehei (var. Cooney et emerson)*	Production of cheese if the enzyme was obtained from a pure culture fermentation.

> **Page 24 of Biocatalysts**

Appendix 3.

Genetically Modified Organisms

Genetically Modified Organisms (GMOs) are increasingly being used for production. There are many reasons for this, but some of them are:

- The production of purer enzyme products.
- Shorter development times for new enzymes.
- Reduced usage of energy and raw materials for production, giving reduced production costs.

In some countries, such as Germany, there has been a large negative reaction to GMOs. From a scientific point of view, there are no reasons for this negative response to GMOs for enzyme production.

The actual enzyme itself is identical whether it is produced by a wild-type organism or a GMO, although the end product will contain less impurities. In addition, enzyme end products do not contain any of the production organism, so the consumer is not exposed in any way to the GMO.

At the moment Biocatalysts Ltd. does not manufacture any of its enzyme products from GMOs, although it has several new enzymes under development which will be produced from GMOs. The first enzyme produced from a GMO is expected to be launched in 1999. These new enzymes will need special literature and a clear policy for communications.

The use of GMOs for enzyme production appears to offer many benefits; they are safe and efficient to use, and pose no threat to the environment or the end consumer. The end-user should be fully informed and promotional literature should clearly state if the production organism is a GMO.

Page 25 of Biocatalysts

Diagram to Show how GMOs are Made:

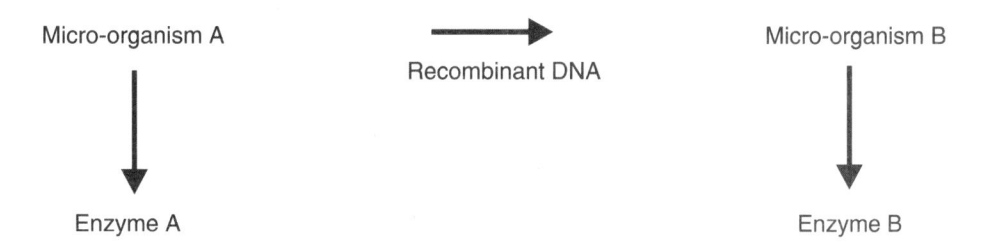

Micro-organism A → Recombinant DNA → Micro-organism B

↓ ↓

Enzyme A   Enzyme B

A Typical Genetic Engineering Sequence

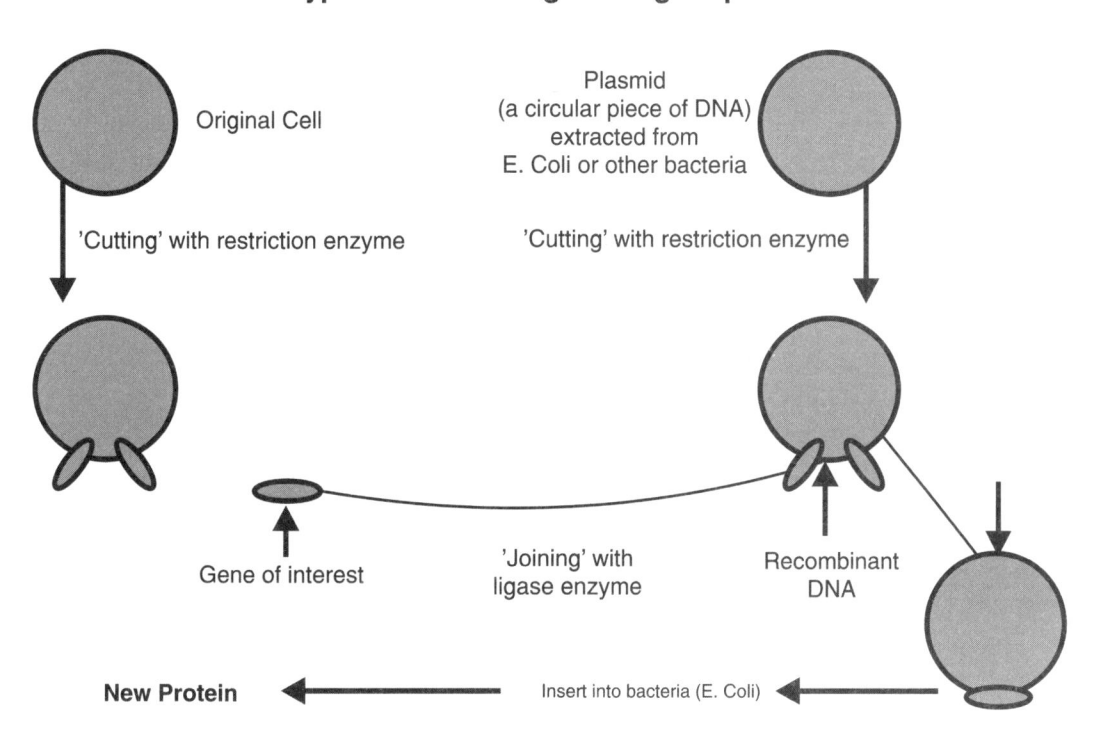

Original Cell

Plasmid (a circular piece of DNA) extracted from E. Coli or other bacteria

'Cutting' with restriction enzyme   'Cutting' with restriction enzyme

Gene of interest — 'Joining' with ligase enzyme — Recombinant DNA

New Protein ← Insert into bacteria (E. Coli) ←

One trait of living matter is the presence of genes which give a particular set of individual characteristics. Most genes are composed of DNA – deoxyribonucleic acid – which has a highly complex structure, consisting of the amino acids adenine, cytosine, guanine and thiamine, together with carbohydrate and phosphate groups, arranged in the pattern of a double helix. It is now possible to extract a fragment of DNA from one living micro-organism (e.g. plant cell or bacterial culture) to a second micro-organism, thus altering the genetic properties of the second micro-organism. Popularly this process is known as 'genetic engineering'; a technically more accurate term is 'recombinant DNA research'.

The new altered micro-organism would naturally possess different characteristics and, more importantly, different enzymatic properties. The way in which this is achieved is shown above.

Part B: The sample case: Biocatalysts

Page 26 of Biocatalysts

FINANCIAL TIMES WEEKEND FEBRUARY 13/FEBRUARY 14 1999

COMMENT & ANALYSIS

An uncontrolled experiment

Concern is growing over genetically modified food, write Clive Cookson and Vanessa Houlder

Might genetically modified foods become the next mad-cow crisis? Plants with altered genes are already pervasive in the food chain (see below). The view of mainstream scientists is clear: genetically modified foods that have been approved for human consumption are extremely unlikely to damage your health.

But the scientific wisdom was just as clear 10 years ago about mad-cow disease: the risk of BSE infecting people was negligible. The few maverick scientists who warned that the infection might cross the species barrier from cattle to people were attacked as irresponsible and received little attention. Unfortunately, they have turned out to be right.

The spectre of BSE haunts the current debate over genetic foods. Again, the vast majority of scientists pooh-pooh the view that eating genetically modified crops could pose any threat.

But this time consumer groups and politicians are listening to the minority who claim that added genes and the proteins they produce could pose a danger both to the environment and to human health.

"BSE has made people in Europe very sensitive to new technologies in the food supply industry, and very wary of scientists and government attempts to reassure them," says John Durant, professor of public understanding of science at Imperial College, London.

"It could be that the price of the BSE fiasco will be even greater outside the beef industry than inside it, if it makes the European public resist GM crops."

Public concern intensified yesterday after 20 international scientists signed a memorandum in support of controversial research that showed rats fed with an experimental kind of genetically modified potato suffered damage to their immune systems and changes to the size of their livers, hearts and brains.

Some of the findings were rapidly disowned by the Rowett Research Institute in Aberdeen, the institute where the work was carried out. It described the presentation of the work as "misleading" and asked Arpad Pusztai, the scientist involved, to retire.

The scientists who this week rallied round Dr Pusztai say his concerns are justified. Stanley Ewen, a pathologist at Aberdeen University medical school, says the work might even have disturbing implications for modified crops already in use, such as maize. Vivyan Howard, toxicopathologist at Liverpool University, says the growth retardation seen in young rats at the Rowett has serious implications, since underweight babies might show behavioural problems.

The researchers challenge the adequacy of the existing regulatory system in the UK and, by extension, the rest of the world. Dr Howard says: "The regulatory process needs to be more thorough, more objective and to ask the right questions." He and other scientists are calling for a moratorium on the use of genetically modified foods.

However, the fact is that such concerns remain those of a minority. Other scientists vigorously defend the existing system which, they say, involves detailed, case-by-case studies including feeding trials where necessary.

Professor Derek Burke, a biologist and former chairman of the UK government's advisory committee on novel foods, is "absolutely confident" about the safeguards in the existing system. The suggestion that the findings have any implications for existing GM crops is "absolute rubbish", he says. There was never any question that the particular genetic modification in the Rowett experiment - the potato contained a toxin - would enter the human food chain.

Lastly, he claims, the British regulatory system is more safety-conscious than that of the US.

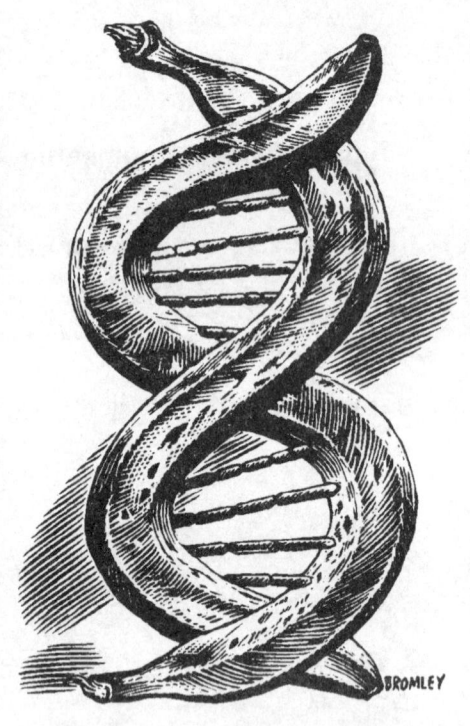

"On medicine and drugs we are more relaxed. On food it is the other way round. It's a different attitude to risk."

One reason why the Europeans may be risk-averse is widespread ignorance both of how much genetically modified food there is and what has been done to the plants. While genetically modified plants are restricted in Europe to experimental field trials, commercial crops are marching across the fields of North and South America and east Asia, facing little consumer or political resistance. The total area planted worldwide has risen from 2.8m hectares in 1996 to 12.8m hectares in 1997 and an estimated 30m hectares last year.

Soya and maize are leading the way. The main modifications introduced so far enable plants either to kill insect pests or to resist a specific herbicide (so the farmer can spray the field with it to kill all the weeds without harming the crop).

Apart from the uncertainty over the facts, another barrier to public acceptance has arisen: all the benefits so far seem to have accrued to the farmers and the companies supplying them, while all the risks are born by consumers and the environment. More obvious public benefits – such as improved food qualities and gigantic improvements in productivity – remain promises.

Large-scale public surveys, such as those conducted by Prof Durant at Imperial College with George Gaskell at the London School of Economics, consistently show far more consumer opposition to genetically modified food in Europe than in North America. But the contrary is true of medical biotechnology; more Americans than Europeans express opposition to genetic testing. "We should avoid the stereotyped view that Americans are gung-ho about new technology and Europeans are not," Prof Durant says.

Besides BSE, which has not affected the US, he cites the very different views of agriculture on opposite sides of the Atlantic. "When Europeans think of wildlife and the rural environment, they think of farmland, and for them GM technology appears to be the next step in an unwelcome intensification of agriculture," he says. "Americans, in contrast, think of the wilderness areas in their national parks; they regard their farmland as part of the industrial system."

Whether the European concern or the American enthusiasm for crop engineering is more justified may not become clear for decades. Dr Howard says it will be extremely difficult to monitor the public for ill effects from GM food.

"Maybe, after 20 to 30 years, things might come to the fore," he says. "But you won't have any unexposed population against which to measure it. It is an uncontrolled experiment."

A fridge full of modified genes

John Willman reports on what vegetables, fruits and foods life science groups have altered

A wide variety of genetically modified crops has been developed by the leading life sciences groups, ranging from potatoes and cauliflowers to lettuces and raspberries. They offer benefits such as better insect resistance, tolerance to chemical spray, better nutritional content and longer shelf lives after harvesting.

Only four are in use in the UK food industry and two of these have relatively restricted applications.

One is the genetically modified enzyme used to make vegetarian cheese, replacing rennet which is extracted from calves' stomachs. It is now increasingly used in making hard cheeses for general consumption.

The second is the genetically modified tomatoes used to make tomato paste. These tomatoes are less likely to rot on the plant and remain firmer after picking, producing a higher yield when turned into purée. As a result, the paste is cheaper and – according to Safeway, the supermarket chain – scores higher in consumer taste tests.

The other two are soyabeans and maize, both of which largely originate from the US. They are used much more widely – and in the case of soya increasingly hard to find in a non-modified form.

Soya is an ingredient in many products, including cakes and biscuits, chilled foods and vegetarian textured meat products as well as soya sauce and cooking oil. It is used in about 60 per cent of processed foods, though in some cases in very small quantities.

Most of the soya used in the UK comes from the US where genetically modified crops made up about a third of the harvest last year and the share is rising rapidly. Bulk shipments routinely mix modified and non-modified, and any food product that may contain modified ingredients must be labelled as such in Europe.

Maize is also used as a basic ingredient in many food and drink products, including breakfast cereals, crisps and snacks, petfood and processed foods. It is also a source of fructose used in soft drinks and confectionery. Europe is able to produce much of its maize needs so it is easier to keep genetically modified grain out of the UK food chain.

Under EU rules, a food using any genetically modified ingredient must be labelled accordingly. The only exception is derivatives of soya that contain none of the protein – such as oil.

The real question, however, is whether food manufacturers always know whether GM ingredients are in their products. One food company – which does not want to be identified – found traces of genetic modification in 14 out of 20 products it believed to be GM-free.

Genetically modified products

Ingredient	Used in
Enzymes to replace animal rennet	Vegetarian cheese and other cheeses
Tomatoes	Tomato paste
Soya	Chilled foods, cakes and biscuits, vegetarian textured meat products, processed foods
Maize	Crisps and snacks, cereals, pet food, processed foods

> Page 27 of Biocatalysts

Appendix 4.

Vegetarian Enzyme Modified Cheese

Important changes in the dairy industry over the last ten years or so, have seen a significant move away from animal derived enzymes, such as calf stomach rennet, used in cheese manufacture, to microbially derived rennets. A similar, but more recent move has also occurred in the production of cheese derived flavour ingredients, such as Enzyme Modified Cheese (EMC) – an important and growing sector of the flavours market. The move away from animal derived products allows the cheeses and EMCs to be offered with both vegetarian, and kosher status – important and growing niche markets in the food industry.

Extra impetus has been given by recent concerns over possible BSE and swine fever transmissions. Many food and flavour suppliers are now starting to look for non-animal alternatives. However, much processed cheese is still made containing EMC, manufactured with animal derived enzymes. It is now generally agreed that there is a pronounced change occurring in the demand for EMC with vegetarian (and kosher) status, requiring the use of microbially derived enzymes in its manufacture. Of course, EMC is not only used in processed cheese but can be found as a flavour ingredient in a rapidly expanding selection of cheese flavoured snacks and convenience foods. It is even used in some pet foods!

Biocatalysts Ltd. is at the forefront of these changes, especially in EMC production. Whilst Biocatalysts Ltd. offers the conventional animal derived enzymes, it has always specialised in microbially derived enzyme products for vegetarian and kosher status EMC. Biocatalysts Ltd. offers a comprehensive range of well-developed formulations for a variety of cheese flavours, and has an active R&D programme for the introduction of new, microbially derived enzymes for new flavours. Biocatalysts Ltd. also offers a unique tailor-made formulation service if a customer has specific requirements that standard products do not fully satisfy.

Page 28 of Biocatalysts

Appendix 5.

Biocatalysts Ltd. Organisation Chart

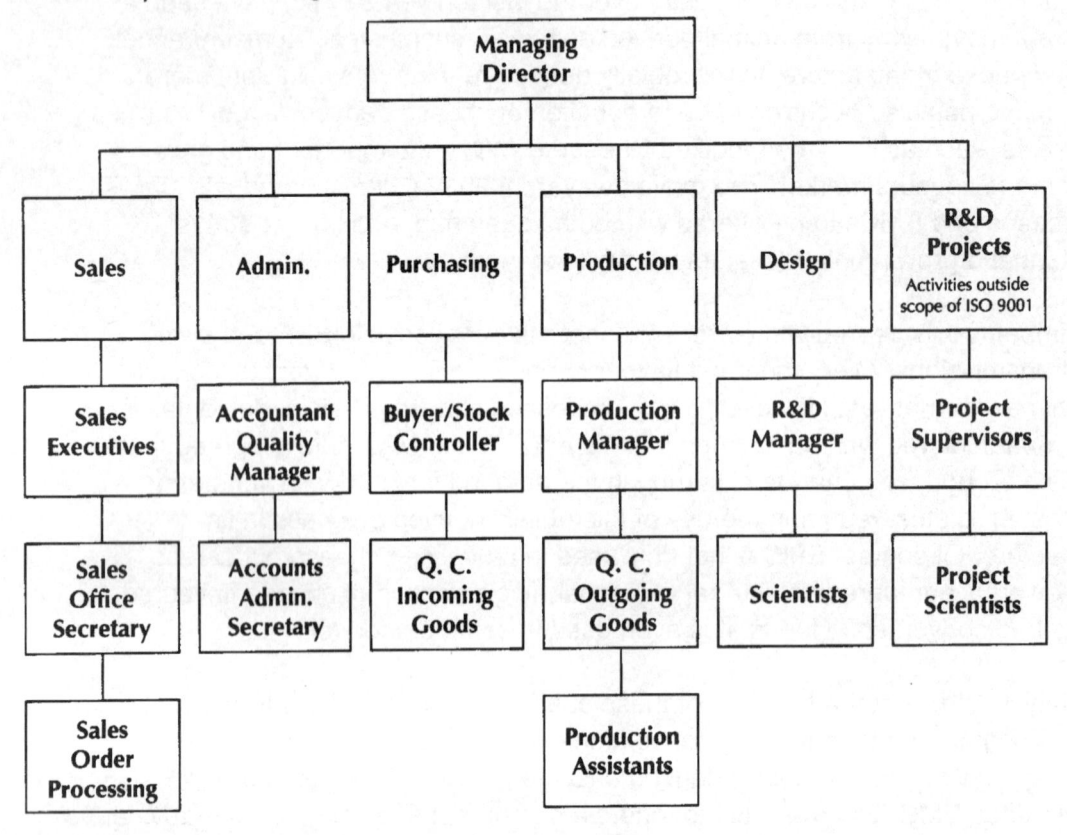

```
                            Managing Director
                                   |
  ┌──────────┬──────────┬──────────┼──────────┬──────────┬──────────┐
 Sales     Admin.   Purchasing  Production  Design    R&D Projects
                                                      (Activities outside
                                                       scope of ISO 9001)
   |          |          |          |          |          |
 Sales    Accountant  Buyer/Stock Production  R&D       Project
Executives  Quality  Controller   Manager    Manager  Supervisors
           Manager
   |          |          |          |          |          |
 Sales    Accounts    Q.C.        Q.C.                  Project
 Office    Admin.   Incoming    Outgoing   Scientists  Scientists
Secretary Secretary  Goods       Goods
   |                              |
 Sales                        Production
 Order                         Assistants
Processing
```

Q. C. = Quality Control
R&D = Research and Development

Appendix 6.

Biocatalysts Ltd.
Abbreviated Balance Sheet

	1997 £	1997 £	1996 £	1996 £
Fixed assets				
Tangible assets		177,667		173,671
Investments		2		3
		177,669		173,674
Current assets				
Stocks	157,877		188,466	
Debtors	783,623		517,462	
Cash at bank and in hand	12,122		30,987	
	953,622		736,915	
Creditors: amounts falling due within one year	(508,073)		(399,078)	
Net current assets		445,549		337,837
Total assets less current liabilities		623,218		511,511
Deferred assets		10,138		10,138
Net assets		633,356		521,649
Capital and reserves				
Called up share capital		500,000		405,511
Capital reserve		–		7,089
Profit and loss account		133,356		109,049
Total shareholders funds		633,356		521,649
Attributable to: Equity shareholders		633,356		521,649

These financial statements are prepared in accordance with the special provisions of Part VII of the Companies Act, 1985, relating to small companies.

(Information supplied by Biocatalysts Ltd.)

Page 30 of Biocatalysts

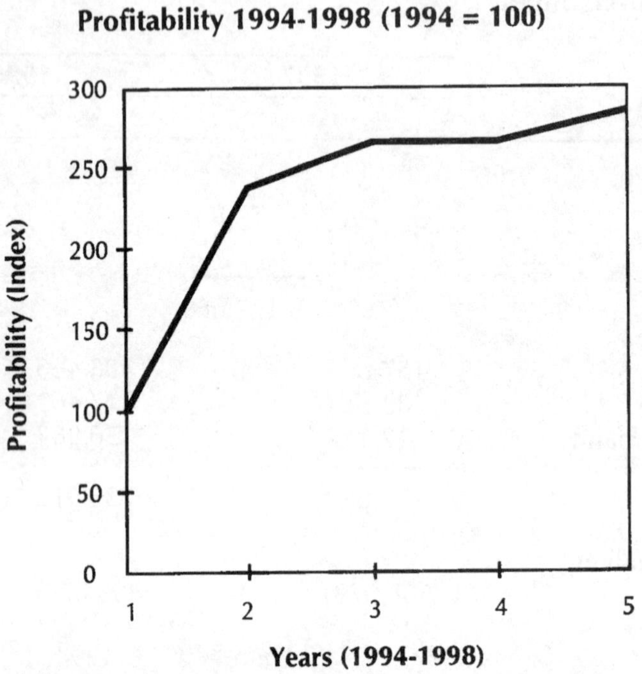
Profitability 1994-1998 (1994 = 100)
Profitability (Index)
300
250
200
150
100
50
0
1
2
3
4
5
Years (1994-1998)

The company turnover is approximately £2.5 million.

Previous Years' Business Ratios

	1994	1995
Current Ratio	2.3	2.2
Acid Test	1.4	1.5
Stock Turn	4.9	4.8
Stock Holding (Days)	75	72
Payment Period	75	72
% Profit	4.9	8.2

The company is growing at 20-30% per annum. The sales profile follows the normal Pareto effect with 80% of the customers providing only 20% of the sales.

> **Page 31 of Biocatalysts**

Appendix 7.

Biocatalysts Ltd. and Trading

Trading in the Euro (€), £s and $s

There is strong worldwide interest in how the new European money system based on the Euro €, is actually working (even if it is only how to get a computer keyboard with the new Euro symbol as part of the standard layout!).

More than two thirds of Biocatalysts' annual turnover is from export sales and it is used to working with different currencies. Biocatalysts Ltd. appears to be fully prepared for trading in the Euro. Biocatalysts Ltd. is able to offer quotations, take orders and, most importantly, accept payment in the Euro (€), American Dollars ($), and UK Pounds Sterling (£). All other currency transactions are usually 'translated' into one of the above three currencies.

> **Page 32 of Biocatalysts**

Appendix 8.

Management Buyout History

1983 Biocatalysts Ltd. name registered.

1985 Work started on a new enzyme facility in South Wales.

1986 Biocatalysts Ltd. starts trading under the ultimate ownership of Grand Metropolitan.

1987 Management buyout financed by the Welsh Development Authority and Welsh Venture Capital Fund when Grand Metropolitan started to divest non-core businesses.

Collaboration with Universities

Biocatalysts Ltd. collaborates with around 8 different UK universities (Food and Biochemistry) and several European universities. In general, basic research is done at the universities (screening, gene cloning, new enzyme developments) before the laboratory processes are brought in for scale-up applications work. In addition, Biocatalysts Ltd. sponsors CASE awards at some universities on more speculative areas of enzyme research.

Appendix 9.

BIOCATALYSTS LIMITED
A manufacturer of speciality enzymes and formulator of enzyme complexes

- BAKING
- BREWING
- FRUIT AND VEGETABLE PROCESSING
- FLAVOUR
- PROTEINS
- DIETETICS
- TEXTILES (GARMENT WASHING)
- DIAGNOSTICS
- PHARMACEUTICALS
- ENVIRONMENTALS

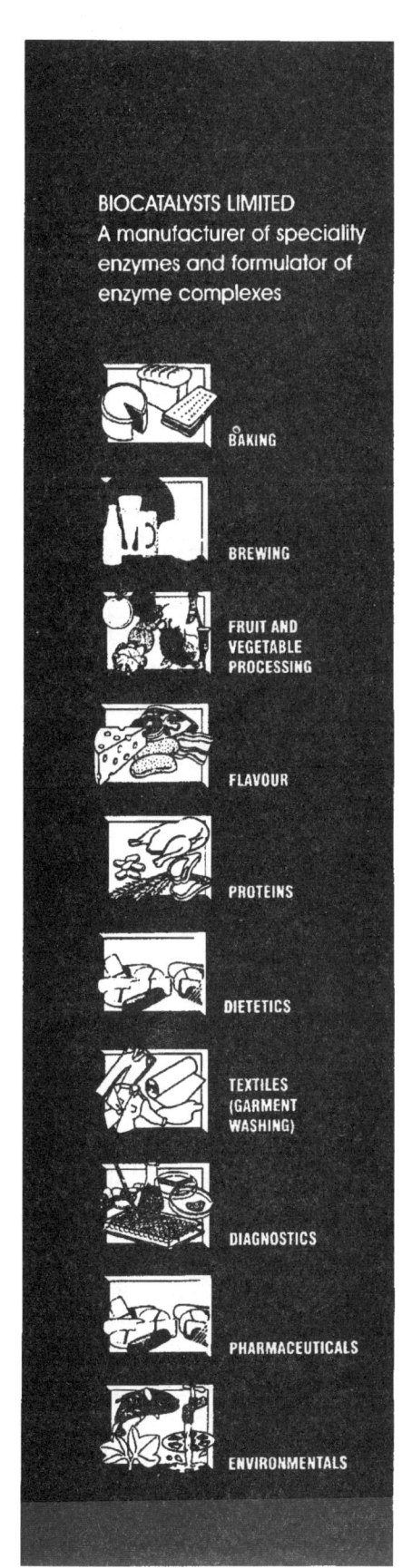

Biocatalysts Ltd is unique amongst the world's enzyme companies. Our willingness to supply custom-tailored products for our clients means that the whole company focus is directed towards our customers and towards giving total customer satisfaction. This customer focus has resulted in Biocatalysts Ltd growing at more than twice the industry average over the past 10 years.

Biocatalysts Ltd is an independent company, located just outside Cardiff, the capital city of Wales. Biocatalysts, as our company name suggests, only makes and sells enzymes. We are not a division of a larger chemical, food ingredients or pharmaceutical company.

Biocatalysts Ltd has many exclusive agreements with blue chip companies around the world, who value the products and technical services we supply. But we are also happy to deal with both small and medium sized companies and our customer base has a full spectrum of company sizes.

Biocatalysts Ltd does not make or sell high volume commodity enzymes, such as those used in the detergent or starch processing industries. We operate in selected parts of the enzyme market where our technical support and willingness to work with customers on a one-to-one basis is highly valued. These enzyme sectors usually require not single enzyme entities but enzyme complexes where the ratios of each of the components are crucial to the efficacy of the whole enzyme product and our customer's process. We do not believe in our customers making do with compromise enzyme products just because that is the way they come off the fermenter! Our own fermentation for the manufacture of our enzyme products is sub-contracted out. This, we believe, allows us to be more flexible, our focus is on investing in enzyme technology – not stainless steel!

Our R&D programme is focused on the development of new enzymes and enzyme complexes mainly identified to us by our customers. We have many allegiances with leading British Universities where most of our basic research into new enzymes is carried out. This allows us to focus our in-house scientists onto the needs of our customers, whilst keeping fully up to date with the latest developments in bio-research.

If you are not sure that you are getting optimum performance from your current enzymes, or if you think your process could benefit by the use of enzymes, why not give Biocatalysts a try and find out what makes us unique amongst the world's enzyme companies.

BIOCATALYSTS

Part B: The sample case: Biocatalysts

Page 34 of Biocatalysts

ENZYMES FOR THE FOOD INDUSTRY

BAKING

PRODUCT	CODE	PRINCIPAL ACTIVITIES	APPLICATION NOTES
AMYLASE	A011P	Amylase	Fungal alpha amylase, protease free, full range of activities to 100,000 SKB.
CATAMYL PLUS	C380P	Mixed amylases, Pentosanase	Anti-staling for bread.
COMBIZYME 261P	C261P	Alpha amylase, Proteinase, Pentosanase	For improving loaf volume, crumb texture & retarding staling in bread.
COMBIZYME 275P	C275P	Proteinase, Alpha amylase, Pentosanase	Protein modifier for biscuits & crackers.
COMBIZYME 359P	C359P	Pentosanase	Bromate replacer.
COMBIZYME 365P	C365P	Xylanase, Proteinase	Viscosity control in batters.
COMBIZYME 366P	C366P	Proteinase, Pentosanase	Metabisulphite replacer in biscuits & crackers.
► COMBIZYME 485P	C485P	Amylase, hemicellulase & protease	Metabisulphite replacer in biscuit manufacture.
DEPOL 112P	D112P	Glucanase, Xylanase	Viscosity control in batters.
DEPOL 222P	D222P	Pentosanase	Amylase free pentosanase.
DEPOL 267P	D267P	Alpha amylase, Pentosanase	Amylase/pentosanase formulated at working strength for direct incorporation into baking flour.
DEPOL 333P	D333P	Xylanase	High activity, amylase free hemicellulase.
DEPOL 364P	D364P	Xylanase, Cellulase	For viscosity control in batters & use in doughnut manufacture.
DEPOL 414P	D414P	Alpha amylases	Speciality amylase for French type bread.
► DEPOL 453P	D453P	Hemicellulase	Aspergillus hemicellulase without amylase for bread improvers.
► DEPOL 454P	D454P	Hemicellulase (xylanase)	Endo-xylanase for bread improvers.
PROMOD 223P	P223P	Proteinase	Bacterial protease for biscuits & crackers.
PROMOD 388P	P388P	Proteinase	Fungal proteinase for improving dough handling & bread texture.
PROMOD 451P	P451P	Proteinase	Fungal proteinase/peptidase for improving dough handling & crumb texture.

BREWING

PRODUCT	CODE	PRINCIPAL ACTIVITIES	APPLICATION NOTES
► AMG BC300	D339L	Glucoamylase	Production of lite beers.
► COMBIZYME 108L	C108L	Protease, Alpha amylase, Beta glucanase	High activity formulation for yield improvements in brewing.
► GLUCANASE 1XL	G011L	Beta glucanase	Improved mash & fermentation performance (run off & solubles) in brewing applications.
► GLUCANASE 5XL	G015L	Beta glucanase	Concentrated (5X) glucanase for improved mash & fermentation performance in brewing applications.
► PROMOD 144L	P144L	Papain	Beer clarification, removal of chill haze.

FRUIT AND VEGETABLE PROCESSING

PRODUCT	CODE	PRINCIPAL ACTIVITIES	APPLICATION NOTES
► CELLULASE 13L	C013L	Cellulase	Cellulose hydrolysis.
DEPOL 40L	D040L	Cellulase, Pectinases, Beta glucosidase	Versatile formulation for maceration, viscosity reduction & extraction of a wide range of fruits & vegetables including mangoes.
DEPOL 220L	D220L	Alpha amylase, Glucoamylase	Hydrolysis of starches during fruit processing.
► GLUCOSE OXIDASE	G168L	Glucose oxidase	Oxygen removal from fruit flavoured drinks.
MACER8 FJ	M263L	Pectinases	Improved performance in a wide range of fruit juice extraction applications (high pectin lyase, low pectin esterase).
MACER8 O	M265L	Pectinases	Significantly improved yield of olive oil & easier to handle waste.
MACER8 W	M264L	Pectinases	Improved extraction performance & flavour enhancement for white wine.
PECTINASE 62L	P062L	Pectinases	General depectinising applications & broad spectrum depolymerisation activity, particularly in fruit.
PECTINASE 444L	P444L	Pectinases	Highly active formulation for general depectinising applications.
CITRUS FRUIT PEELER PECTINASE 152L	P152L	Pectinases	Cost effective peeling of citrus fruits (automation aid).
► TANNASE	T510P	Tannase	Removal of tannins.

BIOCATALYSTS

New Products are Shown with ➡

104

3 ♦ The process case: the ten steps

Page 35 of Biocatalysts

ENZYMES FOR THE FOOD INDUSTRY

PRODUCT	CODE	PRINCIPAL ACTIVITIES	APPLICATION NOTES

FLAVOUR

PRODUCT	CODE	PRINCIPAL ACTIVITIES	APPLICATION NOTES
DEPOL 40L	D040L	Cellulase, Pectinase, Beta glucosidase	Versatile formulation for maceration & extraction in a wide range of vegetables including vanilla, carrots, tea etc.
DEPOL 112L	D112L	Glucanase, Xylanase, Beta glucosidase	Flavour extraction from fibrous botanicals.
FLAVORPRO 192P	F192P	Peptidases	Debittering of protein hydrolysates.
FLAVORPRO 373P	F373P	Glutaminase (Bacillus)	Conversion of glutamine into glutamate in protein hydrolysates.
LIPOMOD 187P	L187P	Esterase	Protease free microbial lipase for enzyme modified cheese (EMC) production. Cheddar type flavours. Kosher certification available.
LIPOMOD 224P	L224P	Esterase (protease)	Enzyme modified cheese (EMC) production. Cheddar type flavours.
LIPOMOD 299P	L299P	Esterase (protease)	Enzyme modified cheese (EMC) production. Cheddar type flavours.
LIPOMOD 29P	L029P	Esterase, Lipase (protease)	General fat hydrolysis & enzyme modified cheese (EMC) production.
LIPOMOD 338P	L338P	Esterase	Protease free microbial lipase for enzyme modified cheese (EMC) production. Blue cheese type flavours. Kosher certification available.
LIPOMOD 34P	L034P	Lipase, Esterase	Protease free, high activity lipase for hydrolysis of oils, tallow & fats including butter fat. Kosher certification available.
PEPTIDASE 436P	P436P	Aminopeptidase, Carboxypeptidase	Debittering of protein hydrolysates. Contains proline peptidase activity. Kosher certification available.
PEPTIDASE 433/4P	P433/4P	Aminopeptidase, Carboxypeptidase	Broad spectrum peptidases for debittering of protein hydrolysates.
PROMOD 215P	P215P	Endo-proteinase, Peptidase	For use with protease free lipases in enzyme modified cheese (EMC) production. Introduces protein notes. Kosher certification available.
PROMOD 446P	P446P	Endo-proteinase, Peptidase	For use with protease free lipases in enzyme modified cheese (EMC) production. Introduces protein notes. Kosher certification available.

PROTEINS

PRODUCT	CODE	PRINCIPAL ACTIVITIES	APPLICATION NOTES
➤ BC PEPSIN 1:3000	P389P	Acid protease	Protein hydrolysis at acid pH values.
DEPOL 20L	D020L	Pectinase	For viscosity reduction of soya polysaccharides.
PROMOD 144L	P144L	Proteinase	Papain liquid 100 TU.
PROMOD 144P	P144P	Proteinase	Papain powder 100 TU.
PROMOD 184P	P184P	Proteinase	Bromelain powder.
PROMOD 192P	P192P	Endo-proteinase	Acid fungal protease with exo-peptidases.
PROMOD 194P	P194P	Proteinase	Neutral fungal protease with exo-peptidases.
PROMOD 24L	P024L	Proteinase	Neutral bacterial, general purpose liquid proteinase.
PROMOD 278P	P278P	Proteinase	Mixed fungal & bacterial proteinases for Stage 1 in the Biocatalysts eHVP (enzyme hydrolysed vegetable protein) Cascade: the bulk hydrolysis stage.
PROMOD 279P	P279P	Proteinase, Peptidase	Fungal proteases & peptidases for Stage 2 in the Biocatalysts eHVP Cascade: the debittering stage.
PROMOD 280P	P280P	Proteinase, Amylase	Mixed fungal & bacterial enzyme activities for Stage 3 in the Biocatalysts eHVP Cascade: the filtration aid stage.
PROMOD 298L	P298L	Proteinase	Broad spectrum bacterial proteinase, will rapidly reduce viscosity of soya protein pastes.
PROMOD 31L	P031L	Proteinase	Neutral bacterial, broad spectrum liquid proteinase.

DIETETICS

PRODUCT	CODE	PRINCIPAL ACTIVITIES	APPLICATION NOTES
AMYLASE	AD11P	Amylase	Aid for digestion of dietary starch. Ready for tableting.
➤ BC PEPSIN 1:3000	P389P	Pepsin	Animal derived acid enzyme to aid protein digestion.
➤ BROMELAIN 1200GDU	P523P	Bromelain	Broad spectrum plant protease to aid protein digestion.
CELLULASE CP	C013P	Cellulase	Aid for digestion of dietary cellulose. Ready for tableting.
DEPOL 333P	D333P	Xylanase	Aid for digestion of dietary hemicellulose. Ready for tableting.
HEMICELLULASE 334P	H334P	Glucanase, Cellulase, Xylanase	Aid for the digestion of dietary fibre. Ready for tableting.
LACTASE	L017P	Lactase	Aid for digestion of dietary lactose. Ready for tableting.
LIPASE, Rhizopus sp.	L036P	Lipase, Esterase	Aid for digestion of dietary fats & lipids. Ready for tableting.
PANCREATIN 4XNF	P211P	Amylase, Lipase, Protease	General aid for digestion. Ready for tableting.
PROMOD D24P	PD024P	Protease	Broad spectrum proteases for aiding the digestion of dietary proteins. Ready for tableting.

New Products are Shown with ➤

Part B: The sample case: Biocatalysts

Page 36 of Biocatalysts

NON-FOOD GRADE ENZYMES

PRODUCT	CODE	PRINCIPAL ACTIVITIES	APPLICATION NOTES

TEXTILES (GARMENT WASHING)

PRODUCT	CODE	PRINCIPAL ACTIVITIES	APPLICATION NOTES
→ CATALASE	C495L	Catalase	Inactivation and removal of hydrogen peroxide.
DESIZE 277L	D277L	Amylase	Very high activity bacterial amylase for cost effective garment & textile desizing applications. Can be diluted.
→ DESIZE 569P	D569P	Amylase	Very strong desizing amylase powder.
→ DESIZE (NON-ENZYMATIC)	D574L	Non-enzyme product	Desizing fabrics with difficult sizes or where minimal backstaining is required.
INDIFADE 7.5L	I07.5L	Cellulase	Range of liquid acid cellulase activities from medium to high activity. Ready to use,
INDIFADE 9L	I009L	Cellulase	cost effective formulations for bio-washing applications.
INDIFADE 11L	I011L	Cellulase	
INDIFADE 13L	I013L	Cellulase	
→ INDIFADE 9 LAS	I480L	Cellulase	Acid cellulase with anti-redeposition chemistry.
INDIFADE 426P	I426P	Cellulase	High activity, buffered mixed acid & neutral cellulase powder.
INDIFADE 501P	I501P	Cellulase	High activity, buffered acid cellulase powder with added anti-redeposition chemistry for an economical, near neutral type of stone wash effect.
→ INDIFADE 555P	I555P	Cellulase	Boosted cost effective neutral cellulase.
→ INDIFADE AGER	I478L	Non-enzyme product	Gives antique look to denims.
→ INDIFADE BRIGHT	I476P	Non-enzyme product	Optical brightener.
→ INDIFADE COLD	I539L	Cellulase	Cellulase for use in cool water (40 - 45°C).
INDIFADE LAS	I014L	Cellulase	High activity, liquid acid cellulase with added anti-redeposition chemistry for an economical, near neutral type of stone wash effect.
INDIFADE NC-1G	I001G	Cellulase	High activity, unbuffered neutral cellulase granules.
→ INDIFADE SOFT	I477L	Non-enzyme product	Specially formulated softener for denims.
INDIFADE SUPER	I474P	Cellulase	Highly cost effective, buffered neutral cellulase powder.
INDIFADE SUPER PLUS	I475P	Cellulase	Cost effective, buffered neutral cellulase powder with added anti-redeposition chemistry.
SOFTZYME	S425L	Cellulase	Bio-softening, anti-pilling formulation for cellulosic fibres (Tencel®).

DIAGNOSTICS

PRODUCT	CODE	PRINCIPAL ACTIVITIES	APPLICATION NOTES
ALKALINE PHOSPHATASE	A500L	Alkaline phosphatase	High stability reagent for immunodiagnostics.
GALACTOSE DEHYDROGENASE	G471P	Galactose dehydrogenase	For determination of galactose in blood of neonatals.
MANNITOL DEHYDROGENASE	M093P	Mannitol dehydrogenase	For determination of mannitol in sugar permeability test in human gastric disorders.
MYROSINASE	M044P	Myrosinase	Determination of glucosinolates in rape seed meal.
PHENYLALANINE DEHYDROGENASE	P098P	Phenylalanine dehydrogenase	For determination of phenylalanine in blood of neonatals.
→ GLUCOSE OXIDASE	TP 574P	Glucose oxidase - catalase free	Determination of glucose - available summer 1998.
→ GLUTAMINASE	G420P	Glutaminase	Determination of glutamine.
→ PEROXIDASE	P558P	Peroxidase	Immuno-diagnostics.

PHARMACEUTICALS

PRODUCT	CODE	PRINCIPAL ACTIVITIES	APPLICATION NOTES
LIPASE, Candida sp.	L034P	Lipase	Stereoselective hydrolysis of esters.
LIPASE, Pseudomonas sp.	L056P	Lipase	Stereoselective hydrolysis of esters.
LIPASE, Pancreatic	L115P	Lipase Esterase	Stereoselective hydrolysis of esters.
SEC ADH 300	S300P	Alcohol dehydrogenase	Synthesis of chiral alcohols.
TRYPSIN 250	T069P	Proteinase	Standard formulation for mammalian cell culture.
TRYPSIN IRRAD.	T070P	Proteinase	Irradiated formulation for mammalian cell culture.
TRYSIN SVF	T071P	Proteinase	Certified specific virus-free trypsin for cell culture.

ENVIRONMENTALS

PRODUCT	CODE	PRINCIPAL ACTIVITIES	APPLICATION NOTES
GREASE BIOSOLVE (COMBIZYME 209P)	C209P	Broad spectrum lipases & carbohydrases	High activity enzyme formulation for reduced fouling of grease traps & drain maintenance.
LATRINE DEODOURISER (COMBIZYME 253L)	C253L	Broad spectrum enzymes	High activity product for significant odour reduction in many waste treatment applications.
ODOURWAY 10X	OO73L10	Mixed, broad spectrum	10X concentrated version. Available with a choice of perfumes.
ODOURWAY 20X	OO73L20	Mixed, broad spectrum	20X concentrated version. Available with a choice of perfumes.

BIOCATALYSTS

New Products are Shown with →

3 ♦ The process case: the ten steps

Page 37 of Biocatalysts

CUSTOM TAILORED PRODUCTS: This catalogue contains our standard products that are sold regularly to our customers. In addition we have many other products that have been developed exclusively for individual customers. If you do not think your current enzyme product is optimised for your process or would like an exclusive enzyme product (not available to your competitors) then contact the Sales department at Biocatalysts to find out how we can develop new enzyme products exclusively for your company.

If there are any enzyme activities that you are interested in that are not mentioned in our standard listing then please enquire; we have many new enzymes under development for release in the near future.

WORLD-WIDE SALES AGENTS: Biocatalysts has an extensive network of agents and distributors in over 40 countries right around the world. Our most recent list is given in our company newsletter 'IN BRIEF'. This is sent out routinely to all clients on our database. If you would like to be added to our mailing list then please fill out a reader reply card included with this catalogue.

PACKAGING: Biocatalysts products are packaged by weight (not volume) according to the following:

Powders (designated 'P' in product code)
Standard packaging   25 kg in fibre kegs or Lesac* lined square boxes.

Liquids (designated 'L' in product code)
Standard packaging   25, 215 and 1000 kg

Granules (designated 'G' in product code)
Standard packaging   25 kg

Other pack sizes are available including 1 and 5 kg on request.

DATA ACCURACY: Whilst Biocatalysts makes all practicable efforts to ensure the accuracy of the information it gives, the data might be subject to change without notice. Biocatalysts cannot guarantee performance in any end application. Prior to carrying out any commercial application, clients should ensure that they are not infringing third party patent rights.

SAMPLES: Product samples for trials are generally available on request. Please fill out and return an enquiry card included with this catalogue or contact the sales department at Biocatalysts.

PRODUCT DATA SHEETS: Further information is available for each of the products listed in this catalogue. Please contact Biocatalysts for individual Product Data Sheets.

HEALTH AND SAFETY: Always read and retain the Health and Safety data sheets supplied with each product, before use. If you are in any doubt about recommended product handling and safety, please contact Biocatalysts before use. Generally, when handling enzymes avoid contact with the skin and eyes and do not breathe dusts or aerosols containing them.

TECHNICAL SUPPORT: Biocatalysts offers a Technical Support Service for all its products.

Page 38 of Biocatalysts

KOSHER STATUS: Most Biocatalysts products are available with Kosher or Kosher Parve certification in accordance with current Orthodox Union requirements. Kosher certification requirements must be specified with order as retrospective certification cannot be issued.

TRADE MARKS: COMBIZYME, DEPOL, INDIFADE, LIPOMOD, MACER8, PROMOD and the Biocatalysts logo including the cat symbol are trademarks of Biocatalysts Ltd.

ENZYMES FROM GENETICALLY MODIFIED ORGANISMS (GMOs): Genetically modified organisms (commonly called GMOs) are being increasingly used by many companies for enzyme production. There are many reasons for this, but some of them include:
- the production of purer enzyme products
- shorter development times for new enzymes
- reduced usage of energy and raw materials for production giving reduced production costs

At the moment none of our products listed in this catalogue is derived from a GMO. We expect to launch our first enzyme produced from a GMO in 1999. All literature regarding these new enzymes will clearly state that they have been produced from GMOs. This is now the norm for the enzyme industry. It is our belief that the use of GMOs for enzyme production offers many benefits and that they are safe and efficient to use, and that they pose no threat to the environment or the end consumer.

ANIMAL DERIVED ENZYMES: None of the enzymes listed in this catalogue is derived from a bovine (cow) source. One of our specialisations is to offer microbial derived alternatives to commonly available animal enzymes (e.g. our alkaline phosphatase). By not processing or dealing with bovine derived products we can ensure that there is no risk whatsoever of any of our products being contaminated with BSE.

The only animal derived enzymes included in this catalogue are from porcine (pig) sources. No primary processing of animal glands is carried out at Biocatalysts Ltd. All partially processed animal derived material comes from animal certified as healthy at the time of slaughter. Our premises are inspected annually by an Officer of the British Ministry of Agriculture, Fisheries and Food (MAFF) and an Approval certificate issued (copy available on request).

HACCP (HAZARD ANALYSIS AND CRITICAL CONTROL POINT SYSTEM): As well as operating under ISO 9001 Biocatalysts Ltd also has additional operating procedures which conform to HACCP.

If you would like product datasheets, quotations or samples of any of the products in this catalogue or would like to be added to our database, please fill in the reply card and post or fax it back to Biocatalysts.

Step 1: Overview of Biocatalysts

Chapter Topic List	
1	What are we trying to achieve at the overview?
2	Bringing order to the case material
3	Adding context to turn information into intelligence
4	The pitfalls
5	The practice: completing the overview for Biocatalysts

Introduction

☑ This chapter shows how to get started on a case study and how to establish the context of a case study. By the end of this stage you will be able to describe and explain the implications of:

- Your role and what you have been asked to do
- The company, its size, sector and key capabilities
- The main environmental challenges
- The customers
- The competitors

Skills and knowledge reminder: techniques and tools at overview

☑ The analysis tools you have already studied will help you to organise and assimilate information quickly. You can identify those you will be able to use during the overview stage and apply them at the inview stages. During this chapter you will see two techniques applied to this case study:

- A mind map used to help sort out the data about enzymes (see 2.9)
- A schematic pulls together a picture of the stakeholders and their needs and interests (5.5)

If you are unfamiliar with any of the basic tools and techniques we use here, take time to review your Diploma notes.

Part B: The sample case: Biocatalysts

1 What are we trying to achieve at the overview?

1.1 There are few people, students or tutors, who do not feel nervous at the prospect of tackling a major exam case. CIM cases do tend to fall with a thud on the doormat when they are delivered and, like Biocatalysts, they are typically 16-20 pages of narrative followed by a similar volume of appendices. They represent a considerable piece of work: the challenge is where to start. The **overview** begins the process of bringing order and method to the case study.

1.2 The mistake at this stage is to keep reading the case without picking up a pen and actually doing something with the data it contains. Simply rereading the case will only give you a superficial picture: you need to really understand the business and the implications of what you are being told. You should **first** sort and **then** analyse the clues and data provided, turning it in the process into relevant information which will eventually help you to make and justify a credible strategy. So, what needs to be done?

1.3 You have already read Biocatalysts and thought about the business: now you are going to start work on it.

1.4 If you are not familiar with the sector (like most students), the challenge of tackling issues generated by an unknown sector can itself be daunting. Remember we will bring order to the chaos of any business by applying our planning processes, objectively and rigorously.

1.5 What did you find out?

Action Programme 1

Even after one read of the narrative, you can probably answer these questions. Try and do this without referring back to the case.

(a) Is this a B2B or B2C case study and what are the implications of that?
(b) What is the product Biocatalysts are producing and why is it a challenging business?
(c) Who are you and what is your role in the case?
(d) What is the role of agents in Biocatalyst's market?

Turn to the end of this chapter to check your answers with ours.

1.6 Before you start getting down to any more detailed work on the overview, just take a few minutes to **familiarise yourself with the appendices**. What do they contain? Again do not try to do anything with this data, but simply assess what sort of information might be available to you once you analyse and cross analyse the various appendices. For example, Appendix 6 on page 29 gives you some headline financial information and, considered against some of the competitor information in Appendix 1 (from page 17), you can see how small the Biocatalysts operation is and that you will be able to assess its financial strength. Clearly Biocatalysts is a very small fish in a big and turbulent global pond.

2 Bringing order to the case material

2.1 You won't understand the case study yet and shouldn't expect to but you are at least beginning to get a sense of the **scenario and scale**. There is no shortage of information but at this stage it is scattered throughout the narrative and appendices. In your overview you need to sort out:

- Information about the industry and its fortunes
- Information about Biocatalysts and its business
- Information about products and markets (sorting the general from the Biocatalysts specific)

2.2 Do not be surprised if the material seems muddled at first. As you work with it and sort it into relevant groups it will start to make more sense. Do avoid rushing into ad hoc analysis: it pays to work through the case thoroughly and logically, so that you can be sure that you have stripped out all the relevant data.

2.3 This next step in the overview process could take you two to six hours, depending on the complexity of the case. Take this task in two or three short bursts and don't worry at this stage about what you are going to do next.

2.4 **Note. You must not do any research outside the Case Study as this will be penalised by the Examiner.** Additional information would only confuse the issues, so just use you own knowledge and the information given. In this instance, the Examiner has especially addressed the issues of anomalies which may be found in the case. There are likely to be some, so do not get bogged down in them, or in the detail of the case. You are working at the broader strategic level: flag up any assumptions you need to make and move on. However, the issue of websites is addressed in the case and it doesn't seem unreasonable for you, as a consultant, to visit Monsanto's website to get a 'feel' for the competitors and a flavour of the industry. **However,** do **not** get sidetracked by additional data; it is simply to help you understand more about the product. In reality, there is relatively little material that we spotted on our surfing of the web that would be of any obvious value, so don't worry if you don't have access or time. Certainly you must not bring 'facts' from any external search to bear on your answer in the exam. The world is as described by the examiner for the duration of the case.

2.5 **Reminder**

As you work through the case, keep an **information shopping list** so that you can use it later if you need to prepare for a research question.

Part B: The sample case: Biocatalysts

2.6 Head up pages with key areas for analysis to help you sort through the case.

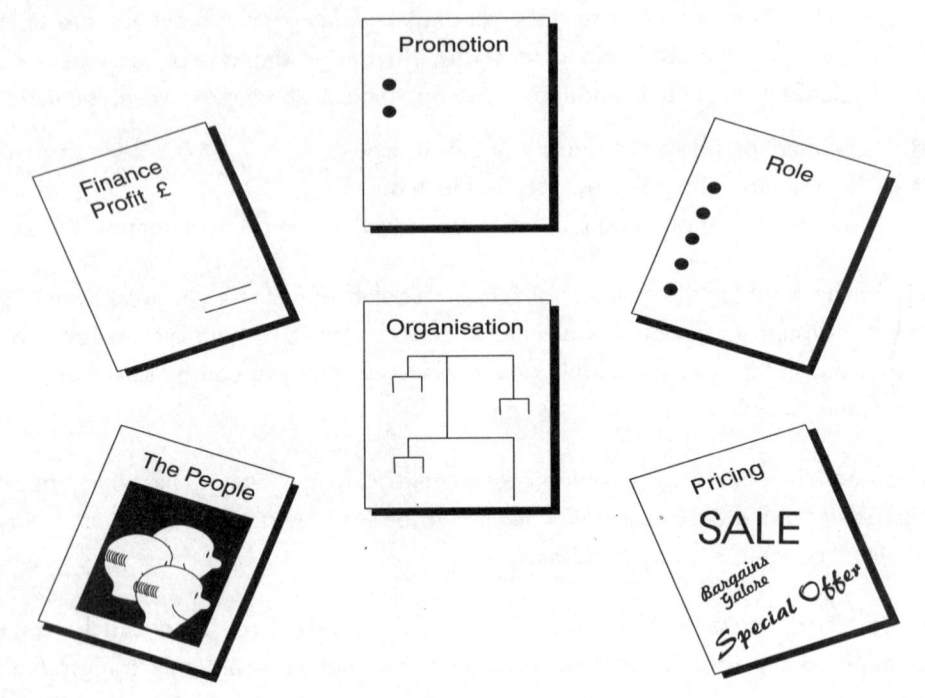

Examine every line and categorise all the significant information under a relevant heading.

- People
- Products
- Current performance, profitability etc
- Organisational structure
- Competitors
- Customers/audiences
- Potential environmental change, eg legislation or customer attitudes to GM products
- Brand and competitive position

The aim of the overview is to familiarise yourself thoroughly with Biocatalysts.

Take a further sheet of paper and use this to record information about the **consultancy role you have and make key notes about your client Stewart North**, his needs and interests and the expectation of the Board.

2.7 Note that with different cases you will need different headings. You will choose these based on what seem to be the key issues in the case. For example, if there was a lot of information on the brand or the sales force, you would pull that information together.

2.8 The idea is that at the end of this process you have, for example, all the financial information or macro environmental information together on one sheet.

Tutor Tip

- Do not be tempted at this stage to make decisions and/or jump to conclusions. Collect all the information and analyse it carefully before you start changing things.

- Try not to work in a mechanistic way as though this were an academic exercise; play your part. What questions do you think Stewart and the Board will want to ask? What extra information would you want if you were the consultant? Remember to add these to your list of information needs – it may be invaluable later.

- Take care with the appendices: currencies change – some are quoted in dollars, others in sterling, you may expect additional information in Euros. We are apparently geared up to work in Euros. Does that imply a strategy is needed for Europe?

- Do not just rely on what is written. Think about the business; try and picture it in your own mind.

- What do you know about the characteristics of marketing in an international business to business sector?

- Enzymes are raw material products, consumables used in the production process and they play a role in determining the quality of the customer's finished product. Their value is potentially high, and price is relatively insignificant as a percentage of total costs. Customers will tend to be relatively price insensitive (inelastic), but ensuring they understand the basis of comparison between different offerings is, it seems, a key issue.

- Channel management, promotion, particularly in relation to presenting GM products and pricing, all seem to be issues which could be on the Examiner's agenda: certainly the service element of the marketing mix is key to differentiating Biocatalysts's offering.

2.9 As you pull the materials together at this overview stage, you will find that the business becomes clearer. When you are faced with detailed and complex narrative in a case study, as we are in this case about enzymes, you might find that a mind map helps to bring various strands together in a way that helps build the bigger picture.

Part B: The sample case: Biocatalysts

A Mind Map of Enzymes and their Market
Catalysts of the Living World

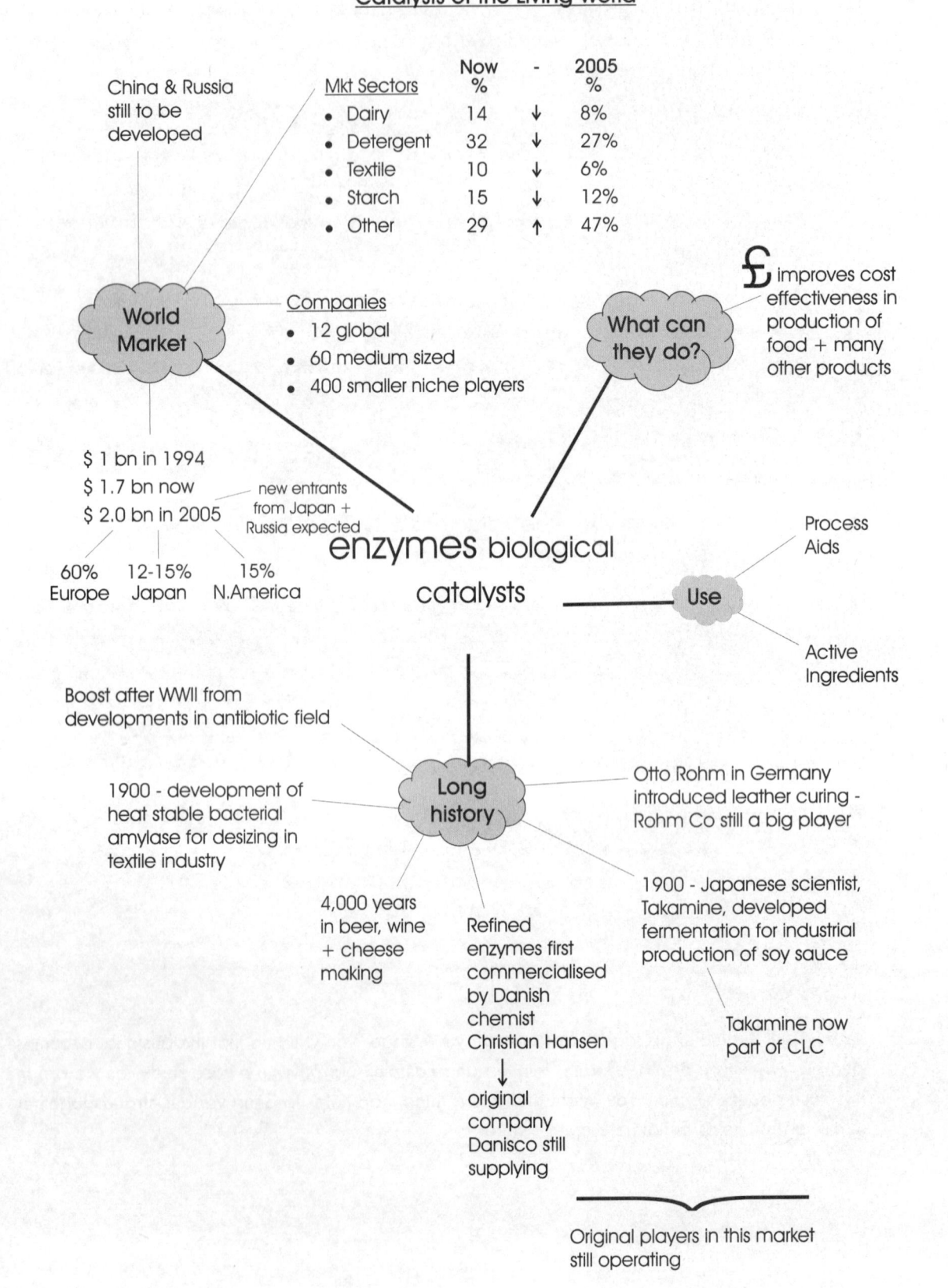

World Market

China & Russia still to be developed

Mkt Sectors	Now %	-	2005 %
Dairy	14	↓	8%
Detergent	32	↓	27%
Textile	10	↓	6%
Starch	15	↓	12%
Other	29	↑	47%

Companies
- 12 global
- 60 medium sized
- 400 smaller niche players

$1 bn in 1994
$1.7 bn now
$2.0 bn in 2005

new entrants from Japan + Russia expected

60% Europe   12-15% Japan   15% N.America

enzymes biological catalysts

What can they do?
£ improves cost effectiveness in production of food + many other products

Use
- Process Aids
- Active Ingredients

Long history

Boost after WWII from developments in antibiotic field

1900 - development of heat stable bacterial amylase for desizing in textile industry

4,000 years in beer, wine + cheese making

Refined enzymes first commercialised by Danish chemist Christian Hansen
↓
original company Danisco still supplying

Otto Rohm in Germany introduced leather curing - Rohm Co still a big player

1900 - Japanese scientist, Takamine, developed fermentation for industrial production of soy sauce

Takamine now part of CLC

Original players in this market still operating

3 Adding context to turn information into intelligence

3.1 Being a consultant or a case study student is a little like being a detective. You can't take the evidence at face value but need to read between the lines to really appreciate what is being said. Let's look at two extracts from the paragraph on page 14 under **targeting.**

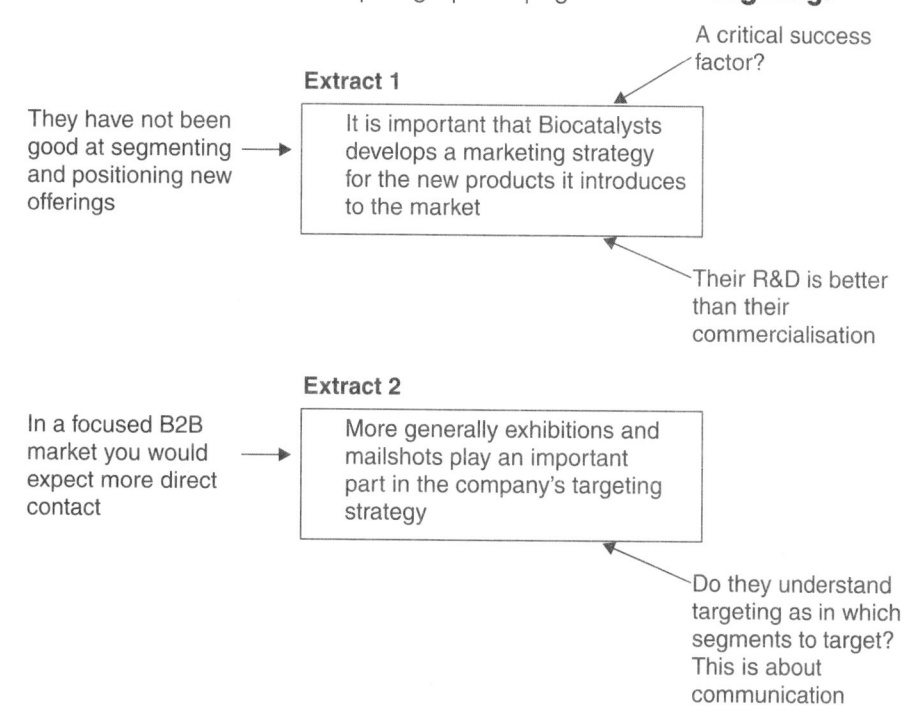

Extract 1

They have not been good at segmenting and positioning new offerings → It is important that Biocatalysts develops a marketing strategy for the new products it introduces to the market

- A critical success factor?
- Their R&D is better than their commercialisation

Extract 2

In a focused B2B market you would expect more direct contact → More generally exhibitions and mailshots play an important part in the company's targeting strategy

- Do they understand targeting as in which segments to target? This is about communication

3.2 Data never becomes intelligence unless you consider it in terms of the case context, ensuring that contextual focus is very much the role of the overview. It provides firm contextual footings on which the rest of the detailed analysis can be built.

Action Programme 2

Adding the context

Looking at this piece of data from the case study page 13:

The products are sold all around the world and 70% are exported. Biocatalysts has a presence in 35 countries.

(a) What do you think about this, what impression does it create, what picture do you now have of Biocatalysts?

(b) Now what do you think about it in the context of the case study. Biocatalysts had a turnover in 1998 of approximately £2.5m (page 30).

(c) Would your assessment change if Biocatalysts was exporting low value/high weight products like bricks rather than enzymes and technology?

Compare your thoughts with our comments at the end of this chapter.

Part B: The sample case: Biocatalysts

3.3 Remember that commercial credibility is key to your exam success and that credibility will be assessed by how relevant and appropriate your strategy is when judged in terms of the business context.

4 The pitfalls

Not too deep, not too shallow

4.1 One of the hardest things about case study is getting the analysis, both overview and inview, right. Analysis can be very reassuring, particularly when the alternative is to move on to the much more challenging and scary decision making!

4.2 You need to avoid analysis for its own sake. Ask yourself **why** am I analysing this – what kind of information will it generate and what will I do with it? Look for example at Appendix 9. You can use it to show a number of things:

- It provides some clues about the company's communication skills
- It shows how many new products they have as a proportion of the portfolio
- It identifies their key markets
- It provides clues about their potential differential advantages

Which of these pieces of information are important to you? In this case they probably all are, so you can analyse the information accordingly, but **be discerning**.

4.3 Typically, students fall into two camps:

(a) **Characterised by the superficial approach**: this person is likely to go into the exam with the headline picture of a **big** international player because they haven't identified from the analysis how **thinly Biocatalysts** are spread in terms of both products and markets. The additional information in the exam room is a real challenge to this candidate who often fails to see its relevance and is likely to jump to an obvious but wrong conclusion.

(b) **Characterised by 'too much analysis'**: this candidate is likely to suffer from the dreaded Analysis Paralysis – never able to move on from the calculator and so goes into the exam room with little decision-making done before the exam. Their tendency is to repeat to the examiner or client what was told to them in the case, adding little of value. Before the exam, it is the case anomalies which really cause concerns for this candidate. The detail of numbers to three decimal places are scrutinised and considered, when all we really need is the big picture. In the exam room the killer for these over-prepared students is time – there is simply not enough of it to either:

- Work through their vast files of information and data , or
- Move on from the analysis to answering the questions set.

4.4 Which category are you most likely to fall into?

Superficial ☐

Bogged down in detail ☐

Take a few minutes to recognise your most likely pitfall. Think about a strategy to overcome it.

(a) **For the superficial**, we advocate a timetable and clarity about the depth and breadth of analysis. Don't forget the value of cross referencing materials and, if possible, work with others to share ideas. Be sure to give at least two weeks out of the four to your analysis.

(b) **For the potentially bogged down,** work to keep an holistic view; the bigger picture is critical in this strategic paper. Again a timetable helps – you **must** move on to decision making. Finally, make yourself a promise **not** to get too concerned about anomalies. Make **assumptions** where necessary and move forward.

5 The practice: completing the overview for Biocatalysts

5.1 It is very difficult to undertake the case overview for you – it **must** be done by each individual to give you a meaningful view of the case. Below we have pulled some observations and comments together to help your overview analysis. You may like to have a go at this yourself before moving on.

5.2 **About the company**

(a) **Biocatalysts** is well established in this industry, formed in 1986 and located in Wales. However, it has already had two transformations, starting life as a wholly owned subsidiary of Grand Metropolitan and, in 1991, becoming an independent company following a management buyout from Shell Ventures. (Page 2)

(b) A leading developer and producer of specialist enzymes, the question seems to be **whether it has got the same ability to commercialise these innovative solutions**. We are told (page 2 paragraph 3) that the wide geographic sales and broad spread of sectors served gives a balanced portfolio with steady profitable, income streams. The question is do we believe this? With only £2.5 million turnover, this is a **small** company. You need to stay aware of this scale context as you work through the case, because the narrative reads as a much bigger global player operating in 35 countries and with pages of product offerings and a customising service for big and small companies.

(c) It is certainly an interesting and topical sector; if you live in Europe, the ongoing controversy about genetically modified (GM) foods seems to roll on and on. There are some clear indications that, in your role as consultant to Biocatalysts, you may need to advise on how to handle the communication and PR challenges currently faced by biotechnology companies wanting to use GMOs in their production (Case Study page 24 paragraph 4). The organisation chart on page 28 shows a functionally organised business with no reflection of the international aspects of the business. R&D, design and production all seem to be involved in doing their own thing.

5.3 **Your role**

(a) **Your role is clear**. You are an **independent consultant**, Joseph Mendes, apparently of some repute. (You must strive not to damage that hard earned reputation with your response to Biocatalysts' problems!)

(b) You have been invited to develop a marketing report, to be presented to the Managing Director, Stewart North, prior to a piece of strategic work. Unfortunately, this brief (page 1) is not presented with as much clarity as we would like. It seems the Case Study itself represents this first stage in this process, the report, which has been sent in advance of the Board Meeting to Stewart North. It seems likely that in response to this you will get some additional information from Stewart and be asked your views on the strategic issues

Part B: The sample case: Biocatalysts

which will frame the next stages of presentation to the Board and preparation for the strategic exercise.

(c) What you might be asked to report on is less clear than it has been in other CIM exams but you can assume the emphasis will be strategic not tactical. You **need to be able to discuss corporate positioning and competitive strategy as well as market segmentation,** short and longer term marketing plans, developing international markets, managing channels as well as the communication issues facing GM products.

5.4 Performance

(a) At first read of the case, Biocatalysts comes over as successful (20% growth, achieving double the industry average over the last 10 years: page 16) and seemingly very customer oriented. **However, for such a small business they seem very over-stretched.** Operating in 35 countries might mean they are trying to be all things to all people. They seem to be reactive to customers' needs, customising their offerings, but less successful at proactively developing a segment of the market as in the case of the olive farmers.

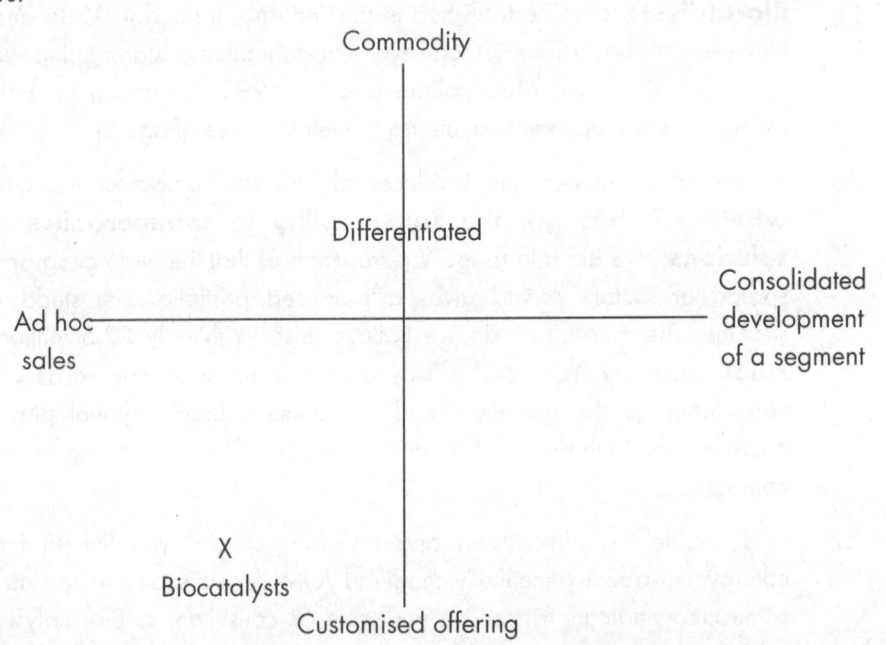

```
                        Commodity
                            |
                            |
                     Differentiated
                            |
                            |                  Consolidated
          Ad hoc            |                  development
          sales             |                  of a segment
        ────────────────────┼────────────────────
                            |
                            |
                            |
                            |
                            X
                       Biocatalysts
                     Customised offering
```

(b) It seems the company is mainly involved in a **niche of the market**, offering customised services, and it is said that this is a unique service, providing an important basis for sustainable competitive advantage. However, this is an **expensive process if additional demand is not generated**. In the last pages of the case you will see the listings of products offered by this company and there are a **large number of new products** in the list.

(c) The question of the product portfolio's balance is an obvious one to consider. Are there too many question marks/problem children and stars and not enough cash generated from the cows to fully exploit them? Certainly we know that 80% of sales come from 20% of customers (page 30), so an analysis of profitability by product and customer would I'm sure reveal some poor contributors. And the challenges of successfully commercialising innovations should be a framework for some of your planning.

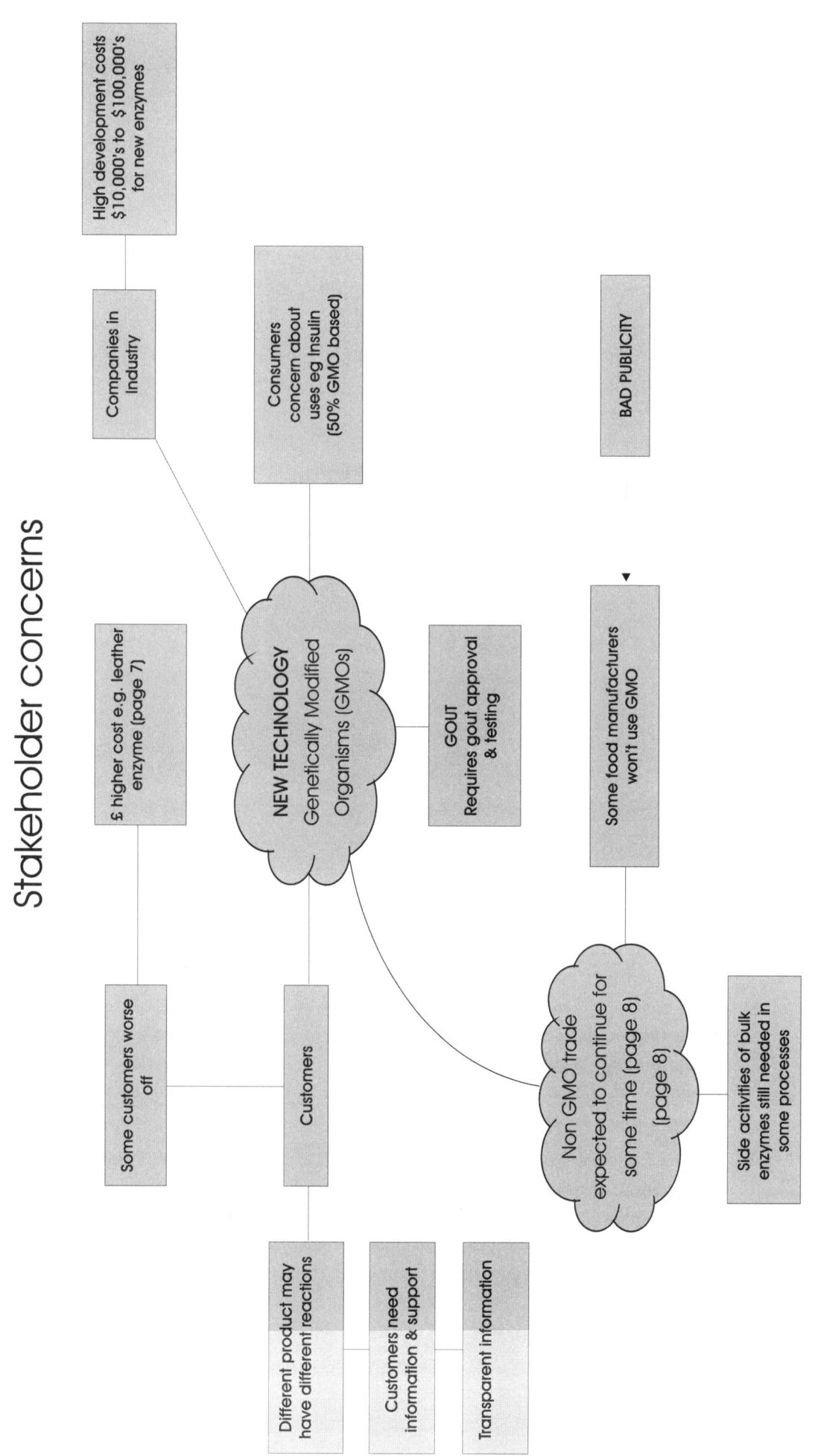

4 ♦ Step 1: Overview of Biocatalysts

Stakeholder concerns

- High development costs $10,000's to $100,000's for new enzymes
- Companies in Industry
- Consumers concern about uses eg Insulin (50% GMO based)
- BAD PUBLICITY
- **NEW TECHNOLOGY** Genetically Modified Organisms (GMOs)
- GOUT — Requires gout approval & testing
- Some food manufacturers won't use GMO
- £ higher cost e.g. leather enzyme (page 7)
- Some customers worse off
- Customers
- Non GMO trade expected to continue for some time (page 8) (page 8)
- Side activities of bulk enzymes still needed in some processes
- Different product may have different reactions
- Customers need information & support
- Transparent information

Part B: The sample case: Biocatalysts

5.5 Stakeholder concerns

The following schematic demonstrates how using models and diagrams can help you capture a lot of related data in a simple to review format.

5.6 Products and markets

The company launched 26 new products last year. 30% of sales are domestic and 70% are international.

The total product concept shows Biocatalyst's perception of the product offering.

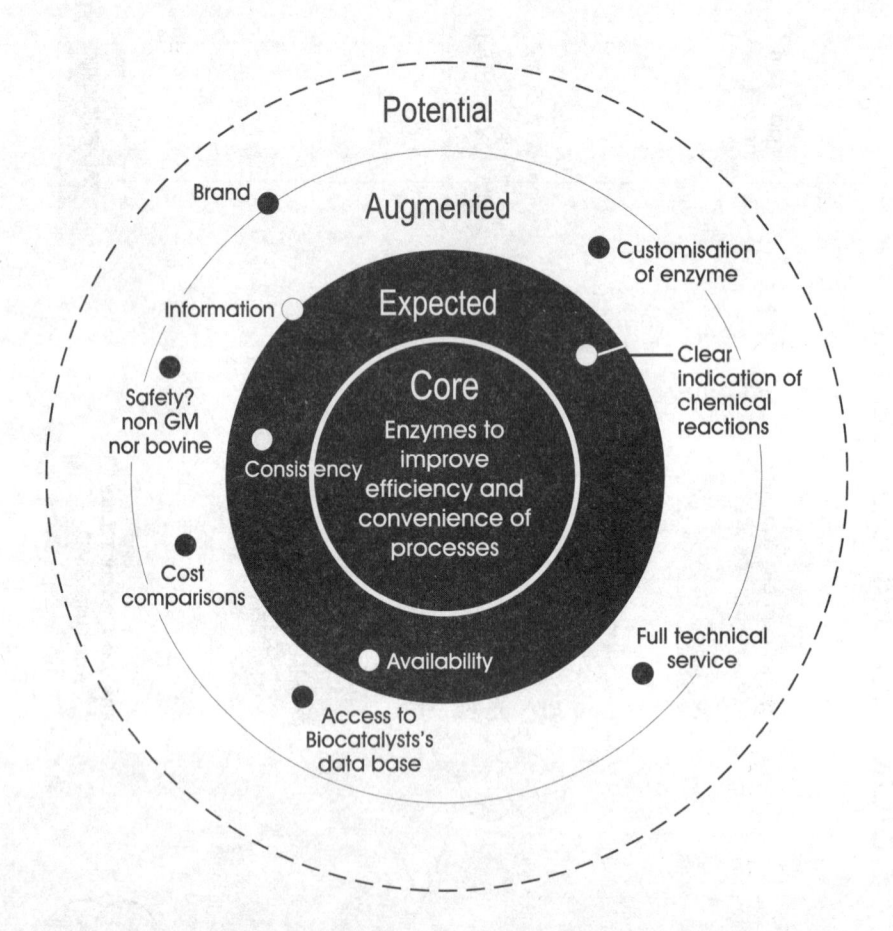

Diagram: Concentric circles showing the total product concept — Core (Enzymes to improve efficiency and convenience of processes), Expected, Augmented, Potential. Labels around the diagram: Brand, Information, Safety? non GM nor bovine, Consistency, Cost comparisons, Availability, Access to Biocatalysts's data base, Full technical service, Clear indication of chemical reactions, Customisation of enzyme.

(a) The company is at the high value, low volume end of the market, offering catalysts which improve process performance across a range of sectors. They are a niche player, able to offer a customised solution to their clients and a full technical service, which should help them avoid price battles and commoditisation as the industry shakes down, with medium-sized players expanding or specialising.

(b) The niche sectors could get crowded, but it is a growing market. Potential is different in the various segments and you will need to sort this out. For example, the Diagnostics Market offers good margins and repeat business (as there are high switching costs) but Biocatalysts is one of three UK suppliers. Some segments like textiles are more price sensitive and protecting these customers from competitive action may be more challenging.

(c) This seems like a company well positioned for future success, with all the essential requirements:

- A unique service offering
- Excellent network of innovators and researchers
- A 'customer focused' culture
- Presence in markets across the world

5.7 The Marketing Mix

There are issues about all elements of the marketing mix which will need sorting out. Remember that, typically, the final case question is about one of the more tactical elements of the case.

(a) **Promotion**
- Dealing with publicity issues relating to use of GMOs
- Developing the 'brand' values and positioning as an expert in the field
- Finding a solution to keeping agents overseas up to date, perhaps the internet and the new website offer an opportunity here

(b) **Pricing**
- Establishing a value/price positioning and avoiding the slide towards commoditisation

(c) **Place**
- Selecting and organising overseas sales

(d) **Product**
- Managing the innovation and NPD process
- Commercialisation of new products

(e) **The service mix**
- Likely to be critical in this knowledge based and customised market: processes and people are going to be key

5.8 The Challenges

The challenges are:

- Turning stars into cash cows
- Establishing a clear focus for activities, not trying to be all things to all people
- A strategic plan: prioritising products and markets, and segmenting those markets is needed
- International distribution needs reviewing and options evaluating
- A clearer positioning is essential: whilst Biocatalysts have the opportunity to carve out a clear niche with customised services, their promotion comes across as an 'off the shelf' product catalogue.

Part B: The sample case: Biocatalysts

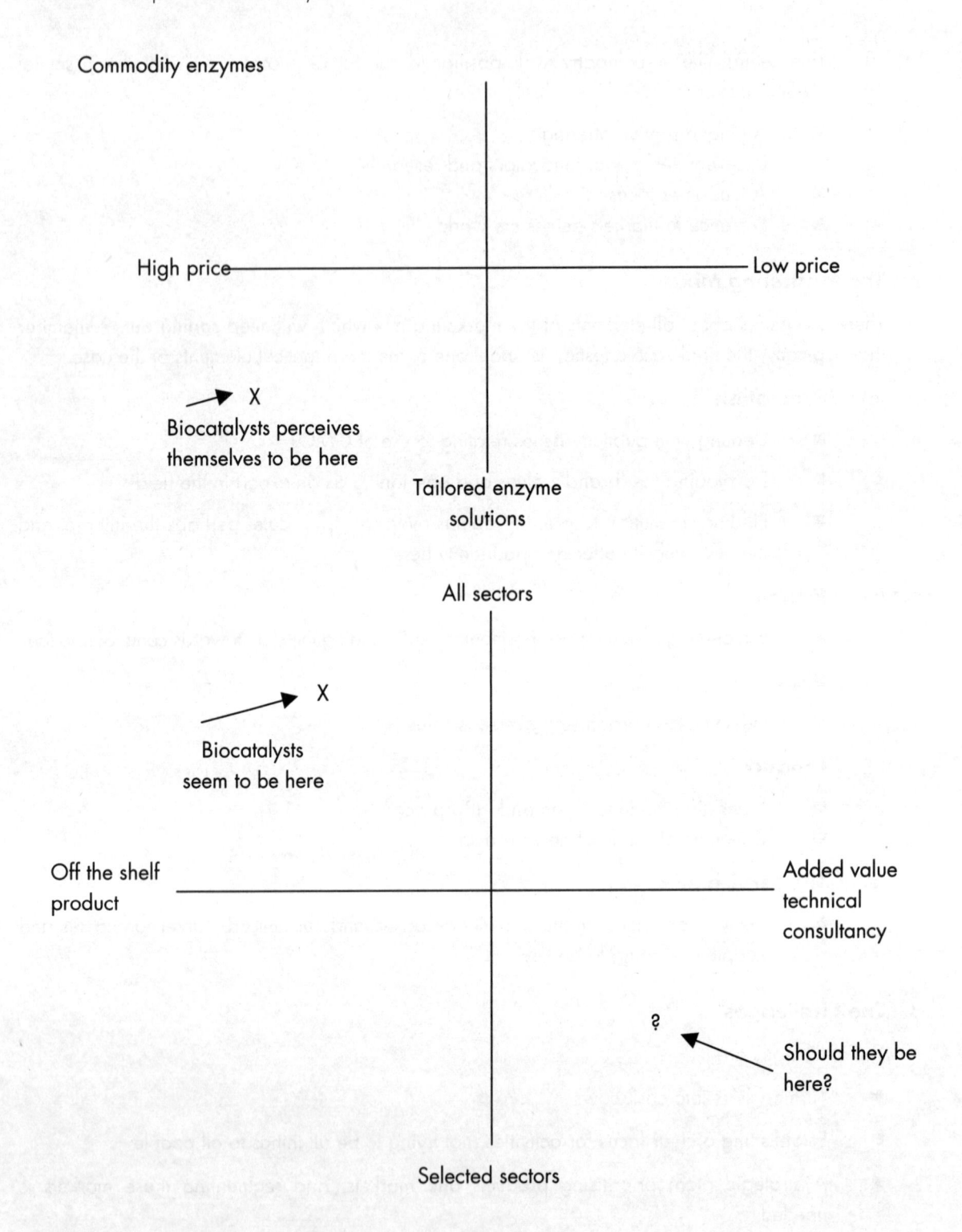

Commodity enzymes

High price ─────────────────────── Low price

→ X
Biocatalysts perceives
themselves to be here

Tailored enzyme
solutions

All sectors

→ X
Biocatalysts
seem to be here

Off the shelf   Added value
product   ──────────────────────   technical
                                                        consultancy

? ← Should they be
        here?

Selected sectors

Where are you now?

5.9 By now you should have a much clearer picture of:

- Biocatalysts – the company and their business in terms of products and markets
- Current performance – financial, operational etc
- The company's competitive position and competitive advantage, actual and potential – focusing on the marketing mix
- The current organisation and the environment it is in
- The enzymes market, developments and challenges

4 ♦ Step 1: Overview of Biocatalysts

- The market place for these products – now and in the future
- New product development at Biocatalysts
- Who the customers are and what matters to them
- The international markets

You should now feel much more ready to tackle the more detailed inview analysis but before you do, test your current understanding of the case.

Action Programme 3

SO YOU THINK YOU KNOW THE CASE..?

QUESTIONS

1. Who are you? What is your role?
2. How would you describe Biocatalysts Ltd?
3. What is the extent and current state of Biocatalysts's international business?
4. How is the product development work managed and paid for at Biocatalysts?
5. What is the value forecast for the structure of the world enzyme industry?
6. What sector of the market is Biocatalysts active in and what is happening to it?
7. What makes Biocatalysts unique?
8. What are the limitations to growth for Biocatalysts?
9. What is the customer's view of price in this market?
10. What is the PR dimension of communication which the company needs to face?

Action programme review

1. (a) This is a business to business market (page 2); this means communication strategies are likely to be sales led and key account management and relationship marketing could be key aspects of Biocatalysts's approach to the market. As you might expect from a B2B firm Biocatalysts has a smaller number of higher value clients and corporate reputation rather than emotional brand values will be important.

   (b) Biocatalysts develops and produces speciality enzymes for industry. It is a challenging global business because it is growing and developing rapidly, but the advent of new genetic engineering techniques and new applications have created their own marketing problems (page 16).

   (c) You are Joseph Mendes, a marketing consultant who (like you) has no experience of this sector. This report is the output of Joseph's initial analysis into the firm and the market – you can expect to be asked to use this to help recommend future strategies.

   (d) Agents are largely involved in export markets.

Part B: The sample case: Biocatalysts

2 Adding the context

(a) It creates the picture of a large successful global player with a number of international markets. Its ethnocentric strategy could be explained by the high knowledge content of its services and the need to customise its services.

(b) Instead of its global expansion being a strength, suddenly it seems more of a weakness. Here we have a business that has stretched itself too thin when it comes to its geographic markets at least. Only an average of 2% of its income, some £50,000, is generated from each country. Clearly there has been little market penetration strategy operating. You start to get a picture of a reactive and opportunist company more like the one we described in a) and the challenge would be to improve penetration and performance in their chosen markets.

(c) An exporting strategy would probably be better replaced with local production, close to eventual markets, thus lowering distribution costs and either improving profitability or local price performance.

SO YOU THINK YOU KNOW THE CASE..?

ANSWERS

1 You are Joseph Mendes, you are a marketing consultant working with Biocatalysts Ltd.

2 A small Welsh-based independent company producing speciality enzymes for a range of industrial clients. They are in the low volume/high value end of the market.

3 70% of sales are exported currently to over 35 countries. Business is managed by agents, who are difficult to control and mainly motivated by finances. The agents earn a 5% commission.

4 Most of the basic research is handled by UK universities where they have many contacts. In-house scientists can focus on customer needs. Funding for higher margin products in diagnostics and pharmaceuticals comes from profits and from European and UK grants.

5 A rapidly growing market:

1994 $1 billion
1997 $1.3 billion
1998 $1.7 billion
2005 $2.0 billion

A polarising market: 12 big global payers with clear positioning/distinct ranges; 60 medium-sized companies and 400 smaller players being forced out because of economies of scale. New competitors from Russia and China forecast.

6 The 'other sector' – likely to be worth over $500m by 2005 (representing 70% of the total market growth).

7 It provides custom-tailored products for its clients.

8 Current capacity would allow output to double. Further growth requires investment funds.

9 We are told price is always an issue, yet enzymes represent a small part of costs (so should be price inelastic) and liability and service is more important. Price comparisons are difficult and Biocatalysts offers a unique customisation service.

10 Genetically modified organisms are increasing by being used for enzyme products (page 24) and Biocatalysts has several under development. A clear communication plan and policy on communications is needed.

Step 2: The Inview – Internal Analysis

Chapter Topic List	
1	Introduction to planning route maps
2	Skills and knowledge reminder
3	Biocatalysts: product analysis
4	Biocatalysts: situation analysis
5	The pitfalls

Introduction

☑ In this chapter we will:

- Review the knowledge and skills you will use in the internal analysis
- Identify the strengths and weaknesses of the Biocatalyst marketing audit
- Identify the strengths and weaknesses of the Biocatalyst business
- Consider the pitfalls at this stage of the process

1 Introduction to planning route maps

1.1 Throughout the file we will be guiding you through the process of analysis and decision with the use of the planning route maps. These maps enable you to quickly assess where you are now in the process and what the next stage is.

Purpose

1.2 At these second and third case steps we will be working on further but deeper case analysis. We need to really get to grips with the information available to us. Because our overview provided us with a real sense of the case context, we will be much better able to make sense of and appreciate the implications of our evaluations and assessments.

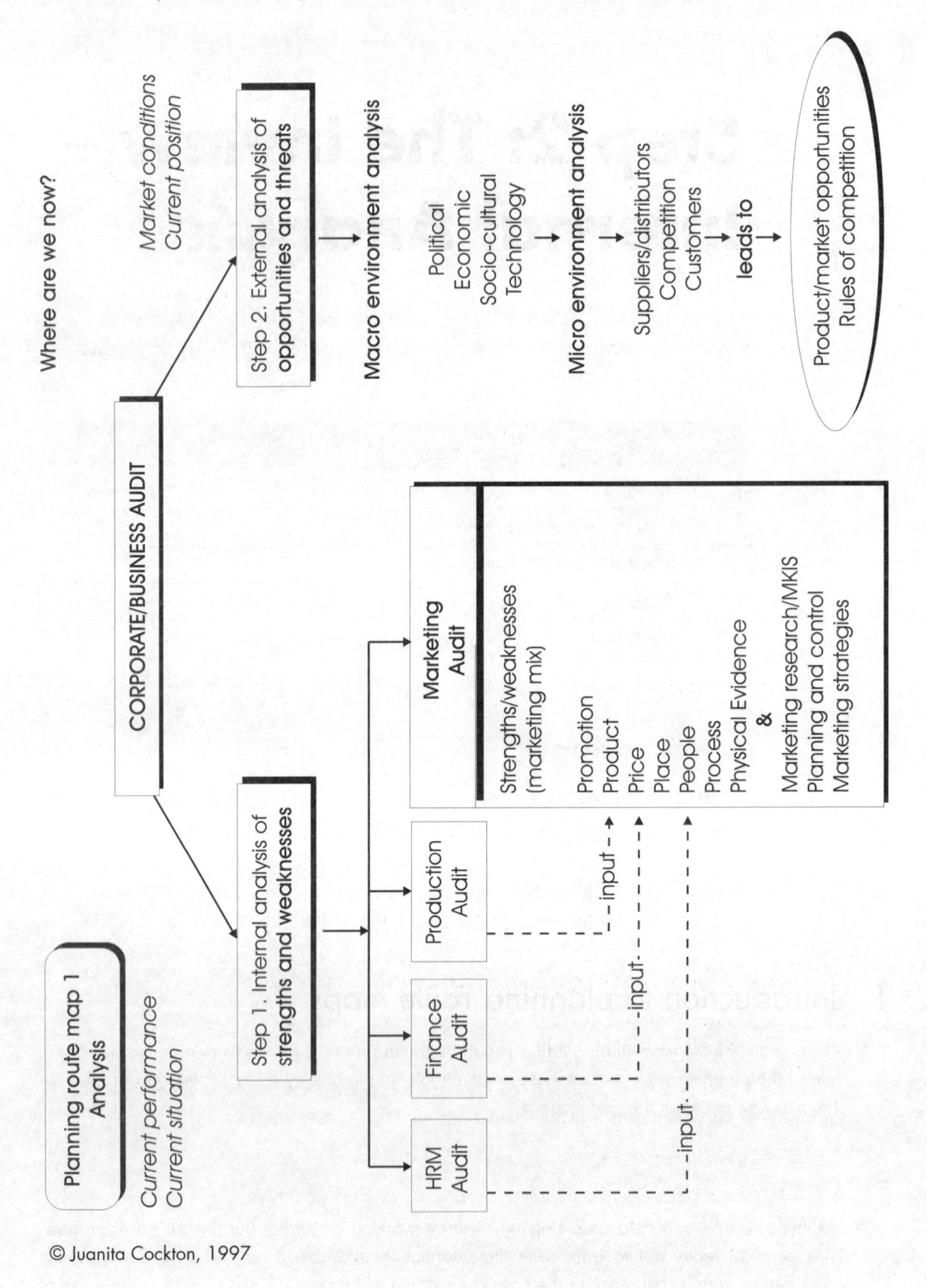

Part B: The sample case: Biocatalysts

Planning route map 1
Analysis

Current performance
Current situation

CORPORATE/BUSINESS AUDIT

Where are we now?

Market conditions
Current position

Step 2. External analysis of opportunities and threats → Macro environment analysis (Political, Economic, Socio-cultural, Technology) → Micro environment analysis (Suppliers/distributors, Competition, Customers) → leads to → Product/market opportunities, Rules of competition

Step 1. Internal analysis of strengths and weaknesses

- HRM Audit
- Finance Audit
- Production Audit
- Marketing Audit

Marketing Audit

Strengths/weaknesses (marketing mix)

- Promotion
- Product
- Price
- Place
- People
- Process
- Physical Evidence
- &
- Marketing research/MKIS
- Planning and control
- Marketing strategies

inputs from HRM Audit, Finance Audit, Production Audit

© Juanita Cockton, 1997

126

5 ♦ Step 2: The inview – internal analysis

Tutor Tip

As we said in Chapter 3, in practice, analysis steps are likely to be undertaken simultaneously. Amongst academics there is some debate as to whether it is most appropriate to undertake an internal analysis before or after the external one. Our overview alleviates that issue to some extent but in reality this audit stage can be sequenced however you like, as long as the internal position is then considered in the context of the external and *vice versa*. For example, at the end of our internal analysis, we would expect to be able to summarise our findings in a weighted and rated table of strengths and weaknesses. To do this, the external perspective must be taken into account because the assessment of strengths and weaknesses must be made against competitor's performance ie bench marked.

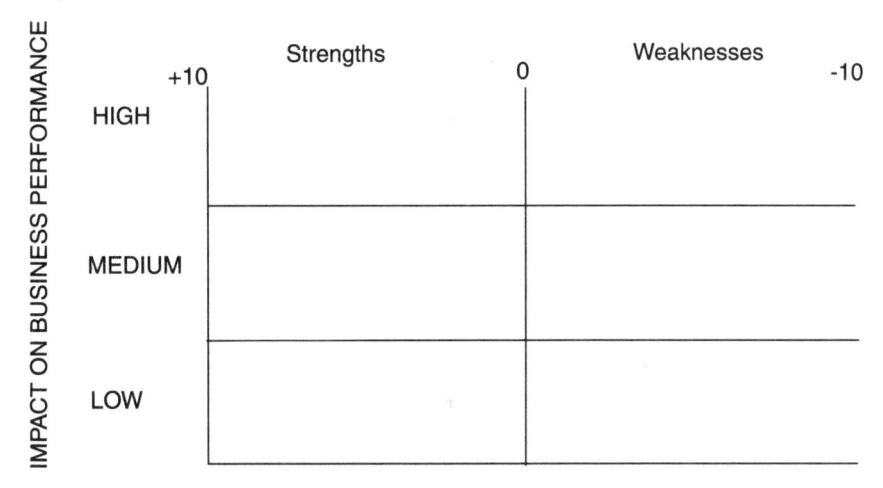

```
                    Strengths              Weaknesses
IMPACT ON        +10              0                    -10
BUSINESS
PERFORMANCE
         HIGH

         MEDIUM

         LOW
```

Point 0 indicates equal to the competitor(s). In this way we can review internal assessments in an external context. We will only be able to interpret our analysis in this way after both internal and external audits are complete, so we will do this in Chapter 7 as a stepping stone to establishing the critical success factors.

1.3 In case step 2, we will be taking the internal analysis first and our purpose is to assess the:

- Core competences
- Capabilities of the business

It is these factors which will both provide the basis for building a competitive advantage but will also help us establish that any recommendations are realistic and credible.

By the end of this chapter we will:

(a) Have used the tools of portfolio analysis to help assess the Biocatalysts's product range
(b) Completed an analysis of Biocatalysts's marketing
(c) Undertaken a broader situational analysis of the business

Part B: The sample case: Biocatalysts

> **Tutor Tip**
>
> The case study is a very challenging paper for marketing students. Its completion requires you can demonstrate not just an understanding of your own discipline, but that you have a broader understanding of all business functions. In order to complete an internal analysis, you must therefore review financial, operational and HR issues facing the business and understand them and their strategic implications. As in the real world, you do not necessarily need to do this alone. You can work with others to break this analysis task down but, as we have indicated, you will need to think about managing that team and sharing the information you produce.

2 Skills and knowledge reminder

2.1 It is at the analysis stage where the tools of planning and control really come into their own. Different cases will lend themselves to different tools and you need to learn to be selective and not to worry if you have incomplete information:

- Use what you have
- Make assumptions if you need to, to fill gaps
- Remember to note the gaps on your information shopping list

2.2 Typically the tools and techniques you might need to use at this stage of a case study will include the following. (Again you will need to take time out to refresh your memory on how each of them is used if you have any doubts or knowledge gaps.)

- Ratio Analysis
- Benchmarking
- Product Life Cycle
- Boston Matrix
- GE Matrix
- Strength and Weaknesses Analysis

What needs to be done

2.3 What needs to be done and how much work is involved at this stage very much depends on the case study. You may have a lot or a little information on the products, marketing or resources of the business. You may have already done quite a bit of work at the overview stage which now needs incorporating or building upon. In this case study though, you can see the distinction between the **overview** and **inview** quite clearly.

(a) At **overview,** we looked at the generic enzyme products and tried to understand what they were and did

(b) We also had an **overview** of the Biocatalysts range – recognising its size, the proportion of new products and its sector focus

(c) At **inview** we need to get even more depth, looking for example at product profitability, if we have enough data

Tutor Tip

You may have already begun to appreciate how much paper can be generated when working on a case study and why file management is such a key skill for the successful student. To help keep your stress levels down by minimising lost pages and work, you should really take positive steps to organise your analysis now.

Steps 2 and 3 are the most paper-intensive, particularly if you are working with a syndicate. You can start by organising your overview into internal and external factors and then working under specific headings like Product, Finance etc within these sections of your decision file.

2.4 By the end of this step we will be able to assess:

(a) Strengths and weaknesses of Biocatalysts's marketing activities
(b) Strengths and weaknesses of Biocatalysts's business situation

2.5 Remember internal analysis assesses the current situation, warts and all!. If staff morale is low, that is what needs to be identified. The fact a new incentive scheme is planned for next year or next month is not relevant. Our task is to evaluate the situation as it is **today**.

2.6 **The distinction between internal and external analysis is decided by controllability.** Low morale, profitability or brand perceptions are all internal controllable factors. Changing them may be difficult, take time and require investment but they can all be tackled. Factors like a declining birth rate, economic recession or introduction of a new technology are external and outside the control of the business.

3 Biocatalysts: product analysis

3.1 We will begin by looking in detail at the Biocatalysts's product portfolio.

Auditing the performance of products

This is undertaken by conducting product portfolio analysis. The intention is to determine which products are performing well and which are not in terms of their profitability, market share performance etc. A number of models can be used.

BOSTON CONSULTING GROUP (BCG)
Relative market share

	High	Low
High (Market growth)	Stars	?
Low	Cash cows	Dogs

PRODUCT LIFE CYCLE (PLC)

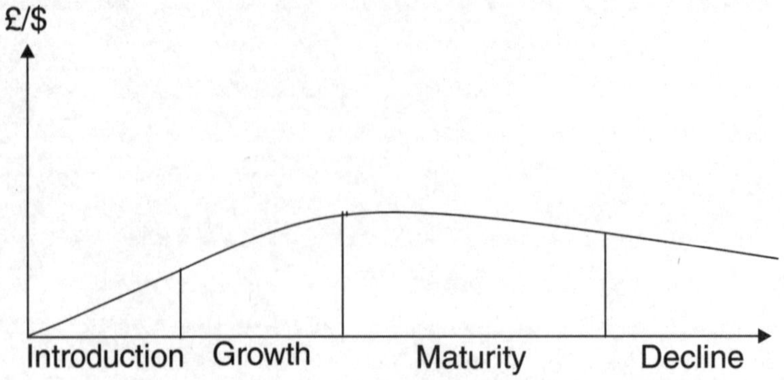
£/$
Introduction
Growth
Maturity
Decline

GENERAL ELECTRIC/MCKINSEY (GE MATRIX)

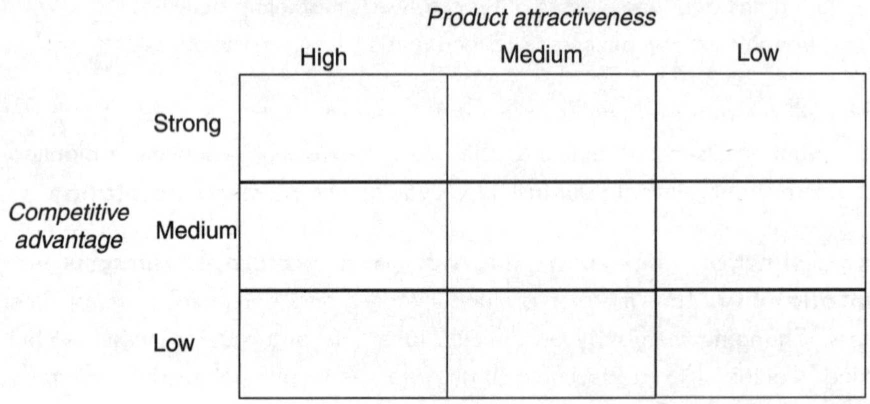
Product attractiveness
High
Medium
Low
Strong
Competitive advantage
Medium
Low

Criteria

Product attractiveness eg	*Competitive advantage* eg
Profitability of ...%	Value for money
Gain market share of %	Reliability
Fit with existing range	Quality (relative
Attract new customers	After sales service
Investment required	Reputation
Repeat purchase	Speed of delivery

The **product attractiveness** criterion is decided by management who then prioritise and weight and rank the criteria. The **competitive advantage** criterion is determined by customers who weight and rank according to their perceptions of importance to them. The results for each product are plotted on the matrix. The results can determine which products should be invested in.

3.2 The market context

(a) We are working in a relatively new technology-driven and global market. We can use a Boston Matrix to help us assess the various Biocatalysts's products/markets within the whole sector.

5 ♦ Step 2: The inview – internal analysis

A MODIFIED BCG MATRIX

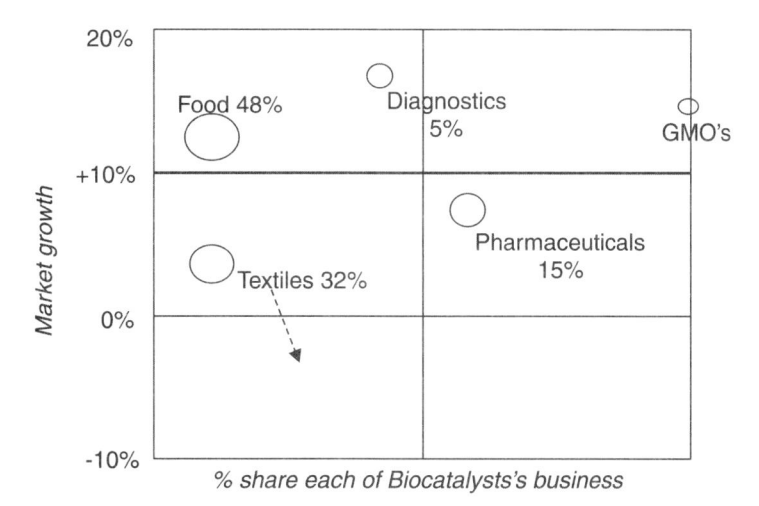

[Chart: Market growth (y-axis, -10% to 20%) vs % share each of Biocatalysts's business (x-axis)
- Food 48% (upper left, ~+13% growth)
- Diagnostics 5% (upper middle, ~+15% growth)
- GMO's (upper right, ~+13% growth)
- Textiles 32% (middle left, ~+3% growth, with arrow pointing down)
- Pharmaceuticals 15% (middle right, ~+6% growth)]

(b) You can see why these tools are so valuable, when you look at this grid and think about what it tells you.

Action Programme 1

Take five minutes to review this indicative BCG Matrix of Biocatalysts's portfolio and identify what this information is telling you. Turn to the end of this chapter to compare your interpretation with ours. You may be wondering where we got the information to apply to our modified Boston Matrix.

Tutor Tip

It is quite acceptable to modify the various tools and models but do make it clear with your labelling. In this case we have used the extended grid which adds warhorses and dodoes to indicate products where the total market is in decline rather than growth. Because Biocatalysts is such a small player, we have used the relative share of their own market rather than relative market share.

Biocatalysts are too small to be market leader so all their products would turn up in right hand cells if assessed against market competitors.

(c) To build this matrix we needed information about:

- Biocatalysts's products
- The product/market sectors

Take a few minutes to look at where we found this and check it against the case study. You can see from this illustration how you need to cross relate data to turn it effectively into information, and then the intelligence we gleaned earlier.

Part B: The sample case: Biocatalysts

> **Tutor Tip**
>
> *You will remember we indicated that internal analysis could only be considered when viewed in an external context. The market information is just that in this example. We will also show how competitor information helps to give us some insight into Biocatalysts's position.*
>
> *Biocatalysts's Product Information*
>
> *Information on pages 34-36 in Appendix 9 is most helpful when you try to sort out the Biocatalysts's portfolio.*

Biocatalysts product range

1	Baking Brewing Fruit and veg Flavour Proteins Dietetics	**Food industry** **48%**
2	Textiles (garment washing)	**Textile Industry** **32%**
3	Own specialist enzymes No npd	**Pharmaceutical industry** **15%**
4	Phen Dehyd Glactose Peroxidase etc	**Diagnostics industry** **5%**

Market information

3.3 Food Industry (from page 34)

(a) 12.5% of all new Biocatalyst's products/investments are in the food sector.

(b) In total, they have 71 old and 14 new products in this area.

(c) 48% of revenue means it represents the largest percentage of sales and Biocatalyst appear to get high margins in this sector.

(d) Their competitive advantage lies in:

- Niche production of specialist enzymes
- Kosher
- Tailored offering
- Safety

(e) This is where GMOs are currently causing concerns and in the UK and Europe the backlash of BSE etc is having a considerable impact.

(f) On average, each product in this part of Biocatalyst's portfolio represents 0.5% of total revenue.

5 ♦ Step 2: The inview – internal analysis

(g) In the UK the closest competitor is Amano (Appendix 1).

```
                    Optimum performing
            Biocatalysts*


                         *Amano
  High value  ─────────────────┼───────────────── Low value


                    Multiple bulk process
```

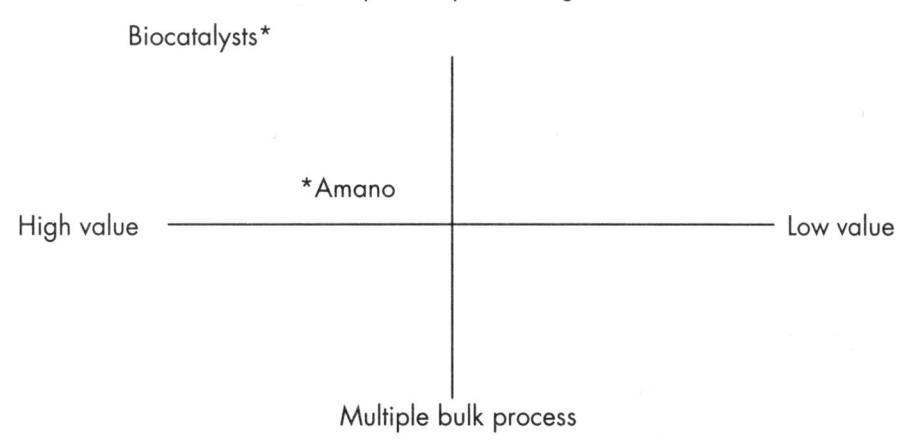

3.4 (a) The Textile industry

(i) 21 products in total, and 9 are new (ie 43%). It is clear that Biocatalyst are investing heavily in this sector, with cost implications.

(ii) Yet this is a declining market.

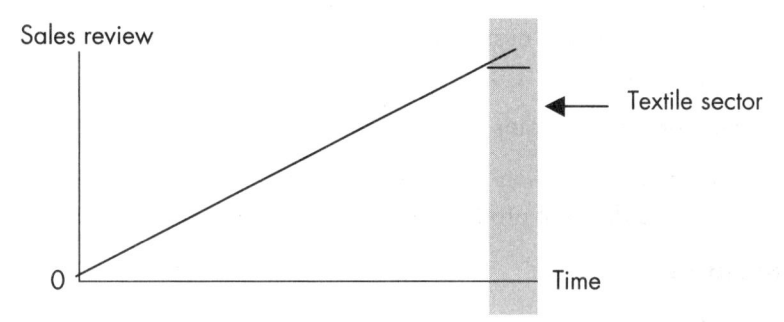

```
  Sales review
       │                                ┌──→ Textile sector
       │                           ╱
       │                      ╱
       │                 ╱
       │            ╱
       │       ╱
       0 ─────────────────────── Time
```

(iii) Gaining a share in a declining market is not an obviously strong strategy. The market, once mature, will commoditise and differentiation will be increasingly difficult and expensive. Biocatalysts will need to decide whether the level of investment needed to stay in this market is worthwhile.

(iv) Textiles represent almost one third (31%) of Biocatalysts' business

(b) **Competitors**

(i) Genzyme and Biozyme do not appear to offer many (if any) textile products.

(ii) What about Rhone-Poulenc: does it have textile products? More information is needed here.

(iii) There appears to be no major competitor in this sector, perhaps this is why Biocatalysts has commanded such a high share of sales from this market.

3.5 (a) Pharmaceuticals

(i) No new products out of a total of 7 offered – so no new investment. Why?

(ii) These represent 15% of total sales.

(iii) We have no real information on positioning or share in this sector.

(iv) Pharmaceuticals are not featured in the world market (page 4). Why not?

(v) Biocatalysts could be a niche player in a small market with high potential profitability.

Part B: The sample case: Biocatalysts

        (vi)   Its competitive advantage would be unique enzymes which could command higher prices.

  (b) **Competitors**

        (i)   Genzyme: what does 'healthcare' cover?

        (ii)   Biozyme: more information is needed

        (iii)   Amano: 51% of their sales are from pharmaceuticals. How does that translate to market share?

        (iv)   Gist Brocades: largest antibiotics producer in the world

3.6 (a) **Diagnostics**

        (i)   8 products in total – 3 of them are new

        (ii)   They represent just 5% of revenue

        (iii)   Biocatalyst is a monopolist in PD enzyme (page 10)

        (iv)   In this sector customers become a captive audience with high switching costs that essentially tie them into a deal.

        (v)   This is another niche market which again does not feature in world figures.

        (vi)   There are new US customers which might lead to growth but also stimulate new competitors.

        (vii)   There are high margins to be made here and it is a profitable product range.

        (viii)   Biocatalyst is investing here and operates in several diagnostic areas and so can offer some depth of product range and experience.

  (b) **Competitors**

        (i)   Amano: 10% of their sales in Diagnostics which amounts to $9.2m a very large player in a small market

        (ii)   Biozyme: more information needed

        (iii)   Genzyme: more information needed

3.7 **GMOs**

Biocatalysts has two genetically modified organisms in development which they are due to launch next year.

Tutor Tip

As you pull your analysis together you will see how the picture builds and those information gaps close up.

3.8 Consolidating information

There are no short cuts to working through case information but you will find it easier if you find ways to summarise and consolidate it.

Product group	Sub Group	Number of products	Number of new products
Food	Baking	18	3
	Brewing	5	5
	Fruit & Veg Processing	11	3
	Flavour	14	0
	Protein	13	1
	Dietetics	9	2
Non Food	Textiles	21	9
	Diagnostics	8	3
	Pharmaceuticals	7	1
	Environmentals	4	0
		110	**27**

(a) A simple table shows the company's spread of activity – 110 products (plus 2 GMOs in development) offered to 10 sectors across food and non food based clients.

(b) Of the 110 products, 27 are new. Five of these are within brewing, a market the company has had no previous experience of. You do need to ask the question **why**?

(c) Has this come about because a researcher wants to work in this sector? If so, we would be worried about the product orientation this demonstrates.

or

Is this development in response to customer requests which shows the company as reactive? In this case we would want to look at the **screening process** for such requests. Does the company simply respond to the scientific challenge rather than assess the commercial feasibility of the new products being developed?

Tutor Tip

The analysis alone is not enough, you must think about what it is telling you. What are the implications?

Part B: The sample case: Biocatalysts

(d) Again mind maps and charts can help you to summarise and consolidate information.

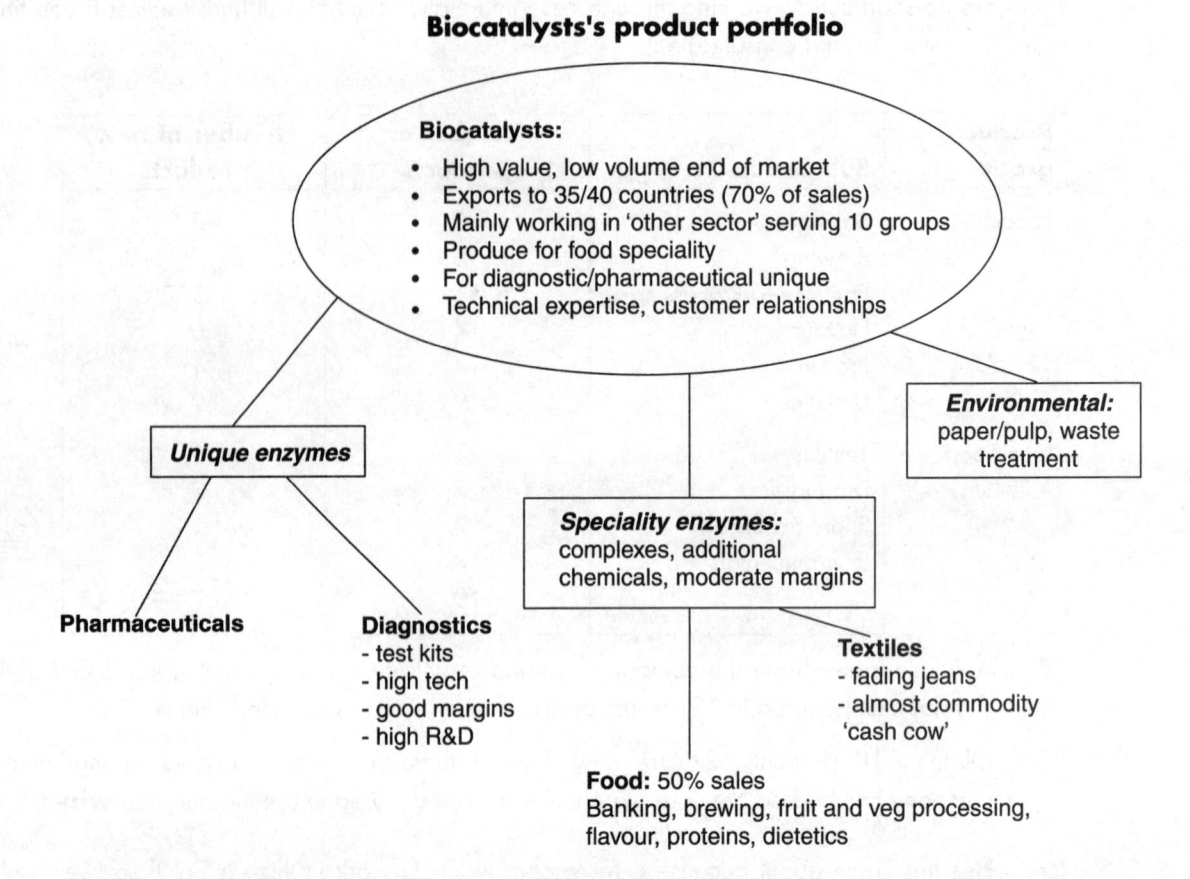

Biocatalysts's product portfolio

Biocatalysts:
- High value, low volume end of market
- Exports to 35/40 countries (70% of sales)
- Mainly working in 'other sector' serving 10 groups
- Produce for food speciality
- For diagnostic/pharmaceutical unique
- Technical expertise, customer relationships

Unique enzymes

Pharmaceuticals

Diagnostics
- test kits
- high tech
- good margins
- high R&D

Speciality enzymes: complexes, additional chemicals, moderate margins

Food: 50% sales
Banking, brewing, fruit and veg processing, flavour, proteins, dietetics

Textiles
- fading jeans
- almost commodity 'cash cow'

Environmental: paper/pulp, waste treatment

3.9 We often find positioning maps useful for clarifying information as well as communicating options and you can see in the one provided here how, in terms of its product, Biocatalyst appears to be uncertain about 'what business they are in' and how to position themselves.

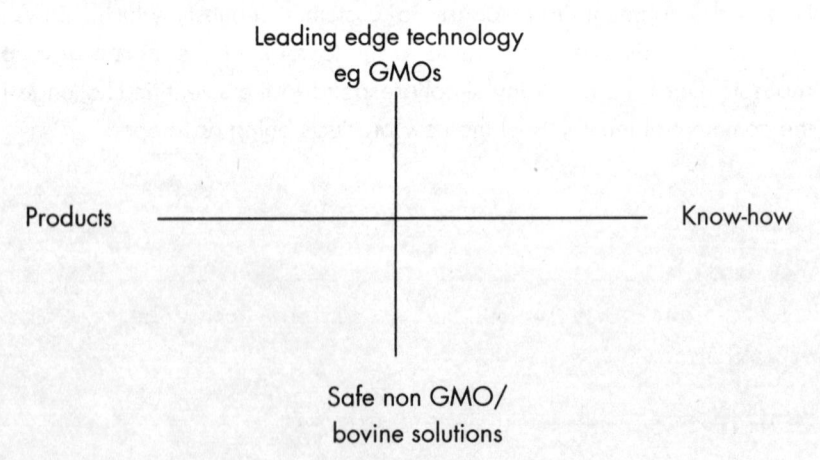

```
        Leading edge technology
              eg GMOs
                 |
                 |
Products --------+-------- Know-how
                 |
                 |
          Safe non GMO/
          bovine solutions
```

3.10 Any position could be tenable but for a very small business, such a big portfolio has them stuck in the middle of the road.

5 ♦ Step 2: The inview – internal analysis

Action Programme 2

Auditing the rest of the marketing mix

Having looked in some detail at the 'product', take no more than 30 minutes to review your case materials and complete a summary strengths and weaknesses analysis for the remaining 6 'P's of the mix.

Tutor Tip

Remember: case studies are never complete, so do not be surprised to find gaps or limited information under certain headings.

Strengths	Weaknesses
Place	
Price	
Promotion	
People	
Physical evidence	
Processes	

Turn to the end of this chapter to compare your analysis with ours.

4 Biocatalysts: situation analysis

4.1 To tackle a case study effectively, you need to address yourself to the whole business **not** simply the marketing activities. This requires that our internal audit is broadened to include:

(a) Financial perspective

(b) Operational overview

(c) People overview

(d) Pan-company issues, including culture, management skills, management information planning processes and new product development

Part B: The sample case: Biocatalysts

4.2 When added to the marketing analysis, you then have a complete situational analysis which will enable us to:

- Assess available resources
- Consider issues of capacity
- Identify any limiting factors
- Establish corporate capabilities which could be used as a basis for establishing a competitive advantage

Tutor Tip

If you are working with a syndicate, you may rely on others to complete parts of your audit analysis for you. That is quite acceptable but you must take the responsibility of owning and understanding the output of that process. In the exam room you could, for example, be faced with additional financial information and you need to know where it has come from and how to use it.

Optional activity

4.3 Before moving forward in this chapter, you might like to practise your analysis skills by pulling together an analysis of these other business areas.

Financial perspective

4.4 Biocatalyst's chosen market is one which requires **high investment** but **delivers high returns** as a result. New products are currently funded from profits and grants from the government and Europe. (The impact of losing grants is a pressing issue.)

4.5 The industry as a whole is growing steadily with sales raising from $1bn in 1994 to $1.3bn in 1997. This is expected to top $2bn in 2005.

4.6 With 70% of sales revenue coming from exports, the company is used to handling different currencies (although it usually only handles $s, £s, and Euros).

Creditors increased in 1997 over 1996 (up 27% or £109k); however debtors have increased by 51% (266k) in the same period.

4.7 Cash flow does not appear to be a problem at the present time. This is assisted by the company policy against stockpiling of finished goods: only raw materials and work in progress is generally held as stock.

- Current ratio > 2:1
- Acid test > 1:1

4.8 The business is growing by 20-30% pa but profitability (page 30) is not improving. There is a danger Biocatalysts is working harder rather than smarter.

Analysing financial information

During your studies of strategic marketing management, you will have covered financial ratios. There has been criticism of marketers' lack of financial skills and the Senior Examiner of Analysis and Decision has made it clear that this area will be tested. We have seen an increase in the financial data and need to be able to work the numbers and interpret financial information. There are many financial ratios but here is a reminder of the key ratios you are most likely to use.

Liquidity and working capital ratios

- Current ratio $\quad \dfrac{\text{Current assets}}{\text{Current liabilities}}$

- Quick ratio (acid test ratio) $\quad \dfrac{\text{Current assets}}{\text{Current liabilities}}$

Efficiency and turnover ratios

- Asset turnover ratio $\quad \dfrac{\text{Sales}}{\text{Average total sales}}$

- Debtor days (average debt collection period) $\quad \dfrac{\text{Sales}}{\text{Debtors}}$

- Average stock turnover period (days) $\quad \dfrac{\text{Sales}}{\text{Stock}}$

Profitability ratios

- Return on capital employed (ROCE) $\quad \dfrac{\text{Earnings before interest and tax}}{\text{Capital employed}}$

- Return on investment (ROI) $\quad \dfrac{\text{Net operating income}}{\text{Operating assets}}$

- Return on sales (ROS) (net profit as a percentage of sales – net margin) $\quad \dfrac{\text{Earnings before interest and tax}}{\text{Sales revenue}}$

- Gross profit as a percentage of sales (gross margin) $\quad \dfrac{\text{Gross profit}}{\text{Sales}}$

- Return on net assets (RONA) $\quad \dfrac{\text{PBIT}}{\text{Sales revenue}} \times \dfrac{\text{Sales revenue}}{\text{Net assets}}$

Debt and gearing ratios

- Debt ratio $\quad \dfrac{\text{Total debt}}{\text{Total assets}} \text{ or } \dfrac{\text{Long term debt}}{\text{Shareholder equity}}$

- Gearing ratio $\quad \dfrac{\text{Total debt}}{\text{Total assets}}$

- Cash flow ratio $\quad \dfrac{\text{Earnings before interest and tax} + \text{depreciation}}{\text{Interest} + [\text{payment}/(1-\text{tax rate})]}$

Part B: The sample case: Biocatalysts

Tutor Tip

Knowledge check: how many of these ratios are familiar to you? Skills check: can you use these ratios? You will need to be able to for the case study.

4.9 There are nearly always discrepancies in the numbers, for example, Biocatalysts's claim to have achieved growth of 20% to 30%. Is it 20%, 30% or somewhere in between? This is one of those occasions when we have to make an assumption before we can start working the figures. Anything from 20% to 30% is acceptable but once you decide what figure you are going to work with, you must remain consistent.

4.10 On page 30 there is reference to the company turnover being approximately £2.5 million. It does not tell us in what year. Again we must make an assumption and, at the time of working the case study, we assumed 1998. We can then work this figure backwards, using whichever figure we have assumed as growth, to give us a turnover figure for 5 years.

4.11 This page also has what is called a profitability index. It is not, in fact, a profitability index but a profit chart.

Action Programme 3

Using appropriate financial ratios, analyse Biocatalysts's financial data. Remember, information is scattered around the case study material, so make sure you collate all the information before you start.

Biocatalysts – working the numbers/key numbers sheet (pages 29/30)

4.12 Remember your figures might be different depending on what growth rate, and therefore turnover, you identified.

Liquidity/working capital

	1994	1995	1996	1997
Current ratio $\dfrac{\text{Current assets}}{\text{Current liabilities}}$			$\dfrac{736{,}915}{399{,}078}$	$\dfrac{953{,}622}{508{,}073}$
	2.3	**2.2**	**1.8**	**1.8**

(Good, 1.8 to 2.3 so fairly sound)

	1994	1995	1996	1997
Acid test $\dfrac{\text{Current assets, less inventory}}{\text{Current liabilities}}$			$\dfrac{548{,}449}{399{,}078}$	$\dfrac{795{,}745}{508{,}073}$
	1.4	**1.5**	**1.4**	**1.6**

(Good, greater than 1 so fairly sound)

Efficiency (productivity) and turnover

		1994	1995	1996	1997
Assets/T/O $\dfrac{\text{Sales}}{\text{Average total assets}}$				$\dfrac{1,601,562}{910,589}$	$\dfrac{2,002,952}{1,131,291}$
				1.8	**1.8**
Debtor days $\dfrac{\text{Sales}}{\text{Debtors}}$				$\dfrac{1,601,562}{517,462}$	$\dfrac{2,002,952}{783,623}$
	(days)	75	72	**118**	**143**
(Poor risk bad debt/cash flow)					
Stock turn $\dfrac{\text{Sales}}{\text{Stock}}=$				$\dfrac{1,601,562}{188,466}$	$\dfrac{2,002,952}{157,877}$
	(days)	**4.9**	**4.8**	**8.5**	**12.6**
(Depends on 6 week lead time)					
Creditor days	(days)	**75**	**75**	**91**	**93**

4.13 This enables you to use very specific case material and therefore provides you with the opportunity to added value and offer insights into financial performance.

Tutor Tip

Have a look at the figures on page 30. This is a good example of how you need to take care with years and comparisons. The table makes you think profit margins are improving significantly: from 4.9% in 1994 to 8.2% in 1995.

There are two issues with this:

(a) Is 8.2% a reasonable return on investment in a high risk, high tech sector? Would the shareholders be better off putting their money in a bank?

(b) It isn't 1995, it is 1998. If you now look at the profitability index you can see the improved performances in 1994 – 1996, but profitability in 1997 and 1998 has levelled off or only increased marginally over the last twelve months.

The available financial analysis is weak. We have no profit analysis by:

- Country
- Product
- Sector
- Agents
- Sales people

We do know that 80% of business comes from 20% of the customers but we do not know whether this also represents 80% of the profits.

Part B: The sample case: Biocatalysts

4.14 Remember the marketer's impact on gross profit

Marketing decisions impact directly on the gross profit margins of the business. Appreciating the implications of your decisions is critical to your ability to share responsibility for the financial health of the business.

(a) **Changing the customer mix**

Different market segments will have different gross profit potential. Large customers may be more or less profitable than small ones. There are no hard and fast rules, just the margins are likely to be different. Before deciding which segments to target, marketers must know which segments are most profitable.

(b) **Changing the product mix**

Different products will have different profit margins. Knowing which are your most profitable offerings is fundamental to decisions at a strategic and tactical level.

(c) **Changing the marketing mix**

Discounts or increased advertising might increase sales revenue and total profit but will depress gross profit margins. Decisions to change any element of the marketing mix will have financial consequences: marketers need to be aware of these and budget for them.

Tutor Tip

Improving Profitability

Biocatalysts is unlikely to be the last case where we are faced with a need to improve profitability and it would be useful for you to ensure you are familiar not only with how marketing can impact on profitability, but on how it can be improved by actions across the business.

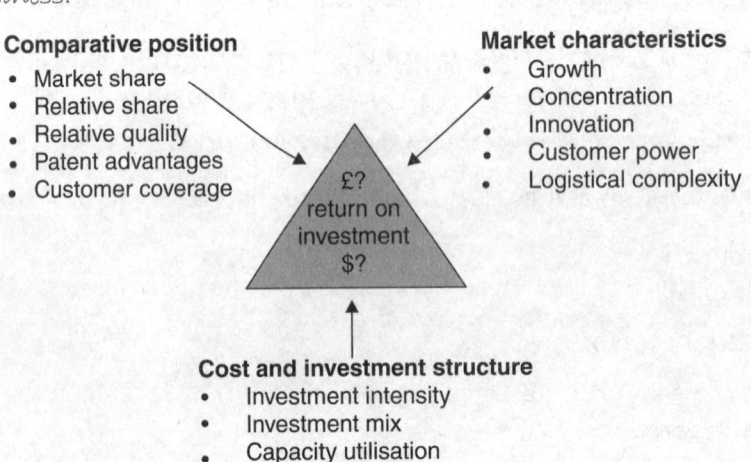

Comparative position
- Market share
- Relative share
- Relative quality
- Patent advantages
- Customer coverage

Market characteristics
- Growth
- Concentration
- Innovation
- Customer power
- Logistical complexity

£? return on investment $?

Cost and investment structure
- Investment intensity
- Investment mix
- Capacity utilisation
- Productivity
- Vertical integration

Porter's value chain can be a useful model to help identify and communicate profit drivers from across the business.

5 ♦ Step 2: The inview – internal analysis

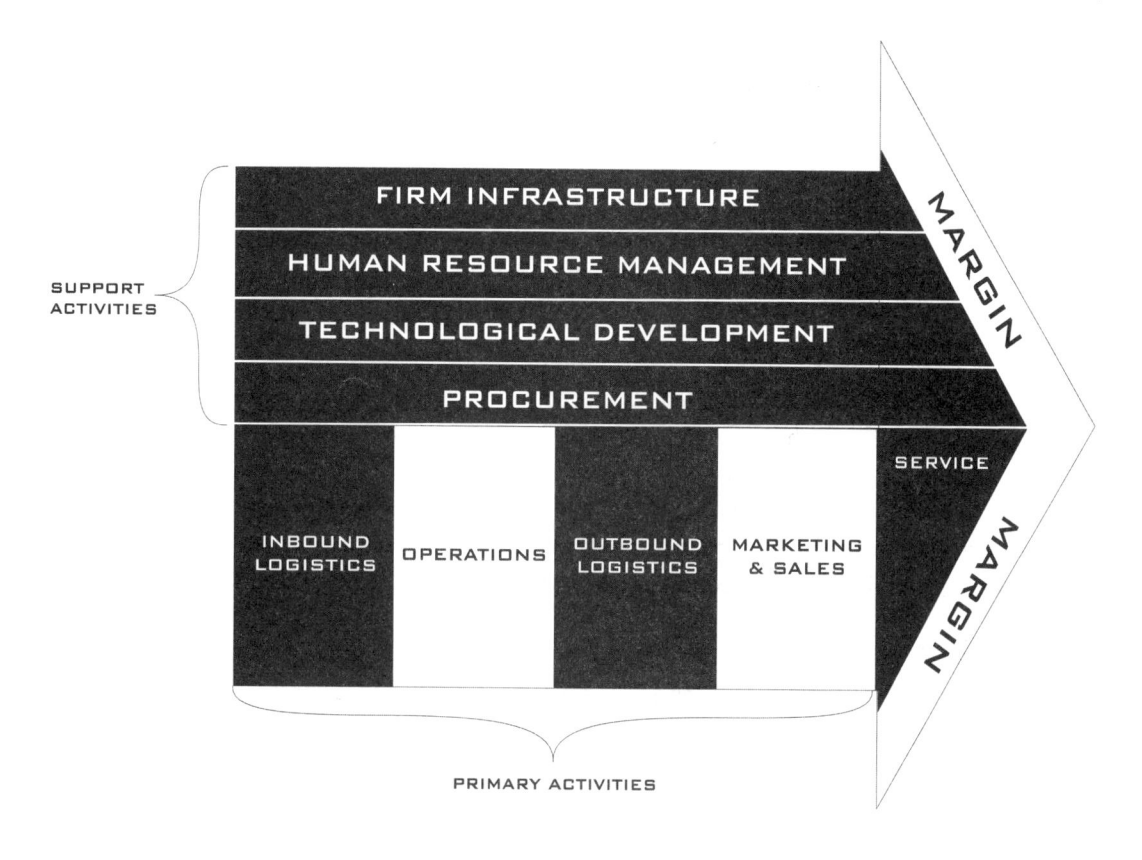

Porter's Value Chain diagram:
- Support Activities: Firm Infrastructure, Human Resource Management, Technological Development, Procurement
- Primary Activities: Inbound Logistics, Operations, Outbound Logistics, Marketing & Sales, Service
- Margin

Operational overview

4.15 Biocatalysts Ltd have only one site: this is in Wales and is an 8,000 square feet modern factory unit. Facilities include:

- Liquid and powder blending facilities
- Small scale fermentation/filtration equipment
- Pilot chromatographic purification and drying units

4.16 Batch sizes for all in-house production is flexible and the company is ISO 9000 compliant, enforcing the highest levels of quality control. All of the above machinery is fully depreciated but envisaged to be capable of another five years' output before replacement is necessary.

4.17 Customer requirements are established and the appropriate enzyme solution is researched by the Biocatalyst Ltd scientists (and researchers at various universities).

4.18 Large scale production/fermentation is contracted out. This has both good and bad aspects – good from the point of view of flexibility for the place/country of production and removal of the need for capital expenditure (for purchase and maintenance of facilities) but bad from the point of view of control. Quality control amongst other things can fall short of the required standards, facilities may not be available when needed and so on.

4.19 A £1m investment would enable all fermentation processing to take place in-house for the next five years (taking into account the sales growth we can expect). It should be noted that this could

Part B: The sample case: Biocatalysts

produce logistical problems in the transport of the finished product that would add to the costs of production and delivery of the final product.

4.20 Currently facilities already in place are not fully utilised. It has been calculated that in-house production could double with limited investment and only one or two more production staff.

4.21 Heavy investment after five years will be needed.

4.22 No fermentation takes place on site.

People overview

4.23 Currently there is a very simple structure in place with small teams for Sales, Administration, Purchasing, Production, Design and R&D projects. The structure is not marketing oriented at present which will need addressing.

4.24 Marketing/Sales is made up of five people including the MD (Stewart North). They look after new product development and long-term strategy. Of these five, there are three dedicated sales staff who spend 80% of their time directly involved with sales. This team of three is responsible for the relationship with the agents who conduct Biocatalyst's business to business sales.

4.25 Nearly all overseas sales are generated by agents and distributors. This has inherent problems such as that agents are not solely representing Biocatalyst Ltd and may sell competitor products in preference to Biocatalysts's; they need constant review, the quality of individuals varies. They are hard to monitor and they are not always motivated to educate the customers as they should.

4.26 Scientists are not full time employees and so their availability and commitment could be an issue.

4.27 There may be an element of 'pet project syndrome' when it comes to evaluating new opportunities.

4.28 High staff costs are minimised by using a project approach.

4.29 Contact with overseas sales teams is inadequate. A newsletter is sent out every six months to all distributors and customers. This details R&D advances and other changes in current products. Training sessions are held every year to bring agents up to speed with the current portfolio. Unfortunately many agents are absent from these meetings, drastically reducing their impact.

4.30 More and more, specialised/narrow niches are emerging and pressure is rising to provide dedicated sales teams who work only for Biocatalyst. Although it would be a challenge to replace all agents with dedicated staff in all countries, there are certain areas where potential volumes demand them, eg the Olive Oil sector and the PKU diagnostics enzyme recently approved for use in the USA.

5 ♦ Step 2: The inview – internal analysis

5 The pitfalls

5.1 For the marketing student, the inview analysis can cause problems and there are a number of pitfalls you need to avoid:

(a) Focusing only on the **marketing aspects** and ignoring other **business issues and factors**.

(b) **Ignoring the numbers**: yes we know it's tempting but the numbers will provide you with the keys to setting objectives and controls so work with them **not** around them.

(c) Failing to consolidate and summarise your analysis so that there are pages of information but you fail to use it as intelligence because it cannot be easily assimilated.

Action Programme 4

Having worked through the internal analysis you should now be in a position to share your understanding of Biocatalyst with others.

Take no more than 20 minutes to prepare some brief notes in answer to a colleague's questions about Biocatalyst. Try and do this without referring back.

1 What are the key points you would make about the company's products?

Key Points

■

■

■

2 How would you summarise the strengths and weaknesses of Biocatalysts in relation to its current markets?

Strengths   *Weaknesses*

3 How would you summarise the company's overall weaknesses?

Check your answers with ours at the end of this chapter.

Part B: The sample case: Biocatalysts

Action Programme Review

1. (a) Over half of Biocatalysts' product/markets are high growth – net cash users not generators.

    (b) The company is operating in four main sectors – so it begs the question, 'are they spread too thinly?'

    (c) The main cash cow, textiles, is a market going into decline.

    (d) GMOs are a classic. They could be highly profitable or, if rejected by customers, immediately become a dog. They should be concerned about future cash flow and funding the effective commercialisation of new products.

2. Auditing the rest of the marketing mix

    Strengths

    Place

    - Network of agents and direct sales covering 35 countries
    - Direct sales team, but it's very small

    > **Implications**: Little control over agents or access to the customer in international markets.

    Price

    - Euro may resolve our exchange problems for Europe in the future
    - Some new sectors and markets are attracting premium prices

    > **Implications**: A one-size fits all pricing strategy will not maximise returns for this business.

    Promotion

    - Key account handling exists in principle if not always in practice
    - They feel mailshots and exhibitions are important

    > **Implications**: There is more of a B2C feel to the communications thinking. Networking and relationship marketing need to be cornerstones for this sector.

    People

    - High calibre scientific staff
    - Flexibility in staffing should enable the right people for the right task and keep costs down
    - Links with University staff
    - 80% of five sales and marketing people's time dedicated to sales

    Physical evidence

    > **Implications**: In a service business physical evidence can add tangibility and value. It needs to be included in our thinking.

    Processes

    > **Implications**: Another black hole with no real insights but would be critical in ensuring customer satisfaction

Weaknesses

Place

- Inconsistent ability of agents to add value
- Training and updating: Biocatalysts' business has limited commission value to agents
- Shipping costs
- Agents will be driven by commission
- No website

Price

- Pricing strategy is not delivering profits expected
- Some sectors are commoditising and prices are low
- Pricing strategy doesn't support the company's positioning
- How are exchange rates impacting on prices – benefits or takes the hit?

Promotion

- Personal sales coverage is weak due to limited resources
- Brand values are undefined and positioning is confused
- Communication with agents is patchy and unfocused
- No website for communication
- The literature is product led, offering few benefits and not focused on the various sectors with very different needs!
- Bad PR related to GM products

People

- No obvious marketing experiences
- There are question marks over the agents' motivation and capability
- Training not taken seriously
- High technical support promised but is it given?

> **Implications.** Selling know-how is dependent on the people. There is a question as to the commitment and availability of this academic community

Physical Evidence

- No mention of any tangible aspects of the brand eg packaging, product literature, van livery, etc

3   The answer is given in the text.

Part B: The sample case: Biocatalysts

4

1 Key points about the Biocatalysts' products

- Positioned at high value, low volume end of market, need to build strong positioning to counteract threats from changes in the market
- Have unique products: however need to protect them – intellectual property
- Diagnostics = good margins: however low percentage of current sales
- New product development led by customers – lack of focus
- Research part funded by grants – what if these were withdrawn
- Over represented in declining product sectors, many new products being produced in these
- GMO's could present both opportunity and threat: need to consider implications in terms of PR and marcomms
- Threats from competitors: they are producing products in a very attractive niche of the market
- Technical ability – but product led

2 Biocatalysts' markets: strengths and weaknesses

Strengths	Weaknesses
Experience in many markets	Overstretched serving too many sectors and countries
Diagnostic high margin	Never fully exploit sector/product potential
Food sector expertise and high growth area	Textiles in decline
Pharma high margin	Fragmented
Seeks niches	Three players have 75% of market
Monopoly of PKU testing	No market analysis
	No environmental screening
	Very competitive – many players
	Commoditisation of some markets
	8% profitability very low – some markets very unprofitable
	Little in-house overseas knowledge

3 Overall weaknesses

- Reliance on other parties for sales and for R&D
- Resources spread thinly in over 35 countries
- Lack of production facilities leaving Biocatalysts at the mercy of other companies (time frames etc)
- Independent sales advisers are used who do not have it in their main interests to promote Biocatalysts's products all of the time(extended portfolios etc). These staff have no one to answer to.
- Lack of sales channels
- Communication channels to existing sales channels are unacceptably poor

Step 3: External Analysis

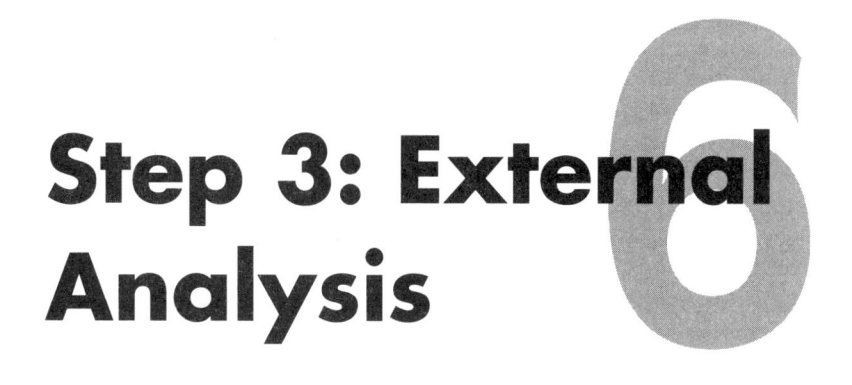

Chapter Topic List

1	Mapping the context: skills and knowledge
2	Building a market map for Biocatalysts

Introduction

In this chapter we will cover:

- ☑ The micro analysis for Biocatalysts covering market analysis, competitor audit and customer analysis
- ☑ The macro analysis for Biocatalysts

1 Mapping the context: skills and knowledge

1.1 Organisations **do not exist in a vacuum and so therefore they cannot plan in one.** It is the **changes** in their external macro and micro environments which create the **opportunities and threats** which drive their fortunes. Those who only look inwardly will be caught out by the environmental threats and will fail to respond to the opportunities. In today's fast moving and dynamic markets, the environmental impact can be swift and significant. Only those really aware of their markets and environments can effectively capitalise on emerging opportunities or minimise the impact of the threats. The smaller the business, like Biocatalysts, the fewer resources they have to weather an environmental storm, and the enzyme market is one where change is a fact of life.

1.2 You need to look **outside** the business to establish the **external context** and conditions facing the case company.

1.3 In the situation analysis, you needed to assess the current position but in the **environmental audit you need to address the future.** Planning is about tomorrow, not today, so we need to look forward and prepare the business for the markets of one, three, five or even ten years time. **This planning horizon will often be clear from the case.** A business struggling to survive might expect to be concerned with short term strategy, whereas a capital intensive industry may be planning for a longer term future.

Part B: The sample case: Biocatalysts

> **Tutor Tip**
>
> This immediately gives us a problem in case study. The CIM tells you not to look outside the case study, yet you are unlikely to have been furnished with environmental forecasts. You may be able to establish environmental trends from case information but you can also use your common sense and experience to make reasonable assumptions about the future.

1.4 By the end of this chapter you will have:

(a) Created a market map for Biocatalysts

(b) Recognised the value of Porter's Five Forces and competitive strategies models in evaluating the micro environment

(c) Undertaken an environmental audit

(d) Considered the international aspects and the implications of different external environments on planning and strategy for a business such as Biocatalysts

Skills and knowledge reminders

1.5 There are a number of tools and models which are helpful when completing the external audit. You may need to familiarise yourself with the following before approaching this chapter.

(a) A **market map** is a useful visualisation of who's who in the market place and lets you look at who is working with whom and so on.

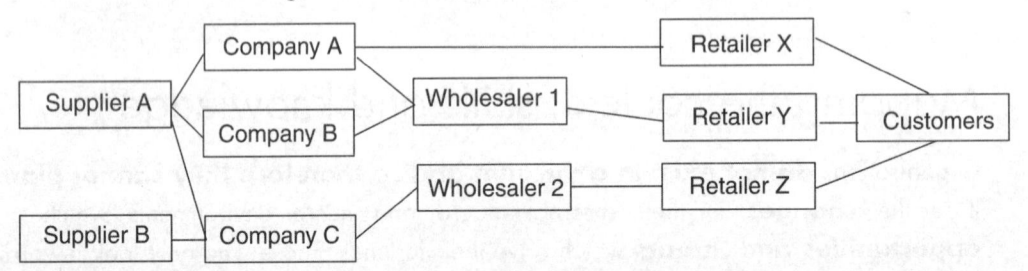

```
                    ┌───────────┐                   ┌───────────┐
                  ┌─│ Company A │───────────────────│ Retailer X│─┐
┌──────────┐      │ └───────────┘     ┌───────────┐ └───────────┘ │
│Supplier A│──────┤                 ┌─│Wholesaler1│─┬─────────────┤
└──────────┘      │ ┌───────────┐   │ └───────────┘ │ ┌─────────┐ │ ┌──────────┐
                  └─│ Company B │───┤               └─│Retailer Y│─┤─│Customers │
                    └───────────┘   │                 └─────────┘ │ └──────────┘
                                    │ ┌───────────┐ ┌───────────┐ │
                                    └─│Wholesaler2│─│ Retailer Z│─┘
┌──────────┐      ┌───────────┐       └───────────┘ └───────────┘
│Supplier B│──────│ Company C │
└──────────┘      └───────────┘
```

(b) A **positioning map** is a very effective framework for identifying who the closest competitors are.

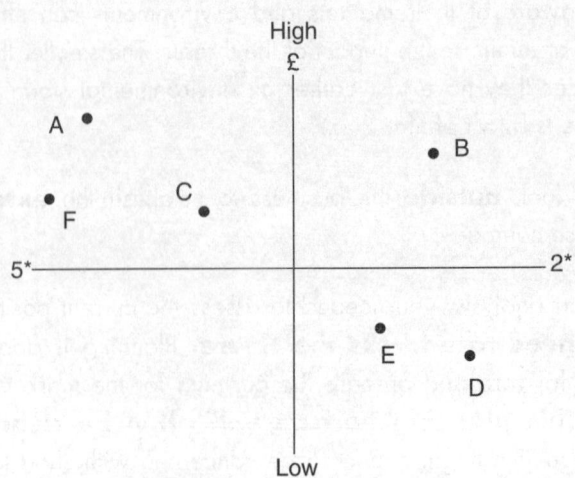

```
                     High
                      £
                      │
          A •         │
                      │         • B
              • C     │
           •          │
           F          │
    5*────────────────┼────────────────2*
                      │
                      │
                      │       • 
                      │       E  •
                      │          D
                      │
                     Low
```

(c) Porter's *generic strategies model* encourages you to identify the strategy being adopted by the market players.

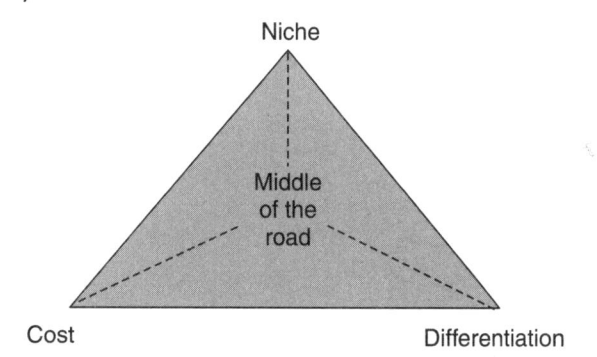

```
              Niche
               /\
              /  \
             / Middle \
            /  of the  \
           /    road    \
          /_____\
        Cost          Differentiation
```

(d) *Porter's Five Forces model* will help you to assess the changes in market dynamics and forecast the likely direction of gross profit margins.

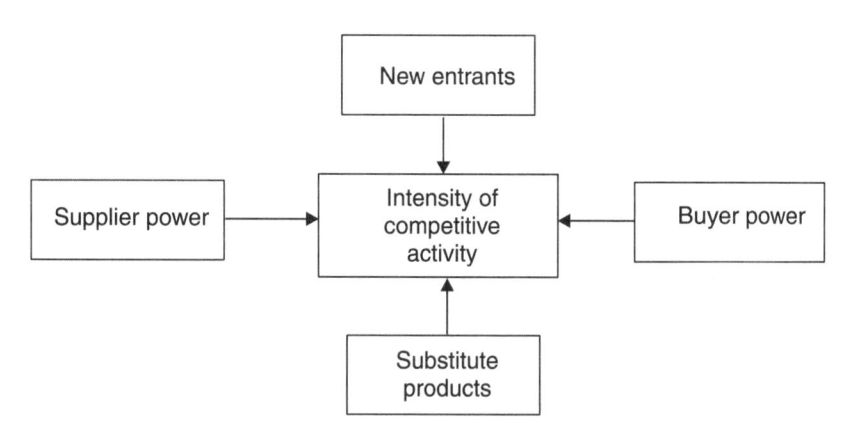

```
                    ┌─────────────┐
                    │ New entrants│
                    └──────┬──────┘
                           │
                           ▼
┌──────────────┐    ┌─────────────┐    ┌──────────────┐
│Supplier power│───▶│ Intensity of│◀───│ Buyer power  │
│              │    │ competitive │    │              │
└──────────────┘    │   activity  │    └──────────────┘
                    └──────▲──────┘
                           │
                    ┌──────┴──────┐
                    │  Substitute │
                    │   products  │
                    └─────────────┘
```

(e) The diffusion of innovation curve show statistical patterns in buyer behaviour.

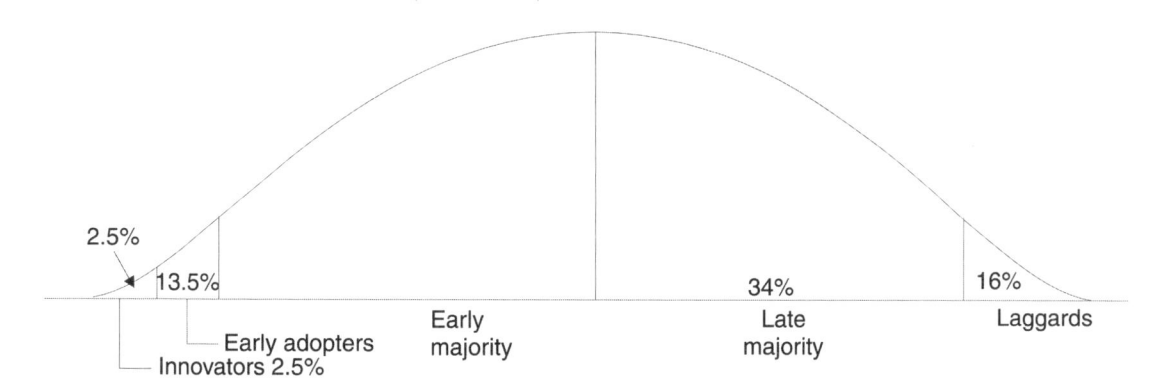

2.5% | 13.5% | 34% | 34% | 16%

Innovators 2.5% — Early adopters — Early majority — Late majority — Laggards

Part B: The sample case: Biocatalysts

What needs to be done

1.6 What and how much needs to be done depends on the actual case you are working on. In some, we have a lot of external information and in others very little. However, the principles will stay very much the same.

Step 1. Build a **Market Map**. You may need two or three if the company is active in different sectors facing different market conditions. If you have already used this framework at the inview stage, you could add detail now.

Step 2. Market dynamics are important in understanding the business. Try to extend the market map into a Porter's **Five Forces Analysis** and assess the implications.

Step 3. A **competitor analysis** is essential to any future strategy. Sort out who is active in what markets and what strategies they are adopting. (We began to collect some of that information when we were looking at the key Biocatalyst product markets in the last chapter.)

Step 4. As customers are key, we need to assess who they are, how the market is segmented and who is in the DMU. We will need to think of channels as customers in this process. We want to assess how customers are changing: what are the emerging needs or concerns?

Step 5. We need to consider the external macro environment, PEST or SLEPT or PESTLE analysis. Your terminology is not important so long as you have considered all the key factors and influences facing the business:

- Political and legal
- Economic and demographic
- Social and cultural
- Technological and environmental

Step 6. **Market structure analysis – a check list**

Every market will differ in its characteristics. However, the following general analytical framework can be applied to most markets or segments. You should identify:

- What are the **market parameters**? In other words, what are its boundaries? The UK domestic market's parameters are the borders of the UK.
- The size of the market within these parameters
- Whether the market is **growing,** stable or declining
- How the market is **segmented**?
- To what extent **each segment** is growing, stable or declining
- The **key players** in the market/segments (eg manufacturers, distributors, others).
- The **key success factors** in this market or segment
- The **buying behaviour characteristics** of this market/segment
- The **major market/segment competitors**, their distinctive competences
- **Future environmental factors** affecting this market/segment
- How **easy** or **difficult** is the market and/or segment to **enter** or **exit**

6 ♦ Step 3: External analysis

2 Building a Market Map for Biocatalysts

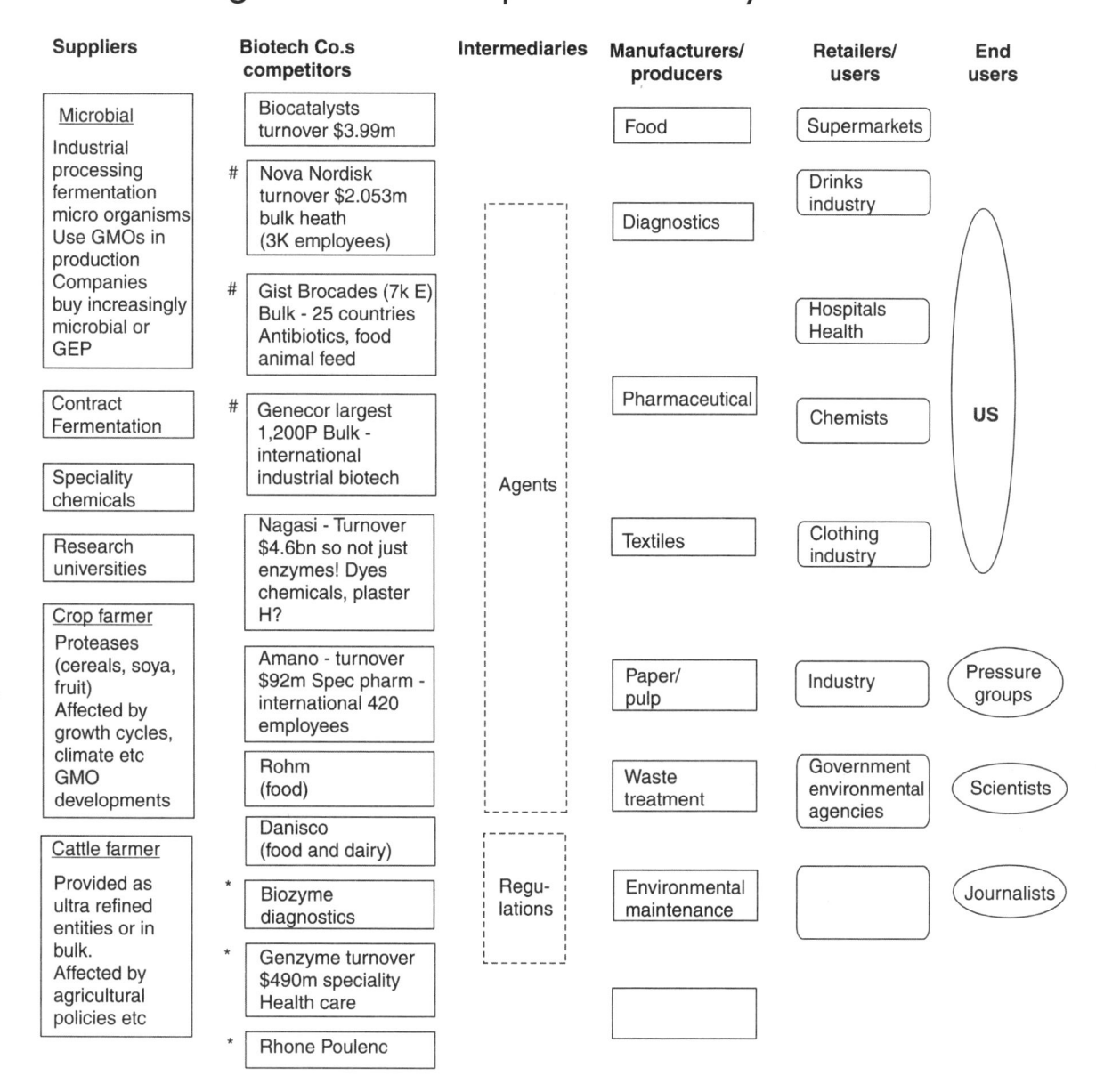

Suppliers	Biotech Co.s competitors	Intermediaries	Manufacturers/ producers	Retailers/ users	End users
Microbial — Industrial processing fermentation micro organisms. Use GMOs in production. Companies buy increasingly microbial or GEP	Biocatalysts turnover $3.99m		Food	Supermarkets	
	# Nova Nordisk turnover $2.053m bulk heath (3K employees)		Diagnostics	Drinks industry	
	# Gist Brocades (7k E) Bulk - 25 countries Antibiotics, food animal feed		Pharmaceutical	Hospitals Health	US
Contract Fermentation	# Genecor largest 1,200P Bulk - international industrial biotech	Agents		Chemists	
Speciality chemicals	Nagasi - Turnover $4.6bn so not just enzymes! Dyes chemicals, plaster H?		Textiles	Clothing industry	
Research universities					
Crop farmer — Proteases (cereals, soya, fruit). Affected by growth cycles, climate etc. GMO developments	Amano - turnover $92m Spec pharm - international 420 employees		Paper/ pulp	Industry	Pressure groups
	Rohm (food)		Waste treatment	Government environmental agencies	Scientists
	Danisco (food and dairy)				
Cattle farmer — Provided as ultra refined entities or in bulk. Affected by agricultural policies etc	* Biozyme diagnostics	Regu- lations	Environmental maintenance		Journalists
	* Genzyme turnover $490m speciality Health care				
	* Rhone Poulenc				

2.1 In practice, you are unlikely to just sit down and complete a perfect market map for the case: you build it up and evolve it as you collect more information. This one is simple; it lists competitors but does not show how each of them is operating in terms of suppliers or access to customers. As we build our knowledge of competitors and customers through this step, you will be able to add more detail to the map.

Understanding market dynamics

2.2 Here is a table summarising the dynamics of the Biocatalysts market as produced by a student group working the case. It gives an idea of how you might synthesise this information, but compare it with the visual communication of the same material using the model. You can see how this gets information across quickly and can be a real asset in the exam room when time is at a premium.

Part B: The sample case: Biocatalysts

Market analysis

Porter's model

Category	Remarks	Rating
Competitive activity	**General:** ■ Biocatalysts Ltd is a small company turnover just £2.5m – 70% export sales. ■ Biocatalysts Ltd provides full technical support, exclusive agreements and 1 to 1 relationship this high dependency relationship makes **switching** less likely ■ Biocatalysts Ltd operates in food 48%, textiles 31%, diagnostics 5%, pharmaceuticals 15% and other 1% ■ 12 major global producers all with relatively distinct offerings ■ 60 smaller range global producers ■ 400 very limited industrial quantity global producers ■ Geographically – 60% production in Europe, 15% in North America and 12-15% in Japan ■ Russian market large but undeveloped ■ Chinese market large (especially for food enzymes) but relatively 'closed' **Medical/diagnostic** (used for testing for abnormalities in humans) **sector:** ■ Japan weak in bulk enzymes but strong in speciality, especially medical diagnostics ■ Growth market ■ High margins **Textiles** (used for fading jeans) **sector:** ■ A near commodity business with little or no R&D required: this appears totally alien to Bio's offering ■ Moderate margins ■ Declining market **Food** (used to increase yields and quality) **sector:** ■ Moderate margins	Textiles: HIGH Other: MEDIUM
Buyers	**General:** ■ Price as a % of customers' production costs will be very low so price likely to be inelastic ■ A lot of product ignorance leading to some buyers focusing on price ■ Business to business market ■ Customers will often be very large and powerful ■ The needs of the deferred customer, the public, need to be considered ie fears in Europe leading to supermarkets not stocking ■ Agents selling many company products	Textiles: HIGH Other: MEDIUM
Suppliers	**General:** ■ Other enzyme producers (patents often in place) ■ University knowledge base ■ Fermenters (as this is outsourced)	MEDIUM

6 ♦ Step 3: External analysis

Category	Remarks	Rating
New entrants	**General:** ■ Growth market which is likely to attract others but high technical expertise may well act as a discouragement ■ Due to GMO option, R&D is lower, so ease of entry is higher ■ In-house option ■ Under-developed countries ie China and Russia	MEDIUM
Substitute products	**General:** ■ Traditional/natural production methods – but these are inefficient and of poor quality ■ Remember the GMO (lower R&D)/non-GO (higher R&D) option	LOW

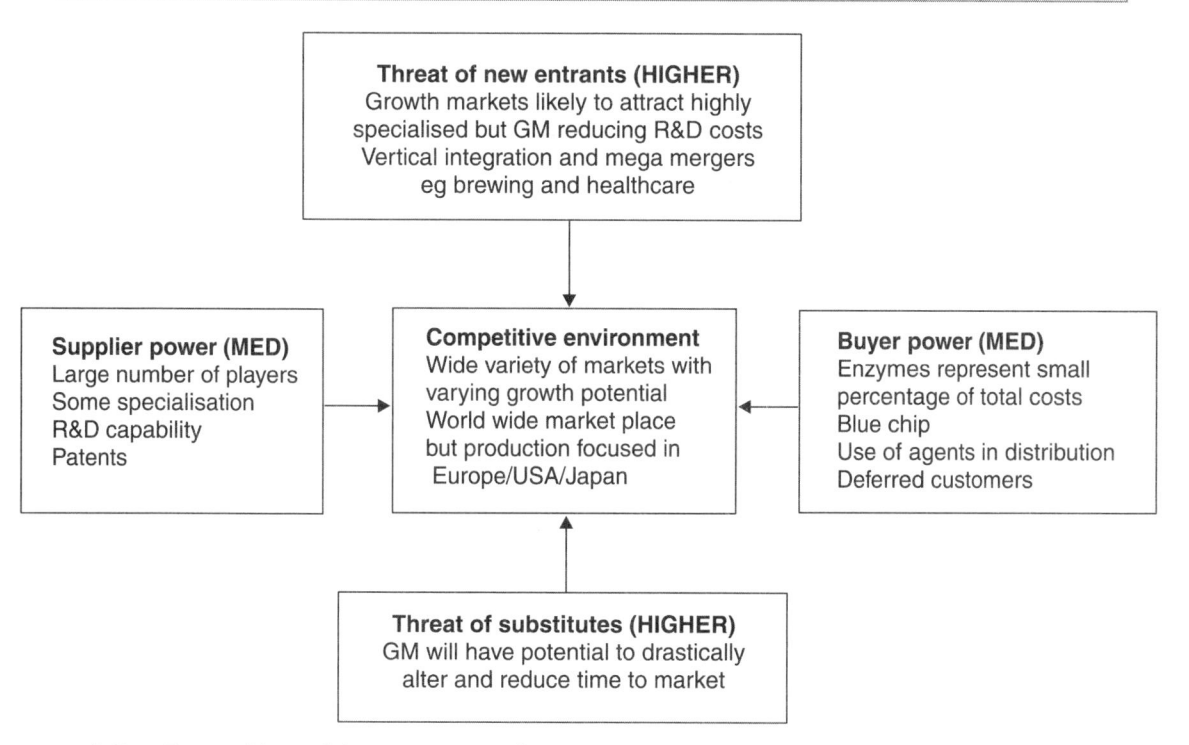

Threat of new entrants (HIGHER)
Growth markets likely to attract highly specialised but GM reducing R&D costs
Vertical integration and mega mergers eg brewing and healthcare

Supplier power (MED)
Large number of players
Some specialisation
R&D capability
Patents

Competitive environment
Wide variety of markets with varying growth potential
World wide market place but production focused in Europe/USA/Japan

Buyer power (MED)
Enzymes represent small percentage of total costs
Blue chip
Use of agents in distribution
Deferred customers

Threat of substitutes (HIGHER)
GM will have potential to drastically alter and reduce time to market

A Five Forces Map of the Enzyme Market (version 1)

Tutor Tip

You should also be aware that in case study there is no single correct answer. The examiners are looking for rigorous process and justification which is credible but not some pre-determined standard approach. Sample answers and our approach should therefore be viewed as indicative rather than prescriptive. You can see this by looking at this alternative version of Porter's Five Forces developed by a different group – equally valid and accurate but perhaps you can see how you might choose the modified content in a model you were presenting if the questions or additional information were different.

If the focus was on international markets and developments, then the first version might be most useful but if the extra information was about a merger between key competitors, the second would have more impact.

Part B: The sample case: Biocatalysts

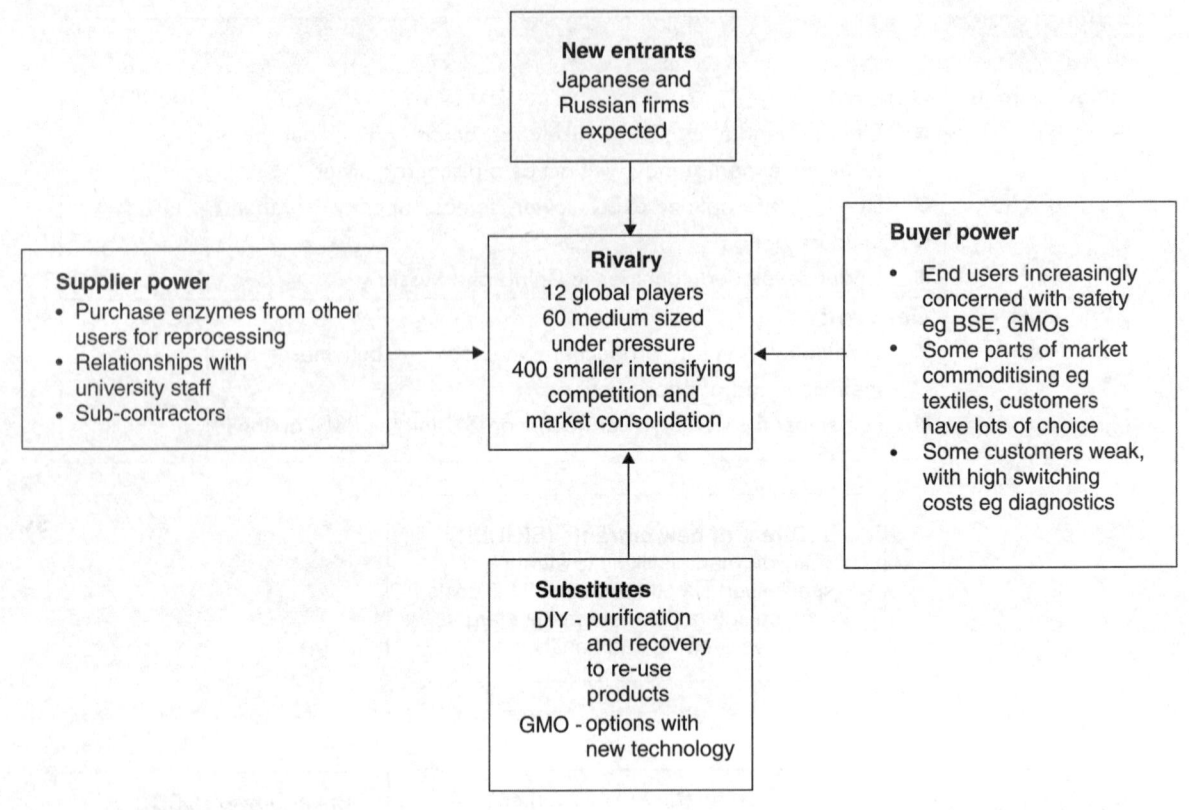

```
                    ┌─────────────────┐
                    │  New entrants   │
                    │  Japanese and   │
                    │  Russian firms  │
                    │    expected     │
                    └────────┬────────┘
                             │
                             ▼
┌──────────────────────┐  ┌──────────────────┐  ┌──────────────────────────┐
│   Supplier power     │  │     Rivalry      │  │      Buyer power         │
│ • Purchase enzymes   │  │ 12 global players│  │ • End users increasingly │
│   from other users   │→ │ 60 medium sized  │← │   concerned with safety  │
│   for reprocessing   │  │ under pressure   │  │   eg BSE, GMOs           │
│ • Relationships with │  │ 400 smaller      │  │ • Some parts of market   │
│   university staff   │  │ intensifying     │  │   commoditising eg       │
│ • Sub-contractors    │  │ competition and  │  │   textiles, customers    │
│                      │  │ market           │  │   have lots of choice    │
│                      │  │ consolidation    │  │ • Some customers weak,   │
│                      │  │                  │  │   with high switching    │
│                      │  │                  │  │   costs eg diagnostics   │
└──────────────────────┘  └────────▲─────────┘  └──────────────────────────┘
                                   │
                          ┌────────┴─────────┐
                          │   Substitutes    │
                          │ DIY - purification│
                          │     and recovery │
                          │     to re-use    │
                          │     products     │
                          │ GMO - options    │
                          │     with new     │
                          │     technology   │
                          └──────────────────┘
```

Porter's Five Forces (version 2)

Add the competitor dimension

2.3 Business would be a lot easier without competitors.

Action Programme 1

Assessing Competitor Responses

Take a few minutes to think about what you already know about competitors and how this knowledge could help you get a more detailed insight into how competitors in a case context might behave.

1. Who are likely to be the most aggressive competitors – those operating in a growing or mature market place and why?

2. If a new entrant, moving into a market which was itself in late growth or early maturity, wanted to avoid head to head competition with the existing players in that market, what strategy should they adopt?

3. Who would you expect to be the most aggressive competitor in an established market place: the market leader, market challenger or one of the other players?

4. Are there any circumstances when a smaller firm might respond more aggressively to a competitive threat?

5. In the Biocatalyst case, how do you expect competitors like Amano and Rhom to respond to changes in Biocatalysts's strategies?

Check your answers with ours at the end of the chapter.

Who are the real competitors?

2.4 In a large marketplace, not every competitor is a major threat (although it will probably mean they could be a potential one). You need to identify the closest competitors: positioning maps are an easy framework to use for this.

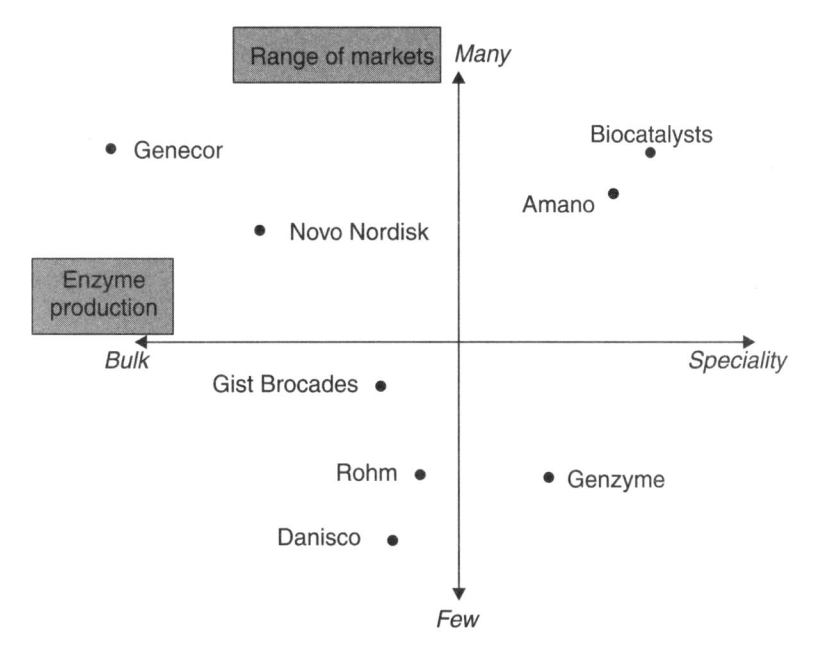

Positioning Enzymes

2.5 Of these players, Amano is the closest competitor (hence their potential interest in acquiring Biocatalysts' expertise). Companies like Genencor and Novo Nordisk are really in a quite different part of the market with expertise in volume production.

Understanding competitor strategy

2.6 Having identified the competitors, you want to understand their competitive strategies. Porter's Generic Strategies model provides a simple framework for this. The analysis below is too kind to Biocatalysts: although a niche player, their lack of product or market focus leaves them vulnerable and 'stuck in the middle'.

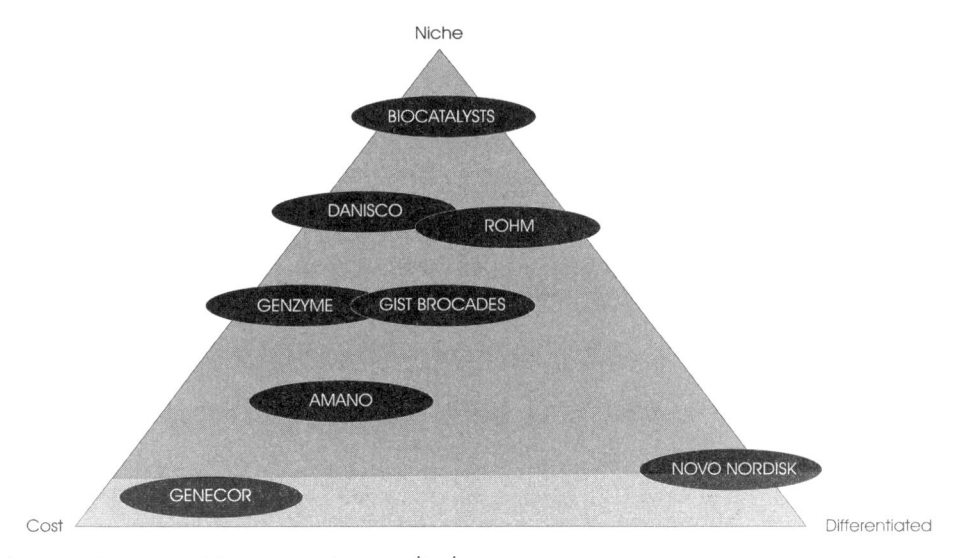

Porter's generic competitive strategies applied to enzymes

Part B: The sample case: Biocatalysts

Adding the customers

2.7 As marketers, it is fundamental that we remember to add the customer dimension. Changes in buyer behaviour can have significant impact on business success and we need to bring our understanding and knowledge of the customer to any strategic assessment or decision-making.

2.8 This is the work which will eventually provide the basis for effective **segmentation**. At a macro level, we will need to define the markets and understand their needs and, at a micro level the decision making unit. You can see here how a student group tackled this part of the analysis for Biocatalysts.

Understanding the Markets

The world market for enzymes is growing, doubling in the 10 years from 1994.

World market for industrial enzymes:

1994	$1 billion
1997	$1.3 billion
1998	$1.7 billion
2005	$2 billion

The Biocatalysts customers come from a number of industries.

Distribution of enzyme sales by product sector:

Year	Other	Detergents	Diary	Textiles	Starch
1994	29%	32%	14%	10%	15%
2005	47%	27%	8%	6%	12%

The 'Other' market is growing. The rest are in decline.

Breakdown of 'other' market:

- Alcohol
- Animal feed
- Baking
- Chemical biotransformations
- Diagnostics
- Fats and oils
- Flavour
- Fruit and wine
- Leather
- Protein (for milk coagulation, flavour and detergents)
- Pulp and water
- Water

The 'other' sector is becoming increasingly significant to Biocatalysts. so this is worth some further review and analysis

---

Action Programme 2

Mind mapping 'other'

Take 20 minutes and produce a mind map or schematic which consolidates the information and analysis we have available about 'other' customers.

Compare your analysis with ours at the end of this chapter.

2.9 Analysis of customers by industry

(a) Biocatalyst's customers are in 35 countries including:

- UK   29%
- Spain   17%
- South America   7%
- Asia Pacific   7%
- Japan   2%
- Europe   9%
- USA   7%
- Other   22% (28 countries)
                 100%

- Sales in Food   48%
- Textiles   31%
- Diagnostics   5% (now 10%)
- Pharmaceuticals 15% (all figures from 1997)

These customers include blue chip, medium and small accounts, buying products and services. The **pareto** rule applies with 80% of the sales going to 20% of the customers.

(b) **Food**. Biocatalysts' products are used as a processing aid. Competitive advantage is function, security and cost in use. This includes baking (bread, biscuits, crackers, batters), brewing, protein modification, fruit and flavouring.

(i) **Decision Making Unit (DMU)**: mainly industrial businesses involved in food and beverage processing of ingredients to produce branded consumer goods. Examples are Hovis, Premier biscuits, Ryvita, Tetley, Robinson's. Also flavourings for snack food and cheese manufacture with Enzyme Modified Cheese (EMC).

People involved are food technologists, industrial buyers, process production and quality staff.

(ii) **Critical issues**
- Consistent quality for customers' production efficiency
- Cost in use is competitive
- Complies with legislation and consumer trends (GM and bovine safety)
- Communication between technical service, agents and customers

(c) **Textile**. Products are used as washing agent that causes the stone-washed effect on jeans. The competitive advantage is low with a declining fashion based market buying on price as a commodity.

(i) DMU: industrial buyers and production staff

(ii) Critical issues
- Correct product specification as set
- Competitive pricing at time of purchase

Action Programme 3

Analysing diagnostics

Take 15 minutes to complete the same analysis of the diagnostic sector. Compare your answer with ours at the end of this chapter.

Part B: The sample case: Biocatalysts

- (d) **Pharmaceuticals**. Cell cultures and hydrolysis of esters. Competitive advantage unknown.
    - (i) Critical issues
        - Technical service support
        - Consistency and quality of product
    - (ii) DMU: similar to diagnostics market with less due diligence
- (e) **Environmental**. Waste water treatment for odour reduction and lower drain maintenance. Competitive advantage unknown.
    - (i) DMU: the customer, the local drainage and sewerage authorities (these civil servants include maintenance managers and procurement officers). The workers will feed back the performance and ease of use of the product and packaging.
- (f) **Other markets**

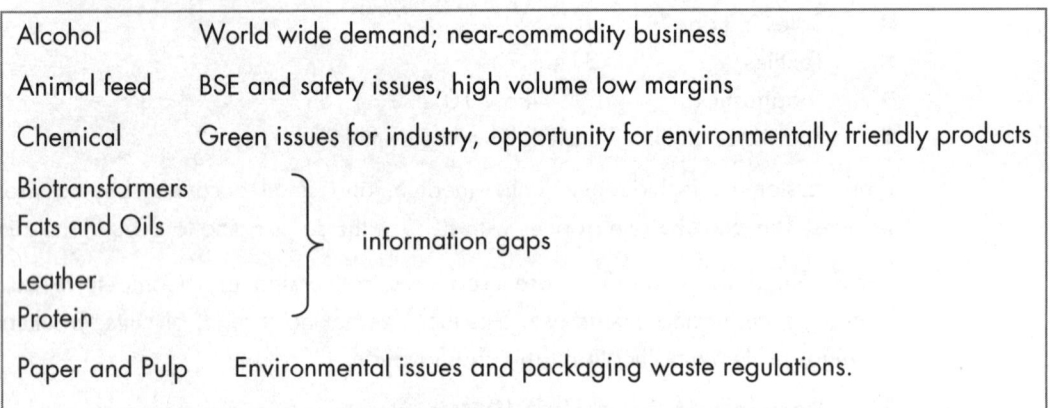

Alcohol	World wide demand; near-commodity business
Animal feed	BSE and safety issues, high volume low margins
Chemical	Green issues for industry, opportunity for environmentally friendly products
Biotransformers	
Fats and Oils	information gaps
Leather	
Protein	
Paper and Pulp	Environmental issues and packaging waste regulations.

Combining product/market information

2.10 From this next chart, you can see how a student has linked product information with end use to give us a further perspective on the variety of customers the company is trying to satisfy.

Biocatalyst's current products by sector

Sector	No. of Products	New Product	End use
Baking	19	3	Bread, biscuits, crackers, batters
Brewing	5	5	Beer
Fruit and Veg	12	3	Fruit juice, wine, citrus fruits
Flavourings	14	0	Vegetables, fibrous botanicals, ECM
Proteins	13	1	Bacterial proteinase Soya
Dietetics	10	2	Aid for digestion ready for tableting
Textile	21	9	Stone-wash, cost effective development
Diagnostics	8	3	Immuno-diagnostics, food testing
Pharmaceuticals	7	0	Cell cultures, hydrolysis of esters
Environment	4	0	Waste odour reduction, drain maintenance

Table 1 Products by sector

6 ♦ Step 3: External analysis

Competitor	Geographic focus	Target markets/ product range	Market share (of $1.7bn	Supplier to Biocatalysts	GMO	Summary
Novo Nordisk	Worldwide (RBCDs)	Industrial and technical enzymes including textiles	[50%]	✓	?	RBDCs allow flexibility to adapt to local conditions Also in healthcare Cost cutting and productivity improvements
Genencor	Worldwide	1,200 patents	[12.5%]	✓	✓	Largest company devoted exclusively to industrial biotechnology State of the art production capability
Genzyme		Medical-diagnostics, therapeutics and surgical			?	Mainly healthcare $490m turnover
Amano	Production in Japan/ USA/UK	Pharmaceutical/food/ diagnostic 50 patents	[7%]	✓	?	'World No 1 speciality enzyme producer' Surface fermentation?
Gist Brocades	Worldwide especially in growth areas of Asia and South America – 70 sites	Food and agriculture Very active with patents	[12.5%]	✓	?	
Nagase					?	Part of $4.6bn turnover company
Biozome		Baking/food		✓	?	
Rohm		Food/sweeteners		✓	?	
Danisco					?	
					?	FDA approval for PKU test in USA

Table 2 Competitor summary

Part B: The sample case: Biocatalysts

Adding the macro dimensions

2.11 Finally, to complete your external audit, you will need to build up the picture of the changing external environment for the enzyme market. Here you can see such an environmental audit completed and prioritised helping you to summarise and consolidate the many clues provided within the case study.

Political/legal	Economic	Social/demographic	Technological
■ Food sector – politicians increasingly responding to public's concerns ■ Food and medical sectors – tight legislation controlling release of new products ■ Food sector – packaging disclosure laws ■ All sectors – employment laws ■ All sectors – worldwide trade agreements/barriers/embargoes	■ Food sector – higher yields could lead to an over-capacity and an agricultural recession in the medium term ■ All sectors – large parts of Wales classed as Economic Development Areas inc grant assistance ■ All sectors – strong pressure on industry from analysts/city to improve productivity ⇒ performance enhancing technology (ie enzymes) will be in demand. ■ All sectors – worldwide trade so UK's involvement in EMU could be important ■ Exchange rate risk from trading across 3 currencies – $, £ and the euro ■ Worldwide recessions eg instability in Asia ■ Merging of large Blue Chip companies ■ China and Russia	■ Food sector – expected population growth will require higher food yields. ■ Food sector – widespread anti-GM feeling in European society building on BSE scare. This includes well organised pressure groups. Far less the case in other continents. ■ All sectors – increasingly 'green' sensitive society in developed countries ■ Food sector – developing countries however want reliable food sources and are not 'green' ■ Textile sector – some linkage to fad and fashion through involvement in textile industry ie faded jeans ■ Medical sector – people becoming more health conscious so medical and diagnostic trade will become more important ■ Increasing demand for global brand foods ■ Global warming ⇒ medicines required and reliable crops	■ All sectors – high new product R&D costs but reducing where GMOs are used. ■ Food sector – strong growth area ⇒ an agricultural revolution is taking place as important as that in electronics ■ Food sector – GM food is actually already widespread ■ All sectors – reliance on universities for research ■ All sectors – Internet makes them more accessible, including deferred customers' products

Table 3 PEST analysis

Moving on

2.12 You have now completed the detailed inview and overview analysis essential to providing the detailed understanding of the case context. In the next chapter we will look in more detail at how you take the next steps to action by sorting and refining the internal and external analysis and identifying the critical success factors.

Before moving on, take a few minutes to reflect on what you have learnt about the process of analysis and how it can best be completed. Look at the pitfalls we have identified and take the time to tackle this end of chapter activity.

Pitfalls

2.13 The most common pitfalls when completing the external audit

(a) Focus on PEST analysis and forget to really work on the micro analysis of competitors and customers

(b) Try to do **two steps** at once during the macro analysis so instead of

- threat of recession

the student says

- falling sales because of recession

This is going from the **external factor** to the **product/market implication**. This is a mistake because an environmental change could generate **both** product market opportunities and threats.

```
                        Recession
                       /        \
        Falling sales in our     Opportunity to launch
        luxury ranges            an economy product
```

Make sure at this step you stick to the uncontrollable and external PEST factors, and leave the translation into product/market implications until Step 5.

2.14 Failure to think ahead. The external analysis requires that we try to think ahead even though forecasting is **not** a very precise art. Keep it reasonable and realistic but use your own knowledge and look ahead.

Part B: The sample case: Biocatalysts

Action Programme 4

We have handled a lot of data and information in this step of the case process. Are you using this to build a clearer picture of Biocatalyst and its challenges?

Take a few minutes to work through the following questions which might help you consolidate your thoughts.

1 Why would a change in Government policy regarding the funding and support of biotechnology be significant to Biocatalyst?

2 Competitor Amano has 400 products and an income of £92m. How might this information help us set an objective for Biocatalyst?

3 Is a differentiated strategy an option for Biocatalyst?

4 Why are GMOs an important issue for Biocatalyst and what impact might decisions about them have on strategy?

5 Why is the 'other' sector of the enzyme market potentially attractive to Biocatalyst?

6 Take 10 minutes to produce a checklist of questions to pose about competitors which you could use in future cases.

Compare your answers with ours before moving on.

Action Programme review

1 *Assessing Competitor Responses*

1 Those working in a mature market because winning new business means taking customers away from someone else.

2 They should target the 'laggards' who will be the only new customers still entering the market place. In this way they can win market share without taking customers from someone else.

3 The market challenger normally who will be focused on winning market share and can often best do this by taking on smaller players rather than the market leader.

4 Yes, if this was its core market and more important to it or if the challenge being made was a direct head to head one.

5 Probably hardly at all. They are significantly bigger and Biocatalyst is a small niche player. Amano may, however, be interested in acquiring them for their expertise and patents but that would probably be the extent of things.

2 Mind mapping 'other'

The 'other' sector of the Enzyme Business

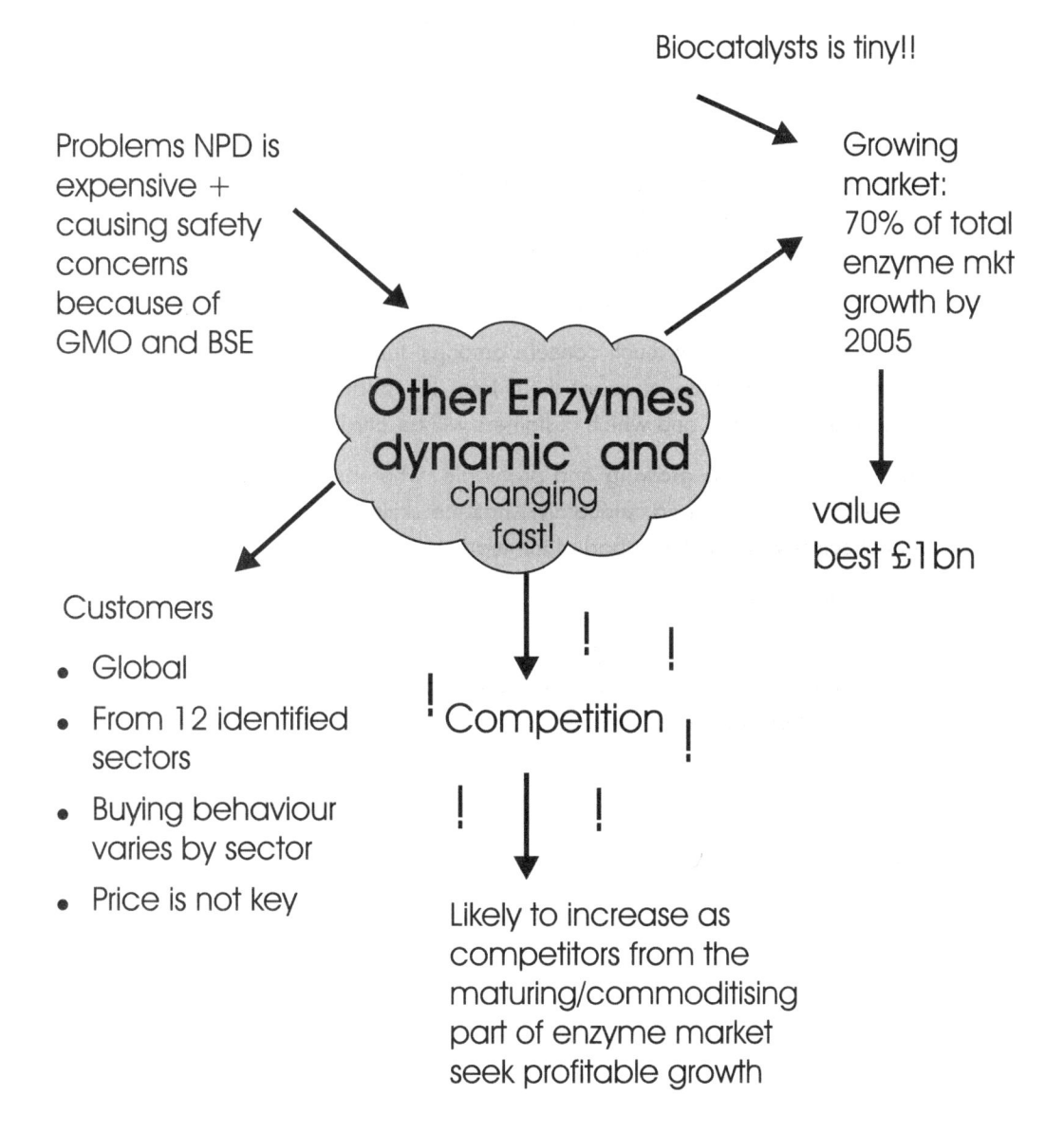

Other Enzymes dynamic and changing fast!

- Biocatalysts is tiny!!
- Problems NPD is expensive + causing safety concerns because of GMO and BSE
- Growing market: 70% of total enzyme mkt growth by 2005 → value best £1bn
- Customers
  - Global
  - From 12 identified sectors
  - Buying behaviour varies by sector
  - Price is not key
- Competition: Likely to increase as competitors from the maturing/commoditising part of enzyme market seek profitable growth

3 Analysing Diagnostics

Diagnostics. Medical applications for determination of presence and immuno-diagnostics. The competitive advantage is technology-based with partnership agreements.

Testing for genetic disorder, blood tests, gastric disorders, determination of glocosinates in rape seed meal.

DMU. This is a highly scientific environment with leading edge technology transformed into commercial reality. The DM is protracted with extensive independent testing and field trials before approval; these include medical bodies, associations and FDA approval. This work would be championed by the drug companies looking to supply the diagnostic kits via the medical profession. Dealing with scientists, doctors, professional supply chain managers, process engineers and marketing.

Part B: The sample case: Biocatalysts

Critical Issues
- Unique formulation and confidentiality agreements
- Quality and consistency of product and process performance
- Medical approval for targeted markets
- Technical support and partnership approach

4   1   Much of Biocatalysts's work attracts grants which could be reduced or stopped. The Government could also influence the extent of support provided by university research if their priorities changed.

2   This means Amano (based in the same sector of the market place) earns some £230k per product compared with approx. £22k per Biocatalyst product. This is a useful benchmark indicating how product rationlisation and improved marketing of say 30 instead of 112 products could increase revenues to say £7m.

3   Not really – it is too small a player, a niche or multi-niche approach feels more credible.

4   GMOs are the cause of much concern amongst the general public, particularly in Europe. The decision to include or reject them from the portfolio will strongly influence both the corporate positioning and which customers will be attracted to the company.

5   Because this sector is growing and profitable, whereas others like textiles are increasingly mature and commoditised. Biocatalyst has the skills, competence and experience to focus very effectively on this £1bn part of the market.

6   A competitors checklist

A great deal can be accomplished in understanding competitors by relatively simple numerical analysis and financial and market review. Here is a checklist of questions about competitors you should find answers to.

Question	Answer
(a) How many?	
(b) Size?	
(c) Growing or declining?	
(d) Market shares and/or rank orders?	
(e) Likely objectives and strategies?	
(f) Changes in management personnel?	
(g) Past reaction to:	
(i) price changes	
(ii) promotional campaigns	
(iii) new product launches	
(iv) distribution drives?	
(h) Analysis of marketing mix strengths and weaknesses	
(i) Leaders or followers?	
(j) National or international?	
(k) Analysis of published accounts?	

Step 4: Prioritisation and Critical Success Factors

Chapter Topic List	
1	Prioritising analysis
2	Prioritising strengths and weaknesses
3	Prioritising opportunities and threats
4	Critical success factors (CSFs)

1 Prioritising analysis

1.1 Professional marketers have a duty to present analysis in a way that is of value to senior management and the organisation. This requires going further than just establishing SWOT; it requires making connections and inferences, drawing conclusions and, ultimately, providing insights that ensure decision making is based on valued information.

1.2 During analysis, the SWOT and other auditing techniques help to determine the current situation. For the results of the audit to be of any value, SWOTs etc must be **prioritised to ensure the organisation is focused on those issues that matter most**, for example the weaknesses and threats that will impact on organisational success.

1.3 A long list of SWOT terms might provide an improved understanding of the current situation but it can be a daunting step to move from this list to decisions. There are also always constraints on resources, money, time, processes and people, and so priorities must be established to determine what is important and must be invested in, and what can wait.

1.4 There are some helpful techniques for prioritising analysis. We will now describe others.

2 Prioritising strengths and weaknesses

2.1 It is of course helpful for employees to comment on the organisation's strengths and weaknesses. However, much more important are the **external** perceptions and opinions on the organisation's performance.

Part B: The sample case: Biocatalysts

2.2 Customers, suppliers, distribution channels and other stakeholders should be canvassed for their opinions. For example, a technique that can help identify what is important to customers and prioritise its importance is the **semantic differential**.

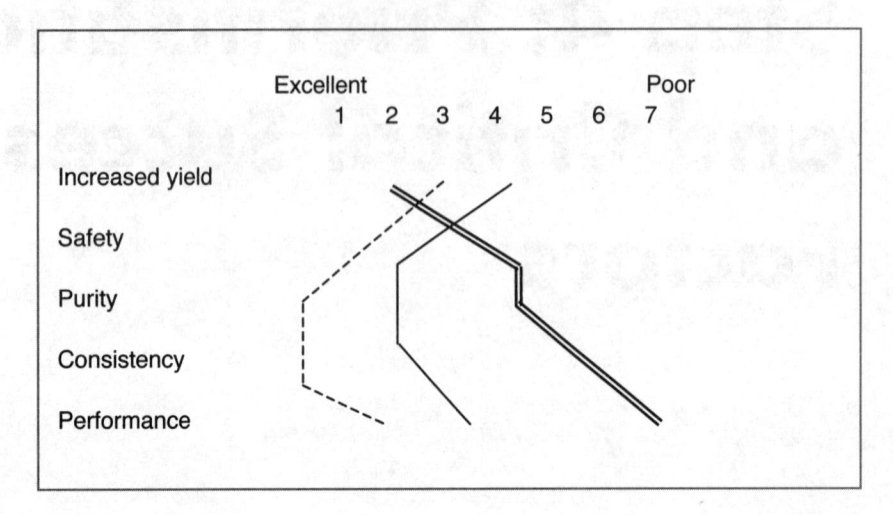

```
                    Excellent                    Poor
                    1    2    3    4    5    6    7
Increased yield
Safety
Purity
Consistency
Performance
```

Biocatalysts   ─────────
Competitor A   ═════════
Competitor B   ─ ─ ─ ─ ─

2.3 Please note, this is not meant to suggest that this is how Biocatalysts's results would look. We do not have the information to enable us to do this. It is an example of how we might be able to identify performance if we did have the information.

2.4 Management can then use this information to rank activities as strengths and weaknesses and to establish some understanding of the importance of each activity to customers. There is no point in an organisation identifying a weakness and allocating resources to improving performance if it is of no importance to the customer. Resources must be used where they will do the most good, or where there is an opportunity to maintain or develop competitive advantage.

2.5 Activities can be weighted and rated to enable marketers to determine whether a strength is major, medium or low.

Activities	Prioritising strengths and weaknesses								
	Strength			Weakness			Importance		
	Major	Medium	Low	Minor	Medium	Serious	High	Medium	Low
Promotions reach									
People technical skills service skills									
Process simple									

168

7 ♦ Step 4: Prioritisation and critical success factors

2.6 When prioritising weaknesses, consider the effort involved in dealing with the weakness. Is it a simple matter of investing more money, (eg a computer)? Or will a major change be required in processes, people skills, organisation structure and so on?

	Performance		
Importance (to customer)	Excellent	Average	Poor
High	Maintain	Improve	Urgent attention
Average			Improve
Low	Over investing	Monitor	Monitor

2.7 Speed may also be a factor. How quickly can the organisation solve the problem? Can it be solved within the planning period and in time to make a positive difference to the organisation?

3 Prioritising opportunities and threats

3.1 Prioritising **threats** forces us to consider the **likelihood** of something happening and how **serious** the threat is. Constraints on resources prevent us from developing contingency plans for every likely threat: it would be impractical. To avoid or at least reduced a 'crisis management' syndrome, we do need to establish threats which are most likely to occur, during the planning period.

(a) **Threats matrix**

	Likelihood of occurrence		
Seriousness	High	Likely	Unlikely
Very			
Average			
Low			

(b) The aim is to make sure we are focused on threats that could damage our prospects and jeopardise business performance. This technique forces us to consider the likelihood of something occurring and how serious it is. We can then decide whether resources should be allocated to develop contingency plans or whether we simply monitor the situation.

3.2 In the same way, we cannot pursue every opportunity that presents itself, and often it is not appropriate for us to do so if it does not fit with our strategic objectives and goals.

Part B: The sample case: Biocatalysts

Opportunities matrix

```
                    Probability of success
                 High      Medium      Low
         High  ┌────────┬────────┬────────┐
               │        │        │        │
               ├────────┼────────┼────────┤
Attractiveness Medium   │        │        │
               ├────────┼────────┼────────┤
         Low   │        │        │        │
               └────────┴────────┴────────┘
```

Action Programme 1

Try to complete both threats and opportunities matrix for Biocatalysts. Compare your answer with ours at the end of the chapter.

3.3 Realities of the case study analysis

(a) Usually we do not have the right, or enough, information to enable us to prioritise analysis, and in the case study we cannot go out and obtain the information we want. Therefore we must make some **intelligent and reasonable assumptions**. A professional job on analysis will generate information for us to make reasonable assumptions, and to justify them with evidence.

(b) One of your objectives is to pass the examination. **If we get the Critical Success Factors right, we will identify, broadly, the question areas**.

4 Critical success factors (CSFs)

4.1 The terminology varies from company to company (eg Significant Performance Indicators (SPIs), Key Results Areas (KRAs)), but Critical Success Factors is widely used.

4.2 The stepping stone from analysis to decision is agreeing **critical success factors** which can only be determined from the results of analysis. These are the factors that will impact on the organisation's ability to pursue the opportunities it has identified and intends to implement.

4.3 Critical success factors are any factors essential to the success of organisation and strategy.
- Profitability and cash flow
- Market development and market position
- Productivity
- Identifying/developing competitive advantage and new product development
- Marketing orientation, employee attitudes and public responsibility
- Marketing management skills and personnel leadership
- Competitive positioning and product leadership

7 ♦ Step 4: Prioritisation and critical success factors

Underpinning each CSF are some key issues. Examples are given below.

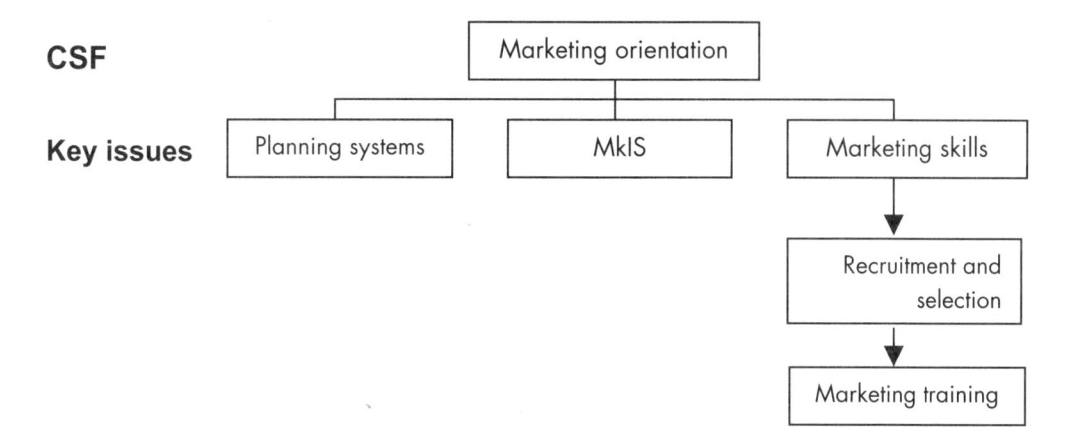

```
CSF                        Marketing orientation
                    ┌──────────────┼──────────────┐
Key issues   Planning systems    MkIS       Marketing skills
                                                  │
                                                  ▼
                                          Recruitment and
                                             selection
                                                  │
                                                  ▼
                                          Marketing training
```

4.4 Identifying and agreeing CSFs ensures corporate decisions are focused on the issues that will produce the desired results. Major problems/obstacles to success must be dealt with. Resources must be allocated to support **critical success factor outcomes**.

Action Programme 2

From your analysis, identify the Critical Success Factors you believe Biocatalysts face, and compare them with ours at the end of the chapter.

Part B: The sample case: Biocatalysts

Action Programme review

1 *Threats matrix*

Likelihood of occurrence

	High	Likely	Unlikely
Very	Growing anti GMOs	Government withdraw funding	
Average	Competitors merge / Legislation	Russia or China enter market	
Low			

(Row labels under **Seriousness**: Very, Average, Low)

Some of the issues that emerge can be both opportunities and threats depending on the organisation's ability to identify and address the opportunity or threat.

Opportunities matrix

Probability of success

	High	Medium	Low
High	Diagnostics / Food		
Medium		Environmental products	
Low		Changing fashions eg faded jeans	

(Row labels under **Attractiveness**: High, Medium, Low)

7 ♦ Step 4: Prioritisation and critical success factors

Biocatalysts' CSFs

CSFs	and	Key issues
■ Competitive positioning		Competitive strategy Brand/values Marketing skills
■ Distribution		Agency skills/expertise/knowledge New channels/Web
■ New Product Development		Processes Marketing information Marketing skills
■ Communications		Strategic and integrated Marketing skills Brand Changing perceptions
■ Marketing information		International problems
■ Relationship marketing		Stakeholders/nurture relationships
■ International market entry		Level of involvement
■ Funding/cash flow		Cost efficiency, profitability, growth

Step 5: Establishing Strategic Direction. Corporate/Business Decisions

Chapter Topic List	
1	Establishing strategic direction
2	Biocatalysts: what needs to be done

Introduction

In this chapter we will:

- ☑ Turn our environmental analysis into a forecast, set quantified objectives and so establish a planning gap for Biocatalysts

- ☑ Assess the role of vision and mission, and develop them for Biocatalysts

- ☑ Use the Ansoff matrix and others to identify strategic options for the business

- ☑ Develop and use criteria for evaluating and selecting strategies to fill the planning gap

- ☑ Consider the potential pitfalls for students working at this critical case stage

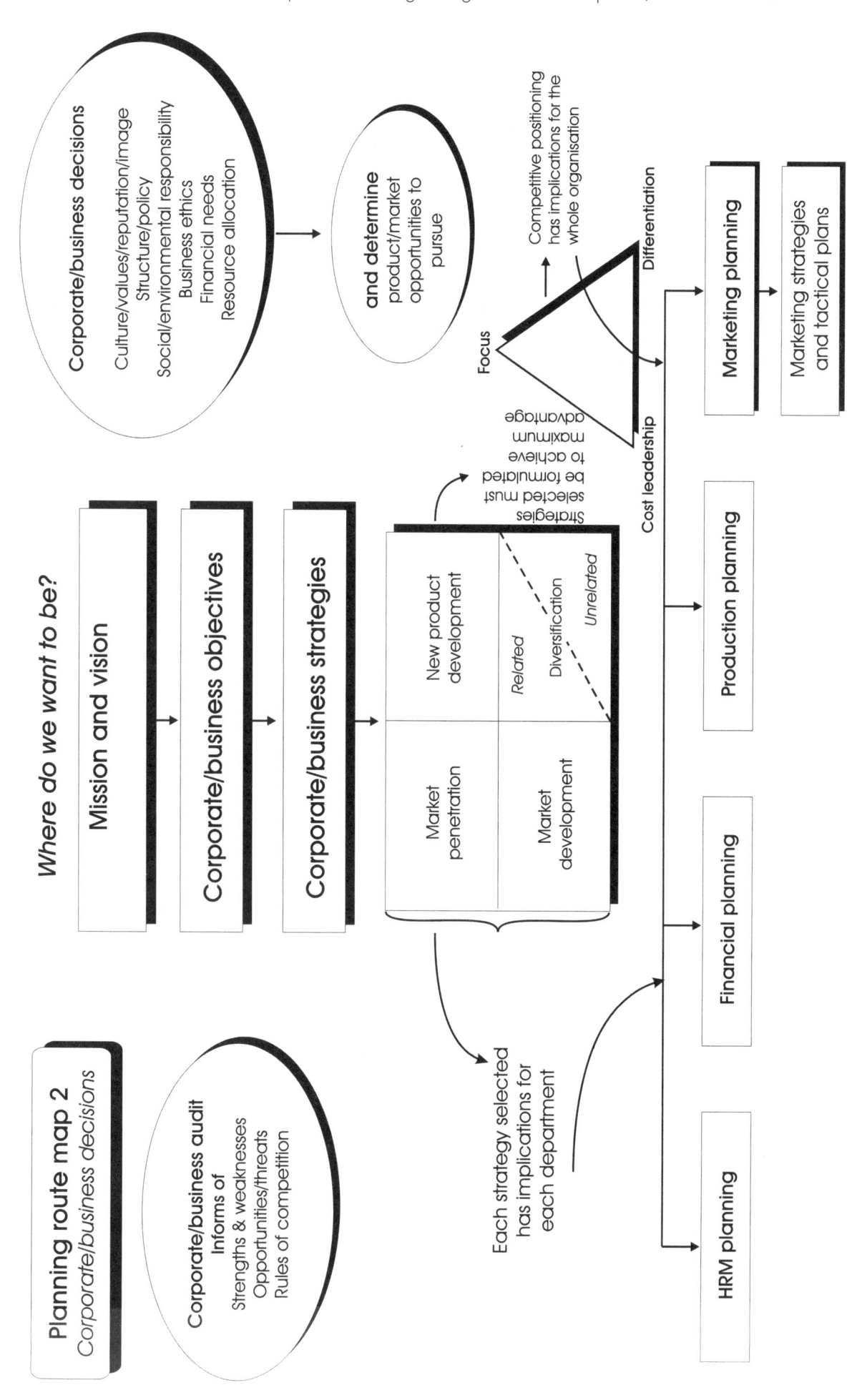

8 ♦ Step 5: Establishing strategic direction. Corporate/business decisions

Planning route map 2
Corporate/business decisions

Corporate/business audit
Informs of
- Strengths & weaknesses
- Opportunities/threats
- Rules of competition

Corporate/business decisions
- Culture/values/reputation/image
- Structure/policy
- Social/environmental responsibility
- Business ethics
- Financial needs
- Resource allocation

→ **and determine** product/market opportunities to pursue

Where do we want to be?

Mission and vision → Corporate/business objectives → Corporate/business strategies

Ansoff Matrix:
Market penetration	New product development	
Market development	Diversification	*Related* / *Unrelated*

Strategies selected must be formulated to achieve maximum advantage

Porter's Generic Strategies: Focus / Differentiation / Cost leadership

Competitive positioning has implications for the whole organisation

Each strategy selected has implications for each department

→ Marketing planning → Marketing strategies and tactical plans
→ Production planning
→ Financial planning
→ HRM planning

Part B: The sample case: Biocatalysts

© Juanita Cockton, 1997

1 Establishing strategic direction

1.1 So far we have been working to establish the current position of Biocatalysts' business. You have seen a number of tools, techniques and models employed to help us really get to grips with the 'where are we now' question for this business. Case step 5 is the one which will allow us to answer 'where are we going?'. It is the first real step down the path of decision making. Many students (and, in fairness, managers) find this a difficult step to take. Analysis is comforting and reassuring. It keeps you busy and productive but at some point you must move forward. This is that point, and from now on you will be faced with uncertainty and assumptions which have to be addressed if decisions are to be made. Try not to worry too much about this; it reflects the real world but remember that assumptions can be monitored by your control systems and that we are only working through the planning process. The planning process is iterative, and decisions made now can still be modified or addressed later if they prove unworkable at the operational planning level.

Skills and knowledge reminders

1.2 You will see a number of tools and models during this step of the case process.

Gap analysis

1.3 By comparing the objectives with the current forecast, it is possible to measure the **gap**, in other words the **discrepancy** between what the firm wants and what it is likely to achieve. A task of corporate planning is to identify gaps and propose strategies whereby the gaps may be closed. In the diagram below, let us assume that re-examination of the current forecast shows that one of the major products will not achieve sales targets (perhaps due to technological developments in market, increased competition and so on).

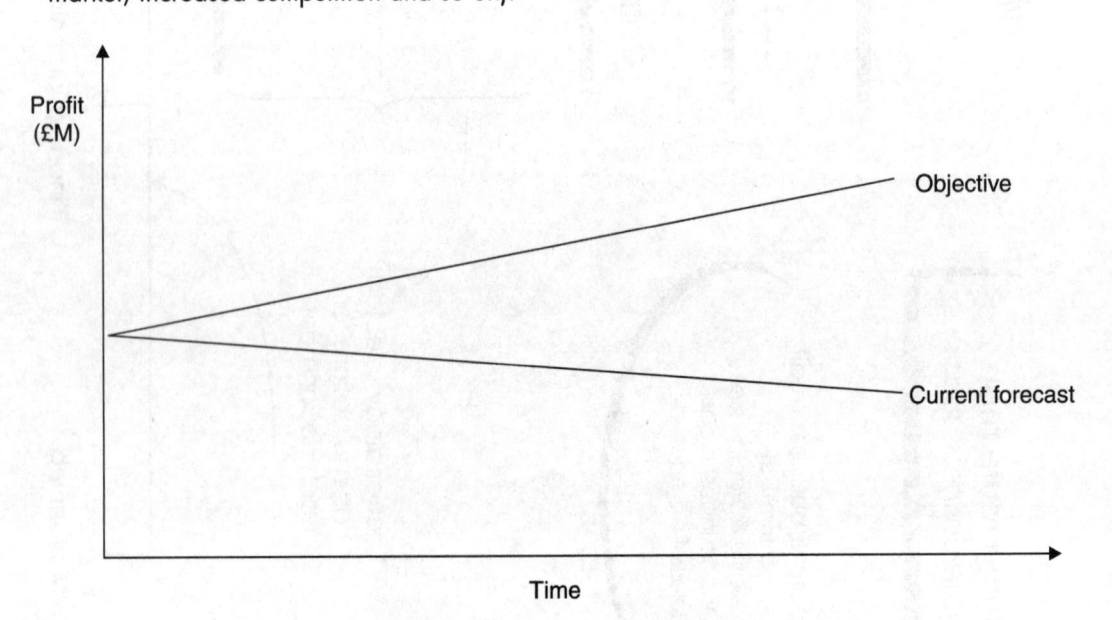

1.4 Ansoff matrix

	Existing products	**New Products**
Existing markets	Market penetration strategy 1. More purchasing and usage from existing customers 2. Gain customers from competitors 3. Convert non-users into users (where both are in same market segment)	Product development strategy 1. Product modification via new features 2. Different quality levels 3. New product.
New markets	Market development strategy 1. New market segments 2. New distribution channels 3. New geographic areas eg exports	Diversification strategy 1. Related 2. Unrelated

The Ansoff matrix is an excellent framework for helping you to identify and communicate the strategic options facing an organisation. It can usefully be modified to create a nine box grid which logs existing, **modified** and new products (and markets).

1.5 Trade-offs inevitably occur between levels of risk and levels of return. When considering entering new markets or new market segments for example, (Ansoff's market development strategy) the following trade-offs are likely.

	Low exit barrier	**High exit barrier**
Low entry barrier	Low stable returns	Low risk returns
High entry barrier	High stable returns	High risk returns

1.6 A variety of matrix analyses can be used. You can invent your own according to your particular product and market situation or, better still, the one in the case study. However, here are some established matrices which have a degree of universality as well as a history of success.

1.7 The multi-factor decision matrix

(a) To be customer focused, organisations must make all decisions based not just on what they want but also on what makes sense from the customer's view. There may be a very attractive opportunity in the market but whether it is right for your business to exploit it is determined, essentially, by the customer's perception.

(b) This model helps the company assess:

- The quality of the opportunity
- The potential competitive advantage they would gain by exploiting it

Part B: The sample case: Biocatalysts

Strategy attractiveness

	High	Medium	Low
High (Competitive advantage)	■	■	
Medium	■		
Low			

(Competitive advantage / Business strengths)

In this exam, the examiners are interested in process and so want to see the criteria you develop from the case study to drive the model.

1.8 Other models can help you assess what approach to adopt once a strategy has been selected.

(a) The **directional policy matrix** matches the amount of competition against the attractiveness of the opportunity (but takes no account of customers, and so is less useful).

(b) The **Arthur D Little** model looks at the stage of the industry life cycle against competitive advantage and so does consider the customer but not the firm's objectives and needs.

1.9 No one tool will do everything for you: each can add to the picture, so be prepared to call on any if it helps a particular case.

(a) **The directional policy matrix (George Day)**

The directional policy matrix (George Day)

Market attractiveness	Strong	Medium	Weak
High	**PROTECT POSITION** • Invest to grow at maximum digestible rate • Concentrate effort on maintaining strength	**INVEST TO BUILD** • Challenge for leadership • Build selectively on strengths • Reinforce vulnerable areas	**BUILDS SELECTIVELY** • Specialize around limited strengths • Seeks ways to overcome weaknesses • Withdraw if indications
Medium	**BUILD SELECTIVELY** • Invest heavily in most attractive segments • Build up ability to counter competition • Emphasize profitability by raising productivity	**SELECTIVITY/MANAGE FOR EARNINGS** • Protect existing program • Concentrate investments in segments where profitability is good and risk is relatively low	**LIMITED EXPANSION OR HARVEST** • Look for ways to expand without high risk otherwise, minimize investment and rationalize operations
Low	**PROTECT AND REFOCUS** • Manage for current earnings • Concentrate on attractive segments • Defend strengths	**MANAGE FOR EARNINGS** • Protect position in most profitable segments • Upgrade product line • Minimize investment	**DIVEST** • Sell at time that will maximize cash value • Cut fixed costs and avoid investment meanwhile

Degree of competition

8 ♦ Step 5: Establishing strategic direction. Corporate/business decisions

(b) **Arthur D Little matrix**

Stage of industry maturity

		Embryonic	Growth	Mature	Ageing
Competitive position	Dominant	Grow fast Build barriers Act offensively	Grow fast Aim for cost leadership Defend position Act offensively	Defend position Increase the importance of cost Act offensively	Defend position Focus Consider withdrawal
	Strong	Grow fast Differentiate	Lower cost Differentiate Attack small firms	Lower costs Differentiate Focus	Harvest
	Favourable	Grow fast Differentiate	Focus Differentiate Defend	Focus Differentiate Hit smaller firms	Harvest
	Tenable	Grow with the industry Focus	Hold-on or withdraw Niche Aim for growth	Hold-on or withdraw Niche	Withdraw
	Weak	Search for a niche Attempt to catch others	Niche or withdraw	Withdraw	Withdraw

Establish a vision and mission

1.10 These are important starting points for any planning process and both need to be developed to provide the parameters of our planning.

(a) **Visions** are aspirational: to be No. 1 or the recognised expert in a particular field. They will help inform our objective setting.

(b) **Mission statements** answer the question 'what business are we in?' and will help us in the selection of appropriate products and markets.

Tutor Tip

You have already given some consideration to visions and missions in order to do your analysis. You cannot identify competitors or draw market maps if you haven't defined the business. What you are addressing now is:

WHAT BUSINESS SHOULD THEY BE IN?

Take care with cases which supply you with visions and missions: they can be product focused or just red herrings. We would advise you to carefully review and if necessary challenge any 'statements' which might have been made earlier.

Part B: The sample case: Biocatalysts

Revisit our analysis to help us quantify our planning gap

1.11 Auditing the present and forecasting the future

(a) It is only when we have a clear picture of where we are now (and how we've come to arrive here) that we can decide, realistically, where we want to be in the future. This relationship between auditing and forecasting can be seen in the following diagram.

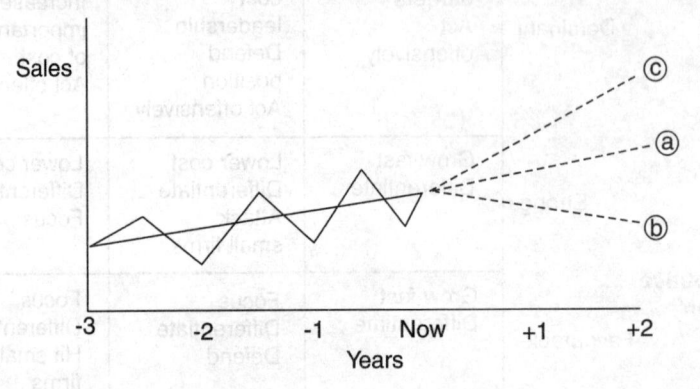

Auditing and forecasting

(b) Here you can see how sales for the last three years have been plotted and a line of 'best fit' added. One approach is to simply extend this line indicating where (all things being equal) the business could expect to be in two years (a).

However all things are not equal. Some people might argue that the more recent past is a more reliable indicator of the future than the more distant past and so weight the last year accordingly. Furthermore one or more of the external environmental factors may be on the verge of radical change.

- The collapse of Amano or a sudden surge in consumer support for enzyme based products could boost Biocatalyst sales to (c).
- A backlash of opinion about GMOs or a sudden economic recession could make (b) a more likely scenario.

(c) Your external analysis (completed at Step 3 and reviewed in the opportunities and threats matrices in the last chapter) will inform this bottom line forecast of your planning gap. In essence, you are trying to add the forecast of how profitable the business **would be** if we stuck with the current products in the current markets.

(d) Having established the bottom line, we now need to add the **top line**, created once you have set a realistic objective.

Again this decision should not be made until the external analysis is complete. You may want to double your profits this year but is that realistic given the market and environmental conditions?

In the following diagram, the economy may be booming (leading to a 'high' objective for sales) but competitive activity may be intense, leading to poorer forecast results.

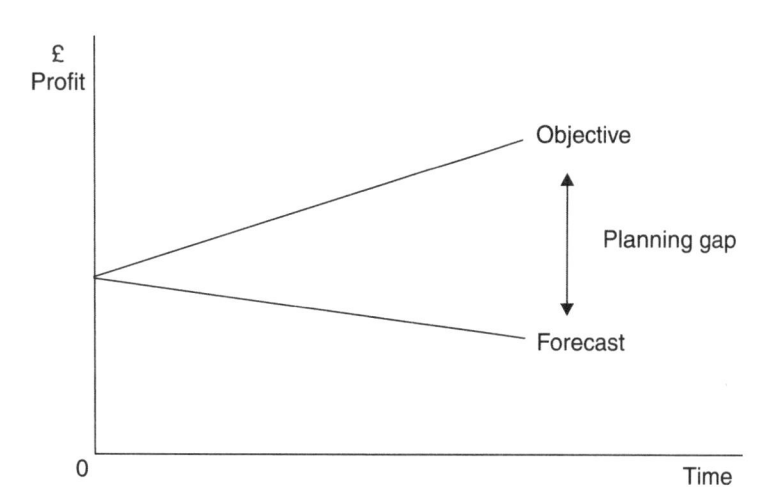

8 ♦ Step 5: Establishing strategic direction. Corporate/business decisions

[Graph showing £ Profit on y-axis and Time on x-axis, with two diverging lines from a common origin point: upper line labeled "Objective" and lower line labeled "Forecast", with a double-headed arrow between them labeled "Planning gap"]

(e) We will now have established a planning gap which is realistic and credible because it was informed from analysis rather than wishful thinking.

Tutor Tip

In practice, the objective will often be a trade off between what the stakeholders aspire to achieve and the assessment of what is realistic or reasonable. There are two things you should bear in mind when writing up a case answer:

(a) Acknowledge the stakeholder's expectation

(b) Justify your objective

It is conservative because ....

It is bullish because ....

Complete your Ansoff matrix

1.12 The opportunities identified in your environmental audit should now provide us with the context for identifying product market opportunity:

(a) Technology breakthrough creates the opportunity for new diagnostic products
(b) Political change provides funding for new development of GMO products
(c) Business growth increases demand for textile and food based products

Completing the Ansoff matrix requires you to look at your environmental analysis and say 'so what'? If this changes, what are the product market implications?

Selecting strategies

1.13 This is the heart of decision making and examiners will be looking hard at how you do this. Decisions made need to be:

- Objective
- Customer focused
- Justified

Part B: The sample case: Biocatalysts

The multifactor matrix criteria will be scrutinised and it **must** be **case specific**:

Not detailed enough	But
Increase revenue	The potential to generate at least £220k per opportunity; this is 10 times more than currently achieved but reflects the 'best of breed' competitor Amano

Notice in this example the criterion is not only **quantified** and **case specific** but **justified**. You leave the examiner in no doubt that you understand what you need to do and how to do it.

Filling the planning gaps

1.14 Once the criterion is determined, the various strategic options can be applied. You do **not** need to show **the calculation** of **weighting** and **rating,** just acknowledge it has been done.

Strategy attractiveness

[Matrix diagram with Competitive advantage (High/Medium/Low) on vertical axis and Strategy attractiveness (High/Medium/Low) on horizontal axis. Option 1 in High/High, Option 2 on border of High/High-Medium, Option 3 in High/Medium, Option 4 in Medium/Medium, Option 5 in High/Low, Option 6 in Low/Low.]

1.15 The strategic options in the **high** and **high/med** boxes are those you will implement in order to fill the planning gap.

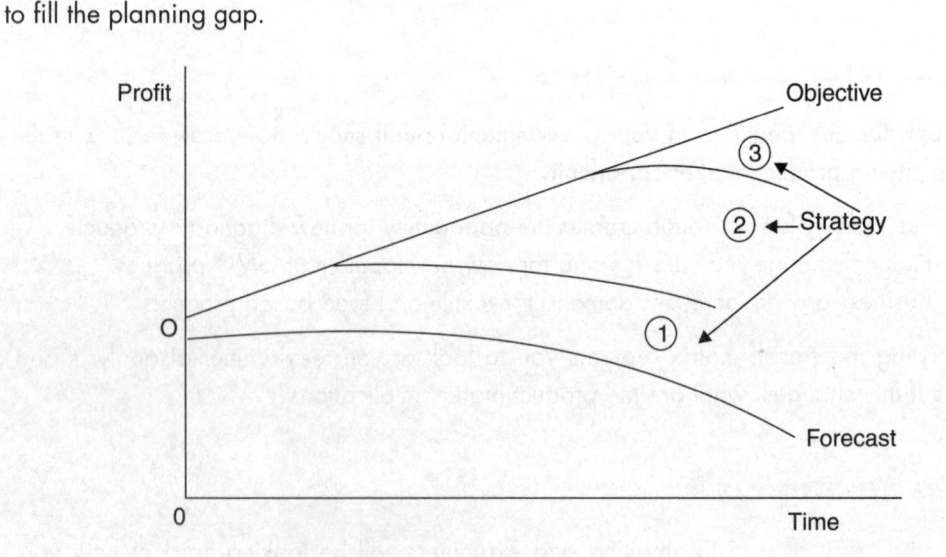

[Graph showing Profit vs Time, with lines for Objective, Strategy (points 1, 2, 3), and Forecast]

1.16 All the business has to do now is:

(a) **Assess the business implications** of selecting these strategies (see step 6)

(b) Develop the **operational plans** to implement the selected strategies (Step 7)

8 ♦ Step 5: Establishing strategic direction. Corporate/business decisions

Action Programme 1

A knowledge review

Before we complete this step for Biocatalysts take a few minutes to check that you are completely happy with the process and tools which underpin this stage.

1. How will you decide on a reasonable objective for the case company?
2. Where will the criteria for assessing the strength of competitive advantage come from?
3. What do you do if the potential contribution of the strategies in the high/med cells of the matrix are insufficient to fill the planning gap?
4. What characteristics would you expect the examiner to be looking for in a 'good' mission statement?

The pitfalls

1.17 This is the case step which perhaps causes students the biggest problems and not surprisingly there are a number of potential pitfalls which need to be avoided.

1. **Not making decisions is perhaps the most obvious pitfall.** Students are often unwilling to decide on an object or preferred strategies because they are worried their decisions will not be in line with the examiner's opinions. Instead they try and sit on the fence. You can spot scripts of these candidates by the 'weasel' words they employ:

    - Perhaps
    - On the one hand
    - On balance
    - Maybe

    As we have said before, there are no single correct answers to a case study, so the examiner will not have fixed ideas about the right strategy. What he or she will be looking for is evidence that you have worked through a logical process resulting in :

    - Clear decision making
    - Justified decisions
    - Convincing arguments in favour of those decisions

Tutor Tip

If you are not confident about the recommendations you are making, it is unlikely you would convince the case organisation or the examiner. The successful selling of strategy in business is being directly tested in how you present your case proposals.

2. **Failing to add the numbers.** We appreciate most marketers hate the thought of numbers, but trust us, it is essential. Objectives and decisions criteria need quantification and those numbers must be drawn from the case study. You must understand them and be able to work with them.

Part B: The sample case: Biocatalysts

3   **Failing to use the analysis to inform decision making**. Too many candidates fall into the trap of treating each case step in isolation and the result is commercial nonsense.

There is no point in recommending a strategy of expansion through acquisition if a business has no cash.

Neither is a long-term product development strategy sensible if there is a short-term survival strategy required.

2 Biocatalysts: what needs to be done

Tutor Tip

You are now ready to start making decisions and you will need to 'own' these in the exam room. If you are working in a syndicate group, it has been quite appropriate for you to share your work up to now but take care from here on in. If the examiner gets twenty scripts from the same centre with a word perfect mission statement, he or she is likely to assume a group answer, which will result in an automatic fail. Discuss and review together by all means but the words need to be yours.

A vision

2.1 Remember the vision is an aspiration. It needs to be realistic and something which will inspire the organisation to strive for its achievement. A good vision can act as something of a 'crie de coeur' for the business.

Action Programme 2

Establishing a Vision

Take a few minutes to look at the following possible visions for Biocatalysts. Which would you reject and why? Which would you choose?

1   It is our vision to be the global leader in the development and production of enzyme solutions for industry.

2   We are in the business of providing enzyme solutions to our clients.

3   We want to be the first choice provider for organisations who have 'other sector' clients who have enzyme problems or opportunities.

4   We want to be the biggest producer of bulk enzymes in the food and textile industries of Europe.

5   We want to be the acknowledged technical leader in UK based enzyme research.

Turn to the end of the chapter for our comments.

8 ♦ Step 5: Establishing strategic direction. Corporate/business decisions

2.2 Take another 10 minutes to craft your own vision for Biocatalysts.

> A Vision for Biocatalysts

Check it for:

- Relevance
- Realism

What business is Biocatalysts in?

Mission

2.3 We must now tackle the mission statement. What do you think of this for Biocatalysts?

> We are in the business of helping our globally-based customers improve the efficiency and effectiveness of their processes through the provision of tailor made enzyme solutions, employing leading edge technology, combined with over 13 years of experience and expertise.

Comments

....

....

....

It is a little longwinded but it incorporates the **customer benefits** of 'efficiency and effectiveness'; it has focus; it is for processes and there is a hint of differentiation built around the technology in safe hands.

Part B: The sample case: Biocatalysts

An alternative mission

2.4 | We will be the leading global supplier of specialised enzymes to diagnostic, food processing and GMO sectors within five years.

2.5 Again take 10 minutes to craft your own mission

A Mission for Biocatalysts

Check it for:

- Distinctiveness
- Focus on customer benefits

Tutor Tip

When using a vision or mission in the exam, do first check it makes sense in the light of the additional information and questions set. For example, if you set out to be No. 1 in Europe and the extra information is about opportunities in Japan, you will need to review your vision.

Action Programme 3

Establishing the Planning Gap

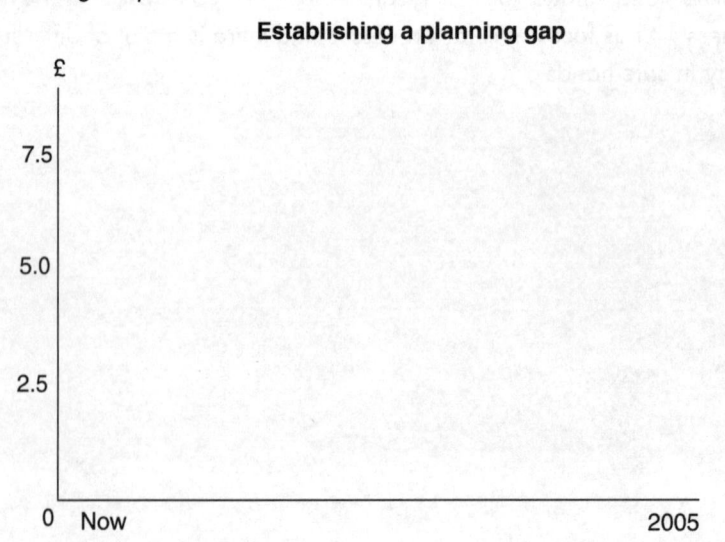

Establishing a planning gap

£

7.5

5.0

2.5

0   Now   2005

Before you turn to the end of this chapter to look at our thoughts on a possible planning gap, have a go at producing one for yourself:

1   Check out current revenue and profit

2   What do you think will happen to both if Biocatalyst continues to operate as it has with the same products and markets?

3   Next, think about the future environment and what the shareholders might expect, and try and set a realistic objective

4   Can you justify your decisions?

Do not agonise about these decisions: be brave and a little bold. Remember you are in essence quantifying the added value marketing might give to this business.

Now turn to the end of the chapter to see our planning gap but remember there will be many variations equally acceptable. Ours is only a sample developed to show you the process.

The strategic options

2.6 The only problem now we have established the planning gap, is to decide how to fill it.

2.7 The first step is to identify the options. The company can only expand its business with combinations of products and markets. Its strategic options are based around four strategies:

- Market penetration
- Product development
- Market development
- Diversification

Action Programme 4

Ansoff options

We have begun to populate the Ansoff Matrix for Biocatalysts – what can you add?

Products

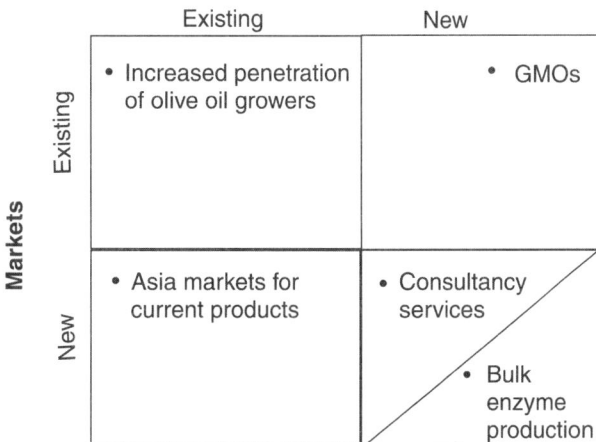

	Existing	New
Markets: Existing	• Increased penetration of olive oil growers	• GMOs
Markets: New	• Asia markets for current products	• Consultancy services • Bulk enzyme production

Part B: The sample case: Biocatalysts

2.8 Having identified the strategic **alternatives open to a business**, the next step is to decide which are **most attractive** for the business. Remember there may be an excellent opportunity in the market, but your firm may **not** be suited to exploiting it.

2.9 You are looking for opportunities which are both attractive to the business and where the business has the propensity to deliver a competitive advantage.

Making strategic decisions

2.10 The **multifactor matrix** is an excellent framework to ensure you have taken account of both the attractiveness of the opportunity and the potential competitive advantage.

2.11 Examiners will be looking for evidence that you can adapt the theory to meet the specific context of the case. That means case specific criteria are needed. What you do **not** need to do is add the weighting and rating to calculate each strategic option. It is highly unlikely you would have the data to do this in a meaningful way anyway.

2.12 What you **do** need to do is explain that you would, or indeed have, weighted and rated the alternatives and then demonstrate the assumed or potential outcome on a multifactor framework.

Action Programme 5

Biocatalysts Decision Criteria

Take ten minutes to think about the criteria you could use for assessing Biocatalysts' options.

You only need 5-6 in each list, but make them as case specific as possible.

Strategy market attractiveness	Competitive position
1...	1...
2...	2...
3...	3...
4...	4...
5...	5...
6...	6...

Our example is provided for you at the end of this chapter.

8 ♦ Step 5: Establishing strategic direction. Corporate/business decisions

Biocatalysts' strategy attractiveness

	High	Medium	Low
High	• Environmental waste Industrial enzymes •	• Environmental solutions • Olive growers	GMOs •
Medium	• Diagnostics • Knowledge brokers	• Pharmaceuticals	
Low		• Japan/Russia	

(y-axis: Competitive advantage)

2.13 Note that there is **no single right or wrong answer as to where to log opportunities on this matrix**. The examiners will be looking for your thought process and in the exam you would want to highlight the selected strategies and comment on their justification. You may like to conclude your strategy section with a completed planning gap, showing how your selected strategies will fill it.

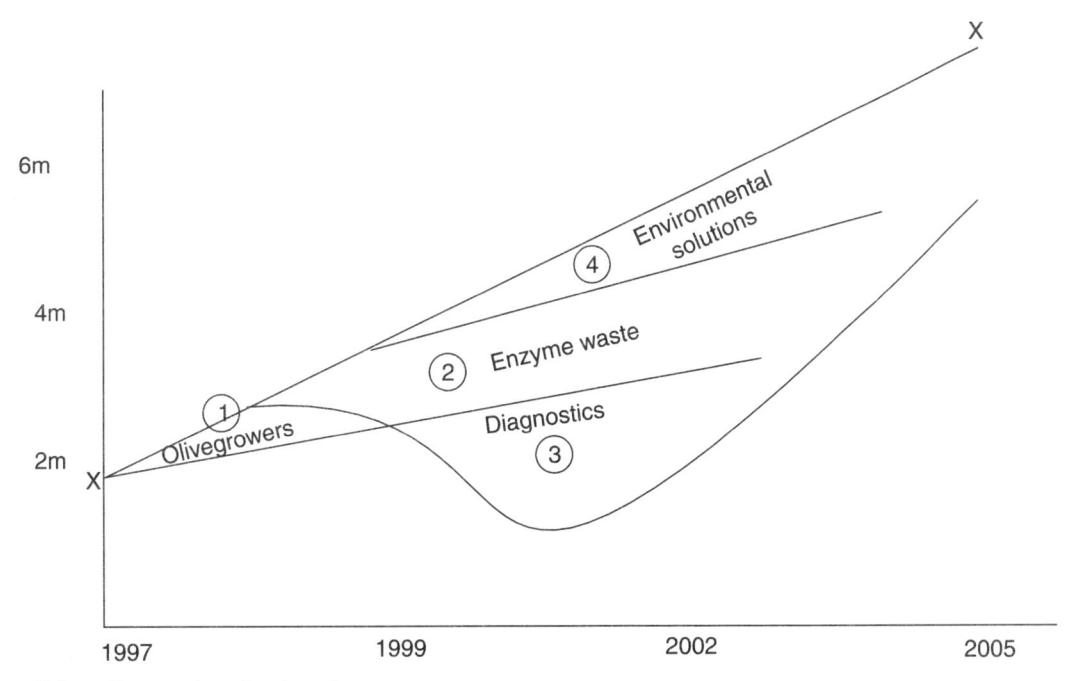

Filling Biocatalysts's planning gap

(Graph showing planning gap from 1997 to 2005, with strategies: ① Olivegrowers, ② Enzyme waste, ③ Diagnostics, ④ Environmental solutions; y-axis from 2m to 6m)

Part B: The sample case: Biocatalysts

Action Programme review

1 *A knowledge review*

   1 By considering likely stakeholder expectations, current and past performance and what competitors seem to be achieving. These to be considered against the general state of the market but there can be many different views. The important thing is to be specific and able to justify the objective set.

   2 It should come from the customers buying criteria so always an aspect of the marketing mix. So for Biocatalysts:

   - Safety
   - Customisation
   - Technical support

   may all be more important than price

   3 There are two options:

   - Either the objective needs to be reviewed downwards
   - Less attractive med/low strategies can be reconsidered and a decision made about their potential to review or re-engineer to make them more attractive. For example, if this strategy was unattractive to the firm because of the high levels of investment needed, perhaps a partner could be found.

   4 Simple, distinctive and based on customer benefits **not** product features

2 *Establishing a vision*

   1 Simply unrealistic – Biocatalyst is a tiny global player.

   2 No, this is a mission statement, not a good one as it has no source of differentiation incorporated in it.

   3 This is quite good – it provides a niche focus 'other sector' and would need the company to build a reputation for problem solving. It is a vision which might appeal to the scientists who make up the Biocatalyst community.

   4 This is not the business Biocatalysts are in; bulk production is a different sector and is not one in which they operate with core competence.

   5 This could be appealing to the staff but is too narrow a focus to provide commercial returns in this global market.

The problem, as we saw in our analysis, is that profits are not growing although revenue is. The business is currently spread too thin in terms of products and markets and new products are developed but not exploited.

However they are positioned to increase revenues if the global distribution is sorted and some pro-active marketing is added – so a slightly bullish objective of £6m or even £8m revenue could be justified.

Notice that, at approximately £250k per new enzyme, this would need 14 launches over 1998 – 2005: less than last year!

The real key though is the profit. If you assume a 15% gross profit margin this needs to be increased from its current low level to £1.5m by 2005.

8 ♦ Step 5: Establishing strategic direction. Corporate/business decisions

Rationalisation of products and markets will be needed to get rid of unprofitable activity. Such a strategy would make the planning gap look like this:

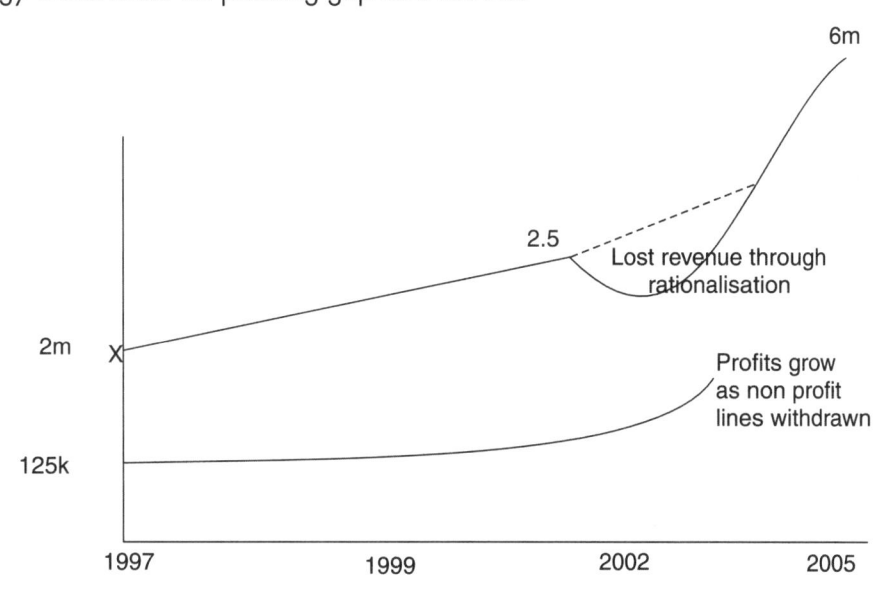

[Graph showing planning gap with rationalisation strategy, 1997-2005. Key points: 2m at X in 1997, rising to 2.5 in 2002 then 6m by 2005. "Lost revenue through rationalisation" shown as dashed curve. Lower line from 125k showing "Profits grow as non profit lines withdrawn".]

Tutor Tip

Look at how adding legends to your diagrams helps with the process of justification and explanation

3 Establishing the Planning Gap

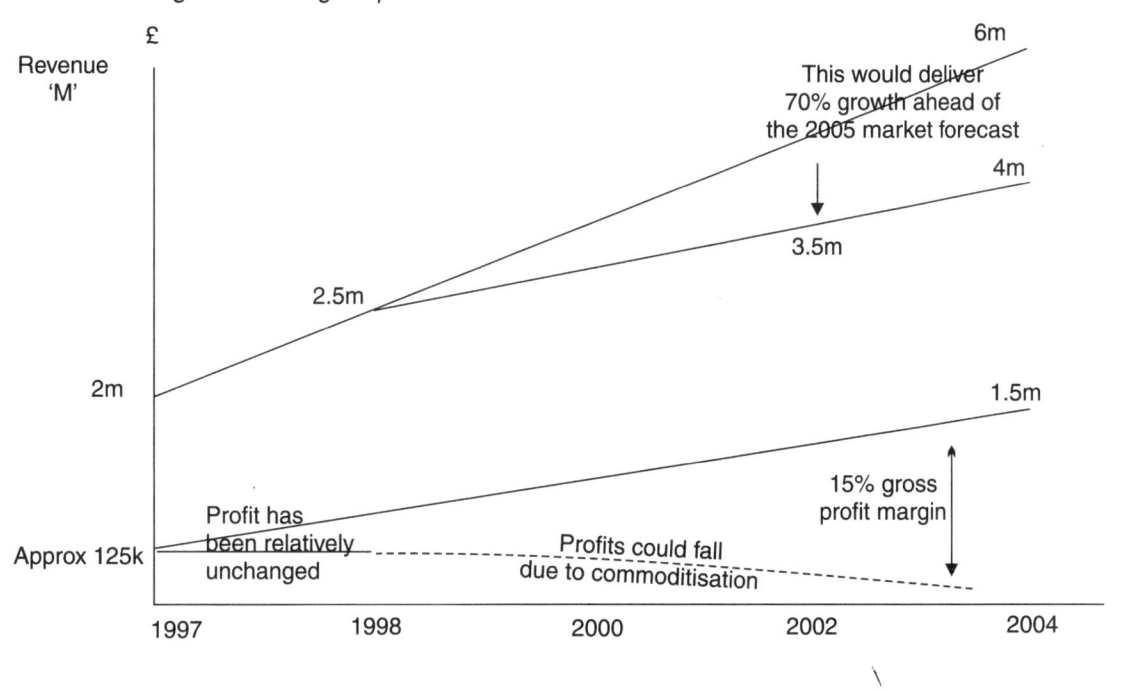

[Graph: Revenue 'M' (£) vs years 1997-2004. Upper line rises from 2m to 6m, labelled "This would deliver 70% growth ahead of the 2005 market forecast". Middle line rises to 4m via 2.5m and 3.5m. Lower line rises from Approx 125k to 1.5m with "15% gross profit margin" marked. Annotations: "Profit has been relatively unchanged", "Profits could fall due to commoditisation" (dashed line).]

You can see we have included both the profit and revenue picture on one graph. You may prefer to do it on two.

Part B: The sample case: Biocatalysts

4 Ansoff options

A number of options emerged during analysis.

	Products Existing	**Products** New
Markets Existing	Environmental maintenance Waste treatment Textiles Health care Unique speciality foods Alcohol, baking, fats/oils Fruit/wine, flavour, protein Animal foods, leather Paper/pulp Chemical biotransformation	More testing kits GMOs By-products High tech diagnostic New Tech foods Full consultancy service Technical backup service

Markets New	Geographic - eg Russia
	  China
	  USA
	  Japan
	New industries/sectors
	Oil spillage
	Pharmaceutical
	Licensing
		Knowledge brokers
		
		Backward
		Forward
		integration

5 Biocatalysts' decision criteria

Evaluation of strategic options

Each strategy must be evaluated for its attractiveness to the business and the competitive advantage/position it offers. The best evaluation tool for this purpose is the GE matrix. Management will agree and prioritise the criteria for strategy attractiveness and research on customers can determine the competitive position. We already have some information on why customers buy which would form this criteria, for example:

Strategy/market attractiveness

1. Profitability of net less than X%
2. Marketing growth potential
3. Levels of competition
4. Investment required of not more than X%
5. Synergy with existing operations
6. New skills required
7. Speed to implement
8. Degree of risk

Competitive position

1. Improving efficiency
2. Cost effectiveness
3. Convenience
4. Safety
5. Availability
6. Consistency and quality
7. Value for money
8. Technical support

Weighting and rating the criteria enables us to plot the strategies on the matrix to reveal which strategies are worth pursuing and should be rejected.

Biocatalysts need to plan for the short- and medium-term. In this fast changing, dynamic market longer term strategies can be difficult to identify. Strategy selection will need to provide immediate profits given our financial position, followed by medium-term strategies that will grow the business and establish a competitive position.

Step 6: Marketing Management and Business Implications

Chapter Topic List	
1	Business implications of marketing plans
2	Marketing orientation
3	Structure
4	Strategic role of the brand
5	Strategic and integrated marketing communications (IMC)
6	International marketing strategy
7	Pitfalls

1 Business implications of marketing plans

1.1 Marketers developing marketing strategies and plans to meet the challenges and demands of the business environment must think of the **implications to the business of developing and implementing their plans.** These implications will usually be to the business as a whole as well as to marketing. Marketers who fail to consider these issues are not thinking or acting strategically and jeopardise the chances of success. **Business implications include:**

- Culture of the organisation (eg marketing orientation)
- Structure
- Financial and funding
- Processes
- People
- Communications and information systems

1.2 Marketing implications are inevitably interlinked with business implications and are those strategic issues associated with marketing activities which include:

(a) **Customer focus** (implicit in a marketing orientation and dependent on good marketing intelligence, marketing information systems and the ability to segment markets)

Part B: The sample case: Biocatalysts

(b) **Product/services** offered and the quality, benefits and value they represent to the customer (including e.g. accessibility – place, value for money – price)

(c) **Customer service** (implicit in the people, processes and physical evidence policies)

(d) **Communications**, positioning and the brand

> **Tutor Tip**
>
> With some case studies more time would be spent on this than with others, depending on how obvious or serious the business implications are. With Biocatalysts, for example, clearly there were business implications, and a few notes need to be made on what these are. Some might come up as a question eg establishing a marketing information system, or might need to be referred to briefly, if relevant, within a strategic marketing plan question.

2 Marketing orientation

2.1 A marketing orientation ensures that management's key tasks are to determine the needs and wants of selected target markets, and to adopt appropriate structures and design activities to meet those needs. Marketing research is a key activity and marketing intelligence forms the basis of decision making. Marketing programmes are tailored to meet the needs of specific, selected groups of people with similar needs and characteristics.

Clues to marketing orientation

People

2.2 **Board level/senior management**

Marketing is represented at board level by qualified marketing professionals. The Chief Executive, from whatever background, has a marketing qualification or training.

2.3 **Staff**

People are valued and trusted by the organisation and this is reflected in internal policies and procedures, and in management attitudes to employees.

Culture and structure

2.4 The values of the organisation are reflected in the way staff are treated, how responsive the organisation is to the local community and the responsibility assumed for social and environmental issues.

2.5 Customers are not considered the sole responsibility of marketing and sales, but the responsibility of everyone in the organisation. All employees understand their role and contribution in delivering benefits to customers; they know who their customers are and what is important to them.

2.6 Organisational structure is designed to meet the challenges of external demands rather than internal convenience. Continuous improvement is a corporate goal that is assimilated into departmental, team and individual objectives.

Tasks and processes

2.7 Strategies

Senior management are concerned with the long-term future and direction of the organisation and developing strategies that reflect the reality of the market place. Marketing plays a pivotal role in determining what product market opportunities the organisation pursues. Financial resources for marketing are determined by objectives to be achieved, not spare cash left over.

2.8 Marketing information

(a) There is a **formalised** Marketing Information System (MKIS) feeding into a Management Information System (MIS) and **primary marketing research is regarded as an essential activity**. Management decisions are based on the results of marketing research activities and reflect business strengths and competitive positioning.

(b) The business understands its business environment, the likelihood and nature of opportunities and threats and how well it is performing compared with competitors. It understands customer behaviour and the values customers attribute to the organisation's brand(s).

2.9 Co-ordination and integration

(a) Planning and control is recognised as the most efficient and effective way to use limited resources and organise activities. Activities across the organisation are co-ordinated and integrated by senior management to ensure consistency of delivery and take advantage of maximising value-added opportunities.

(b) Departments understand each others' problems and needs, and work in partnership to solve problems and accomplish overall departmental and corporate objectives.

(c) This partnership philosophy extends to suppliers, distribution channels and other stakeholders who are included in the planning process and whose activities are assimilated into the organisation's plans.

2.10 Communications

Communications, internal and external, with employees, customers and all stakeholders, incorporate values and positioning, and reflect the needs of different target groups. Two-way communications are encouraged, with mechanisms for listening as well as talking.

2.11 New product/service development

New product development involves the customer either directly or through marketing intelligence and customer contribution to this process is considered fundamental. Customer service is designed in at the start, developed with the product or service and is seen as key to competitive advantage and customer retention. Different customer needs are reflected in different products, and services are designed to meet those needs.

Part B: The sample case: Biocatalysts

2.12 Measuring effectiveness

Setting targets and standards is regarded as pivotal to successful outcomes and measuring effectiveness as an integral part of planning. Employees have customer satisfaction performance targets as well as the usual easily quantified targets. Evaluation of successes and failures determines the nature of future plans.

2.13 Training and development

Training and development of employees is recognised as key to ensuring business success, and marketing and customer service training is **not confined to marketing personnel.** Appraisals form part of continual improvement, and the development and motivation of employees is seen as a significant management task. Training and development is also seen as the most effective way of ensuring employees are prepared and able to accept and implement change in response to market conditions.

Innovation and organisation culture

2.14 An important aspect of marketing orientation is innovation. This is the only way businesses can stay ahead. Central to innovation is an **environment that allows creativity**. Control therefore, must be flexible and is able to adapt when circumstances demand a different approach.

2.15 A key driver of innovation is **attitude**.

(a) People in the organisation are not interested in following but in leading, wanting to be first. This attitude will also affect the type of innovation.

(b) Incremental innovation is less risky, costly and more likely to succeed due to its nature. The business learns as it evolves and, because the innovation is usually built on something the customers already know and understand, they are likely to appreciate the 'new' benefits.

(c) Innovation can be revolutionary and involve 'megaprojects' or 'do everything'. This requires heavy investment, the 'unknowns' are greater including the market's response and the learning curves are far steeper. It is only usually an option if it is a matter of business survival (due to falling so far behind the competition) or the innovation is known to meet a significant identified need and has guaranteed commercial viability.

Continuous improvement

2.16 An attitude of, and systems for, continuous improvement is also essential in developing an innovative culture and environment. Change can be very disruptive and threatening.

2.17 Change can be gentle and continuous, a part of everyday life, so people are used to it and work with it. This requires flexibility in structures, systems and processes so that events can evolve gradually, but continuously, where appropriate. An attitude of wanting to improve on what is done now is encouraged through rewards and recognition. Continuous improvement is included in personal and team targets.

3 Structure

Key factors affecting organisation design/structure

3.1 Internal influences

- **Mission**: corporate objectives and strategies
- **Culture**: management style/attitudes to control will be reflected in design
- **People**: skills requirements and levels
- **Task**: the product made and the way work is organised
- **Processes**: technology

3.2 External influences

(a) **Location**: some industries are affected by their necessity to be in a certain geographic location eg mining industry and this will affect structure

(b) **Customers**: organising around customers can be driven by necessity or a desire to differentiate

(c) **Legal/political**: eg organisations producing dangerous or toxic products.

Centralised versus decentralised operations

3.3 The extent of centralisation and decentralisation depends on a number of factors including size of organisation, number of markets it operates in, industry type, products and processes. Usually the more complex and competitive the environment the greater the need for decentralisation.

Advantages of centralisation	Advantages of decentralisation
■ Facilitates the co-ordination of marketing	■ Allows local responses
■ Can dilute low management expertise in some areas	■ Improves effective local performance
■ Should result in better control	■ Improves management development
■ Ensures transfer of ideas across teams	
■ Avoids duplication of effort and therefore reduces costs	

3.4 Structural options

- Functional eg finance, marketing, product
- Territory eg north, home countries
- Product
- Market
- Process/technology
- Knowledge/skills eg paediatrics, radiology
- Matrix

4 Strategic role of the brand

4.1 The brand plays a more significant role than ever before. Its value to the organisation as a source of competitive advantage and means of securing customer loyalty has been recognised and the nature of brand management has changed as a result.

Part B: The sample case: Biocatalysts

Brands and their strategic role

4.2 Managing brands at a **tactical** level has always been easier than at strategic level. It did not require co-ordination across the organisation or consideration of integrating business activities.

4.3 The role of the brand has become much more 'strategic' in the last decade. This has been driven by brands appearing on balance sheets as assets. Suddenly organisations realised the financial value of brands. To build and maintain financial value requires a strategic approach which, in turn, requires long-term commitment to the brand, investment and innovation.

4.4 All business activities must be co-ordinated to represent the desired meaning and values of the brand.

Objectives and benefits

4.5 Objectives and benefits of brand management include:
- Building demand and building/holding margins
- Protection (eg reputation and quality)
- Added value
- Competitive advantage
- Customer loyalty and repeat purchase

What is a brand?

4.6 A brand is more than just a physical product or service; it can help build relationships with customers. This is particularly important in markets where the organisation has no face to face contact with customers (eg fmcg). A brand is also more than just the component parts that make up a product, it has **additional values attributed** to it by customers.

4.7 A brand adds value to the product. Added value often has more potential to differentiate one product from another than core and expected functional benefits.

Where is value added?

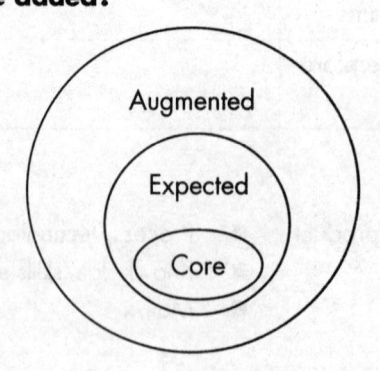

The brand (and its values) represents the total benefits received from offering both tangible/functional benefits and intangible/emotional benefits

(Diagram: three concentric circles labelled Augmented, Expected, Core)

Brands and corporate image/reputation

4.8 Image and reputation come from a number of sources. How the business performs in its markets can help build a positive image and reputation (or not). Customers' views and perceptions, and competitor actions, will also affect image and reputation.

4.9 A key factor in building a positive image and reputation will be the **effectiveness** of the organisation's **communication activities**. Fundamental to this will be the brand and what it has come to represent. The brand can be (and increasingly is) the company name or product names.

4.10 The communications effort, amongst other things, should be concerned with promoting **positive associations** with the brand that are meaningful and valued by customers. Sony is a good example of a brand that is perceived as trustworthy and reliable, with high quality performance. This reduces the customer's need to take time deciding between brands: the Sony brand is trusted and so the **perceived risk** is lessened.

Brands, corporate culture and customer service

4.11 Corporate culture can affect perceptions of the brand either positively or negatively. An organisation that receives bad publicity for the way it treats its staff is likely to damage its image in the eyes of its publics. An organisation that values its staff and is perceived as a good place to work will add value to the brand. This also extends to its role in the local community, society and environmental responsibility.

4.12 Customer service, increasingly a source of competitive advantage, is one of the most difficult elements of the marketing mix to manage. Variability in service affects customers' perceptions of the value of the brand.

4.13 To ensure consistent and desired customer service levels, the right people need to be recruited, employees need to feel valued and receive the appropriate customer service training if the desired levels of service are to be achieved and maintained.

Brands, positioning and the marketing mix

4.14 The marketing department does not have **control** over all of the marketing mix: the whole organisation is involved. The marketing department should, however, have **significant influence** over the marketing mix, particularly if the brand is to perform effectively and provide a source of competitive advantage.

4.15 The entire marketing mix must represent and reflect the brand values. Any inconsistencies confuse customers and damages the brand's reputation and performance. The marketing task is to ensure that, in the first place, it understands the brand values as perceived by customers and, secondly, manages the mix to build positive brand values and effectively position the mix in the market.

Action Programme 1

What brand values would you recommend Biocatalysts consider? Think about what they do well and how they need to build a niche position in the future.

There is no feedback for this Action Programme.

Part B: The sample case: Biocatalysts

5 Strategic and integrated marketing communications (IMC)

5.1 Key to achieving a unique position in the market place, and managing the strategic role of the brand, is ensuring that all the ways in which the organisation communicates with its publics, both directly and indirectly, are consistent. Everything the organisation does and the way it does it reinforces the positioning values. There should be no confusing or conflicting messages.

5.2 This requires a strategic approach and planning and the rewards include:
- Improved effectiveness of communications with selected targets
- Improved efficiency in use of resources
- Improved profits as a result of above two
- Improved competitiveness

5.3 The organisation does not simply communicate through its marketing mix promotional activities. There are four main levels at which the organisation communicates, spanning strategic and tactical levels.

5.4 **Strategic communication levels** are the industry (or institutional) and company levels and include:
- Corporate actions (eg social responsibilities, influencing industry and government)
- Corporate identity – brand values
- Management style and behaviour
- Corporate strategies
- Positioning

5.5 Integrated communications require vertical and horizontal co-ordination of activities.

Corporate vision, mission and communications

5.6 **The company's mission statement defines the purpose of the business**. The role of strategic marketing communications is to **signal that purpose** to the market and reinforce the message through regular, planned promotional activities. The company's aspirations are defined in the vision and this also is communicated to the market. The messages signal future intentions and aspirations to the market.

5.7 Fundamental to the success of these messages is that the **market believes** what is communicated. Developing credibility is core to messages of business purpose and vision: therefore the organisation's know how and capabilities are given prominence.

Corporate culture and communications

5.8 The **culture of the organisation** is expressed through the **behaviour of the people** within the organisation, both management and staff. The culture is the personality of the business and increasingly culture is playing an important role in adding value to the corporate brand. The organisation's reputation may be built through quality, reliability, innovation and so on, and these become part of what the company is known and respected for. Positive attributes become core communication messages.

5.9 The values and attitudes held by people in the organisation are reflected in the way people are treated, both internally and externally. They also reflect attitudes to risk, and influence strategic choices. These values and attitudes communicate the sort of 'personality' the organisation has, and will have a positive or negative impact.

Management style and communications

5.10 **The culture of the organisation significantly affects the style of management.** The extent to which management trusts and respects employees is demonstrated in the extent of supervision and control. Rules, regulations and procedures all reflect attitudes towards employees perceived capabilities and how they are valued (or not). This trust and respect is passed on to customers through employee attitudes to service. Customers will either feel they have been processed or that they have been served. The result of this communication with the customer is either an impersonal experience that resulted in the customer feeling uncomfortable, unhappy and/or unsatisfied or a personal experience where the customer felt valued and expectations were at the very least met or exceeded.

Corporate image/identity and communications

5.11 Corporate image is achieved through the combination of:

- Culture: its personality, values and attitudes
- Visual cues: the physical evidence e.g. buildings, logos, colours
- Behaviour: performance (eg competitive and reliable) and integrity (conducting business, eg with awareness of, social and environmental responsibilities, ethics)

All these organisational issues are interwoven.

Corporate strategy, positioning and communications

5.12 **Competitive positioning** and growth strategies depend on effective marketing communications to achieve the overall goal. Customers may position a company in their minds but it is up to the organisation to influence that position positively and in line with their strategic goals. This position follows on from the mission and vision, and is reinforced through the company's performance in the market.

5.13 Growth strategies depend on identification of specific market segments to target with specific products. The success of these strategies depends on the effectiveness of the marketing mix including communication messages targeted at those existing and new segments. Different strategies will require different messages; for example, market penetration messages are targeted at existing customers with whom a relationship has already been built. This will differ from market development where messages are targeted at new customers who will not be so familiar with the organisation.

6 International marketing strategy

6.1 The same processes and frameworks are used in international marketing. The difference is the complexity and increased need for co-ordination and integration of strategies, particularly if global strategies are to be pursued.

Part B: The sample case: Biocatalysts

6.2 As well as vertical planning systems, there is a need for horizontal planning systems, a framework for senior management to co-ordinate and harmonise Strategic Business Unit plans. The goal is to maximise competitive advantage through sharing best practice and skills and develop coherent global strategies.

International business operations

6.3 Structure and control present problems for international companies, and structuring and re-structuring has become part of normal life for the multi-national in a bid to find the 'best' structure for managing international activities. Organisations have centralised control and decentralised control and back again.

6.4 There are no easy answers or perfect solutions. The international market place is changing rapidly, not least because of the impact of technology. Organisations must therefore remain flexible and ensure that continuous improvement and adaptation is part of day to day operations.

Managing across borders

6.5 Organisation culture and the influences of national culture affect both management style and communications. Marketing is responsible for responding to the needs of external customers and stakeholders. Marketing management must therefore respond to the needs of internal employees to ensure those external customers and stakeholders receive what they want.

   (a) **Staffing policy**. Decisions include whether to recruit locally, post home country staff to overseas appointments or a combination of both. There are advantages and disadvantages to recruiting local people (see your international notes). Staff should receive support and training for overseas assignments and communications systems should ensure employee/s feel as in touch as they did before moving abroad. This requires extra effort from the organisation, not the same effort. Motivation must take account of differences for example, while Maslow's hierarchy of needs is still valid, the order of the needs changes depending on the culture.

   (b) **Training programmes**. Factors to consider include and learning styles and expectations, training methods available, training skills available and attitudes to training. If training is not common practice in a culture, it may be seen as threatening, a criticism of performance. It is important to communicate the purpose and benefits of training and ensure people perceive training positively.

   (c) **Communication programmes**. Factors to consider include language and interpretation, style and tone, expected forms of communications, technology availability, symbolism and cultural influences e.g. meaning of colour and use of humour. In high power distance cultures employees will expect to be 'told' what to do and communications are one-way. If the manager wishes to encourage two-way communications and involve employees, plans will be needed to change employee expectations and perceptions of their role in decision making. In low power distance cultures, two-way communications will be the norm. Employees expect to be allowed to clarify instructions and challenge actions.

Action Programme 2

Consider the implications of Biocatalysts' business and strategic marketing. What might affect their ability to implement strategic marketing plans and what changes may they have to make?

6.6 All of these issues impact directly or indirectly on marketing planning. Marketers need to ensure they have taken account of the impact and incorporated, where appropriate, actions to address the business and marketing implications of the mission, vision, corporate objectives and strategies selected.

6.7 In this chapter we have discussed the business implications that may arise as a result of developing strategic marketing plans. In fact, for Biocatalysts, all of these issues are relevant. For example they need to adopt a **marketing orientation** if they are going to achieve their goal of being a respected **niche player**. This cannot be achieved with their current business and marketing planning skills.

6.8 Strategic and integrated marketing communications will also be essential to success. Particularly as Biocatalysts do not have much cash to fund communications activities and so must ensure that everything they do will maximise results.

6.9 Their international development has been unmanaged and appears to be ad hoc. There is no clear strategy and, given their financial performance, they cannot afford to operate in this way any longer. Again, to produced successful results they need to develop coherent international plans and this may require re-structuring the business.

7 Pitfalls

7.1 Sometimes the exam questions do not ask specifically for you to identify implications for the business of the recommendations you have made. The danger is of failing to incorporate these vital issues within your answers even if they have not been specifically asked for. We do not suggest that you spend much time discussing them but, for example, if adopting a marketing orientation or customer focus is essential to the success of building a brand or integrated communications strategy, you should briefly refer to the need to change the culture to a marketing orientation.

Part B: The sample case: Biocatalysts

Action Programme review

2   There are many factors you might include here:

- The lack of customer orientation
- Shortage of funding and uncertainty of funding
- Lack of marketing skills
- The product focus of technology staff
- The product focused business structure
- Lack of information

Changes which would be needed:

- To restructure around customer groups
- To establish an effective marketing information system
- To establish internal marketing skills

Step 7: Marketing Strategy and Marketing Mix Plans

Chapter Topic List	
1	Marketing planning
2	Marketing objectives
3	Marketing strategy: segmentation
4	Marketing strategy: positioning
5	Marketing strategy: targeting
6	International marketing strategy
7	Separating process from plan
8	Implementing marketing strategy
9	Product strategy
10	Price strategy
11	Place strategy
12	Promotions strategy
13	Customer service and customer relationship management
14	International marketing mix issues: some reminders

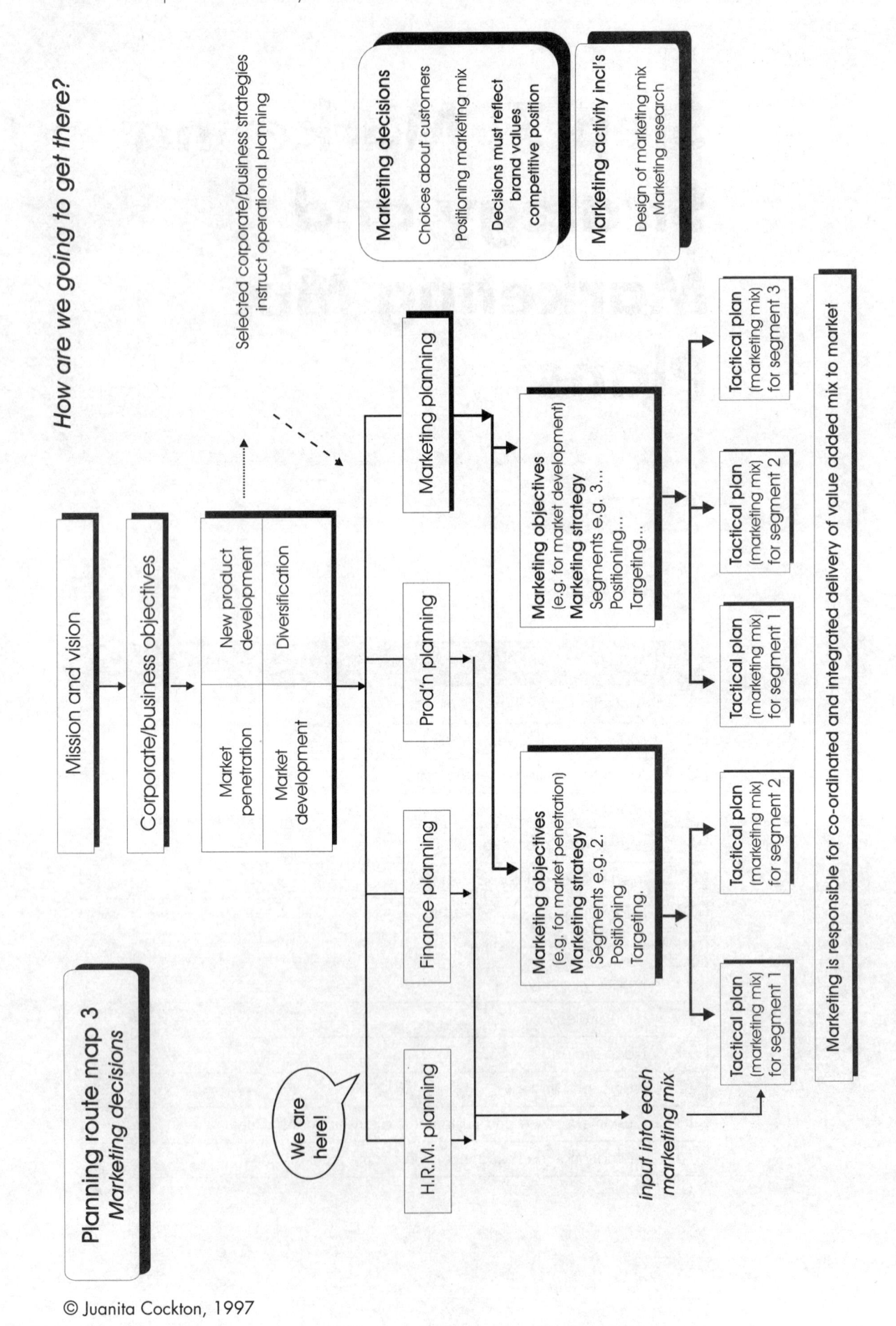

Part B: The sample case: Biocatalysts

Planning route map 3
Marketing decisions

How are we going to get there?

Marketing decisions
- Choices about customers
- Positioning marketing mix
- Decisions must reflect brand values competitive position

Marketing activity incl's
- Design of marketing mix
- Marketing research

Selected corporate/business strategies instruct operational planning

Mission and vision → Corporate/business objectives → [New product development / Diversification / Market penetration / Market development]

Branches: Marketing planning, Prod'n planning, Finance planning, H.R.M. planning

"We are here!"

Marketing objectives (e.g. for market development)
Marketing strategy
Segments e.g. 3...
Positioning...
Targeting...

→ Tactical plan (marketing mix) for segment 1
→ Tactical plan (marketing mix) for segment 2
→ Tactical plan (marketing mix) for segment 3

Marketing objectives (e.g. for market penetration)
Marketing strategy
Segments e.g. 2.
Positioning
Targeting.

→ Tactical plan (marketing mix) for segment 1
→ Tactical plan (marketing mix) for segment 2

input into each marketing mix

Marketing is responsible for co-ordinated and integrated delivery of value added mix to market

© Juanita Cockton, 1997

1 Marketing planning

1.1 Marketing objectives and marketing plans cannot be developed until the organisation has made decisions on which broad product market opportunities it intends to pursue. You will see from the planning route map that marketing plans need to be developed for each business strategy selected and, for each segment identified, tactical plans will be developed and implemented.

2 Marketing objectives

2.1 When senior management have communicated their decisions, marketing can set marketing objectives for each business strategy selected by the business.

2.2 The marketing objective is translated from the business objective. So for example a business objective of £1.2 million profit and forecast gross profit margin of 10% can be translated into a marketing objective of £12 million revenue. If we are able to value customers and/or markets in financial terms then marketing objectives can also be interpreted in these terms.

This will be cascaded further when we get to tactical plans. For example products sold, brand awareness, and customer numbers can all be calculated from your revenue objective.

Action Programme 1

Using your analysis and business objectives, set a marketing objective for each strategy you have selected.

Check that the figures work and that it is an interpretation of the business objective. Also is it realistic given Biocatalysts' strengths and market conditions? Please note we do not give feedback for this.

3 Marketing strategy: segmentation

3.1 As markets become more competitive, there are increasing constraints on **budgets**. At the same time, consumers having more choice. How can resources be used more efficiently and effectively to ensure consumers make the 'right' choices? Segmentation achieves this by identifying target groups for marketing purposes.

Key Concept

Segmentation is the process of splitting customers into different groups, or segments, within which customers with similar characteristics have similar needs. By doing this, each one can be targeted and reached with a distinct marketing mix.

Part B: The sample case: Biocatalysts

3.2 Successful segmentation can be a key source of competitive advantage. Unfortunately, of those businesses that do bother to segment their markets, few consciously adopt an approach that maximises their competitive advantage, opting instead for traditional methods of segmentation.

> **Knowledge brought forward**
>
> Here is a brief reminder of segmentation techniques
>
> **Traditional methods of segmentation**
>
> **Geographic**
>
> - Postcode, city, town, village, rural, coastal, county, region, country, climate
>
> **Demographic**
>
> - Age, sex, family life cycle, family size, religion, income, occupation, ethnic origin, socio-economic group
>
> **Psychographic**
>
> - (AIO) Personality traits, attitude, family life cycle, lifestyle, VALS, product specific
>
> **Behavioural**
>
> - Benefits sought, purchase behaviour, purchase occasion, usage
>
> **Geodemographic**
>
> - Combines geographic and demographic **plus** overlay of psychographic **and** patterns of purchasing behaviour; most well known are ACORN and MOSAIC
>
> **Business to business**
>
> - SIC codes, process or product, geographic, size of company, operating variables, circumstances, purchase methods
>
> Increasingly organisations are developing segmentation models combining the above, the DMU and personality characteristics (eg loyalty, attitudes to risk, beliefs and values).

3.3 Decision Making Unit – (DMU)

Users - those who will use product

Influencers - often help define specifications, provide information

Buyers - formal authority for selecting supplier, arranging terms of purchase

Decision Making Unit DMU

Deciders - have power to decide on product requirements and/or suppliers

Gatekeepers - have power to prevent sellers or information reaching members of buying centre

Approvers - authorise proposed actions of deciders

Action Programme 2

Who is the customer?

How many of the roles in the DMU above can you identify for Biocatalysts?

Decision making units are also valid in consumer markets.

The company's own segmentation techniques

3.4 As well as using some of the more traditional methods of classifying the information, organisations should be gathering more precise information about their customers, tailored to the exact needs of the organisation. This information should provide answers to needs and motives. It can then inform product and promotion development and insights into achieving competitive advantage. It requires systematic gathering of information on their motives/needs from customers over time.

Action Programme 3

Segmental analysis

Choose one or two of Biocatalysts' markets and think about:

- Who buys
- What is bought
- Where
- When/how
- Why

You may have gaps or have to make assumptions but complete what you can and turn to the end of the unit for a Biocatalysts Segmental Analysis.

Tutor Tip

We often do not have as much information as we would like to segment markets effectively. We will have broad industry sectors and sometimes we will have some information about business to business customers or consumers. We can make realistic assumptions about segments and identify any information gaps that would help us improve segmentation.

We should be able to make recommendations on how we can improve segmentation. This is when the segmental analysis process and the identification of information gaps can help us.

Part B: The sample case: Biocatalysts

4 Marketing strategy: positioning

4.1 **Positioning takes place in the minds of customers**. They evaluate and compare companies, products and services, and position them according to the values they attribute to them based on their experience. Companies have influence over positioning, through communications, product quality and customer service. Positioning is critical to competitive advantage. The more value customers perceive, the greater the competitive advantage.

4.2 **Positioning is based on rational and emotional evaluations**. The functional benefits of a product are easily copied by competitors and provide little opportunity to differentiate. Emotional evaluation, often intangible values attributed to the product such as status, can offer much more opportunity to differentiate the product offering to appeal to customers.

4.3 **Successful positioning requires a realistic approach**. To aim for a 'world leader' position when there is no chance of this happening, particularly if resources and marketing skills are lacking, is unproductive. However realism should be balanced with vision. It is realistic to aim for a 'lead' position, for example, a leader in a segment/s, in industry or a particular process or technology.

4.4 **Successful positioning requires commitment, investment and sustained effort.** Leave it up to the customers and they may not bother. Worse, the competition may decide to position you, for example, Qualcast very successfully re-positioned Hover mowers.

Positioning and the competition

4.5 Know your position. Are you a market **leader, follower, challenger or a nicher?** These positions will affect the strategies adopted. Decisions influence the position and resources will be allocated and strategies designed to build and maintain actual position. Know where you are going. There may be a need or desire to change position. This will require a change in strategy.

Firms A, C, F

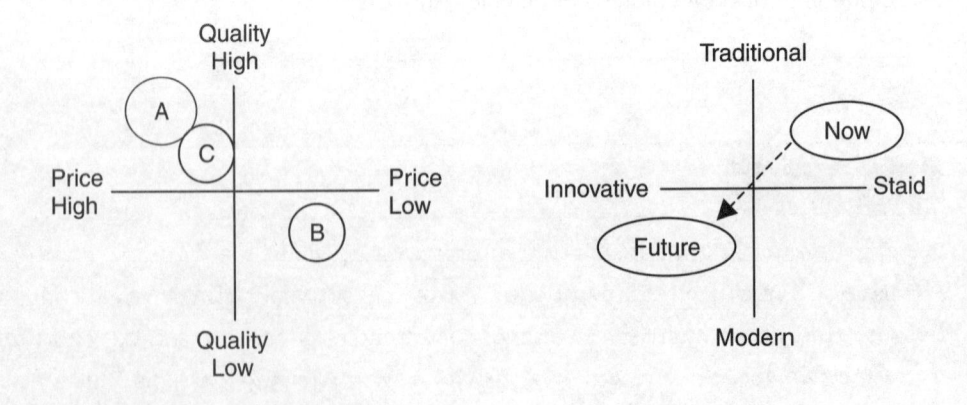

Action Programme 4

Decide how you would position Biocatalysts for the Diagnostic sector. Remember the buying criteria identified during analysis: what matters to customers, on what basis do they make decisions on which product/services to buy? Compare your answer with ours at the end of the chapter.

Step 7: Marketing strategy and marketing mix plans

Blank positioning maps for you to use

Part B: The sample case: Biocatalysts

5 Marketing strategy: targeting

5.1 The word **'targeting'** is too often confused with **'targets'** (segments). Targeting makes the connection between the segments identified, the positioning strategy and the design of the marketing mix. The targeting strategy is simply a statement on how the marketing mix is used eg undifferentiated to the whole market or differentiated to identified segments.

5.2 Information acquired during analysis will determine which targeting options are viable both in terms of business operations and marketing effectiveness.

5.3 The choices are these.

Undifferentiated strategy (one marketing mix unchanged for entire market)

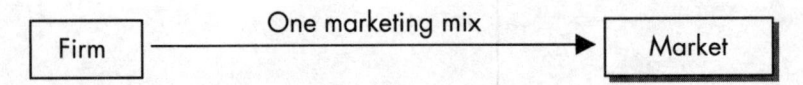

Firm → One marketing mix → Market

Differentiated strategy (tailored to meet needs of selected segments)

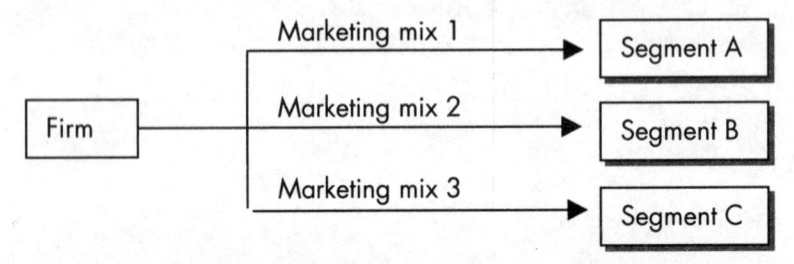

Firm → Marketing mix 1 → Segment A
Firm → Marketing mix 2 → Segment B
Firm → Marketing mix 3 → Segment C

Concentrated strategy (undifferentiated for a niche)

Firm → One marketing mix → Segment F

Tailoring the mix

5.4 To maximise effectiveness, the marketing mix is tailored to meet the specific needs of selected customers. Ideally, to maximise efficiency, marketing mixes should be standardised and so provide opportunities to achieve economies of scale.

5.5 To be efficient in business operations **and** effective in the market place there must be a balance between standardisation and adaptation: only change elements of the marketing mix that will have impact. Often this can be achieved by promotional messages alone or small changes to the product.

Action Programme 5

Assessing target options

Take 10 minutes to assess the suitability and implications of these targeting alternatives for Biocatalysts.

Turn to the end of the chapter for our feedback.

6 International marketing strategy

Marketing planning: planning for differences

6.1 In some instances, differences will have to be accepted and planned for: in fact these differences, from a marketing perspective, may be essential to success.

(a) Customer service is significantly influenced by culture. What is expected in one culture is not necessarily expected in another. For example, self-service has become part of Western life. In other parts of the world, customers do not expect to serve themselves in any exchange with a business.

(b) When selling, in some cultures the price is publicised and that is the price people expect to pay. In other cultures the expectations is that you will always bargain over price. In some parts of the world fast and direct negotiations are the norm; in others, time is taken over building a relationship before any negotiations can begin.

6.2 The same frameworks and tools can be used to develop marketing plans. There are, however, some extra considerations.

(a) **Country selection** should be an objective process (Harrell and Kiefer matrix).

(b) **Methods of entry** must also be evaluated for their suitability in terms of levels of involvement as well as managing control. An increasingly important trend is SAs, JVs, M&As as a means of developing international markets. It is also significantly affecting the nature of competition.

(c) **Segmentation**: standard techniques can be used in many markets such as identifying strategically equivalent segments (SES) and acknowledging similarities and differences across rather than within markets. Segmentation can be based on consumers not countries. In some markets, however, it cannot be assumed that the same customer characteristics apply. Geodemographic Euromosaic, VALS 2 (Europe) and Euro-styles, RISC Euro type.

(d) **Positioning**: changing markets can mean having to change position. For example product use might change (Japanese using strimmers to cut lawns) and benefits may be sought for different reasons (eg four wheel drive in most European countries and part of the USA is often about adventure; in other parts of the world durability and reliability really do matter if you are driving through difficult terrain. Decisions on global, regional, country, market or segment positioning.

7 Separating process from plan

7.1 All the activities described in this chapter so far are part of the **process** we go through to reach effective marketing decisions. The outcomes of these decisions are then recorded in the marketing plan. Plans are communication documents. They inform people of decisions made, actions to be taken, by whom, when and where.

Tutor Tip

Reference has been, and will be made to the need for communications in the examination to be persuasive. When developing outline plans for the exam, as with the real world, we must explain and justify our decisions and recommendations. Recommendations usually require senior management to allocate resources, people, time and money and they will only be prepared to do this if we can justify that what we proposed will result in successful outcomes. The Examiner will be looking for justification.

7.2 The outcomes of the marketing planning process are decisions recorded in the plan; your activities in this chapter have been reaching those decisions. So you will now have:

- Marketing objectives
- Segments identified to target
- Positioning of the marketing mix
- Targeting strategy adopted

The marketing plan must reflect the competitive position of the business strategy.

Marketing strategy: statements (decisions) for marketing plan document

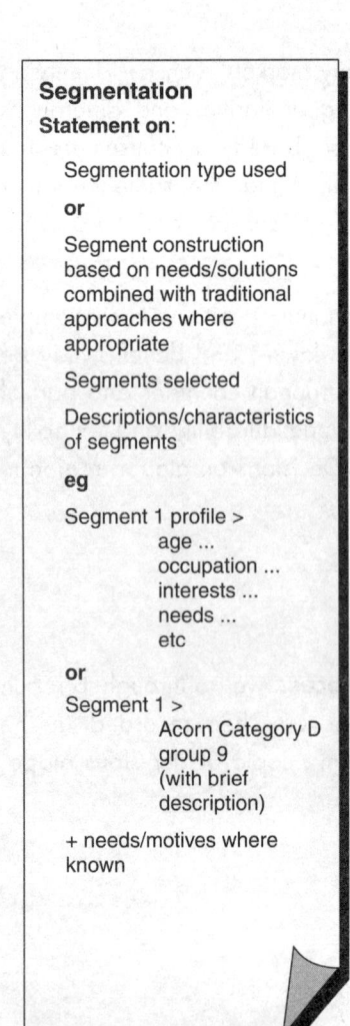

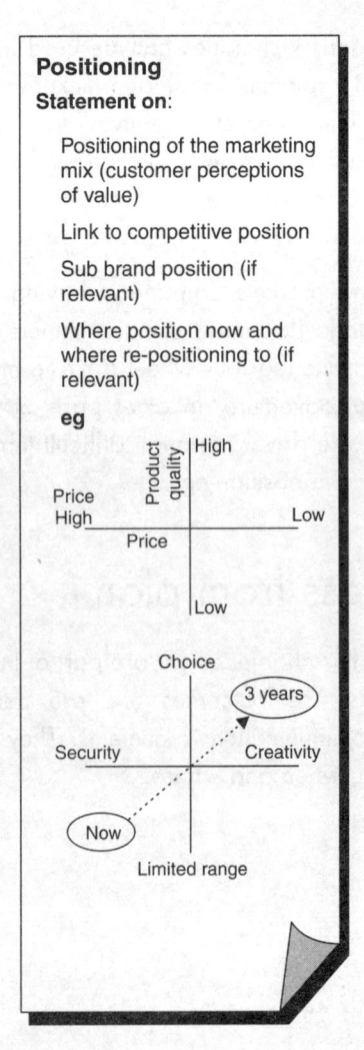

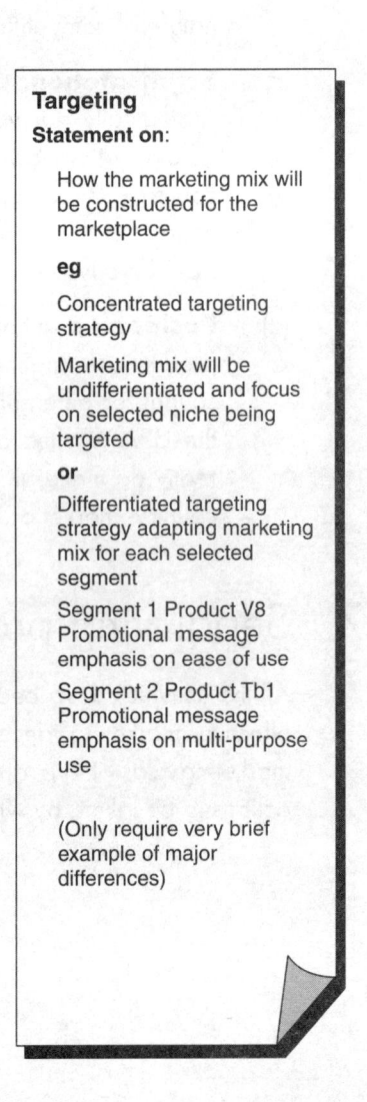

Segmentation

Statement on:

Segmentation type used

or

Segment construction based on needs/solutions combined with traditional approaches where appropriate

Segments selected

Descriptions/characteristics of segments

eg

Segment 1 profile >
age ...
occupation ...
interests ...
needs ...
etc

or

Segment 1 >
Acorn Category D group 9 (with brief description)

+ needs/motives where known

Positioning

Statement on:

Positioning of the marketing mix (customer perceptions of value)

Link to competitive position

Sub brand position (if relevant)

Where position now and where re-positioning to (if relevant)

eg

Product quality
High
Price High
Low
Price
Low

Choice
3 years
Security
Creativity
Now
Limited range

Targeting

Statement on:

How the marketing mix will be constructed for the marketplace

eg

Concentrated targeting strategy

Marketing mix will be undifferientiated and focus on selected niche being targeted

or

Differentiated targeting strategy adapting marketing mix for each selected segment

Segment 1 Product V8
Promotional message emphasis on ease of use

Segment 2 Product Tb1
Promotional message emphasis on multi-purpose use

(Only require very brief example of major differences)

8 Implementing marketing strategy

8.1 Implementation is an area that is too often undertaken as an unrelated activity to the business and marketing strategies. The marketing mix tactical plans implement the marketing and business strategies.

8.2 It is assumed you are knowledgeable about developing tactical plans. There are also strategic issues associated with each element of the marketing mix, for example new product development requires a strategic and integrated approach, the type of product or service will affect communications plan at a strategic level, and these will be discussed briefly.

Part B: The sample case: Biocatalysts

Planning route map 4
Tactical decisions

How are we going to get there?

- CORPORATE AUDIT *informs*
- VISION & MISSION → CORPORATE OBJECTIVES → CORPORATE STRATEGIES
- CORPORATE DECISIONS *determine*

Business strategies (long term)

Unit objectives: Marketing Objectives, Production Objectives, Finance Objectives, HRM. Objectives

Unit strategies (medium term): Marketing strategies

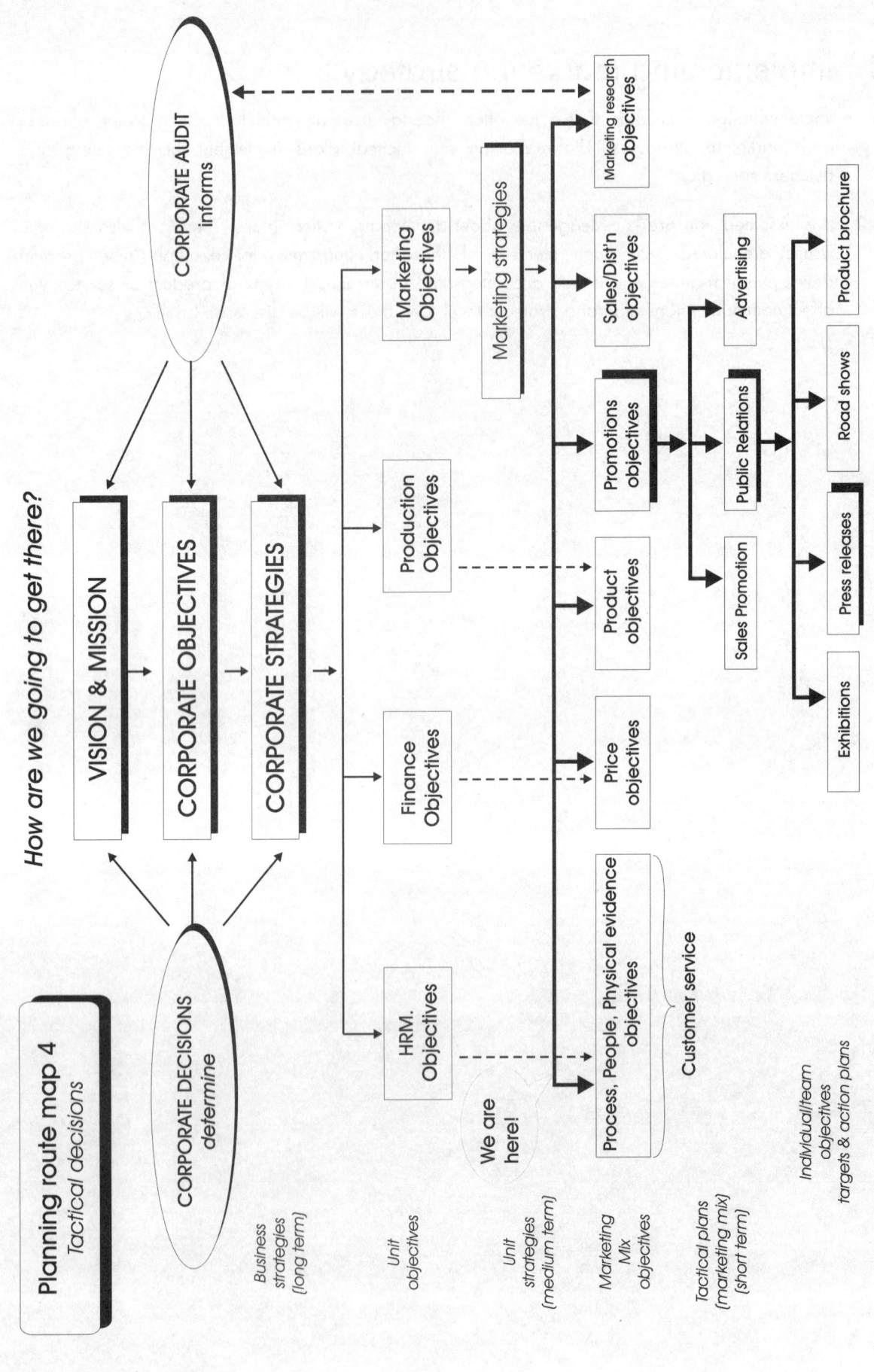

We are here!

Marketing Mix objectives:
- Marketing research objectives
- Sales/Dist'n objectives
- Promotions objectives
- Product objectives
- Price objectives
- Process, People, Physical evidence objectives (Customer service)

Tactical plans (marketing mix) (short term):
- Advertising
- Public Relations
- Sales Promotion

Individual/team objectives targets & action plans:
- Product brochure
- Road shows
- Press releases
- Exhibitions

© Juanita Cockton, 1997

> **Tutor Tip**
>
> You are not expected to spend much time on this part of the plan. The paper is strategic and tactical plans used to demonstrate to the examiners that you know how to implement strategy. They will be looking for consistency and integration of your plans, assuming you have been asked for one.
>
> What is important is any strategic issues associated with the marketing mix. You might cover these under 'Business Implications' or, depending on the question asked, it might be more appropriate in the tactical

9 Product strategy

9.1 Central to the purpose of the business is the product/service provided that meets customers needs. Marketing is not concerned with product features but with the benefits perceived by the customers.

9.2 Meeting customer needs in a competitive business environment is not the only challenge facing marketers, they must do so in a way that either is:

(a) **Unique, innovative**, truly new

or

(b) **Differentiated** in some way from the rest

9.3 **Factors affecting product strategy**

(a) **Quality policy**. This is concerned with, for example, the level of quality (implications for position), physical components (life span, replacements), technology and social preferences (patterns, trends and timescales)

(b) **Product category. Search product**: here the purchase decision is made by evaluation (eg size, colour) and comparison (eg performance against competitors). **Experience product**: the purchase decision cannot be based on sensory perceptions or comparison it must be experienced. **Credence product**: the purchase decision cannot be by comparisons or experience as the product/service will be different each time.

(c) **Product life cycle.** The plc can be very difficult to determine in many industries. The stage the product is at in its life cycle does have implications for the marketing effort, so some endeavour must be made to establish its life cycle stage.

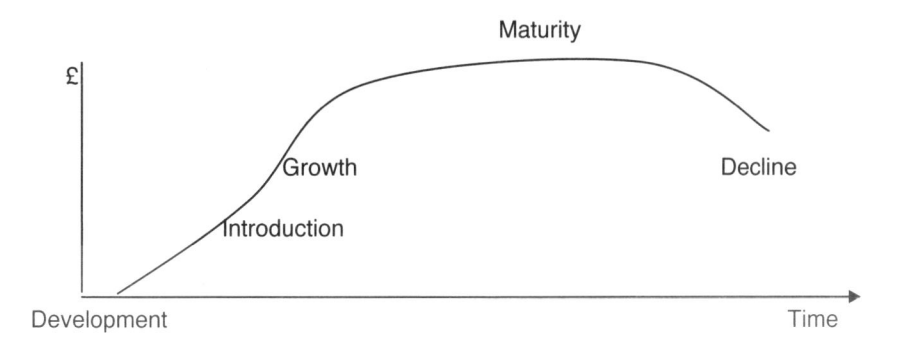

Part B: The sample case: Biocatalysts

Each stage of the product life cycle requires different strategies to ensure maximum profits are achieved. Different industries/products have different life cycles, s can be seen from the following.

The product life cycle and impact on the business

Introduction	Growth	Maturity	Decline
Competition limited	Competition growing	Competition intense	Competition declining
Sales low	Sales rapid	Sales peak	Sales falling
Profits nil	Profits rising	Profits stable	Profits falling

The product life cycle and marketing planning

Introduction	Growth	Maturity	Decline
Product basic	Product extensions	Product modifications	Product rationalise
Price cost-plus	Price penetration	Price competitive	Price cut
Promotions heavy	Promotions heavy	Promotions uniqueness	Promotions minimal
Place selective	Place extend	Place extend	Place rationalise

Total product concept

9.4 If products do not offer some competitive advantage their time in the marketplace will be a short one. Trying to develop competitive advantage is becoming increasingly difficult and the basic product rarely provides opportunities in this area unless it is unique.

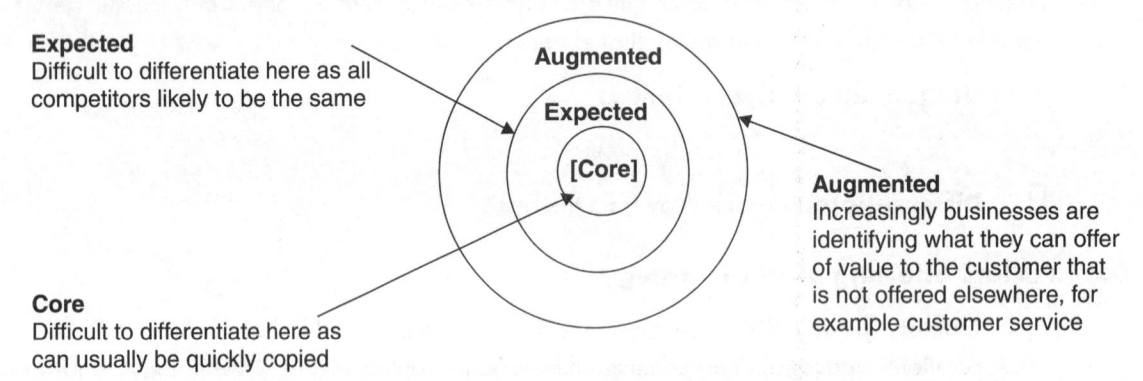

Expected
Difficult to differentiate here as all competitors likely to be the same

Augmented
Increasingly businesses are identifying what they can offer of value to the customer that is not offered elsewhere, for example customer service

Core
Difficult to differentiate here as can usually be quickly copied

'Product' for Biocatalysts

9.5 With Biocatalysts we know that important issues in product development include to increase yield, to improve efficiency, cost effectiveness, safety (track record), expertise, consistent quality and activity, to be kept informed (openness, transparency), guidance on developments, availability, reliability, strength, purity, value for money reflects quality and similar analytical techniques.

Other issues that also need to be planned for include, for example, include where Biocatalysts' products are in the product life cycle.

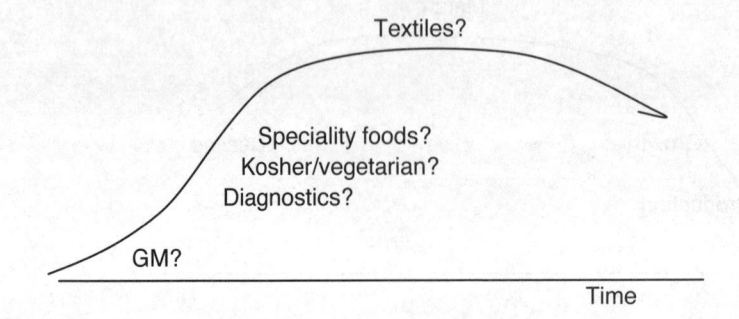

Textiles?
Speciality foods?
Kosher/vegetarian?
Diagnostics?
GM?
Time

9.6 **NPD**. Another issue for Biocatalysts was that of developing new products **reactively in response to any customer** instead of **proactively in response to selected customers** in the context of **business goals and market conditions**.

9.7 Products must also be appropriate to the markets they are developed for including international markets.

New products and market growth

9.8 During the screening process of new product development, one of the tasks for marketing will be to determine the speed of market development. A number of factors will affect new product sales.

Diffusion of innovation process

9.9 Determining how quickly a new product is likely to be accepted by the market requires an understanding of the people most likely to buy and of who in the market will be most likely to purchase the product on its launch. The diffusion of innovation curve or adoption process provides some insight.

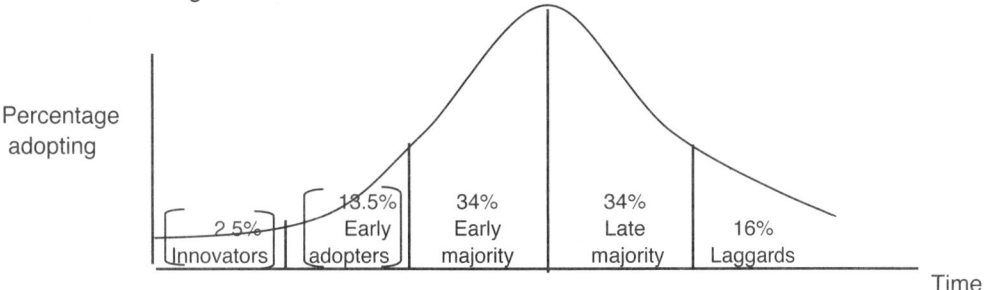

[Diagram: Bell curve showing adoption categories — Percentage adopting vs Time: 2.5% Innovators, 13.5% Early adopters, 34% Early majority, 34% Late majority, 16% Laggards]

9.10 The number of people initially interested in buying innovative products may be small, therefore targeting these people is critical. The marketer's task is to identify the innovators and early adopters and ensure marketing activities are targeted specifically at these people.

9.11 Factors affecting speed of diffusion

- Complexity of the new product (the more complex/different the longer the take-up period)
- Relative advantage (the greater the advantage the faster the take-up)
- Compatibility (with existing lifestyles etc compatibility speeds take-up)
- Ability to try (if it can be used and benefits are experienced the faster the take-up)
- Communications (how easy/difficult is it to promote the benefits: if it is very new and different, it might be difficult to get the message across initially, slowing down diffusion)

New product development

9.12 Staying ahead of the competition requires a company to continually update its product and service range to meet the changing needs of its markets. Customers are more demanding, sophisticated and less inclined to stay loyal to a company that does not provide the benefits sought and service expected.

Part B: The sample case: Biocatalysts

9.13 New product launches have suffered notoriously high failure rates in some industries usually because new product development was internally driven by 'good ideas people' rather than externally focused on identifying customer needs. The process of new product development should be a combination of both and, to ensure the process meets the challenge of speedy 'time to market' demands, the process should ensure several NPD activities are undertaken, at the same time in parallel to reduce the development period.

New Product Development process

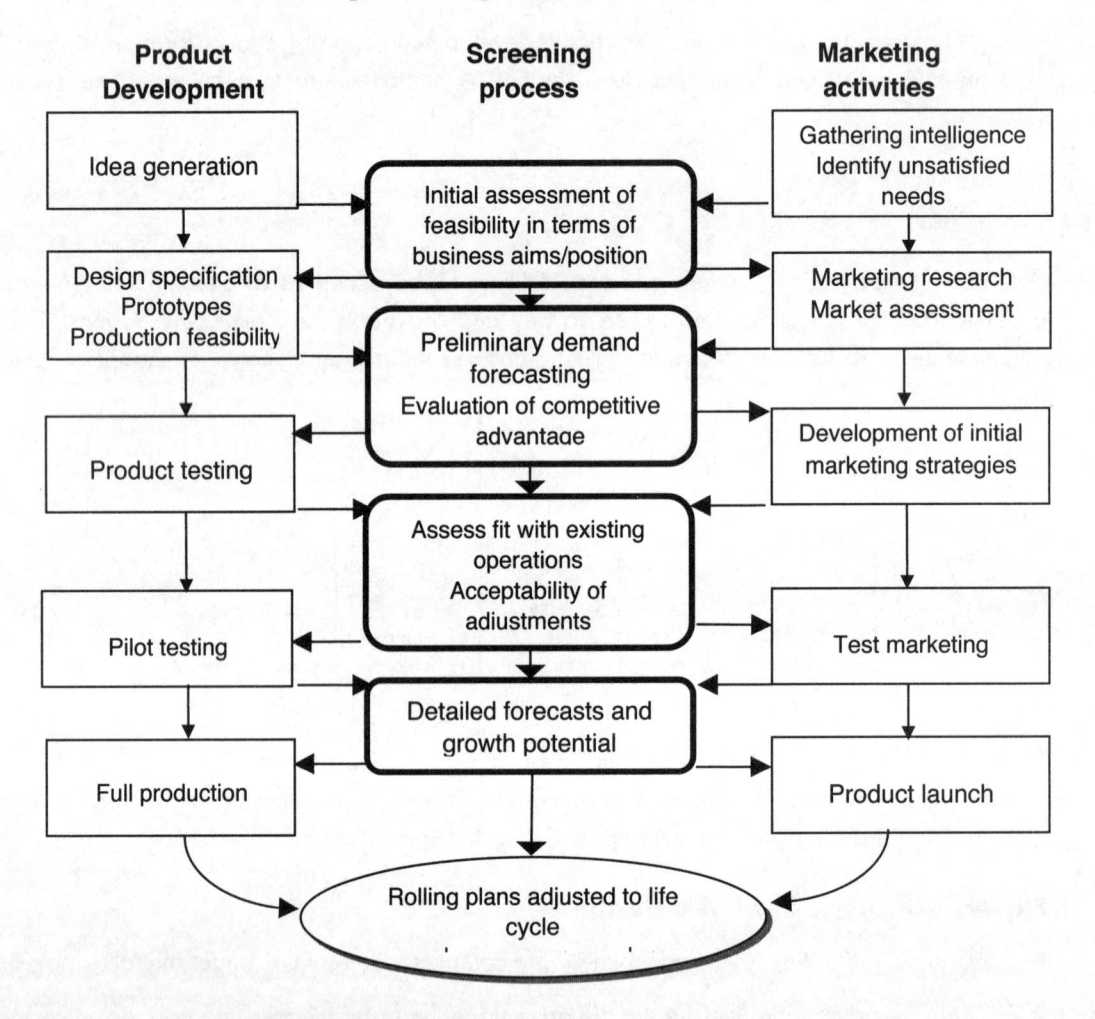

Product Development	Screening process	Marketing activities
Idea generation	Initial assessment of feasibility in terms of business aims/position	Gathering intelligence Identify unsatisfied needs
Design specification Prototypes Production feasibility	Preliminary demand forecasting Evaluation of competitive advantage	Marketing research Market assessment
Product testing	Assess fit with existing operations Acceptability of adjustments	Development of initial marketing strategies
Pilot testing	Detailed forecasts and growth potential	Test marketing
Full production		Product launch

Rolling plans adjusted to life cycle

10 Price strategy

10.1 At a strategic level, decisions on price will include the range and movement of price during the planning period. Price should not be set as a cost plus exercise. This does not take account of market conditions or of the company's vision and positioning.

10.2 Critical factors that define range of strategic pricing options

- Real costs and profits
- Product or service value to customer relative to value offered by the competition
- Market segment differences and positioning
- Likely competitive reactions
- Marketing objectives

10 ♦ Step 7: Marketing strategy and marketing mix plans

- **Positioning: product quality/price**

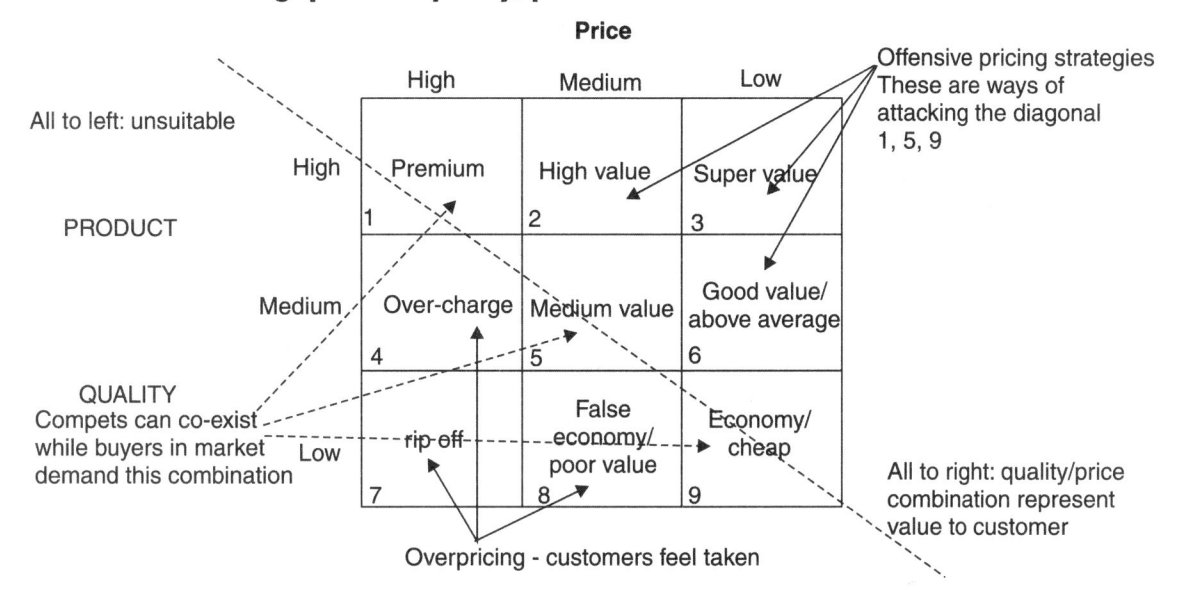

	Price High	Price Medium	Price Low
Product High	Premium (1)	High value (2)	Super value (3)
Product Medium	Over-charge (4)	Medium value (5)	Good value/above average (6)
Product Low	rip-off (7)	False economy/poor value (8)	Economy/cheap (9)

- All to left: unsuitable
- Competitors can co-exist while buyers in market demand this combination
- Overpricing - customers feel taken
- Offensive pricing strategies: These are ways of attacking the diagonal 1, 5, 9
- All to right: quality/price combination represent value to customer

Strategic pricing

10.3 Here are some **examples** of what strategic pricing can achieve.

(a) Gain customer trust by reducing price when costs decline substantially and when the drop is easily noticed

(b) Weaken competitors by choosing key market segments in which to launch price promotions

(c) Win customers from competitors by offering multiple items at low total price (perhaps including products or services not offered by rivals)

10.4 There are two main ways to **implement strategic pricing**.

(a) **Skimming** (gaining high profits)
- **Rapid skimming**: high price, high promotion/gain high returns, high awareness
- **Slow skimming**: high price, low promotion/gain high returns, promotion unnecessary, word of mouth more appropriate eg cult

(b) **Penetration** (market entry or increasing share)
- **Rapid penetration**: Low price, high promotion/gain market share rapidly
- **Slow penetration**: Low price, low promotion/gain market share, low promotion spend typical with own label brands

10.5 International pricing strategies and issues

(a) **Forms**
- **Ethnocentric**: uniform around the world
- **Polycentric**: subsidiaries set whatever price they want
- **Geocentric**: does not fix worldwide price/ignore subsidiary price decisions balance between the two

Part B: The sample case: Biocatalysts

(b) **Techniques**

(i) **Transfer pricing**. Concerned with pricing of goods sold within company: implications on value for cross border taxation purposes; should optimise corporate rather than divisional objectives (cause problems if division is profit centre impacts of profit performance)

(ii) **Gray markets or parallel importing**. Unauthorised importing and selling of products intended for one (high priced) market and sold in another (low priced) market: often arises due to fluctuating value of currencies between countries (other reasons – lower transport costs, fiercer competition, higher product taxes)

(iii) **Incoterms**. International terms of trade (export license, currency permit, packing, transportation, bill of lading, customs export papers, wharfage/storage, invoicing, insurance)

Price for Biocatalysts

10.6 For Biocatalysts, a significant strategic issue is that they have been customising products using their expertise and high technical skills but their **financial performance suggests they are not charging premium prices for premium products**. Decisions will need to be made on pricing in relation to their desired position.

11 Place strategy

Distribution audit

11.1 Reasons for a distribution audit include a need to improve control, improve productivity/performance, improve market effectiveness or establish resource requirements. This audit takes place at the strategic and tactical level.

11.2 A **strategic distribution audit** should take place every two to four years and include a review of **market profile** (structure, existing markets, potential markets PEST factors), **competitor profile** (number, location, strengths and weaknesses, distribution standards, potential competitors), **customer profile** (location, behaviour needs) and **channel profile** (buyer/supplier strengths and power, differential costs and technology use).

11.3 A **tactical distribution audit** should be ongoing and include a review of **product profile** (mix, range, seasonality, patterns, handling, innovation), **process/system** (ordering, delivery, technology, customer experience, logistics, service levels), **cost/efficiency** (order processing, data processing, materials handling, inventory control) and **sales/promotion** (sales force performance, standards and targets, and promotional effectiveness)

11.4 Evaluation criteria: current distribution channels (efficiency and effectiveness)

Financial criteria	Non financial criteria
Order quantities/value/cycles	Delivery times/reliability/condition/materials handling
Profitability	Customer service satisfaction/problem handling
Margins	Inventory management Marketing capability/performance Competitive performance Value added

Distribution channel selection

11.5 Developing strategies will require consideration of channel length and breadth.

(a) **Channel length**: will vary from industry to industry/country to country depending on requirements (market and legal). Consider extent of added value through chain:

- Vertical integration (ownership of distribution outlets) improves ability to differentiate, improves access
- Contractual eg franchising
- Conventional eg agents, distributors
- Direct marketing

(b) **Channel breadth**: meets market coverage needs.

Intensive Distribution	Selective Distribution	Exclusive Distribution
Mass market coverage Low priced products Convenience Impulse buy Sought by mfr. of high volume/low value goods	Balanced coverage Knowledgeable dealers Specialty goods Search characteristic Industrial markets Shopping around in consumer markets	Restricted coverage High priced luxury goods No competing products May require expert advice

(c) **Evaluation criteria: potential distribution channels**

Financial criteria	Non financial criteria
Sales turnover of outlets	No. of outlets/geographical location/accessibility
Pricing policies	Promotional co-operation
Profitability	Competitive products Reputation/quality/size sales force Terms of business/stocking policies Product characteristics. Buyer behaviour Degree of control

11.6 Distribution channel management

Channel management is another area that is too often neglected. Once appointed, there tends to be an attitude of 'get on with it'. Distribution channels are key to success and should provide a source of competitive advantage, but they can only do so if managed properly. Some of the issues include:

(a) Service and support: identifying dimensions of service that customers value and prioritise, and determine costs of providing that service against expected revenues

(b) Agree and set performance standards and targets and monitoring of performance standards and day to day operations

(c) Communications and relationships: partnership approach

(d) Availability, reliability, convenience, speed of delivery, order sizes and product variety

Place for Biocatalysts

11.7 **Biocatalysts have not been managing their channels**. There is clearly evidence in the analysis, of poor revenue generation in some markets, particularly overseas markets. Evaluation of existing channels and of new channels is critical, as will be their need to manage channels more effectively in future. Channel management must also improve international development.

11.8 Given Biocatalysts's weak financial position, they should consider utilising the Internet to their advantage.

12 Promotions strategy

12.1 Promotional activities are the company's key means of communicating with its publics, customers, suppliers, distributors, and so on. Communications are, or should be, mostly under the control of the business and used to best advantage by developing an integrated communications strategy.

12.2 During marketing research, the identification of target markets will have included assessment of the means of reaching the targets through appropriate channels with the appropriate promotional mix.

Key factors affecting promotional mix selection

- Business to business or consumer market
- Mass market, numerous segments or niche
- Product or service
- Technology (both in terms of product/service and media channel)

12.3 The selection of promotional tools will also be determined by the objectives set. A number of response hierarchy models have been developed which attempt to understand the process of buyer behaviour and therefore what we are trying to achieve with our communications.

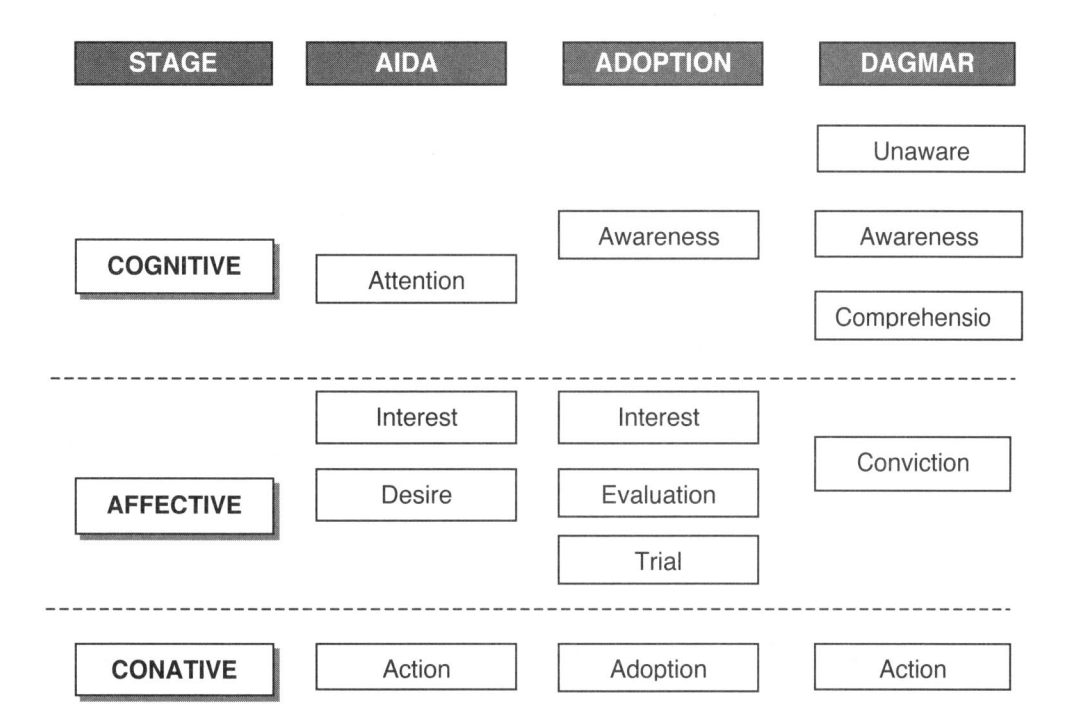

10 ♦ Step 7: Marketing strategy and marketing mix plans

STAGE	AIDA	ADOPTION	DAGMAR
COGNITIVE	Attention	Awareness	Unaware / Awareness / Comprehensio
AFFECTIVE	Interest / Desire	Interest / Evaluation / Trial	Conviction
CONATIVE	Action	Adoption	Action

12.4 Using AIDA for example, if we have achieved **attention,** then the task is to generate **interest** and move potential buyers through the stages of **desire** and **action**. Interest might be achieved through public relations activities, while desire might be created through sales promotion and action through sales. When the task is understood, it is usually easier to estimate the time it may take to achieve the task.

12.5 It is important that promotional design takes account of the targets. At whom are the messages being targeted and therefore what is likely to be the most effective promotional tool and channel to reach them.

12.6 The DMU (Decision making unit) is another useful model for understanding better the people being targeted: identify needs and target messages to their specific problems or benefits sought.

12.7 Another useful model is the well known Maslow's hierarchy of needs. This model identifies needs that motivate individuals. Promotions linked to the target market's needs become much more effective than those that are not related to the target's needs.

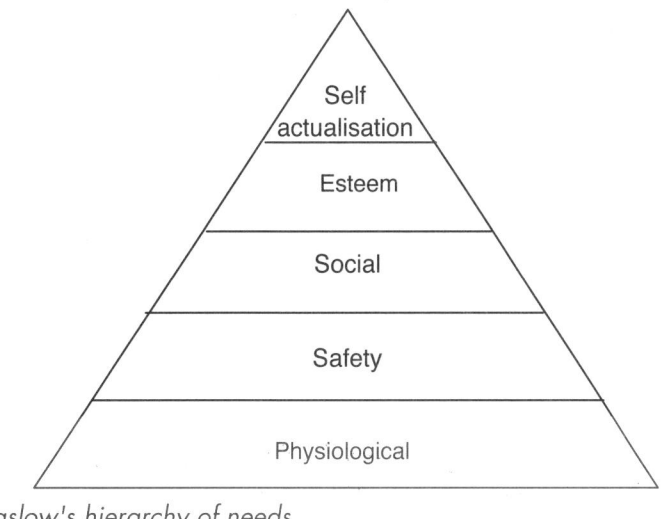

Pyramid (top to bottom):
- Self actualisation
- Esteem
- Social
- Safety
- Physiological

Maslow's hierarchy of needs

Promotional techniques

- Advertising
- Public relations
- Sales promotion
- Direct marketing
- Publicity
- Sponsorship
- Exhibitions
- Packaging
- Point of sale and merchandising
- Word of mouth
- Corporate identity
- Personal selling

12.8 These tools of communications only become truly effective when integrated through the communications plan. However the plan must also take account of publicity not within the control of the business eg bad press, word of mouth. Crisis management is part of communications planning, as is influencing the less obvious communications.

Above and below the line

12.9 Advertising is above the line promotions. It is paid for space eg advertisement in a journal, poster and commission is usually involved. All other promotional activities are below the line with the exception of direct marketing. This has recently repositioned itself as through the line promotions.

Profile, push and pull strategies

12.10 **Profile strategies** are typically concerned with strategic communications and can be targeted at a broad range of stakeholders, both internal and external. Profile strategies will focus on building reputation and status, image and brand values and so on.

12.11 Communications are designed to either **push** the product/service out or **pull** people in. Typically push strategies are used to push products into distribution channels and a sales force is critical to the success of push strategies. Pull strategies are used to pull customers into the outlets to buy and typically advertising is successful for pull strategies. A combination of both is usually required.

Media decisions

12.12 There are two types of decisions facing the marketer:

(a) **Inter media** decisions: which media category to use eg TV or press

(b) **Intra media** decisions: which medium within the category to use eg Daily Telegraph or Times

Media channel/s selection should provide the best access to the target audience the company is trying to reach. The objective is to reach as many of the target audience as possible cost effectively. The development of new channels is opening up opportunities for businesses not before possible.

Promotion for Biocatalysts

12.13 Biocatalysts's promotional activities need to become more strategic and focused. Their major problem is cash so any recommendations must be realistic in terms of budgets and the context of the industry they are in. Business to business promotions need not be expensive activities and most certainly should not be extravagant campaigns.

12.14 Building and maintaining a strong brand over time will be important. Maintaining and building their reputation for quality and expertise are potentially powerful brand values and any promotional activities should be designed to build the brand. Remember that in different countries there are different attitudes to GMOs, for example, and this needs to be considered when building brand values.

12.15 Biocatalysts promotional activities require a strategic and integrated approach to marketing communications including international ones.

13 Customer service and customer relationship management

People

13.1 People impact on customers both directly and indirectly. The marketing manager has to consider the influences and impact on the marketing mix and how it affects overall customer service, impressions, experience and company/product positioning.

Contact

13.2 Firstly the marketing manager needs to determine who directly and indirectly influences the customer's experience. Once the nature of contact is identified, decisions can be made on service, training, operations, policies and procedures appropriate to desired contact outcomes. Too often, outcomes of contact are not considered or prepared for resulting in mixed experiences for customers. It cannot be left to chance as its influence on customer perceptions are significant.

Process

13.3 The role of processes in customer service and product delivery has often been underestimated and usually attention to efficiency has been concerned with cost reductions and internal operations rather than added value and customer satisfaction. People within the organisation who are responsible for delivery, either directly or indirectly, usually rely on processes to support that activity. The processes are often key to the product or service being delivered and take many forms and have a variety of functions.

Design must consider the degree of contact a customer will have directly and indirectly with processes. The higher the contact, the greater the opportunity for problems and inconsistencies and the more difficult it can be to manage and control. Processes should be kept to a minimum and be simple and easy to use.

Physical evidence

13.4 Customers are influenced by many factors when making decisions to purchase a product or service. An important factor, particularly to the service industry, is the role of physical evidence. Often intangible, for example atmosphere, its influence is no less important. It can

Part B: The sample case: Biocatalysts

play a key role in forming impressions and perceptions of a company and the position it holds within the competitive environment.

13.5 Factors such as buildings, furnishings, layout, colour schemes and associated goods such as carrier bags, tickets labels etc. should be considered in positioning and the overall design of the marketing mix. There are two kinds of evidence that customers experience.

(a) **Peripheral evidence**: possessed as part of the purchase but has little or no independent value eg bank cheque book, admission ticket. Peripheral evidence 'adds to' value of essential evidence only as far as the customer values these **symbols** of service. They provide tangible evidence of an exchange.

(b) **Essential evidence**: cannot be possessed by the customer but an important influence. The appearance of a hotel, the 'feel' of the branch of a bank, or of the aircraft are all essential evidence that provide **clues** to quality and standards and are often intangible in nature.

13.6 It is therefore important to pay attention to **external factors** (physical size, shape, frontage of buildings, materials used, outside lighting, entrances, signs and logos, vehicles, parking areas) and **internal factors** (layout, colour schemes, equipment, materials and support materials eg stationery, lighting, space and its use, heating and ventilation).

14 International marketing mix issues: some reminders

14.1 The **international marketing mix** must be designed appropriate to market conditions, particularly cultural. Decisions on the extent of standardisation v adaptation should be balanced with the need for economies of scale, profitability and consistency, and meeting the diverse needs of different markets.

Personal selling in international markets

14.2 Personal selling in international markets is often more important because of the restrictions on promotional techniques, for example bans on advertising or sales promotion and restricted use of media channels.

14.3 Within a country there can be a mix of languages and literacy and a range of cultural diversity, for example in countries where tribes exist. This puts demands on the sales team and requires a high level of diverse skills from individuals and across the team.

14.4 Selling in international markets requires an understanding of the cultural differences in communications and negotiations. In some cultures, people are more willing to trust each other than in others. This needs to be understood because if the willingness to trust is low and people are suspicious, the task of selling becomes much more difficult and potentially complex. Attitudes to change, already discussed, also affects negotiations. In cultures where people tend to resist change, the sales task can become difficult if it requires people to accept something new and/or different.

14.5 **Key factors affecting the success of negotiations**

(a) **Gender**. In some cultures, women are not expected to negotiate contracts or sell goods and services. It can be difficult for women from cultures where this is normal practice to accept they cannot operate in some markets. For example, women from cultures where there is equality between the sexes, such as Scandinavia would be likely to find this difficult.

- (b) **Age**. In Western economies, it is typical for young people to be in responsible managerial jobs, negotiating high value contacts. In other cultures, for example South East Asian, this is not typical or expected. It can cause offence if a young manager is sent to negotiate a contract in, say, China.

- (c) **Status and rank.** The status of those you are negotiating with must be matched with people of equally high rank and authority or again you can cause offence and jeopardise the negotiations.

- (d) **Authority**. In some cultures the person negotiating is the person with the authority to make the decisions, eg Western cultures. In other cultures, the person with authority might not be involved in the negotiations and has to be referred to for decisions and approval, as is typical in China.

14.6 Recruitment, selection and training of personnel selling in overseas markets is key to success. Depending on the complexity of the culture, eg high context, it may be more appropriate to recruit locally or, depending on the complexity of the technology eg highly technical/innovative, it may be appropriate to recruit internally. Either way, recruitment, selection and training will be designed to equip personnel with the skills needed to operate successfully in overseas markets.

Customer service (3Ps) for Biocatalysts

14.7 Customer service in this case study is pivotal in transforming their technical capability into an offer that adds value. Biocatalysts's expertise and ability to advise and guide customers in a way that enhances the customer's performance is central to business success.

Customer service in international markets

14.8 Customer service has become the battleground for attracting customers and building customer loyalty. Most other elements of the marketing mix can be copied and offer little opportunity to differentiate the business from the competition. Customer service in many markets is poor and any organisation that can deliver excellent customer service will have a distinct competitive advantage.

14.9 The problems of customer service are the intangibility and variation of service received. Even within a company, the quality of service can vary from person to person. In an attempt to build brands and reputation and improve performance, many businesses have set service standard goals and implemented customer service training.

14.10 It becomes even more difficult to standardise service when businesses start to operate in international markets. The organisation has to establish whether it is appropriate to standardise customer service. People have different attitudes to customer service in different cultures. For example, attitudes to waiting for service include these issues.

- (a) **Time**. Is waiting for service viewed as wasting time or is it seen positively as an opportunity to socialise? In Europe, time spent in a restaurant is not only for eating but

Part B: The sample case: Biocatalysts

also for conversation and relaxing over a meal. Japanese people waiting for service in a restaurant would view this as poor service.

(b) **Rules**. It is traditional in some countries to 'wait your turn'; in other words queuing for service is typical and this can range from expectations of short queues and time to long queues and time. In other cultures, queuing is not a cultural norm and people expect to fight for what they want.

(c) **Power**. In cultures where power distance is strong, it is seen as acceptable for 'superiors' to bypass the queue. Less powerful people expect to wait longer.

Automation and service

14.11 In Western societies, automation of service has become the norm. We serve ourselves in restaurants, petrol stations, supermarkets etc. In other cultures people expect personal service, time taken to get to know the person providing the service and to understand their requirements; the relationship is important.

14.12 A company's customer service policy must reflect the different cultural expectations and staff development and training should reflect these cultural differences. This can become a problem if the goal is standardisation of customer service to improve quality. However, some aspects of service can be standardised to represent the corporate image and brand values while other aspects specific to culture can be adapted to meet the needs of the local market.

Action Programme 6

You now need to develop tactical plans for each of the marketing strategies you have developed. A tactical plan is needed for each segment. The differences between each plan might be very small, for example the promotional mix messages might be different or service provided, and they will reflect the valued added for that segment.

No feedback is provided for this action programme.

Action Programme review

2   *Who is the customer?*

   Example: food

At company level	Known	Assumed
Approvers		Finance
Buyers		Purchasing managers
Gatekeepers	{ Industry technicians	Standard setters
Deciders		Food technologists
Influencers		{ Industry analysts, Consumer watchdogs
Users		Production staff

   Note. Beyond this industry DMU, there would be the end-consumer and the people influencing their decision to buy GM products or not.

3 Segmental analysis

Biocatalysts – segmental analysis

Who buys	What is bought	Where	When? How	Why
Food and drink industries		Direct	Seasonality foods/drugs	**Buyers** have common needs: Increase yield, improve efficiency, cost effectiveness, safety (track record), expertise, consistent quality and activity, to be kept informed (Openness, transparency), guidance on developments, availability, reliability, strength, purity, value for money reflects quality **Food**: information on animal derived enzymes, safety, guidelines allergenic potential, kosher certified enzymes, reassurance additional chemicals are safe for human consumption, improve/alter texture, extend life of food products, improve processing eg faster fermentation, flavour enhancement, depectinising, peeling, easier to handle waste products **Diagnostic**: high specificity, high sensitivity, stable products, ideally product that can be versatile, stable in small scale and bulk production (for R&D trailing then commercial production). Information on financial stability of firm as one kit been approved Diag Co loath to change a component therefore purchase is quite a large commitment to the supplier **Textile**: product that will maintain its stability in bulk production, wide ranging heat stability
Mass and niche markets Diagnostics*	Enzymes	or through	Initially sample trials	
Textiles		agents	Small batches	
Pharmaceutical Pulp/paper Water Animal feed Environment			Bulk Currency issues	

Other stakeholder needs and objectives

FDA. Needs: ensure product produced safe for consumer, health and safety procedures met, clearly documented procedures
Objectives: protect consumers and promote public health, alert of potential danger, work with government to promote uniform activity in food/drug related matters, assist manufacturer in understanding how to comply with good practice standards, remove unsafe/ unlawful products, work with international harmonisation committees to develop accepted standards, monitor companies with regulations

Investigators and industry analysts: open and transparent information and procedures reputation

Trade bodies/associations/professional societies: access to company documentation, is endorsement sought?, encourage ethical practices, conduct research, represent industry effectively, keep up to date

Many have characteristics in common including buying criteria. Some reasonable assumptions can be made on specific criteria.

Part B: The sample case: Biocatalysts

4   *Positioning Biocatalysts*

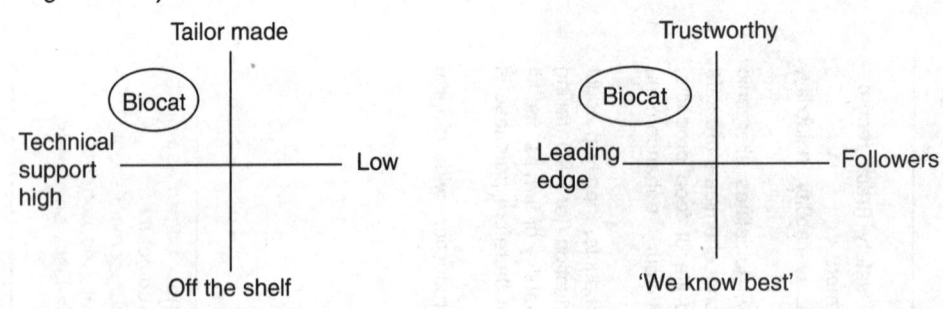

```
              Tailor made                                Trustworthy
                  |                                          |
              (Biocat)                                   (Biocat)
Technical         |                         Leading         |
support    ———————+——————— Low              edge   —————————+————————— Followers
high              |                                          |
                  |                                          |
              Off the shelf                            'We know best'
```

5   *Assessing targeting options*

Undifferentiated

Biocatalysts already offer customised solutions: their strength is their expertise and ability to customise so undifferentiated not a realistic option. Also offers no competitive advantage opportunities.

Differentiated

This requires ability to deliver a broad range to variety of customers. Medium to large size players have strength and resource to do this. Biocatalysts do not.

Niche

Requires expertise and customisation and to work effectively on a global scale can also adopt multi-niche strategies. Works well in highly specialised or narrow markets. This fits well with Biocatalysts's position.

Step 8: Contemporary Issues and Marketing Plans

Chapter Topic List
1   Customer service and relationship marketing
2   The Internet

1 Customer service and relationship marketing

1.1 Before we move on to tactical implementation, there are some other important issues to consider when developing marketing strategies and plans. These are strategic issues and they are influenced by people and policies vertically and horizontally across the organisation.

Customer service and relationship marketing (CRM)

1.2 Organisations are turning to customer service as a way of achieving and sustaining competitive advantage. Customer service, for companies faced with increasing competition and more demanding customers, is no longer a choice but a necessity if they are to survive. Consumer protection is increasing and tolerance of poor service has never been lower.

1.3 The launch of customer service initiatives was beset with superficiality and exemplified by slogans paying lip service rather than being representative of service values. Organisations are now coming to terms with the full implications of what delivering good customer service means.

Part B: The sample case: Biocatalysts

What is service?

1.4 Service involves two key elements.

(a) **The actual product or service** the customer receives, and benefits and solutions to problems. Businesses have steadily improved in this area through efficiency and quality drives.

(b) **The personal service:** way in which the product or service is delivered and the interaction between companies and customers. This is probably the most visible aspect and often the one on which the company is judged. This has been neglected through lack of training the right people with the right skills.

Developing customer service

1.5 Culture has been referred to throughout the file but note in particular that if management distrust employees and believe in high levels of supervision and control, are poor at communicating, giving little understanding to staff of the purpose of the business or of the customers served, then employees will feel de-motivated and undervalued. In these circumstances, establishing a customer care culture will be difficult.

1.6 There may be an atmosphere of trust and respect between management and employees, where the company believes in its social and environmental responsibilities, and staff understand the purpose of the business and customers served, are motivated and feel valued. In these circumstances the company is in a strong position to develop a customer care culture.

1.7 Until the appropriate culture and values have been established, efforts to implement customer care programmes are futile and will result in limited short-term success. They may even do more damage than good if customer and staff expectations are raised only to be disappointed.

The customer's chain of experience (moments of truth)

1.8 Customers come into contact with a company in a number of different ways, at different points and with a number of different people during any transaction. These pre-transaction, transaction and post-transaction activities are the **customer's chain of experience**, and whether or not this experience is good or bad depends on the organisation's efforts to understand the customer and manage the experience.

1.9 The customer will come in contact with both **processes** and **people** and both have the potential to **add value** to what the customer receives, thereby providing opportunities for competitive advantage.

1.10 A review should be undertaken to determine:

- The customer's chain of experience
- The customer's expectations and buying criteria
- Opportunities to improve the experience

1.11 The design of future processes and training of staff should reflect the goal of at least matching experience with expectations or, better, exceeding expectations if any competitive advantage is to be secured.

Customer relationships

1.12 Customer relationships are about the long-term value of a customer and the building of long-term relationships. In many business to business industries, ensuring continued business has always required investing considerable time, over the long term, in building relationships with customers. Reasons vary but include the following.

(a) **Need for trust** and **reduce risk**. This is particularly vital if:

   (i) The product or service has to do with saving, maintaining or improving life, for example in the caring professions

   (ii) Large sums of money are involved, meaning that the investment has to be seen to be of benefit and to solve problems, for example in aerospace companies

(b) **Need for security.** If secrecy, privacy or sensitivity are issues the customer has to believe their interests will be protected, for example in financial services.

(c) **Need for time.** If projects have long time scales (eg 5, 10 even 15 years) businesses have to be patient and think and act in the time scales typical of the industry, for example, in the military.

(d) **Need for co-operation.** Working partnerships with customers are a feature of business operations especially where input from customers is required in product development.

1.13 Many businesses do not operate, or previously have not operated, in this way. While demand exceeded supply there was no incentive to do so. As markets become increasingly competitive, companies are looking for ways to improve customer retention. The answer lies in 'relationship marketing'.

What is relationship marketing?

1.14 Relationship marketing involves the bringing together of quality, customer service and continuous improvement, managed through marketing activities.

1.15 Clues to an organisation's ability to adopt a relationship marketing philosophy and develop relationship marketing strategies have been covered elsewhere, in particular marketing orientation.

The loyalty ladder

1.16 Relationship marketing requires organisations to change the emphasis of their activities from focusing on acquiring new customers to building mutually beneficial long-term relationships with existing customers. This does not mean that there is no strategy for acquiring new customers, just a change in emphasis.

Part B: The sample case: Biocatalysts

Through customer service, the aim is to move customers up the loyalty ladder.

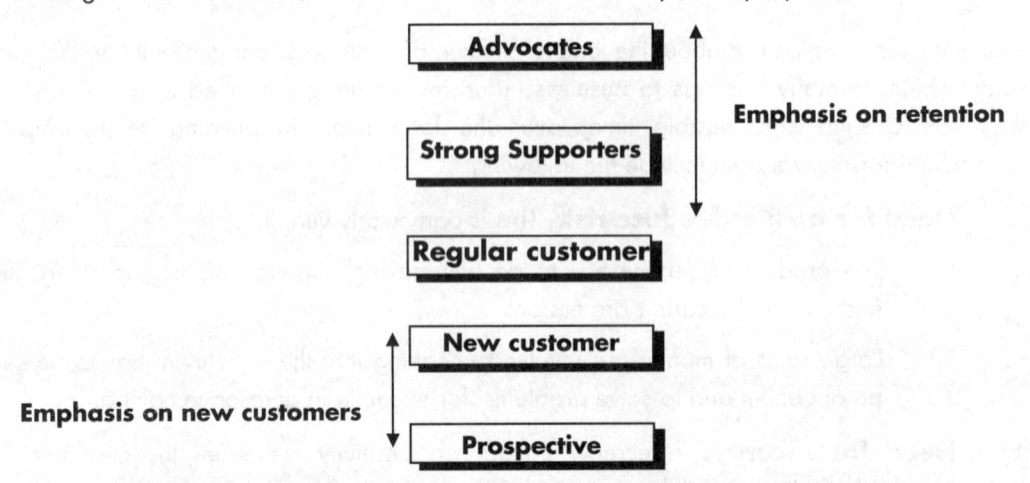

```
                    Advocates
                                    ↑
                 Strong Supporters  │ Emphasis on retention
                                    ↓
                 Regular customer

                  ↑  New customer
Emphasis on      │
new customers    ↓  Prospective
```

Adapted from Christopher, Payne, Ballentyne

Holistic market approach: seven markets

1.17 Relationship marketing does not assume that customers are the only market (or stakeholder) that exists and strategies are developed to build relationships with all its markets.

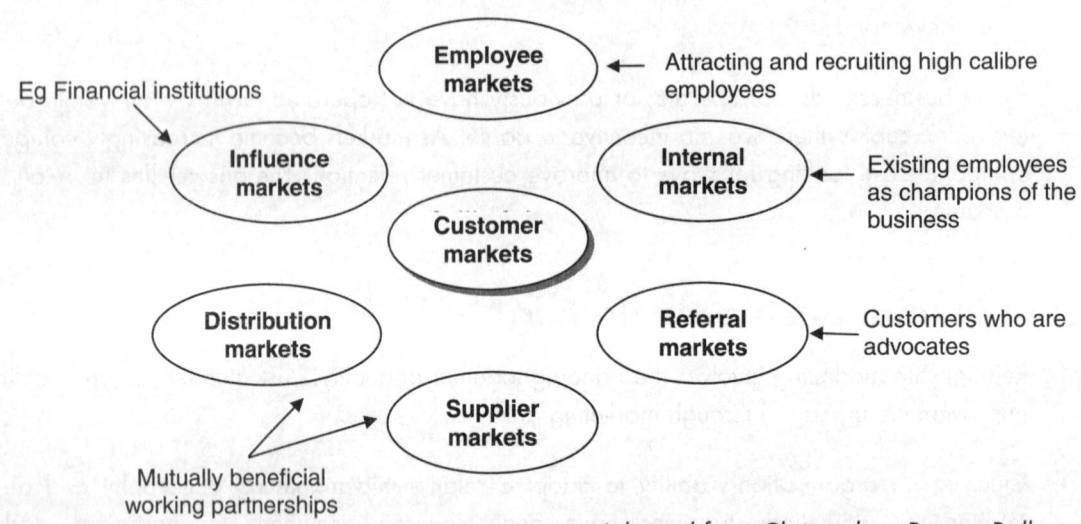

- **Employee markets** ← Attracting and recruiting high calibre employees
- **Influence markets** (Eg Financial institutions)
- **Internal markets** ← Existing employees as champions of the business
- **Customer markets**
- **Distribution markets**
- **Referral markets** ← Customers who are advocates
- **Supplier markets** ← Mutually beneficial working partnerships

Adapted from Christopher, Payne, Ballentyne

1.18 Integrated marketing and communication strategies designed to build long-term relationships with all markets are essential to success.

Relationship transitions

1.19 Relationship strategies must take account of the customer's life cycle and transitions in the relationship. Transitions and stages are points where there is a high risk of losing the customer due to the changes taking place and the different needs that are emerging. The changing needs and relationship need to be understood and strategies designed appropriate to the needs of that stage or transition to help ensure that customers remain loyal and highly satisfied. The emphasis is on working partnerships and two way communications.

Managing expectations

1.20 Managing expectations is one of the marketing manager's key tasks but it is too often disregarded, and promotional activities make claims and promises that little resemble the experience. Customers' expectations are determined both by factors within the control of the organisation and by some which are not.

1.21 Strategies for managing expectations should be incorporated into the marketing plan with marketing influencing areas of the business that impact on both expectations and experience.

The Biocatalysts customer

1.22 You can see in the Biocatalysts Case Study how important customer relationship management is, and how inadequately it is currently being dealt with. Biocatalysts could be developing relationships with:

- Their agents
- Directly with their customers

1.23 If they position themselves in the specialist end of the market, the creation of **advocates** would be essential to establishing preferred supplier status to niche users. It is easy in this case to see Biocatalysts as customer focused but actually they respond to customers' technical problems and challenges in an ad hoc way. There is no evidence of strategic relationship marketing or it would be reflected in their financial performance.

2 The Internet

2.1 It may be worth considering the Internet in a number of contexts.

The Internet and distribution

2.2 An Internet distribution strategy depends on a number of factors.

- Customer groups served – their needs, preferences
- The role and power of current intermediaries
- Size of business and ability to adopt/embrace company-wide technology (structure, operations)
- Culture of the business – innovative, low risk avoidance
- Products/services provided (digital, non digital, value per unit, volumes, level of incorporated technology)

2.3 Internet as a direct distribution channel

The Internet provides an ideal channel for digital product categories (software, text, image, sound). Examples of industries/businesses that can benefit include publishing, information, services, technology companies (computers, software, entertainment games), multi media (films, music etc) and financial services.

Part B: The sample case: Biocatalysts

The increasing ease of the Internet as a search tool is likely to change buyer behaviour from a tendency to be reactive to promotion/sales to being proactive and searching for information and engaging with sellers who can provide what is wanted.

2.4 Internet as an indirect distribution channel: intermediaries

Many products and services cannot be distributed down the line and therefore intermediaries are still needed. The role of the Internet in these circumstances can be:

- Communications and information channel
- Transactions
- Extranet link with intermediaries who distribute goods
- Co-ordinating/monitoring physical logistics

As with any intermediary strategy, a business must have clear objectives of what it expects from its intermediaries. Internet distribution strategies may require the role of the intermediary to be redefined. Is the Internet just extending the chain or adding value? Traditional intermediaries may eventually disappear if they do not redefine the value they add and the role they can play in e-commerce.

Internet communication strategy

2.5 Many of same processes and rules apply for Internet communications as for more traditional media.

- Need for objectives
- Strategy: push, pull and profile
- Positioning and messages: consistent with brand values and targets
- Targets: identifying who talking to
- Promotional techniques: can use on-line brochures
- Controls: measuring effectiveness

2.6 Differences between the Internet and other media are as follows.

(a) Targets are still limited and often poorly defined: assumptions made about who is online

(b) Online communications is interactive and can engage target audiences in a way traditional communications cannot

(c) Dynamic, instantly updating, moving, changing in direct response to customer demands

(d) Different measures for online activities

(e) Role of the database management

(f) Information overload

2.7 Factors to consider

(a) How are (or can) brand values (be) interpreted? Will the Internet affect perceptions in anyway and if so how?

(b) Ensuring it is a two way process: capturing customer information

(c) Matching experience with expectations: ensuring communications are clear, unambiguous, helpful, avoid 'click help' syndrome (ie no help at all)

(d) Because it is dynamic, must engage, interact

(e) Do not use as an alternative to all other forms of communication, in particular if a telephone call will do the job better, make the call.

Step 9: Control

Chapter Topic List	
1	Control: introduction
2	Budgets
3	Financial and human resources implications
4	Scheduling
5	Benchmarking
6	Measuring marketing effectiveness
7	Marketing information and knowledge management

1 Control: introduction

1.1 Controlling business performance and planning activities is as important as the planning process and is, indeed, an integral part of that process, but control will require different skills. Control is about making sure we do what was intended. It is important to start by distinguishing levels of control. Control issues are too often dealt with as a tactical activity. As the focus of planning moves to a strategic focus, so must control.

1.2 There are broadly three levels of control:

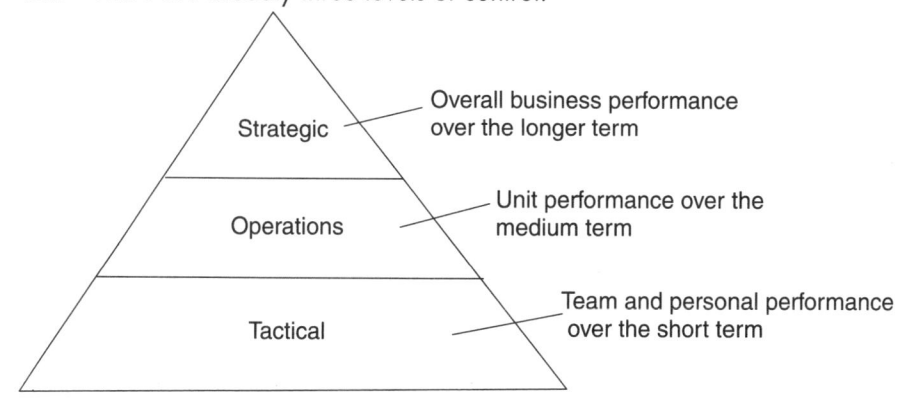

- Strategic — Overall business performance over the longer term
- Operations — Unit performance over the medium term
- Tactical — Team and personal performance over the short term

Part B: The sample case: Biocatalysts

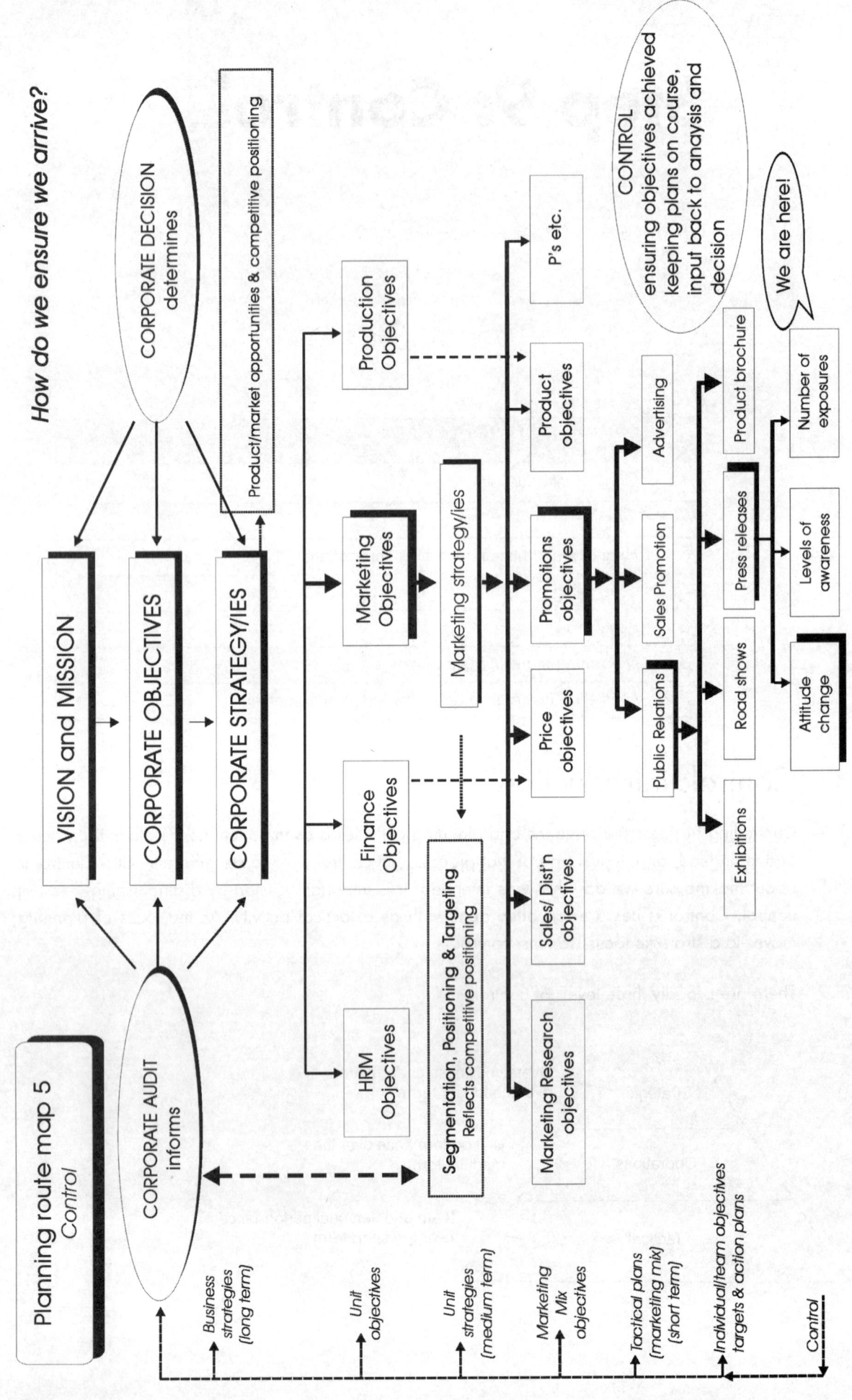

How do we ensure we arrive?

Planning route map 5 — *Control*

- VISION and MISSION → CORPORATE OBJECTIVES → CORPORATE STRATEGY/IES
- CORPORATE AUDIT informs
- CORPORATE DECISION determines
- Product/market opportunities & competitive positioning

Branches from Corporate Strategy:
- Production Objectives → Product objectives → P's etc.
- Marketing Objectives → Marketing strategy/ies → Promotions objectives → Advertising, Sales Promotion, Public Relations → Product brochure, Press releases, Road shows, Exhibitions → Number of exposures, Levels of awareness, Attitude change
- Finance Objectives → Price objectives
- Segmentation, Positioning & Targeting — Reflects competitive positioning
- Sales/Dist'n objectives
- Marketing Research objectives
- HRM Objectives

CONTROL — ensuring objectives achieved, keeping plans on course, input back to analysis and decision

We are here!

Levels (bottom):
- Business strategies (long term)
- Unit objectives
- Unit strategies (medium term)
- Marketing Mix objectives
- Tactical plans (marketing mix) (short term)
- Individual/team objectives, targets & action plans
- Control

240

Key control activities

1.3 Performance measurement

(a) **Setting performance standards and targets**
- Informs employees what is required of them
- Informs employees how they are excepted to achieve it (conditions)
- Informs employees when they have to achieve targets

(b) **Measuring and evaluating performance**
- Compares actual performance against standards set
- Compares performance against the competition
- Compares performance against best practice

(c) **Taking corrective action**
- Monitors performance
- Adjusts performance in line with standards/targets, or
- Revises plan

2 Budgets

2.1 Budgets are required for the planning horizon to determine the cost of implementing the plan against expected revenues. Problems lie in the difficulties of accurately forecasting demand for products and services, so monitoring revenues is vital to ensure the financial stability of the business.

2.2 The availability of resources can sometimes be difficult to predict and managers can be reluctant to commit to a budget.

2.3 Purposes of budgets

- Co-ordinate activities across organisation
- Communicate financial performance
- Monitor effectiveness of performance

2.4 Setting marketing budgets

The most common methods are:

- % of previous year's sales
- % of budgeted annual sales
- % of previous year's profit

2.5 This safeguards the risk of spending more than can be afforded but does not take into account the objectives set.

2.6 **Objective and task method** requires that once the objective is set, investigation on how much it will cost to achieve the objective is undertaken. This then has to be balanced against what can be afforded but if achieving the objective in the long term is vital to business survival and success, profits may have to suffer in the short term.

Part B: The sample case: Biocatalysts

3 Financial and human resource implications

3.1 Any recommendations and plans will have both financial and people implications. Marketers have, in the past, been criticised for ignoring these critical issues when developing plans.

3.2 A review of each recommendation made for its implications on business operations is required. In practice the **justification** for each course of action would play an important role in persuading senior management to accept the proposals made and the same applies to the exam case. Any proposal will cost money and require other resources and senior management have to be convinced the expenditure will see worthwhile returns.

3.3 Financial implications (example)

- Capital investment
- Risk
- Revenue
- Profit, profitability
- Working capital
- ROI/ROCE   Also consider major or new projects
- Creditors/debtors   eg re-organisation/structuring
- Stock   new markets (exporting)
- Liquidity   new product development
- Depreciation   additional costs (patents, legal etc)
- Budgets
- Financial control

3.4 Human resource implications (example)

- Known/expected staff losses due to normal wastage
- Transfers in/out
- New appointments
- Promotion plans
- Current staffing requirements
- Future staffing requirements
- Surplus/shortfall in staffing requirements
- Current skills needs
- Future skills needs
- Training requirements (costs/timing)
- Changes (eg conditions of employment, health and safety)

3.5 A good marketer will make the link between the resource implications and benefits of using these resources, and the consequences of not using them. The task is to use these benefits and expected outcomes to persuade management of the value of the strategies and plans you have developed.

3.6 In the case study, you are using the same process to persuade the examiner that, based on your analysis, you have developed credible plans to ensure the organisation achieves its goals.

4 Scheduling

4.1 All plans have a planning horizon, a time within which the plan must be executed and objectives achieved. Activities are also often dependent on each other: one activity must be completed before another can commence, so scheduling activities to make the best use of time is necessary.

4.2 Gantt charts, and for planning that involves hundreds of activities, critical path analysis, are useful techniques for ensuring activities have deadlines and are scheduled according to sequence.

Simple Gantt Chart

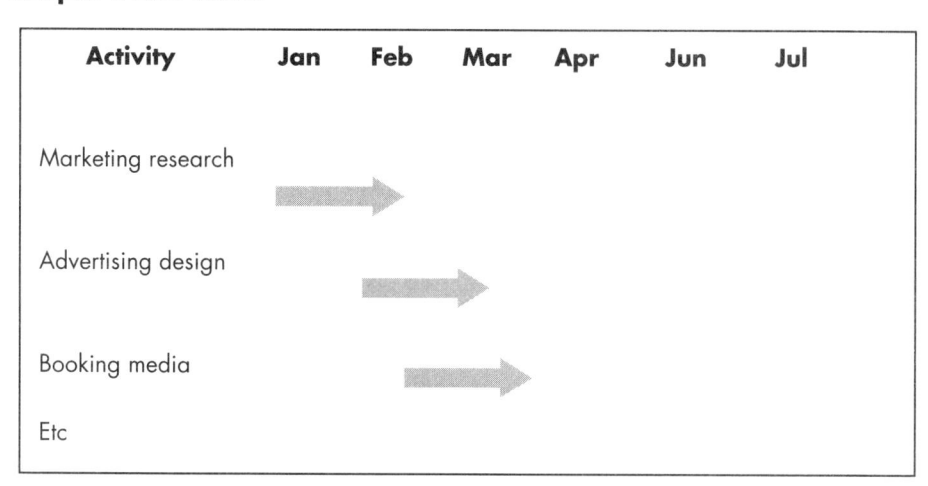

Activity	Jan	Feb	Mar	Apr	Jun	Jul
Marketing research	→					
Advertising design		→				
Booking media			→			
Etc						

Simple Critical Path Analysis

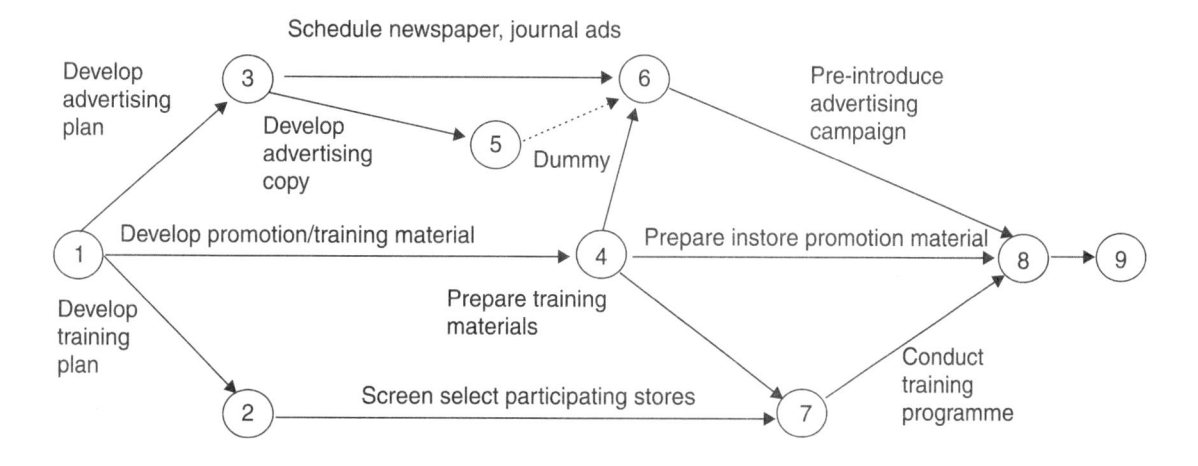

5 Benchmarking

5.1 Increasingly, businesses are looking at the competition to determine how well their own performance compares. Competitive benchmarking requires that a business identifies key performance indicators to benchmark against the competition and against best practice which may be a company outside the company's own industry. This benchmarking forces an external focus on performance and provides opportunities for the company to establish a base with the intention of out-performing the competition in the eyes of its customers.

Part B: The sample case: Biocatalysts

5.2 How easy it is to benchmark the competition will depend on the industry. If it is intense, competitive information will not be easily accessed: in other industries where technology is 'newsworthy', information flows freely. If there are few competitors and they are concentrated in one area it is usually easier to acquire information. Benchmarking partners can be established which requires trust, open communications and mutual exchange of information.

5.3 It may be unrealistic to attempt to be 'the best' but improvement targets are important.

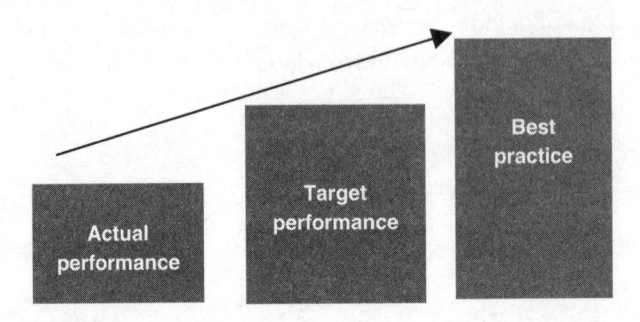

Warning: competitive benchmarking is not about copying the competition, it is about out-performing them, doing things well but differently.

6 Measuring marketing effectiveness

6.1 Quantitative and qualitative measures must be used to establish the effectiveness of marketing.

	Comment
Product	Contribution to sales revenues and volumes, contribution to profit, increasing market share, accessibility to new markets, reliability and durability, adaptability
Price	Impact on profits, impact on sales volumes, perception of value for money, attraction of new sales, customer loyalty
Place	Support and service to us and customer, reliability and consistency, added value (specify), accessibility, claims procedures, condition of goods
Personal selling	Sales by customer and by product, customer call frequency, average sales value per call, average cost per call, number of new customers obtained, customer retention
Promotions	Advertising (queries generated and conversion rates, attitude change – pre, during and post testing), PR (column inches), sales promotion (sales volume and sustainability)
People	Attainment of targets set, productivity, efficiency measures eg order turnaround, problem solving, delivery of training (content, presentation, visuals etc)
Processes	Reliability, speed, simplicity
Physical evidence	Perception of material evidence e.g. atmosphere/impressions created by offices, reception, training support materials, exhibition stands, impact on awareness, recall

	Comment
Customer service	Measure customer complaints (numbers, types), analyse levels of repeat business, analysis of chain of experience (customer contact points)
Marketing research	Methodologies used, accuracy of information, utilisation of information, accuracy in determining future information needs, analysis of usefulness in decision making

6.2 Measuring marketing effectiveness cannot take place without information. Measurement should be in the context of the business environment and should include indications of competitive performance. This requires the design, implementation and management of an effective marketing information systems.

Action Programme 1

Complete your plans by establishing the controls you require. Consider a realistic budget, establish a timetable and confirm what you are going to measure and how. This does not need to be a lengthy activity, keep it brief.

Compare your answers with ours at the end of this chapter.

7 Marketing information and knowledge management

7.1 At the heart of knowledge management is the culture of the organisation. Culture will affect the way and extent to which knowledge can be managed. Beliefs, attitudes and values, management style and communications all influence culture. The culture should also reflect an enthusiasm for learning.

7.2 Potential conflicts include knowledge ownership and management must acknowledge joint ownership, where appropriate, and recognise individual contribution, their intellectual capital, encourage the sharing of knowledge (informed employees are more likely to reciprocate with information), and give rewards and recognition (performance measurement should take account of the value of knowledge).

Three key elements to knowledge management

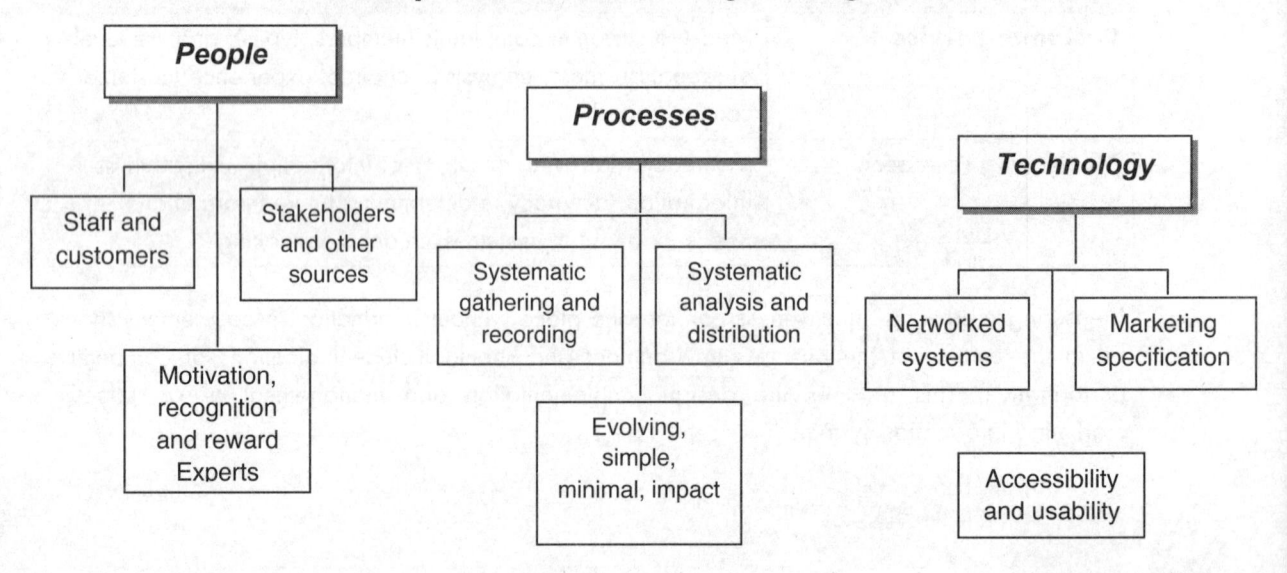

```
         People                          Processes                        Technology
        /      \                         /        \                       /         \
  Staff and   Stakeholders        Systematic    Systematic         Networked      Marketing
  customers   and other           gathering      analysis          systems        specification
              sources             and recording  and distribution
        |                                |                               |
  Motivation,                      Evolving,                       Accessibility
  recognition                      simple,                         and usability
  and reward                       minimal, impact
  Experts
```

J. Cockton © 2000

Marketing information and database management

7.3 Research and gathering information as part of the customer relationship building and maintenance process leads to the need for database management. The strategic goal of database management is quality marketing intelligence that helps to build good long-term relationships that, in turn, lead to 'highly satisfied' and 'loyal' customers and results in profits.

7.4 Database management is not about the technology. It is about the outcomes – customer knowledge. Good database management often means changing the information you gather, moving from product knowledge management to **customer knowledge management.** It requires changing the 'mind set' from concentrating on the products you sell to concentrating on the different kinds of customers who buy. Moving from product expertise to **customer expertise**.

Management and Marketing Information Systems

7.5 Pivotal to control is the establishment of information systems. The monitoring, gathering, analysis and reporting of information allow the business to control its internal operations and be prepared for external opportunities and threats. Most businesses are gathering in information in various forms all the time but the difference between a successful business and the less successful will often be the formality of that information gathering process. Making connections between pieces of information makes the difference.

The role of a marketing information systems in control

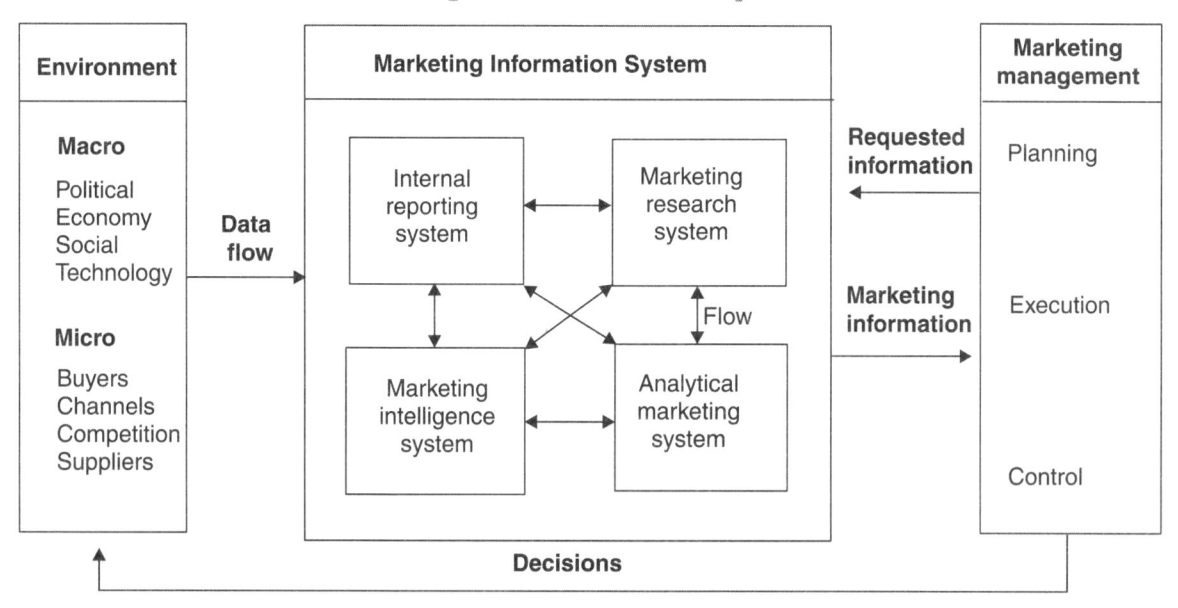

```
Environment          Marketing Information System            Marketing
                                                             management

Macro                                          Requested
Political                                      information   Planning
Economy     Data    Internal      Marketing
Social      flow    reporting  ↔  research
Technology          system         system
                       ↕  ⤢ ⤡  ↕                Marketing
                       ⤡  ⤢                     information   Execution
Micro                              │Flow
Buyers              Marketing      Analytical
Channels            intelligence ↔ marketing
Competition         system         system                    Control
Suppliers

                          Decisions
```

7.6 An MkIS ensures an ongoing information flow that enables the business to be prepared for events as they unfold. It accesses information from numerous sources in a variety of ways to build a complete picture of external opportunities and threats, market characteristics and dynamics.

Action Programme 2

A more strategic control issue is that of management and marketing information systems. Briefly consider the information system needs and how you would tackle them.

Compare your answer with ours at the end of the chapter.

Action programme review

1   Budget – Obviously Biocatalysts's financial constraints are a real problem. You need to think creatively, for example marketing research costs can be significantly reduced by working with customers who will be willing to share information and through participating where appropriate in omnibus research and of course partnerships with universities.

    They are already spending some money on marketing – we could use this to far greater effect with more focused strategies and, as Biocatalysts's financial situation improves, increase marketing spend.

    Schedule – remember Biocatalysts has some short-term survival needs as well as the longer-term vision.

    Measurement – key issues include financial performance and critical cash flow, market position and share, product performance and communication.

Part B: The sample case: Biocatalysts

2 Introduction

- Importance of marketing information (and fast developments in biotechnology)
- Consequences of not knowing/understanding market dynamics (eg changing nature of competition with competitors adopting more strategic positions)
- Biocatalysts current situation re marketing information

Internal information needs

Biocatalysts performance S/W
- Financial performance
- Marketing skills levels
- Management skills levels
- Planning and control systems and processes (product/market selection etc)
- Competitive position and strategy
- Market share and performance by country, industry, segment (value customers)
- Distribution channel performance

Market information needs

- Market characteristics – PEST, life cycles etc growth, sectors
- Competition – who, strategies (response profiles), size, location/market coverage
- Customers – who, demand forecasts, buying criteria, DMUs
- Channels – poor performance and market implications

Potential problems

- Our skills – current information held, lack resources, experience
- International markets – comparability, accessibility, reliability, accuracy
- Cost and time scales – short term little money, increase investment longer term
- Security, sensitivity particularly given nature of industry
- Conflicts of interest – who owns the information e.g. university, Biocatalysts?

Overcoming problems

- Senior management commitment (allocation of resources, responsibilities, set objectives)
- Audit current information and effectiveness how gathered/used etc
- Establish formalised system MKIS – funding
- Role/selection of agents/distributors
- Sources of information – governments, embassies, trade associations etc
- Contacts – formalise network of stakeholders (global) e.g. universities
- Role of interactive website
- Planning process for

Formalised gathering and analysis of information for planning and control purposes

Marketing Information System MkIS

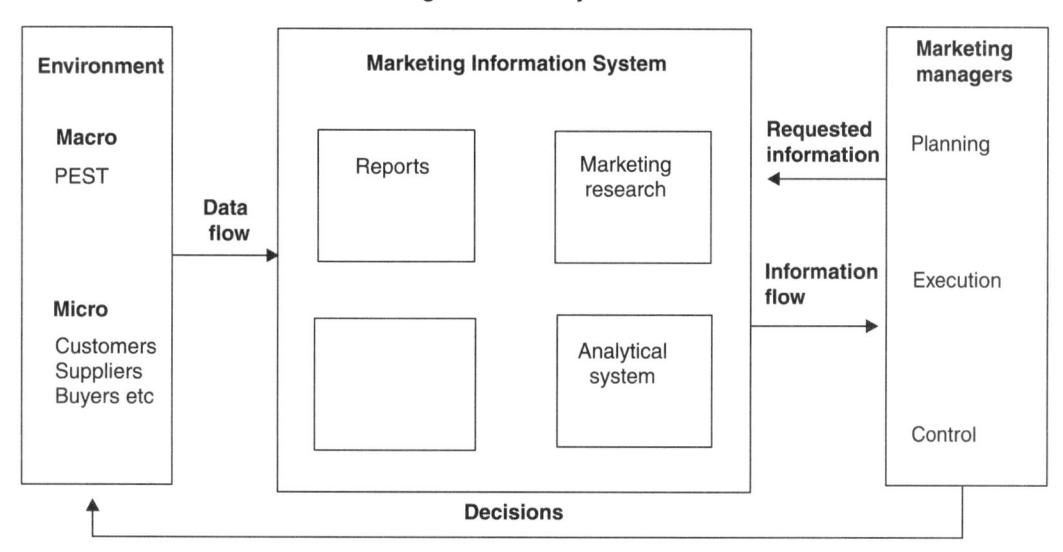

```
┌─────────────┐         ┌──────────────────────────────┐           ┌──────────────┐
│ Environment │         │ Marketing Information System │           │  Marketing   │
│             │         │                              │           │  managers    │
│   Macro     │         │  ┌────────┐   ┌──────────┐   │ Requested │              │
│   PEST      │  Data   │  │Reports │   │Marketing │   │information│  Planning    │
│             │  flow → │  │        │   │ research │   │ ←─────    │              │
│             │         │  └────────┘   └──────────┘   │           │              │
│   Micro     │         │               ┌──────────┐   │Information│  Execution   │
│  Customers  │         │               │Analytical│   │   flow    │              │
│  Suppliers  │         │               │ system   │   │  ─────→   │              │
│  Buyers etc │         │               └──────────┘   │           │  Control     │
└─────────────┘         └──────────────────────────────┘           └──────────────┘
       ↑                          Decisions                                │
       └──────────────────────────────────────────────────────────────────┘
```

Step 1. Design

- Evaluate current information, flows, sources etc. S/W and processes
- Review requirements e.g. use in decision making, identifying, collecting, recording, analysing, reporting, storing, retrieval, removing outdated, use for control
- Involve staff in design – project teams

Step 2. Technology

- Evaluate systems – meet needs of everyone, flexibility, networking

Step 3. Implementation

- Project teams develop implementation plan
- Staff training
- Test run
- Monitoring and evaluating

Step 10: Managing Your Materials and Preparing for the Exam

Chapter Topic List
1   Managing materials
2   Preparing for the exam

1 Managing materials

Organising yourself

1.1 Now you have had the benefit and experience of working your way through a practice case you will be aware of the amount of paper you accumulate. It is essential you manage your material to ensure you work the case study effectively and are properly prepared for the exam.

1.2 Lack of a system or a methodical approach can be your undoing. So much information is scattered across the case that, if you are not organised, you will fail to draw together the clues and make the connections that lead to insights. Decisions risk being flawed or missed altogether if you are not methodical. For the exam case, here is what you should do.

Step 1. ***Draw up a plan*** with a timetable – allocate time to specific tasks, do not leave things to the last minute. For the exam case you should aim to be finished by the beginning of the week of the exam to give yourself time to move away from the case. This way you go to the exam fresh and ready to tackle anything rather than exhausted and still buried in detail.

Step 2. ***Negotiate time*** where needed and gain people's support. If you do not do this you may eventually waste more time and jeopardise your chances of success. There will inevitably be pressure but do not allow it to become stress by lack of planning and communicating your needs to others. You are only asking for four weeks.

Step 3. ***Copy the case*** (or print off website). A second copy is useful (a) just in case original gets lost, and (b) a copy it is much easier to re-organise into logical sections e.g. organisation, customers etc.

13 ♦ Step 10: Managing your materials and preparing for the exam

Step 4. **Organise and create files** with dividers to help bring some order to what you are doing and ensure precious pieces of paper do not go walkabout.

Step 5. **Number paragraphs, reference sections, pages and so on** – This is all the paragraphs and reference to your analysis for quick and easy tracking of where information came from.

Step 6. **Contents** – It is worth doing a 'contents' sheet of where the figures, tables, articles etc. are for quick and easy reference. If you are likely to be working in different places, to maximise use of your time, put your name and address on files so if they are mislaid they stand a chance of being returned to you.

1.3 We recommend your file is structured as follows

- Where are we now – analysis
- Where do we want to be – corporate decisions
- How are we going to get there – marketing decisions
- How to we ensure we arrive – control

You can break your file down further into sub sections, as indicated in the following example, while you are working the case and possibly pull back into the above four sections when you get to the concluding, summarising and making notes stage. Do not expect to be able to comment on everything because of information gaps.

Part B: The sample case: Biocatalysts

WHERE ARE WE NOW? – Analysis contents

1a. Internal audit – strengths and weaknesses

Corporate

- Purpose (mission)
- Profitability
- Structure
- Culture
- Processes/task
- People (management/employees through organisation)
- Competitive strategy
- Market position (or men, money, machines, materials and markets)

Marketing

- Integration of marketing through organisation
- Image/influence of marketing in organisation
- Planning and control systems and processes
- Current marketing strategy effectiveness (segmentation, positioning, targeting)
- MkIS – gathering, analysing and disseminating
- Marketing research

Marketing mix

- Product
- Price
- Place
- Promotion
- People
- Processes
- Physical evidence

Example of models you can use:

- Financial ratios
- Portfolio analysis (Boston, GE, Shell etc.)
- Product life cycle
- Cultural web or McKinsey 7S
- Porter's generic competitive strategies
- Strengths/weaknesses performance/importance matrix
- Positioning maps

1b. External audit – opportunities and threats

Macro environment (SLEPT, PEST, STEEPLE or whatever you prefer)

- Political/legal
- Economic
- Social cultural
- Technology
- Industry structure – (supply chains, vertical or horizontal etc.)
- Market/s

Micro environment – Customers and stakeholders (including channels)

- Who buys
- Intermediaries
- What is bought
- Where is it bought
- When is it bought
- How is it bought
- Why is it bought

Micro environment – Competition

- Main competitors
- Strengths/weaknesses
- Strategies
- Market share
- Product range
- Competitive advantage

Examples of models you can use:

- Porter's five forces
- Threat and opportunity matrices
- Porter's generic competitive strategies
- Positioning maps
- Multifactor matrices
- Market/industry life cycles
- Supply and demand chains

RESULTS AT END OF ANALYSIS – You will be able to describe:

- Company performance
- Market conditions
- Current position in market
- Customer behaviour and issues
- Competitive situation

The summary of analysis should focus on critical success factors, associated key issues and any major problems.

Part B: The sample case: Biocatalysts

WHERE DO WE WANT TO BE? – Corporate decisions contents

2. Vision and mission statements (if appropriate)

- Future direction/what the business aspires to be
- What business we are in/purpose
- Reflect actual or desired position

3. Corporate objectives

- Quantified objectives
- Meet financial needs of business
- Growth needs of business

Example of models that can be used include gap analysis and forecasting techniques

4. Corporate/Business Strategy

To grow the business

- Strategic product market growth options open to business
- Explanation and justification of those solutions selected/rejected
- Selected strategies to be pursued

Example of models that can be used include:

Ansoff matrix (to develop strategic options)

GE matrix (to evaluate strategic options)

To ensure growth strategies are competitive

- Competitive nature of strategies to be pursued
- Competitive actions

Example of models that can be used include:

- Porter's generic competitive strategies (to identify sources of competitive advantage, position)
- Competitive moves (military analogies)

To ensure strategies will succeed

Where appropriate notes/outlines for case specific issues eg:

- Implications for business
- Business and management strategies
- Marketing orientation
- Managing change
- Internal marketing
- Relationship marketing and customer service

Example of models that can be used include:

- Managing change models eg stages people go through
- Culture web or McKinsey 7S
- Relationship marketing Venn diagram

HOW ARE WE GOING TO GET THERE? – Marketing decisions

5. Marketing objectives

- Corporate objectives interpreted as marketing objective

6. Marketing strategy

- Segmentation, positioning and targeting

7. Tactical Plans

- 7.1 Product
- 7.2 Price
- 7.3 Place
- 7.4 Promotion *(UNLESS separate communications plan)*
- 7.5 People
- 7.6 Processes
- 7.7 Physical evidence

Each has an objective/aim (what is to be achieved), briefest details on actions (how it is to be achieved)

Notes/outlines should take account of:

- Constraints – internal and external
- Implications – financial and human resources
- Outline marketing research plan/list of information needs

Briefs on:

- Appointing/briefing marketing agencies
- Commissioning marketing research
- Managing outside resources

Example of models/techniques that can be used include:

- Segmentation – geodemographic, lifestyle and pyschographic, DMU, SIC codes
- Positioning maps
- Quality/price positioning matrix
- Total product/brand concept

RESULTS AT END OF DECISION

You should have:

- Marketing plan notes/outline for each selected business strategy (explained and justified recommended courses of action)
- Management or business plan notes/outline for implications to business (explained and justified recommended courses of action)

Part B: The sample case: Biocatalysts

HOW DO WE ENSURE WE ARRIVE? – Control contents

8. Control

8.1 Budgets

Notes/outlines on financial needs for the planning period

- Expected revenue generation for period of plan
- Expected expenditure for period of plan
- Expected profit for period of plan

8.2 Timetable (Short, medium and long term planning horizons)

- Detailed actions – what will happen when and in what sequence (Gantt)

8.3 Measuring performance (marketing metrics)

Setting targets (often expressed as objectives – revenues, volumes, customer satisfaction)

Financial measures

- Profitability
- Short and long term solvency
- Working capital
- Shareholders' investment

Marketing measures

- Communications
- Sales
- Product and price
- Distribution

People measures

- Setting performance standards (eg quantity, quality, cost, time)
- Monitoring performance (appraisals, customer surveys)

Note: Whatever you recommend in your notes/outlines there should be follow through controls. You should also give some though to implementing and maintaining MkIS

9. Contingency plans

Notes/outlines developed to deal with unlikely events/changes during planning horizon.

Example of models/techniques that can be used include:

- Balanced scorecard
- Gantt charts
- Network analysis

RESULTS AT END OF CONTROL

- Identification and allocation of responsibilities
- Systems and procedures for evaluating performance
- Checks for ensuring plan proceeds on course/time, mechanisms to trigger corrective action

2 Preparing for the exam

Developing a Case Study appendix

2.1 The modified open book examination means you:

    (a) Cannot take a case file into the exam room
    (b) Can develop a six page appendix to attach to your exam answer
    (c) Can take your annotated copy of the case study into the exam

CIM has given relatively little guidance on how best to use this new opportunity.

2.2 You will see in our sample answers to the case one or two examples of these pre-prepared appendices and you will be able to draw some conclusions of your own.

What you should NOT do

2.3 You should not:

    (a) Try to incorporate all your analysis squashed into six sides
    (b) Try to produce a strategic marketing plan in advance of the question and additional information
    (c) Try to second guess the questions; if you are wrong your appendices will be less useful
    (d) Present analysis without added value

What you should do

2.4 You should:

    (a) Think about how best to use your A4 sheets in the context of the case
    (b) Ensure you add the commentary, business implications or links which the examiner understand 'why' this analysis is valuable or relevant and how it might inform strategy
    (c) Use models and frameworks: it will save you time in the exam
    (d) Label them and number them for easy reference in your answer script
    (e) Make your figures and illustrations big enough to be read by an ageing and tired examiner!
    (f) Remember the value of colour and white space
    (g) Go for quality rather than quantity
    (h) Be clear whether your sheets are supporting analysis or decision

The headings and framework given earlier in this chapter for file management will help you organise content logically.

Biocatalysts Ltd: The Examination 14

Chapter Topic List	
1	Exam hints
2	The examination paper
3	Reading the exam paper
4	A sample answer

BIOCATALYSTS LTD

DO NOT LOOK UNTIL YOU ARE READY TO SPEND

THREE HOURS DOING THESE AS A MOCK EXAM

---

1 Exam hints

1.1 Equipment, aids and exam centre

Make sure you have all the equipment you need.

(a) Good quality pens – **not** highlighter or felt tips: use colour for models, underlining etc but **not red**: use a ruler where appropriate when drawing models

(b) Calculator (in the past this has not been needed but take one just in case)

(c) Tipp-Ex fluid or similar (in good condition)

(d) Stencils for drawing charts, boxes, models

(e) Watch/clock

(f) For analysis and decision candidates pre-prepared models (to scale where appropriate) are useful: use black felt tip for pre-prepared examples so you can trace on exam paper.

For Strategic Marketing in Practice candidates you need your six pages of pre-prepared analysis

(g) Copy of case

1.2 Make sure you know where the exam centre is and where you can park (do you need permission, change etc). If travelling by public transport, where is the nearest station etc and how long does it take to walk from the station to the centre, train/bus times and so on.

1.3 Allow plenty of time on the day: you will not be allowed into the exam room 15 minutes after the start. Check with the exam centre when they intend to start the examination and be prepared for there to be other people in the room taking other exams. Their exams may be shorter and they may leave earlier.

1.4 Examination and presentation techniques

(a) **Always** plan your answers. Even if you have prepared well and anticipated questions successfully, you will still need to plan your answers, particularly to take on board the additional information. You must be selective in the material you draw on and it will require modification to meet the specifics, emphasis and slant of the question.

(b) One area where the well prepared student often fails is **poor time management**. Time and again this comes back as a problem. Manage your time and be disciplined about moving on to the next question. If you have run out of time on a question, leave space to go back to it later, if you have time. Just because you have more material to draw upon does not mean you must use it all.

(c) Structure your answer to keep you focused on the question **and** make it easier for the examiner to mark your script. Where appropriate, use headings from the question to help keep you focused. Always use report format, unless otherwise stated.

(d) **Use good communication skills**. Get your points across succinctly: explain and justify where appropriate (never make a recommendation without some explanation and justification). Be persuasive: you would have to use this skill if you were trying to convince senior management of the validity of your recommendations and the same is true for the examiner. Do not allow the examiner to get lost (or worse bored!) in a wall of words that wanders around the point.

(e) **Demonstrate both knowledge and experience**. Do not leave the examiner to fill in gaps and guess whether or not you know the theory or how to apply it: they will not do that, it is not their job. Make the connection and links: the point of the case study examination, in particular, is for you to demonstrate your skills as a marketing professional.

(f) **Do not deliver what you want to as opposed to what the question has asked for**. Unless the question specifically asks for analysis, you are expected to deliver decisions. The quality of your analysis is tested through the quality of your decisions. If a 'current situation' type question is asked for, do not deliver SWOTs. You are expected to give an overview of the current situation that adds value, an interpretation of the current situation that provides insights. A SWOT cannot do this.

(g) Use plenty of white space – aim for 25%. A wall of words is hard on the eyes (and the brain!) and immediately signals to the examiner that report format is not understood.

Part B: The sample case: Biocatalysts

(h) **Always** check your answer: particularly important when you have had to adjust your pre-thinking to take on board additional information. Check for integration and consistency.

2 The examination paper

Additional information to be taken into account when answering the questions set.

Owing to the problems in the South Asian and South American economies, Biocatalysts is likely to face an erosion of margins within its textiles business. Clients are demanding cheaper enzymes for jeans and other textiles production. The agents in the key offices in Hong Kong and Singapore are also finding that they need more time and support from the Head Office in Wales. They are, however, finding that some of the specialist food enzyme demand is growing, although many of the potential customers require high levels of technical support.

Examination questions

Based on your analysis of Biocatalysts' competitive position, and after further discussion with the Managing Director, as the appointed marketing consultant to the Managing Director, you are to prepare a report which should address the following.

Question 1

Produce a strategic marketing plan for Biocatalysts Ltd for the next five years, justifying your recommendations. **(50 marks)**

Question 2

Biocatalysts Ltd sells a diverse range of products into many geographical areas. Critically assess the best possible international marketing strategy that the company should follow, taking into account the generally poor performance of its agents and distributors.

(25 marks)

Question 3

Given the long-term prospects of the development of genetically modified organisms (GMOs) for the production of enzymes, develop a marketing communications strategy for Biocatalysts Ltd.
(25 marks)
(100 marks in total)

3 Reading the exam paper

3.1 Remember exam technique is vital to your success and the first action you need to take is to note the marks for each question and allocate the appropriate time to each question.

3.2 Next you need to read the entire paper, additional information and all questions. Then you need to look for clues on what is being asked for.

Additional information

> 'Owing to the **problems** in the **South Asian** and **South American** economies, Biocatalysts is likely to face an **erosion of margins** within its **textiles** business'

Already you have clues on how you should develop your answer.

We now know there are problems with some economies which will affect Biocatalysts's margins and that textiles is not an attractive option.

> '**Clients are demanding cheaper enzymes** for jeans and other **textiles** production.'

How does this fit with your analysis and decisions, particularly on Biocatalysts' position? Were you intending to stay in textiles? Does staying in textiles fit with Biocatalysts' potential position? How does it fit with their strengths?

> 'The **agents** in the **key offices** in **Hong Kong** and **Singapore** are also finding that they **need more time and support from the Head Office** in Wales. They are however finding that some of the **specialist food enzyme demand is growing** although many of the **potential customers require high levels of technical support**.'

So specialty food enzymes are looking attractive and Biocatalysts's expertise and technical skills can be used to help position them as a premium priced service.

The questions

Question 1 is asking for the strategic marketing plan, question 2 for an international strategy (with specific reference to agents) and question 3 for a communications plan (with specific reference to GMOs).

Question 2 and 3 mean we do not have to spend much time on international issues, 'Place' or 'Promotions' in question 1. We can refer the examiner to questions 2 and 3. It does mean that in question 1 our strategic marketing plan must refer to and reflect an international focus.

4 A sample answer

Planning your answer

Now you have examined the examination paper to determine precisely what you have been asked for, you can start to plan your answer.

Tutor comments on example answers

Please note this is an example only. You may have tackled the question differently. Providing you answered the specifics of the questions and within a marketing framework, there is no reason why your answer is not as good or better.

The most important lesson to learn from this is, how much could you write in three hours (broken down into 90 minutes and 45 minutes × 2)? This is what you need to know before you go into the exam.

Part B: The sample case: Biocatalysts

Contents

> Leave the first page blank, go back when you have finished and complete this page. Normally you would include subheadings but this may be too time consuming in the exam

1   **Five year strategic marketing plan**

1.1   Current situation
1.2   Mission, vision and business objective
1.3   Business strategy and competitive positioning
1.4   Marketing objectives
1.5   Marketing strategy (segmentation, positioning, targeting)
1.6   Marketing mix plans (product, price, technical support)
1.7   Control (budget, scheduling, measurement)

2   **International marketing strategy**

2.1   Country/market selection
2.2   Agents and distributors
2.3   Methods of entry and levels of involvement
2.4   Marketing objectives
2.5   Marketing strategy
2.6   Tactical plans
2.7   Control

3   **Marketing communications strategy**

3.1   Communications objectives
3.2   Communications strategy
3.3   Targets
3.4   Promotional activities
3.5   Control

4.1 Question 1

1. **Five year strategic marketing plan**

1.1 Current situation

1.1.1 Market conditions

The biotechnology industry is young and very dynamic and technology is a key driver of developments and change, both of which occur with increasing frequency. Governments in many countries have supported developments in biotechnology through funding and a reluctance to over-regulate the market. Pressure from consumers may change this.

Economic conditions have been relatively stable in Europe and North America, but as highlighted in the additional information, this stability is not reflected across the globe, with South Asia and South America suffering from economic downturn.

Predicted future market growth in enzymes is from $1.7 billion to $2 billion by 2005. The greatest opportunity is the growth in 'other' eg animal feed, baking, fruit and wine, speciality applications and is predicted to be very rapid and collectively likely to be the largest section of the enzyme market exceeding £500 million sales by 2005. Bulk enzymes will increasingly be produced from GMOs. Some of Biocatalysts' markets are predicted to decline, for example textiles, while value will increase with total growth. Markets need to be examined for future viability.

Market/industry life cycle

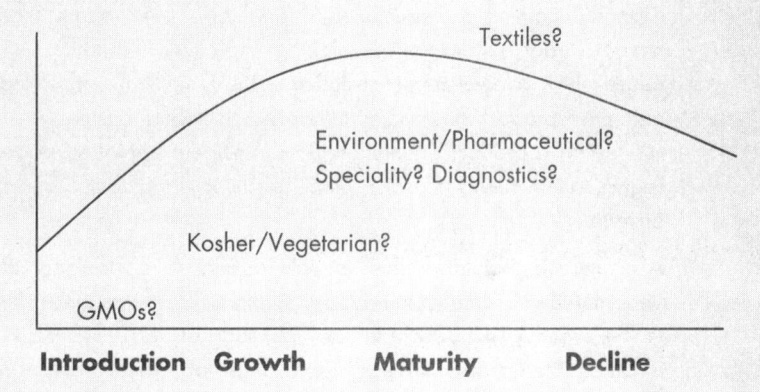

[Graph showing life cycle curve with the following labels positioned along the curve:
- GMOs? (Introduction stage)
- Kosher/Vegetarian? (Growth stage)
- Environment/Pharmaceutical? Speciality? Diagnostics? (Maturity stage)
- Textiles? (near peak, heading to Decline)
X-axis: Introduction, Growth, Maturity, Decline]

1.1.2 Competition

The nature of competition is changing. In this young industry, competitive 'positions' have not been an issue until now. Competitors are now clearly thinking about future positions. This would indicate a move to a more strategic marketing approach and you can expect clear competitive positions to emerge.

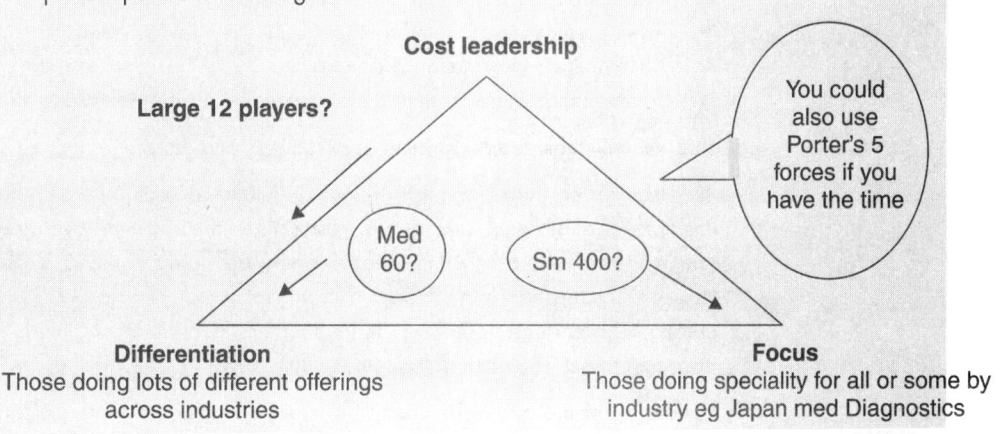

[Triangle diagram with:
- Top: Cost leadership
- Bottom left: Differentiation — Those doing lots of different offerings across industries
- Bottom right: Focus — Those doing speciality for all or some by industry eg Japan med Diagnostics
- Large 12 players? (on left side)
- Med 60? and Sm 400? (inside triangle)
- Callout: "You could also use Porter's 5 forces if you have the time"]

With the competitive information we have, it is difficult to be precise about competitors as we are not always comparing like with like but some assumptions can be made. Novo is a major player with 50% of the market. Gist and Genecor share 25% of the market. These players are most likely to have the potential to develop cost leadership positions. The remaining 25% of the market is shared by the rest of the biotechnology companies so the competition amongst these players is likely to become increasingly intense.

The 60 medium-sized companies are most likely to have enough market share to enable them to segment their markets and adopt differentiated positions. The remaining 400 small players will not have the strength to take on the medium and large players and are likely to look for opportunities to develop niche markets.

1.1.3 Customers

The end consumer significantly influences your customers who are typically manufacturers, producers and retailers and their future decisions will be based on what is acceptable to the consumer.

The industry has a complex network of many stakeholders that influence, directly and indirectly, what the industry does. For example MAFF, universities, industry analysts, FDA, HACCP etc.

1.1.4 Biocatalyst's current position

If adding pre-prepared analysis remember to refer to it here. The business has highly qualified experts providing strong technical competence. With high levels of technical support becoming an expectation, this will be a key strength. Biocatalysts are innovative and have a track record of developing customised products and are good at customer relationships. However the customer focus is tactical not strategic or marketing orientated and new product development has not included business screening or marketing input suggesting a product orientation. This is evident from their poor financial performance. No segmentation seems to take place resulting in Biocatalysts tending to do anything for anyone.

A concern is that three sales people appear to be looking after 35 countries. The poor performance in some of the overseas markets, for example as little as £40,000 from Japan in 1997 and £140,000 from the USA, suggests this is not working. There does not appear to be an international strategy. There does not appear to have been a rigorous process for appointing, managing and evaluating agents and distributors. There is a lack of clear strategy, and competitive position.

Broader issues of market conditions, trends and competitive activities do not seem to be considered. Overall there is a lack of planning and control, evident in:

- Lack of up to date marketing intelligence. (lack of analysis)
- No monitoring of the market (performance, developments)
- Competitor information is patchy
- information is not gathered systematically or analysed methodically

This will inevitably lead to missed opportunities and threats.

An analysis of financial performance indicates a lack of control and is of immediate concern. The business has grown faster than the industry average but profits are low, running at around 6%. At the moment they are fairly liquid and able to cover liabilities. However increased debtors days (75 in 1994 to 143 in 1997), together with paying creditors faster than receiving debts suggests availability of funds and cash flow could become critical. The cash balance has come down to £12,000, down 61% ('96 on '97).

In conclusion the market is changing rapidly, competitors are becoming more strategic in their approach, customers are more demanding and Biocatalysts have some critical issues facing the business.

1.2 Mission, vision and business objective

Biocatalysts need to clarify the purpose of the business and their aspirations. Decisions will include whether or not Biocatalysts intend to pursue GMO production and, if so, the time scales involved. Biocatalysts are not in a strong position to launch a GMO product into the current hostile market without a clear strategy.

1.2.1 Mission statement

Biocatalysts are in the business of providing...

Add your mission and vision here

1.2.2 Vision

To be...

1.2.3 Business objective

A profit objective is recommended to keep the business focused on what it must achieve and to provide a measure.

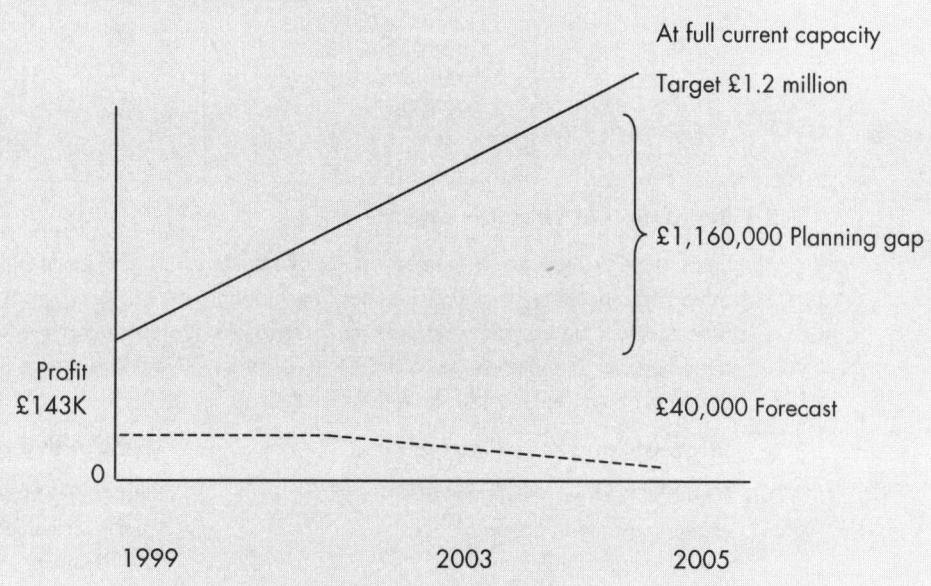

At full current capacity
Target £1.2 million

£1,160,000 Planning gap

Profit £143K

£40,000 Forecast

1999   2003   2005

This profit objective requires an increased margin to 10%.

A company can grow when a market is growing substantially. However, given the rapidly changing nature of the market and increasing competition, to carry on as Biocatalyst is now, the forecast is likely to be a decline. With such low profits, unless a clear strategy and direction is implemented, there is a danger Biocatalysts will not be around in 2005.

Strategies now need to be identified to fill the planning gap.

Part B: The sample case: Biocatalysts

1.3 Business strategy and competitive positioning

A number of options emerged during analysis.

	PRODUCTS	
	Existing	New
Existing	Environmental Waste treatment Textiles Health care Unique speciality foods Alcohol, baking, fats/oils Fruit/wine, flavour, protein Animal foods, leather Paper/pulp Chemical biotransformation	More testing kits GMOs By products High tech foods Full consultancy service Technical backup service
New	Geographic - eg Russia China USA Japan New industries Oil spillage Pharmaceutical Licensing	Knowledge brokers Backward forward integration

MARKETS (row label)

1.3.1 Evaluation of strategic options

Each strategy must be evaluated for its attractiveness to the business and the competitive advantage/position it offers. The best evaluation tool for this purpose is the GE matrix. Management agree and prioritise the criteria for strategy attractiveness and research on customers to determine the competitive position. We have some information on why customers buy. This would form one of the criteria.

Strategy/market attractiveness	**Competitive position**
Profitability of not less than 10%	Improving efficiency
Marketing growth potential	Cost effectiveness
Levels of competition	Convenience
Investment required of not more than X%	Safety
Synergy with existing operations	Availability
New skills required	Consistency and quality
Speed to implement	Value for money
Degree of risk	Technical support

Weighting and rating the criteria enables us to plot the strategies on the matrix to reveal which strategies are worth pursuing and which should be rejected.

Biocatalysts need to plan for the short and medium term. In this fast, changing, dynamic market, longer term strategies can be difficult to identify. Strategy selection will need to provide immediate profits given your financial position, followed by medium term strategies that will grow the business and establish a competitive position.

The information we do have suggests the most attractive strategies are:

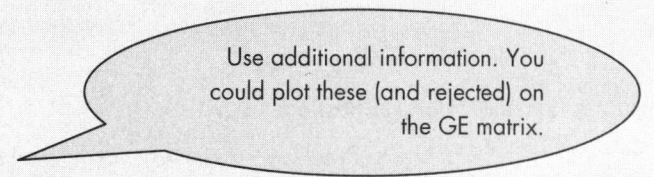

> Use additional information. You could plot these (and rejected) on the GE matrix.

- Short term market penetration strategy diagnostics
- Short to medium term market development strategy – Speciality foods
- Medium term new product development strategy – Technical support with selected products and as stand alone service

> You could indicate how much each strategy will contribute.

More accurate and up to date marketing research will confirm validity of this selection and profitability.

1.3.2 Competitive position

Strategy selection must be more focused than has been the case to date. The mission and vision will guide strategy selection and formulation. Biocatalysts cannot be all things to all people so product rationalisation and customer segmentation is going to be important. When formulating strategy, a clear competitive position should emerge and this can only be established through a co-ordinated effort by the business.

Analysis shows there are 12 major players in this market. Their size makes a cost leadership position possible. This is not an option for Biocatalysts given their size. The investment is too great. Increasingly even large companies are moving towards a differentiation strategy to improve their competitive position. 12 major players and 60 medium sized companies will be vying for positions using a differentiation strategy.

This leaves some 400 small companies, including Biocatalysts, to decide how they are going to compete. Analysis of the market and trends and Biocatalysts's strengths would indicate that a niche strategy would be the best option.

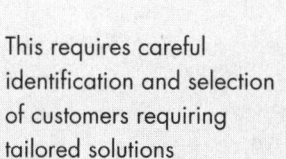

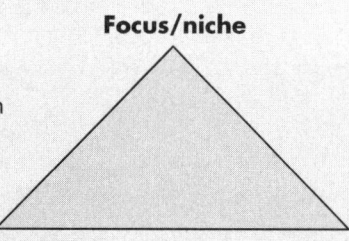

Focus/niche

This requires careful identification and selection of customers requiring tailored solutions

Niches must be assessed for their viability

Cost leadership **Differentiation**

1.4 Marketing objectives

An overall marketing objective is recommended to generate £12 million revenue by 2005 to deliver a £1.2 million profit.

Marketing objectives must then be further broken down by industry/market and for each strategy eg:

Diagnostics 35%   £4.2m (from £100K 1997) at 12% = £504K
Pharmaceuticals 35%   £4.2m (from £300K 1997) at 12% = £504K
Food 30%   £3.6m (from £960K 1997) at 5.3% = £192K

Part B: The sample case: Biocatalysts

1.5 Marketing strategy

A marketing strategy will need to be developed for each business strategy selected. The following plan is for speciality foods.

1.5.1 Segmentation

More information is required to segment the market effectively. However we do have some information, which will enable us to make a start.

Options for segmentation include initial segment bases determined by industry sectors, so for speciality foods, Kosher and vegetarian producers. Product, process and size of company may provide some opportunities for segmentation but none for competitive advantage. We must identify decision making units and needs and motives for buying. Many of these emerged during analysis. For example:

NEEDS	Users	Influencers	Deciders	Buyers	Approvers	Gatekeepers
Purity	X					
Cost efficiency				X		
Increase yield			X			

Research will improve information on precise needs and motives for Kosher and vegetarian foods. The technical support required may also affect segmentation. You may find customers from different sectors have commonalities by which we can segment. The advantage of this type of segmentation is that it can be used again, with small modifications and improvements, across national and industry boundaries.

1.5.2 Positioning

The positioning of the marketing mix should reflect the desired competitive position and customer needs. For example:

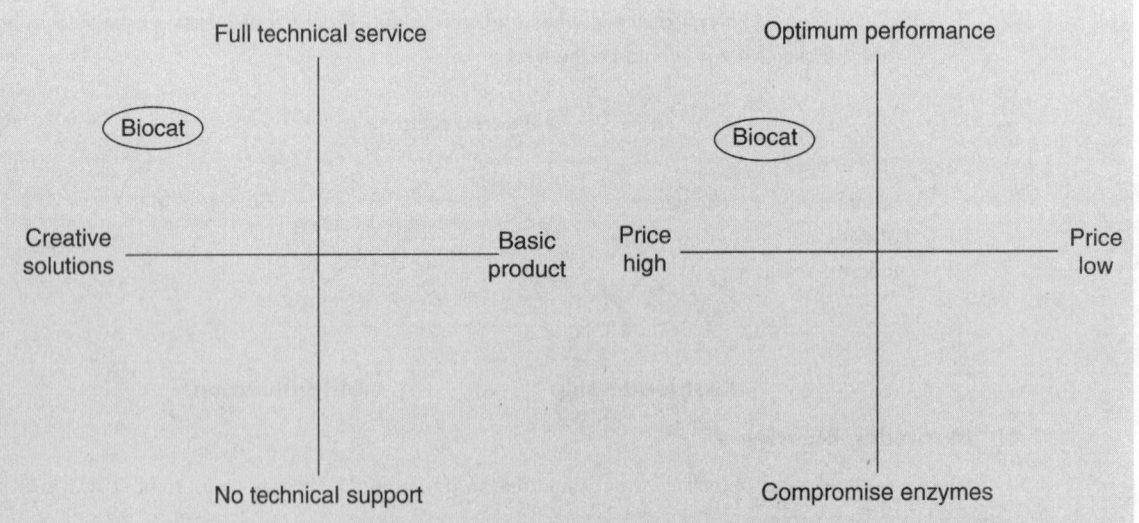

```
              Full technical service                          Optimum performance
                      |                                               |
                      |                                               |
          (Biocat)    |                                   (Biocat)    |
                      |                                               |
  Creative            |         Basic            Price                |         Price
  solutions ----------|-------- product          high  ---------------|-------- low
                      |                                               |
                      |                                               |
                      |                                               |
                      |                                               |
              No technical support                          Compromise enzymes
```

It is important to establish current competitor positions and to monitor this activity and ensure Biocatalysts maintain a position that differentiates itself from the rest.

The role of the brand will be crucial in communicating and establishing desired position.

1.5.3 Targeting

It is recommended that Biocatalyst pursue a multi-niche strategy. It would be risky to pursue only one niche for two reasons. The speed of change might result in a new entrant taking an interest in the niche and a single niche might not support the desired growth objectives.

The targeting strategy will therefore be differentiation. Specific needs of niches will be identified and marketing mixes designed to meet those needs.

1.6 Marketing mix plans

A distinct marketing mix plan will need to be developed for each niche targeted. By way of illustration, this plan is for speciality vegetarian foods.

1.6.1 Product

Objectives: to be determined: number of products sales by sector/market should be established

Actions: To rationalise the product range and ensure focus on profitable niches
To identify precise needs and possible future needs of vegetarian enzymes

1.6.2 Price

Aims: To reflect value for money and added value technical service: to achieve profit objective through premium price that reflects technical service

Actions: Research on price in the market and clarify price sensitive areas, complexities
Review sources of supply
Review impact of currency and exchange rate

1.6.3 Place

See answer 2

1.6.4 Promotion

See answer 3

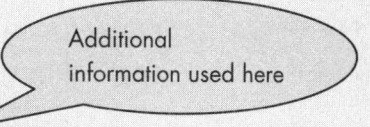

(Additional information used here)

1.6.5 Customer service and technical support (service 3Ps)

Aims: To provide full technical support that will add value and differentiate the company to establish clear competitive position

Actions: Research customers, existing and potential, to establish nature of technical support needed

Evaluate current skills levels, both technical and customer care, and identify training needs

Design training programmes and review recruitment policy to meet above

1.7 Control

1.7.1 Budget

Cash flow is a problem and the reality is this will affect the marketing budget. However with a more strategic, efficient and focused plan, the current budget can be used much more effectively. Biocatalysts should consider alliances with customers on some activities e.g. research to help finance plans. Omnibus research might be of use.

If Biocatalysts are to survive and succeed, money will need to be spent on marketing and a recommended budget of X%.

(You would need to specify)

1.7.2 Scheduling

It is not the intention to detail every activity, these will be included in each plan, but rather to cover broadly key tasks.

Part B: The sample case: Biocatalysts

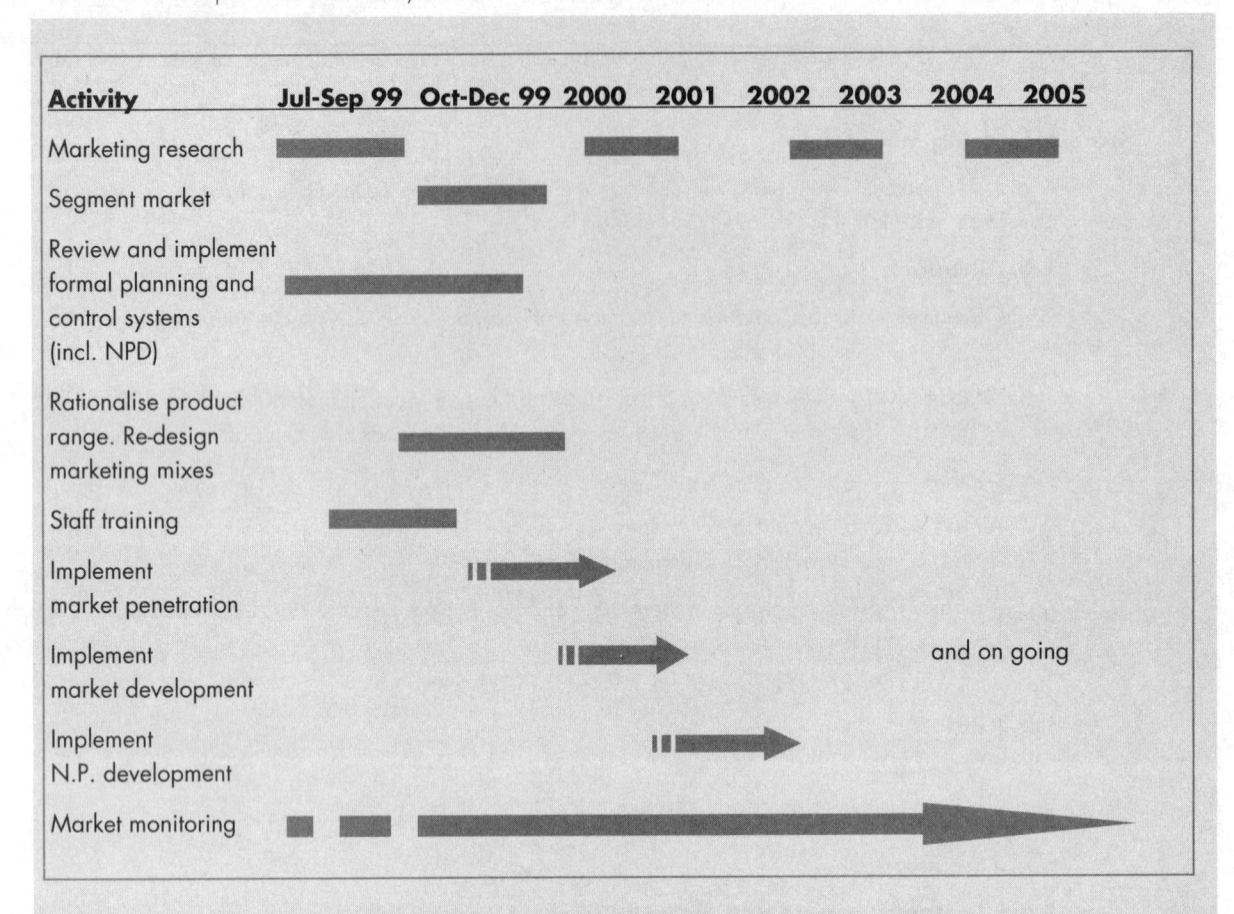

Activity	Jul-Sep 99	Oct-Dec 99	2000	2001	2002	2003	2004	2005
Marketing research	▬▬▬		▬▬▬		▬▬▬		▬▬▬	
Segment market		▬▬▬▬						
Review and implement formal planning and control systems (incl. NPD)	▬▬▬▬▬▬▬▬▬							
Rationalise product range. Re-design marketing mixes		▬▬▬▬▬▬						
Staff training		▬▬▬▬						
Implement market penetration		▬▬▶						
Implement market development			▬▬▶		and on going			
Implement N.P. development			▬▬▶					
Market monitoring	▬ ▬ ▬▬▬▬▬▬▬▬▬▬▬▬▬▬▬▬▬▬▬▬▶							

1.7.3 Measurement

Biocatalysts must track performance and ensure they are on course. Performance measures will include:

- Profits and profitability
- Product sales by sector
- Effectiveness of competitive positioning (customer, supplier, distributor surveys to track attitudes and perceptions)
- Customer satisfaction and loyalty
- Technical support performance

4.2 Question 2

2. International marketing strategy

The strategic marketing plan developed above has outlined vision, mission, business objectives, competitive position and issues on product and some market selection.

The intention in this plan is to recommend how Biocatalysts's international efforts can be very much more effective than they currently are.

2.1 Country/market selection

Not all markets are performing well and decisions need to be made on which markets to develop, particularly in view of Biocatalysts's limited resources.

A useful model for evaluating which countries or regions to operate in is the Harrell and Kiefer model. It works on the same principles as the GE matrix but the dimensions and criteria are different.

Criteria to enable the business to evaluate the attractiveness of the market eg:

Country attractiveness	**Biocatalyst's capabilities**
Political stability, risks and legal requirements	Experience of market
Economic conditions/growth	Investment required
Infrastructure	Management skills
Local technical skills and knowledge	Existing channel performance
Levels of competition	Control issues

We know from the additional information that the South Asian and South American economies have problems. Added to this, these markets have been significant textile markets, a market that appears to be commoditising, possibly in decline.

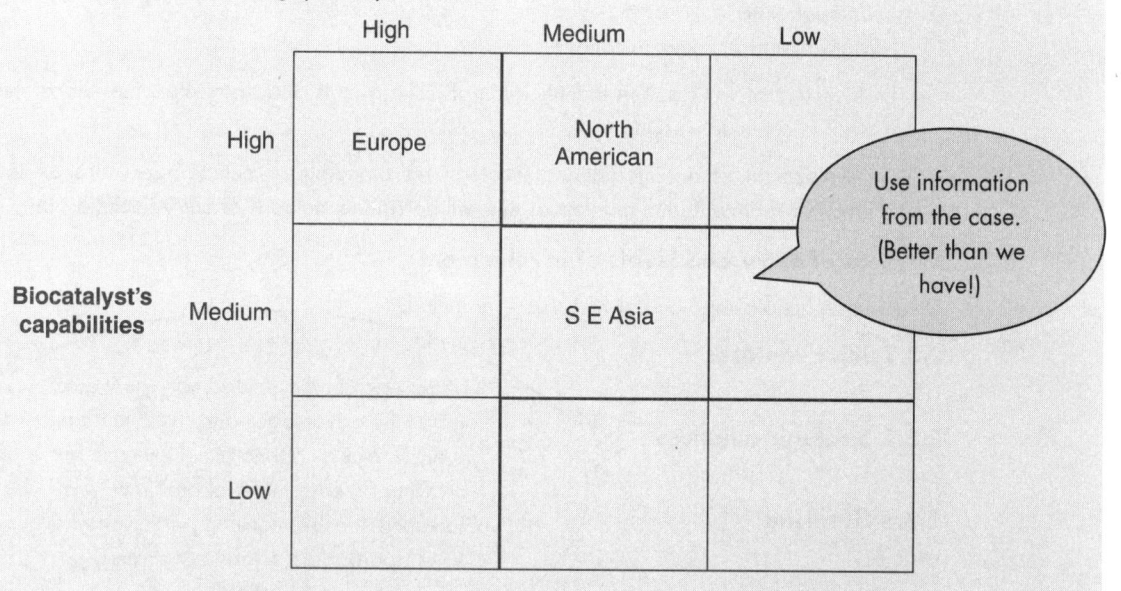

	High	Medium	Low
High	Europe	North American	
Medium		S E Asia	
Low			

(Biocatalyst's capabilities on vertical axis)

Use information from the case. (Better than we have!)

Europe and North American are stable markets where food, particularly specialist food, is a rapidly growing market. North America is very competitive and would be difficult, initially, for Biocatalysts to manage, given their financial situation. Europe, however, is closer to home and showing significant growth.

2.2 Agents and distributors

We must evaluate and rationalise the current network. The results of the analysis suggest performance is mixed. In some markets, Biocatalysts are hardly making enough money to make it worthwhile. The additional information suggests that agents in Hong Kong and Singapore are performing well as they are described as **'key offices'** so both these markets and agents are likely to be part of Biocatalysts's future developments in the medium-term when the economic situation improves. What we must establish for the short- and medium-term is the strength of distribution channels in Europe.

2.2.1 Evaluating current situations

As mentioned in the additional information, market conditions vary and will also need to be taken into account.

The GE matrix is again a very useful tool for evaluating distribution channels. The criteria will be different for evaluating distributors. Criteria will include for example:

Distribution attractiveness/performance

Order quantities/value
Profitability
Delivery performance
Technical know-how, experience, knowledge
Customer technical support capabilities (including problem handling)

Marketing performance (activities)
Market performance (penetration, development)

The customers' view of the effectiveness of distribution channels is important. They should be surveyed and their criteria will be similar to that discussed in part 1.

The evaluation process is two way. Biocatalysts need to establish their performance from the channels' point of view. Their criteria will include:

Reliability
Support – both technical and marketing
Profitability
Consistency
Compatibility
Motivation and communications

This exercise will result in identification of those agents and distributors that Biocatalysts will want to continue working with.

Development of an international strategy for Biocatalysts includes decisions on levels of involvement in different markets as this will determine methods of entry selected.

2.3 Methods of entry and levels of involvement

Other viable options for Biocatalyst to consider include:

2.3.1 Joint ventures

2.3.2 Strategic alliances

2.3.3 Licensing

2.3.4 Wholly owned subsidiary

> Under each of these headings you would discuss the advantages and disadvantages of each, **not** as a theoretical exercise but drawing on case material and in view of Biocatalysts' aspirations. In particular what is appropriate given your strategy selection?

2.4 Marketing objectives

Once countries/regions have been selected and methods of entry identified, marketing objectives by market can be established. Marketing research will clarify market value and therefore what Biocatalysts can realistically aim for. However there will be a minimum acceptable level for the market to be viable.

> Illustrate your quantified marketing objectives by market. Make sure they link back to the business objective

2.5 Marketing strategy

The marketing strategy will be developed along the lines illustrated in the five year plan. Specifically, segmentation will identify similar niches across Europe initially, other regions later, that can be targeted. Positioning should have a broad theme for all niches and each niche will have specific needs and values. Research will identify any market-specific issues.

2.6 Tactical plans

Marketing mix design must reflect the constraints of the country including laws, standards and cultural issues.

> You could expand briefly on the marketing mix but time would be against you

2.7 Control

Span of control increases with market development. Control issues include the extent of centralisation and decentralisation, and managing and motivating channels of distribution.

An important strategic issue will be the structure of the organisation as this impacts on control.

Budgets need to be set by market and measures of control would be similar to those outlined in the five year plan with performance measures for market and channel performance.

4.3 Question 3

3. Marketing communications strategy

Our communications strategy should focus on our customers and key stakeholders. However, as mentioned, in the current situation, there is increasing hostility in the market about GMOs in particular and, more generally, the biotechnology industry is beginning to suffer from some of the backlash. We therefore cannot ignore what is happening in our customers' markets. The responsibility for this hostility lies partly with governments and particularly with biotechnology companies, so we must be part of the solution.

Consumers in developed countries are usually better educated and informed and are more sophisticated and demanding. Governments and large companies have, in the past, presumed they know best and made decisions about goods and services with little, if any, consultation with consumers. Consumers want to be informed and will make decisions about purchases based on that information.

Biocatalysts has the opportunity to build a brand that represents quality, safety and ethical practice so is of value to our customers who in turn have to address the needs of their consumers.

3.1 Communications objectives

Broad aims can include the intention to inform, reassure and if necessary persuade and change attitudes towards biotechnology and GMOs. However it is important to be clear about what is to be achieved. Aims can include the need to raise awareness or attention, generate interest, create a desire and encourage action.

It is difficult to quantify objectives until we have some indication of number of customers and stakeholders we need to influence. Once this has been established we can set quantified objectives. For example:

To raise awareness from X% to X% within three years of the benefits of GMOs

To change attitudes towards GMOs from a negative view of X% to a positive view of X% within five years

3.2 Communications strategy

Because of Biocatalysts' limited financial and marketing resources, some realistic decisions will have to be made about the development of communications strategy.

Biocatalysts should have a push and profile strategy. It is essential to ensure effective use of all resources and maximum impact on the marketplace.

A pull strategy is unrealistic and must be left to your customers. Biocatalyst's role could be to provide evidence and information to help customers communicate more effectively with consumers.

Part B: The sample case: Biocatalysts

This support might encourage customers to return the support and help with the funding of some communication activities.

Biocatalysts customers' pull strategies will play a significant role in dealing with negative perceptions and cannot be ignored.

3.2.1 Push

This strategy will be designed to encourage and persuade existing and new distribution channels and business to business customers to purchase Biocatalysts's enzymes and services.

3.2.2 Profile

This strategy is intended to promote broader issues to a wider audience, the complex and very influential stakeholders involved in this industry.

The communications strategy will build the brand and competitive position over time.

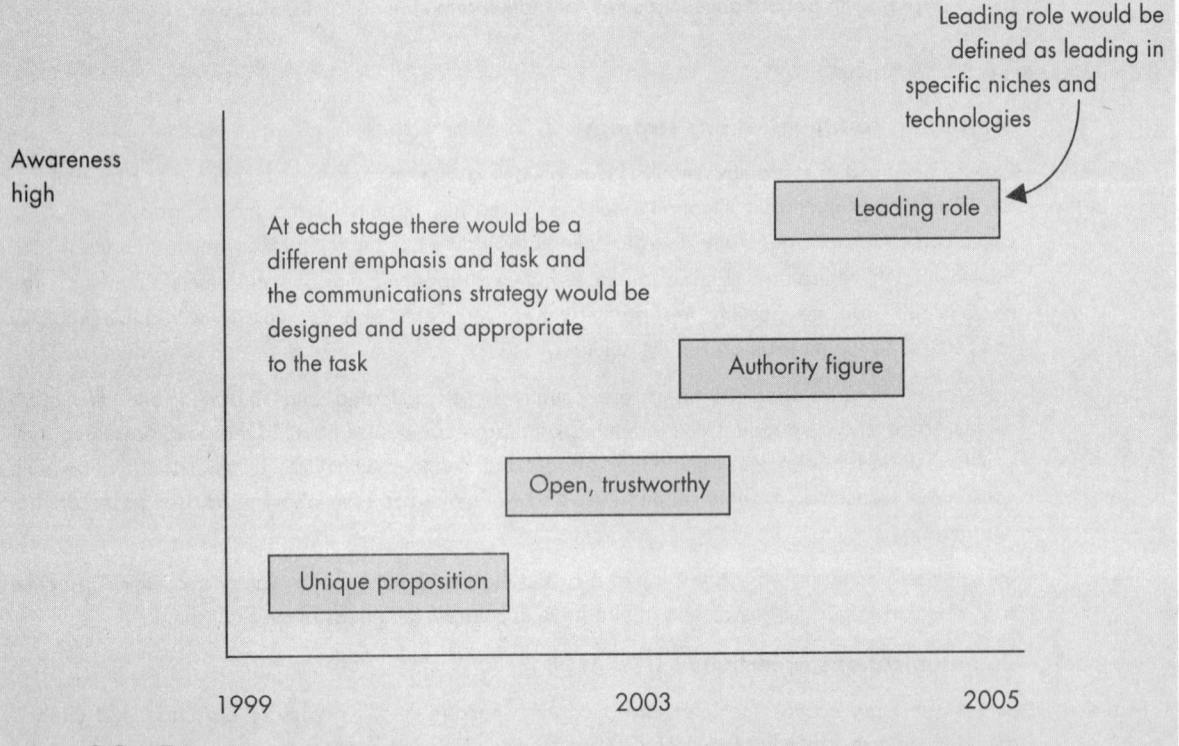

At each stage there would be a different emphasis and task and the communications strategy would be designed and used appropriate to the task

Leading role would be defined as leading in specific niches and technologies

Awareness high

- Leading role
- Authority figure
- Open, trustworthy
- Unique proposition

1999   2003   2005

3.3 Targets

The targets for communications will be broader than the marketing strategy. The reason for this is the need to influence the significant number of stakeholders involved that in turn influence, directly or indirectly, developments in the biotechnology industry. These stakeholders include:

Performance network - stakeholders directly influencing include:

- Suppliers, MAFF, FDA, universities, agents/distributors, industry producers, consumers, competitors, employees

Support network - Stakeholders that indirectly influence include

- Pressure groups, industry analysts, investigators, scientists, journalists, trade bodies, religious groups, slaughterhouses, environment agencies, food and drug agencies, governments

All stakeholders need to be targeted with clear, tailored messages and promotional mixes to ensure effective communications.

3.4 Promotional activities

3.4.1 Positioning and messages

The key issue to address in this business is that of trust. Consumers have lost faith with businesses and governments and no longer trust them to make decisions that are in the best interests of consumers.

This is an opportunity for Biocatalysts to position themselves as trustworthy and as the biotechnology company that puts safety first. Testing procedures would take account of consumer concerns, not just the profit motive. Creativity is going to be vital and Biocatalysts, while able to provide the information, do not have the creative communications skills. An agency will need to be considered.

```
                    Reputation for trust and safety
                                |
              (Biocat)          |
                                |
    Rigorous testing            |            Minimal testing
    procedures      ------------+------------ procedures
                                |
                                |
                                |
                    Disregard for public concern
```

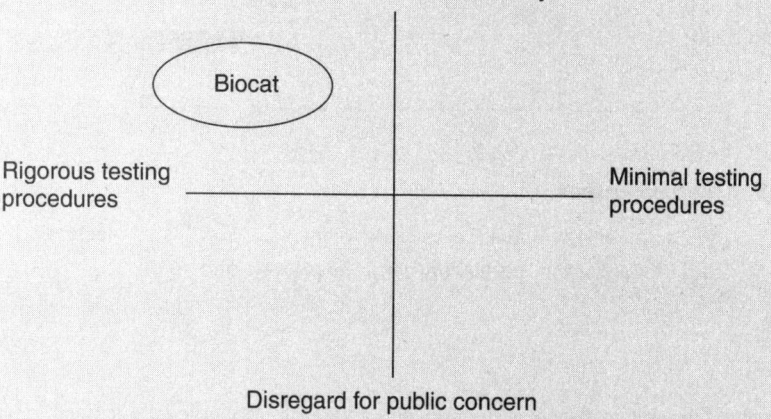

3.4.2 Promotional mix

Because of limited financial resources, the promotional budget will have to be used creatively. PR will be a main feature, which is in Biocatalysts favour because of its credibility and the current interest. Identifying newsworthy items will be crucial.

There has never been a better opportunity to tap into the 'human interest' story and encourage media to print.

Push strategy – sales force, technical support team, brochures, exhibitions, trade press

Profile strategy – PR, papers at seminars and conferences, explore opportunities for sponsorship

3.5 Control

3.5.1 Budget

[Margin note: You would need to specify]

Biocatalysts's cash flow problems means that, until improved market penetration leads to improved profits, the communications strategy, though crucial, will have a slow start. However until research is completed the design of the campaign cannot start in earnest.

Other sources of funds should be reviewed and allocation of existing marketing budgets examined for more effective use. This can be used in the short term with more funds allocated as profits improve.

A budget of £X is recommended for the first year, increasing to £X for years 2 – 4. By year 5 the success of the campaign should lead a lower volume of funds being required. However the communications effort will remain vital and should be sustained.

Part B: The sample case: Biocatalysts

3.5.2 Schedule

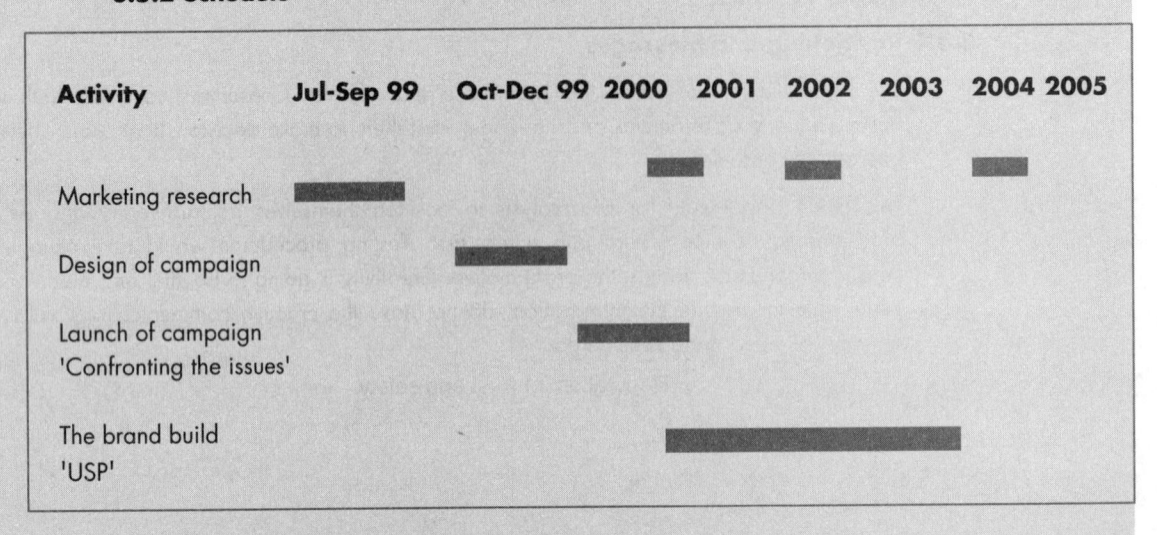

Activity	Jul-Sep 99	Oct-Dec 99	2000	2001	2002	2003	2004	2005
Marketing research	■■			■	■		■	
Design of campaign		■■						
Launch of campaign 'Confronting the issues'			■■					
The brand build 'USP'				■■■■■■■■■■■■				

3.5.3 Measurement

Measurements will include tracking attitudes to GMOs, biotechnology companies generally and Biocatalysts in particular, awareness levels and so on.

Appendices

For Marketing Strategy in Practice students six pages of appendices will be added here. Remember the more you have related these to your report the more marks you will get.

Part C

Practice Cases

Tackling a Practice Case: Reiss

Chapter Topic List

1	Introduction
2	Reiss: text and appendices
3	Step 1: Initial overview
4	Step 2: Completing your overview
5	Step 3: Assessing your overview
6	Highlights from the overview
7	Summary

1 Introduction

Tackling a Practice Case: Reiss

1.1 You have already been practising your case study skills by working the Biocatalysts case study, as we demonstrated the approach in Section B. This second case is one you really should work through yourself, using the materials we have provided as samples against which you can monitor and benchmark your own output. Simply reading the material is really not good enough. Case study analysis, as you have seen, is made up of a series of techniques which you need to develop and practice for yourself so that by the time the exam case is issued, you are confident about tackling it, whatever the business or sector.

1.2 In the second half of this manual, you will find two more cases. We have included the next, Reiss, with analysis and decision material developed by student groups actually working the case study. The final case study, Centrica, is to give you a final rehearsal case and is supported only with general guidance and some tutor comment.

1.3 For Reiss, we will remind you at each stage of the case of the steps you should be following and then present you with our material and any necessary tutor comments. We will not be reminding you of 'how' to tackle each step, so if you are in doubt, you will need to refer back to section B.

By the end of this chapter, you will have:

(a) Read the Reiss case
(b) Completed your overview analysis
(c) Compared your analysis with our tutor comments and feedback
(d) Tested your understanding of the case

Part C: Practice cases

> **Case Step 1**
>
> *Complete the overview*
>
> Consult Chapter 4 for detailed 'how to' guidance.
>
> (a) Read the case study
>
> (b) Stop and think about the case context
>
> (c) Sort out the case narrative into topic areas eg finance, marketing environment etc
>
> (d) Identify what is included in the Appendices and what information their analysis might generate
>
> (e) Remember to start your information shopping list

2 Reiss: text and appendices

The Chartered Institute of Marketing

Case Study
December 2003

Strategic Marketing Management: Analysis & Decision

Reiss

© The Chartered Institute of Marketing

… Part C: Practice cases

Case Study – December 2003

Strategic Marketing Management: Analysis & Decision

Important Notes for Candidates

The examiners will be marking your scripts on the basis of questions put to you in the examination room. Candidates are advised to pay particular attention to the *mark allocation on the examination paper and budget their time accordingly.*

Your role is outlined in the candidates' brief and you will be required to recommend clear courses of action.

You WILL NOT be awarded marks merely for analysis. This should have been undertaken before the examination day in preparation for meeting the tasks which will be specified in the examination paper.

Candidates are advised not to waste valuable time collecting unnecessary data. The cases are based upon real world situations. No useful purpose will therefore be served by contacting companies in this industry and candidates are **strictly instructed not to do so as it may cause unnecessary confusion.**

As in real life, anomalies will be found in the information provided within this case. Please simply state your assumptions where necessary when answering questions. The CIM is not in a position to answer queries on case data. Candidates are tested on their overall understanding of the case and its key issues, not on minor details. There are no catch questions or hidden agendas.

Additional information will be introduced in the examination paper itself, which candidates must take into account when answering the questions set.

Acquaint yourself thoroughly with the case study and be prepared to follow closely the instructions given to you on the examination day. To answer examination questions effectively candidates must adopt a report format.

The copying of pre-prepared "group" answers, including those written by consultants/tutors, is strictly forbidden and will be penalised by failure. The questions will demand analysis in the examination itself and individually composed answers are required to pass.

Page 1 of Reiss

Candidate's Brief

You have been appointed as a Marketing Consultant to the Senior Management Team at Reiss. Reiss have recently more than doubled the size of their retail operations by entering the lucrative womenswear sector of the clothing market in September 2000. In 2002 they opened their first international store in Dublin, and they are using this operation as a test-bed for further expansion internationally. The company considers itself to have a unique place in the market being a "bridging brand" between high priced designer labels and lower priced mass-market clothing brands. Fashion markets are notoriously fickle and consumers have become more demanding, expecting value for money with design led fashion. Parents dress more like their children these days than like their own parents at their age, and lifestyle is often more important than age in targeting fashion markets. As a consequence traditional market segmentation is more difficult to apply in this market. Reiss realise that they are only just beginning to move towards their long-term goal of establishing the brand internationally as well as in the UK. Careful planning, investment in design, product development, purchasing, production and supply management, merchandising, store environments and marketing are the keys to their success. During the past six months a graduate employed by the company prepared the attached report on the fashion industry, Reiss, and its recent developments. You have been asked to prepare for detailed questions about future marketing strategies posed by the Senior Management Team at a meeting on the 5th December 2003.

Important Notice

This case material is based on an actual organisation and existing market conditions.

Candidates are strictly instructed NOT TO CONTACT Reiss or any other companies in the industry. Additional information will be provided at the time of the examination. Further copies may be obtained from The Chartered Institute of Marketing, Moor Hall, Cookham, Maidenhead, Berkshire, SL6 9QH, UK or may be downloaded from the CIM student web site www.cimvirtualinstitute.com

---

© The Chartered Institute of Marketing

Page 2 of Reiss

Reiss

Reiss is a retailer of "own brand" quality fashion menswear and womenswear. It is a profitable company that established itself in London and the South East in the 1970s. During the past five years the company has grown organically and rapidly. In 2000, Reiss developed a womenswear brand to complement the long established menswear brand. The entrepreneurial owner David Reiss is the driving force behind the business.

This report begins by explaining the company and its development and the fashion industry context before discussing the designerwear market in more detail.

Reiss the Entrepreneur

David Reiss was born in London in the 1950s. He took over his father's business (wholesaling menswear) in the early 1970s and for some time owned a factory in Yorkshire where he produced his own collection. It was in 1980 that the first Reiss store opened on the King's Road, Chelsea, and it proved an immediate hit with customers. Reiss continued to open new stores in the 1980s and sold a mixture of wholesale garments and his own designed collection.

In 1987 the emphasis switched completely to retailing collections designed in-house. This was a bold move; one which David thought would guarantee the future. Establishing and developing a brand was important for Reiss. However, the final years of the decade became turbulent times for all retailers, and the recession that hit the high street hard led to a rationalisation of the company and its structure. Inventory control, careful buying, and cash flow management were essential to the survival of the business and for building a solid base for the future. Today the company has a wholesale side, 25 retail stores, and owns some prime city-centre properties. In 1997 David won the Menswear/FHM Retailer of the Year Award, and Reiss received "highly commended" from readers of Maxim in their 2001 style awards.

David's vision, energy, imagination, flair and creative abilities have driven the business forward in a determined manner. In 1998 David recognised the opportunity in the fashion market between the high street and the international designer brands and decided to target this gap. The strategy proved so successful he decided it was time to fulfil the same niche role in the womenswear market. An external agency helped to gather market research information prior to the launch of the womenswear brand.

Reiss the Stores

From its roots selling Italian suits in 1971, essentially over the next 25 years Reiss remained a small menswear business, although a number of new stores were added. With the opening of the Bond Street Store in London in 1997 the business entered a period of rapid growth and change. There were four new store openings in 1998 in Newcastle-upon-Tyne, Brighton, Trafford Park (Manchester), and Hampstead (London), and three additional stores were added in 1999 at the Bluewater Shopping Centre (just outside London), Nottingham, and Glasgow, Royal Exchange.

Page 3 of Reiss

In 2000 Reiss made a radical departure from its roots in menswear and entered the highly competitive and lucrative womenswear market for the first time. Following significant investment in a womenswear division, womenswear was introduced into 13 of the company's 19 stores in September 2000. Womenswear accounted for 21 per cent of turnover in 2001 and increased to around 30 per cent by the end of 2002, (see Appendix 1 for financial summaries). With the successful launch of its womenswear brand, Reiss opened its Central London flagship store at Kent House, Market Place, spanning three floors with over 6,000 square feet of selling space. This was a significant step in raising the profile and perception of the Reiss brand. More store openings followed in major city locations and the first non-UK store, Dublin, was added in 2002. Three concessions were added in 2002, selling Reiss products through House of Fraser Stores at Bluewater, Glasgow and Birmingham. A fourth concession at House of Fraser (King William Street, London) was added in 2003.

During the last three years Reiss has worked with London architects Lever and Hopley to completely redesign the stores' image to project a fresh, modern style (see Appendix 4 showing Reiss stores). With all clothing and accessories designed in-house, the clothing, graphics, displays and interiors can achieve continuity and directness in design. The signature style mixes rough with smooth, creating an urban look – sandblasted walls set against smooth steel, floating oak and steel staircases, limestone floors, clear and sandblasted glass, exposed steel rafters and raw steel tables. These are combined with geometric form wall openings, counters in pebble resin, and floating wall mountings with glowing surrounds. Each store retains original features where possible to combine character with clean, modern styling. Historical stores include Glasgow, which is in a Grade 1 listed building spanning three floors, including an original Victorian staircase restored to its original shape and structure. Nottingham is also a Grade 1 listed building, formerly a dining hall for 19th Century lace workers. The original wrought-iron glazed roof and the Gothic arched frontage were fully restored. The Liverpool store, situated in the heart of the Cavern Quarter, features an impressive five-metre-high doorway, structurally cut into the building to expose both floors, and making the second floor appear to be suspended.

Page 4 of Reiss

Table 1. – Reiss Stores, August 2003

Number	Name	Date Opened	Square Footage
001	King's Road	1977	3,680
002	Birmingham	1979	Relocated
004	Manchester King Street	1984	2,163
005	Long Acre	1985	3,612
009	Glasgow Princes Square	1988	925
007	Bond Street	1997	3,292
008	Newcastle	1998	2,052
010	Brighton	1998	1,219
011	Trafford Park	1998	1,743
012	Hampstead	1998	1,505
013	Bluewater	1999	1,722
014	Nottingham	1999	4,767
015	Glasgow Royal Exchange	1999	2,755
016	Kent House	2000	6,147
017	Liverpool	2001	1,800
018	Chester	2001	2,701
033	Lowry	2001	1,800
032	Livingston	2002	1,148
790	House of Fraser Glasgow©	2002	500
791	House of Fraser Bluewater©	2002	800
792	House of Fraser Rackhams©	2002	450
019	Cambridge	2002	2,000
020	Kingston	2002	2,000
021	Regent Street	2002	3,000
400	Dublin	2002	3,000
022	Leeds	2003	3,200
023	Manchester Shambles	2003	4,000
024	Birmingham	2003	4,000
025	Broadgate	2003	1,100
026	Canary Wharf	2003	3,000

© = concessions

Source: Company files

Thirteen stores have been opened in the past three years, together with the three concessions in House of Fraser. Guildford is the latest new store to open in 2003, bringing the total to fourteen in three years. Store development and visual marketing remain a priority in the progression of the Reiss business.

Improvements have continued in 2003 with significant increases in trade. Also the product range in both menswear and womenswear is expanding to include accessories. Turnover in 1999 was around £17 million, and is forecast to be £35 million in 2003. The company is now poised to capitalise on its market domestically and internationally.

Reiss ceased wholesaling in 2001, enabling the company to have complete control over where its clothes are sold and also to give total commitment to the expansion of the retail division.

Page 5 of Reiss

The Management Structure

The rapid expansion of the business in the past three years has led the company to develop a professional management team that can take the business forward to its next stage of growth. Figure 1 gives details of the new management structure.

Figure 1.

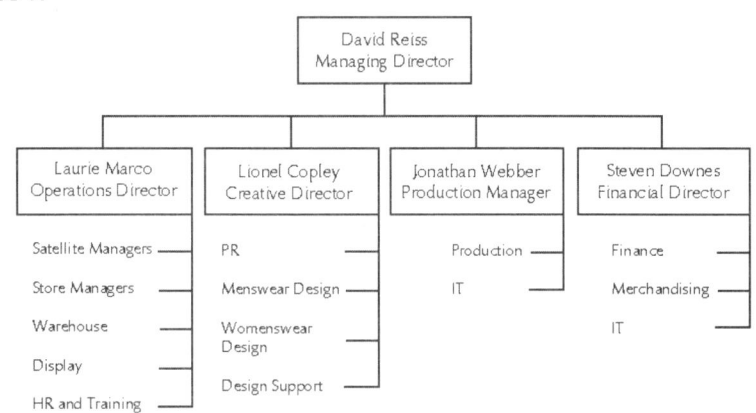

```
                        David Reiss
                     Managing Director
    ┌───────────────┬──────────────┬──────────────┐
 Laurie Marco   Lionel Copley  Jonathan Webber  Steven Downes
 Operations     Creative       Production       Financial
 Director       Director       Manager          Director

 Satellite Managers   PR                Production       Finance
 Store Managers       Menswear Design   IT               Merchandising
 Warehouse            Womenswear                         IT
 Display              Design
 HR and Training      Design Support
```

Source: Company files

Steven Downes, Financial Director (FD), has wider responsibilities than one might expect of the traditional FD. One important function that Steven manages is merchandising. Essentially this function is key to managing retail stocks and product throughput. The Merchandising Department was established in 2003 and has had a significant impact on improving the flow and management of the product in the business. Sales volumes and margins have improved and inventories have lowered substantially in the last year. In the coming year the intention is to focus management effort on reviewing stock levels at stores relative to space and store turnover.

Merchandising is a critical role for most fashion retailers. The preparation of seasonal buying plans with other key members of the team through thorough analysis of historical sales data and an understanding of future trends is key. Retailers must establish Key Performance Indicators (KPIs) that cover sales, stock intake phasing, margins, stock-turn, mark-down and terminal stock. Monitoring trading and in-season changes requires attention if retailers are to maximise profitability and reduce risks.

The rapid growth of the management team has put a premium on office space inside Reiss, and the plan is to move to new offices at Oxford Circus, located beneath the Kent House store in January 2004. The possible synergies from the interaction of different departments are expected to bring a number of benefits. It is envisaged that the move will help the business to develop and improve its internal communications. Having staff located in one place will mean that meetings can take place on a single site and people will be available. It may also help the creative processes become more effective.

Page 6 of Reiss

Jonathan Webber is the Production Manager and his job entails turning a designer's sketch into the finished products that are delivered to the warehouse. The product then becomes the responsibility of the Operations Director, who gets the products to the stores. Designers primarily source the fabric for a style they have in mind. However, the Production Manager often has to cross-source the fabric as designers are usually not very commercially aware. This is an important decision in developing fashion products because the price at which fabrics can be bought determines the price points retailers set in store. Fabrics are sourced from a variety of countries, depending on the properties of the particular fabric required. China (including Hong Kong), South Korea, Japan, Romania, Italy and Turkey are regular sourcing destinations. Turkey, for example, has moved up the scale in terms of cotton fabric supply in recent months. Previously these cotton fabrics would probably have been sourced from Italian mills, who may have in turn sub-contracted the work to Turkish mills. Where possible Reiss go direct to Turkey and avoid the "Italian middle-man". Nevertheless, fabric is really the domain of the Italians when it comes to the special fabrics, fabrics with special treatments and finishes that Reiss requires for its "edgy fashion". For example, bonded fabrics would be bought from Italy. Double twisted ("doppio retorto") fabrics to accommodate and minimise perspiration would be supplied from Italy. Standard cottons can be obtained anywhere, and the Italians tend to go to Turkey or China and buy it in to supply rather than produce it themselves. It is not simply specially treated fabrics but the size of fabric order that is an important constraint on sourcing. Asia Pacific fabric suppliers only wish to supply 2,000-3,000 metres of fabric as a minimum quantity. For some lines Reiss is able to meet these minimum order quantities, but only when the fabric can be shared across mens' and womenswear, covering two or three styles in two or three colours. However, this is a rarity.

Unlike many large clothing retailers, Reiss does not have many continuity lines that repeat season in and season out. As a consequence they do not tend to buy large quantities of "greige" fabric, which is what some larger retailers tend to do with the aim of printing designs and colours when demand is known. It is easy to do this if the fabric itself is relatively less important. Reiss however does not tend to buy the same fabrics continuously because they are a fashion company trading designerwear, and pride themselves on offering the customer something new in terms of style, colour and fabrics. The fashion in fabrics changes over time. For Reiss, greige fabric would not exceed 10 per cent of its total fabric purchases.

Trims are another important aspect of purchasing for Reiss. Trims are the responsibility of one specialist inside the business who sources for both mens and womenswear. Although trims are small, they are a major part of a fashion garment. If the trim is wrong it will prevent the sale and if it is right it can help sell it. Womenswear is significantly more trim orientated than menswear. Reiss has had to develop and learn to manage this important aspect, especially since entering the womenswear market. It is another consideration when planning production.

One of the biggest influences affecting sourcing is exchange rates. If the exchange rate deteriorates between the placing of an order and the receipt of finished garments, it adversely impacts upon cost and hence the forecast profit margins. With the opening of its Dublin store Reiss will also need to monitor the effect of exchange rates on its retailing activities.

Page 7 of Reiss

The Fashion Industry Context

The fashion industry at retail value in 2002 was worth £26 billion in the UK, excluding footwear and leather (footwear and leather goods account for nearly £4 billion). European apparel was worth $324 billion and $314 billion in the USA in 2002. Retail supply chains span the globe in the search for the right fabrics, trims, and for the manufacturers who can deliver the right products, at the right price, at the right time. In the UK the fashion industry accounts for around 7 per cent of the Gross Domestic Product (GDP).

The fashion industry is notoriously fickle. A glance at the daily newspapers and trade press will indicate just how fickle fashion can be. Lead times in sourcing and production inevitably create their own pressures, adding to the uncertainty of a highly risky retail environment. Time to market can be critical. Whenever sales fall retailers provide a list of reasons why they have not been as successful in selling this season's ranges. Weather is nearly always top of this list. For example, worse than expected weather during a summer season can lead to a fall in sales of light summer clothing, or a warmer than expected autumn period can lead to a downturn in the sale of autumn and winter outerwear ranges. There are also differences in purchases by country and by region, owing to external factors other than mere fashion trends. For example, London accounts for a substantial proportion of total expenditure on formal wear, suits, overcoats, hats, gloves, ties and traditional leather shoes. A partial explanation for this might be found in the large numbers of people employed in professional offices travelling by public transport. In provincial cities, where more people tend to travel by car, the need for overcoats, hats and gloves is lower than that demanded in London. Additionally, retailers who have tried to expand their business to international locations have to be sure that they understand the market drivers behind the purchases. Southern Europe, where climates are generally warmer, may not appreciate the ranges that a retail store in Glasgow or Edinburgh would offer! Demographic trends and physical attributes also contribute to the complexity experienced by the fashion retailer. Average shirt collar sizes, waistlines, chest sizes and leg length have all become bigger in the UK since the 1960s. The UK population has grown by around 10 million since 1960, and the make-up of that population has changed over time. People live longer and the numbers over the age of fifty is set to increase to over 50 per cent by 2020. All of these factors contribute to the changing nature of fashion and retailing.

Page 8 of Reiss

Table 2. – Size of Apparel Segments in the UK 1997 (£m)

Women's outerwear	11,785	
Lingerie	1,675	
Hosiery	508	
Womenswear total	**13,968**	56.60%
Men's outerwear	6,036	
Men's underwear	610	
Menswear total	**6,646**	26.93%
Childrenswear	4,064	16.47%
Total	**24,678**	100.00%

Source: UK Fashion Report, EMAP/MTI 1999

Table 2 gives an indication of the size of particular market segments, split between women and menswear in 1997. The womenswear segment is more than double the size of menswear. This is an interesting statistic because more men are in employment and generally male disposable income is higher.

Within the UK, clothing retailing is highly concentrated in the hands of a small number of large retail chains who dominate the market (see Table 3). The so called "middle market" in particular has been saturated in recent years, with too many retailers chasing the same customers, with very little difference in the product offer apart from price. As a consequence some high profile "exits" from the high street have occurred (C&A, Littlewoods), whilst some new entrants from international retailers (Zara, Mango, Hennes & Mauritz), and non-traditional retail sectors such as supermarket chains (George at Asda Wal-Mart, Tesco and Sainsbury), have developed their clothing offers. Nevertheless, other specialists, including independent retail outlets, still accounted for 26 per cent of the market. Reiss is a retailer that falls into this latter category.

Page 9 of Reiss

Table 3.

UK Clothing Market Shares 1999

Specialist Retailers	(%)
Marks and Spencer	11.00
Arcadia	8.20
Next	4.50
C&A*	2.20
BhS	2.20
New Look	1.60
Matalan	1.30
Littlewoods*	1.10
River Island	1.10
Gap	0.90
Etam	0.80
Monsoon	0.60
Oasis	0.50
Austin Reed	0.40
Others	26.00
Total Specialists	**62.40**

Source: EMAP/E-business

Total UK Clothing Market

All Retailers	(%)
Specialists	62.40
Grocers (Supermarkets)	4.90
Department Stores	12.30
Mail Order	12.30
Other	8.10
Total	100.00

Source: Verdict/E-business

* These two retailers exited from the UK High Street market in 2000 after many years.

The smaller independent retailers face a number of challenges. They do not generally have large selling spaces by comparison with their large counterparts, and as a consequence they find it difficult to achieve any economies of scale. In fact they may suffer from quite the reverse. These firms have to make decisions about merchandise that determine and define their market position more clearly. For example, should they offer established designer brands, and more importantly, will the brand allow them to? If they choose this route they may be constrained by the brands in terms of promotion, pricing, products, and how and what they can sell. Should they offer non-branded goods? Should they contract their own clothing ranges? Should they establish their own brand label? There are no easy answers to these questions.

Page 10 of Reiss

The Specific Market Sector – Designerwear in the UK

Designerwear is defined as haute couture and diffusion, off-the-peg ranges, where usually the label is a designer name. The latter are often called "bridge collections". This report focuses on the latter category, where Reiss is competing with other bridge collections. Designerwear products are priced at a premium and consumers are more likely to buy such items when levels of discretionary income are high. In this respect a rise in the number of working women (from 12.04 million in 1997 to 12.74 million in 2001, a rise of almost 6%) has contributed significantly to the recent growth of this sector. The most fashion-conscious age group are the 15-24 year olds. This age group is forecast to expand by 7% between 2001 and 2006 (Mintel, 2002). The number of 55-64 year olds is also set to grow, but this group have more traditional tastes that may impact negatively on the designerwear market unless the products offered meet the needs of these customers as they experience a different lifestage.

The UK designerwear market is highly fragmented in nature, represented by a large number of small players and relatively few large suppliers. According to Mintel (2002), the ten most desirable brands are in rank order: Calvin Klein (26%), Giorgio Armani (26%), Gucci (25%), Versace (18%), Christian Dior (15%), Ralph Lauren/Polo (15%), Burberry (14%), Hugo Boss (13%), Yves St Laurent (13%), and Chanel (11%).

In recent years designers have been prepared to extend their market coverage by entering partnerships with retail stores. Debenhams was the first store to enter agreements with 26 designers under its "Designers at Debenhams" initiative. Marks and Spencer (M&S) launched the "Autograph" collection in February 2000, hoping to emulate the success of Debenhams and recapture some of its lost market with designers such as Betty Jackson (womenswear) and Timothy Everest (menswear). M&S also launched "Per Una" in partnership with George Davis. These initiatives have broadened the appeal of designerwear and the retail partnerships have made the clothes more accessible.

A number of key factors influence the size and structure of the UK market for designerwear. Demographic, social and economic factors, as well as fashion trends, play a large part, as do availability of product, pricing, and advances in retail distribution.

Demographic Trends

According to the Office of National Statistics (ONS) data and Mintel, the working population is increasing whilst the number of people unemployed is falling and will remain low in the foreseeable future. Steady growth in the numbers of women in employment has led to greater financial independence, and more women are in professional employment where they need to wear smart clothing. Women as a grouping also tend to spend more on clothing and have a higher propensity than their male counterparts to spend on fashion. Working women are often time-poor, which leads to a boost in retail activity at the outlets most convenient to shop at. This includes supermarkets, some of which now open 24 hours a day. Convenience and availability are paramount to women when purchasing clothes.

Page 11 of Reiss

Table 4. – Workforce in Employment in the UK, by Gender and Employment Level, 1997-2006

	Men m	%	Women m	%	Total m	Index	Unemployed m	Index
1997	14.99	55	12.04	45	27.07	100	2.09	100
1998	15.19	56	12.13	45	27.32	101	1.83	88
1999	15.33	55	12.32	45	27.64	102	1.81	87
2000	15.53	55	12.47	45	27.99	103	1.70	81
2001	15.66	55	12.74	45	28.41	105	1.50	72
2003 (est)	15.62	55	12.87	45	28.49	105	1.65	79
2006 (proj)	15.85	55	13.07	45	28.92	107	1.60	77

(Data may not equal totals due to rounding.)

Source: National Statistics/Mintel

Table 4 indicates that the workforce is composed of 55 per cent men and 45 per cent women. Unemployment was at its lowest level for five years in 2001, and the numbers in employment rose by 5 per cent over the period, with female employment rising at a faster rate than male employment. This is good news for fashion retailers whose market is dominated by female expenditure. More women in work increases the demand for smarter, more fashionable, workwear as well as leisurewear. Consumer expenditure surveys show that women are more inclined to spend their income on designerwear than their male colleagues, although younger males spend more than their older colleagues. One consequence is that the increase in the number of women working will have a positive effect on the designerwear market. Table 5 shows the number of young people in the age band 15-24 year old is set to rise by 7 per cent between 2001-2006, and it is widely reported that this group are more likely to spend a higher proportion of their income on branded fashionwear.

Table 5. – Trends and Projections in UK Adult Population, by Age Group, 1997-2006

	1997 000	%	2001 000	%	2006 (proj) 000	%	% change 1997-2001	% change 2001-06
15-19	3,602	8	3,727	8	3,995	8	+3	+7
20-24	3,628	8	3,635	7	3,903	8	-	+7
25-34	9,360	20	8,679	18	7,857	16	-7	-9
35-44	8,294	17	9,213	19	9,645	19	+11	+5
45-54	7,696	16	7,877	16	8,028	16	+2	+2
55-64	5,783	12	6,248	13	7,229	14	+8	+16
65+	9,272	19	9,369	19	9,585	19	+1	+2
Total	47,635	100	48,747	100	50,239	100	+2	+3

(Data may not equal totals due to rounding.)

Source: National Statistics/GAD/Mintel

Page 12 of Reiss

Social and Economic Change

Consumer behaviour is constantly changing. Personal Disposable Income (PDI) rose by 11% between 1997 and 2001, and there is a further projected increase of 13% between 2001 and 2006 according to Mintel (2002). PDI is the greatest influence on people's propensity to spend. PDI generates a "feel good factor". For example, if mortgage payments reduce, payments on loans reduce, taxes reduce, and incomes rise, people feel happier about spending more. As Table 6 indicates, PDI increased by 11 per cent between 1997 and 2001 and consumer expenditure grew by 16 per cent.

Table 6. – PDI and Consumer Expenditure, 1997-2006

	PDI at 1997 Prices £bn	Index	Consumer Expenditure at 1997 Prices £bn	Index	Savings Ratio %
1997	577.6	100	523.0	100	9.5
1998	575.9	100	542.6	104	5.7
1999	594.5	103	566.2	108	4.8
2000	619.5	107	587.9	112	5.0
2001	641.1	111	605.3	116	5.1
2003 (est)	672.3	116	634.1	121	6.6
2006 (proj)	722.5	125	683.5	131	5.6

Source: National Statistics/Mintel

As PDI rises there has also been a trend for people to want to spend more on themselves. This is good news for fashion retailers because they become beneficiaries of the trend. People have a tendency to want to trade up when they have more disposable income, and they spend more on branded fashionwear. Consumers are spending rather than saving, and many spend beyond their current PDI using credit cards and other loans when they "feel good" about their current position.

People also spend more on leisure than their counterparts in earlier generations. For example, people generally spend more time and disposable income on holidays (including short-breaks), eating out, shopping, and going out generally than previous generations did.

Page 13 of Reiss

Fashion Trends

Each new collection of branded fashion garments is created to satisfy a predicted target consumer demand. Consumer demand predictions are based on target market research, past sales analysis, and input from experienced product merchandisers, designers and buyers. The collections are influenced by trends observed in fashions (e.g. textiles, shoes, accessories, home furnishings), and other fashion related industries (e.g. automobiles, music, entertainment, sports, leisure activities), as well as wider environmental movements (e.g. political, social, cultural, ecological, technological, economic). All of these elements combine to help determine concepts and themes for a new season. Relevant textile materials, colour palettes and silhouettes are developed and selected accordingly. Trims and details are added as further embellishments to the garment. These former and latter design elements are co-ordinated and grouped into product lines that meet cost, production and delivery time requirements.

The introduction of new colours and styles by designers is critical in maintaining consumers' interest in keeping up with the latest fashion and hence encouraging spending. From spring 1996 to summer 1999 there was little change in styling, with urban and minimalist trends dominant. This together with a predominantly dark colour palette did little to stimulate the market according to Mintel (2002).

The product development process is complex. Figure 2 illustrates typical sources and criteria for various decisions in developing a concept. Once a concept has been developed this is only the beginning. Lines then need selection and approval before they are fully developed for ranges in the retail store.

Figure 2.

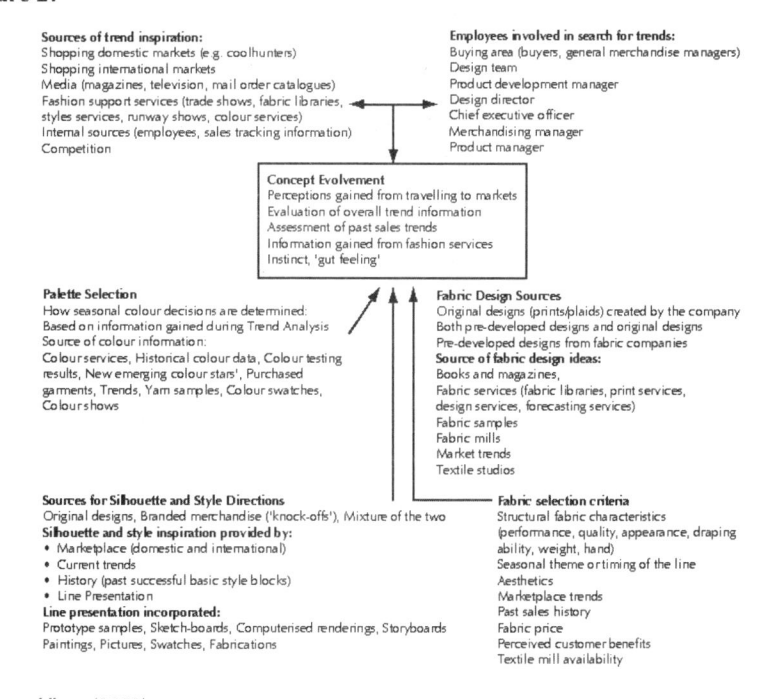

Sources of trend inspiration:
Shopping domestic markets (e.g. coolhunters)
Shopping international markets
Media (magazines, television, mail order catalogues)
Fashion support services (trade shows, fabric libraries, styles services, runway shows, colour services)
Internal sources (employees, sales tracking information)
Competition

Employees involved in search for trends:
Buying area (buyers, general merchandise managers)
Design team
Product development manager
Design director
Chief executive officer
Merchandising manager
Product manager

Concept Evolvement
Perceptions gained from travelling to markets
Evaluation of overall trend information
Assessment of past sales trends
Information gained from fashion services
Instinct, 'gut feeling'

Palette Selection
How seasonal colour decisions are determined:
Based on information gained during Trend Analysis
Source of colour information:
Colour services, Historical colour data, Colour testing results, New emerging colour stars', Purchased garments, Trends, Yarn samples, Colour swatches, Colour shows

Fabric Design Sources
Original designs (prints/plaids) created by the company
Both pre-developed designs and original designs
Pre-developed designs from fabric companies
Source of fabric design ideas:
Books and magazines,
Fabric services (fabric libraries, print services, design services, forecasting services)
Fabric samples
Fabric mills
Market trends
Textile studios

Sources for Silhouette and Style Directions
Original designs, Branded merchandise ('knock-offs'), Mixture of the two
Silhouette and style inspiration provided by:
• Marketplace (domestic and international)
• Current trends
• History (past successful basic style blocks)
• Line Presentation
Line presentation incorporated:
Prototype samples, Sketch-boards, Computerised renderings, Storyboards
Paintings, Pictures, Swatches, Fabrications

Fabric selection criteria
Structural fabric characteristics
(performance, quality, appearance, draping ability, weight, hand)
Seasonal theme or timing of the line
Aesthetics
Marketplace trends
Past sales history
Fabric price
Perceived customer benefits
Textile mill availability

Source: Hines (2003)

Page 14 of Reiss

Final line decisions are based on:

- Saleability judgements.
- Testing results.
- Perceived customer reaction.
- Cost.
- Selling history.
- Co-ordination with other apparel product groups.
- Marketplace trends.
- Other factors such as newness, variety, lead time, quality, colour, instinct or "gut feeling" as it is often expressed by people in the industry.

The current trend in womenswear towards "mixing and matching" garments, means that women are buying designer items and complementing them with high street brands, to make their appearance casually formal. As a consequence, clothing accessories are experiencing a dramatic increase in sales, as women buy them to enhance and complement their outerwear.

During the latter part of the 1990s there was a noticeable move towards casual clothing. There was also a relaxation in office dress codes. Men are increasingly looking for greater flexibility and a certain amount of mixing and matching takes place similar to the womenswear market. No longer is a white shirt the only accepted office shirt. There has also been a discernable trend in the decline of formal wear. There is a wider acceptance of different and brighter-coloured shirts within the workplace. Trends in the rest of Europe have led the way, whereby a greater variety of colours have been acceptable for many years as a means of individual self-expression.

Other Fashion Influencers

One of the greatest influences on fashion during the last decade has been the proliferation of magazine titles, particularly in the target group aged 25-34. Male magazines such as *Loaded, Maxim, FHM* and *GQ* have led the way. It is offered as one reason why younger men have become more fashion and brand conscious. There have also been a number women's magazine titles launched, with fashion-oriented titles such as *Glamour* and *In Style* providing further avenues for advertising, editorial review and promotion. Fashion promotion through the media is very important for retail brands.

A further important influence, particularly in the younger age groups (apart from peer pressure) has been celebrity endorsement. Film stars, pop idols and sports stars have become fashion leaders. In some cases, for example David Beckham, the soccer star has become a fashion icon. Magazines such as *Hello!* and *OK!* run numerous stories on the personal lives of these celebrities, with accompanying pictorial imagery. These lifestyle magazines have become influential in what people wear and want to wear.

Page 15 of Reiss

Fashion has also become more widely available. More retailers sell fashion, even in the mass-market, which was once the province of commodity clothiers. There is more square footage devoted to fashion and there are more places to buy. The rise in the number of designer factory outlets has made designerwear more accessible to the public at large. Often these designer retail outlets offer end of line or seconds stock at a discount. Discounts vary, but typically the product will be sold at 60-70 per cent of the full price. Attractive prices, ease of accessibility, and free parking make these retail outlets particularly attractive to consumers. In 2000 there were 34 factory outlet schemes operating in the UK, offering over 400,000 sq m of selling space. There are also large retail parks located on the fringe of large cities or conurbations like Trafford Park in Manchester and Bluewater in Kent. These retail parks offer a variety of designerwear amongst a much larger clothing and non-clothing offering. Many of these retail outlets offer consumers a different shopping experience from traditional stores. Family shopping visits and even days out are planned around these venues.

Even market traders offer designerwear. Some of this may be genuine, acquired legitimately on the "grey market" whilst some of it may be illegal, counterfeit products. The Anti-Counterfeiting Group (ACG) estimated the loss to brand owners to be in the region of £3 billion in 2000. Brand owners are not simply concerned about lost sales revenue, but also the damage that these products might do in tarnishing the brand image. Anecdotal reports from some lesser developed countries cite incidents where a customer can enter the store, purchase an item of clothing, and be asked the question "which brand logo would you like to have on it?". In the UK, market Trading Standard Officers from the local authorities remain vigilant to the problem, and it is likely to be less of a problem in the UK than elsewhere.

Fabric trends also help in the development of new fashionwear. For example, Du Pont has developed fabrics with moisturising cream. There have been developments with fabrics that change colour in response to changes in body heat. Intelligent fabrics that offer health benefits are also expected to become readily available within the next five years. Transfer of technologies from space exploration, such as Teflon-coated fabrics, have been used for several years to offer people stain resistant clothes and easy removal of difficult stains, including red wine, which was notorious for staining cloth. Men's shirts, ties and trousers have all benefited from Teflon coatings. There is also expected to be an increase in machine washable fabrics, offering convenience to time-poor professionals who will have the opportunity to put their clothing (including suits) into domestic washing machines.

Phillips, the electronics company, amongst others have been working on intelligent garment technologies for aerospace projects for several years. Intelligent garments that offer a range of inbuilt custom electronics may also become popular with younger consumers as fashionwear. Telephones, cameras, radio, digital music and thermal controls could all be contained within intelligent garments. Radio Frequency Tags (RFT) are already being used in clothing to store product and sales data. The cost of RFTs has fallen dramatically in the past few years, making it viable to place them in everyday wear. It is possible that garments with RFTs could contain washing instructions, and combined with bluetooth technology, in an intelligent washing machine the only human intervention necessary would be to place the garment in the machine. The rest would be performed automatically.

Page 16 of Reiss

Market Size and Trends

Towards the end of the 1990s, the clothing industry did not perform as well as some other market sectors, as increased discretionary expenditure was diverted to other areas of the economy. Sectors that benefited were travel and tourism, DIY, IT and mobile phone products. During this period much of the potential spend on clothing was channelled into lifestyle home products. As a consequence many clothing specialists diversified into home products, such as bed linen and other soft furnishings, in the hope of recapturing the revenue. Furthermore, middle-market shoppers looked towards added-value products on the one hand, and on the other to the discount clothing market at the value end for everyday purchases. As a result many retailers in the middle market felt the pinch, and as a consequence responded by lowering prices and having never-ending sales. The effect of this was price deflation in the sector. Customers expected more for less. Suppliers also got caught in the cross fire, and often bore the brunt of retailer discounting through lower prices for their goods to the retailer.

Table 7. – UK Retail Sales of Men's and Women's Designerwear, 1997-2002

	£m	Index	£m at 1997 Prices	Index	$m	Index
1997	1,186	100	1,186	100	1,771	100
1998	1,230	104	1,237	104	1,831	103
1999	1,249	105	1,291	109	1,899	107
2000	1,312	111	1,410	119	2,155	122
2001	1,360	115	1,523	128	2,190	124
2002 (est)	1,417	119	1,656	140	2,168	122

Source: Mintel (2002)

Table 7 shows that the real increase in expenditure on designerwear between 1997-2002 is 40 per cent. This increase was fuelled by consumers becoming more brand conscious and more fashion aware. Consumers moved away from the middle market. Middle market retailers found themselves squeezed between branded fashion and discounters.

The market split between men and women is given in Table 8.

Table 8. – UK Retail Sales of Designerwear, by Type, 1997-2002

	1997 £m	%	1999 £m	%	2001 £m	%	2002 (est) £m	%	% Change 1997-2002
Women's	729	61	756	61	790	58	810	57	+11.1
Men's	457	39	493	39	570	42	607	43	+32.8
Total	1,186	100	1,249	100	1,360	100	1,417	100	+19.5

Source: Mintel (2002)

Page 17 of Reiss

It is interesting to note the change in the gender mix between 1997-2002 and the trend towards more menswear as a proportion of total designerwear sales. The male share of this market has grown by nearly 33 per cent since 1997. Overall market growth for the period is just under 20 per cent.

Reiss the Brand

Reiss established a fashion brand in the early 1970s. Today, Reiss fashion can only be purchased through Reiss stores, unlike many fashion brands who sell through other distributors. The Reiss brand has become recognised as a progressive, fashion-led retail company, designing and producing own-label ranges targeted towards style-conscious men and women aged 18-40 years. It offers an individual and aspirational look at affordable prices, successfully combining good design, quality and value.

Table 9.

AW03 Womenswear Price Points

Jackets	£135-£175
Leather Jackets	£295
Trousers	£79-£110
Skirts	£69-£110
Dresses	£89-£130
Shirts	£65-£75
Cottons	£25-£79
Tops	£65-£89
Knitwear	£59-£79
Coats	£129-£195
Shoes	£95-£115

AW03 Menswear Price Points

Shirts	£69-£89
Trousers	£79-£89
Sweaters	£59-£89
Cottons	£28-£49
Suits	£295-£495
Outerwear	£159-£450
Shoes	£89-£120
Belts	£39-£59
Ties	£39-£45

AW = Autumn/Winter

Source: Company files

Significant effort has been put into the visual imagery to support the brand. Window displays and in-store graphics have helped communicate a strong brand image for Reiss.

Reiss aims to develop an aspirational, fashion-led men's and womenswear brand, with a clear identity that can be expanded domestically and internationally. Key values underpin the brand's image and these may be summarised with words such as: creative, contemporary, essential, comfortable, affordable and directional. The brand has established a reputation for good quality, fashion forward, and price competitive offerings, sold in a well-considered retail environment.

Page 18 of Reiss

The company recognises that international expansion needs careful consideration. The Dublin store (see Appendix 2) will provide a microcosm laboratory from which the management team can learn. They already recognise that perhaps Northern European markets may be easier to serve than Southern European ones, focusing on fashionable consumers with similar tastes to UK customers, and markets with similar climatic, social and cultural environments. The company is keen to exploit the brand and new market opportunities, and has identified the USA and Japan as possibilities in the future in addition to Europe.

Under Creative Director Lionel Copley, the design teams produce clothes that are individual, stylish and sexy. Key to the brand's success is a contemporary and directional product. Reiss fashion has a definitive look, which aims to lead rather than follow trends. Since the clothing product itself is not overtly branded, it is important that other aspects of the trading format complement and enhance the brand in four main areas: location, store design, marketing and store environment.

Location and Store Design

Since the product is aspirational, stores are chosen in prime, quality locations nationwide. Generally new stores are larger (in excess of 3,000 sq ft) to accommodate the combined offer of men's and womenswear. Where possible buildings with individual architectural features are chosen, which help make the stores unique.

The actual store design is undertaken by a retained architect to enhance and complement the environment, whilst achieving the Reiss signature. Key to design is the ability to use materials, lighting, and textures conveying warmth and vibrancy.

Marketing

Following a management review in 2001 it was decided to refocus marketing resources into making sure more emphasis was placed on store windows and campaign graphics. The seasonal campaigns aim to promote menswear and womenswear, ensuring they represent the combined brand. A greater emphasis has been placed on imagery to match the brand statement: individual, stylish and sexy. Fashion shoots need to have an artistic merit that reflects and refines the brand identity, and locations can be as diverse as Blackpool and Zanzibar.

In addition, the display team has expanded and a dedicated Visual Manager creates the window displays with a team that implements plans, ensuring that the windows match the creativity of the campaigns and the product.

Page 19 of Reiss

Public Relations (PR) is another key activity for Reiss and this is now under the control of Lionel Copley, the Creative Director, and has been developed significantly in the last three years. It was noted in 1998 that BT spent more on advertising than all the clothing retailers in the UK did (Jones, 2002, p242[1]). However, it is equally important to recognise that the growth of style and celebrity fashion magazines has quadrupled since the mid 1990s, and fashion editors and journalists need to fill the newly created spaces. This has presented many fashion retailers with opportunities to gain press coverage for their brands. This is an area that Reiss have been reasonably successful at exploiting in the past three years since they entered the womenswear market. Fashion, being a visual medium, allows it to gain easier press interest without spending on advertising.

Store Environment

Reiss aims to communicate a consistent creative marketing message through their stores. The store environment is carefully considered with staffing, merchandising, music and seasonal graphics as key elements of the mix. Service levels, staff presentation and training are imperative to Reiss's success. All staff attend induction programmes where they learn about the brand and its history and receive an intensive introduction to the Reiss customer service ethic.

All the stores are individually merchandised to take account of the specific context of the store, its local market, and to ensure that each store has its own personality within the Reiss offer. The music is selected to enhance the environment and changes to reflect the mood required. During each season the internal graphics are changed, including pictures, wallpaper, and handpainting, with the intention of communicating the current season's messages. London stores now also sell a selection of books and CDs in line with the Reiss brand.

In summary Reiss is a unique proposition being the only men's and womenswear brand that bridges the market between the high street and international designer brands. This is achieved by focus upon the design of product, complemented and reinforced through the store environment and individual store aesthetics.

Reiss Customers

Table 10. – Reiss Customers

Age	Person Type	Purchase Type
18-25	Young student	Limited purchases
25-35	Professionals	Buying larger range
35 +	Older fashionable	Aspirational

Source: Company files

---

[1] The Apparel Industry – Richard Jones (2002).

Reiss Competitors

Table 11. – Reiss Competitors

Position	Men	Women
Above	Paul Smith/Armani	Joseph
Par	BOSS/DKNY	Jigsaw/Whistles
Below	Ted Baker/FCUK	FCUK/Zara

Source: Company files

The company refers to its brand as a "bridging brand", by this they mean it bridges the gap between higher priced fashion from the likes of Armani and Paul Smith at one end of the spectrum, and Ted Baker and FCUK at the lower priced end for menswear. They have established a similar position for womenswear, sitting between Joseph at the top end and FCUK and Zara at the lower end of the price ranges.

Reiss Web Site

Reiss has established a non-transactional web site (see Figure 3). The web site provides store information, product ranges, and new season collections information for customers, and information for job applicants. One recent innovation allows visitors to the site to enter and walkthrough selected store locations. The main aim of the web site is to attract footfall to the "bricks and mortar" stores. Although the management team think the web site is important to their overall market strategy, they do not consider the web site important as a transactional tool. Unlike many retail ventures, the market for fashion is one that is difficult to pursue through electronic marketing strategies. This is because fashion is a tactile business and consumers like to try clothes for style, fit and colour before purchase.

15 ♦ Tackling a practice case: Reiss

Page 21 of Reiss

Figure 3.

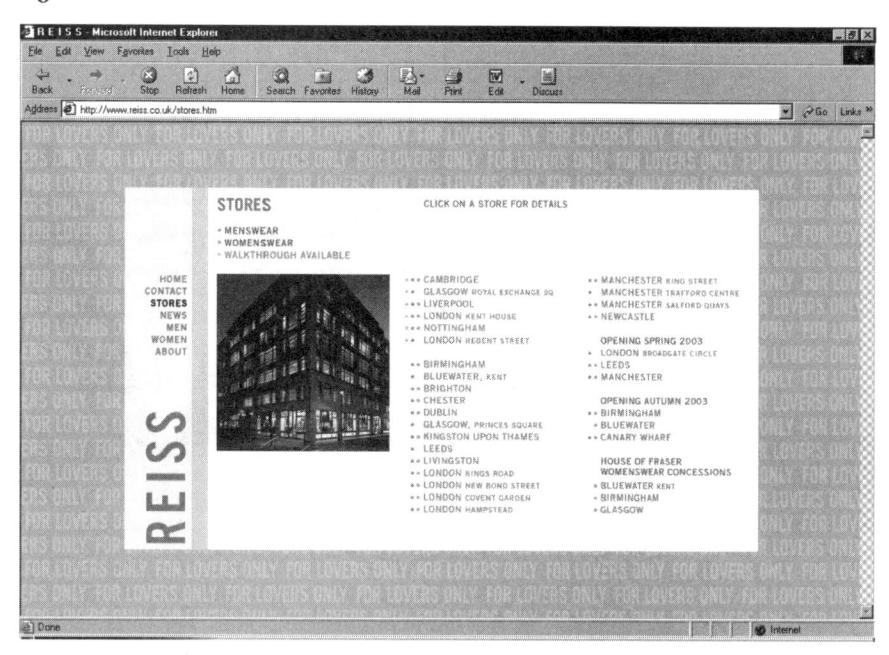

Source: Reiss web site

Fashion Branding

According to a report by KPMG (2002), creating customer loyalty by means of branding is becoming ever more important for companies' survival in all price ranges of the fashion business. This applies in equal measure to retailers and producers. Only strong brands are able to serve the customers as fixed points and to awake their interest in associated product features and stories. However, from time to time there are success stories such as Tommy Hilfiger, who hyped the brand and spent huge amounts on advertising. Sometimes customer satisfaction may not lead to loyalty, as the timing and the availability of goods may be more important. Customers tend to be fickle and may be willing to swap brands regardless of satisfaction levels. Better measures of loyalty are needed. Research carried out in Germany showed the following influences (Figure 4).

Page 22 of Reiss

Figure 4.

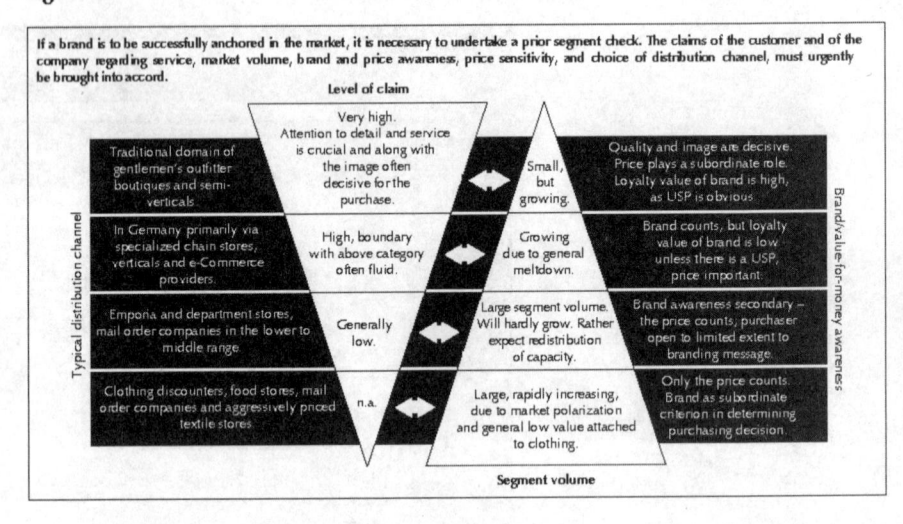

If a brand is to be successfully anchored in the market, it is necessary to undertake a prior segment check. The claims of the customer and of the company regarding service, market volume, brand and price awareness, price sensitivity, and choice of distribution channel, must urgently be brought into accord.

Typical distribution channel	Level of claim	Segment volume	Brand/value-for-money awareness
Traditional domain of gentlemen's outfitter boutiques and semi-verticals.	Very high. Attention to detail and service is crucial and along with the image often decisive for the purchase.	Small, but growing.	Quality and image are decisive. Price plays a subordinate role. Loyalty value of brand is high, as USP is obvious.
In Germany primarily via specialized chain stores, verticals and e-Commerce providers.	High, boundary with above category often fluid.	Growing due to general meltdown.	Brand counts, but loyalty value of brand is low unless there is a USP, price important.
Emporia and department stores, mail order companies in the lower to middle range.	Generally low.	Large segment volume. Will hardly grow. Rather expect redistribution of capacity.	Brand awareness secondary – the price counts; purchaser open to limited extent to branding message.
Clothing discounters, food stores, mail order companies and aggressively priced textile stores.	n.a.	Large, rapidly increasing, due to market polarization and general low value attached to clothing.	Only the price counts. Brand as subordinate criterion in determining purchasing decision.

Source: KPMG

The brand is a very important part a retailer's armoury and that promise needs to be sustained. However, the means of establishing a clear brand presence can vary according to the emotional values that have been established by each brand in the marketplace.

Figure 5.

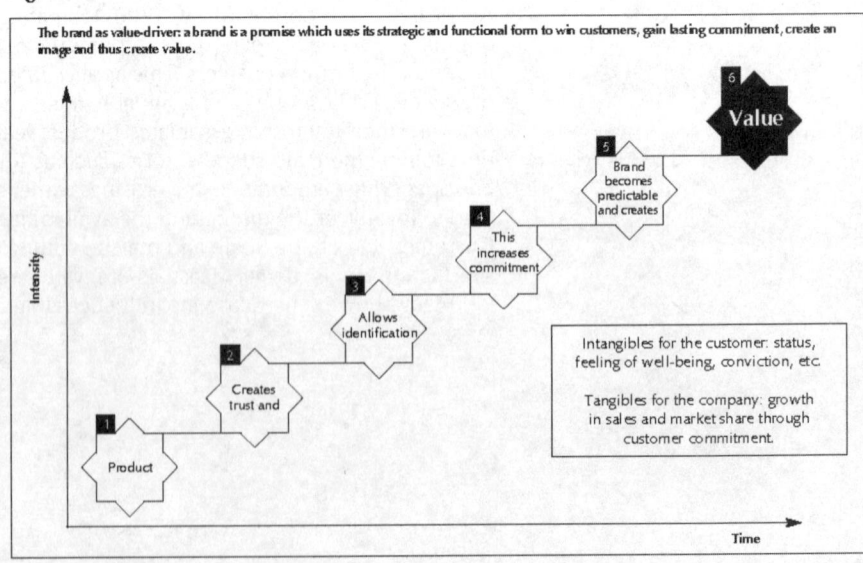

The brand as value-driver: a brand is a promise which uses its strategic and functional form to win customers, gain lasting commitment, create an image and thus create value.

Steps (Intensity vs Time):
1. Product
2. Creates trust and
3. Allows identification
4. This increases commitment
5. Brand becomes predictable and creates
6. Value

Intangibles for the customer: status, feeling of well-being, conviction, etc.

Tangibles for the company: growth in sales and market share through customer commitment.

Source: KPMG

15 ♦ Tackling a practice case: Reiss

> **Page 23 of Reiss**

Summary

Fashion retailing is now one of the most challenging areas of business activity in the developed world, as there is intense competition, smaller profit margins, and variable selling seasons, with delivery times getting longer in some instances. Typically a fashion season is marked by a bell-shaped curve (see Figure 6).

Figure 6. – Fashion Life Cycles

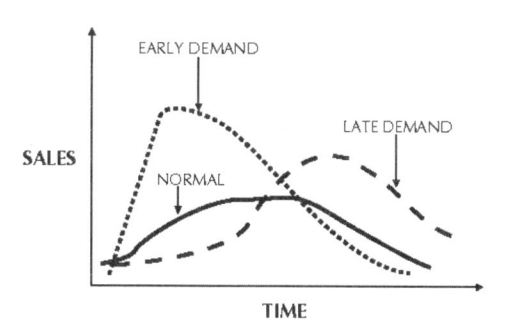

Source: Ranchhod (2003)

The differing demand patterns need to be understood, as price points need to be established at each level. Often the demand at each price, in each period of the season, is uncertain, and price sensitivity to particular items may also vary. Goods left over at the end of the season lose their value dramatically and the demand may completely disappear! Thus companies such as Reiss need to monitor price levels and stock levels as accurately as possible. Discounting could cause a heavy demand resulting in poor stock levels, or vice versa, marking-down too late or too little could also cause heavy losses. Each market is likely to react in different ways, so the company needs both localised and globalised information systems. Reiss is at an important stage in its development, with its rapid expansion programme throughout the UK and ambitious plans to become an international brand. The company needs to consider what the next stages of development might be. A number of strategic options are available to Reiss. It is a small, strong brand in a very large market, and it therefore needs to leverage this position effectively in the marketplace and establish a presence beyond the United Kingdom. It also needs to consolidate its position in its current main market. These issues are exercising the directors who are now considering the best strategies the company should pursue.

Appendix 1.

Reiss Financial Statements

Profit and Loss Account

Date of Accounts Y/E	31st Jan 2003	31st Jan 2002	31st Jan 2001
Total Sales	20,883,000	18,138,000	17,653,000
Cost of Sales	6,752,000	6,658,000	6,131,000
Gross Profit	14,131,000	11,480,000	11,522,000
Operating Profit	1,977,000	1,255,000	1,201,000
Exports	N/A	129,000	252,000
Non-trading Income	119,000	119,000	125,000
Interest Payable	289,000	328,000	322,000
Pretax Profit	1,807,000	1,046,000	1,004,000
Taxation	588,000	441,000	276,000
Profit After Tax	1,219,000	605,000	728,000
Retained Profits	1,219,000	605,000	728,000
Value Added	8,509,144	6,778,768	6,070,712
Capital Employed	7,008,000	6,362,000	5,788,000
Net Worth	4,545,000	3,321,000	2,710,000
Working Capital	-2,396,000	-1,441,000	-1,497,000
Employee Remuneration	4,886,000	4,267,000	3,603,000
Director Remuneration	299,000	277,000	272,000
Audit Fees	25,000	27,000	27,000
Non-audit fees	7,000	4,000	12,000
Depreciation	1,138,000	813,000	892,000
No. of Employees	325	276	234

Page 25 of Reiss

Balance Sheet

Assets

Date of Accounts	31st Jan 2003	31st Jan 2002	31st Jan 2001
Tangible Assets	9,356,000	7,750,000	7,226,000
Intangible Assets	48,000	53,000	59,000
Total Fixed Assets	9,404,000	7,803,000	7,285,000
Stocks	2,985,000	2,179,000	2,450,000
Debtors	70,000	55,000	162,000
Cash	41,000	860,000	692,000
Misc. Current Assets	1,376,000	1,024,000	1,167,000
Other Current Assets	1,417,000	1,884,000	1,859,000
Total Current Assets	4,472,000	4,118,000	4,471,000
Fixed Assets	9,356,000	7,750,000	7,226,000
Total Assets	**13,876,000**	**11,921,000**	**11,756,000**

Liabilities

Date of Accounts	31st Jan 2003	31st Jan 2002	31st Jan 2001
Creditors	1,310,000	1,171,000	1,867,000
Bank Overdraft	400,000	400,000	400,000
Misc. Current Liability	5,158,000	3,988,000	3,701,000
Other Short Term Finance	1,253,000	1,087,000	1,587,000
Due to Group, Current	1,000	1,000	507,000
Other Current Liabilities	3,905,000	2,901,000	2,114,000
Short Term Loans	1,653,000	1,487,000	1,987,000
Long Term Loans	2,320,000	2,853,000	2,857,000
Long Term Bank Loan	0	400,000	800,000
Other Long Term Finance	2,320,000	2,453,000	2,057,000
Due to Group, Non-current	1,539,000	1,539,000	1,161,000
Other Long Term Liabilities	95,000	135,000	162,000
Total Current Liabilities	6,868,000	5,559,000	5,968,000
Total Long Term Liabilities	2,415,000	2,988,000	3,019,000
Total Liabilities	**9,283,000**	**8,547,000**	**8,987,000**

Part C: Practice cases

Page 26 of Reiss

Liabilities	31st Jan 2003	31st Jan 2002	31st Jan 2001
Called Up Share Capital and Sundry Reserves	266,000	266,000	266,000
Profit and Loss Account Reserve	4,327,000	3,108,000	2,503,000
Shareholder Funds	4,593,000	3,374,000	2,769,000
Called Up Share Capital	266,000	266,000	266,000
Net Assets	**7,008,000**	**6,362,000**	**5,788,000**

Source: Reiss

> **Page 27 of Reiss**

Appendix 2.

I haven't got a thing to wear! Why are so many men badly dressed? Because high-street menswear is rubbish, says Gareth McLean

The Guardian – United Kingdom; June 06, 2003

I am standing in Zara menswear, surrounded by a dizzying array of drawstring linen-ish trousers, highly patterned (and, I imagine, highly flammable) short-sleeved shirts, and non-descript knitwear. There are fleets of tan sandals, knots of ties, and a clot of blue sleeveless rayon grandad shirts. They are very Gala bingo. Some curious Christian country music is playing and there's that Zara smell, the odd aroma that is cold on the nostrils like an overly air-conditioned holiday apartment.

'This,' says my friend Gill, with whom I am shopping, 'is where DJ Sammy buys his clothes.' We pause to consider the Euro-disco DJ who recently murdered the 80s soft-rock classic Boys of Summer. Gill has a point. Even without the multitude of kaftan tops (the preponderance of which I blame entirely on David Beckham), there is something very Eurotrash about Zara menswear.

Zara womenswear isn't quite so bad, but womenswear never is. Women have the best shops. They have Topshop, feted for taking catwalk trends and translating them into high-street apparel in a matter of weeks. Men, on the other hand, have Topman. It is the preserve of 19-year-old mobile phone salesmen, thirtysomethings who think buying a T-shirt emblazoned with the words "Doggy Style" makes them appealing to the opposite sex, and boys who consider Avril Lavigne an attractive older woman. I've always found French Connection to be a store with delusions of grandeur, and you may as well hook yourself up to Dr Nitschke's suicide machine if you're going to frequent Next.

Granted, there is Gap, but there are only so many classic T-shirts a boy needs (sometimes I get to work, realise I am dressed head to toe in Gap and feel so boring that I contemplate getting a tattoo. On my neck). There's always Marks & Spencer, but it has only made a half-hearted attempt to engage with the under-40s, doing such a good job of hiding the decent bits of its Autograph range that Indiana Jones would have trouble uncovering them. We simply shan't be mentioning its Blue Harbour brand-within-a-brand.

You wonder why so many men are so badly dressed? I'll tell you why. High-street menswear is rubbish. The best thing you can say about it is that it's consistent. And that's just another word for monotonous.

Now, I am aware that pessimism isn't exactly an attractive attribute, so I decided to give the high street the benefit of the doubt. I identified key trends in designer fashion and tried to find them in the likes of Topman, H&M, River Island and Zara. There must be at least a hint on the high street of neon as used by Helmut Lang on vests and T-shirts, Miu Miu's biker-lite, multi-buckle, many-zipped jackets, and Junya Watanabe's Jamaican-themed, logo-tastic, acid-coloured T-shirts.

Part C: Practice cases

Page 28 of Reiss

In Topman, there are neon sweatbands and a not bad print of neon squares on some T-shirts, but the sweatbands are reminiscent of the aforementioned Avril and the T-shirts are as boxy and shapeless as the million other pounds 15 Topman T-shirts. There is a biker-ish denim jacket with zips and buckles priced at pounds 45, but it's just nasty, Miu Miu's idea horribly mutated. Of all that Topman has to offer – and, as the Oxford Circus store is the flagship, the choice is better than the average branch – a white suit jacket and some Marimekko-esque striped T-shirts stand out as, if not must-haves, then certainly may-buys.

H&M, conversely, was a complete wasteland. There were plenty of bad jeans, worse shirts and saggy-necked T-shirts, but no echoes of the designer trends. My lack of faith in the shop – I have always viewed it as a glorified jumble sale in which the occasional nice item is hidden, lucky dip-style – was vindicated.

Meanwhile, someone should do the world a favour and burn every branch of River Island to the ground.

Even in the posher shops – Reiss, for example – everything is terribly subdued and decidedly non-fashionable, preferring instead to be stylish. There is nothing wrong with this: Reiss has lots of lovely things. Yet most of its wares are slightly too expensive, seemingly designed to appeal to the man wealthier than I, someone who buys signature items to add to his shades-of-grey capsule wardrobe. Aspirational rather than everyday-wearable. Suave rather than fun.

And that is the fundamental problem. Shopping for men's clothes can be incredibly dull, not an adjective you could reasonably attach to the Topshop experience. For many men, shopping is a means to an end, not an end in itself. Men don't enjoy shopping and, crucially, don't think when they shop. This gives retailers the latitude to be lazier when assembling their men's collections. They go for a lower common denominator and provide less choice because they assume their male customers aren't interested in browsing; making a day of it. Men want to go into a shop, get what they want and leave quickly.

But I am not convinced that, given the choice and the right environment, modern man would not happily wander round surveying what's on offer. It is true that the majority of men aren't as fashion-conscious as women, so there isn't the demand for a male Topshop. Women spend more – and more often – on clothes, while men tend not to care about seasonal trends other than vests-in-summer, jumpers-in-winter. And, of course, men's fashion isn't as dynamic as women's. Such is the dominance of jeans, all the action tends to play itself out on our top halves (unless we're talking tracksuit trousers, which, let's face it, don't suit everyone).

Men who are interested in fashion tend to buy labels from smaller shops – your Duffers, Diesels, Boxfresh and Carhartt – and there's a lot to be said for it. A pair of Carhartt trousers will last you for years, a Duffer hooded top is a classic. But there are times when I don't want a pair of timeless trousers. Sometimes I want a pair that will be smashing for two months then distinctly not. Amid the reliable Diesel jeans and Boxfresh sweatshirts, a bit of fickle fashion would be marvellous, something that is not H&M-cheap but not Reiss-expensive. Now that choice would be a real treat.

Source: The Guardian – United Kingdom; June 06, 2003

Page 29 of Reiss

Reiss finds pink is not big on Green

Financial Times Information Limited – United Kingdom; April, 2003

UK designer David Reiss has brought his upmarket store to Ireland and is optimistic that our fashion fans will ensure the success of the stylish venture.

AFTER five years of trying to open in Dublin, David Reiss, founder of the upmarket British women's and men's fashion company Reiss, recently opened a store at a prime location, opposite St Stephen's Green.

He describes getting prime retail space in the city as "close to impossible" and when the company took over the lease of the store it was reported that a new level for Dublin retail rents had been reached.

The company then spent GBP750,000 on the fit of the Irish store, which marks its first step in international expansion.

'Our end of the market is all around the Grafton Street area, and it's quite a tight space if you're quite specific about where you want to be. What we've finished up with is probably the ideal,' said Mr Reiss, who started the business in the mid-70s.

However, the shape of the premises was not ideal, even though it has about 3,500 sq ft of trading space.

'We tend to have big frontages which make a powerful statement and this is a relatively small frontage and it opens out at the back, so we've had to be very creative,' he said.

The company chose to set a precedent with its new Dublin store, with a new format which will be reflected in seven more stores opening in Britain later in the year.

The company worked with three architects to get what they wanted, using lighting specialists and an architect who has just finished working on British designer Alexander McQueen's New York store.

Explaining the investment in Dublin and his appetite to open here, Mr Reiss said: 'Dublin is a vibrant city, one of the most exciting cities in Europe. We just felt very strongly that it was an area where we would compete.'

'It lacks the normal intense competition you get in big cities. I'm quite surprised, actually, that at our level, other than Brown Thomas, there didn't seem to be an awful lot on offer.'

Reiss is at the mid to upper end of the market, with most items priced at 100-plus and the label is described as a "bridge", covering the gap between the high street and designer stores.

The best comparison already operating in Ireland is Karen Millen, which is in a similar price range but differs in style.

Mr Reiss describes as "phenomenal" the initial response of Irish shoppers to the store and said that within the first few minutes of the opening in November, between 60 and 70 people were inside.

Page 30 of Reiss

'What really surprised us when we opened the store was it pretty much took off from the first day, and that may well have been because people were waiting for something new to happen,' said the designer.

'We certainly had a very strong initial reaction, which doesn't always follow through with the opening of a new store,' he added.

The shop opened during the fashion business's peak time, with November, December and January all strong months.

Mr Reiss said that business has slowed since that but should build up again into the summer.

He will be closely watching the profitability of the shop. 'We normally look for quite a quick return from all our stores,' he said.

Other store openings are possible, with the developers of the new shopping centre in Dundrum very interested in involvement from Reiss.

'They're pushing hard certainly to open in Dundrum. What I've told them is, give us a year.'

'One of the things that's becoming apparent on the men's side is that Irish men are probably more conservative than customers we get in the UK. So we're having to tweak it slightly,' he said, with pink proving not to be a very popular colour with Irish men.

'Certain things which are strong sellers in the UK are not such strong sellers here,' he said.

Despite the economic slowdown, Mr Reiss is optimistic that his label will fill a niche in the Irish market.

'What's happening (economically) in Ireland is happening all over the world,' he said.

'All I can tell you is that so far we've no complaint and we're certainly well above budgets that have been set, so we're very happy.'

Source: Financial Times Information Limited – April, 2003

15 ♦ Tackling a practice case: Reiss

Page 31 of Reiss

Commercial Property (Retail): Retail steady as outlook remains positive – Consumers are still consuming, so the retail sector is holding up in spite of the uncertain economic climate; some retailers are seeking to expand, and Zone A rents in Grafton Street and Henry Street are on the way up. Edel Morgan reports

The Irish Times – February 12, 2003

The consumer mattress-money spending spree that accompanied Euro-changeover last year – bringing with it an unrealistic buoyancy to the retail market – has proven a tough act to follow for many retailers.

However, all things considered, feedback from traders has indicated that sales over the Christmas period and January went reasonably well this year, says Fintan Tierney of Lambert Smith Hampton.

'Out-of-town shopping centres such as Liffey Valley and Blanchardstown probably fared better than Dublin city centre, with some people opting to avoid the hassle of city gridlock and the scramble for parking, although some suburban centres were also choked with traffic,' says Tierney.

There is still an appetite for expansion among existing retailers – for example Next is actively seeking suitable locations.

However, the scarcity of prime retail space continues to be a problem as vacancy rates remain negligible.

'Dundrum shopping centre and Mahon Point in Cork are among the few new shopping centres coming on stream in 2004 and they are filling up already,' he says.

Blanchardstown centre's extension will also provide much needed space, as will Stack A which is under construction on Dublin's docklands and will be aimed at high-end retailers.

Despite continuing demand for high-profile locations, retailers are not as aggressive as in previous years as caution prevails in an uncertain climate.

'There is still plenty of demand with substantial rental premiums being paid at prime locations such as Grafton Street and Henry Street. Saying that, it's a strange time; we don't know if there's going to be a a war, and some retailers are taking a more short-term view.'

The continuing growth in Zone A rents will surprise many when a number of rent reviews are completed on Grafton Street in the coming months. Already, the ICS Building Society is paying a rent of E5,260 per sq m for its shop premises fronting on to both Grafton Street and Nassau Street. Another shop off the top of Grafton Street, 1 St Stephen's Green, was let to the UK fashion retailer Reiss at a Zone A level of E5,188 per sq m.

Marie Hunt of Gunne's commercial division says a number of European retailers have been looking to enter the Irish retail market since the Euro was introduced.

Part C: Practice cases

Page 32 of Reiss

While Spanish fashion chain Zara is due to open in Roches Stores, for other operations such as French cosmetics giants Sephora and Louis Vuitton (LVHM), a division of Moet Hennessy, a high street premises has proven elusive.

UK companies Gap and Space NK have also been on the lookout for suitable premises.

'There are retailers that have been looking to gain a foothold in the Irish market for years but can't. Gap, for instance, won't go into out-of-town centres, it will only consider a prime shopping street,' says Hunt.

While Christmas trading was generally positive for retailers – with an estimated maximum of 10-15 per cent drop in footfall in the city centre – it did not take off until the second week in December – with November being a quiet month.

John Reynolds, CEO of the Henry Street/Mary Street partnership, says this is accounted for by more cautious spending patterns, given the downturn in the economy.

A survey on consumer spending conducted by the IIB Banks and the ESRI found that consumer confidence picked up in January, but pointed out the significance of this should not be overestimated.

The outlook for the rest of 2003 is quite positive, says Marie Hunt, with 'demand continuing to outstrip supply. Even in a slower economic environment, the outlook for retail consumption is positive.'

Source: The Irish Times – February 12, 2003

> **Page 33 of Reiss**

Appendix 3.

Fashion Retailing at a Crossroads

Published: 3rd May, 2000

The UK high street in the year 2000 is a microcosm of trends that will impact retailing worldwide. Middle market retailers are being squeezed at both ends by designer labels from above and value-for-money operators from below. Retail is changing painfully because of the increasing sophistication of the consumer; the self-created problems of retail space and profitability; and the globalisation of retailers and their suppliers.

Although this could lead to more merchandise variety in the high street, the variety will be supplied through fewer and fewer mega-big retail conglomerates and major groups striving to operate worldwide. The evidence is that we are entering a "buy or be bought" retail era. Malcolm Newbery reports.

UK Fashion Retailers In Turmoil

Although there always has been change in fashion retailing, the pace of that change has undoubtedly been accelerating. The established and secure major players are no longer that. Marks and Spencer has undergone an "annus horribilis" in 1999, and staff are still bailing out. The women's wear brands of Sears fell into the hands of Philip Green, who promptly sold them on to Arcadia. Arcadia, having just managed to avoid insolvency by doing a new financing deal with its banks, has now announced the disposal of 350 stores and the axing of three brands, SU214, Principles for Men, and Wade Smith Jnr. The last was only bought in 1998 for £17.3 million. And BhS has been bought by the same asset-stripper Philip Green, who says he intends to keep and run the retail fascia, but will either drive it upmarket or down!

To add to the confusion in the high street, the middle ground (variety stores, multiple chains, and mass market brands) is being attacked from above and below. Label conscious consumers are deserting St Michael for designer names with "street cred" such as Calvin Klein. "Value for money" shoppers are heading the opposite way to buy George at Asda. As a recent trade press article put it: 'cheap and nasty has become cheap and clever'.

The reason this has happened now is because of the confluence of three factors:

1. The increasing sophistication of the consumer.

2. The self-created problems of retail space and profitability.

3. The globalisation of retailers and their suppliers.

Page 34 of Reiss

The Consumer

Retailers used to sell on a good gross margin at full price for 46 weeks of the year, and discount to move old stock twice a year. Now there are sales and offers in store at least six times a year: January and July, mid-season and special events. The consumer has learnt to wait for these, and has become adept at buying at discounted prices.

Moreover, the growth of factory outlets and off-price shopping centres has sharpened consumers' desire for a bargain. Many brands now deliberately make products obsolete in order to make them available to outlet stores.

Space and Profitability

Across the same period, in almost all developed countries, "organised retail" (the chains) built square meters of space faster than they grew sales. The combination of this and the squeeze on gross margins as a result of consumer opportunism has cut profits to the bone.

Globalisation

The third factor impacting on the retail scene in all developed countries is globalisation. Retail was presumed in the past to be national, with national preferences restricting cross-border activities. That is no longer the case. In food, electricals and fashion, multi-national retailers are growing at the expense of those with a purely domestic franchise. Very recent examples from the fashion sector are: Zara with more than 900 stores in over 30 countries; Hennes & Mauritz, whose stock is currently valued at £12 billion, and is stepping up its store expansion plans in Europe and the USA; and Gap, which will roll out the Old Navy format in the UK later this year, with Banana Republic to follow. J Crew, the USA mid-market chain with 120 stores, has announced a start-up in the UK next year.

Brands are also becoming international, whether they are part of a massive luxury stable such as LVMH (Louis Vuitton Moet Henessey), or a quick-on-their-toes minnow like Ted Baker. The perceived wisdom is that a brand cannot survive in one market, not even in one as big as the USA.

And to complete the story, although it is primarily in food, the takeover by Wal-Mart of Asda looks likely to lead to the sale of value-for-money George clothing in the States. These global retailers and brands will sell globally and source globally.

Where Will It End?

The shopping mall is looking more and more like a shopping "maul", with the global retail giants struggling for domination of the high streets around the world. As events prove that there is no effective domestic defence against the aspirations of the multi-nationals, lessons can and should be learned from other industries such as chemicals and automobiles.

Page 35 of Reiss

In the chemicals business, the major players bought and sold (in some cases swapped) their investments in different types of chemical, in order to become the market leader worldwide in a particular sector. In cars, the famous Boston Consulting theory of the 1960s has been proved right over the last three decades. You use your investment muscle to become the biggest. You use that to drive down costs and kill the competitors. You then either buy the weakened competitor or leave it to die, and then, like a vulture, pick over its corpse (collect its market share). This inevitably has meant fewer and fewer car manufacturers. In the UK in the month of April alone, we have seen BMW retreating from Rover, and Ford announcing the end of car assembly at Dagenham.

Buy or Be Bought

If the analogy with automobiles is sound, and it would appear to be so, then the reaction of food and fashion companies with genuinely global aspirations is clear. It's "buy or be bought!" Certainly Kingfisher thought that way, when in April 1999, it tried to merge with Asda. But the party was spoilt by the speed with which Wal-Mart moved to secure Asda and provide itself with a launchpad for Europe.

More recently, the French merger of Promodes and Carrefour has created a genuine European food and fashion giant, capable of playing in the same league as Wal-Mart.

Such is the confusion amongst food and fashion retailers in the UK at the moment that absolutely anyone, including blue-chips like M&S, is deemed to be "in play". One thing is certain; in today's edgy environment, there will be some more surprising mergers and acquisitions in retail before long.

Accreditation

just-style.com is the leading global textile, apparel and footwear web site, giving industry professionals easy access to the latest industry news, hundreds of valuable feature articles, and over three years of archive material. The site's unique content is researched and produced via our dedicated editorial team and a worldwide network of correspondents. In addition, the new just-style.com research store provides you with instant access to over 300 reports, books and research products from leading market information providers.

To browse just-style.com and discover how you could benefit, go to:
www.just-style.com

Source: just-style.com

Page 36 of Reiss

European Apparel Retailers Face Rocky Road

Published: 25th March, 2003

Continued sluggish retail sales growth in 2003 across much of Western Europe will exacerbate the already tough competitive environment for apparel retailers, according to a new study of the region's clothing and footwear retail industry.

Total consumer spending on apparel, footwear and accessories in Western Europe in 2002 was around 324 billion euros, roughly the same as the entire US market at $314 billion. However, new Retail Forward research shows the growing trend for ageing consumers to spend cash on homes, personal care, savings or leisure time, means apparel retailing in Europe is going through major structural change.

The study, entitled Apparel Retailing in Western Europe, says several factors are transforming apparel retailing in major countries such as Spain, France, Germany, Italy, Sweden, Portugal, the UK and the Netherlands, like never before.

But despite the difficult environment, it says major European clothing chains, and particularly multi-national specialty operators, are succeeding by taking market share through innovative, fast-changing product offers and lower cost, more efficient business models.

'The ability of these specialty chains to implement faster and more flexible supply chains is giving them a real competitive advantage,' said Ira Kalish, director of Retail Forward's Global Intelligence Program.

Changing Face

Kalish said the factors seen as transforming fashion retailing in Western Europe over the next few years and early part of this century are:

- Weakening demand – while apparel spending in Western Europe grew at an annual rate of 3.8 per cent from 1997 to 2000, the industry's share of total consumer spending is declining as the economy decelerates and consumer confidence slips.

- Rapid consolidation – although apparel distribution channels and the concentration of apparel sales are still quite different across Europe, rapid consolidation reflects growing market maturity.

- Greater internationalisation of styles – multi-national retailers like H&M, Zara, and Mango, have moved toward greater internationalisation of styles and more disposable fashion through low prices and fast rotation of inventory.

- Supply chain flexibility and speed to market – faster and more flexible supply chains are the principal drivers of the retail apparel industry in Europe, and are key to the success of these specialty apparel chains.

'Consolidation, internationalisation, and the speed of the fashion cycle will continue to drive change in the structure of European apparel retailing,' Kalish explained.

Page 37 of Reiss

Size and Growth of Western European Apparel Market
Total Apparel Spending by Country
€ billions, ranked by 2000 Spending

Country	1997	1998	1999	2000	2001	1997 to 2000 CAGR[1]
Germany	69.5	69.6	70.7	71.6	72.0	0.9%
Italy	58.0	62.2	63.9	64.4	68.3	4.2%
UK	44.8	47.4	50.9	56.3	58.2	6.8%
France	37.2	37.7	38.2	39.0	NA	1.6%
Spain	20.6	21.8	23.5	24.9	NA	6.6%
Netherlands	10.1	10.9	11.5	12.0	NA	6.0%
Greece	8.9	9.0	9.7	10.0	NA	4.0%
Austria	7.2	7.5	7.7	7.7	NA	2.5%
Belgium	6.5	6.7	6.7	7.0	NA	2.1%
Switzerland	6.1	6.2	6.4	6.6	NA	2.8%
Portugal	4.7	5.1	5.4	5.8	NA	7.0%
Norway	3.8	3.7	3.9	4.2	4.4	4.0%
Denmark	3.8	3.9	4.0	4.0	4.1	1.8%
Sweden	3.2	3.2	3.5	3.8	3.6	3.5%
Ireland	2.4	2.7	2.9	3.4	NA	12.1%
Finland	2.5	2.6	2.7	2.8	NA	4.5%
Luxembourg	0.4	0.5	0.5	0.5	0.5	2.3%
Total	289.5	300.6	312.0	324.0	NA	3.8%

[1] Germany, Italy, UK, Norway, Denmark, Sweden and Luxembourg growth is from 1997 to 2001.

Source: Retail Intelligence and Retail Forward, Inc.

According to Kalish, the most significant issue transforming the retail apparel industry in Europe is fast response. 'Speed and integration of the supply chain will continue to shape the future of the retail apparel industry in Europe by enabling more flexible, demand-driven fulfilment,' he said. 'The hallmark of successful apparel retailers is an ability to create distinctive product ranges that are responsive to quickly changing consumer expectations.'

Under Pressure

The ability of specialty chains to implement fast response is placing pressure on traditional retailers, including independents and department stores. Their explosive growth is shifting apparel market share and is changing the structure of apparel distribution across Europe, argue the report's authors.

Recent tough market conditions have favoured those retailers who can respond to consumer demand more quickly and at lower cost. A handful of specialty retailers such as Sweden's Hennes & Mauritz (H&M) and Spain's Zara (part of the Inditex fashion empire), continue to defy the global economic downturn. 'These companies are particularly adept at understanding what consumers buy – and want to buy – in real time and responding quickly to sales trends and customer feedback,' Kalish added.

The explosive growth of these chains also is driven by diversification and international expansion. As a growth strategy, they are capitalising on the heightened interest in their brands by extending them into new product areas, new customer segments, and new formats.

Page 38 of Reiss

UK: Apparel Retail Concentration
Sales of Top 10 Apparel Specialty Retailers, 2001/2002

Rank	Retailer	2001/2002 Sales (£m)	1996/1997 Sales (£m)	1996/1997 to 2001/2002 CAGR	2001/2002 # Outlets	Operation(s)
1	Arcadia	1,925	1,102	11.8%	2,750	Menswear/womenswear
2	Next Retail	1,359	730	13.2%	331	General Clothing
3	Matalan	847	185	35.6%	143	General Clothing
4	New Look (UK)	527	218	19.3%	487	Womenswear
5	Primark Stores	376	111	27.6%	67	General Clothing
6	Mothercare UK	375	395	-1.0%	252	Womenswear and Childrenswear
7	Gap UK	368	112	26.9%	184	General Clothing
8	Alexon Group	341	108	25.9%	1,242	Clothing and Footwear
9	River Island Clothing Co.	301	285	1.1%	195	Menswear/womenswear
10	TK Maxx (USA)	254	48	39.6%	69	General Clothing
	Total Sales of Top 10	6,673	3,294	15.2%		
	Total Apparel Specialty Retail Sales	16,984	13,289	5.0%		
	Top 10 Retailers % of Total	39%				

Source: Retail Intelligence and Retail Forward, Inc.

Flexibility the Key

The report says the secret to the rapid rise of these vertically integrated, multi-national corporate chains is flexibility – flexible supply chains, the flexibility to price aggressively, flexible product ranges, and flexible retail formats. The winners are taking market share through a combination of innovative, fast-changing product offers and lower cost, more efficient business models. Supply chain advantages are giving these retailers a price advantage, which leads to market share gains, as well as the opportunity to improve gross margins, both of which support further expansion of the concept.

Page 39 of Reiss

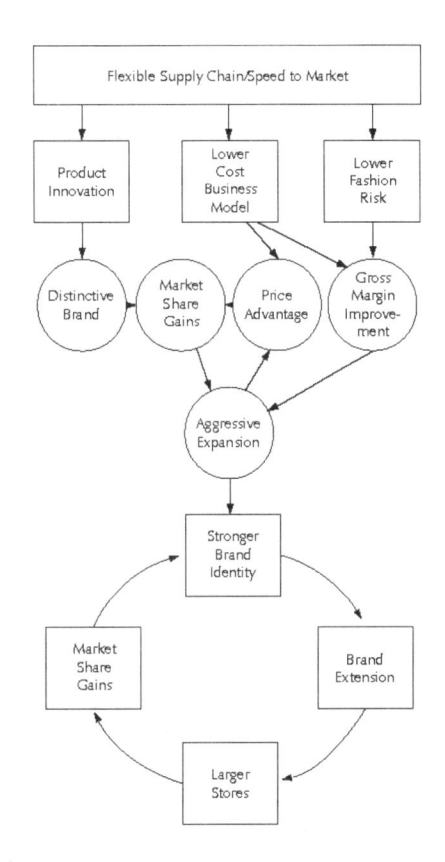

```
                    ┌─────────────────────────────────┐
                    │ Flexible Supply Chain/Speed to Market │
                    └─────────────────────────────────┘
                         │            │            │
                         ▼            ▼            ▼
                    ┌─────────┐  ┌─────────┐  ┌─────────┐
                    │ Product │  │  Lower  │  │  Lower  │
                    │Innovation│  │  Cost   │  │ Fashion │
                    │         │  │Business │  │  Risk   │
                    │         │  │ Model   │  │         │
                    └─────────┘  └─────────┘  └─────────┘
                         │        │     │         │
                         ▼        ▼     ▼         ▼
                      ( Dist- ) (Market)(Price )(Gross  )
                      (inctive) (Share )(Advan-)(Margin )
                      (Brand ) (Gains )(tage  )(Improve-)
                                                (ment   )
                                    │
                                    ▼
                              (Aggressive)
                              (Expansion )
                                    │
                                    ▼
                              ┌──────────┐
                              │ Stronger │
                              │  Brand   │
                              │ Identity │
                              └──────────┘
                              ↗          ↘
                     ┌────────┐          ┌────────┐
                     │ Market │          │ Brand  │
                     │ Share  │          │Extension│
                     │ Gains  │          │        │
                     └────────┘          └────────┘
                              ↖          ↙
                              ┌──────────┐
                              │  Larger  │
                              │  Stores  │
                              └──────────┘
```

Source: Retail Forward, Inc.

It cites H&M and Zara as great examples of the competitive advantages and benefits of greater speed to market. The secret to their success is the ability to provide the latest fashion trends to their customers. Zara, seen to be more at the cutting edge of fashion than H&M, has maintained a lead in its ability to respond rapidly to fashion trends. It puts fashion ranges together in 7-30 days and can replenish bestsellers in the stores in five days. H&M can respond in 30-60 days. This compares to as much as 40-50 weeks from design to delivery for a typical clothing retailer.

The explosive growth of these chains also is driven by diversification and international expansion. As a growth strategy, they are capitalising on the heightened interest in their brands by extending them into new product areas, new customer segments, and new formats.

Product offers are being broadened to include categories such as childrenswear, lingerie, fragrance and personal care products, and homewares. Many have launched petite, large size, and maternity ranges. Bigger stores are then justified to accommodate the expanded product ranges. To further appeal to different customer groups, some chains adopt a portfolio strategy to extend their reach through the development or acquisition of multiple branded concepts.

With either approach, the impact of these retailers on the competitive landscape is becoming more pervasive. International expansion is slowly but surely leading to the homogenisation of European high streets.

Rosy Retail Future?

Economic and retail sales growth has slowed across much of Western Europe since the turn of the millennium, with the softness in the economy driven in large part by cyclical factors such as reduced exports amid global weakness. However, in countries such as Germany and Italy, the economy also suffers from structural barriers to growth, such as a rigid labour market and a strict regulatory environment. Among Europe's five largest economies, the outlook for retail sales growth is mixed.

Retail Forward forecasts that retail sales in Germany will continue to fall this year following a 2.3 per cent slide in 2002. In France, retail sales growth has been on a slowing trend since 1999 and sales are forecast to grow at a moderate 2.4 per cent pace in 2003 as the economy recovers from the recent slowdown.

Following several years of rapid growth in the UK, sales are expected to slow, registering about a three per cent increase. Despite the slowdown in the Italian economy, the retail sector grew nearly two per cent in 2002, the strongest increase in more than 10 years. However, growth is expected to ease below one per cent in 2003. Retail sales grew an estimated 2.9 per cent in Spain last year and that growth is expected to improve slightly in 2003 to more than three per cent.

Accreditation

just-style.com is the leading global textile, apparel and footwear web site, giving industry professionals easy access to the latest industry news, hundreds of valuable feature articles, and over three years of archive material. The site's unique content is researched and produced via our dedicated editorial team and a worldwide network of correspondents. In addition, the new just-style.com research store provides you with instant access to over 300 reports, books and research products from leading market information providers.

To browse just-style.com and discover how you could benefit, go to: www.just-style.com

Source: just-style.com

No part of this publication may be copied, reproduced, stored in a retrieval system, or be transmitted in any form by any means electronic, mechanical, photocopying, recording or otherwise without the prior permission of the publishers. All material published within this report is copyright Aroq Limited.

This report is provided for individual use only. If you would like to share this report with your colleagues, purchase additional copies or sign up for a company wide licence please contact Will Johnston:
Tel: +44 (0)1527 573 608. Fax: +44 (0)1527 577 423. Email: will@aroq.com

Aroq Limited
Registered in England no: 4307068
Seneca House, Buntsford Hill Business Park, Bromsgrove, Worcs, B60 3DX, UK.
Tel: +44 (0)1527 573 600 Fax: +44 (0)1527 577 423 Web: www.aroq.com

© 2003 All content copyright Aroq Limited. All rights reserved.

> **Page 41 of Reiss**

Appendix 4.

Cambridge Store

Source: Lever and Hopley

Part C: Practice cases

Page 42 of Reiss

King's Road, London Store

Source: Lever and Hopley

15 ♦ Tackling a practice case: Reiss

> **Page 43 of Reiss**

Leeds Store

Source: Lever and Hopley

Part C: Practice cases

Page 44 of Reiss

Newcastle Store

Source: Lever and Hopley

Page 45 of Reiss

The Chartered
Institute of Marketing

Moor Hall, Cookham
Maidenhead
Berkshire SL6 9QH, UK
Telephone 01628 427120
Facsimile 01628 427158
Web site: http://www.cim.co.uk

Part C: Practice cases

3 Step 1: Initial overview

3.1 As you can see, this Case is about a family business, started by David Reiss's father, selling Italian suits for men. Over the years the business has moved around the supply chain. At one time Reiss owned a factory in Yorkshire and, until 2001, the company had a wholesale as well as a retail business.

3.2 By 2001, not only had Reiss moved into women's fashion but had also focused on retail. This market development strategy has given the company a 'unique' position as the only 'bridging brand' catering for both men and women. You will need to consider how strong a differentiator this is (or could be) and how valuable a benefit it may be to customers.

3.3 Clothing is a consumer durable product. We are all familiar with it so you should have no difficulty in relating to the Case context.

> **Consumer durables are not Fast Moving Consumer Goods**
>
> Do not confuse FMCG's with durables – that is a mistake you should not make. Durables, as their name implies, have a 'life' and so are purchases made infrequently – washing machines, watches, furniture, cars and of course, clothes. Shopping behaviour can vary, but would usually be based on a shopping trip to see what is available, before making a selection. **Branding** is not so much about loyalty, as it is in a frequently-purchased FMCG market, but about **reassurance** or **prestige** in an area the customer may feel unfamiliar with because purchases are infrequent. In fashion markets, the brand adds value. As for prestige – think about the premium prices paid for Lacoste, Nike or Chanel products.

3.4 This Case is strongly based on the UK but you need to take care not to ignore the international dimensions.

(a) Exchange rates impact on supply costs

(b) The fashion market is increasingly global with strong international competitors eg Zara, who now have 900 stores in 30 countries (some 30 times the size of Reiss) [Case page 34, paragraph 4]

(c) Reiss have global ambitions and the Dublin store is being treated as a pilot for developing other international outlets.

3.5 The Ireland pilot could provide the context for extra information - perhaps you will be given the results of the first year of trading in Dublin. This can help you formulate an international expansion strategy.

3.6 So, you need to ensure your analysis covers home and overseas opportunities. You will need to take your time but don't worry if you have little experience of the sector. Case technique remains the same, as does the planning process, irrespective of size or sector.

3.7 Remember, the analysis you undertake before the exam provides the foundation for your recommended strategies - but analysis alone will not get you a pass. Case exams emphasise a longer-term customer-oriented business strategy and the need for commercially credible proposals. You must be prepared to present these to the examiner in a professional way and make your recommendations persuasive and convincing.

4 Step 2: Completing your overview

4.1 This first step in the case process is an important one. It allows you to familiarise yourself with the case content and really understand the context established both by the industry and the scenario set. It is the essential foundation for your detailed in-view analysis. At this stage, try not to worry about what you will be asked to do, but focus instead on understanding the material available to you and make a note of the information gaps.

4.2 Try to sort out the products, segments, the current activities and positioning of Reiss. Take it in a couple of short bursts if you start to get muddled. Sort out all the information on the fashion market in general and then move on to the specific information on the company and its portfolio. You may keep information on men and women's fashion separate.

(a) Do not just rely on what is written. Think about the business; try to picture it in your own mind, a visit to the Reiss website or store would help.

(b) What do you know about the characteristics of marketing in an international consumer market?

(c) The design and fashion industry is varied and complex. The company has it seems, successfully added geography and women's ranges to its core business. It seems to be extending into other 'products'. How far can this be stretched? Will its values and look export well?

(d) Brand strategy is critical but how robust is it? Will it date? How well is it differentiated and communicated?

(e) Channel management, branding and new product development all seem to be issues which could be on the examiner's agenda - certainly the service element of the marketing mix is key to differentiating the company's offering. What is the shopping experience like?

(f) Contemporary issues in this case include customer relationship management and the short life cycles/need for effective NPD strategies with as many as eight seasons in the fashion industry.

4.3 Faced with an increasingly competitive market and demanding customers, Reiss will need to be clear about who they are serving and what benefits they are offering.

4.4 The following notes are tutor comments that will help you to assess your overview. Before reviewing them, complete your own overview of the case study. You need to practice handling case material and be able to assess whether or not you are working in both the breadth and depth needed in the case exam. Note page references given refer to page numbers within the case study.

Part C: Practice cases

5 Step 3: Assessing your overview

The industry and Reiss's position in it

5.1 The fashion industry is both fascinating and complex, as is the retail industry, and Reiss is active in both.

5.2 Reiss is however a small player. The UK fashion industry was valued at £26 billion (page 7) in 2002 and Reiss had sales of almost £21 million in the year ending 31st January 2002 (page 24), representing less than 0.08 per cent of the market. This is just under one tenth of one per cent of the UK market, so it seems reasonable to place Reiss as a niche player, contrasting with operators such as George at Asda acting as cost leaders.

Generic strategies in the fashion market

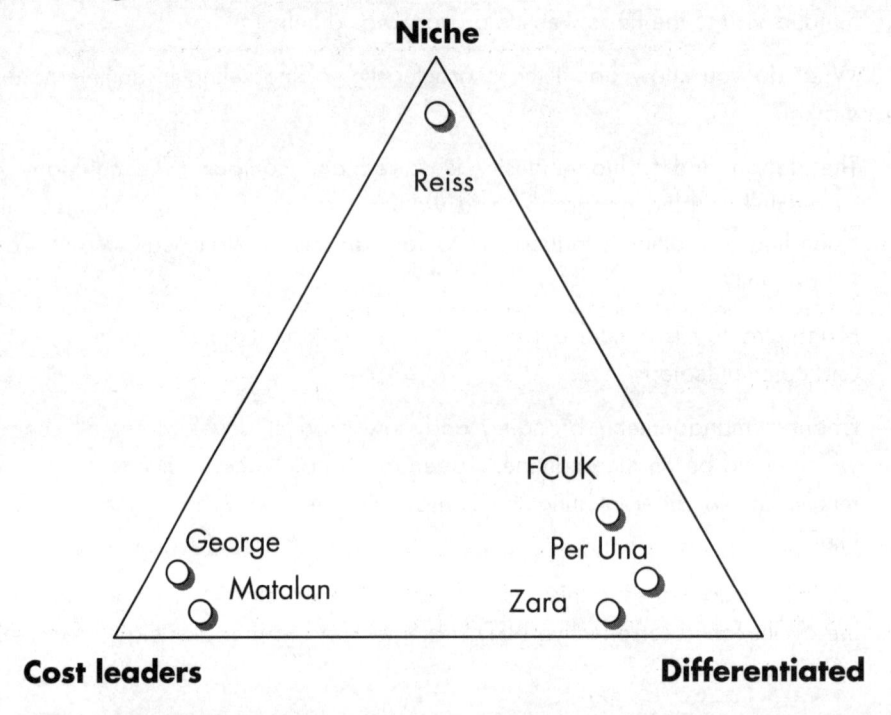

```
                    Niche
                      ○
                    Reiss




                              FCUK
                               ○
              George         Per Una
               ○              ○
              Matalan        Zara
               ○              ○
  Cost leaders                    Differentiated
```

5.3 You may have a different perception of where key players have positioned their strategy but use the models to help you capture and communicate your assessment. We may find that Reiss themselves have drifted into a 'middle of the road' position.

Defining the market

5.4 One of the problems with any Case Study is determining precisely the market space we need to be concerned with. There are a number of dimensions to this.

- Geography
- Classification/position
- Segment/sector
- Current/future

5.5 When you start to focus your questions more specifically, you find the market space better defined and therefore the value of case data and information clearer. In a sense, you are answering two questions.

(a) What market is Reiss in today?
(b) What market might Reiss be in tomorrow?

15 ♦ Tackling a Practice Case: Reiss

	Today	Tomorrow
By geography:	UK Ireland	UK Ireland International
By segment/sector:	Men's Women's	Men's Women's Children's?
By classification:	Designer wear/off the shelf Accessories	Designer wear/off the shelf Accessories Lifestyle products and services

Within the men's and women's designer-wear market, Reiss is known as a 'bridging brand', as it bridges 'high' and 'high street' fashion, and men's and women's products.

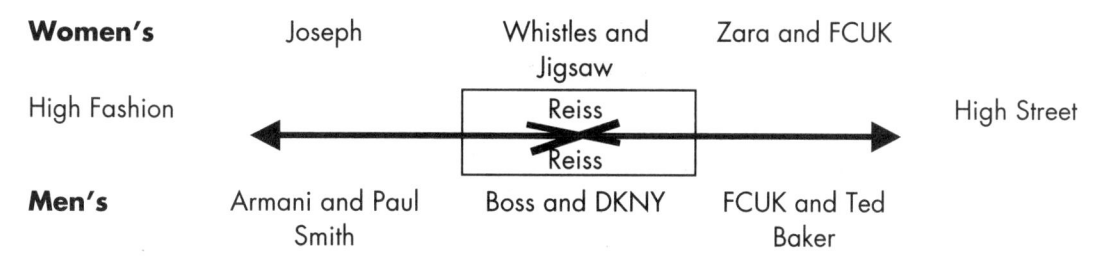

Women's Joseph   Whistles and Jigsaw   Zara and FCUK

High Fashion ←———————— Reiss / Reiss ————————→ High Street

Men's Armani and Paul Smith   Boss and DKNY   FCUK and Ted Baker

For both male and female fashion, Reiss is positioned between high fashion and high street fashion.

5.6 It offers a retail experience and an aspirational lifestyle brand, which is reflected in its prices and retail outlets, several of which are housed in listed buildings. It is classified as part of the independent retail sector – which represents 26 per cent of UK fashion retail (page 8).

About the extra information

5.7 You should not bring additional information into your Case analysis but if you are unfamiliar with the Reiss brand, a visit to their website (or a store) will really help you visualise and get to grips with their positioning. The website lets you look at images from a store as well as examples of their product range.

Tutor Tip

*Additional information and its prohibition always causes case students concern. You should **not** do specific external research, but you **can** use your own general knowledge and experience. Do **not** quote specific data and numbers, but use your knowledge particularly of the macro environment to help your understanding and analysis.*

About the company

5.8 Reiss is a company which, on the face of things, seems successful. Reiss is growing rapidly and has further growth ambitions. In the last three years they have doubled their retail outlets from 13 to 31 (including Guildford, which we can assume opened after August 2003, see page 4 and a fourth concession in King William Street, London see page 3). That is a new store every three months or so, quite a challenge for the team to manage.

Part C: Practice cases

In total, the company has about 75,000 square feet of retail space. The average store sizes are increasing to accommodate men and women's ranges (see page 4).

Note however, that average size is reduced by much smaller concessions.

5.9 Appendix 1 and Table 1 represent some key data in this Case Study. Take care not to get confused between financial years (ending 31st January) and calendar years. You can assume that the trading results reported at January 2003 relate essentially to business in calendar year 2002.

Stores opened during that year will not contribute a full year's trading and you are presenting to the Senior Management Team only six weeks before the 2003 results are reported.

5.10 As square footage has increased, so have sales from £17 million in 1999 to a forecast £35 million in 2003 (page 4). Effectively this means double the stores and the turnover. However, you will notice when you look at the financial statements on page 24 that revenue in 2002 was only £20 million. This implies revenue is forecast to grow by £15 million (some 75 per cent) in one year. Some of this could be explained by new stores – five opened by August 2003 (page 4) but not all of these will add a full year to the trading figures. We may need to bear in mind the possibility that this forecast is 'bullish' and the reality may be less buoyant.

Tutor Tip

As you get into your own Case analysis you will be able to draw your own conclusions but it is worth remembering that just because something is written in the Case, doesn't necessarily make it true. Question and check numbers and data from elsewhere in the Case where possible and ask yourself whether figures and forecasts or objectives are credible. We will return to the numbers later in more detail during the inview analysis at Stage 2.

The company structure

5.11 You will find you need to look for clues about the company and its culture. Reiss has been a family business and David Reiss is the entrepreneurial driver behind its progress. That can be a weakness as well as a strength. What would happen without him? Laura Ashley really struggled when their founder died, but Body Shop has not suffered since the retirement of Anita Roddick. The question is, to what extent do the values and vision belong to the individual or are they shared by everyone?

5.12 Staff numbers are increasing in line with the expansion. Between 31st January 2001 and 2003, numbers increased from 234 to 325 (page 24). If you make allowances for staff turnover (traditionally fairly high in retail), you might assume that less than 1:3 of the staff have been with the firm for more than two years. In itself that may not be a problem but managing fast expansion and ensuring coherent culture and values is harder. Internal communications is likely to be a challenge.

5.13 Marketing is not in evidence as a function within Reiss (page 5). The activities of strategic marketing have been divided up across the senior team.

New product development	Creative director
Merchandising	Finance director
Display	Operations director
PR	Creative director

Comments on page 18 indicate that a corporate view of marketing is limited to store windows and graphics, perhaps campaign involvement, but little more.

5.14 Your overview should leave you asking **a lot of marketing questions**.

   (a)   Who is responsible for customer research and forecasting?

   (b)   Who decides on positioning and is managing the brand?

   (c)   Who has/is decided/deciding on segmentation and ensuring the Reiss offer and experience meets evolving clients' needs?

   (d)   Who is analysing market opportunities?

   (e)   Who is ensuring integrated communications activities?

5.15 Your list could go on and on. You might suspect that Reiss is a design rather than customer-led company. We have almost no specific customer data – in terms of age/profile/average spend/frequency of visit and so on. Is this because the data does not exist?

5.16 Are Reiss' female clients worth double a male client in line with average spend (page 8)? Are men's and women's products equally profitable and are the clients equally loyal?

5.17 Create yourself an information shopping list and add to it as you work through the Case. You always need to be prepared for a question on marketing information system proposals and with the evident gaps in this Case it wouldn't be an unreasonable question to ask a consultant.

Your role

5.18 Your role is clear. You are a marketing consultant appointed by the Senior Management Team at Reiss. The material you are working from comes from a report produced by a graduate employed by Reiss (page 1).

What is less clear is what you will be expected to answer questions on. There are a number of possibilities:

- International expansion
- Stronger, more differentiated branding and communication
- UK marketing strategy
- Improving sales per square foot or average client value.

5.19 There is evidence that the finance director has worked hard to ensure the efficiency of the operation (page 5), so focus going forward is likely to be on improved effectiveness – building loyalty, a broader client case and maximising earnings per square foot. Currently this is falling and it is a key measure of marketing effectiveness so you can be fairly certain neither David Reiss, not the senior management team will be very happy with this situation.

Part C: Practice cases

6 Highlights from the overview

6.1 Use the following notes as guidance to help you as you access your overview analysis. They are presented to highlight rather than direct and you will need to decide for yourself how important each point is, but do take note of points you may have missed – keep asking yourself 'so what'? – it is interpretation of analysis that adds insights.

Page 1

6.2 The candidate brief – we have already indicated the significance of you being positioned as a **consultant**. This brief is long on company background and short on the specifics of what you will be required to do. But successful marketing is, it seems, one of the critical success factors and you can be expected to face questions about future marketing strategies from the SMT.

Page 2

6.3 Historically, we find that Reiss has followed a strategy of organic growth. Growth, over the last five years, has been rapid and driven by managing director, David Reiss. The first anomaly is found in paragraph 4 where we are told 'today the company has a wholesale side' which contradicts page 4 paragraph 3, 'Reiss ceased wholesaling in 2001'.

About anomalies

6.4 You need to make an assumption about which of these is correct and then work with it consistently. As we have no other data on wholesale performance, our preference is to go with the page 4 version. Do not let such problems distract you, they are a characteristic of case work – make your judgement, stick to it consistently and move on.

6.5 It is reassuring to see that before launching the women's wear brand, some market research was undertaken (page 5) but we do not seem to have access to its findings.

6.6 We also get the sense of how the company took a long time building the solid foundations that would be the platform for its future growth. They opened only about five stores in 25 years but then the growth strategy driven by David Reiss kicked in.

Page 3

6.7 Notice the impact of the market development strategy highlighted in paragraph 1. Although only launched in 2/3^{rds} of the stores by September 2000, women's wear represented 21% of 2001 turnover and 30% by the end of 2002. We have no information on whether it is in all stores by 2003 and its continued roll out could explain the high revenue forecast for 2003.

6.8 The strategy of growth is clear in this page – geographic expansion (including a first international opening) plus the new women's market.

6.9 Concessions in House of Fraser stores (page 4) have been added, perhaps to build the brand profile as well as offering a cost effective alternative to expanding their own retail networks. Unfortunately, we have no information on performance of concessions versus stores. Presumably it is much harder to control the environment and build the exclusive brand image in a concession

15 ♦ Tackling a Practice Case: Reiss

and the available space is much smaller than the 3,000 square foot space now preferred to house both men's and women's ranges.

6.10 Store openings require purchase or lease of property, concessions will require rent and commission.

6.11 It is also clear form this page how important design within the environment of the stores is. Choosing listed buildings does not make retail investment either cheap or simple – it should however create a 'unique' shopping experience. The stores themselves could be a differentiator – the question is, are they?

Page 4

6.12 Notice the stores list only goes up to August 2003 and we know Guildford has been added since then (paragraph 1) and a fourth concession (page 3).

6.13 You can play with these numbers to compare year on year store growth with the increase in square footage. Average store sizes are growing (excluding concessions). These are fixed costs and the value of property investments will be considerable but it gives a strong asset base to the business and would be useful if it needed to support borrowing.

6.14 By comparing square footage and sales income (page 24) you can calculate a sales per square foot as a metric but take care – we do not have specific dates for store openings and so you can't assume a whole year's trading in the year of opening.

6.15 You can however get a rough estimate to work with. We took the number of trading units of each year end and then took an 'average' between each year which allows for the new units to contribute, on average six months trade in its first year.

Year ending 31st January

	2000	2001	2002	2003	2004
Number of trading units at year end (financial)	12	13	16	24	31
Average number of units that year		12.5	14.5	20.0	27.5

6.16 In the same way you can calculate trading space at the financial year end and an average. This enables you to consider average sales per square foot.

6.17 We learn in paragraph 2 of further product development into accessories – the withdrawal from wholesale (and why) and the extent of forecast growth, £35 million in 2003.

Paragraph 4

6.18 A new office move is planned for next month (January 2004) and we are told that one benefit will be improved internal communications. This could be a clue about a communications question and it is one worth being prepared for. Pull out a stakeholder map for the business; employees, shareholders, fashion critics, store managers and staff etc. You will then be able to think about communication strategies for each stakeholder group.

Part C: Practice cases

Page 6

6.19 You will need to sort out the information on this page to help you understand and perhaps chart the new product development process. A few points are worth highlighting, the company, it seems, cannot benefit from cost economies of bulk fabric purchases from Asia Pacific.

6.20 In paragraph 2 we have another point of differentiation identified '.......pride themselves on offering the customer something new in terms of style, colour and fabric'.

6.21 In the final paragraph there is the comment on the exchange rate. Currently with a stronger Euro and the UK not yet a member of the 'Euro club' there is a reason for the management team to take steps to manage currency fluctuations to avoid profits being damaged by exchange rate changes. However, this should not be too problematic if currencies are purchased when orders are placed etc.

Page 8

6.22 Women spend more than men on clothes (now there's a surprise!).

6.23 The question is, is diversifying into children's wear a strategic option, à la Baby Gap? That strategy may not 'fit' with the image of the brand but it is an option to add to your Ansoff Matrix (note these are 1997 figures – do take care when using secondary data, even in a case exam).

6.24 We are told the middle market for fashion in the UK is saturated. We know competition here is fierce not just because of C&A and Littlewoods departures but the problems M&S has had with getting its fashion offer right.

6.25 New entrants include other retailers like the supermarkets and international players like Zara. You can begin to build up your Porter's Five Force's picture of increasing competition and threatened margins.

6.26 Reiss is one player in the independent retailer sector making up 26 per cent of the total market.

Page 9

6.27 These retailers face problems which are examined on page 9. Reiss have their own brand and so avoid some of the problems but this sector is likely to get squeezed. If they fail to offer customers a truly differentiated and valued service, customers will be less and less likely to pay the premiums needed to support smaller independents.

Page 10: About designer wear

6.28 You will find background to the designer wear market on this page. You can see that Reiss is active in designer wear with 'off the peg' ranges where the Reiss label is an important differentiator. Reiss is in competition with other bridge collections. We find the retail market is fragmented but supplier power is relatively strong with only a few large suppliers.

6.29 You might note the success of retail partnerships like 'Per Una' at Marks & Spencer – does this provide a model for international expansion?

6.30 This is a luxury market dependent on discretionary spend, income levels as well as social and demographic factors.

The customers

6.31 Across the Case you will find information about population statistics. You will need to pull these together to build a complete picture. Reiss needs to decide how it is then going to position itself.

(a) The under 24's are most fashion conscious but have less disposable income.

(b) Over 55's are growing but more sceptical about the value of designer wear.

(c) Working men and women could be a target (ie working wardrobes rather than leisure) or they could provide all clothing needs for a specific lifestyle and age range.

Page 12

6.32 Although it seems the savings ratio has been increasing since a low in 1999 it is projected to fall between now and 2006. You might wonder why, with the increasing emphasis on saving for our own pensions etc – remember forecasts are just that. When completing your PEST analysis you will need to complete your opportunities and threats matrix:

(a) What is the environmental change?
(b) How likely is it to happen?
(c) What impact would it have on Reiss or designer wear if it did?

Page 13

6.33 In this market place the brand's success is dependent on each season's collections (you might remember that many observers blamed the failure of a 'grey' season for the demise of much of M&S's fashion business).

6.34 The new product development process is therefore a real interest and importance to the business. Create your own mind map of the influences and processes. How could market research, mystery shopping or environmental scanning help inform process?

Page 14

6.35 We are offered the criteria by which new range decisions are assessed (more input for multi-factor matrices). It seems there is a growing market for accessories and it seems many potential clients will be occasional buyers rather than regular loyal shoppers.

6.36 It may be sensible to keep your notes on men's and women's markets separate. There are clearly differences in buyer behaviour and potential and it is possible you will need to respond to information about one or other sector.

The media

6.37 Managing publicity to raise the brand profile is an important aspect of the communications strategy for a fashion brand and being seen in the right publications will be important. Unfortunately, we have no information about current promotional activities or their effectiveness

– however, the advantage of this is that you have something of a blank sheet of paper to work with.

Page 15

6.38 The content about the mix continues with some insights about pricing. Note Reiss already has concessions in form for example, Bluewater.

6.39 This page is a good example of the 'mix' of facts in a Case narrative. New technology in fabric is a PEST factor whilst counterfeit products is a threat.

Page 17

6.40 The core men's market for Reiss would seem a strength if this is the more rapidly growing sector – 33 per cent since 1997.

The brand

6.41 Reiss is an exclusive brand with a target audience of men and women ages 18-40. You will note that this is still a fairly broad segmentation for a £35 million company and more targeted segmental analysis may help.

6.42 You have some examples of prices (this could help us check the credibility of any growth objective) and it gives you an indication of the current portfolio.

At the bottom of page 17 the brand values are spelled out.

Page 18

6.43 Clearly Reiss has ambitions for establishing a global brand. They have their eyes on Southern Europe, the USA and Japan. Obviously they will need to be careful about not spreading themselves too thinly but their interest in an international strategy is clearly high on the agenda so it is a question we need to be ready for.

The P of place

6.44 The stores are as well designed as the clothes and clearly add to the brand experience. The difference between concessions and owned or leased stores has already been flagged up. Remember, that increasing the proportion of concession based outlets would influence the ROCE, as less capital is needed to open a concession.

Marketing

6.45 Marketing seems to be viewed as communications only, so your strategic approach may need justifying. A strategy to build the brand profile is another question area you will need to be prepared for.

6.46 Reiss has a design-based culture, so integration and consistency across the mix is already understood and applied (whether or not it is labelled marketing). They also seem to understand

15 ♦ Tackling a Practice Case: Reiss

the value of 'thinking global but acting local', which will be valuable as they expand internationally.

6.47 Note the portfolio extension into branded CDs and books – we do not know the justification for this nor the sort of revenue generated.

6.48 Customer segmentation is clearly a bit thin and the information on competitors likewise.

Page 20

6.49 It is external information but the website is slow and the unwillingness to use it for transactions may need challenging. In fact, a lot of clothes are bought by mail order and off websites. For loyal customers who know the brand, this could be an attractive, time-saving option and certainly it could be a shop window for accessories. It is perhaps an option which should be considered.

Pages 21 and 22

Branding

6.50 If you needed any clues of a possible branding question they occur on these pages.

6.51 Note Reiss's strong brand strategy, a family brand based on the retailer (not the designer). Revise your communication notes on brand building and brand strategy.

Page 23

6.52 The lifecycles developed by the Senior Examiner are not totally clear. Fashion life cycles are usually not the normal 'S' shaped curve but much more exaggerated.

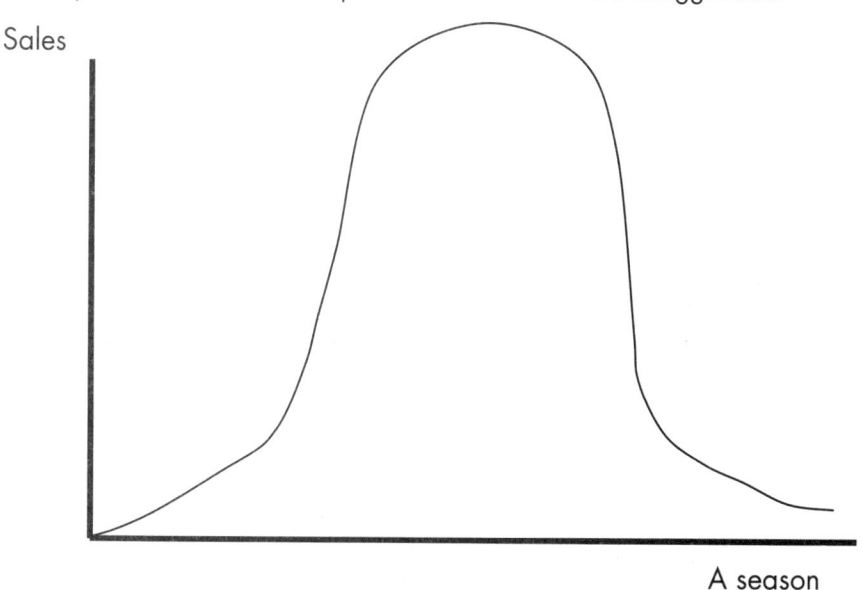

Sales vs. A season

(a) Early, late and normal demand could refer to customer types eg innovators and laggards etc.

(b) Timing is key at the launch and at the end of a range. Price can be used to help influence sales volume but price elasticity will vary across products.

Part C: Practice cases

(c) Make a note of the strategic priorities of the most recent three lines (and so question areas are pretty clear).

Appendix 1

> **Tutor Tip**
>
> *Will all non-numerate marketers try not to panic! You will need to understand these numbers. Get help from a friend if you need to or talk to a friendly accountant at work. It is essentially a strong profitable operation.*

6.53 You may find the presentation of some of the financial data confusing because the grouped elements and subtotals are not clear. Do not get hung up on the tables. They do not add up because they are extracts and are not intended to do so, but you can get some useful metrics and insights from them.

Year ended	31.1.2003	31.1.2002	31.1.2001
	£'000	£'000	£'000
Tangible Fixed Assets	**9,356**	**7,750**	**7,226**
Current Assets	4,472	4,118	4,471
Current Liabilities	(6,868)	(5,559)	(5,968)
Working Capital	**(2,396)**	**(1,441)**	**(1,497)**
Long Term Liabilities	**(2,415)**	**(2,988)**	**(3,019)**
Net Worth	4,545	3,321	2,710
Add: Intangible assets	48	53	59
Less: Long Term Liabilities	2,415	2,988	3,019
Capital employed	**7,008**	**6,362**	**5,788**

There are some assumptions and facts to note for yourself:

(a) The company probably owns the freehold of most of its stores, although you can't be certain. This would account for £9.3 million invested in fixed assets.

(b) The ability of the business to meet its day-to-day commitments is stretched. Its working capital position is negative in all three years. It will need to concentrate on judicious control of its cash flows.

(c) As a retail business its debtors will mainly be credit card companies.

(d) Turnover per square foot has fallen, as have operating costs by some 20 per cent +. These figures give you a potential basis for objective setting. Turnover per employee is also down - so though still a profitable business it is less effective than previously.

6.54 Work through your analysis and be certain you have a key numbers page, which you understand and recognise the implications of.

Pages 27 and 28

6.55 This appendix gives us a clue about the lack of competition and opportunity for men's products. Work through this to pick up details on competitors and so on.

Pages 29 and 30

6.56 Information on the Irish store, an investment of £750,000 for 3,000 square foot (notice the anomaly between table 1 and this press article - I assume the company records are accurate). We are given clues about the need for quick profit on new stores and again the examiner could be setting the scene for those first all important results.

Pages 31 and 32

6.57 There is an opportunity for a second Ireland store, this could be a decision the SMT have to make soon.

Pages 33, 34 and 35

6.58 This is an older article (May 2000) but provides us greater insight into the fashion retailing market, much of it re-affirming material you will already have assimilated. You will however, pick up extra facts and figures about the importance of earnings per square foot and the general feelings about the importance of global branding.

Pages 36, 37 and 38

6.59 Here you are given some background for the European opportunities and marketplace. The flow chart on page 39 is very useful in describing the recommended strategy for success in this sector. You might consider where and how marketing could help implement this.

Your Case finishes with some of the Reiss images, how strong do you find the brand?

7 Summary

7.1 We are faced with a rapidly growing and successful company with a fairly sound financial base and global as well as growth ambitions.

7.2 Managing the brand, cash flow and the portfolio are likely to be critical to long-term success. There is a need for even stronger differentiation and positioning if the Reiss brand is to be noticed in an increasingly competitive marketplace. Notice how the middle of the road players like Marks & Spencer are moving into the designer wear space.

7.3 Managing growth is the focus for our strategy. They are already doing well, you will need to demonstrate how marketing can help them do even better. Notice that a £10 per square foot increase in revenue adds some £750,000 revenue to the business and currently sales per square foot measure seems to be declining – working harder rather than smarter is never a good idea.

Part C: Practice cases

7.4 By this stage, you should have a much greater sense of the Reiss business and the challenges it faces.

Problems and opportunities

7.5 As you work through the Case you will begin to see problems and opportunities.

(a) The problem – at home:

  (i) Increased competition, due to polarisation of the fashion market and growth of cheaper as well as prestige brands

  (ii) Changing buying behaviours for example, increased importance of department stores and propensity to mix and match

  (iii) Reiss is extending its portfolio, women's fashion, accessories, books and CDs. Is there a danger of causing confusion about the brand image? It could end up as a 'middle of the road' player

  (iv) The possibility that the brand will be less popular if spending power falls or fashions change

  (v) Currently, growth is rapid and organic. Is there a danger they may spread themselves too thin?

(b) The opportunity – at home:

  (i) Increase brand awareness and profile
  (ii) Extend UK market coverage through new stores, concessions or e-sales
  (iii) Expand the portfolio eg children's fashion or lifestyle products.

(c) The problem – overseas:

  (i) Only one store currently

  (ii) No clear strategy for the brand overseas, no decisions about which markets offer the best opportunities

  (iii) Possibly in danger of spreading itself too thin – too many countries and products

  (iv) Cost of market entry in terms of brand awareness etc likely to be high.

You can test your own grasp of the Case basics by tackling the Action Programme which follows, before moving on to see how previous students pulled the case information together to complete an inview analysis for Reiss.

15 ♦ Tackling a Practice Case: Reiss

Action Programme

1. Who are you and what is your role?
2. Who is David Reiss and what is his influence on the organisation?
3. Look at this Ansoff Matrix depicting the Reiss business in 1999, how has it changed?

MR = Men's retail

MW = Men's wholesale

Products

	Existing	New
Existing (Markets)	MR, MW	
New		

4. What is the forecast turnover for Reiss in 2003?
5. Who is Steven Downes and what is his role and areas of responsibility?
6. How would you define the sector of the market Reiss operates in?
7. What is happening to competition in the UK fashion market?
8. How does the magazine market impact on the Reiss business?

Action Programme Review

1. Marketing consultant to Reiss.

2. Managing Director and the entrepreneurial driver of the business – his vision, energy, imagination, flair and creative ability are seen to be key in driving the business forward (page 2).

3.

   MR = Men's retail

   MW = Men's wholesale

	Products	
	Existing	New
Markets Existing	MR / MW	
New		

   It entered women's retail in 2000, left wholesale in 2001, moved into Ireland in 2002, has begun to look at other predicts – accessories/books/CD's etc.

4. £35 million

5. He is the FD but also responsible for merchandising and IT.

6. Designer wear off the peg/'bridge collections'.

7. Polarisation and globalisation, some consolidation is expected.

8. Their editorial influences fashion trends, they offer PR and advertising space which is tightly targeted. The number of titles is growing.

Reiss: Analysis Steps 2-4

Chapter Topic List

1	Completing the analysis for Reiss
2	Step 2A: Internal audit
3	The strengths and weaknesses of Reiss's marketing
4	Step 2B: Situation audit
5	Step 3A: External analysis
6	Step 3B: External analysis: competition
7	Step 3C: Market and customer analysis
8	Step 3D: Stakeholder analysis
9	Step 4: Critical success factors

Introduction

In this long chapter you will:

- ☑ Work through the internal and external analysis for Reiss
- ☑ Compare your approach with that of the other students to help you assess and improve your own technique
- ☑ Prioritise activities and establish Reiss's critical success factors

1 Completing the Analysis for Reiss

1.1 Once you have a broad understanding of the case study you are much better placed to tackle the more detailed audits and analysis. This is the time consuming part of your case work and remember, if working with others, you can share the work load.

1.2 For each step in the process we have provided you with some sample material and tutorial comments. We suggest you take this practice case a step at a time; complete one part of the analysis and review our feedback before moving on to the next step. Utilise the tools and models because they will help not only to pull material together for you but also to communicate your assessment to others.

Part C: Practice cases

1.3 By the end of this chapter you will have:

(a) Undertaken and reviewed the internal analysis of Reiss
(b) Undertaken a macro and micro external audit
(c) Consolidated your analysis into a SWOT framework
(d) Identified the critical success factors facing Reiss

2 Step 2A: Internal audit

> **Case step 2A: the internal audit – strengths and weaknesses of marketing**
>
> This first part of your analysis requires you to assess the strengths and weaknesses of the marketing activity at Reiss. Work under the marketing mix headings when you have completed it. Compare our work with the preventions of analysis provided below. These were taken from the work of candidates preparing for the Reiss exam, and you will find tutor comments where necessary.

3 The strengths and weaknesses of Reiss's marketing

3.1 Influence/image of marketing

Strengths	Weaknesses
■ David Reiss – influence of founder	■ No marketing director
	■ No marketing department
	■ PR, display and merchandising handled by three different directors
	■ Product/distribution orientated – not consumer disorientated
	■ Focused on efficiency not effectiveness

3.2 Planning and control

Strengths	Weaknesses

■ Conducted market research prior to entering women's market
■ Planning for the new office
■ Evidence of planning in production/logistics:
  – Stock control
  – Cross sourcing of fabric to get best prices
	■ Vague view about the European market
	■ Evidence that there is a vision (David's) but there are no long term objectives or plans to support the vision
	■ Silo mentality/over the wall approach – production dept hands over to ops dept
	■ No SMART objectives
	■ Planning – founder's gut feeling (entry into Dublin – pink men's wear and lots of surprises!)
	■ No control in terms of tracking performance versus competition
	■ No strategic planning
	■ No marketing audit – no proactivity to deal with competition

3.3 Current marketing strategies

Strengths	Weaknesses

■ Bridging brand strategy
■ Growth strategy based on
  (a) increasing stores/distribution
  b) entering new sectors (women)
Declared strategy – create new stores
	■ Consumer targeting strategy appears vague – demographic segmentation is broad but untargeted. (18-25, 25-35, 35+, young student, professional, older fashionable)
	■ 'One club' strategy (because no clear objectives)
	■ Under utilisation of the marketing mix

3.4 Brand and values

Strengths	Weaknesses
■ Reiss Signature in stores ■ Bridging brand ■ Aspirational and fashion leader/not follower ■ Premises – strong brand – unique, quirky, urban look, rough smooth, old/new juxtaposition ■ Drive branding and values through induction programmes	■ Stylish but boring – subdued (reporter) ■ Lack of consistent branding across premises and product mix ■ Reiss branding is understated on product ■ Low number of stores therefore low visibility of branding ■ Not a global brand (versus backdrop of competitors) ■ No supply chain 'buy in' into brand values – sourcing of materials, ethical debate, etc.

3.5 MkIS

Strengths	Weaknesses
■ Used external agency to research ladies' market ■ Awareness of positioning versus competition	■ No evidence of structured MkIS ■ No ongoing research ■ No evidence of a database although they have a website ■ Under-utilisation of website

3.6 Product

Strengths	Weaknesses
■ Expanding product range ■ Men 70% sales – women 30% sales ■ Limited continuity lines (exclusive) ■ Stylish ■ Aspirational ■ High quality	■ Product range too exclusive? ■ Non fashionable, subdued, too expensive (journalist) ■ Limited continuity lines = costly ■ Product mix is not consistent across stores = non availability ■ No evidence of NPD

3.7 Price

Strengths	Weaknesses
■ Premium pricing ■ Affordable designer wear ■ Wide price brands ■ Compete favourably with competitor stores – Zara, DKNY, Jigsaw	■ High price could alienate potential consumers ■ Can premium pricing be justified in low awareness/low disposable income areas against a backdrop of declining sales in Europe?

3.8 Promotion

Strengths	Weaknesses
■ PR (FHM/Maxim) ■ Website ■ Window displays ■ In-store graphics ■ Evidence of campaigns and fashion shoots	■ No evidence of integrated communications plan ■ No structure within Reiss that handles communications

3.9 Place

Strengths	Weaknesses
■ Rapid expansion – 29 stores and 3 concessions ■ Prime quality locations ■ Stores individually merchandised ■ Complete control over own sales as all sales go through own stores – guaranteed route to market ■ Signature look ■ Property ownership = huge asset base	■ Limited accessibility because products only available through Reiss outlets ■ High occupancy cost – prefer listed buildings ■ Does store mix (concessions and high street) send right brand imagery? ■ Distribution costs will be high due to city centres ■ Store locations – the correct place? ■ Is there an over-emphasis on store location versus other elements of marketing mix?

3.10 People

Strengths	Weaknesses
■ Good training ■ David Reiss = entrepreneurial ■ Professional management team ■ Good inductions ■ Relocation of team to Kent House to improve internal communications and creative processes	■ Designers not commercially aware ■ Multi role of some directors leading to inconsistency and lack of focus ■ Over-reliance on David Reiss ■ £15k per employee remuneration? ■ No international expert if they have aspirations to go international ■ No facilities manager/director in charge of property/assets ■ People = Brand. No evidence of 'Reiss Champions' in store

3.11 Process

Strengths	Weaknesses
■ Customer service ethic	■ No evidence of who or where products are made ■ No evidence of NPD process – Reiss do not follow any of the stages illustrated in the product development process (fig 2 page 13) ■ Generally there appears to be very little formalised processes in place – 'the way we do things around here' mentality

3.12 Physical evidence

Strengths	Weaknesses
■ Individual store aesthetics ■ Window displays ■ Staffing, merchandising, music, seasonal graphics	■ Understated versus competition ■ Inconsistency/low visibility of external appearance/branding – Cambridge store looks like a bank (more welcoming than Barclays)

> **Tutor Tip**
>
> *This is a logical approach which ensures all key areas are covered but doesn't give us a sense of the relative importance of various strengths and weaknesses.*

3.13 Information gaps

- No evidence of mission, vision and corporate objectives
- Sales split between products – what is best seller – ranking etc
- Average spend per visit
- No customer profile – who is buying what?
- Discounts/promotions
- Competitor information
- Marketing spend
- Level of advertising
- Type of advertising
- Type of PR
- Nature of personal selling in store
- Sales turnover conflicting info – £21 million/£35 million
- Do they still have wholesale operation?
- Awareness levels of Reiss
- Number and distribution of competitor outlets
- After-sales service
- Internal culture of organisation
- Information regarding manufacturing of products
- Sales per store – possible Pareto effect 80/20
- No evidence of CRM

> **Tutor Tip**
>
> *Note how thorough this information shopping list actually is – it could be very useful later.*

3.14 Positioning maps

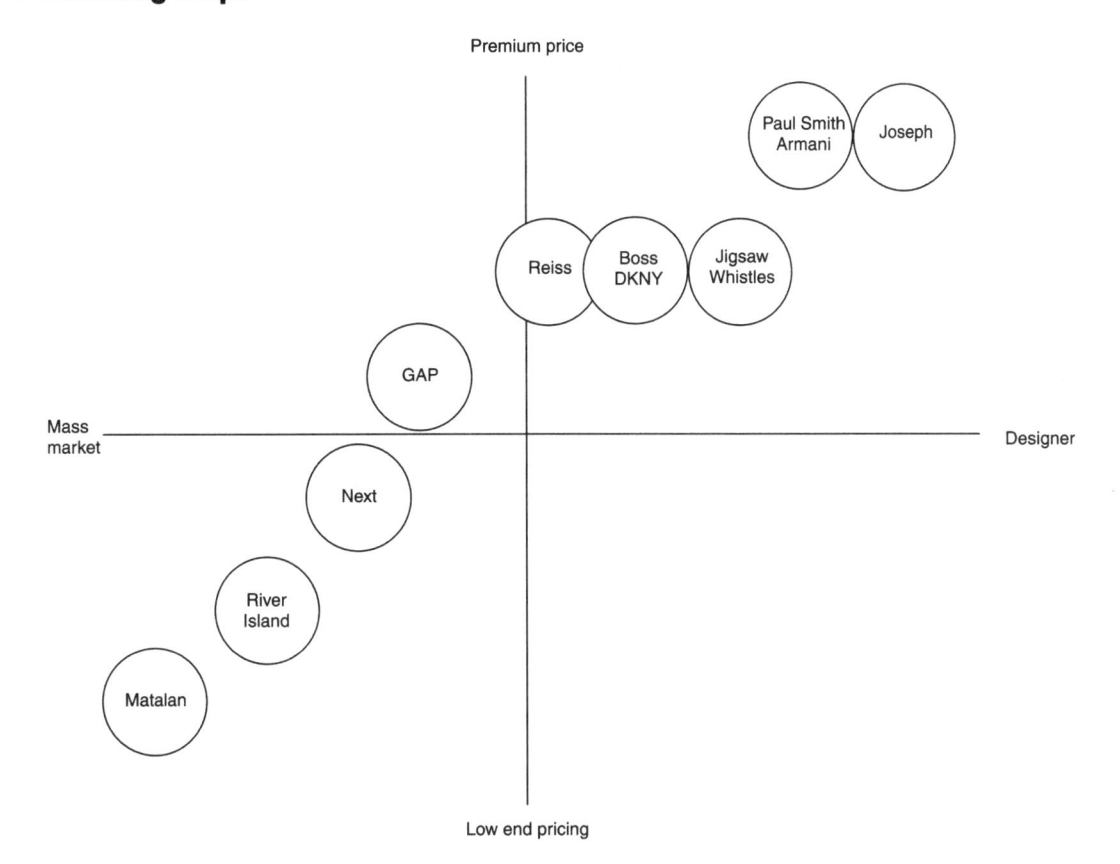

```
                    Premium price
                          │
                          │         ┌──────────┐  ┌──────┐
                          │         │Paul Smith│  │Joseph│
                          │         │  Armani  │  │      │
                          │         └──────────┘  └──────┘
                          │    ┌─────┐ ┌────┐ ┌───────┐
                          │    │Reiss│ │Boss│ │Jigsaw │
                          │    │     │ │DKNY│ │Whistles│
                          │    └─────┘ └────┘ └───────┘
                          │      ┌───┐
                          │      │GAP│
                          │      └───┘
 Mass ────────────────────┼──────────────────────────── Designer
 market                   │
                          │   ┌────┐
                          │   │Next│
                          │   └────┘
                          │ ┌──────┐
                          │ │River │
                          │ │Island│
                          │ └──────┘
                          │┌───────┐
                          ││Matalan│
                          │└───────┘
                          │
                    Low end pricing
```

Tutor Tip

Positioning maps are excellent for communication but if they get too crowded use colour to ensure the key brand stands out.

Part C: Practice cases

3.15 Total product concept

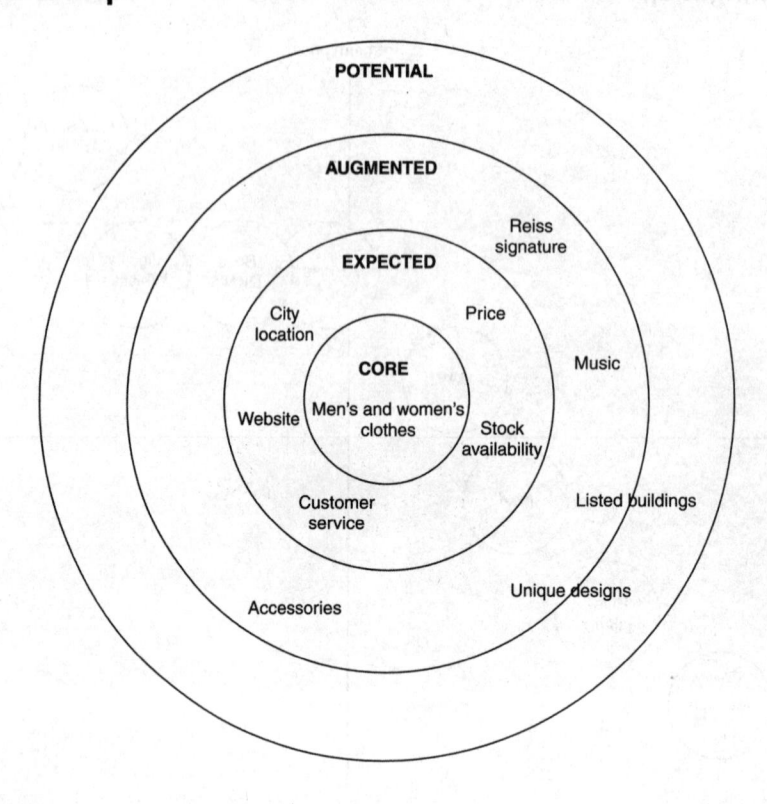

Core: Men's and women's clothes

Expected: City location, Price, Website, Stock availability, Customer service

Augmented: Reiss signature, Music, Listed buildings, Unique designs, Accessories

Potential:

> **Tutor Tip**
>
> Kotler's total product concept model helps identify potential and current differentiators and is a great way of communicating your proposed offer within a strategy recommendation

3.16 Product life cycle

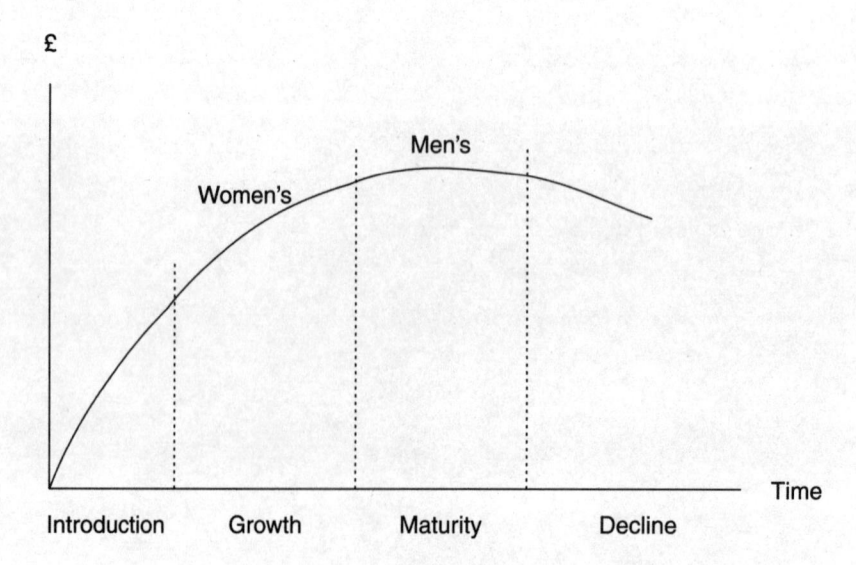

Stages along the curve: Introduction, Growth, Women's, Maturity, Men's, Decline (Time on x-axis, £ on y-axis)

Market share

Market share

High ─────────────────── Low

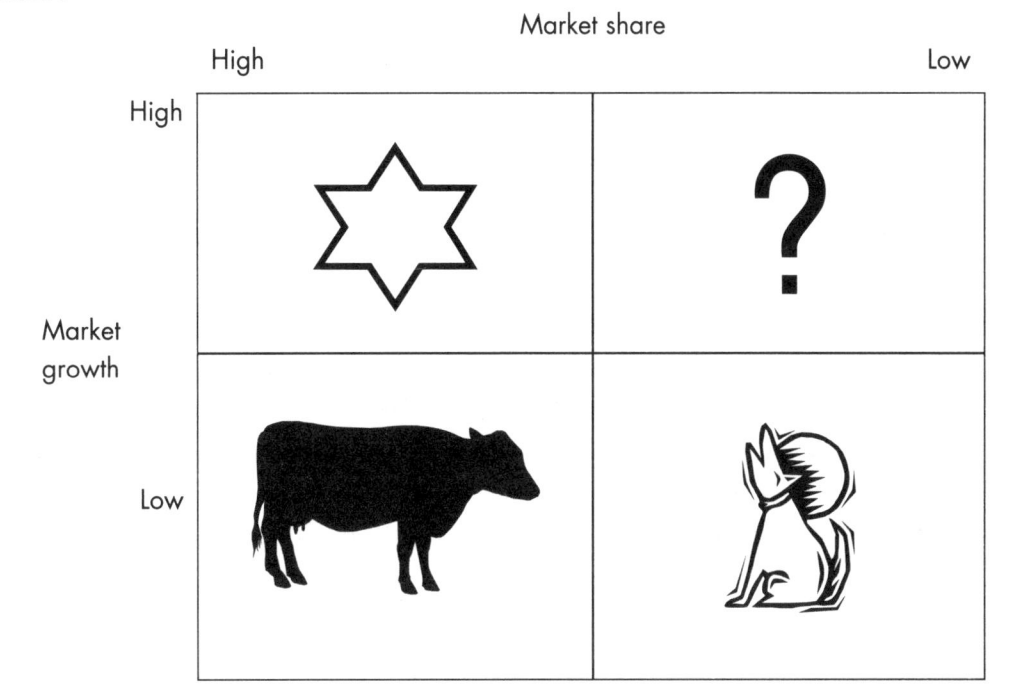

```
          High
                ┌─────────────┬─────────────┐
                │             │             │
                │     ★       │     ?       │
                │   (Star)    │ (Question)  │
                │             │             │
   Market      ├─────────────┼─────────────┤
   growth      │             │             │
                │   (Cow)     │   (Dog)     │
                │             │             │
                │             │             │
          Low   └─────────────┴─────────────┘
```

3.17 Summary

(a)	No evidence of marketing influence within Reiss
(b)	The company has developed through the 'gut feel' of David Reiss
(c)	Founder's vision is not translated into clear mission or objectives
(d)	No strategic planning and control within this company
(e)	They have pursued a niche strategy
(f)	Their aspiration is to grow and they have achieved this through entering the women's sector and by opening new stores
(g)	No evidence of any MkIS
(h)	Internal perception of brand positioning is negative
(i)	However brand development appears to be limited to product and place
(j)	Product offering is based on style, aspiration and high quality, and the company are fashion leaders
(k)	Pricing is premium but bridges gap between high street and mainstream designer wear
(l)	No evidence/limited promotional activity – profile building but little push/pull strategy
(m)	Brand building achieved through place
(n)	Professional and well inducted
(o)	Little evidence of formal process – doing things efficiently but not effectively

Tutor Tip

How well did your analysis measure up to this group's? Don't be surprised if it is not as detailed; people work particularly hard on the exam case.

Part C: Practice cases

Tutor debrief

This marketing audit has the advantage of being clear about where the strengths and weaknesses are and being comprehensive in approach.

Sometimes it is difficult to agree whether something is a strength or weakness and you must take care to contextualise your conclusions. For example, Reiss had established a niche position and if they intend to remain niche (or exclusive) their limited locations and exposure are not necessarily a weakness. Their marketing of this position however is a weakness.

It is important to draw on and use the case material. On page 5 specific KPIs (Key Performance Indicators) used by retailers were mentioned. It is not clear whether or not Reiss use these or whether they are a strength or weakness. It does give us some context and we should raise it as a question.

An important conclusion from the internal audit is that recent decisions made by Reiss, eg moving into womenswear and competing internationally, have changed their position. They are slipping from niche into the middle of Porter's triangle of generic competitive strategies.

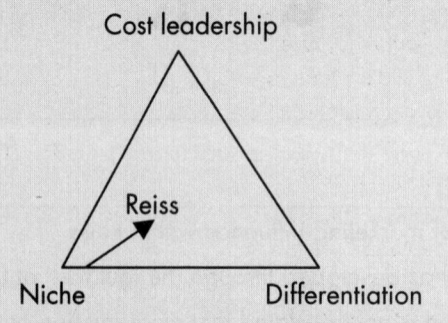

```
              Cost leadership
                    /\
                   /  \
                  /    \
                 /      \
                /  Reiss \
               /    ←     \
              /_____\
          Niche          Differentiation
```

The launch of womenswear does not appear to have included a clear strategy on branding of the womenswear.

The analysis of 'place' would have been strengthened by some reference to store and square footage performance over recent years during the rapid and dramatic expansion programme. The impact of focusing on one aspect of the marketing mix has had a serious impact on financial performance, particularly cashflow.

A really good effort has been made to use some of the models in this analysis. Some points to consider:

- When using positing maps try to use more than the usual price/quality positions. For example, are Reiss exclusive and distinct or common and ordinary?

- The total product concept was very helpful. Remember that perceptions are from the customers' point of view: do 'listed buildings' matter to them? 'Unique designs' should be in augmented or they are not unique.

- It is important in this case to remember the timescales. When using, for example, a product life cycle, we are working in months and weeks not years. We also have to include the 6-8 seasons that now exist in the fashion industry.

4 Step 2B: Situation audit

4.1 The corporate strengths and weaknesses analysis is often one of the more challenging areas for marketers but understanding the organisation's capabilities and competencies overall is key to delivering commercially credible strategies. Complete yours before reviewing the work of this exam syndicate.

Reiss – situation audit

4.2 An internal analysis of Reiss strengths and weaknesses across the key functional areas of the business would normally include a marketing audit but as we have already covered this separately this audit will concentrate upon: finance, human resources, culture/brand, operations and planning systems.

Functional area	Strengths	Priority	Weaknesses	Priority
Finance	■ Profitability has grown significantly by over 3% which means Reiss are generating profits to reinvest in their expansion plans	High	■ Sales per sq foot has fallen significantly from a high of £708 in 2001 to £470 in 2003	High
	■ The return on capital employed is good at 29% for every £1 invested – the owners would not be able to achieve this return by investing in the Stock Market	Medium	■ Reiss is illiquid and would be unable to pay all current liabilities from current assets – the business will need to monitor this position closely	High
	■ GPM is increasing indicating Reiss are carefully controlling their cost of sales which is one of their Key Performance Indicators (KPIs)	High	■ Reiss are paying their creditors faster than in previous years – this could be to obtain better discounts or it may reflect the move away from manufacturing	Low
	■ The gearing level of debt to assets is good indicating they could gear up further to fuel their investment plans	Medium	■ Presentation of the financial information could be improved – we know that Reiss do have some forecasts so it would be nice to see some management accounts with the actual performance against budgets	Medium
			■ Reiss may need to review the capital structure of the business to try to reduce the current liabilities – refinancing onto long term loans would improve liquidity	Medium

Part C: Practice cases

> **Tutor Tip**
>
> Note the inclusion of a priority rating, which is really useful and some key numbers.

Functional area	Strengths	Priority	Weaknesses	Priority
People/HR	■ Reiss recognise the importance of having a strong senior management team (SMT) and have restructured it across four key functions: operations, production, finance and creativity.	High	■ There does not seem to be a dedicated marketing function as marketing responsibilities are spread across the other functional areas, eg finance look after merchandising, creative look after PR	High
	■ Strong design theme and resource has been invested in store layout and window display with the appointment of a visual display manager to ensure the creativity of their campaigns is reflected in the window display	High	■ Reiss highlight staffing issues: – internal communication – synergy between departments – making the creative process more efficient	High
	■ Reiss understand how important their staff are and all staff attend an induction programme to learn about the brand, history of Reiss and the customer service ethic	High	■ HR function is also spread out across the SMT	Medium
	■ Reiss is an aspirational design led company and design is a key strength	Medium	■ The report does not give us any information about the skills/ qualifications of the people in the SMT – CVs of key staff would be helpful	Medium

16 ♦ Reiss: Analysis: Steps 2–4

Functional area	Strengths	Priority	Weaknesses	Priority
Culture/brand	■ Reiss recognise the importance of building a strong brand and their brand statement is: individual, stylist and sexy	High	■ The report refers to the brand in many different ways: individual, aspirational, affordable prices, comfortable, good design, quality, value, sexy, essential, contemporary – Reiss need to tighten up on this and establish a clear language otherwise it will give a mixed message about the brand	High
	■ Reiss is an aspirational fashion led brand – it is important that they lead the fashion rather than follow fashion trends	Medium		
	■ Reiss have a clear view on fashion – that it is a tactile business and consumers prefer to try on clothes for fit, style and colour prior to purchase	Medium		
	■ Very receptive to change – refitting the stores at the change of each season to ensure the atmosphere is right	Medium	■ Culture of Reiss is very design orientated and they believe all customers should visit their bricks and mortar stores to make purchases – hence they have not pursued an electronic marketing strategy	Medium
	■ Progressive strategy to establish the Reiss brand in the UK and then look to develop the brand internationally	Medium		

Functional area	Strengths	Priority	Weaknesses	Priority
Operations	■ Reiss have an operations director with clear responsibility for the products once they are in the warehouse	High	■ Difficult to fully understand the Reiss operations as the report does not go into detail – such as whether they have their own logistics, haulage etc	High
	■ Reiss have demonstrated they are efficient at operations as they have undergone a rapid expansion programme and are planning to open seven stores throughout 2003	High		

Part C: Practice cases

Functional area	Strengths	Priority	Weaknesses	Priority
Planning systems	■ We now that Reiss have a rapid expansion programme for the UK and plans to have an internationally recognised brand	High	■ Reiss lack a formal marketing information system – the graduate report does not mention any of the control systems Reiss have in place	High
	■ The appendices in the graduate report do indicate that Reiss are astute and lead fashion trends as well as pulling together some competitor analysis	Medium	■ Research on customers, fashion trends appears to be missing – how is this undertaken?	High
	■ A significant amount of research/understanding was done before Reiss entered the Dublin market evidenced by the statements that: – Dublin lacks normal intense competition seen in major cities – Brown Thomas are the only key competitor to Reiss	High		
	■ Reiss understand the need to adapt their product for different markets, eg Irish more conservative than UK customer	Medium		
	■ Reiss describe their KPIs as: – Sales – Stock intake phasing – Margins – Stock turn – Mark down – Terminal stock	High		

Tutor Tip

The students have presented a good summary of some of the key strengths and weaknesses at corporate level. It would have been improved by including some conclusion on the purpose of the business and structure, for example.

Corporate/business audit

STRENGTHS	WEAKNESSES
Purpose (vision, mission, direction)	
No obvious stated vision or mission	
Aims and goals P1 'long term goal establishing brand internationally'	
Structure P5	Established 1970s (30 years)
	P5 Merchandising est 03 under FD?
P4 Had vertical integrated system (VMS) but not now? No longer wholesaling (01)?	
P4, P21 – 26 stores, 3 concessions, 3 to open	
P5 New management structure	
Culture	
Entrepreneurial and creative	
Innovative?	
Mixed with product orientation?	

Tutor Tip

Some students attempted to analyse Reiss using the value chain framework. This was very useful, particularly as the value chain is so critical in the retail industry. However there were many gaps making it difficult to reach conclusions.

What was useful was that using this framework highlighted the confused structure the organisation and with a fragmented marketing function and the conclusion from this was that Reiss could not be as integrated or co-ordinated as they assumed.

Take care when using words such as 'significant'. Is it significant and particularly for this industry? Also avoid confusion between 'profitability' and 'profits'; profits can be rising while profitability is either static or falling.

The following is the more detailed financial analysis from another student with useful 'key insights and observations'.

Part C: Practice cases

1 **Shareholder/stakeholder management**

Key ratios	1/01	1/02	1/03
Gearing (borrowings as a % of net worth)	400%	308%	209%
Current ratio (current assets to current liabilities)	0.8	0.5	0.4
Stock as a % of sales	13.9%	12%	14.3%

1.1 **Observations**

- Amount of borrowed money in the company relative to the net worth of the company is reducing from an uncomfortably high level of 400% as at 1/01 to 209% at 1/03.

- Current ratio (otherwise known as the liquidity ratio, viz the ability to pay current liabilities from current assets) is showing a deteriorating trend over the thee years to 1/03.

1.2 **Key insights**

- A 209% gearing is still high, reflecting the expansionist strategy of the company, which has seen the square footage *double* over the last three years. This expansion has been financed by increased borrowings and from retained profits (see 2 below). The company's current and future bullish expansionist plans make it imperative that the company's external financiers (bank, shareholders, loan-note holders) as key stakeholders are fully consulted and agree with Reiss's plans. Detailed business plans with supporting budgets and cash flow forecasts are a 'must', not least because the company's plans need to be captured in SMART objectives – sales, by gender mix, profitability and market share relative to chosen competition.

- With a reducing current ratio, the company has instigated remedial action in 2003 through its merchandising department in focusing upon product/inventory flows to manage cash flow and levels of current/redundant stock. Against the backdrop of further planned expansion, this remains a critical are and warrants further focus of management attention, with time-relevant MI to monitor trends and instigate necessary actions.

2 **Profitability trends**

Key stats/ratios	1/01	½	1/03	F.
Sales	£17.6m	£18.1m	£20.9m	£35m
		+2.8%	+15.5%	+67%
Sales per sq foot	£421	£331	£298	£500
NPAT	£728k	£605k	£1,219k	
GPM	65.8%	63.3%	67.7%	
Per capita employee costs	£15,400	£15,460	£15,033	

2.1 **Observations**

- Sales growth 2001-02 at 2.8% was sluggish, being less than latest market growth figures available for the period at 4.2%.

- Gross profit margins robust – no issues.

- Per capita staff costs stable, but will need to rise reflecting company's expansion.

2.2 Key insights

- Forecast 2003 sales figure of £35m places these ratios/statistics into a healthy context. Specifically, a resultant impressive rise of 68% in sales per square foot (£298 to £500) confirms success. This figure needs to be benchmarked against comparative data from Reiss's identified competitors (Boss/DKNY for men, Jigsaw/Whistles for women), if available. This will place this metric into context.

- The company broke through the £1m profitability barrier for the first time in 2002. It paid away 32% of this (£588k) in taxation. Tax planning to mitigate this is a requirement.

- At £290k, interest paid is 15% of operating profit. With interest rates now rising, and set to continue thus over the planning cycle, the company should explore options for confirming *fixed* interest rates on its longer-term borrowings.

3 Foreign exchange policy

- The company is currently £-based, with international aspirations, building upon its 3,000 sq ft Dublin store which opened in 2002 at a cost of £750,000.

- The company sources its fabrics from a number of countries, trading in foreign currencies thus:
    - China (US $?)
    - S Korea (US $?)
    - Japan (Yen)
    - Rumania (Euro?)
    - Italy (Euro)
    - Turkey (Euro?)

    The Dublin store, in sq footage terms, accounts for 4.3% of total retail space. As a rough proxy, this equates to sales of £1.5m thus becoming available as income in Euros.

- Foreign currency (predominantly Euros) will be required to finance the company's international expansion plans, if confirmed.

- All of the above points to the need for the development of a cross-currency treasury function within the company, matching Euro inflows (Dublin store) and outflows (Rumania, Italy and Turkey fabric suppliers), together with purchasing of Yen and US $.

- In addition, currency movements and the relative strengths of £, require a clear policy of covering forward to protect the company's foreign currency exposures.

3.1 Key insight

Is the company's finance department geared up to mange this challenge? Does the FD have the time to focus on the critical element of the company's operations whilst also managing the companies equally – critical merchandising function and managing the company's financial stakeholders? (see 1 above).

Part C: Practice cases

5 Step 3A: External analysis

5.1 Your next task is to complete the external audits, at micro and macro levels.

Work through what you know about the markets, customers and PEST environment, before reviewing the analysis examples provided below.

Opportunities and threats

5.2 Economic

Opportunities	Threats
UK ■ Low unemployment, increasing PDI and high consumer confidence will lead to continued growth in the UK fashion industry – long term planning can assume this trend will prevail for the foreseeable future ■ Exchange rate fluctuations will positively affect profit forecasts **Europe** ■ Consumer confidence is picking up in Ireland – this can be exploited **Globalisation** ■ Reiss can capitalise on the homogenisation of fashion on European high streets – especially as their products are based on international designers	**UK** ■ Fashion industry sector does not continue to grow as predicted or growth will slow ■ PDI does not continue to grow or even declines ■ Number of women working will have reached a plateau ■ Exchange rates will adversely affect profits ■ Reiss will become attractive to a predator **Europe** ■ Signs of an upturn in Irish consumer confidence may be premature ■ Irish entry into the Euro will attract other competitors from the Euro zone **Other** ■ Seasons, weather, climate – pattern may alter or not be predictable ■ Frequent sales and discount may not be sustainable

> **Tutor Tip**
>
> Note how it can help to keep your analysis organised into home and overseas markets if you may be questioned on different aspects of your international strategy.

5.3 Social/demographic

Opportunities	Threats
■ Target new segments which reflect demographic/societal trends: – age groups – physical attributes – lifestyle ■ Time poor – offer convenience shopping ■ Product ranges – Formal wear for women – Leisure wear – men and women – Business casual ranges – Holiday wear – Overalls – Accessories – Lifestyle home ■ Discount outlet – hook to upgrade to full price stores ■ Storecard ■ Publicity and advertising ■ Establish link with a celebrity endorser	■ Growing age groups may not be interested in DW – so target audience may actually diminish rather than expand as population increases ■ Potential and existing customers may be enticed away to other brands through celebrity endorsement ■ Magazines/celebrities come to exert disproportionate power on the market ■ Cannot control any publicity derived through style and celebrity magazines ■ Consumer spending/PDI may be diverted to other consumables and fashion wear ■ Consumer borrowing comes to a halt ■ Consumers refuse to pay full price

5.4 Technological

Opportunities	Threats
■ Use new generation fabrics ■ Link up with a manufacturer developing intelligent washing machines ■ Introduce electronic tags to manage stock controls/sales and control store theft ■ Develop interactive website	■ New fabrics could cause problems for consumers – rashes, allergies – or not work – threat of litigation

5.5 Legal and political

Opportunities	Threats
	■ Counterfeiting ■ Euro zone competitors could find it easier to expand ■ Barriers to entry in Germany and Italy ■ Interest rates and taxes may increase – affect PDI and feelgood factor need for growth ■ War

5.6 Underlying observations

Economic	Social/demographic
Employment - Numbers in employment are increasing - Unemployment falling and will remain low for foreseeable future **UK economy** - PDI has increased significantly and will continue to do so - Spending on credit suggests consumers have confidence **UK fashion industry** - Sector has been growing. It accounts for 7% GDP (2002) - The growth is linked to rising numbers of working women - Surfeit of retail capacity - Acquisitions, mergers and consolidation prevalent both in the UK and Europe **Business cycles** - Linked to seasons and climate – weather determines demand for seasonal ranges - Peak season, Nov, Dec and Jan - Shift from discounting old stock twice a year, to sales and offers six times a year or more **Irish economy** - Moved to the Euro in 2002 - Has experienced a recent downturn – climate uncertain - Cautious spending patterns - Signs in Jan 2003 that consumer confidence could be picking up **European economy** - Weakening demand – fashion industry share of apparel spend is declining - Economy decelerating - Consumer confidence slipping **Globalisation** - Of retailers and suppliers (global sourcing) - Internationalisation of brands – homogenisation of European high streets **Exchange rates** - Fluctuations affect costs and profit forecasts	**Population and demographics** - UK population is growing as people are living longer - 15-24 age group will grow by 7% 2001-6 - 55-64 age group also growing – 50% of population will be over 50 by 2020 **Physical attributes** - Physical attributes are changing and average sizes have increased since 1960s **Female employment trends** - Female employment is rising faster than male, and increased by 6% between 1997-2001 - Women form 45% of the workforce, and that workforce is growing - More women are in professional employment **Money rich, time poor** - Women as a group have gained greater financial independence - As women have less time, there has been a growth in retail outlets which offer convenience (24 hour opening, parking, retail parks) **PDI – personal disposal income** - Men have more PDI than women, but women spend more of their PDI on clothes – but men's share of DW market is growing faster than women's **Consumer spending habits** - Consumers are more sophisticated and opportunistic - Consumers are spending rather than saving, using borrowing and credit cards to spend beyond their PDI - People tend to trade up when they have more PDI and spent more on branded fashion wear - They spend more on leisure than their predecessors - There is a trend towards spending more on themselves - In late 1990s, consumers began channelling their PDI into lifestyle home products, travel, tourism, DIY, IT and mobile phones

Economic	Social/demographic
	Lifestyle factors ■ People in cities use public transport whilst in the provinces they are more inclined to use cars ■ Office dress codes relaxed since 1990s ■ A trend for colour and free expression has come in from Europe ■ Internationalisation of styles **Publications and celebrity endorsement** ■ Proliferation of magazines targeted at men and 25-34 age group and lifestyle magazines – style and celebrity mags have quadrupled since late 1990s ■ Men have become more fashion conscious ■ Celebrity endorsement and fashion leaders have considerable influence particularly among younger groups

Underlying observations

Political/legal	Technological
European countries ■ Germany and Italy have rigid labour markets and strict regulatory regimes ■ Planning restrictions **UK** ■ The UK is outside the Euro zone ■ Implication that taxes and interest rates are low **Preventing counterfeiting** ■ ACG operates in UK (pressure group?) ■ Trading Standards Officers in UK ■ Lesser developed countries counterfeiting appears to be more acceptable **War** ■ Possibility of war	**Current fabric developments** ■ With moisturising cream ■ Which change colour with body heat ■ Teflon coated fabric – stain resistant, easy clean – mostly men's clothing **Future fabric developments** ■ Intelligent fabrics which offer health benefits (5 years) ■ Machine washable fabrics for formal wear ■ Intelligent garment technologies with built-in electronic gadgets **Radio frequency tags** ■ Which store product and sales info – cost has been falling ■ In future could be used in conjunction with intelligent washing machines **Internet** ■ Internet is widely available

5.7 European retail forecasts

Country	2002 %	2003	Trend	Comment
Germany	−2.3		↓	Declining
France		2.4	← →	Growth slowing
Italy	2	1	← →	Improvement easing
UK		3	← →	Growth slowing

Part C: Practice cases

Country	2002 %	2003	Trend	Comment
Spain	2.9	3+	↑	Growth improving

5.8 Country analysis

UK clothing market		1999	2002	2006
Total market £m	%	35,100	42,900	55,700
Grocers (supermarkets)	4.9	1,720	2,102	2,729
Dept stores	12.3	4,317	5,277	6,851
Mail order	12.3	4,317	5,277	6,851
Other	8.1	2,843	3,475	4,612
Specialists	62.4	21,902	26,770	34,757
	100.0			

Marks & Spencer	11.0	3,861	4,719	6,127
Arcadia	8.2	2,878	3,518	4,567
Next	4.5	1,580	1,931	2,507
C&A*	2.2	772	944	1,225
BHS	2.2	772	944	1,225
New Look	1.6	562	686	891
Matalan	1.3	456	558	724
Littlewoods*	1.1	386	472	613
River Island	1.1	386	472	613
Gap	0.9	316	386	501
Etam	0.8	281	343	446
Monsoon	0.6	211	257	334
Oasis	0.5	176	215	279
Austin Reed	0.4	140	172	223
Others (inc. REISS)	26.0	9,126	11,154	14,482

* gone since 2000

	Projected	
	2002	2006
REISS sales	20.9	69.3
Market share estimate	0.05%	0.12%
Men's/Women's only	0.06%	0.15%

Segments		1999	2002	2006
	%			
Men's	26.9	9,452	11,553	15,000
Women's	56.6	19,867	24,281	31,526
Children	16.5	5,781	7,066	9,174
	100.0			
M/W	83.5	29,319	35,834	46,526

Total apparel spending by country

Country	1997 €bn	1997 £bn	1998 €bn	1998 £bn	1999 €bn	1999 £bn	2000 €bn	2000 £bn	2001 €bn	2001 £bn	Projected 2002 €bn	Projected 2002 £bn	Projected 2006 €bn	Projected 2006 £bn	1997 to 2000 AGR %	1997 to 2000 GR %
Germany	69.5	48.0	69.6	48.0	70.7	48.8	71.6	49.4	72.0	49.7	72.6	50.1	75.3	51.9	0.9	3.6
Italy	58.0	40.0	62.2	42.9	63.9	44.1	64.4	44.4	68.3	47.1	71.2	49.1	83.8	57.8	4.2	17.8
UK	44.8	30.9	47.4	32.7	50.9	35.1	56.3	38.8	58.2	40.2	62.2	42.9	80.7	55.7	6.8	29.9
France	37.2	25.7	37.7	26.0	38.2	26.4	39.0	26.9	39.6	27.3	40.3	27.8	42.9	29.6	1.6	4.8
Spain	20.6	14.2	21.8	15.0	23.5	16.2	24.9	17.2	26.5	18.3	28.3	19.5	36.1	24.9	6.6	20.9
Netherlands	10.1	7.0	10.9	7.5	11.5	7.9	12.0	8.3	12.7	8.8	13.5	9.3	16.8	11.6	6.0	18.8
Greece	8.9	6.1	9.0	6.2	9.7	6.7	10.0	6.9	10.4	7.2	10.8	7.5	12.6	8.7	4.0	12.4
Austria	7.2	5.0	7.5	5.2	7.7	5.3	7.7	5.3	7.9	5.4	8.1	5.6	8.9	6.1	2.5	6.9
Belgium	6.5	4.5	6.7	4.6	6.7	4.6	7.0	4.8	7.1	4.9	7.3	5.0	8.0	5.5	2.1	7.7
Switzerland	6.1	4.2	6.2	4.3	6.4	4.4	6.6	4.6	6.8	4.7	7.0	4.8	7.7	5.3	2.8	8.2
Portugal	4.7	3.2	5.1	3.5	5.4	3.7	5.8	4.0	6.2	4.3	6.6	4.6	8.7	6.0	7.0	23.4
Norway	3.8	2.6	3.7	2.6	3.9	2.7	4.2	2.9	4.4	3.0	4.6	3.2	5.3	3.7	4.0	15.8
Denmark	3.8	2.6	3.9	2.7	4.0	2.8	4.0	2.8	4.1	2.8	4.2	2.9	4.5	3.1	1.8	7.9
Sweden	3.2	2.2	3.2	2.2	3.5	2.4	3.8	2.6	3.6	2.5	3.7	2.6	4.2	2.9	3.5	12.5
Ireland	2.4	1.7	2.7	1.9	2.9	2.0	3.4	2.3	3.8	2.6	4.3	2.9	6.6	4.5	12.1	41.7
Finland	2.5	1.7	2.6	1.8	2.7	1.0	2.8	1.9	2.9	2.0	3.1	2.1	3.6	2.5	4.5	12.0
Luxembourg	0.2	0.3	0.5	0.3	0.5	0.3	0.5	0.3	0.5	0.3	0.5	0.4	0.6	0.4	2.3	25.0
Total	289.7	199.9	300.7	207.5	312.1	215.3	324.0	223.6	335.2	231.3	348.1	240.2	406.2	280.3	3.8	

Part C: Practice cases

UK designer wear (M/W)

	1997		1998		1999		2000		2001		2002		2003		2004		2005		2006	
	€m	£m	€m	£m	€m	£m	€m	£m	€m	£m	€m	£m	€m	£m	€m	£m	€m	£m	€m	£m
Men's	1,708	1,186	1,771	1,230	1,799	1,249	1,889	1,312	1,958	1,360	2,040	1,417	2,123	1,474	2,208	1,533	2,295	1,594	2,388	1,658
	666	463	691	480	701	487	756	525	823	571	877	609	955	663	1,015	705	1,102	765	1,170	812
Women's	1,042	723	1,080	750	1,097	762	1134	787	1,136	789	1,163	808	1,167	811	1,192	828	1,194	829	1,218	846
	%		%		%		%		%		%		%		%		%		%	
Share (M)	39		39		39		40		42		43		45		46		48		49	
Share (W)	61		61		61		60		58		57		55		54		52		51	

	Up			Men's	32%	Women's	12%
1997-2002	Up	19.5%		Men's	33%	Women's	5%
2002-2006	Up	17.0%					

	Projected	
	2002	2006
REISS sales	20.9	69.3
Designer market share estimate	1.47%	4.18%

368

> **Tutor Tip**
>
> There is some excellent analysis here. Figures on market values etc have not just been reproduced but have added insight, more information. Presenting figures in table form can be problematic, particularly if you were required to do so in the exam. Bar and pie charts can be a better, and certainly quicker, way of getting this information across and these could be a summary of the table of figures.

Using market maps

5.9 Market maps are also useful for helping you get a helicopter vision of the key actors in the market place. The example here is of the domestic market. You can add in different aspects of the external analysis, to make the map rich in information.

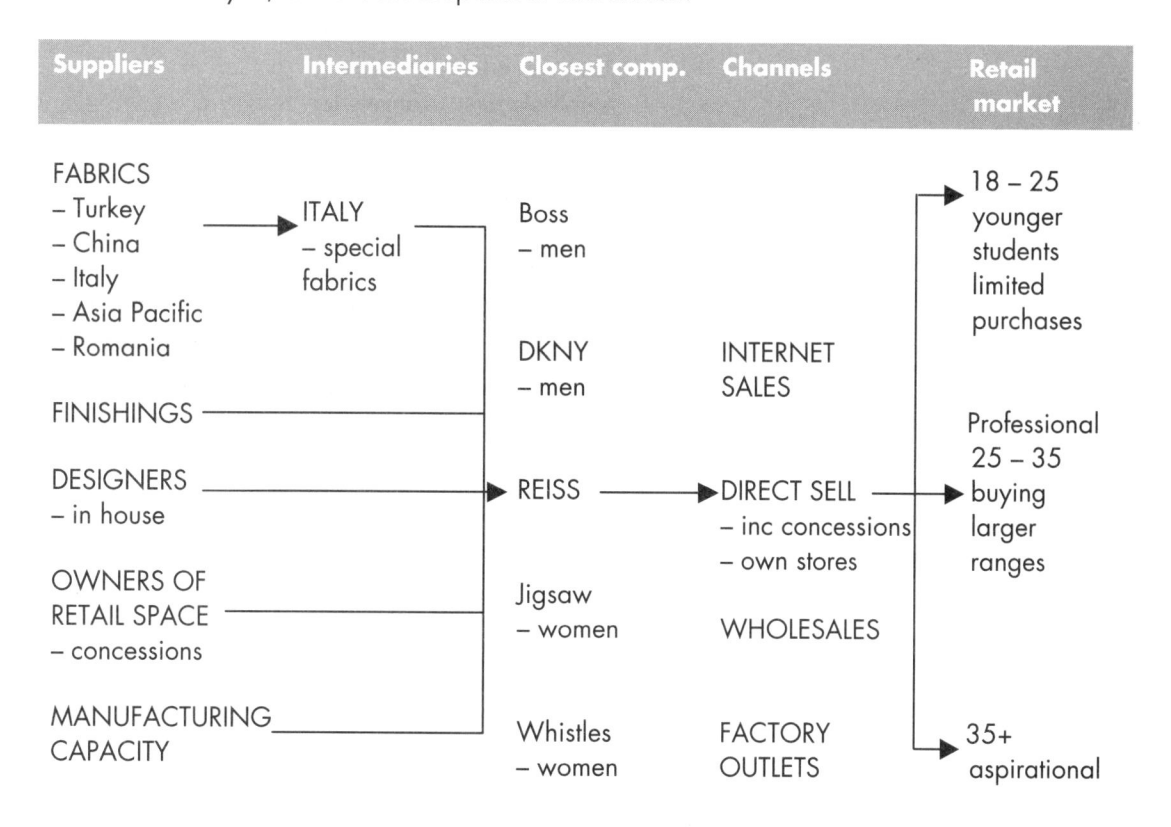

Suppliers	Intermediaries	Closest comp.	Channels	Retail market
FABRICS – Turkey – China – Italy – Asia Pacific – Romania	ITALY – special fabrics	Boss – men		18 – 25 younger students limited purchases
FINISHINGS		DKNY – men	INTERNET SALES	
DESIGNERS – in house		REISS	DIRECT SELL – inc concessions – own stores	Professional 25 – 35 buying larger ranges
OWNERS OF RETAIL SPACE – concessions		Jigsaw – women	WHOLESALES	
MANUFACTURING CAPACITY		Whistles – women	FACTORY OUTLETS	35+ aspirational

6 Step 3B: External analysis: competition

6.1 Sorting out the competitor information in a case study is often difficult. This example shows how diagrams and models can help. Sorting material in this way means you do not have to keep reorganising it as your analysis progresses.

Part C: Practice cases

6.2 Competition: five forces

New entrants
Global players/brands
Non clothing companies
Non fashion, eg sports
Designer outlets
Web-based providers
J. Crew

Industry rivalry

P8 clothing retail highly concentrated in hands of small number of large retail chains who dominate market

P9 breakdown, brands listed

P10 Designer wear highly fragmented, large number small players, relatively few large players

P15 growth in designer retail outlets that sell products at 60-70% of full price (easy access and parking) 34 schemes in UK in 2000 offering over 400,000 sq m space

P15 plus large retail parks: Trafford Park, Manchester; Bluewater, Kent; Lakeside, Essex; Merryfield, W. Midlands

P31, 32 competitors opening in Ireland

P34 competitors sell and source globally

P35 'buy or be bought'. Competitor strategies to survive – lessons from

Suppliers
P6 Fabrics – China, S. Korea, Japan, Romania, Turkey, Italy (often act as middleman, treat cotton, provide specialised fabrics), Asia Pacific supply 2k-3k metres as minimum quantity can only order this if can sell across different lines in different forms

Property owners
Production?

Buyers
Consumers – see customer analysis

Substitute products
- Holidays and travel
- Hobbies and activities
- Cinema, theatre
- Eating out
- Technology products
- The home and DIY
- Jewellery
- Cosmetic surgery

P16 clothing specialists diversified into home products (bed linen, soft furnishings) in response to diverted income into substitute products.

Student notes

- Supplier power is medium for materials where no value is added, and high value is added (for example, Italian suppliers).
- Buyer power (consumers) is high as collectively competition is intense and differentiation low.

Tutor Tip

Keeping the case references in even at this stage really helps when it comes to discussion but you would not add them in your exam models.

6.3 Competitor analysis – what is known

Tutor Tip

Tables help you to summarise and spot the gaps.

Part C: Practice cases

Who	What products?	Where (markets)	Size T/O	£$€	Competitive position/adv
10 most desirable brands Calvin Klein 26% Giorgio Armani 26% Gucci 25% Versace 18% Christian Dior 15% Ralph Lauren/Polo 15% Burberry 14% Hugo Boss 13% Yves St Laurent 13% Chanel 11% **P20 Reiss competitors** BOSS*/DKNY M Jigsaw/Whistles W **Above** Paul Smith M/Joseph W **Below** Ted Baker M Zara W FCUK H&M Gap Banana Republic J Crew (USA) Designers partner with retailers Debenhams (26 designers) M&S 'Autograph' Betty Jackson, Timothy Everest 'Per Una' George Davis Asda George clothing in USA		over 30 countries Europe, USA USA, opening UK		£12bn	P34 900 stores P34 120 mid market stores USA

6.4 Competitor strategies in fashion market

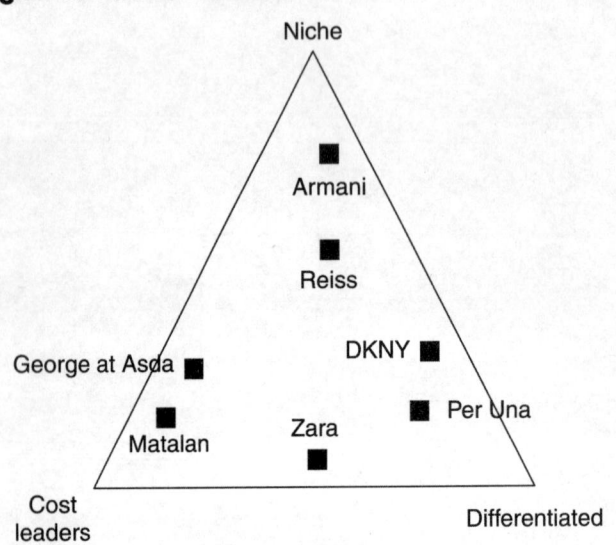

Niche / Cost leaders / Differentiated triangle with positions:
- Armani (near Niche, slightly right)
- Reiss (below Armani)
- DKNY (middle-right)
- George at Asda (left, cost leaders side)
- Matalan (bottom-left, cost leaders)
- Zara (bottom-middle)
- Per Una (bottom-right, differentiated)

6.5 Strategic groups in fashion industry (UK)

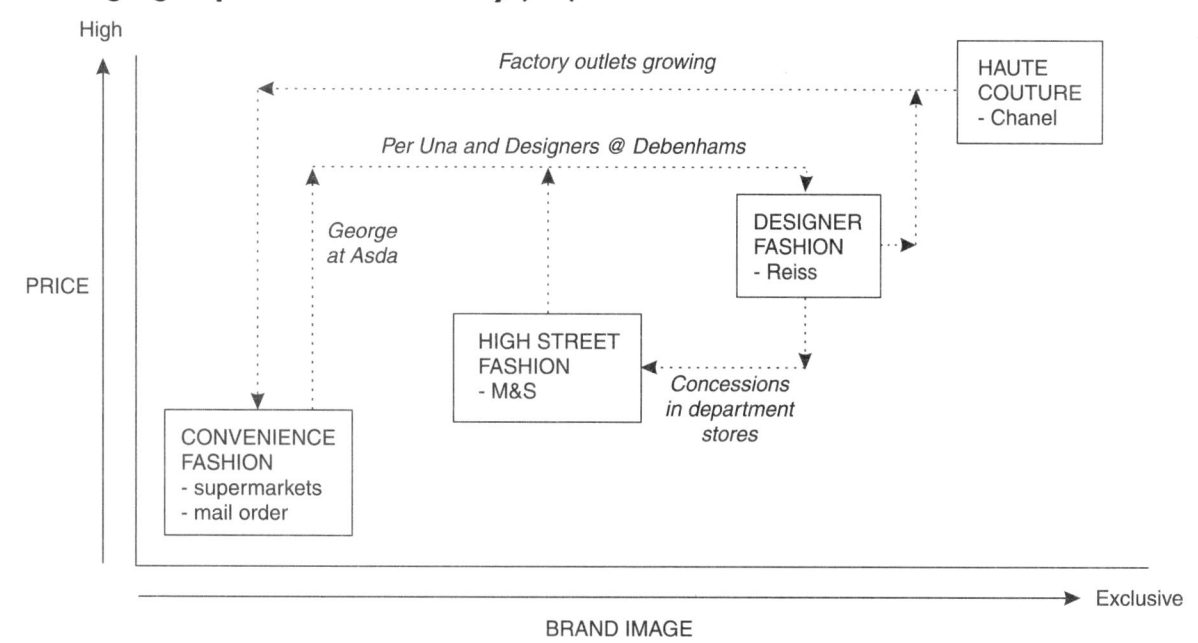

```
High
 ↑
 |         Factory outlets growing           ┌─────────┐
 |   ←---------------------------------→    │ HAUTE   │
 |                                           │ COUTURE │
 |         Per Una and Designers @ Debenhams │ - Chanel│
 |   ←------------------------→              └─────────┘
 |                                    ┌──────────┐
PRICE  George                         │ DESIGNER │
       at Asda                        │ FASHION  │
 |                                    │ - Reiss  │
 |                                    └──────────┘
 |                  ┌──────────┐
 |                  │HIGH STREET│
 |                  │ FASHION  │  Concessions
 |                  │ - M&S    │  in department
 |                  └──────────┘  stores
 |   ┌────────────┐
 |   │ CONVENIENCE│
 |   │ FASHION    │
 |   │-supermarkets│
 |   │-mail order │
 |   └────────────┘
 |_____→ Exclusive
              BRAND IMAGE
```

Blurring between strategic groups as new markets sought

> **Tutor Tip**
>
> *A really useful summary of the market.*

Tutor note

6.6 While it was possible to do a Porter's five forces and reach some conclusions the information on competitors was patchy. There is the usual problem of not knowing who the business is really competing with, as opposed to who the business *thinks* it is competing with and the information that has been gathered provides no real insights into competitive strategies and advantage.

6.7 However, the important conclusion here is that Reiss are in danger of losing their niche position due to their move into womenswear and desire to become an international player. They need to interpret these actions and aims playing to their strengths not going head to head with much bigger competitors who have strong global brands.

7 Step 3C: Adding the market and customer analysis

Tutor comment

7.1 A strategy cannot be customer-focused if marketers are unable to provide the insight into **buyer behaviour** that will enable effective segmentation.

7.2 There were lots of gaps in customer information so this group's effort was really excellent in trying to make sense of what we knew about customers. The pie for the size of the UK apparel market is useful but would have been better with values added.

Part C: Practice cases

7.3 What follows is a customer analysis done in report format.

Reiss case study

Customer analysis – notes

1. Size of market(s)
2. The Reiss customer
3. Customer segmentation
4. Consumer behaviour and spending
5. Info gaps and summaries
6. Threats and opportunities

(Non-italics = gathered from case study; italicised = own points)

1   Size of total UK apparel market

Size of UK apparel market £m

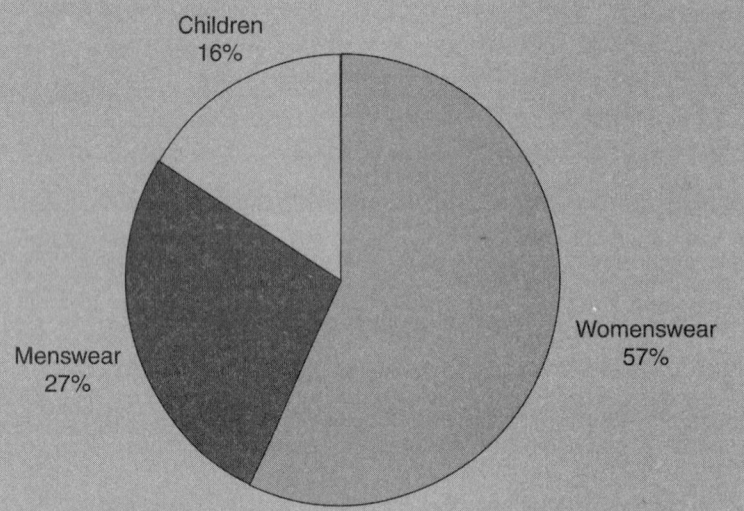

- Children 16%
- Womenswear 57%
- Menswear 27%

Projected growth in UK apparel retail market 3% in 2002. (p.40)

Designerwear as percentage of total apparel market

Using 1997 figures (p.8 and 16)

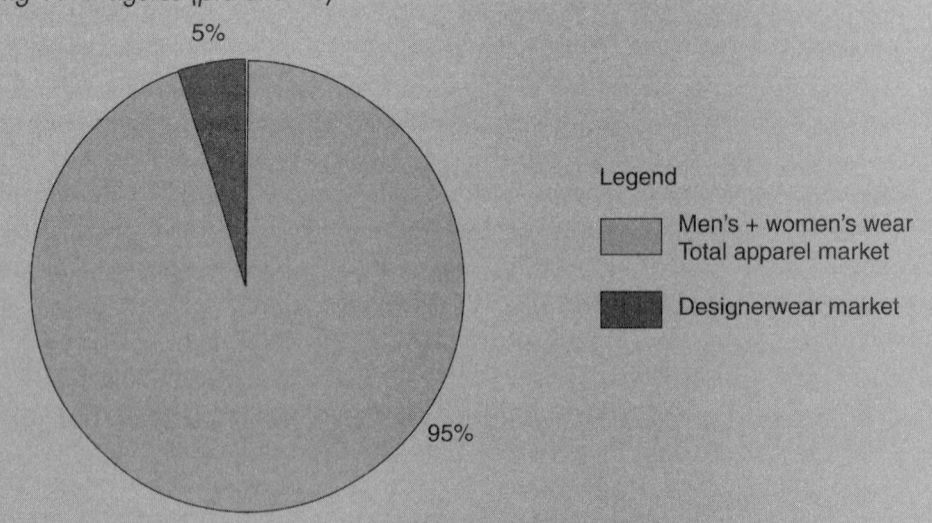

- 5%
- 95%

Legend
- Men's + women's wear Total apparel market
- Designerwear market

- *Total UK apparel market (excl children): £20,614m*
- *Total UK designerwear market £1,186m*
- *Designerwear accounted for 5.75% of total UK apparel market in 1997*

Size of designerwear market (p.16)

- Value 31,417m at 2002 prices
- Reiss share not known
- Total market value has increased by 40% (at 1997 prices) over 5 years
- *No projection for growth available*

Gender split of designerwear market (p.16)

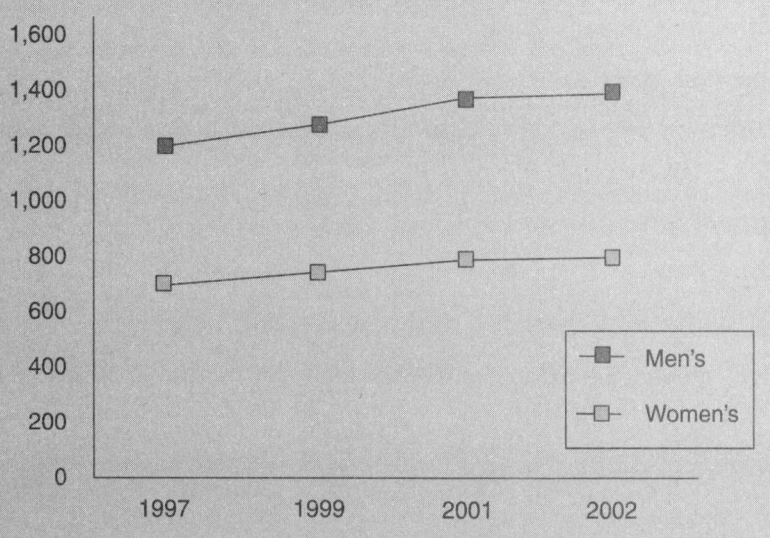

[Line chart showing Men's and Women's designerwear sales from 1997 to 2002. Men's values rise from approximately 1,200 in 1997 to around 1,400 in 2002. Women's values rise from approximately 700 in 1997 to around 800 in 2002. Y-axis scale: 0 to 1,600.]

- In 2002 (est) womenswear accounted for 57% of designerwear market
- Between 1997-2002 (est), menswear sales increased by 33% - from 39% of total designerwear market in 1997 to 43% in 2002

> From the above we know that:
> - Designerwear is a niche market (small relative to total apparel market)
> - Men's designerwear sales have grown fast
> - Childrenswear is a significant proportion of total apparel market

2 The Reiss customer

2.1 **Reiss' perception** of its target customer: (p.17)

- Style-conscious men and women, aged 18-40
- Aspirational; want to express individuality
- Valuing good design, quality and value at affordable prices

2.2 **Actual Reiss customer** – *not known*

- **Information gap** – *no profile given for Reiss customers. Information needed includes:*

  - Age?
  - Income?
  - Spending pattern?
  - Buying behaviour (brand loyal)?
  - Repeat customers or one-off shoppers?
  - Occupation?
  - Lifestyle?
  - Customer satisfaction?
  - Geographic?

3 Customer segmentation

3.1 Men

- A smaller segment than women, but growing faster (p.16). Sales of designerwear to men up by 33% between 1997-2002
- Designerwear customers have high disposable income (p.10)
- Looking for greater flexibility and move to mix and match (p.14)
- Declining demand for formal wear (p.14)
- Influence on fashion and style from Europe leading to demand for greater variety of colours and individual style (p.14)

3.2 Working women

- Growth slowing with projected rise of 2.6% between 2001 and 2006
- High disposable income, financially independent (p.10)
- Tend to spend more disposable income on clothing (and designerwear) than men (p.10)
- Demanding smarter, more fashionable, workwear and leisurewear (p.11)
- Tend to be time-poor; convenience and availability are paramount (p.10)
- Are buying more accessories (p.14)
- Want to mix and match designer items with high-street brands and accessories (p.14)

3.3 **Segmentation by age**

Age range 15-24	Age range 25-34	Age range 35-44	Age range 45-54	Age range 55-65
Projected growth: +7% between 2001-2006 (p.11)	Projected growth: –9% between 2001-2006 (p.11)	Projected growth: +5% between 2001-2006 (p.11)	Projected growth: +2% between 2001-2006 (p.11)	Projected growth: +16% between 2001-2006 (p.11)
Most fashion-conscious age range (p.10)	*(This is in the middle of Reiss's target age.)*		Higher disposable income?	High disposable income – 'empty nesters'
More likely to spend a higher proportion of income on branded fashionwear (p.11) *(But likely to be lower income levels, more price conscious – shopping at discount, value end of market.)* Influenced by celebrity endorsement (p.14)	Particularly influenced by mags such as GQ, Loaded, etc (p.14)		Ageing consumers spending on homes, personal care, savings or leisure time (p.36)	Traditional tastes but dressing younger (pp.1, 10) Ageing consumers spending on homes, personal care, savings or leisure time (p.36)
Size (7,230m)	Size Largest (9,360m)	Size (8,294m)	Size (7,696m)	Size Smallest (5,783m)

Summary points

- While UK consumer expenditure is forecast to grow by nearly 13%, the retail apparel share of this expenditure is forecast to slow (3% growth expected for 2003). However, this UK retail growth is still one of the highest expected in Western Europe. Others to note are: Eire, Spain, Portugal, Italy, Netherlands. International expansion?

- Reiss's own target age group is 18-49 year olds. The population of the age range 25-34 (the largest group) will fall by 9% by 2006. The age range 15-24 will grow, but does this group have the necessary high disposable income for Reiss clothes? Are Reiss clothes fashionable enough? (p.28 – perception of Reiss as 'grey' and 'not fashionable'.)

- The rise in the number of working (professional) women who typically spend more of their disposable income on clothing and designerwear will slow down. This segment values convenience and availability. Reiss' current town centre strategy may put them at a disadvantage – Whistles, for example, already sell through factory outlets and retail villages.

- Sales of designerwear to men are growing. This large segment needs to be further analysed to make sure Reiss is meeting consumer needs and expectations.

Part C: Practice cases

Opportunities	Threats
Growth in designer menswear spend **A**	Slowing growth in working women segment (projected 2.6% 2001-2006) **A**
Working women demanding smarter, more fashionable workwear **B**	Lack of out of town presence (convenience and availability) **B**
European influence = demand for greater flexibility, colours, style **C**	Consumers becoming more price conscious **C**
Accessories (already recognised) **D**	Women tending to mix and match designerwear with cheaper high-street buys **D**
Consumers more brand/fashion aware **E**	Consumer needs constantly changing **E**
Forecast increase in consumer expenditure: nearly 13% to 2006 **F**	Spending moved from clothing to lifestyle and leisure products **F**
Polarisation (discount vs designerwear) **G**	Polarisation (discount vs designerwear) **G**
Spain, Italy, France, Netherlands showing expected retail growth **H**	

Tutor Tip

Again see how summaries really help to bring the analysis together.

8 Step 3D: Stakeholder analysis

Tutor Tip

It was essential to undertake a stakeholder audit. So many stakeholders can influence Reiss's performance they need to be understood. This was a good structure and comprehensive effort. Other stakeholders could have included local government, trading standards and consumer pressure groups.

Where needs can be identified or reasonably assumed they should be. When we get to decisions, understanding the needs makes it easier to develop communication messages.

Group	Stakeholder group	Reason for importance
Marketing communications	Celebrities	For endorsement use
	Magazine journalists	To increase sales through good PR
	Musicians	To use complementary music in stores to help sell product
	Media agencies	To ensure audiences are reached through the most effective and efficient communication channels with effective encoding and of messages
Finance	Banks	For investment loans to open new stores. To discuss the state of the economy re disposable income remaining for retail purchases
Technology	IT companies	To understand how technology advances will affect both design software and clothing advances. To understand how technology can best be used for communications distribution (not sales), as well as stock control (eg RFID tags)
Product	Research agencies or trend analysis	For a clearer understanding of demographic and lifestyle pattern shifts, both affecting the sales of fashion items
	Fabric manufacturers	Can stop production, and therefore sales, instantly
	Asian Pacific manufacturers	Will no doubt be used more and more in the future
	Haute couture fashion houses	To take catwalk designs and translate them into cheaper high street versions
	Accessory and shoe manufacturers	To understand complementary fashion
Property	Retail mall owners (eg Bluewater)	Make decision on whether to allow retailer to rent space in mall
	Commercial estate agents	Can inform board of up and coming strategic property sites for purchase
	Architects	To help design the most innovate and complementary stores

9 Step 4: Critical success factors

9.1 There is one final step in this unit; it is the one which bridges the analysis and decision making and involves establishing the **critical success factors** and key issues.

Remember these are the things the firm **must** get right if it is to be successful. These factors are often also the basis for the examination questions.

You now take the time out to identify your critical success factors for Reiss, before checking them against the list below.

Part C: Practice cases

9.2 Reiss's critical success factors

In conclusion the key critical success factors are as follows.

Critical success factors	Key issue
■ Marketing orientation	Planning and control systems
■ Profitability/cashflow	Store utilisation/marketing mix
■ Competitive position	Brand values, customer needs
■ Brand building/communications	External and internal
■ International development	Country selection, product mix
■ SCM	Stakeholder management, value
■ Marketing information and metrics	Measuring loyalty
■ NPD and creativity and innovation	Process for NPD

Reiss: Decision Making: Steps 5-10

Chapter Topic List	
1	Step 5: The corporate and business decisions for Reiss
2	Step 6: Business implications
3	Steps 7 & 8: Marketing strategy and tactical planning
4	Step 9: Control
5	Step 10: Final preparation and managing of materials

Introduction

☑ In this chapter of the Reiss practice case, you will work from the completed analysis to the end of the decision-making processes. This prepares you for tackling the exam paper.

1 Step 5: The corporate and business decisions for Reiss

Vision and mission

1.1 You have completed your analysis of Reiss but still need to do a lot of work. The analysis and your interpretation of that analysis are simply the foundations for making decisions, which will move the business forward. It is very easy to get 'stuck' in the analysis phase of case work; in some ways it is a safe place to be – taking decisions is risky. But if you are to be prepared for the exam and of any help to David Reiss and his team, you must move forward and develop strategies and solutions that will help Reiss achieve their aims and ambitions.

1.2 The first decisions needed provide the sense of direction and purpose for the business:

- The vision – establishing future direction and competitive position
- The mission – clarifying their position and decisions about what business they want to be in. Currently it seems they are trying to do too much for too many customers – how do you see them in the future?

Part C: Practice cases

Action Programme 1

What vision and mission would you recommend for Reiss?

Vision:

Mission:

Check your ideas with the feedback which includes a student example, as well as our comments.

Setting corporate objectives

1.3 Setting specific, quantified targets is one of the most challenging areas of planning and case work. To make it easier for yourself, think of this step as part of the process – this objective is a 'stake in the ground'. What if we were to set our objective of £x – what would we need to do – how realistic is it? Remember later in the process you could revise that goal in light of different or better information.

1.4 There is not a single correct objective – but you need to be able to justify your recommendations based on case analysis. With the same case, different students may set objectives which are:

Ambitious	Justified by significant company advantages and market conditions
Prudent	Justified by moderate advantages and market conditions
Cautious	Justified by limited company advantages and market conditions

1.5 Just remember that you will need to 'sell' your strategy to David Reiss – you need to demonstrate that a market oriented approach will make a difference even if this is in the longer rather than shorter term.

1.6 You can use the planning gap framework to set objectives.

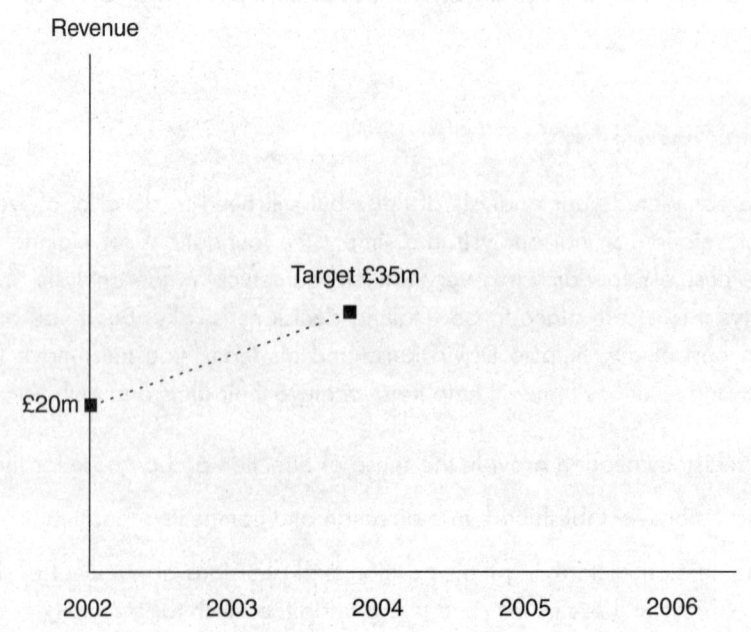

```
Revenue



                                            Target £35m
                                               ■


       £20m ■

        2002    2003    2004    2005    2006
```

One of the challenges in this case is that we know revenue in 2002 was £20m and there is a target of £35m in 2003, but we don't know if that will be delivered or not. You can assume it is

17 ♦ Reiss: decision making: Steps 5–10

or isn't – but you need to have a view of what can be achieved, both from the current square footage and assuming continued expansion.

Tutor Tip

Think about the sales per square foot now and as a target against current square footage and then the impact on revenue as square footage increases.

Action Programme 2

Now set your own planning gap for Reiss.

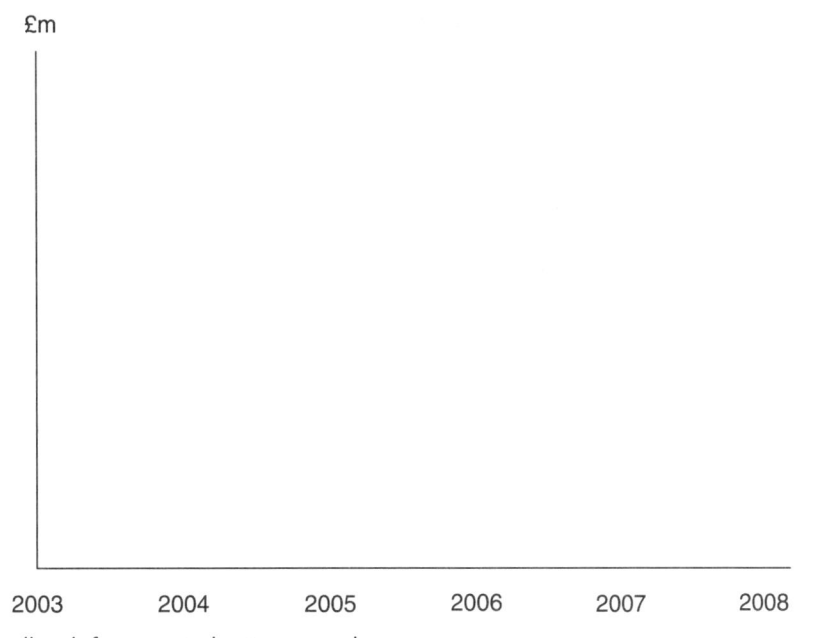

£m

2003   2004   2005   2006   2007   2008

Check the feedback from a student's example.

Strategic options and evaluation

1.7 It is one thing to set the objectives, another to deliver them. Your next task is to identify how Reiss can achieve its growth targets and then set criteria for evaluating and selecting the strategies they should focus on.

Determining business strategy

1.8 Reiss are not short of options. How does your Ansoff analysis compare with this student's ideas?

Part C: Practice cases

	PRODUCTS	
	Existing	New
MARKETS Existing	• Increase spend per customer • Increase store visit frequency • Increase store traffic	• Customised design wear • Dry cleaning services • New accessories • Stock other designers products • Sportswear
New	• 2nd store in Dublin • New UK stores • Stores in Europe • Stores elsewhere – Japan/US • Large sizes	• Children's stores • Fabrics and furnishing • Perfumes

Remember, at this stage you are identifying the options, not choosing between them.

1.9 The business **cannot pursue all these strategies** and some will be unsuitable for its desired positioning. You need to develop criteria to evaluate and select from these any other options you have developed, both in terms of its:

- Attractiveness to Reiss
- Potential competitive advantage

Tutor Tip

Criteria must be case specific for example, not just potential revenue but the potential to deliver a minimum of £540 per square foot.

Action Programme 3

Setting these criteria is an important step in the case process – so have a go for Reiss.

Strategy attractiveness	Competitive position
■ ■ ■ ■ ■ ■	■ ■ ■ ■ ■ ■

Check your list with the suggestions provided at the end of this section.

17 ♦ Reiss: decision making: Steps 5–10

1.10 You would need to describe weighting and rating these options, but you do not need to show any calculations – instead you show a completed matrix.

Strategy Attractiveness

	High	**Med**	**Low**
High (Competitive Advantage)	Business professionals		
Medium	Europe; Children's market; Japan; Fabrics and furnishing		
Low	18-25		

Use the strategic options to populate your matrix.

Part C: Practice cases

Filling the planning gap

1.11 At the end of this process you should be in a position to fill your planning gap.

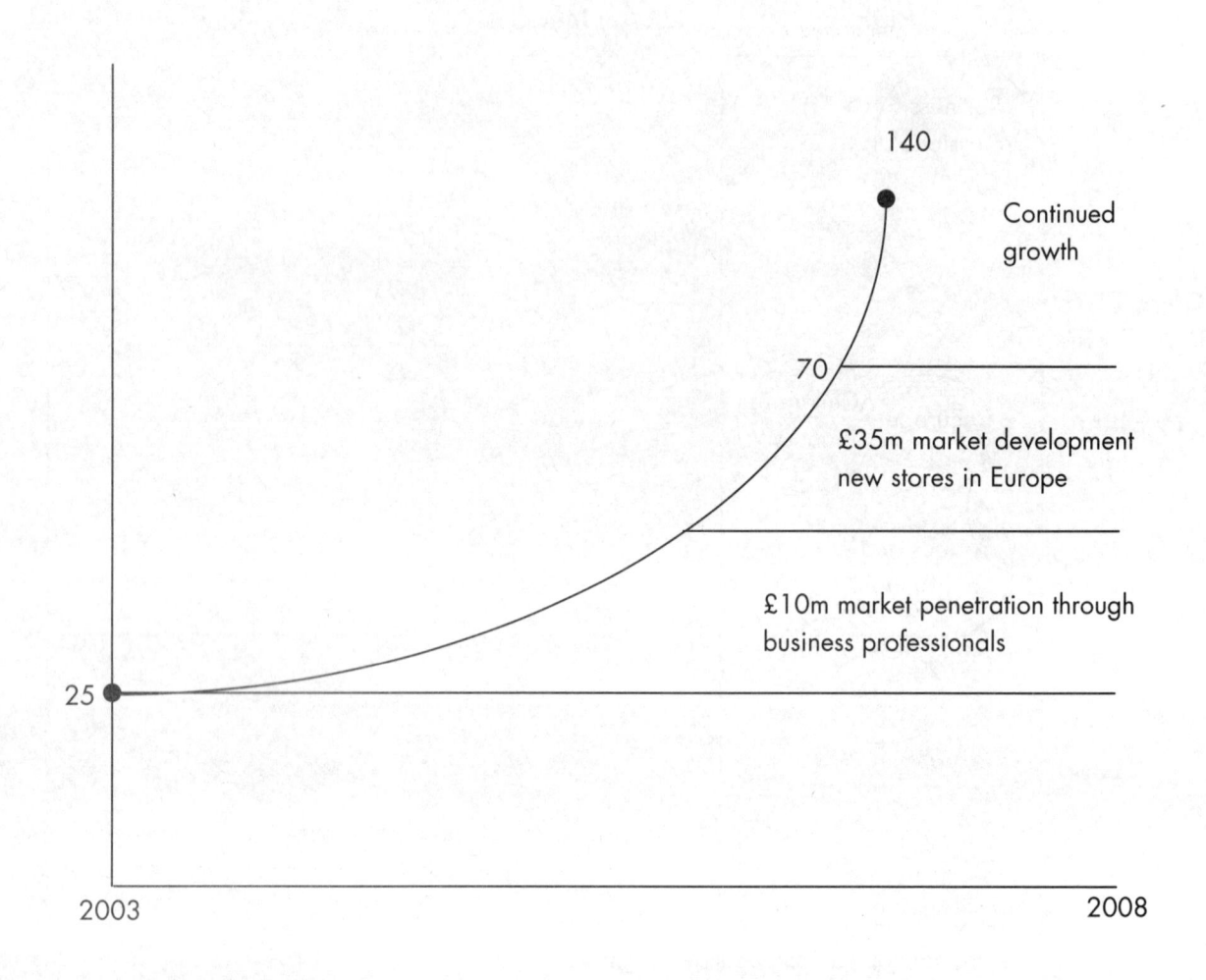

```
                                           140 ● Continued
                                                  growth

                                        70 ┤─────────────
                                              £35m market development
                                              new stores in Europe
                                           ─────────────
                                              £10m market penetration through
                                              business professionals
         25 ●──────────────────────────────────────────
         2003                                      2008
```

> **Tutor Tip**
>
> *This is an excellent communications tool and for every specified strategy you will need to be able to present an operational marketing plan.*

Competitive position

1.12 Reiss need to re-assert themselves as unique with a niche position supported by a distinct style and designs.

Establishing a competitive position and brand development strategy for Reiss

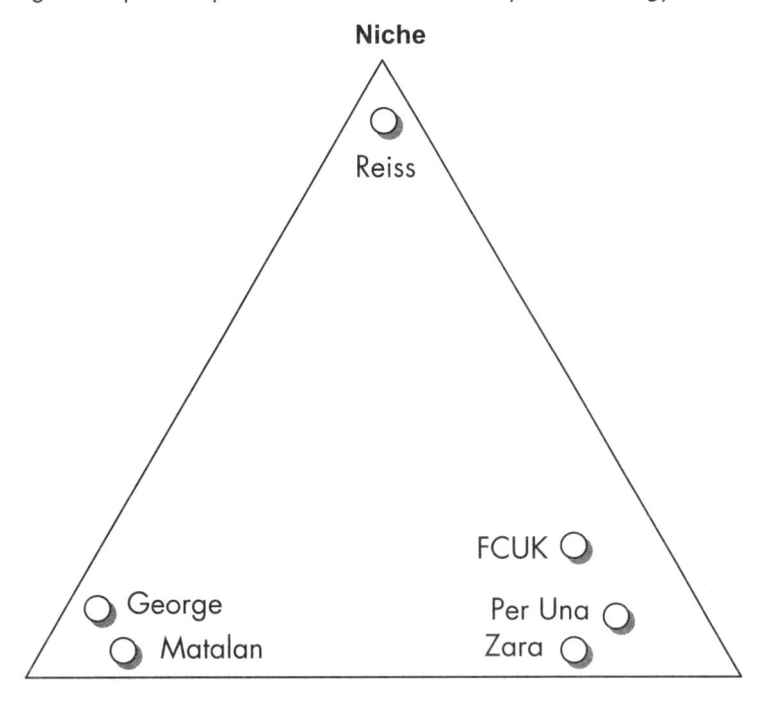

```
                    Niche
                      ○
                    Reiss



                              FCUK ○
              ○ George        Per Una ○
                ○ Matalan     Zara ○
```
Cost leaders   **Differentiated**

1.13 The menswear range was distinct and womenswear needs to establish its own clear position but one that fits with the Reiss brand. This will mean interpreting brand values that embrace both menswear and womenswear.

2 Step 6: Business implications

2.1 These corporate decisions have implications for the business. The key implications are outlined in the paragraphs below.

2.2 Marketing orientation – Reiss need to consider the structure of the business in terms of integrated and co-ordinated marketing activities. This will require centralising some of the marketing activities that are currently spread across different departments.

2.3 Strategic marketing planning – the focus to date has been on product and more recently on place, the stores. Other elements of the marketing mix have been ignored resulting in lack of awareness or clarity of the Reiss brand, lack of distinct positioning and lack of a more comprehensive use of the promotional mix. Measuring marketing effectiveness should also be part of this planning process.

2.4 Segmentation – Reiss need to know more about their customers and build a database that informs decision-making. Basic demographic information is not enough, consumer needs and motives for buying is essential information, particularly for a niche player.

2.5 Marketing information system – that gathers quality information rather than just data. Interpreting information for decision-making is more likely to lead to successful outcomes.

Part C: Practice cases

3 Steps 7 & 8: Marketing strategy and tactical planning

3.1 So, for every selected strategy you need to be prepared to describe how it will be achieved, ie an operational marketing plan, to deliver it. In the case of Reiss you have two strategies – a market penetration strategy, which will require you to segment the UK market for business professionals and develop an offer including perhaps customised tailoring on-line personal shopper, early opening hours and city centre locations, but you also need an international plan. Look at the following example developed by a student preparing for the case. Look through it and note the structure and comments under each of the P's – think about how you might build on or improve it.

International Marketing Strategy for Reiss

1   Introduction

Reiss currently has 0.08% of the UK market and is expanding rapidly. It already has one international outlet in Dublin and should seek to expand more geographically in order to create the status of a worldwide brand.

2   Situation Analysis

- **Customer/Markets**

    As established in the strategy marketing plan, I recommend that Reiss targets young professionals. This customer segment crosses geographic borders and will be large enough to sustain Reiss's aggressive growth – but specific enough to establish a credible niche position.

- **Competitive position**

    The designer market internationally is extremely competitive, with global brands operating at the designer and high street ends. These brands dwarf Reiss in terms of outlets eg Zara is 30 times larger than Reiss.

    Market is showing signs of maturity as consolidation is rife.

3   Core competencies or capabilities

Reiss's heritage is in design and quality garments that will translate well across international borders.

Reiss's strengths in the UK have been based on the store environment. It is an entrepreneurial company which is not averse to innovation.

4   Chances or Opportunities

- Opportunities exist within Europe for innovative fast-changing product offers and lower cost, more efficient business models.
- Size of the European market is E324bill, almost the same as the US market.
- Growth strategies include extending brands into new product area.
- Internationalisation of styles across Europe.

5   Critical success factors/problems to be overcome

- Time to market needs to be addressed.
- Apparel market is growing in Western Europe increased 3.8% ' 97 – 00, but the share of consumer spending is declining.

- Reiss needs to consolidate branding strategy if it wishes to take market share away from established players.
- Increase in 'grey' market and counterfeiting.

6 Constraints

- Reiss is a small company with small budgets in comparison to the global brands. The current organic growth of the company is an expensive proposition for entering international markets.
- Exchange rates will have an impact on international expansion.

7 Mission

Reiss shall lead international style by creating high quality clothing and accessories for global professionals. Our relationships with customers are key and with them, we will innovate through excellence in design.

8 Target markets

The chosen segment in the marketing plan – young professionals – both male and female, was partly selected due to the fact that it does cross international borders. Reiss should focus marketing effort on identifying territories that also have a large proportion of the population in professional employment so that their needs will be similar to the UK segment.

9 Foreign market selection criteria

- Market potential: size, competition, resources, customer demand, wants, income
- Similarity: geographical proximity, psychological proximity
- Urbanisation
- Similar climate
- Comprehensive structure

Accessibility: geographic, psychological (especially important for the emotional branding), political distance, delivery time, management, communications

Using the above criteria in the Harrall & Keefer's model, the following countries were opportunities:

Primary: Germany, France and Italy
Secondary: Netherlands, Spain
Tertiary: Greece

I would suggest a more thorough analysis is undertaken with up-to-date data, which includes the markets outside of Europe.

Using Doole & Lowe's 12 Cs model, a robust information system will allow the targeting to be more methodical.

This will include data on:

- Country
- Choices (competitors)
- Concentration (market segments – in the case of Reiss, it is very important to note the concentration of young professionals)
- Culture/consumer behaviour (such as decision-making and shopping habits eg high street versus malls)
- Consumption (growth patterns, substitute products)

Part C: Practice cases

- Capacity to pay
- Currency
- Channels (particularly the department stores that are well positioned to take Reiss concessions)
- Commitment
- Communication
- Contractual obligations
- Caveats

10 International Marketing Strategy and Objectives

Increased market coverage

Objective	Enter 5 new markets by 2009
Distribution strategy	Research potential targets with attractive size of young professional segments

Market entry

Objective	To enter new markets in most efficient way
Entry strategy	Establish an alliance with a European partner of similar stature as House of Fraser and replicate concession strategy in UK. Develop franchising documentation in order to maintain that outlets maintain the Reiss brand. Assign alliance managers to work with local markets

Technical efficiency

Objective	To harness technology systems developed for sales internationally
Effective strategy	Allow international sales to take place via website as low cost market entry. Monitor success of products overseas in order to mine data for further market penetration.

Phasing

These strategies are phased in order to have the lowest initial investment. Given Reiss's low financial liquidity at this time, it is evident that the UK strategy of organic growth cannot be replicated immediately and the lower risk and investment of alliances/franchises will enable Reiss to monitor success of chosen markets and grow at a profitable pace.

11 Implementation

Tactically, there are further considerations for entering international markets. In addition to the added complexities of marketing internationally, some elements of the marketing mix will need to be considered:

Price

In Euros but will need to take into consideration relative prices across territories.

Promotion

Concessions limit the possibility of in-store displays that Reiss has relied on in the UK. I would recommend a strategy that incorporates push (to establish relationships with the European department stores) pull (brand awareness campaigns) and profile strategies for market entry. Local agencies will be best placed to advise on this, or to have one agency with outlets in the key territories in order to gauge the local knowledge.

Cultural differences will also play a part in promotion, which is where the knowledge of local agencies will be key.

Product

May require different colours and sizing, different ranges.

Place

Covered above in distribution strategy. It is important to stress that Reiss will have less control over store environments and will therefore have to rely on other means of physical evidence to strengthen the brand.

In order to satisfy the professional segment, city-centre locations should continue to be pursued.

People

In line with UK recruitment and training – ambassadors of the brand.

Process

International logistics in place for timely deliveries.

Physical evidence

Consistent branding which is sensitive to cultural issues.

12 Conclusion

International expansion is fundamental as part of the GAP analysis for corporate strategy and revenue targets.

Expansion into new markets will be key in securing further revenue growth and the consistent targeting will pave the criteria for selecting which markets to enter.

Electronic business and distribution channels will reduce the cost of sales and satisfy consumer needs in a cost effective manner.

Tutor Comment

This piece of preparation covers most of the key steps and points – it is long on the intro and context which you may already have covered in an earlier questions. Use the tactics to remind you of how you will use or modify the mix to expand your offer to new customers. The strategy could have been a little more on the international philosophy ie standardised but with what brand values – promoting 'UK' or a global positioning?

Part C: Practice cases

4 Step 9: Control

4.1 You will notice that in this outline plan there are no notes on control. It is an easy piece to miss out but it will cost you dearly.

4.2 Take time to think through a rough timetable of activities.

Identify 5 target store locations

Roll programme of store openings

And so on..............

6 months

Time

At the same time give some thought to budgets and measurements and feedback systems.

Tutor Note

4.3 Students were encouraged to develop a number of strategic marketing plans, for example for the UK and internationally and for different growth strategies, including market penetration, market development and new product development. We also got students to prepare a strategic communications plan – variations of this included to build the brand and to build stakeholder relationships (CRM). We also encourage students to think about supply chain management and implications to the business.

All of these plans were in outline only.

5 Step 10: Final preparation and managing materials

Final preparation

5.1 The following notes represent a last minute briefing which will help you as you consolidate your notes and thoughts before moving on to tackle the exam paper as a practice.

5.2 **Remember, when tackling the questions**, keep your work clear, strategic and justified, add budgets, timetables and comments about control and feedback

Task

5.3 Now take the time to pull your notes and materials together and plan a time when you can sit down and tackle these questions. Ideally, work in exam conditions – in the three hours. Time management is always a problem in exams, but it is particularly difficult in the Case study – one of the main reasons why well prepared students fail.

As you try out this practice paper, think again about how well organised your materials are. How could you prepare better?

Open book	**Closed book**
Analysis & Decision	Marketing Strategy in Practice
How well ordered is your file? Can you find material?	What would you choose to include on your six A4 sheets? How helpful are they in light of the question?

5.4 You are now ready to move onto the exam paper itself, but before you move on, take a few minutes to look at these final questions to help you consolidate your Case preparation skills.

Action Programme 4

Checking case preparation skills

1. It is unlikely you will have enough information to be certain about decisions: how then can you justify setting a quantified objective in a Case study?
2. Examiners are interested in what strategy you recommend, not how you decide on the strategy. True or False?
3. Visions and missions are mainly a PR exercise for the business, but the best way of generating them is to brainstorm one with your college syndicate group. True or False?
4. Evaluation criteria need to be Case specific – examiners are looking for quality not quantity of factors. True or False?
5. The best way to be prepared for the exams is to write your plans out in full. Then, all you have to do is copy them out in the exam room. True or False?

Check your answers with ours at the end of this chapter.

Part C: Practice cases

Action Programme Review

1 Vision

Student example

To be an internationally recognised brand, bringing design wear to all.

Comment

Clearly this reflects David Reiss's international ambitions – but it does need to be believable and the 'to all' target is stretching it for a company of this size.

Alternative

To be an international brand recognised for its skill in bringing design to business wear.

Comment

This is much narrower, but it reflects more of a niche positioning, it is a less competitive sector of the fashion market and builds on the traditional core competencies Reiss had in tailoring.

Mission

Student example

We are a retailer making aspirational, high quality designer wear accessible to our customers through an international brand, using prime site locations and knowledgeable, motivated staff to serve our valued customers.

Comment

Again, this is generally OK but a bit too broad and woolly – it doesn't differentiate Reiss from other competitors like Zara.

Alternative

We are in the business of helping our time poor customer base of business professionals have access to the benefits of a stylish design inspired wardrobe which meets their functional and aspirational needs.

Comment

Again, by being more specific, the mission can be more meaningful and specific – it is more of a 'call to arms' and would give staff and customers a clearer sense of the company's position in the market.

2 Corporate objectives

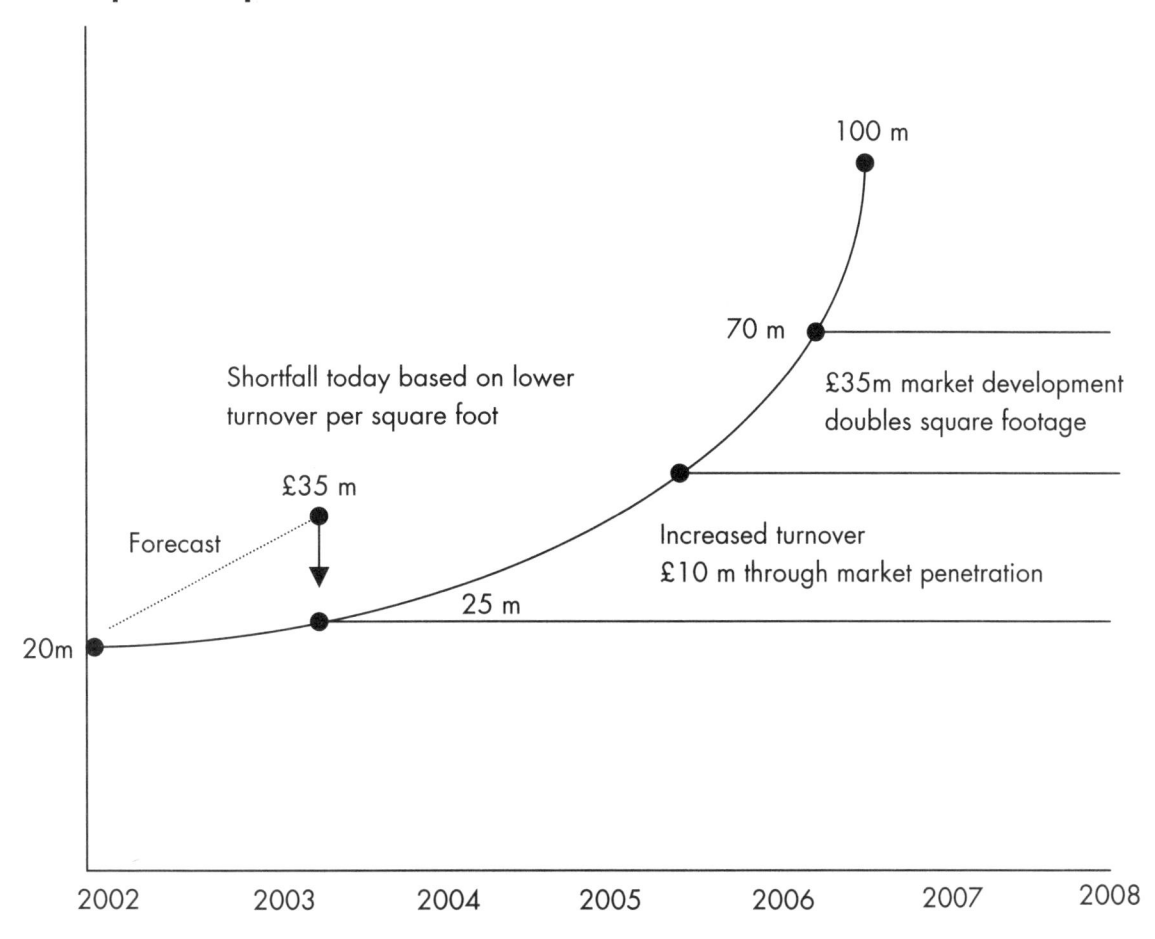

(Graph showing revenue growth from 2002 to 2008, with key points: 20m in 2002, £35m forecast with shortfall down to 25m in 2003, £10m increased turnover through market penetration, £35m market development doubles square footage reaching 70m by 2006, growing to 100m by 2007/2008)

This sample assumes that £35m won't be achieved in 2003 based on the lower sales turnover (falling from £543 in 2001 to £432 in January 2003) – to hit £35m by January 2004 the 2001 level would need to be achieved again.

Assuming therefore the lower level of £25m is achieved, this student is going for a dual strategy to 2005.

£10m from market penetration regains a £543 per square foot level on current sites.

£35m by doubling square footage at a £543 revenue level.

Over the longer term continued expansion should fuel steady organic growth – perhaps £100 or £140m by 2008 (doubling every 3 years).

Comment

These are revenue objectives – you can use the current or improved profit margins to turn them into a profit based business objective.

Part C: Practice cases

3 **Evaluating and selecting strategies**

Strategy attractiveness	Competitive position
Profit margin of at least 68%	Value for money
Demand	Style and quality
Investment required	Availability
Utilisation store capacity	Access
Synergy with range	Service
Synergy with customers	Distinct and exclusive

4 1 Set an approximate, but realistic figure.

    2 False. Process is as important as outcomes. Explain the steps through the structure of your answers.

    3 Develop your own mission and vision, the cornerstones of the planning process. Reproducing a group mission or vision could be evidence of a syndicated answer.

    4 True

    5 False

The Reiss Exam

Chapter Topic List

1. The exam
2. The examiner's review of the questions
3. Sample script 1
4. Sample script 2

Introduction

In this chapter you will:

- ☑ Work the Reiss case under exam conditions (allow 3 hours)
- ☑ Have the opportunity to review student sample answers to the exam
- ☑ Consider tutor comments and examiner feedback for Reiss

Part C: Practice cases

1 The exam

> **Tutor Tip**
>
> Reiss exam paper and sample answers
>
> In this chapter, you will have another opportunity to tackle the actual exam paper under exam conditions, no matter how much or little of the analysis you have completed.
>
> Independently, we would strongly advise you to take the time out to tackle an actual paper.
>
> To be of value, you really need to do this under exam conditions.
>
> Once you have prepared yourself, make the time to tackle the paper, ideally in:
>
> - An undisturbed environment
> - A single three hour sitting
>
> If that is not possible, tackle it in two or three timed sessions. Do not cheat and give yourself any longer: managing time is one of the biggest obstacles to case success and the more prepared you are, the harder it is to fit everything in.
>
> For Reiss, we have offered a shorter section on guidance, but this is supplemented by the sample scripts, with the examiner's comments, showing how you could have earned marks and giving you an insight into the examiner's perspective.
>
> By the end of this chapter, you will have:
>
> - Seen the Reiss question paper and considered the additional information
> - Undertaken Reiss as a practice exam paper
> - Reviewed your own exam technique and approach
> - Considered two sample scripts as a comparison for your own work and to show you what others were able to achieve in the exam room
> - Seen the examiner's comments about this paper

The Chartered Institute of marketing

Postgraduate Diploma in Marketing

Strategic Marketing Management: Analysis & Decision

9.54: Strategic Marketing Management: Analysis & Decision

Time: 14.00 – 17.00

Date: 5th December, 2003

3 Hours Duration

This paper requires you to make a practical and reasoned evaluation of the problems and opportunities you have identified from the previously circulated case material. From your analysis you are required to prepare a report in accordance with the situation below. Graphing sheets and ledger analysis paper are available from the invigilators, together with continuation sheets if required. These must be identified by your candidate number and fastened in the prescribed fashion within the back cover of your answer book for collection at the end of the examination.

Read the questions carefully and answer the actual questions as specified. Check the mark allocation to questions and allocate your time accordingly. Candidates must attempt ALL parts. Candidates should adopt a report format; those who do not will be penalised.

© The Chartered Institute of Marketing

Reiss

Examination Paper

Additional Information

> Reiss has been very successful in implementing its UK expansion strategy in the current year. In future, developing European and International markets will require better customer intelligence. One aspect that requires further attention is the way in which the company might build stronger relationships with customers, in order to target particular fashion offers to particular market segments. The company is looking at how it can capture customer data to achieve this objective, and then use to communicate offers effectively to particular customer groups in ways that build the brand image, increase turnover, and improve profitability.

Examination Questions

As a newly appointed Marketing Consultant for Reiss, you have been asked to prepare answers to the following issues by the Managing Director:

Question 1.

Develop a three-year strategic marketing plan for the company.

(40 marks)

Question 2.

Evaluate the current web strategy and propose a Customer Relationship Management (CRM) strategy for the company.

(30 marks)

Question 3.

Propose a European market-entry strategy for Reiss, concentrating on brand development.

(30 marks)

(100 marks in total)

Note the distribution of marks and allocate your time accordingly.

Postgraduate Diploma in Marketing

54: **Strategic Marketing Analysis & Decision
REISS – Examiner's Report**
Date: **January 2004**

Introduction

Cases are always difficult to analyse and take apart. This paper shows the indicative answer scheme that was utilised for understanding and marking answers from candidates. The indicative answer scheme is wide ranging and allows candidates to come up with novel and interesting strategies. Within this scheme, the strengths and weaknesses of the candidates' answers to each section is given.

The case

This case represents an important departure from the more conventional marketing dilemmas and offers an insight into the challenges faced by retailers. The case is based on an SME that is becoming well established in the designer clothing niche within the UK. The company finds that it has been quite successful in the UK and that it would seem reasonable to emulate this elsewhere in Europe. The company has a loyal following and the Reiss brand is often featured in the clothing sections of the major magazines (male and female) and the Saturday and Sunday magazines of the major papers such as the Guardian and the Sunday Times. Its organic growth is a testimony to its success. The reasons for its success are complex and manifold. Part of this is design, part niche marketing and part store design. The company has a good eye for new trends and designs and the move to retailing has meant that it has had to give up its wholesale arm. In recent years the company has grown very rapidly and has reflected the general trend of prosperity within the UK. This is a very positive outcome as it competes in a messy and fickle market. The clothing market in the UK is huge - around £25bn. Reiss with a £35m turnover is a tiny but significant niche player in a market dominated by major players such as M&S, Debenhams and medium sized concerns with fashionable but medium priced clothing such as Zara and Mango. At the same time unconventional players such as Asda (George) and Sainsburys are becoming entrenched in the market. Given the range of issues such as supply chain management, marketing and competition, the company now has to position itself to take advantage of the opportunities and to minimize the risks associated with international expansion.

Key Issues

a) This is a medium sized company with a turnover of approximately £21m.

b) The company is profitable, but the profits in relation to the turnover are low but indicating an upward trend (around 4% net profit in 2001 to 5.8% in 2003).

c) The stock levels are quite low indicating good operations management.

d) The assets of the company are 50% more than the liabilities, largely because of the fixed assets (the retail premises).

e) The UK market is intensely competitive offering a range of options to the consumer who wishes to purchase clothes.

f) The company has just launched its first shop outside the UK in Dublin.

g) The UK clothing market is quite fragmented and the niche that Reiss operates in needs to be monitored continuously in order to meet challenges from the likes of Zara and the highly regarded marques such as Christian Dior.

h) The company faces the biggest threats from more moderately priced shops as indicated in the Guardian article.

i) The shop in Ireland appears to be a success, but it is high cost and will need to be monitored effectively.

j) As disposable incomes increase then more people could be drawn into purchasing clothing from Reiss.

k) The company is still very much a niche operator and is not really very well known as a brand.

l) Store management and design are great assets and the importance of this is highlighted in figure 4, when building brands.

m) The company now has many opportunities in the large womenswear market.

n) The company has begun to diversify into other merchandise in the London Stores (books, CDs etc.)

o) The company needs to consider the mix of its communication strategies.

p) The company needs to be continuously creative and lead trends.

The New Information and Brief

Reiss has been very successful in implementing its UK expansion strategy in the current year. In future, developing European and International markets will require better customer intelligence. One aspect, which requires further attention is the ways in which the company might build stronger relationships with customers in order to target particular fashion offers to specific market segments. The company is looking at ways in which it can effectively capture customer data to achieve this objective, and then use it to communicate offers effectively to particular customer groups in ways that build the brand image, increase turnover and improve profitability.

The Answers

This case is fairly complex and candidates need to understand the market sector that the company is operating in. It is important, therefore, that the following issues are considered:

1. The application of theory.

2. The amount of international and communications marketing theory/application that the students can apply to the case.

3. The candidates should be thinking strategically not tactically.

4. The answers given must be realistic and practical.

5. A degree of innovation and lateral thinking should be rewarded.

6. It is important that the questions are answered within the given context.

7. The additional information offers some insights into managing customer relations.

Examination Questions

As the newly appointed Marketing Consultant for Reiss, you have been asked to prepare answers to the following questions by the Managing Director:

a) Prepare a three-year strategic marketing plan for the company.

40 marks

b) Evaluate the current web strategy and propose a Customer Relationship Management (CRM) strategy for the company.

30 Marks

c) Propose a European market entry strategy for Reiss, concentrating on brand development.

30 Marks

Question One

a) Prepare a three-year strategic marketing plan for the company.

This question requires students to use many of the strategic planning models used by marketers. They therefore need to consider

a) The shorter-term objectives that they wish to set for Reiss.

b) Take into account the challenges from retailers such as Zara.

c) Take advantage of its strong cult following, brand and store design.

d) An understanding of how web technology can be enhanced for marketing purposes.

e) The company may need to undertake regular market research in order to understand the changing nature of consumer tastes.

f) The strategy should take into account the financial status of the company. Any well-developed strategy will require sound financing. The company's net profitability is not particularly exciting, but it has enough reserves to push for expansion.

g) What market positioning strategies should the company adopt?

h) Operations management and inventory management are critical to the success of the company

i) How far should the company move towards other retail items (books CDs etc)?

j) How much is the company constrained by the amount of fabric it orders?

k) How far will the company be exposed by exchange rates, especially as the UK has not embraced the Euro?

j) Models such as Porter, Ansoff, BCG, GEC, Shell Directional and GAP could be used in the analysis of the case.

n) What are the constraints to the chosen strategy?

o) Which markets are the key priorities and why?

p) What possible organisational structure could be developed from the current one shown?

With such a low market share, the company needs to

a) Continue innovating;

b) Keep developing the brand;

c) Build on the retailing strengths.

Points in the marketing plan:

1) Set objectives.

2) Identify target markets.

3) Set marketing objectives.

4) Develop marketing strategy and tactics.

5) Organise control systems.

Given the points above, the best answers will show a clear grasp of the following

1. A good analysis of the current position.

2. The development of a marketing plan with
Fully developed implementation strategies.

3. A good justification of the strategies to be adopted.

Strengths and weaknesses of the answers

Although this question is generally predictable, more than 20 % fail this question. Many do not master the elements of a plan and the application of relevant concepts from the Planning and Control module. Often there is a failure to provide adequate explanation and justification for strategies. The setting of sound clear objectives remains a challenge for many candidates. Weaknesses range from a lack of quantification (poor data analysis) through the absence of sensible time scales to wild figures for growth that are more relevant to a company with much larger resources. The treatment for segmentation was weak in many scripts, showing a distinct lack of understanding of the topic, especially psychograhics. On the plus side many candidates made good use of Porter, Ansoff, the GE Matrix and Harrel and Keifer.

Question 2

Evaluate the current web strategy and propose a Customer Relationship Management (CRM) strategy for the company.

(30 Marks)

It is clear that the company is using the website for informational and not transactional purposes. The issues surrounding this are important to discuss, especially in the light of the 'bricks n' clicks' debate. The company has got rid of its wholesaling arm and is very tight on stock control as this may not be very helpful if transactions are carried out via the Web.

Evolutionary Paths of a Web Site

MNCs

Information ⟶ Transaction Model

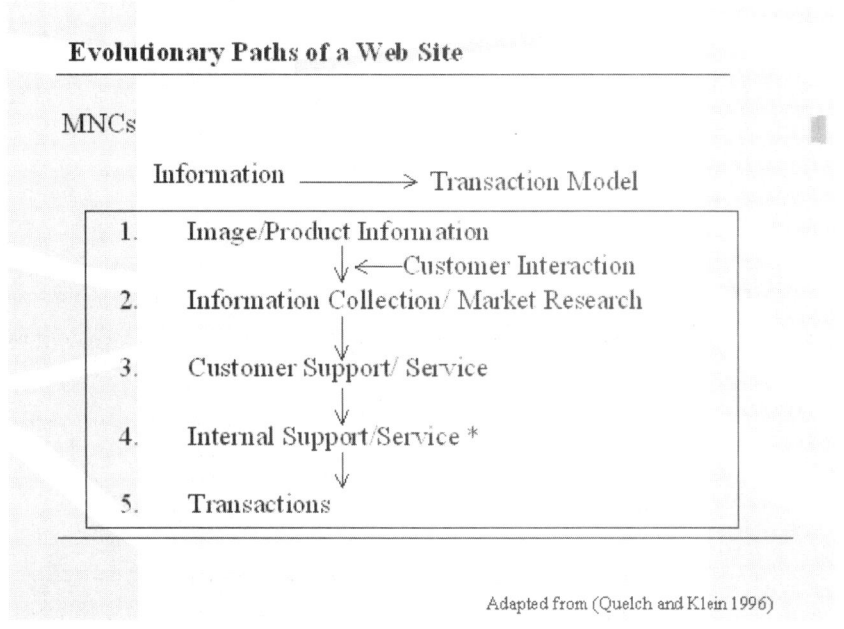

1. Image/Product Information
   ↓ ⟵ Customer Interaction
2. Information Collection/ Market Research
   ↓
3. Customer Support/ Service
   ↓
4. Internal Support/Service *
   ↓
5. Transactions

Adapted from (Quelch and Klein 1996)

Figure 1

For many companies the Web is an important part of building a CRM strategy. This is because many of the functions can be automated and companies can manage to track customer preferences and needs. The diagram above shows the path that Reiss could follow in the way it can develop its web site in the future.

At the same time classic relationship marketing requires the company to attract and retain customers. For this to happen customer information needs to be captured. This is not easy unless a database is involved. The best way to do this through direct and web based marketing. A purely transactional site is limiting. The figure below highlights the key strategies for developing a CRM strategy. At the same time the benefits of such a strategy will allow the company to build brand equity as shown in figure 3.

Part C: Practice cases

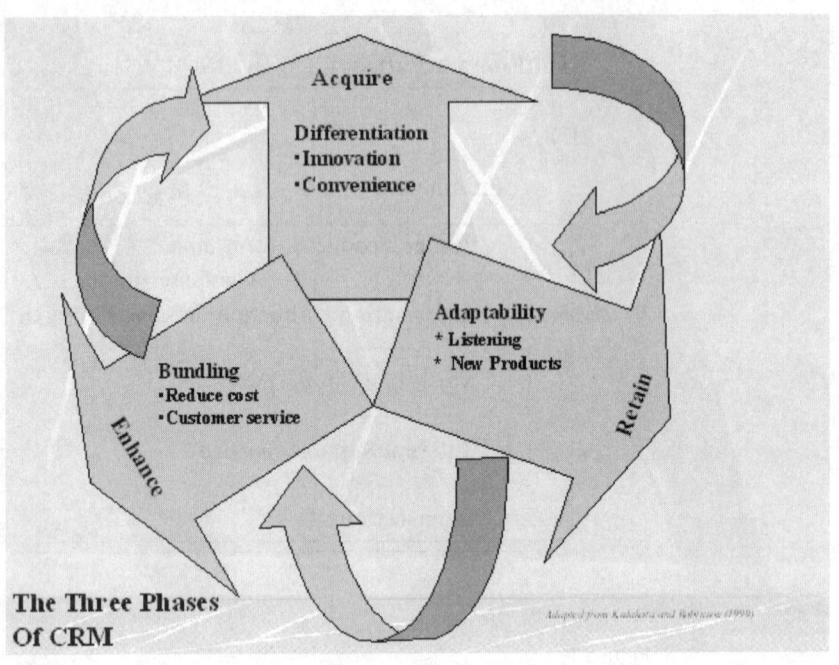

Figure 2

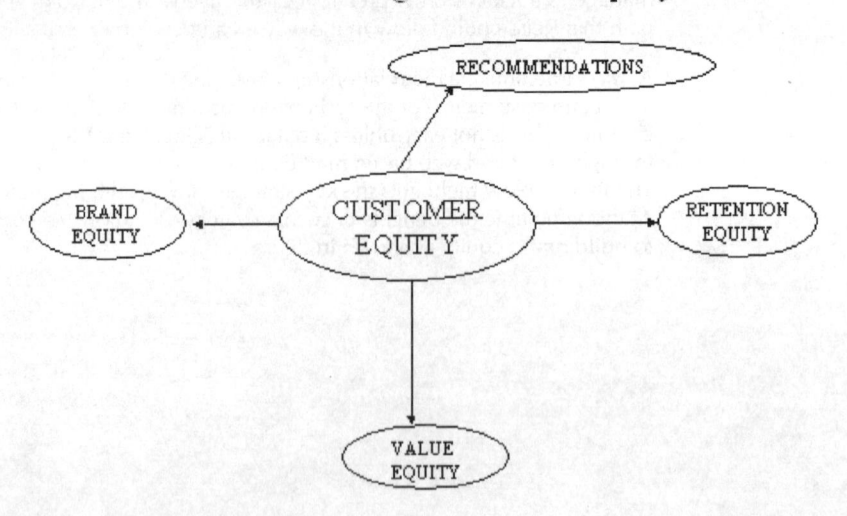

Figure 3

A good CRM strategy will help the company to build its Customer profitability profiles and retention levels.

Answers should therefore contain:

A good evaluation of current strategy

The development of a CRM strategy

Strengths and Weaknesses of Answers to Question Two

The quality of answers to this question varied greatly. The majority of candidates were unable to introduce relevant concepts for the CRM and Internet topics even though examples were given within the case. This resulted in fragmented and superficial answers with many candidates failing to produce coherent strategies. Often theory was trotted out without an understanding of its application. In general, apart from some good candidates who tied up web development with CRM, this question was poorly handled.

Question 3

Propose a European market entry strategy for Reiss, concentrating on brand development.

30 Marks

When answering this question, candidates should be able to discuss some the key factors shown below, as well as some others they may have considered:

a) The high rental paid for the shop in Dublin.

b) The initial success in Dublin.

c) The development of the brand image in the EU.

d) The possibility of offering different styles in different markets.

e) The high growth markets after UK and Ireland appear to be Portugal, Spain and the Netherlands.

f) The largest market, Germany, is experiencing slow growth or stagnation.

g) Overseas expansion will need a more dedicated marketing team.

h) The utilisation of the Internet within the international context.

i) Entry strategies based first on site purchase or rental agreements?

Part C: Practice cases

According to the article in the appendix,

Speed and integration of the supply chain will continue to shape the future of the retail apparel industry in Europe by enabling more flexible, demand driven fulfilment.... The hallmark of successful apparel retailers is an ability to create distinctive product ranges that are responsive to quickly changing consumer expectations.

Students need to bring this out in their answers as well as the models contained within the case regarding brands.

If a brand is to be successfully anchored in the market, it is necessary to undertake a prior segment check. The claims of the customer and of the company regarding service, market volume, brand and price awareness, price sensitivity and choice of distribution channel must urgently be brought into accord.

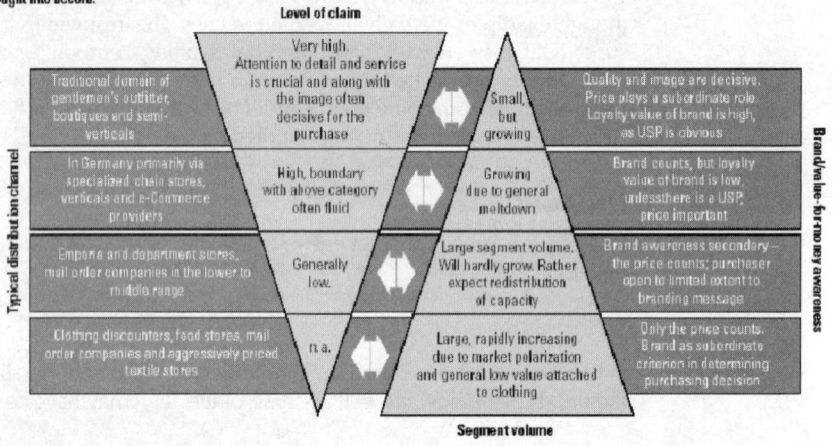

Typical distribution channel	Level of claim	Segment volume	Brand/value-for-money awareness
Traditional domain of gentlemen's outfitter, boutiques and semi-verticals	Very high. Attention to detail and service is crucial and along with the image often decisive for the purchase	Small, but growing	Quality and image are decisive. Price plays a subordinate role. Loyalty value of brand is high, as USP is obvious
In Germany primarily via specialized chain stores, verticals and e-Commerce providers	High, boundary with above category often fluid	Growing due to general meltdown	Brand counts, but loyalty value of brand is low, unless there is a USP, price important
Emporia and department stores, mail order companies in the lower to middle range	Generally low	Large segment volume. Will hardly grow. Rather expect redistribution of capacity	Brand awareness secondary – the price counts; purchaser open to limited extent to branding message
Clothing discounters, food stores, mail order companies and aggressively priced textile stores	n.a.	Large, rapidly increasing due to market polarization and general low value attached to clothing	Only the price counts. Brand as subordinate criterion in determining purchasing decision

The brand will have to convey a strong coherent image throughout Europe in order to develop recognition and trust. It is also important for the company to segment and target specific markets.

Entry ought to be preceded by brand building exercises and full utilisation of Web strategies.

Students should consider the issues above as well as offer their own ideas of how the company could enter the European market based on its experience in Dublin. Candidates should also analyse which markets are the best ones to enter in the early stages. They also need to consider the need for market research.

Candidates were marked on the following:

- Entry strategy
- Brand Development

18 ♦ The Reiss exam

Strengths and Weaknesses of Answers to Question Three

This question was the downfall of many candidates who often just trotted out an International marketing strategy and failed to answer the question set. Few candidates mentioned brand development in the context of international markets, even though branding issues were discussed in the case. Cultural issues were ignored and the country detail provided within the appendix of the case was also ignored. Good answers took account of the best markets and the best possible entry strategies that would be cost effective. They also considered the lessons that could be learnt from the Irish adventure. At the same time links with an integrated strategy for brand development were considered.

Summary

This case allows for a range of innovative and creative answers. The fashion market is fickle and difficult. Candidates need to understand this as well as the need for Reiss to build a convincing brand. Candidates should also give convincing strategies for CRM development. They should also utilise the growth figures within the European market. The financial results are simply represented and these should be used in the answers.

In all answers we look for the usual, justification, strategic thinking, coherence and detail of information when marking the answers.

There is still a disappointing reliance on 'formulaic' answers that have been pre-prepared. There is also a reliance on theory without application to the actual case and the data within it. Candidates need to guard against this tendency and come to the examination with an open mind and answer the actual questions that have been set and not what they think have been set!

```
                    STRATEGIC THINKING
                           /\
                          /  \
                         /    \
                        /      \
                       / COHERENCE \
                      / and links between \
                     /      answers       \
                    /_____\
        DETAIL UNDERPINNING         JUSTIFICATION OF
        STRATEGIES ADOPTED          STRATEGIES ADOPTED
```

A Final Practice Case: Centrica 19

Chapter Topic List	
1	Introduction
2	Guidance notes for Centrica
3	About Centrica
4	Overview analysis comments
5	Your role
6	Contemporary issues
7	Problems and opportunities
8	Starting your inview analysis
9	Templates to help decision making
10	The exam paper
11	Extracts from the Examiner's report

Introduction

In this chapter you will:

☑ You will be able to work through a final practice case, further developing your own skills and case technique in advance of the exam.

Part C: Practice cases

1 Introduction

1.1 In this chapter you will find a final practice case study – Centrica set in 2004. This is a contrast to Reiss, because it is a large complex multinational organisation with some challenging contemporary issues.

Tutor Tip

You might find it helpful to create templates of tools, checklists for each stage in the process which will provide you with your own customised DIY guide to help you when the final case arrives.

1.2 You will find in this section:

- The Centrica Case
- Some guidance notes to get you started
- A sample answer and Examiner's comments

Action Programme 1

Start by reading the Centrica case as far as the end of the narrative and turn the pages to see what is included in the Appendix. You will see this is quite a different sector – complex but also essentially a consumer market focus

19 ♦ A final practice case: Centrica

The Chartered Institute of marketing

Case Study
June 2004

Strategic Marketing Management: Analysis & Decision

Centrica Plc

© The Chartered Institute of Marketing

Part C: Practice cases

Case Study – June 2004

Strategic Marketing Management: Analysis & Decision

Important Notes

The examiners will be marking your scripts on the basis of questions put to you in the examination room. Candidates are advised to pay particular attention to the *mark allocation on the examination paper and budget their time accordingly*.

Your role is outlined in the candidates' brief and you will be required to recommend clear courses of action.

You WILL NOT be awarded marks merely for analysis. This should have been undertaken before the examination day in preparation for meeting the tasks which will be specified in the examination paper.

Candidates are advised not to waste valuable time collecting unnecessary data. The cases are based upon real-world situations. No useful purpose will therefore be served by contacting companies in this industry and candidates are *strictly instructed not to do so* as it would simply cause unnecessary confusion.

As in real life, anomalies will be found in this Case situation. Please simply state your assumptions where necessary when answering questions. The CIM is not in a position to answer queries on Case data. Candidates are tested on their overall understanding of the Case and its key issues, not on minor details. There are no catch questions or hidden agendas.

Additional information will be introduced in the examination paper itself which candidates must take into account when answering the questions set.

Acquaint yourself thoroughly with the Case Study and be prepared to follow closely the instructions given to you on the examination day. To answer examination questions effectively candidates must adopt a report format.

The copying of pre-prepared "group" answers, including those written by consultants/tutors is strictly forbidden and will be penalised by failure. The questions will demand analysis in the examination itself and individually composed answers are required to pass.

Page 1 of Centrica

Candidate's Brief

You have been appointed as a Marketing Consultant to the Board of Centrica Plc. The company initially started life as British Gas, but is now a multinational, diversified energy company. As the deregulation of the energy market continues apace throughout the world, the company is attempting to take full advantage of the opportunities this offers. At the same time, as a large company attempting to give the consumer a range of services related to the home, it is keen to understand and develop customer relations to a high degree. The energy market is a complex market involving both the distribution and storage of energy in a global arena. The company's main market is the UK at present, but it has designs to expand in Europe and North America. The global energy market has been tainted by the Enron affair, so developing trust is important. The company has been very active in acquiring a range of companies, such as the UK's Automobile Association (AA) and a range of energy companies. It also launched Goldfish, a credit card with related financial services. However, it has now divested itself of this venture as it was loss making. The company has major rivals in the UK, Europe, and in America. As a company, its market capitalisation is not as high as some of the major players. It also has to develop an image which is more in tune with the 21st Century, rather than the old British Gas image. The biggest challenge facing the company is in establishing a substantial and unique brand presence in the UK, Europe and North America. Centrica is a company with a range of different products and services. In each market different brand names are prevalent. In order to help the company develop a market focus for the next decade, you have been hired to work closely with the Board and the marketing team. Your name is Yasmin Viccars and you have previously worked in the telecommunications sector. Based on an initial request, you have prepared the following short report on the key marketing issues facing the company. At a later meeting, scheduled for 5th June 2004, you will be asked to elaborate on this report to the Board of Directors who will pose specific questions to you based on your current findings.

Important Notice

This Case material is based on an actual organisation and existing market conditions.

Candidates are strictly instructed NOT TO CONTACT Centrica Plc or any other companies in the industry. Additional information will be provided at the time of the examination. Further copies may be obtained from The Chartered Institute of Marketing, Moor Hall, Cookham, Maidenhead, Berkshire, SL6 9QH, UK, or may be downloaded from the CIM student web site www.cimvirtualinstitute.com

---

© The Chartered Institute of Marketing

Centrica Plc

Introduction

Centrica Plc was formed in 1997, following the demerger (dismantling by the UK Government) of British Gas Plc. As a result of deregulation and the demerger, opportunities for developing new business areas opened up for Centrica. Initially the group comprised of the gas supply, services and retail businesses of British Gas, selling white goods and related items, together with the gas production business of the North and South Morecambe gas fields in the UK. It also retained ownership of the Goldfish (credit card) brand. Centrica then took operational control of Accord Energy, previously a joint venture between British Gas and NGC Corporation of Houston, USA. Accord Energy is a major player in the short-term gas trading and wholesaling market in Great Britain. Later in the year, Centrica and Thyssengas in the Netherlands signed a contract to supply gas through the UK-Continent Interconnector pipeline. Under the agreement, Centrica agreed to sell to Thyssengas up to 3 billion cubic metres of gas over a period of seven years. Deliveries started in October 1998 when the Interconnector pipeline opened. The company also entered into agreements with Amerada Hess, Enterprise Oil, OMV, Mobil North Sea Limited, ARCO British Limited and Eastern Natural Gas (offshore Ltd) to terminate gas sale and purchase contracts. This made it possible for the company to purchase and sell gas on the open market. The company expanded its gas export sales to the Netherlands. Centrica also launched its first financial product to complement the Goldfish credit card. A home and contents insurance package offering average savings worth £75 was launched under the British Gas and Goldfish brands. In 1998, Centrica ceased to be a monopoly supplier, as gas competition completed its roll-out across Great Britain. The last tranche of the roll-out opened up competition to 3.1 million homes in Greater London and Surrey. In the same year, the first set of domestic customers received their electricity supply from British Gas. This was again an energy distribution opportunity for the company as a result of deregulation in the UK energy market. More than 400,000 customers had signed up for electricity by the time the market opened in the Canterbury, Chester, Hull and Norwich areas. On the 12th of October, 1998, Centrica made its first upstream acquisition, buying PowerGen's gas and oil company, PowerGen North Sea Limited (PGNS) for £248 million. The acquisition involved interests in eight producing fields and several undeveloped gas fields in the Southern North Sea and the East Irish Sea, close to Centrica's existing Morecambe fields. In 1999, competition for domestic and business electricity customers intensified across Great Britain, with nearly 1.5 million customers choosing British Gas as their electricity supplier. As a result of difficult High Street trading conditions, the company closed its 243 British Gas Energy Centres, ending the retail arm of its operations.

Acquisitions

In 1999, Centrica acquired the UK's Automobile Association (AA). This gave the company a foothold in the car insurance and distress rescue market. In 2000, the AA was the UK's top-ranked roadside assistance provider, following a survey of 25,000 drivers. Centrica made a major step towards launching a telecommunications service by announcing it had entered into a strategic alliance with Vodafone UK Limited, to provide mobile telephone services across Great

Page 3 of Centrica

Britain, and reached agreement with Torch Telecom and Cable & Wireless Communications for the provision of residential telecommunications services. Later in the year, the company acquired Direct Energy Marketing Limited (a Canadian energy supply business), including its 27.5% interest in Energy America (a joint venture with Sempra Energy), which trades in the United States. The company also bought Avalanche Energy Limited, a privately held Canadian gas and oil production company. The purchase of Sempra Energy's 72.5% stake in Energy America gave the company full ownership and management control. Over the next two years Centrica continued to create strategic alliances, acquire energy and service companies, and purchase customer bases in the USA and Canada. Much of this is captured in Figure 1.

Figure 1 – Centrica's Growth Path

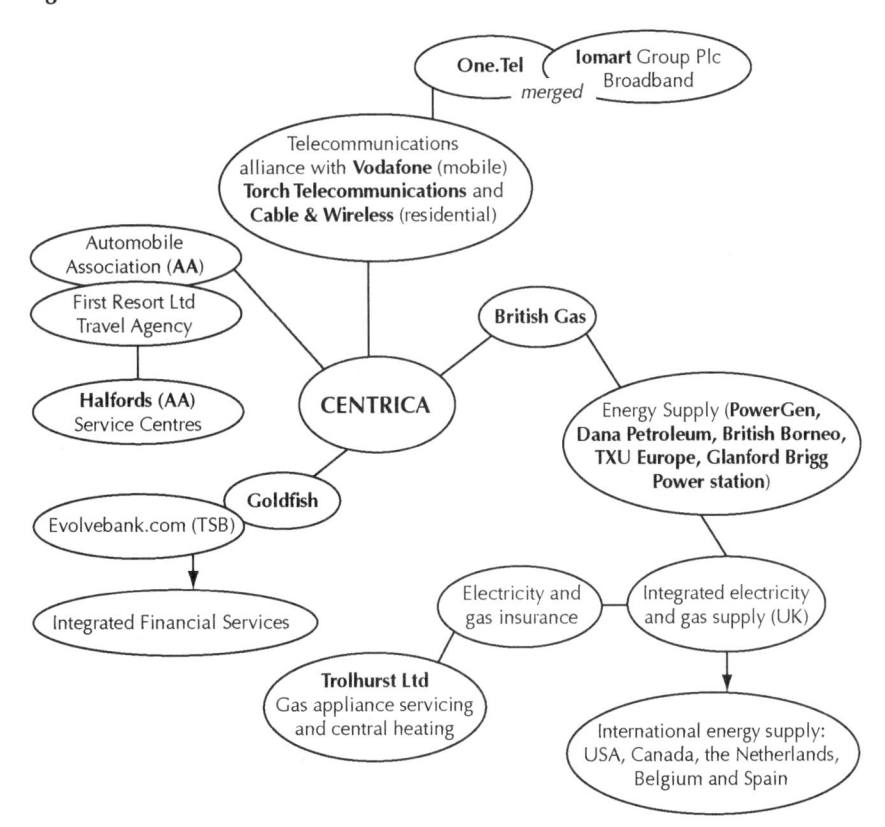

```
                    One.Tel ─── Iomart Group Plc
                         merged    Broadband
                              │
                    Telecommunications
                    alliance with Vodafone (mobile)
                    Torch Telecommunications and
                    Cable & Wireless (residential)
                              │
    Automobile                │
    Association (AA)          │
         │                    │          British Gas
    First Resort Ltd          │              │
    Travel Agency             │              │
         │                    │          Energy Supply (PowerGen,
    Halfords (AA)  ───── CENTRICA ─────  Dana Petroleum, British Borneo,
    Service Centres           │          TXU Europe, Glanford Brigg
                              │          Power station)
                           Goldfish
         │                    │              │
    Evolvebank.com (TSB)      │       Integrated electricity
         │              Electricity and    and gas supply (UK)
         ▼              gas insurance          │
    Integrated Financial Services              │
                              │                ▼
                        Trolhurst Ltd    International energy supply:
                   Gas appliance servicing  USA, Canada, the Netherlands,
                    and central heating      Belgium and Spain
```

Source: Ranchhod (2003)

Detailed information on the company's history is provided in Appendix 1. The key brands that are under Centrica's wing are shown in Figure 2. Figure 3 shows the key business areas associated with each brand.

Part C: Practice cases

Page 4 of Centrica

Figure 2 – Key Centrica Brands

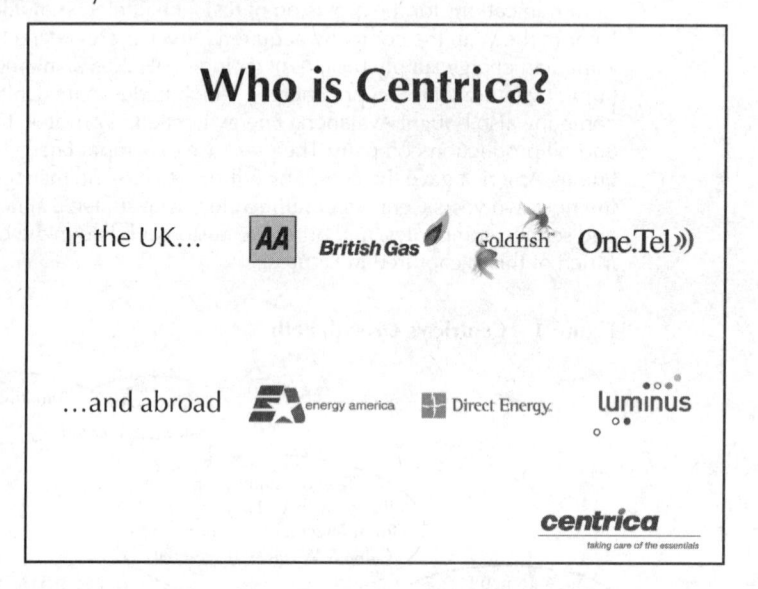

Who is Centrica?

In the UK... AA British Gas Goldfish One.Tel

...and abroad energy america Direct Energy luminus

centrica
taking care of the essentials

Source: Centrica

Page 5 of Centrica

Figure 3 – Key Brands and Business Areas in the Centrica Portfolio

British Gas — www.house.co.uk

Gas: We supply gas to homes throughout Britain, under the British Gas and Scottish Gas brands. Against the background of a highly competitive energy market, millions of customers continue to choose us as their gas supplier.

Electricity: Since the residential electricity market opened to competition in 1998 we've become one of the largest suppliers of electricity in Britain.

We are committed to providing our customers with excellent service and great value for money.

Telecommunications: British Gas Communications was launched in September 2000, and offers customers fixed line, mobile and internet services.

Home services: We continue to be the largest provider of gas central heating installation and servicing in the country. We also offer our customers the reassurance of protection in other areas of the home, providing services for kitchen appliances, plumbing and drains, electrical wiring and home security systems.

British Gas
Scottish Gas
Nwy Prydain

The AA — www.theaa.com

Roadside services: We provide reassurance and services to motorists in the UK and Ireland through the AA. The roadside assistance service remains at the core of our activities, with members choosing the level of cover that best suits their needs.

Personal finance: We are the UK's number one independent insurance intermediary, and we are a growing provider of personal loans and financial services.

Other AA services: AA Service Centres offer a range of maintenance and repair services to motorists across Britain.

We are the only national driving school exclusively using fully qualified driving instructors.

AA

One.Tel — www.onetel.co.uk

With a fresh and innovative approach, we provide a range of landline, mobile and internet services across the UK.

Our mobile service offers one of the lowest monthly line rental charges in the country.

One.Tel

Goldfish Bank — www.goldfish.com

Building on the success of the Goldfish card, we have launched the Goldfish Bank in partnership with Lloyds TSB to develop a wide range of financial services products.

New products include a savings account, personal loans and a guaranteed savings bond.

Goldfish

North America and Europe — www.directenergy.com / www.energyamerica.com / www.luminus.be

North America: Through Direct Energy in Canada and Energy America in the US we supply energy to homes and businesses in several provinces and states.

Our Direct Energy home services division provides heating and ventilation installation and maintenance services.

Europe: Our joint venture energy business, Luminus, is an active participant in the liberalising Belgian market.

Direct Energy
energy america
luminus

Source: Centrica

Company Values

For a company with such a diverse portfolio, it is important to have a set of values that incorporate the many different aspects of the business. The company's actions are therefore based on attitudes such as a passion for customers, pride, support for customers, developing and maintaining trust, and continuous improvement (see Figure 4).

Figure 4 – Company Values

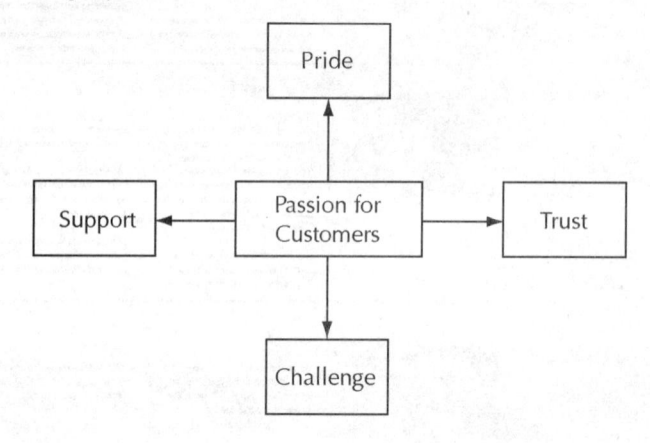

```
                    Pride
                     ↑
                     |
  Support  ←  Passion for  →  Trust
               Customers
                     |
                     ↓
                  Challenge
```

Source: Centrica

Passion for Customers

This is undoubtedly the most important aspect of the company's philosophy as most of its business is service related. The company's ethos is to deliver outstanding customer service, anticipating customer needs, giving value for money, and delivering efficient and effective products and services.

Pride

Company pride is derived from customer satisfaction and delivering good-quality products and services. The company is proud of staff achievements and success is rewarded.

Trust

The company is keen to build trust with its customers, by empowering and respecting their employees. Integrity is central to building this trust with all stakeholders.

Challenge

The company strives for continual improvement, engaging in constructive dialogue with both advocates and critics from within and outside the company. The challenge is to deliver competitive advantage and consistently outstanding shareholder returns.

Page 7 of Centrica

Support

Employees are fully supported to meet challenges through teamworking and knowledge. The company is happy to provide the tools and training required to maintain outstanding performance.

Company Performance

The company has generally performed well and its share price currently stands at around 250p. This results in a market capitalisation of around £10 billion. It is generally impressive that the company has outperformed the stockmarket index by 187% between 1997 and 2002. Company earnings increased by £155 million to £478 million in 2002. The operating profit for the company was £932 million. The return on capital employed was 32%, or 7.9% on the average market capitalisation. Figure 5 shows how Centrica's fortunes have fared from 1996-2002. (Appendix 1 contains all the key financial reports pertaining to the various businesses operating under Centrica).

(Appendix 1 – Company Report).

Figure 5 – Centrica's Fortunes – 1996-2002 (£m)

Year	2002	2001	2000	1999	1998	1997	1996
Profit Breakdown							
UK Energy Supply	738	652	553	461	248	275	211
Home Services	61	36	26	20	9	-49	-196
Road Services	73	37	25	-3	N/A	N/A	N/A
Financial Services	-40	5	9	-9	-5	N/A	N/A
Retail	N/A	N/A	N/A	-25	-31	-45	-66
Telecoms	-33	-97	-49	N/A	N/A	N/A	N/A
Other Activities/CBS/ North America	133	46	-24	-16	-7	N/A	N/A
Total Profit	932	679	540	428	214	181	-51
Total Turnover	14,315	12,611	9,933	7,217	7,481	7,842	8,125
Profit %	6.5	5.4	5.4	5.9	2.9	2.3	-0.6

Source: Centrica

Figure 5 – Profit by Business Area

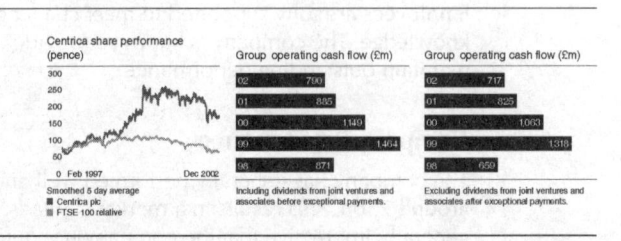

Source: Centrica

What is Centrica?

Centrica has various businesses, each dedicated to servicing different sets of customers that in many instances overlap. According to Deutsche Bank:

*'Centrica is one of the few pure customer 'hubs' to which investors can get exposure... its structure is unique... it is essentially a **'customer hub'** offering an enlarged range of utility services into the home... the domestic gas customer base forms the core, and without a customer base how can a company cross sell? Hence the long - term issue to Centrica's core gas customer base is the level of sustainable margin.'*

The common theme for the company is the service provided to each home. These can be listed as:

a. Gas, electricity and Liquid Petroleum Gas (LPG).
b. Home related finance and other services.
c. Travel and traffic services.
d. Telecommunications via mobiles, fixed lines and the Internet.
e. Savings, investments and credit.
f. Gas and electrical appliance servicing, offering appliance cover and home security.
g. Roadside recovery, vehicle checks and car service centres.
h. Motor insurance, home insurance and travel insurance.

The number of UK customer relationships is continually growing and this is illustrated in Figure 6. Each area of business offers opportunities and threats for Centrica. These areas of business and customer perceptions are now considered in detail.

Page 9 of Centrica

Figure 6 – Centrica: UK Customer Product Relationships

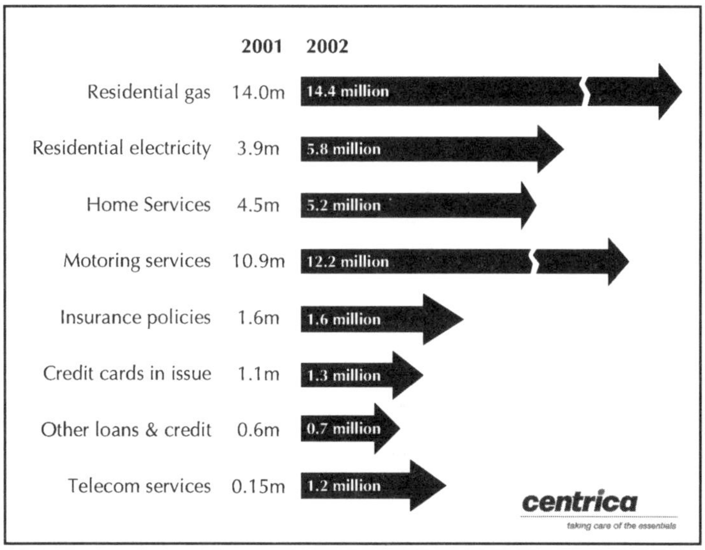

	2001	2002
Residential gas	14.0m	14.4 million
Residential electricity	3.9m	5.8 million
Home Services	4.5m	5.2 million
Motoring services	10.9m	12.2 million
Insurance policies	1.6m	1.6 million
Credit cards in issue	1.1m	1.3 million
Other loans & credit	0.6m	0.7 million
Telecom services	0.15m	1.2 million

centrica — taking care of the essentials

Source: Centrica

British Gas

In May 1999, when a brand audit was carried out, customers felt that British Gas would become better and that customers would benefit accordingly. However, as deregulation has progressed, it has allowed an emerging market for energy/utility brands where viable alternatives are present. Customers are now more willing to accept utility supplies from one 'meta-supplier' that can not only offer multiple utilities, but can also adopt products from non-traditional suppliers. This leaves British Gas in a good position as a result of its alliances and acquisitions. It is able to supply electricity, gas, LPG and telecommunications. Market research carried out by the company shows that as far as British Gas is concerned, the public do not discern big changes, but are aware of the changing environment (Figure 7).

Part C: Practice cases

Page 10 of Centrica

Figure 7

The key elements of the current British Gas brand based on all respondents: generally consumers perceive there have been no big changes but there is a range of small but highly significant developments.

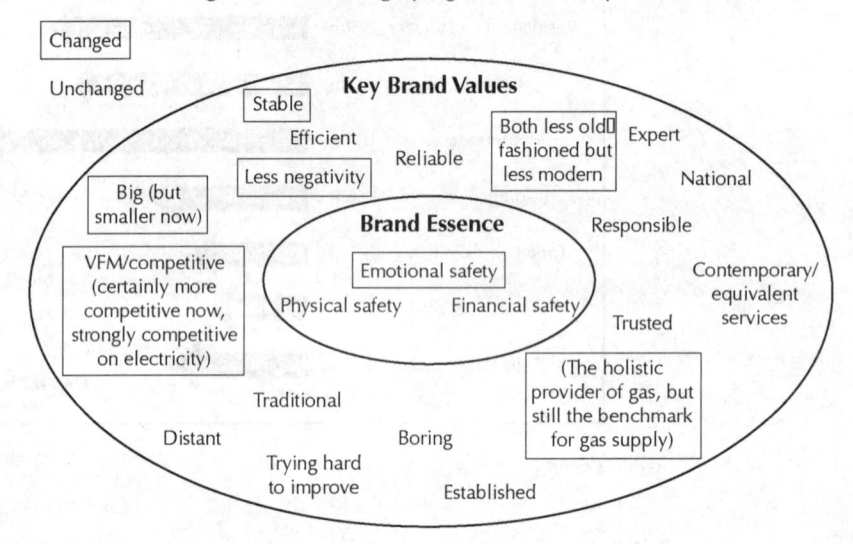

```
Changed
Unchanged              Key Brand Values
              Stable
              Efficient           Both less old
                         Reliable fashioned but    Expert
         Less negativity          less modern
 Big (but                                          National
 smaller now)               Brand Essence
                                              Responsible
 VFM/competitive         Emotional safety
 (certainly more                                 Contemporary/
 competitive now,   Physical safety  Financial safety  equivalent
 strongly competitive                              services
 on electricity)                          Trusted
                                       (The holistic
                    Traditional        provider of gas, but
                                       still the benchmark
          Distant         Boring       for gas supply)
                   Trying hard
                   to improve   Established
```

Source: Centrica

Gas and electricity are typically seen as boring and low involvement services by customers, as there is very little that is tangible to attach emotions to. However, utilities are now part and parcel of modern existence in developed countries such as the UK. Utility companies such as PowerGen and nPower are taking steps to make the utilities more 'exciting'. Figure 8 illustrates the way in which British Gas is perceived, offering the company some opportunities to brand themselves differently.

Page 11 of Centrica

Figure 8 – Consumer Perceptions of Change in British Gas

The ideal British Gas brand is more different than it was two years ago but this is mainly due to consumers being clearer in what they want.

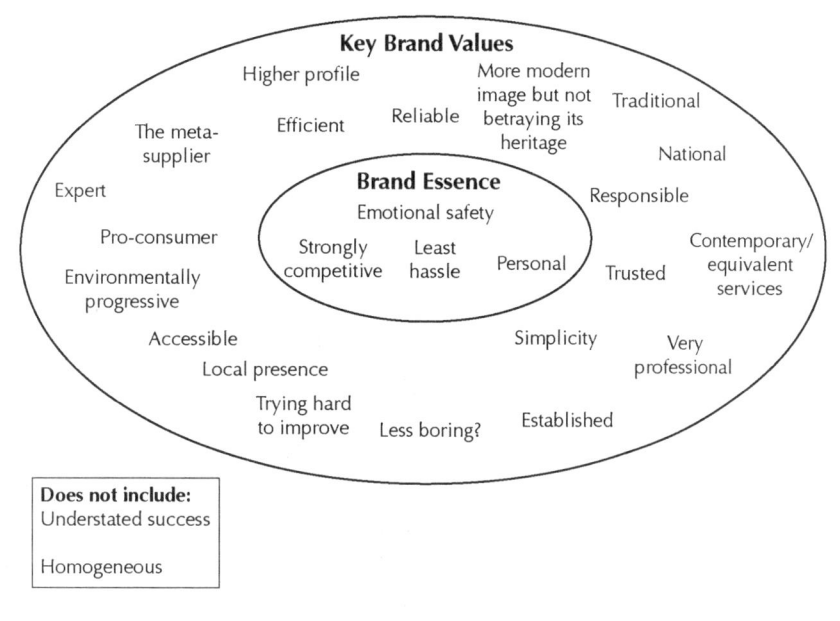

Key Brand Values: Higher profile, More modern image but not betraying its heritage, Traditional, The meta-supplier, Efficient, Reliable, National, Expert, Responsible, Pro-consumer, Contemporary/equivalent services, Environmentally progressive, Trusted, Accessible, Simplicity, Very professional, Local presence, Trying hard to improve, Less boring?, Established

Brand Essence: Emotional safety, Strongly competitive, Least hassle, Personal

Does not include:
Understated success
Homogeneous

Source: Centrica

Many consumers, having seen the deregulation of energy and utility companies are now much more open to accept:

- One bill for all utilities.

- Meta-packages (offering packages with a range of different services).

- Easy and fast recourse to a pleasant person.

- Sense of stability in the energy/utility market – (reduction in confusion about who owns who and what is happening in the market)

- Easy cost comparisons between suppliers (this now easily possible on the Internet).

- Easy access to a credible advisory body.

- Reassurance of empowering help for gas.

Page 12 of Centrica

The utility market is now complex with many different service offerings. The marketing stances adopted by each provider and the public perceptions of each major supplier are shown in Figure 9. Figure 10 shows the way in which consumers think when they actually purchase brands.

Figure 9 – Comparison between British Gas and other Energy Providers

Overall perceived similarity between British Gas, PowerGen and npower

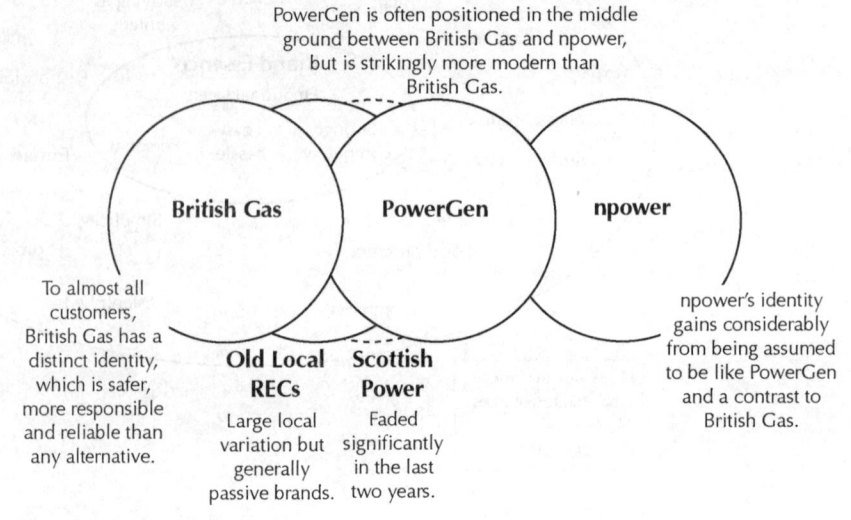

PowerGen is often positioned in the middle ground between British Gas and npower, but is strikingly more modern than British Gas.

British Gas   **PowerGen**   **npower**

To almost all customers, British Gas has a distinct identity, which is safer, more responsible and reliable than any alternative.

Old Local RECs – Large local variation but generally passive brands.

Scottish Power – Faded significantly in the last two years.

npower's identity gains considerably from being assumed to be like PowerGen and a contrast to British Gas.

Source: Centrica
(* REC = Regional Electricity Company)

Figure 10 – Purchasing Behaviour of Consumers

For most consumers there is a rough hierarchy of alternatives for gas and electricity

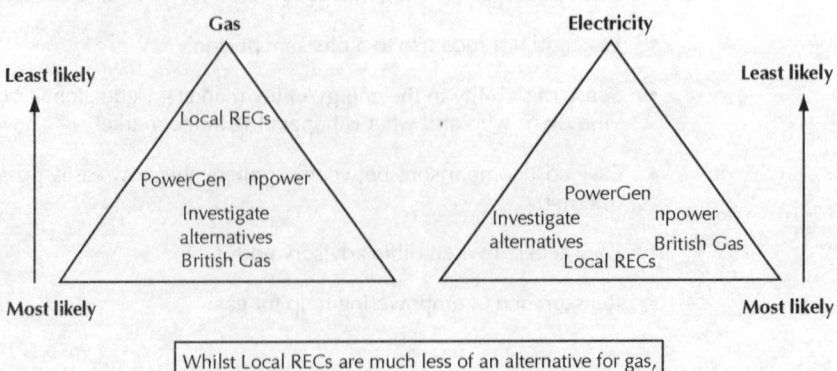

Gas (Least likely → Most likely):
- Local RECs
- PowerGen   npower
- Investigate alternatives
- British Gas

Electricity (Least likely → Most likely):
- PowerGen
- Investigate alternatives   npower
- British Gas
- Local RECs

Whilst Local RECs are much less of an alternative for gas, they are certainly part of the scrum for electricity

Source: Centrica

Page 13 of Centrica

British Gas, under Centrica, has many opportunities to provide customers with a range of services, including finance and home servicing. However, under Centrica the brand has a chance to develop globally.

One.Tel and British Gas Telecommunications

Currently under Centrica there are two brands offering telecommunications:

- British Gas Telecommunications – offering fixed, mobile and narrowband Internet service, with telecommunications as a key part of the 'essential services' package. The company has 400,000 'active customers'. Most of these customers have an existing relationship with British Gas.

- One.Tel – offering fixed, narrowband and broadband services, with a mobile service to be launched soon. It has over 800,000 'active' customers, billing around 18% of the residential international call minutes. The company tends to attract younger, 'sophisticated' telecommunications users, with 30% self serving through the Virtual Customer Service Centre.

One.Tel is an interesting entrant into the telecommunications market. It made its initial mark as a low-cost telephone services provider after the BT monopoly was opened up through UK Government regulation. Customers either dial a prefix to current numbers or purchase set-up boxes which direct calls through One.Tel, undercutting BT. After the acquisition by Centrica, more opportunities have opened up for the brand, through British Gas telecommunications and also broadband services for the Internet. The biggest challenge for the brand is to provide customers with a comprehensive package dealing with mobiles, land-based communication and Internet communication. Research carried out by the company indicates that One.Tel is a serious contender within the telecommunications market, but is not necessarily really well-known. This is illustrated by Figures 11-13.

Figure 11 – Total Awareness of Companies that Provide Fixed/Landline Telephone Services

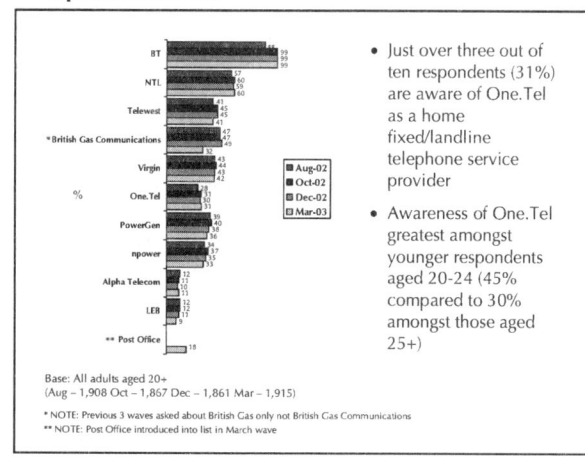

- Just over three out of ten respondents (31%) are aware of One.Tel as a home fixed/landline telephone service provider
- Awareness of One.Tel greatest amongst younger respondents aged 20-24 (45% compared to 30% amongst those aged 25+)

Base: All adults aged 20+
(Aug – 1,908 Oct – 1,867 Dec – 1,861 Mar – 1,915)

* NOTE: Previous 3 waves asked about British Gas only not British Gas Communications
** NOTE: Post Office introduced into list in March wave

Source: Centrica

Part C: Practice cases

Page 14 of Centrica

Figure 12 – Total Awareness of Companies that Provide Mobile Telephone Services

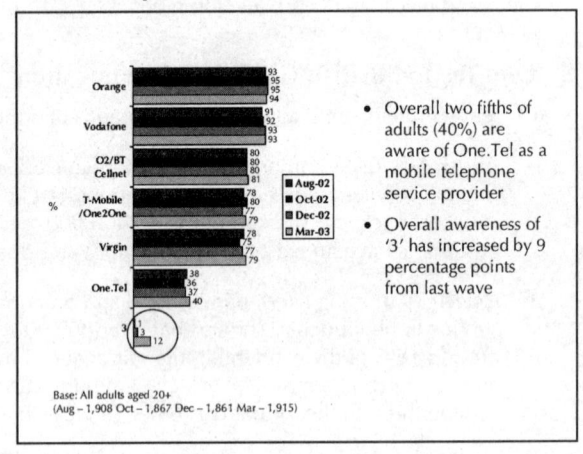

- Overall two fifths of adults (40%) are aware of One.Tel as a mobile telephone service provider
- Overall awareness of '3' has increased by 9 percentage points from last wave

Source: Centrica

Figure 13 – Total Awareness of Internet Service Providers

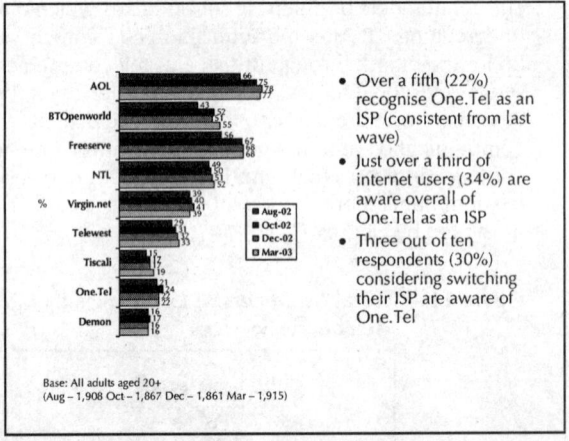

- Over a fifth (22%) recognise One.Tel as an ISP (consistent from last wave)
- Just over a third of internet users (34%) are aware overall of One.Tel as an ISP
- Three out of ten respondents (30%) considering switching their ISP are aware of One.Tel

Source: Centrica

In each telecommunications area, some old brands have an advantage as they are well known. However, many individuals are now more willing to try new providers if they can get better service and cheaper deals. None the less, reliability of service will always be a key issue for many customers. For mobile users in particular the complexity of the tariffs is often a daunting prospect, with no clear idea of the best value propositions. Until 1992 telecommunications service supply was restricted to the original duopoly of BT and Mercury (now known as Cable & Wireless Communications). Deregulation within the UK market has lead to a massive influx of alternative competitive activity, ranging from licenced Public Telecommunication Operators (PTOs), similar to BT and Cable & Wireless Communications, to switched and switchless resellers and wholesalers, aggregators etc.

Page 15 of Centrica

With rapid changes in technology, ever increasing wireless communications, and the advent of broadband, the global telecommunications market is estimated to be in excess of $1,000 billion (1 trillion US dollars). The UK is a very profitable market, with BT dominating the sector. However, with deregulation, their market share is gradually being eroded by players such as One.Tel. In order to curb BT's dominant position, OFCOM (the UK telecommunications regulatory body) decided to impose caps on BT's charges, giving competitors a chance to offer the public the most competitive tariffs possible. Competing suppliers are now able to offer services and tariffs that significantly undercut BT without any compromise on quality or innovation. The lowering of costs to businesses and domestic customers has created in the UK one of the most buoyant markets in Europe.

Broadband

The residential market for broadband access will be worth around $88 billion by 2007, an estimated sevenfold increase in revenue over the next five years (www.theregister.co.uk). Industry consultancy ARC Group estimates that by 2007 almost 300 million business and residential premises worldwide will be wired up to broadband. By 2007, broadband will become the norm rather than the exception, ARC forecasts. DSL will account for almost a third of all connections closely, followed by cable. Satellite, fibre and fixed wireless will all represent a smaller proportion of the market "due to cost and availability factors", according to ARC. Competition for customers is likely to be very intense, as each provider tries to woo customers over from narrowband provisions. Complexity will also increase as 'triple-play' packages of voice, data and digital television can be on offer.

The Automobile Association (AA)

The AA started life as a road recovery company. Over the years it has built an excellent client base and an excellent reputation with the public. The motorist vehicle breakdown services market has three main sectors. They are the ad hoc vehicle breakdown sector, the retail or private breakdown sector, and the commercial breakdown sector, provided through third party organisations such as affinity groups and car distributors. The breakdown service sector has grown at a fast rate as motorists regularly use them for roadside assistance. At the same time, drivers are less conversant with engines and cars have also become more complex. Intense competition between the main players (the AA and RAC) slowed down the growth in the market. However, since 1999 the sector has been revitalised as a result of changes in ownership (e.g. the acquisition of the AA by Centrica). The nature of the consumer has also changed as they increasingly look for reassurance. The main motoring organisations, including the Automobile Association (AA), Royal Automobile Club (RAC) and Direct Line Rescue, have strategies that are designed to offer more than just vehicle breakdown services. The idea behind the strategies is to develop a much closer relationship with their customers (Keynote publications, 2001). The AA strategy is to generally maintain Road Services as the foundation of its brand equity and utilising the customer base for participation in other markets. It can continually create motoring products and services exploiting the AA Service Centres. At the same time, it has the ability to significantly expand its presence in related financial services (Figure 14).

Part C: Practice cases

Page 16 of Centrica

Figure 14 – AA Brand Propositions

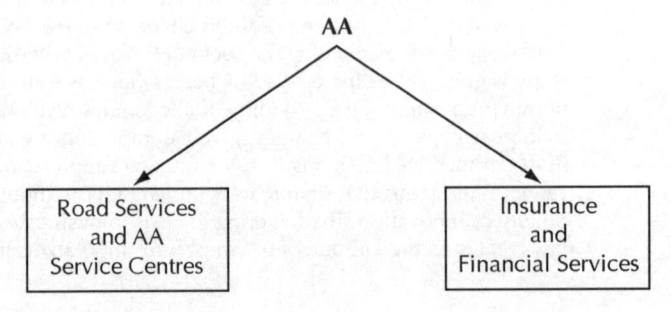

```
                    AA
                   /  \
                  /    \
        Road Services   Insurance
        and AA          and
        Service Centres Financial Services
```

Source: Centrica

Goldfish

Goldfish, initially a credit card developed through Centrica, has been generally aimed as a service to the general consumer. However, the British Gas image also helped to reach a wider audience. Initially this link was with HFC. The financial services market is a difficult market at the best of times, and the company has to deal with many competitors in the marketplace. However, as a newcomer to the market it has some advantages, as shown in Figure 15.

Figure 15. – Goldfish Brand Values

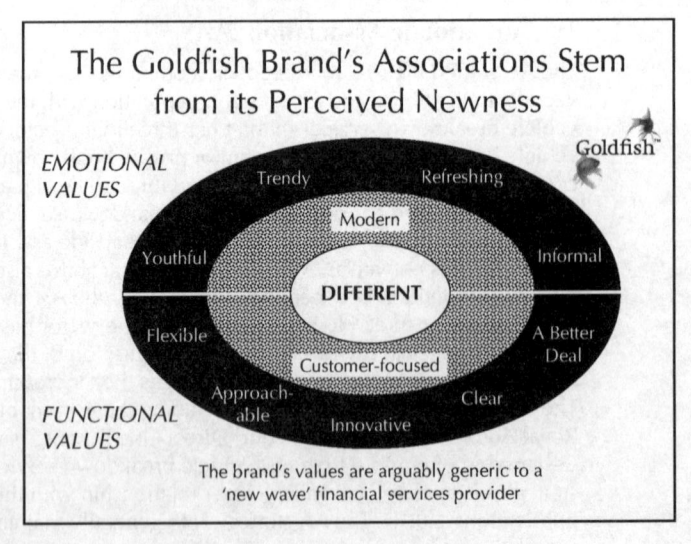

The Goldfish Brand's Associations Stem from its Perceived Newness

EMOTIONAL VALUES: Trendy, Refreshing, Modern, Youthful, Informal

FUNCTIONAL VALUES: Flexible, A Better Deal, Approachable, Customer-focused, Innovative, Clear

Centre: DIFFERENT

The brand's values are arguably generic to a 'new wave' financial services provider

Source: Centrica

> **Page 17 of Centrica**

The Goldfish card is generally regarded as fun and appeals to a younger audience. In the long run, the company has to decide whether it becomes a multi-line financial services business. **Centrica recently announced that it has sold the brand for around £112 million. This releases cash for the company (see Appendix 4).**

International Companies

The continuing deregulation of the US and European markets has offered opportunities to a range of companies, such as Vivendi from France and Enron in the USA. However, Enron has been a disaster with its bad corporate governance and has left many shareholders and employees with huge losses. Centrica, however, has managed to get a foothold in many diverse international markets such as Canada, USA, Belgium and Spain. These companies are:

- **Direct Energy and Energy America**

    Direct Energy is based in Canada and supplies electricity to Canadian consumers. The company has a growing customer base and presence in the Canadian utility market. Likewise, Energy America has a growing presence in the USA. Details are given in Appendix 2.

- **Luminus**

    Luminus was formed to take advantage of the growing deregulation within the European markets. However, different countries are likely to be deregulated at different times. This makes planning even more important (see Appendix 3). Belgium, Holland and Spain are key markets that Centrica have entered. Details are provided in Appendix 1.

Corporate Social Responsibility (CSR)

By being in a market that offers services to the home, Centrica has opportunities to demonstrate the level of responsibility not only to key shareholders, but also to the weaker stakeholders such as the general consumer. The company places a great emphasis on helping within the community, on issues such as environmental protection, sustainability, charitable donations and employee welfare. This is done through the various companies that operate under the Centrica umbrella (see Appendices 1 and 4). The company's emphasis on CSR has earned it a place on the FTSE4Good index.

Branding Relationships

With a range of different products and services that the company can offer to the consumer, it is important that Centrica considers the type of relationships it wants to build with consumers. Part of understanding consumer needs is building an elaborate and sensitive customer database. Currently, the company is spending £450 million on customer relationship projects for British Gas and the AA. As energy companies begin to develop competitive positions within a deregulated global environment, they need to build brands and trust with long-term trusting relationships. Often branding is more than price related. It is about trust and confidence. Centrica is a relatively new brand name, whereas its associated

Page 18 of Centrica

companies have well established brand names such as the AA and British Gas. One.Tel is also a new brand, though it is becoming fairly well established in its own right. Trust breeds loyalty, and this is extremely important as it is six times cheaper to retain customers than to acquire them. Realising this, Centrica has embarked on its expensive CRM programme that is being closely scrutinised by the City. The theory is that creating a centralised Customer Hub means that there is a single view obtainable of customers and their relationships with the various providers such as the AA, British Gas, and One.Tel. Figure 16 poses a question as to the possibilities that may evolve from developing a CRM hub.

Figure 16 – Developing a Decentralised Customer Hub

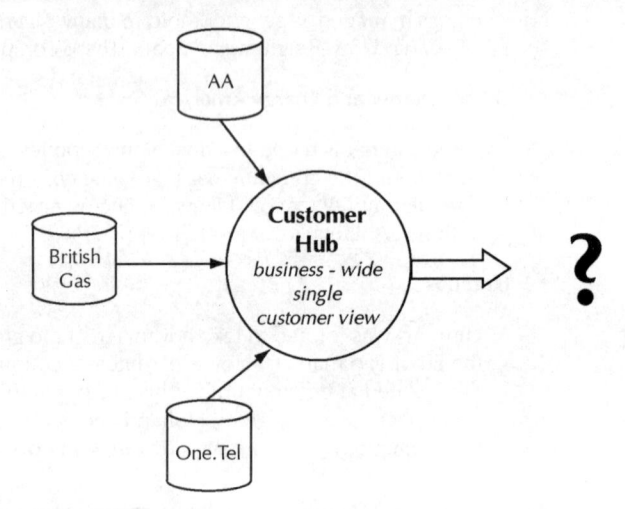

Source: Adapted from Centrica

This type of strategy also requires customer permission and 'buy-in', so that the company can offer different services to each customer. In the long run this also poses the question of how important the Centrica brand is, as opposed to individual brands such as the AA, British Gas, and One.Tel. As Appendices 2 and 3 show, there are many competitors both in the European and the American markets. As deregulation grows globally, many companies are positioning themselves to take advantage of new markets. At the EU Summit, in Barcelona, an agreement was reached on the key principles for a competitive market:

a. Separation of transmission and distribution from production and supply.

b. Non-discriminatory network access with transparent and published tariffs.

c. A regulatory function in each member state.

Non-household gas and electricity markets are to open in 2004, equating to 60-70% of the market by volume. The entire market is expected to be open by 2006/7, but with many markets are now ahead of this deadline (details in Appendix 2).

Page 19 of Centrica

Centrica is not as big as some of its competitors, and as a global player it may need to operate under a single brand identity which is as easily recognisable as Coca-Cola or Sony (see Appendix 4).

At the same time, even with the most elaborate systems, the length of customer-business relationship is difficult to measure in the present economic environment, characterised as it is by unpredictability and rapid change. Many companies are using relationship data as their main tool for prediction, utilising the analysis of historical data about the past behaviour of their customers, identifying specific segments, and extrapolating the behaviour of these segments into the future. This method can be used successfully only in relatively stable market environments because it assumes that:

- customers will repeat their past behaviour in the future.

- market conditions will not change significantly.

However this is difficult in a dynamic, fast-changing market environment. With a range of competitors in the market, it is possible that customers' perceptions will change fast, and also as better offers appear in the marketplace they may become less wedded to one supplier and become more promiscuous. Under these circumstances, developing a valued brand is even more important. If trusted, a customer is likely to become loyal, and most methods start from developing a sense of Customer Lifetime Value (as shown in Figure 17).

Figure 17 – Customer Lifetime Value

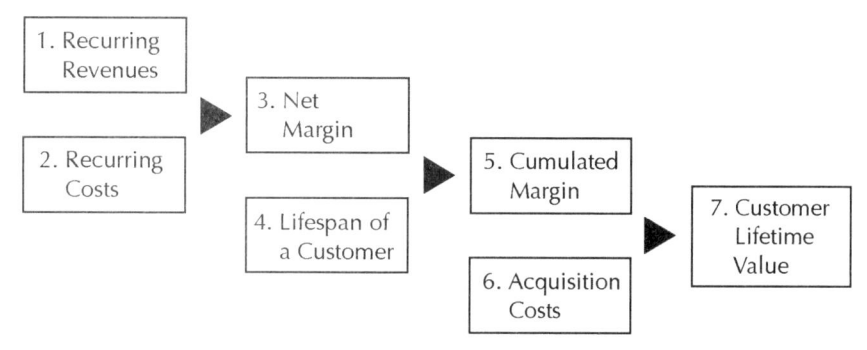

1. Recurring Revenues
2. Recurring Costs
3. Net Margin
4. Lifespan of a Customer
5. Cumulated Margin
6. Acquisition Costs
7. Customer Lifetime Value

Source: Bacuvier et al., 2001

Part C: Practice cases

Page 20 of Centrica

Summary

Given the rapid expansion of Centrica and the various brands under its umbrella, it is now important that the company addresses its *'raison d'etre'*. The expansion into the global market is slowly beginning to pay dividends, and the European market is poised for expansion. As the company begins to consolidate its position in the UK market and begins to understand the links between the various businesses, it is faced with further expansion in the global arena. The question remains as to how the company consolidates its UK market effectively, and at the same time devotes enough energy into expanding its presence in international markets. At the same time the company needs to reassure its shareholders that the company can manage the complex portfolio and post good profits. The company has an effective marketing structure (see Appendix 1) that needs to be utilised in other markets.

Page 21 of Centrica

Appendix 1

Our History

2003

23 December 2003

Centrica acquires additional offshore windfarm sites from AMEC Investments Ltd

11 December 2003

Centrica announces appointment of a new Chairman - Roger Carr

9 December 2003

Centrica named Utility Company of the Year in the Utility Industry Achievement Awards.

30 September 2003

Sale of Goldfish credit card and personal loan businesses to Lloyds TSB

12 September 2003

Centrica agres a joint venture with DONG, the Danish energy group, and Statkraft, the Norwegian power company, to acquire Barrow Offshore Wind Limited (BOW), which has the rights to develop a 90MW offshore electricity windfarm in the East Irish Sea.

15 August 2003

Centrica secures contract to develop gas reception facility adjacent to its Easington terminal, which will receive gas imported primarily from the Norwegian sector.

1 August 2003

Sales of Goldfish credit card and personal loan business agreed.

24 July 2003

Centrica entered into an agreement to acquire the 240MW Barry power station in South Wales from AES Barry Limited and AES Barry Operations Limited, wholly owned subsidiaries of AES Corporation.

14 May 2003

The group's portfolio of power stations increased to five with the acquisition of the Roosecote gas-fired station in Barrow-in-Furness, Cumbria. The plant adjoins the Barrow gas terminals.

Page 22 of Centrica

7 February 2003

Centrica signs electricity purchase contracts with British Energy.

2002

10 December 2002

Centrica announces plans to acquire 988,000 customers in Alberta, Canada, from ATCO Group.

14 November 2002

Centrica acquires Rough storage facility.

4 November 2002

Sale of Centrica's LPG business.

5 August 2002

Commercial customer base grows through the acquisition of Electricity Direct.

1 August 2002

Acquisition of over 200,000 New Power natural gas customers in Ohio and Pennsylvania completed.

28 June 2002

Glanford Brigg power station adds 240 MW to Centrica's generating capacity.

7 May 2002

Centrica completes acquisition of the home and business services operation of Canada's Enbridge Inc.

17 April 2002

Centrica agrees acquisition of more than 800,000 customers in Texas.

21 February 2002

Centrica placed 200.7million new ordinary shares at 215 pence per share, raising approximately £426 million, net of expenses.

9 January 2002

Centrica acquires the broadband business of iomart Group plc.

Page 23 of Centrica

2001

5 December 2001

British Gas acquired the energy customer business and certain assets of Enron Direct Ltd.

30 November 2001

Centrica announced an agreement to acquire Trolhurst Ltd, a provider of gas appliance servicing and central heating in Britain.

19 October 2001

Centrica extended its portfolio of generation plant with the acquisition of the operating leases of gas-fired power stations at King's Lynn and Peterborough from TXU Europe.

1 September 2001

Centrica acquired the garage business of Halfords. The garages are being converted into AA Services Centres.

3 July 2001

Centrica became the largest provider of indirect telecoms services in the UK with around one million active customers, following the acquisition of One.Tel plc.

29 June 2001

Centrica plc announced its first step into the liberalising energy markets of Continental Europe with the purchase of a 50 per cent share in Luminus N.V., a newly created energy supply business in Belgium.

28 June 2001

British Gas extended its electrical servicing business into 80,000 more households across Britain with the acquisition of National Homecare. British Gas Services now provides cover for over four million heating and kitchen appliances.

29 May 2001

Centrica entered the power generation business with the acquisition of a 60 per cent share in Humber Power Ltd – operator of a gas-fired power plant at Stallingborough, North Lincolnshire.

19 March 2001

The AA entered into a strategic alliance with The First Resort Ltd, one of the UK's leading online travel agents.

Page 24 of Centrica

2000

13 December 2000

Centrica and Lloyds TSB agreed to form a joint venture between Goldfish, Centrica's financial services brand, and evolvebank.com, Lloyds TSB's standalone Internet banking operation, to offer a broad range of integrated financial services products.

12 December 2000

Centrica announced that it would assume full ownership and management control of Energy America after acquiring the 72.5 per cent stake of former partner Sempra Energy.

7 December 2000

Completion of the acquisition of Avalanche Energy Ltd, a privately - held Canadian gas and oil production company. The assets were acquired to support Centrica's growing customer base in Canada.

26 October 2000

The AA signed up its 10 millionth member at the Birmingham Motor Show.

16 October 2000

Centrica acquired the UK LPG cylinder business of Shell Gas, strengthening British Gas' position in the domestic LPG market.

28 September 2000

British Gas Communications opens for business, and customers make their first telephone calls using the system.

19 September 2000

Mark Clare was appointed to the newly created position of Deputy Chief Executive, responsible for the Centrica financial services business and the company's e-commerce activities. Phil Bentley succeeded him as Finance Director. Phil joined Centrica from Guinness-UDV, the alcoholic beverages division of Diageo plc, where he was Finance Director.

6 July 2000

Centrica announced its acquisition of the Canadian energy supply business, Direct Energy Marketing Ltd, including its 27.5% interest in Energy America, a joint venture with Sempra Energy, which trades in the United States.

19 June 2000

'For the second year running, the AA is the UK's top-ranked roadside assistance provider, according to a comprehensive survey of almost 25,000 drivers by the international market research company JD Power.

Page 25 of Centrica

25 April 2000

Centrica made a major step towards launching a telecommunications service by announcing it had entered into a strategic alliance with Vodafone UK Ltd, to provide mobile telephone services across Great Britain, and reached agreement with Torch Telecom and Cable & Wireless Communications for the provision of residential telecommunications services.

10 February 2000

Centrica welcomed confirmation that industry regulator Ofgem was to remove price controls for British Gas direct-debit customers from 1 April 2000 and intended to extend this for all customers from 1 April 2001.

1999

7 October 1999

Agreement was reached with Veba Oil and Gas UK and Total Oil Marine to purchase further offshore gas assets in the Southern North Sea.

28 September 1999

Centrica was appointed by OAO Gazprom as its agent for operating its Interconnector capacity. In addition, OAO Gazprom, Centrica plc and Wingas GmbH announced they had reached a tripartite agreement entitling each party to use this capacity.

16 September 1999

Centrica's proposed acquisition of the AA received overwhelming support from members. Of the millions of proxy votes counted, approximately 96 per cent backed the purchase.

19 July 1999

Centrica announced the closure of its 243 British Gas Energy Centres in the face of difficult High Street trading conditions.

15 July 1999

Centrica's work in helping unemployed carers and disabled people enter the workplace was recognised with a major national award presented by the Prime Minister, Tony Blair. He presented Chief Executive Sir Roy Gardner with a Business in the Community Award for Excellence for the group's North West New Deal Project.

5 July 1999

The board of Centrica and the committee of the Automobile Association (AA) announced that they had reached agreement for Centrica to acquire the AA for £1.1 billion, subject to the approval of members.

Page 26 of Centrica

24 May 1999

Competition for domestic and business electricity customers completed its roll-out across Great Britain, with nearly 1.5 million customers having chosen British Gas as their electricity supplier.

8 February 1999

Centrica announced agreements to acquire offshore gas assets from Dana Petroleum and British Borneo.

28 January 1999

A multi-million pound partnership between British Gas and Help the Aged was launched with the aim of combating fuel poverty and cutting the number of older people dying needlessly each winter in Great Britain.

1998

12 October 1998

Centrica made its first upstream acquisition, buying PowerGen's upstream gas and oil company, PowerGen North Sea Limited (PGNS), for £248 million. The acquisition involved interests in eight producing fields and several undeveloped gas fields in the Southern North Sea and the East Irish Sea, close to Centrica's existing Morecambe fields operation.

1 October 1998

Centrica was one of the first companies to flow gas through the UK-Continent Interconnector on the day it opened.

14 September 1998

The first domestic customers received their electricity supply from British Gas. More than 400,000 customers had signed up for electricity by time the market opened in the Canterbury, Chester, Hull and Norwich areas.

16 July 1998

Centrica was chosen to lead an innovative project under the Government's New Deal for Disabled People. The company was one of 10 groups named to receive financial support for its scheme providing work, new job skills and training for disabled people who have been long-term unemployed. The project was the only one selected which provided opportunities for carers as well as those who are sick or disabled.

22 June 1998

Centrica, through its subsidiary Hydrocarbon Resources Ltd, reached agreement with Burlington Resources (Irish Sea) Ltd to transport and process natural gas from its Millom and Dalton fields in the East Irish Sea.

Page 27 of Centrica

23 May 1998

Centrica ceased to be a monopoly supplier as gas competition completed its roll-out across Great Britain. The last tranche of the roll-out opened up competition to 3.1 million homes in Greater London and Surrey.

12 February 1998

An innovative gas contract which links the price of gas to market levels was agreed between Centrica and Enron Europe. Under the 10-year contract, Enron agreed to supply Centrica with more than five billion cubic metres of gas at prices linked to the screen-based International Petroleum Exchange (IPE) Natural Gas Futures Contract.

1997

4 December 1997

Substantial price reductions were announced on Centrica's "Take or Pay" contracts with Conoco and the bulk of its high-priced gas purchase commitments with Elf and Total. As a result of these agreements, together with deals done with other suppliers, Chief Executive Sir Roy Gardner said that Centrica's inherited gas contract exposures had been reduced to a manageable level.

1 December 1997

Centrica launched its first financial product to complement the Goldfish credit card. A home and contents insurance package offering average savings worth £75 was launched under the British Gas and Goldfish brands.

9 October 1997

Centrica announced further Interconnector gas export sales to the Netherlands through the UK-Continent Interconnector pipeline. Under the agreements, Centrica agreed to sell a total of around 0.7 billion cubic metres per annum to EnTrade (a trading joint venture between PNEM and MEGA) and DELTA over a period of eight years.

Page 28 of Centrica

3 October 1997

Centrica launched it first major nationwide advertising campaign to promote the British Gas brand, publicise major price cuts, and announce its entry into the domestic electricity market. The objective was to reinforce the British Gas brand and promote the company's commitment to becoming Great Britain's leading energy supplier.

1 October 1997

Centrica reached agreement with Mobil North Sea Ltd, ARCO British Ltd and Eastern Natural Gas (Offshore) Ltd to terminate the Welland gas sale and purchase contracts. This further reduced Centrica's gas purchase contract commitments.

1 October 1997

Education and Employment Minister, Andrew Smith MP, announced that Centrica would be launching a new employment and training programme as part of the UK Government's New Deal initiative. The programme focused particularly on disadvantaged groups with special needs, such as unemployed disabled people and long-term carers returning to work.

24 July 1997

Centrica reached agreement with Amerada Hess, Enterprise Oil and OMV to terminate gas sale and purchase contracts for the Beryl field. The agreements marked another major step towards Centrica reducing its gas purchase contract commitments.

15 July 1997

Centrica entered its first agreement to supply gas through the UK-Continent Interconnector pipeline direct to a major energy user, rather than a gas trading/transmission company. The agreement to supply the Elsta cogeneration project in the Netherlands was for around 1 billion cubic metres per annum over a period of eight years.

1 July 1997

Sir Michael Perry appointed non-executive Chairman of Centrica plc.

14 May 1997

Centrica and Thyssengas signed a contract to supply gas through the UK-Continent Interconnector pipeline. Under the agreement, Centrica agreed to sell to Thyssengas up to 3 billion cubic metres of gas over a period of seven years. Deliveries started in October 1998 when the Interconnector opened.

19 ♦ A final practice case: Centrica

Page 29 of Centrica

21 February 1997

Centrica took operational control of Accord Energy, previously a joint venture between British Gas and NGC Corporation of Houston, USA. Accord Energy is a major player in the short-term gas trading and wholesaling market in Great Britain.

17 February 1997

Centrica is created following the demerger of British Gas plc. The group comprise the gas supply, services and retail businesses of British Gas, together with the gas production business of the North and South Morecambe gas fields. It also retained ownership of the Goldfish brand.

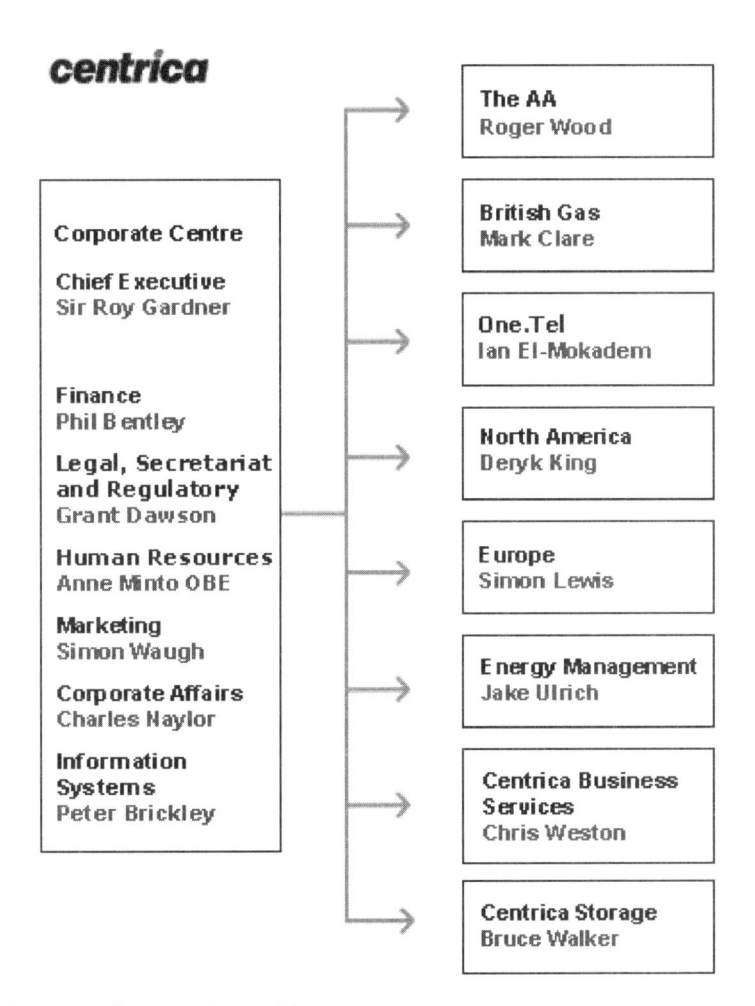

centrica

Corporate Centre

Chief Executive
Sir Roy Gardner

Finance
Phil Bentley

Legal, Secretariat and Regulatory
Grant Dawson

Human Resources
Anne Minto OBE

Marketing
Simon Waugh

Corporate Affairs
Charles Naylor

Information Systems
Peter Brickley

→ The AA — Roger Wood
→ British Gas — Mark Clare
→ One.Tel — Ian El-Mokadem
→ North America — Deryk King
→ Europe — Simon Lewis
→ Energy Management — Jake Ulrich
→ Centrica Business Services — Chris Weston
→ Centrica Storage — Bruce Walker

Source: http://www.centrica.co.uk/index.asp?section=Our_company&area=About_us&content=Our_businesses

Page 30 of Centrica

Operating and financial review

British Gas serves millions of customers every day.

British Gas residential
Improved gas margins and growth in electricity and services

2002 has seen progression in the performance of British Gas residential, driven by improved gas margins, continuing growth in electricity and home services and reduced losses in communications. Aggregate turnover was up 2.3% in 2002, at £6 billion with operating profit at £244 million (2001: loss of £46 million), despite warmer weather. Our energy and home services operations have been integrated to reflect our vision of enhancing customer loyalty through greater understanding and to realise higher revenue and cost synergies. Our investment in the British Gas brand continues to support our leading position in the residential energy and services sectors and allows us to continue to build further multi-product customer relationships, with the aim of becoming Britain's leading home services provider. Our operations will be further supported by our investment in customer relationship management (CRM) infrastructure, enabling improved service levels, a lower cost to serve and lower costs to acquire new product relationships.

At British Gas we're making investments to enhance the quality of service we provide to millions of customers every day. We are now significantly increasing the number of engineers and developing a range of skills and expertise to sustain our competitive edge in the market. Continued investment in development of our employees so that they are able to provide ever improving service standards will lead to durable and profitable customer relationships.

British Gas strongly believes that selling practices across the energy industry must continue to be improved. It has taken a leading position driving the new code of sales practice, removing commission-only sales agents and implementing an independent compliance regime.

At 40%, British Gas's share of the aggregate residential energy customer base in Britain remained steady against the same time last year. Net losses in gas customers were in line with 2001 but reflect a longer term trend of stabilising market share with losses occurring primarily during the few months following retail price increases. Second half losses were 186,000 compared with 426,000 in the first half. Electricity sales growth was reduced by the withdrawal of commission-only sales agents. Churn rates declined in the second half of the year, with the market showing signs of lower switching rates overall. We believe that our premium British Gas brand, improving customer service and breadth of branded home service offerings will continue to afford us competitive advantages in our sectors.

Increases in residential energy gross profits were partially offset by the £26 million expensed investment in CRM infrastructure (2001: £9 million). We expect this will begin to improve our operating profit by reducing the costs to acquire and serve our customers from 2004. We also capitalised £154 million of CRM expenditure during the year (2001: £60 million). General and administrative expenses were higher as a result of higher manpower costs (largely to support a growing home services engineering workforce), higher debtor provisions (£20 million) and increased spending (£25 million) to meet our obligations under the government's Energy Efficiency Commitment.

Most of this spend was incorporated in our 'here to HELP' programme. This programme, created by British Gas, is the country's biggest independent initiative to tackle household poverty. In alliance with local housing providers and seven leading charities, this programme will provide help to 500,000 households over the next three years. This will take the form of energy efficiency measures, benefit checks and a range of services provided by our charity partners.

British Gas's home management website, www.house.co.uk, gives customers online access to British Gas 24 hours a day, every day of the week. Research shows that the site has averaged around 28% of all utility related web traffic in

Key residential energy performance indicators

	2002	2001	Δ %
Customer numbers (period end) (000)			
Residential gas	12,839	13,451	(4.5)
Residential electricity	5,795	5,374	8
Estimated market share (%)			
Residential gas	64	67	(3ppts)
Residential electricity*	22	21	1ppt
Average consumption			
Residential gas (therms)	607	661	(8)
Residential electricity (kWh)	4,132	4,098	0.8
Weighted average sales price			
Residential gas (p/therm)	47.12	43.80	8
Residential electricity (p/kWh)	6.06	5.99	1.2
Weighted average unit costs			
Residential gas (WACOG, p/therm)	21.96	21.90	0.3
Residential electricity (WACOE, p/kWh)	2.47	2.55	(3.1)
Transportation and metering charges (£m)			
Residential gas	1,256	1,508	(17)
Residential electricity	444	342	30
Total	1,700	1,850	(8)
Sales and marketing expenses (% of turnover)	4.2	4.3	(0.1ppts)
Average products per customer ** (period end)	1.53	1.50	2
Turnover (£m)			
Residential gas	3,805	4,029	(6)
Residential electricity	1,380	1,121	23
Total	5,185	5,150	0.7
Gross profit margin (%)			
Residential gas	20	12	8ppts
Residential electricity	26	27	(1ppt)
Total	22	15	7ppts
Operating profit (£m)			
Residential energy	218	19	n/m
Operating margin (%)			
Residential energy	4.2	0.4	3.8ppts

*2001 restated to reflect Ofgem market resizing during 2002.
**British Gas residential brand.

Δ % has been used to express 'percentage change'.
n/m has been used to represent 'not meaningful'.

Source: Centrica plc Report, 2002
© Centrica 2003

Page 31 of Centrica

Operating and financial review continued

We continue to invest in the development of employees.

British Gas residential segmental turnover (£m)

	2002	2001
Residential gas	3,805	4,029
Residential electricity	1,380	1,121
Home services	810	722
British Gas Communications	52	37
Total	6,047	5,909

Britain, up from around only 6% on the old British Gas site.

Residential gas
Turnover decreased by 6% to £3.81 billion. Higher average selling prices were offset by a reduction in sales volumes, reflecting warmer UK weather (operating profit impact £42 million) and the net loss of around 600,000 customer accounts. We believe that our brand and the scale of service we provide support our average revenue per customer being above the average of the competition.

Gross margins recovered to 20% (2001: 12%). The recovery was driven by the increase in average selling prices and a reduction in transportation and metering costs of £252 million compared with 2001, due to lower volume and timing differences. A large portion of the lower costs arose in the early part of the year reflecting a reversal of the over-recovery by Transco in 2001 of National Transmission System (NTS) entry fees with a year-on-year impact of £98 million.

In 2002 we withdrew from the liquefied petroleum gas (LPG) business in line with our strategy of focusing on direct customer relationships as a large portion of the LPG business operated through third party retailers.

Residential electricity
Turnover increased by 23% to £1.38 billion. Our weighted average retail price was slightly higher, as the full year effect of a reduction in prices in 2001 was offset by a shift in our customer mix following growth in the prepayment segment, which operates on higher tariffs given related administrative costs. Average consumption was broadly flat year on year. We believe that our average retail pricing is approximately 8% below the average of the incumbent suppliers and we estimate our market share at year end was 22% (2001: 21%).

Gross profit grew by 21% due to higher volumes, while our gross margin fell one percentage point to 26% due to increased transportation and metering costs being only partially offset by lower commodity costs.

Home services
British Gas home services continued to report strong growth in the year. Turnover increased by 12% to £810 million. Higher central heating volumes, augmented by the impact of our Trolhurst acquisition in late 2001, were complemented by good contributions from our newer products, in particular home electrical care. We are the only major service supplier providing bundled service products under our own brand, using our own people. This integrated offering gives competitive advantage over outsourced products and services marketed by other suppliers and is a strong tool for the retention of energy customers.

A £64 million improvement in gross profit resulted from an increase in volume and average order value along with a higher gross margin due to product mix, increased productivity and the lower price of materials. This was partly offset by increased operating costs, mainly due to higher manpower and home services marketing expenses. The resulting growth of 69% in operating profit illustrated the continuing scalability of our home services business model as we increased both customer numbers and product penetration.

Our engineering staff numbers (including installation engineers) grew by 13%. Securing access to skilled engineering staff is a key challenge and during the first half of the year we announced our intention to recruit and train approximately 5,000 engineers over the next five years: this is already well under way. To this end British Gas has set up its own engineering academy which will co-ordinate all engineering recruitment, skills training and apprentice development across the company. It will also liaise with external bodies including government and the wider industry to promote training and to reduce skills shortages.

British Gas Communications
Turnover in 2002 was up 41% at £52 million (2001: £37 million), due primarily to a higher average number of customers over the 12 month period. Our gross margin increased to 28% (2001: 26%) as call traffic was transferred to the group's switches, managed by OneTel. Our switches allow us to take advantage of the lowest cost routing for each individual call.

The business continues to operate at a loss, mainly due to underlying infrastructure costs and the cost of customer acquisition in an environment of continuing high churn rates. Since the implementation of enhanced carrier pre-selection (CPS) processes in July, all new customer connections are fulfilled using this method. Initial results support our expectation that the average revenue per customer

Key British Gas Communications performance indicators

	2002	2001	Δ %
Customer numbers (fixed line) (period end) (000)	367	400	(8)
Average minutes use per month (fixed line)	340	347	(2)
ARPU (fixed line) (£)	10.52	10.87	(3.2)
Variable gross margin (%)	28	26	2ppts
Sales and marketing expenses (% of turnover)	7	22	(15ppts)
Turnover (£m)	52	37	41
Operating loss (£m)	(35)	(101)	65

Key home services performance indicators

	2002	2001	Δ %
Customer relationships (period end) (000)			
Central heating service contracts	3,482	3,314	5
Kitchen appliances care (no. of appliances)	871	562	55
Plumbing and drains care	905	743	22
Electrical care	367	143	157
Home security	28	28	–
Total relationships	5,653	4,790	18
Central heating installations	102	109	(6)
Turnover (£m)			
Central heating service contracts	398	371	7
Central heating installations	260	255	2
Other	152	96	58
Total	810	722	12
Engineering staff employed	6,036	5,356	13
Sales and marketing expenses (% of turnover)	6	5	1ppt
Gross margin (%)	46	42	4ppts
Total operating profit (£m)	61	36	69
Operating margin (%)	8	5	3ppts

Source: Centrica plc Report, 2002

Part C: Practice cases

Page 32 of Centrica

Centrica Business Services focuses on the needs of small and medium sized enterprises.

CEMG segmental turnover (£m)

	2002	2001
Industrial sales and wholesaling	784	921
Gas production	83	80
Accord energy trading	4,304	3,570
Total	5,171	4,571

(ARPU) will increase and the rate of churn for customers using CPS will reduce. We are continuing to lobby for a converged process for both CPS and wholesale line rental (WLR) in order to make it simpler for customers to switch suppliers but we remain of the view that considerable work needs to be done before a fit for purpose product can be launched.

Significant reductions have been made to operating costs as synergies with One.Tel have been realised. Cancellation and churn rates have improved in the second half through better customer targeting and quality of service. Customer care and billing were transferred onto One.Tel's system in June, reducing information systems spending by approximately £1 million per month.

Centrica Business Services
Profit up 48% with organic growth supported by acquisitions

Centrica Business Services established itself as the number one supplier of energy to the commercial sector in the UK by maintaining its position in the gas market and by achieving strong organic growth in the electricity sector, supplemented by the acquisition of Electricity Direct. The organic growth accounted for almost half of the 53% growth in the electricity customer base since the beginning of the year.

Enron Direct has been successfully integrated, increasing overall business profitability, giving enhanced sales capability across the market and improving service to larger multi-site customers.

Turnover has increased by 67% to £971 million as a result of organic growth as well as a full year's results from Enron Direct and five months' contribution from Electricity Direct. Overall gross margin increased by 3 percentage points to 17% following price rises in gas.

Centrica Business Services has increased its UK commercial energy market share to 27% (2001: 22%, measured by share of supply points), comprising 51% of the gas market and 20% of the electricity market. In gas we seek to defend our market position through focusing on customer service and a value proposition rather than acquiring market share. In electricity, due to the acquisition activity and better targeted organic growth, average consumption per customer has increased by 39%. We believe our pricing is approximately in line with other major branded suppliers.

Key Centrica Business Services performance indicators

	2002	2001	Δ %
Customer supply points (period end) (000)			
Gas	383	389	(1.5)
Electricity	516	337	53
Total	899	726	24
Average consumption			
Gas (therms)	3,276	3,878	(16)
Electricity (kWh)	22,398	16,115	39
Weighted average sales price			
Gas (p/therm)	36.72	34.04	8
Electricity (p/kWh)	4.79	5.49	(13)
Weighted average unit costs			
Gas (WACOG, p/therm)	20.71	20.46	1.2
Electricity (WACOE, p/kWh)	2.25	2.44	(8)
Transportation and metering charges (£m)			
Gas	126	130	(3)
Electricity	170	40	325
Total	296	170	74
Sales and marketing expenses (% of turnover)	2.9	2.1	0.8ppts
Turnover (£m)			
Gas	457	460	(0.6)
Electricity	514	121	324
Total	971	581	67
Gross margin (%)			
Gas	16	12	4ppts
Electricity	18	22	(4ppts)
Total	17	14	3ppts
Operating profit (£m)			
Commercial energy	65	44	48
Operating margin (%)			
Commercial energy	7	8	(1ppt)

CEMG
Upstream gas assets portfolio being enhanced

The Centrica energy management group (CEMG) consists of gas production operations, the newly acquired Rough gas storage facilities, electricity generation (managed for British Gas residential and Centrica Business Services), large volume industrial and wholesale gas sales, and our energy procurement, optimisation and scheduling operations. This unit is fundamental – through its provision of competitively priced energy supplies – to the success of the customer facing operations that are at the core of Centrica's consumer marketing business.

Gas production

Upstream gas profits were adversely affected by the reduction in wholesale prices compared with last year, reducing the average unit sales price (which is linked to market) by 5% in 2002. Production volumes, which represented 27% of our downstream demand, were 5% lower than last year due in part to warm weather in the first and last quarter. Unit production costs increased as a percentage of turnover given the higher volume taken from those fields which attract higher unit depreciation charges and the overall reduction in turnover to cover our fixed cost base.

During the year, a number of upstream gas transactions were concluded in line with our strategy of increasing gas equity ownership beyond the Morecambe fields. In the first, Centrica undertook a strategic swap with Agip in which Centrica acquired uncontracted gas and equity in the large Goldeneye development, and built its equity in the Armada complex in the Central North Sea, together with other small equity parcels and cash. In return, Agip acquired Centrica's equity in the Liverpool Bay development, where the gas is not contracted to British Gas.

Subsequently, an 18% stake in the Seymour development, adjacent to Armada, was acquired from BP. This well, which was drilled late in the year and contains significant quantities of gas and liquids, should be in production in the first quarter of 2003. At the end of the year, Centrica entered into a contract to acquire the remaining 60% equity and overall operatorship in the Rose gas development in the Southern North Sea. The development is expected to deliver its first gas in 2004. Finally, agreement was reached for the sale to Talisman of the R Block

Source: Centrica plc Report, 2002

Page 33 of Centrica

Operating and financial review continued

oil production interests acquired from Agip as part of the swap deal.

In total an estimated 135 billion cubic feet (bcf) (1.3 billion therms) of gas was acquired.

We have also focused on making best use of our asset infrastructure in the East Irish Sea. In November, the Centrica operated Bains field came on stream and now links into our South Morecambe infrastructure. During the year, an innovative drilling project in our South Morecambe field added a small amount of additional reserves to the portfolio. This technique is now being evaluated for future use at our other East Irish Sea assets and offers us the potential of adding reserves cost effectively.

Storage
In November Centrica acquired the Rough gas storage facilities in the North Sea. During the period of Centrica's ownership, turnover was £9 million with an operating profit of £1 million. The Secretary of State for Trade and Industry has to decide whether to clear the acquisition, refer it to the Competition Commission for further investigation or accept undertakings in lieu of a reference.

Industrial sales and wholesaling
Sales volumes were down by 8% against 2001 due to reduced takes under long term interruptible contracts with power stations, and the termination of one European contract. However, better gross margins, a profit of £9 million recognised in the first half of 2002 in connection with the early termination of a gas supply contract, and one-off losses on the termination of other contracts in 2001 contributed to increased profits relative to last year.

Key CEMG performance indicators

	2002	2001	Δ %
Gas production and storage			
Production volumes (m therms)			
Morecambe	3,659	3,892	(6)
Other	397	395	1
Total	4,056	4,287	(5)
Average sales price (p/therm)	21.5	22.5	(5)
Turnover * (£m)	932	1,033	(10)
Turnover (external) (£m)	83	80	3.8
Operating costs (% of turnover)			
Royalties	7	7	–
Petroleum revenue tax	8	8	–
Volume related production costs	25	23	2ppts
Other production costs	12	10	2ppts
Total	52	47	5ppts
Rough operating profit (£m)	1	n/a	n/a
Operating profit (£m)	448	552	(19)
Industrial and wholesale			
Sales volumes (m therms)	5,694	6,215	(8)
Average sales price (p/therm)	19.8	19.5	2
Turnover (£m)	784	921	(15)
Operating profit (£m)	72	5	n/m
Accord			
Traded volumes (physical)			
Gas (m therms)	20,399	18,512	10
Electricity (GWh)	95,329	29,446	224
Turnover (£m)	4,304	3,570	21
Operating profit (£m)	0	16	(100)
CEMG operating profit (£m)	520	573	(9)

*91% was to group companies in 2002.

Electricity generation
We currently have interests in four power stations with peak capacity of 1.7 GW as well as a 0.9 GW tolling agreement with Intergen for the entire output capacity of its Spalding plant, where operations are expected to commence by the end of 2004. The volume of production at our generation plants was 7,662 GWh, an increase of 160% on last year due mainly to the addition of Glanford Brigg and the full period use of the King's Lynn and Peterborough plants. Our stations provided 22% of our annual downstream demand, and 20% of peak requirements. The main value of our plants remains in their flexible mid-merit and peak generation capacity in a less liquid market for peak supplies. However, they also provide strategic upside potential in the event of higher wholesale prices, with the option to increase generation volumes as it becomes more profitable.

Accord Energy
Our Accord trading operations continued to support our strategic procurement requirements and take additional trading positions within strictly controlled limits based on our wholesale market outlook.

Accord broke even on the year, a drop of £16 million on 2001. After a positive first half, we experienced gas trading losses during the unplanned shutdown of the continental European interconnector. Given Centrica's trading positions in Europe, this led to Accord having to procure gas at short notice to meet its obligations, which would have been fulfilled by exports from the UK. Accord's performance also suffered in the power markets through the highly publicised problems of TXU and British Energy, which contributed to high volatility. Accord also provided for a one-off loss of £6 million when TXU went into administration late in 2002. Physical volumes traded during 2002 were equal to 1.4 times the gas and 2.2 times the electricity volumes supplied to our downstream customers.

The AA
Core business growth in roadside and personal finance

2002 saw further progress in the development of the underlying profitability of the AA's core roadside and personal finance operations. Key to the AA's future growth is the ongoing investment in brand repositioning which was launched in May. The 'JustAAsk' message focuses consumer attention on the product range offered by the AA and has increased product awareness beyond roadside assistance from 33% to 43%. Turnover grew 10% to £760 million. Operating profit increased by 1.4% to £73 million with increases in roadside services and personal finance offset by start-up losses for the AA Service Centres. This repositioning of the AA brand will support the AA's continued drive towards end-to-end motoring services to members and cross-sales of the whole product range.

Source: Centrica plc Report, 2002

Part C: Practice cases

Page 34 of Centrica

The 'JustAAsk' campaign launched in May has helped broaden awareness of the AA product range.

Our network of Service Centres has now been fully rebranded.

In addition, the AA is investing in a major CRM infrastructure programme over three years. In 2002, £30 million of expenditure was incurred (of which £26 million was capitalised). This investment is central to developing the AA's cross-selling potential and at the same time achieving cost efficiencies across the business.

The AA's website continues to attract new customers to buy AA products and services online. Judged to be the UK's most popular automotive related site in 2002, the website also brought the AA the award for e-business strategy of the year at the National Business Awards. TheAA.com supplied 16 million route maps in 2002 and was accessed by 21 million visitors.

The AA continues to act as the independent voice of the motorist. Highlights included February's launch of EuroRAP, a system to give a safety star rating to Europe's roads, and the Chancellor's budget commitment not to make any further fuel tax increases.

AA roadside services
Turnover increased by 5% to £476 million, driven primarily by membership growth, and whilst our overall share of the personal and business market marginally increased to 31%, the average price per customer fell by 0.6% due to a change in product mix.

Operating profits increased by 23% to £54 million, as higher turnover was accompanied by tight management controls and initiatives to contain the roadside breakdown costs and increase patrol utilisation.

Investment in roadside assistance continues with the provision of new vehicles, GPS route guidance and improved management systems. The growth in roadside assistance membership has continued and with increased productivity of the 3,600 patrols, customer satisfaction has improved from 66% to 68%. The AA won the JD Power & Associates UK Roadside Assistance Study award for customer satisfaction and was named the UK's best motoring organisation in a Which? magazine survey.

Also, the first tranche of specialised all weather, portable computer systems with fault diagnostic capability were deployed to AA patrols to help maintain their ability to fix faults at the roadside. All patrols will be similarly equipped during 2003.

In the year the AA continued to train patrols and Service Centre technicians at its dedicated training college. Some 125 new patrol recruits were trained during 2002.

AA personal finance
Turnover in personal finance grew by 11% to £172 million. Supported by the 'JustAAsk' campaign, over 70,000 car and personal loans were taken out during the year which, after renewals, left a year end portfolio of approximately 117,000 fixed term personal loans (2001: 77,000) provided through the AA joint venture. At the year end, the fixed term loan book had increased by 54% to stand at a record £661 million (2001: £428 million) with provision levels decreasing by 1% to below 3%. Continued product improvements coupled with specific advertising, emphasised the benefits of getting 'car loans from car people'.

Motor and home insurance commissions grew by 9% on higher policy volume (up to £93 million), with customer renewal rates rising to 78% (2001: 74%). The average annual premium rose by 2% to £261, reflecting general pricing conditions in the industry.

Operating profits increased by 17% to £47 million. Turnover growth of 11% was augmented by close control of support costs with increased efficiency improving the ratio of employees to insurance policy levels.

A tailored motor insurance policy specifically for AA personal members was launched in 2002 and sales of 6,000 have been achieved in its first year. Breakdown history is one of the major factors that form part of the premiums assessment. The number of policyholders of the AA's new insurance product for parts and labour repairs grew from 3,000 in December 2001, following its launch in May to 130,000 by December 2002.

Other AA services
Turnover is up 37% at £112 million, including a full year of turnover from the AA's network of 129 garages acquired from Halfords in September 2001. In 2002 the business rebranded and relaunched the garages as

Key AA performance indicators

	2002	2001	Δ %
Roadside services			
Customer numbers (period end) (000)	12,975	12,194	6
Customer renewal rate (%)	85	85	–
Average transaction value (£)	34	35	(1)
Roadside patrols employed	3,651	3,592	2
Personal finance			
Insurance customers (000)			
Motor	959	906	6
Home	664	618	7
Overall renewal rate (%)	78	74	4ppts
Average annual premium (£)	261	257	2
Motor and home insurance commissions (£m)	93	86	9
Loans (fixed term) book size (£m)	661	428	54
Loans (fixed term) operating profit (£m)	20	17	18
Number of fixed term personal loans (000)	117	77	52
AA Service Centres			
Site numbers	129	129	–
Average turnover per site (£000)	320	n/a	–
Turnover (£m)			
AA roadside services	476	452	5
AA personal finance	172	155	11
Other AA services	112	82	37
Total	760	689	10
Sales and marketing expenses (% of turnover)	10	9	1ppt
Operating profit (£m)			
AA roadside services	54	44	23
AA personal finance	47	40	17
Other AA services	(28)	(12)	(133)
Total	73	72	1
Operating margin (%)	10	10	–

Source: Centrica plc Report, 2002

19 ♦ A final practice case: Centrica

Page 35 of Centrica

Operating and financial review continued

One.Tel now offers a complete telecoms service covering landline, mobile and internet.

AA Service Centres to provide a retail presence for AA members and customers. As a further step towards providing a complete motoring service it also purchased Tyreserve and expanded its own mobile tyre replacement service, which now gives private and fleet customers access to a network of more than 3,000 AA approved fixed and mobile tyre centres.

Other AA services incurred operating losses of £28 million. £4.5 million of this came from the closure of AA workshops, with the Service Centres producing an operating loss of £15 million. £7 million of investment in infrastructure and rebranding of the Service Centres was expensed. We are carrying out various initiatives such as a cost reduction programme, advertising campaigns and offers to the current membership base to increase utilisation and rapidly reduce the ongoing loss.

The AA in the Republic of Ireland contributed a profit of nearly £2 million, an increase of over 80% on 2001, due to growth in both insurance and roadside assistance membership, thereby remaining the leading roadside assistance and personal insurance provider in the country.

Publishing, car data check, the driving school and roadside signs made positive contributions which were offset by start-up investments in Tyreserve and costs in AABuyacar and information services.

AA exceptional item
The group has decided to reduce the operations of Golf England Limited, a subsidiary undertaking, and has recognised a £14 million provision in respect of losses on the disposal of fixed assets.

One.Tel
Improving sector outlook

Our focus for this year has been on increasing the value of the existing One.Tel customer base through enhanced product offerings and operational efficiencies. In the medium term, we believe that this positioning provides us with a sound platform to develop in the UK, assuming recent regulatory proposals are implemented quickly and fully.

In the second half of the year turnover grew by 20% over the second half of 2001 to £78 million, as a result of further growth in the customer base. Our variable gross margin increased by 5% to 52% as we took advantage of opportunities to negotiate improved transmission charges with our carriers. Our switched reseller business model relies on the use of the networks of a variety of infrastructure owners (13 as at 31 December 2002), mitigating the risks associated with network failure or carrier financial distress. Operating profit for the year was £2.1 million reflecting the investment in new products, particularly mobile and a £2 million marketing campaign undertaken in the fourth quarter to raise awareness of One.Tel's transition from a discounted international calls provider to a full communications provider offering landline, mobile and narrow and broadband internet services. To this end, during the second half of the year we launched our first call inclusive package.

Customer acquisition costs increased to £14 million in the second half (full year: £22 million) supporting full year growth in the customer base of 23% from 2001. ARPU increased by 1% against the second half of 2001. With the implementation of the revised industry process for carrier pre-selection (CPS) in July, the level of our new landline sales using this connection method increased to 37% in December.

Mobile sales have been very encouraging with more than 35,000 contracts sold since the launch in July, supported by attractive pricing and expanded retail distribution. The migration of our broadband customers onto the One.Tel customer care and billing system is due for completion in the first quarter of 2003 enabling us to offer a complete customer experience with all our telecoms services charged on a single bill.

Goldfish Bank
Credit card growth from renewed brand building

Goldfish Bank has continued to make progress. Following a review of product strategy by the Goldfish management team, we are focusing increasingly on brand performance through a smaller range of more capital efficient products.

The credit card business was migrated to Goldfish's new infrastructure in November. This was a significant and complex process involving more than one million cards in issue and their associated loyalty points records. The new platform is operating well and customer service, through the new contact centre in Glasgow, has improved significantly. Independent research indicates that brand awareness has remained high in the credit card market and strengthened in the overall financial services business. The key objective has been to generate awareness of Goldfish as a financial services provider, rather than simply a credit card. Spontaneous awareness improved from 6% at the end of 2001 to 12% at the end of 2002, which puts Goldfish towards the top end of non traditional banking brands.

Credit card recruitment performance has strengthened throughout the year following changes to the channel mix and customer management approach. Total card net interest income was up 9% at £36 million despite lower margins prevailing within the industry and higher utilisation of interest free promotional balance transfers. Fee income rose 6% to £54 million, primarily due to higher levels of customer spend. Credit losses remained low at 3% of outstanding balances.

Key One.Tel performance indicators

	2002	2001	Δ %
Customer numbers (period end) (000)			
Fixed line	746	668	12
Other services	216	117	85
Total *	962	785	23
Average minutes used per month (fixed line)	284	277	2.5
ARPU (fixed line) (£)	16.20	15.85	2.2
Variable gross margin (fixed line) (%)	51	47	4ppts
Sales and marketing expenses (% of turnover)	14	8	6ppts
Turnover ** (£m)	153	65	135
Operating profit (£m)	2.1	4	(48)
Operating margin (%)	1.4	6	(4.6ppts)

*30 day tolling
**2001 turnover is from date of acquisition (3 July 2001)

Source: Centrica plc Report, 2002

Page 36 of Centrica

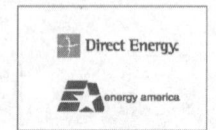

A new internet based savings account was launched during the year.

Key Goldfish Bank performance indicators

	2002	2001	Δ %
Credit cards in force (000)	1,082	1,025	6
Average monthly spend per active card (£)	541	476	14
Gross card receivables	773	677	14
Net interest margin (%)	5.2	5.1	0.1ppts
Credit card income (£m)			
Net interest income	36	33	9
Fee revenue and other income	54	51	6
Total (before deduction of loyalty costs)	90	84	7
Loyalty scheme costs (% of income)	33	31	2ppts
Credit losses (% of receivables)	3	3.2	(0.2ppts)
Credit card profit contribution (£m)	9	12	(25)
Goldfish non-credit card product contribution (£m)	(2.4)	n/a	n/a
Sales and marketing expenses (% of income)	6	5	1ppt
Goldfish operating loss before minority interest (£m)	(40)	(32)	(25)

The number of cards in force has increased by 6% to 1.08 million (2001: 1.02 million). During the year 77,000 new accounts were opened (2001: 27,600), with attrition low at 4.5%. The average monthly spend on the Goldfish card increased by 14% against 2001, making it among the highest in the UK market. The credit card profit contribution of £9 million was £3 million lower than 2001 due to a £4.5 million increase in customer acquisition costs and a £3 million cost relating to the migration to Goldfish's new infrastructure in November.

In the autumn Goldfish entered the personal loan market, focusing initially on generating a high quality applicant pool. The product proposition was based on flexibility featuring no redemption penalties for early settlement. At the year end approximately 1,800 personal loans had been drawn down with total outstanding balances of £14 million. Increased awareness, response and take-up rates will be sought in 2003. Goldfish customers purchased 104,000 additional Goldfish branded products including travel insurance, home insurance and personal accident insurance. This is 69% up on 2001 and is an encouraging indicator of future cross-sales potential. The profit contribution from all non-credit card products was negative: a net loss of £2 million due to the investment of £5 million in customer acquisition during the period.

Goldfish successfully launched its internet based savings account and began active marketing in the autumn. This has proved to have strong appeal with £286 million in deposits and over 11,000 accounts opened of which approximately 50% were customers new to Goldfish. Savings will continue to form part of a diversified funding strategy.

The overall operating loss was £40 million with operating expenses at Goldfish, consisting of brand marketing, banking systems and product development, up 7% at £47 million. A further £46 million investment was capitalised in the development of the IT systems platform. As this nears completion, we expect significantly lower investment in 2003.

Centrica North America
Acquisitions of incumbent positions but slower organic growth

Total North American turnover was £1,118 million in 2002, an increase of 46% over 2001 driven largely by our entry into the Ontario and Texas electricity markets, our entry into the Ontario services market through the acquisition of Enbridge Services Inc and the addition of over 300,000 gas customers through the acquisitions of Enbridge Services Inc and parts of NewPower Company's customer base.

Operating profit fell by 7%, as profits from our home services businesses (£23 million) and reduced losses in our electricity business (by £5 million) were offset by lower profits (by £4 million) in our gas business. Included within the retail energy results are the increase in the cost base (£10 million) due to the development of the infrastructure to support future growth and £21 million of expensed costs incurred in acquiring customers organically. Upstream profits were lower as wholesale prices fell and favourable forward contract prices expired. These results include the adverse currency movements (£4 million), with a 6% decline in the average Canadian dollar exchange rate during the year.

The pace of organic growth slowed in 2002 owing to a combination of slow emergence of competitive markets, restrictive legislative and political developments affecting sales activities, and large fluctuations in wholesale natural gas prices. We are continuing our efforts with governments and regulators at state, provincial and federal levels in support of market liberalisation. We remain of the view that momentum will be regained in the regions that are important to our future, but the timing remains uncertain.

Retail energy

Turnover for the residential gas supply business increased by 12%, driven primarily by higher selling prices and acquisitions. Our Ontario residential gas market share was approximately 26% at year end. In our US gas markets, slower growth caused by high rates of customer churn was offset by the acquisition in August of 212,000 customers in Michigan, Ohio and Pennsylvania from the NewPower Company. We continue to manage our portfolio of US gas customers closely, and will focus our efforts on maximising the value from our current position.

In our first year of operating in the electricity business in Ontario (from May) and Texas, turnover was £189 million with an operating loss of £10 million. Based on operating experience this year, we estimate that average annual consumption for our residential electricity customers would be 11,000 kWh, broadly in line with our expectations and more than twice our UK customer average. The Texas residential electricity market continues to support a positive competitive environment, with the presence of a pricing regime that affords reasonable, sustainable gross margin prospects to both incumbents and new market entrants. Following our entry into this market in January, we served 890,000 retail energy customers by the year end, consisting of both acquired positions (810,000 customers) in southern and western Texas (for which our transaction closed in late December 2002) and organic programmes mainly in the Houston and Dallas/Fort Worth regions.

Source: Centrica plc Report, 2002

Page 37 of Centrica

Operating and financial review continued

The integration of Enbridge Services Inc has allowed us to broaden the range of products we offer.

Our retail energy supply gross profit grew by 14% to £95 million. Our gross margin decreased to 14%. Our current gross margins (other than for our acquired incumbent positions) are largely driven by our historic hedging activities in each local market, through which we have procured the energy commodity at a fixed forward cost, achieving a margin on the quantities supplied to our fixed price retail customers over a contracted period. There are risks to these margins from the complexities involved in accurately forecasting total commodity requirement, linked to rates of consumption, customer acquisition and retention. We are now the third largest electricity retailer in Texas.

Volatility in wholesale gas spot prices remained high, as benchmark gas contract prices moved between US$10/mmbtu and US$2/mmbtu. In markets where we compete against utilities flowing through gas or electricity to customers at wholesale spot cost, this made winning new forward curve-based business extremely challenging and also led to high levels of churn among customers signed up to what became relatively high priced programmes. This cyclical pattern will continue to be a feature of our organic growth. In the latter part of the year, prices returned to levels that we believe are more sustainable in the long term (US$4-5/mmbtu) and conducive to the development of our customer base.

Gross margins for our recently acquired customers in Texas are based upon prices approved by the Texas Public Utility Commission under the 'Price To Beat' structure, which we can apply to have modified twice in any year to reflect changes in gas feedstock costs. Under the acquisition arrangement, Centrica has an economic interest in the profitability of these businesses with effect from 1 September 2002 through to completion on 24 December 2002. These amounts will be credited against amounts payable, under the acquisition agreement, in respect of the sharing of earnings over the next four years. All such payments will be treated as deferred purchase consideration. With effect from 24 December 2002 the full profits have been recognised in the accounts.

Market entry costs this year for Ontario and Texas of £20 million have been expensed. Organic customer acquisition costs were lower, following high levels of Ontario electricity customer acquisition in 2001 and due to slower organic growth in the US market. This, along with the growth in turnover meant that sales and marketing costs as a percentage of turnover reduced by 2 percentage points.

We entered the Ontario electricity market when it opened in May, and successfully converted over 500,000 contracts signed pre-opening to flowing customers. We now have 15% of the residential electricity market. On 11 November, the Ontario government announced that it would cap residential and small business electricity prices at below market rates, to be subsidised by government, effectively suspending competition until 2006. Under this legislation, Centrica remains entitled to receive the market pricing mitigation agreement payment, amounting to £16 million relating to 2002. Margins on residential retail contracts already written are protected, at least to 2006. The regulations regarding business customers are still formative. This electricity customer base of over 500,000 will continue to retain value and be used for cross-selling gas and home services products, but further organic electricity growth is unlikely to be possible until this new legislation expires in 2006.

We continue to seek opportunities to acquire incumbent customer positions from utilities seeking to exit the retail function. Our agreement in December, which is subject to legislative changes and regulatory consents, to purchase the incumbent retail energy business of ATCO Group in Alberta – which currently consists of approximately 820,000 gas and 160,000 electricity customers – will give us an 80% share of the gas market and 14% of the electricity market. We will maintain growth momentum into 2003 as we migrate customers to unregulated energy and services packages.

Home and business services
As part of our strategy to gain competitive advantage and operating leverage from an energy and home services cross-selling platform, the acquisition of Enbridge Services Inc for C$1 billion (£438 million) was completed in May 2002. Enbridge Services Inc made an operating profit of £23 million during the year. We subsequently

Key North America performance indicators

	2002	2001	Δ %
Customer numbers (period end)			
Residential and small commercial gas (000)	1,339	1,230	9
Residential and small commercial electricity (000)	1,416	n/a	n/a
Home and business services (000)	1,627	n/a	n/a
Industrial and commercial energy (sites served)	61	49	24
Average consumption			
Residential and small commercial gas (therms)	1,138	1,154	(1)
Residential and small commercial electricity (kWh)	10,666	n/a	n/a
Industrial and commercial energy (m therms)	19	23	(18)
Gas production and energy trading			
Gas production volumes (m therms)	356	344	3
Average sales price (p/therm)	21.4	27.9	(23)
Turnover (£m)			
Residential and small commercial gas	486	433	12
Residential and small commercial electricity	189	n/a	n/a
Home and business services	159	n/a	n/a
Gas production and energy trading	124	105	18
Industrial and commercial energy	160	230	(30)
Total	1,118	768	46
Sales and marketing expenses (% of turnover)	1.7	3.7	(2ppts)
Gross margin (%)			
Residential and small commercial gas	13	19	(6ppts)
Residential and small commercial electricity	16	n/a	n/a
Operating profit (£m)			
Residential and small commercial gas	16	20	(20)
Residential and small commercial electricity	(10)	(15)	33
Home and business services	23	–	n/a
Gas production and energy trading	33	62	(47)
Industrial and commercial energy	1	1	–
Total	63	68	(7)
Operating margin (%)	6	9	(3ppts)

Source: Centrica plc Report, 2002

Page 38 of Centrica

raised some C$744 million (£303 million) through selling down 58% of our interest in the waterheater assets acquired as part of the transaction by way of the launch of The Consumers' Waterheater Income Fund. Our remaining 42% retained interest had a value of C$218 million (£89 million) at 31 December, which we intend to continue to sell down in 2003. Centrica remains the exclusive installer and provider of maintenance and repair services for our customers' waterheaters and, accordingly, without legal ownership of these assets, retains relationships with approximately 1.3 million households.

In the group's balance sheet the waterheaters are included in fixed assets and the debt financing raised (C$500 million), for which there is no recourse to Centrica, is included in loans, net of expenses. The profit and loss account includes the entire rental income and related costs, including depreciation and interest on the income fund's debt financing from the date of launch of the fund in December. The income fund unit holders' share of profit is reflected in a non-equity minority interest in the profit and loss account. The balance sheet non-equity minority interest includes amounts raised from the sale of units.

The value of the retained businesses together with the cash receipts for the divested assets has created major value for Centrica shareholders. We also remain a leading installer of heating, ventilation and air-conditioning (HVAC) equipment in Ontario, which has a profitable associated financing business and, in addition, some 330,000 of households have contracted with us for HVAC maintenance and protection plans. We now have around 50% share of this home services market and increasing this share is a key objective of 2003. Beginning in 2003 we intend to manage services for our business customers separately.

Upstream gas
Development of our gas fields in Alberta continues. We drilled, completed and began production at 218 wells during 2002, compared with 307 in 2001. Production volumes were up slightly at 356 million therms, representing 24% of our North American downstream gas sales. Operating profit fell by 47%, primarily as a result of a lower wholesale market which led to a 23% decline in our average sales price and the expiry of higher priced forward sales contracts.

Europe

In developing our strategy for Europe, we are focusing on those countries where the speed of market opening and legal and political conditions, including unbundling and independent regulation, are more advanced.

Through Luminus, our joint venture in Belgium, we now have approximately 18% of the electricity market above 1 GWh in Flanders which opened in January 2002. The broader commercial energy market opening in early 2003 will be followed closely by the residential market opening in July 2003 for both electricity and gas. Luminus is positioned as the number two player in the Flemish market. When the residential market opens the business expects to have over 600,000 residential electricity customers and nearly 200,000 residential gas customers.

Our second move in Europe is in Spain, where our initial aim is to enter the small and medium sized business sector of the market and to build a business organically which utilises the skills we have developed in other markets. We are currently testing our proposition with a view to opening for business in the second quarter of 2003.

The operating loss in 2002 was £7 million, reflecting start-up costs in Belgium and Spain.

Note: All current financial results listed are for the year ended 31 December 2002. All references to 'the prior-year period', '2001' and 'last year' mean year ended 31 December 2001 unless otherwise specified.

A major advertising campaign launched Luminus in Belgium.

Source: Centrica plc Report, 2002

Page 39 of Centrica

Group financial review

We aim to grow our earnings and cash flow within a prudent risk management framework. During the year our share price out performed the FTSE 100 by 3.1 % and since demerger in February 1997 to the end of 2002 we out performed the index by 187%.

Centrica's aim is to achieve a total shareholder return (TSR) ranking in the first quartile of UK FTSE 100 companies, taking account of share price growth and dividends received and reinvested over a sustained period. Centrica promotes continuing growth in earnings and cash flow and seeks to maximise the return on capital it achieves within a prudent risk management framework. The remuneration report on pages 25 to 30 summarises our TSR performance over recent years against our FTSE 100 comparator group.

The company's closing share price on 31 December 2002 was 171 pence (31 December 2001: 222 pence), resulting in a market capitalisation of £7.3 billion (2001: £8.9 billion). World stock markets continued to fall in 2002, the FTSE 100 index dropping by 24.5%. The company's share price still out performed the FTSE 100 by 3.1% (2001: 2.1%) and since demerger to the end of 2002 we out performed the index by 187%.

Earnings
Earnings increased by £155 million to £478 million in 2002. This reflected improved operating profits* up £253 million and lower exceptional charges offset by taxation up from £155 million to £250 million and higher goodwill amortisation, up by £35 million to £123 million.

Earnings before exceptional charges and goodwill amortisation were up 32% to £636 million. This represents a return on capital employed over the year of 32% or 7.9% on our average market capitalisation.

Operating profit
Operating profit* was £932 million (2001: £679 million). Most of the improvement came from our UK residential gas supply business, and growth in our business services and home services operations.

Exceptional charges and goodwill amortisation
During the year, non-operating exceptional charges arose of £26 million net of tax (2001: £71 million operating exceptionals net of tax). These related to changes in our Golf England operation and disposal of our LPG cylinder business. In addition, a £9 million (2001: £ nil) exceptional tax charge arose (see Taxation below). The goodwill amortisation charge for the year was £123 million (2001: £88 million), in line with our programme of continuing acquisitions.

Net interest
Net interest charged to the profit and loss account was £62 million compared with £43 million in 2001 and was covered 15 times by operating profit* compared with 16 times a year earlier. The increase in interest payable was due to higher average indebtedness mainly as a result of acquisitions, offset by lower interest rates and the net proceeds of the share placement during the year.

Taxation
The ongoing taxation charge of £243 million for 2002 represents a 28% rate on profits adjusted for goodwill amortisation and exceptionals (2001 comparative rate: 26%). The increase in the effective rate is principally due to the introduction of a 10% corporation tax surcharge on UK offshore gas production, with effect from 17 April 2002. This surcharge increased the tax charge for the year by £12 million and resulted in a restatement of the deferred tax liability of £9 million, which has been treated as exceptional. The overall charge is still less than the UK 30% statutory rate, primarily because previously unrecognised deferred tax assets of £35 million have been utilised during 2002.

Earnings per share and dividends
Basic earnings per share grew from 8.1 pence to 11.4 pence and adjusted earnings per share from 12.1 pence to 15.2 pence. Over the last three years the adjusted performance measure has grown by an average compound growth rate of 24% and facilitated a progressive dividend policy. We are proposing a final dividend of 2.6 pence giving a total of 4.0 pence (2001: 3.1 pence), an increase of 29%.

Cash flow
Group operating cash flow (including dividends from joint ventures and associates, from continuing operations before exceptional payments) was £790 million for 2002, compared with £885 million in 2001. An increase of £299 million in operating profit* before depreciation and amortisation of investments was more than offset by changes in working capital, including growth in trade debtors, the timing of gas transportation payments, petroleum revenue tax (PRT) and gas production royalty payments.

Total capital expenditure was £449 million this year, up from £312 million in 2001. This includes £180 million of costs capitalised for information systems investments associated with our new customer relationship management (CRM) infrastructure. Acquisition expenditures (net of cash and overdrafts acquired) were £989 million in 2002 (2001: £1,204 million), consisting primarily of our purchases of the Brigg power plant and Rough

*Before exceptional charges and goodwill amortisation, including joint ventures and associates.

Source: Centrica plc Report, 2002

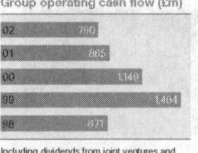

Page 40 of Centrica

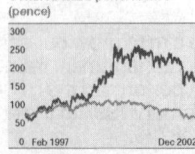

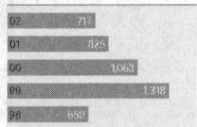

gas storage facilities in the UK, Enbridge Services Inc in Canada and WTU Retail Energy LP and CPL Retail Energy LP in the US. The group's net cash outflow before liquid resources and financing was, as a result, £918 million, against a net outflow of £342 million in 2001.

Balance sheet
The net assets of the group increased during the year from £1,536 million to £2,402 million.

Fixed assets
Net intangible fixed assets of £1,813 million (2001: £1,524 million) represented goodwill, which has arisen on acquisitions. During the year, £466 million (2001: £314 million) was added, including £193 million for the acquisition of Enbridge Services Inc, £167 million for WTU Retail Energy LP and CPL Retail Energy LP and £80 million for Electricity Direct. Goodwill is amortised by way of charges against profits over periods ranging from 5 to 20 years.

Tangible fixed assets, mainly comprising gas field assets and power stations, had a net book value of £2,763 million (2001: £2,058 million). During the year gas field assets, including the Rough gas storage facilities, and power stations totalling £590 million were acquired. At the year end, the proven and probable gas reserves represented by our field interests amounted to 2,846 billion cubic feet (bcf) (2001: 3,232 bcf), which included 404 bcf (2001: 446 bcf) in North America. At the year end, hardware and software costs relating to our major investments in CRM had a net book value of £237 million.

The group's investment in joint ventures stood at £74 million (2001: £112 million), comprising its share of gross assets of £810 million and share of gross liabilities of £736 million, of which £629 million related to borrowings. These investments related principally to the investments in 60% of Humber Power Limited, 50% interest in the AA's joint ventures with HBOS and 50% of Luminus NV.

Working capital
Current assets less current liabilities, excluding net indebtedness and Goldfish funding amounted to a deficit of £243 million (2001: deficit of £625 million). Excluding Goldfish, growth in trade debtors and accrued energy income has given rise to a net increase of £565 million in working capital.

Goldfish Bank
Goldfish Bank debtors, mainly in respect of credit card balances receivable, were £792 million (2001: £673 million), offset by customer savings account balances of £286 million (2001: £ nil). Goldfish Bank borrowings amounted to £430 million (2001: £610 million).

Net debt
Net debt (excluding the Goldfish Bank facility of £430 million and the £196 million of non-recourse debt raised on the water heater assets acquired with Enbridge Services Inc) increased to £529 million at 31 December 2002 from £433 million at the previous year end.

Issue of share capital
In February 2002 £426 million, net of expenses, was raised via the issue of 232 million ordinary shares.

Provisions and other creditors due after more than one year
Together these increased during the year to £1,384 million (2001: £1,218 million). Increases in respect of decommissioning costs, mainly from acquisitions, and deferred corporation tax have more than offset the decrease in provisions for deferred PRT.

Financial risk management
The board has established objectives and policies for managing financial risks, to enable Centrica to achieve its long term shareholder value growth targets within a prudent risk management framework. These objectives and policies are regularly reviewed.

Currency, interest rate, liquidity and counterparty risks are managed centrally by a treasury and risk management team, within parameters set by the board. This team is also responsible for managing the relationships with the agencies setting the company's credit ratings and managing the cost of its debt capital. Energy market price and weather risks are managed by business led energy and risk management teams operating within group established policies. Where appropriate, financial instruments are used to manage financial risks as explained below and in note 29 on pages 59 to 62. Goldfish Bank interest rate risks are managed by a treasury team with Lloyds TSB Bank plc within parameters set by the Goldfish Bank board.

Credit rating
The company's credit ratings from Moody's Investors Service/Standard & Poor's remain unchanged at A2/A (long term) and P1/A-1 (short term) and with a stable outlook.

Currency risk
Through wholly-owned US and Canadian subsidiaries, the group has operational exposure in Canadian and US dollars. Canadian dollar translation exposure is hedged by maintaining a portfolio of Canadian dollar financial liabilities, which approximate to the net asset value of the Canadian operations. US dollar exposure has been hedged by borrowing on a short term basis through a combination of US commercial paper programme and currency instruments. In addition there is an element of exposure to the euro through the 50% interest in Luminus, which has been hedged by selling euro forward on a rolling basis. Exposures to foreign currency movements from operating activities are also hedged through the use of forward foreign exchange contracts. All debt raised in US dollars through the US commercial paper programme, apart from that hedging the US translation exposure, is either swapped into sterling or another functional currency as part of the translation hedging operations described above.

Interest rate risk
Throughout the year, the group's policy has been to maintain approximately 50% of long term borrowings at a fixed rate of interest. This is achieved by using derivative financial instruments, such as interest rate swaps, to adjust the interest basis of the portfolio of long term debt (see note 29 on pages 59 to 62). At the year end debt has been raised on both a fixed and floating rate basis.

Liquidity
Cash forecasts identifying the liquidity requirements of the group are produced frequently. These are reviewed regularly by the board to ensure that sufficient financial headroom exists for at least a 12 month period. The group policy includes maintaining a minimum level of committed facilities and an objective that a proportion of debt should be long term, spread over a

Source: Centrica plc Report, 2002

Page 41 of Centrica

Group financial review continued

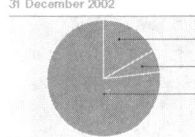

Capital funding
31 December 2002

- Net debt, excluding Goldfish Bank working capital borrowings – £529 million
- Non-recourse debt (Consumers' Waterheater Income Trust) – £196 million
- Equity including minority interest – £2,402 million

range of maturities. Details of the maturity profile of borrowings are given in note 29 on pages 59 to 62. At 31 December 2002, the group had undrawn committed facilities of £1 billion (2001: £935 million), which were used as a backstop for the US commercial paper programme.

Counterparty risk
The board's policy is to limit counterparty exposures by setting credit limits for each counterparty, where possible by reference to published credit ratings. Exposures are measured in relation to the nature, market value and maturity of each contract or financial instrument. Surplus cash is invested in short term financial instruments and only deposited with counterparties with a minimum credit rating of A3/A- or P1/A-1 in Moody's Investors Service/ Standard & Poor's long term and short term ratings respectively. Energy trading activities are undertaken with counterparties for whom specific credit limits are set. All contracted and potential exposures are reported to the financial risk management committee of the board.

Commodity price risk
The key commodity price risks facing the group are first, natural gas and electricity prices both in the short term market and in respect of long term contracts and, secondly, escalation indices on long term gas contracts, of which the most influential are oil product prices and general price inflation.

The group's policy is to hedge a proportion of the exposure for a number of years ahead matched to the underlying sale and purchase risk profiles. The group aims to manage its risk by using financial instruments such as oil and gas swaps and gas derivatives and bilateral agreements for gas and power, as well as asset ownership.

The financial risk management committee regularly monitors the extent of the group's commodity price exposure and the level of hedging activity alongside the availability of forward prices and market liquidity.

The acquisition of the Glanford Brigg power station has further contributed to the company's target to cover around a quarter of its electricity requirement from its own sources in 2002.

Weather risk
Gas sales volumes, and to a lesser extent electricity volumes, are influenced by temperature and other weather factors. In Britain, the weather derivatives market remains relatively immature. We again entered into a number of weather derivative transactions for the winter period October 2002 to March 2003 in order to hedge part of the group's weather exposure.

Accounting policies
The principal accounting policies remain unchanged over last year and are described in note 1 to the financial statements on pages 35 to 37. Where appropriate, wording has been expanded to more fully explain policies, particularly in relation to financial instruments, and energy trading activities.

In keeping with many other major companies, adoption of FRS 17 Retirement Benefits, has been deferred in line with the revised timetable announced by the Accounting Standards Board. Accordingly, the group has continued to report under SSAP 24 Accounting for Pension Costs.

In accordance with FRS 17, additional disclosures are contained in note 26 on pages 55 and 56. If the standard had been fully adopted in 2002, profit would have been reduced by £47 million (2001: £16 million) and net assets would have been reduced by £507 million (2001: £117 million). Full adoption is not mandatory until 2005, but the group will continue to keep this under review.

Phillip Bentley
Group Finance Director

Source: Centrica plc Report, 2002

Part C: Practice cases

Page 42 of Centrica

Corporate responsibility

Centrica community investment

- Older or disabled customers and their carers – 19%
- Other – 6%
- Support for motor related causes – 31%
- Energy efficiency and fuel poverty – 16%
- Education – 19%
- Support for employees and local community – 10%

Bruno Peek OBE, chairman of the Golden Jubilee Summer Party, test-fires the British Gas Jubilee Beacon that illuminated Buckingham Palace during the weekend celebrations.

Energy Angel Eleanor Whitehead whose school, Little Gaddesden Primary, signed on for the next stage of British Gas's award winning 'Think Energy' educational programme.

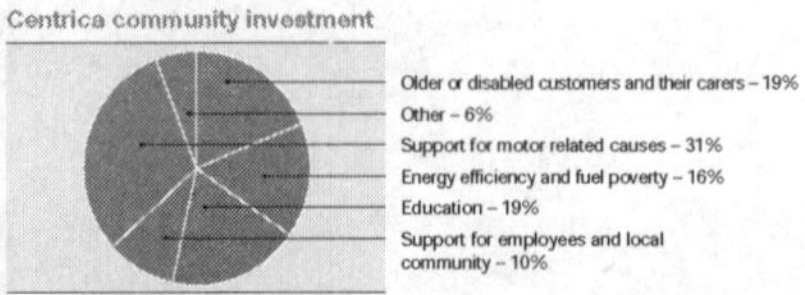

Centrica's community spend is focused on a number of priority areas, linked to issues relevant to our business.

Our businesses are focused on delivering essential products and services to millions of people every day. Continued and sustainable success requires that we accept and respond to our social responsibilities. By understanding our impact on society, the economy and the wider environment, we can develop positive relationships with stakeholders to benefit both business and the community.

Corporate responsibility is integral to all our activities. Our framework is set and co-ordinated by the Centrica corporate responsibility committee that was formed in 2002. Detailed information about our range of corporate responsibility activities is available at www.centrica.com/responsibility.

The effectiveness of our approach was illustrated by Centrica's inclusion in the 2002 FTSE4Good Index and, for the first time, in the Dow Jones Sustainability Indexes for 2003.

We are aware not only of the positive business potential of demonstrating our commitment to corporate responsibility, but also of the negative impact of poor performance in this area.

Corporate responsibility concerns have been fully integrated into the group's risk management structures. These address the financial impact on the business of social and environmental threats as well as the potential impact on the reputation of our brands.

Our corporate responsibility activities fall into four main categories:

Environment
Our prime responsibility is managing the impact of our operations on the environment. We also have a responsibility for helping our customers make informed decisions about using our products and services in a way that minimises any negative impact on the environment. British Gas plays a leading role in helping to achieve the government's fuel poverty and climate change targets through the provision of free or subsidised energy efficiency products. During our Energy Efficiency Standards of Performance (EESoP) programme, which finished in April 2002, British Gas provided 14 million energy efficient products to 585,000 households throughout Britain, in total saving 5,250 GWh of energy.

From April 2002, EESoP was replaced by the Energy Efficiency Commitment, a three year programme with an energy saving target of around 27,000 GWh. British Gas is on target to deliver these savings. Key to this success has been our ability to engage customers through new product innovation and groundbreaking customer propositions. Through our Warm-A-Life programme, more than 70,000 disadvantaged customers have received a range of benefits including free insulation products, benefits assessment to ensure that they are claiming everything that they are entitled to and discounts on British Gas energy bills.

In 2002, we worked hard on delivering our environmental programme. Notable improvements included increasing the recycling in our offices from 18% to 34% and improving their energy efficiency by implementing projects that saved more than 4.5 million kWh per annum. In terms of environmental management, sites that were certified to ISO14001 have completed their reassessment and the British Gas Service Centres and AA Service Centres achieved certification for the first time.

We published our second environment report in March 2002.

We also promoted environmental good practice in the home through our 'Think Energy' education programme for schools. To date, more than 14,000 primary and secondary schools in Britain have signed up for the programme, involving an estimated one million school children between the ages of 7 to 14. The programme will be extended to include 14 to 16 year olds from 2003. During 2002, 'Think Energy' won a British Commitment to the Environment Premier Award.

Community
Our community programme addresses issues relevant to our business and, where possible, we also support our employees' volunteering activities. Communities will benefit most from our investment if there is a sound business case for it, since this provides the best foundation for sustained involvement.

We contributed £5.66 million to community causes in 2002 as measured by the London Benchmarking Group model, which includes both cash and in-kind support.

Our UK charity of the year initiative enables employees across the group to raise funds for a charity chosen by a panel of employees. From April 2001 until July 2002, our partner was the Cystic Fibrosis Trust and our employees raised more than £475,000 to fund vital research and treatment for the UK's most common life threatening inherited disease. The partnership received an Institute of Public Relations Sword of Excellence award in July.

We hope for similar success with our new chosen charity, the Meningitis Trust. Between its launch in September 2002 and the end of the year, employees raised more than £150,000.

In North America, we launched 'Direct in the Community'. The programme seeks to play a leadership role in fostering, supporting and encouraging charitable initiatives that provide services related to safe and affordable housing, especially for adults, families, older people and people with disabilities.

The British Gas partnership with Help the Aged continues to support some of Britain's most vulnerable older people. Since its launch in 1999, British Gas has provided Help the Aged with more than £5.4 million of support and to date there have been 1.6 million beneficiaries of partnership initiatives. The partnership received the Business in the Community Excellence Award for cause related marketing in July.

We have enjoyed a successful association with Carers UK since 1996. In 2002 we sought to identify 'hidden' carers and guide them to information, advice and support. Promotion, including a bill message to more than two million customers, also generated awareness among our employees about Centrica's carer friendly employment policies. Our chief executive is president of the charity.

The AA Accessible Hotel of the Year Awards highlight the importance of ensuring equal access for people with disabilities to hotels and guest accommodation in the lead up to the next phase of the Disability Discrimination Act in 2004. During 2002, AA hotel inspectors assessed 60 hotels and guest houses selected from the results of a detailed questionnaire returned from more than 300 of the

Source: Centrica plc Report 2002

Page 43 of Centrica

Corporate responsibility continued

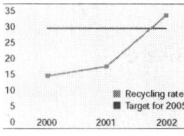

Material recycled from Centrica offices (%)

Recycling rate / Target for 2005 (2000–2002, ranging from about 15 up to 30+)

The success of our recycling initiatives has meant that we have already exceeded our target for 2005, initially set in 2000.

Sir Roy Gardner is joined by meningitis sufferer Samuel Cloke to launch the 'Every Second Counts' partnership – a year-long partnership with our employee charity of the year, Meningitis Trust.

Employees in Cardiff ride the world's largest bicycle to raise funds for Cystic Fibrosis Trust, Centrica employee charity of the year 2001 to 2002.

Rod Kenyon, director of the British Gas Engineering Academy, is joined by a group of trainees to launch the academy.

AA's 8,000 strong list. The awards will be repeated in 2003 to make more establishments aware of the need for improved accessibility.

The AA Foundation for Road Safety Research published reports in 2002 on the safety of young male and female drivers, when and why older drivers give up driving and on safety in pan-European tunnels. During the year, research continued on the effect of surface conditions on road safety and accidents on high speed dual carriageways.

In December, it was announced that One.Tel would be working with the Samaritans, the emotional health charity, to promote its new telephone directory enquiries service. During 2003, One.Tel will donate 1p for every call made to the new service generating vital funds for the charity.

Marketplace
We try to take a responsible approach to the marketing and selling of our products and services. We take care of our customers' daily essentials and provide the necessary access and expertise to ensure they benefit fully from the products and services we offer. For example, we currently provide over 500 communications each day to customers who are blind or visually impaired in the format they require, which includes Braille, large print and audio.

Some of our customers have specific needs. Current services include the Home Energy Care Register, the password scheme, providing information in alternative formats and using access technology such as text phones. We have developed our own website accessibility guidelines based on internationally recognised standards and intend that all our business websites will meet and exceed these standards in the near future.

We have reviewed the needs of hearing- and speech-impaired customers in collaboration with the RNID and the Royal Association for Deaf People. Text phones have been installed throughout the business and the AA has developed a text messaging service so that hearing and speech-impaired members can communicate effectively via their mobile phones.

The British Gas 'here to HELP' initiative was launched in 2002 to help tackle household poverty in the most deprived communities in Britain. From a package of £150 million, British Gas's investment of more than £70 million is supported by additional government and social housing provider funding. Over the next three years, 500,000 homes will be supported in urban, suburban and rural areas through a network of local authorities, housing associations and charity organisations. Households are offered energy efficiency measures and advice along with other services delivered by our charity partners.

Workplace
Relationships with all our employees are based on trust and respect for the individual. We aim to attract, develop, reward and retain high quality people who are motivated to achieve our business objectives. Our employment policies seek to create an environment that motivates and engages all our employees, rewards performance, and satisfies material needs whilst supporting equality of opportunity for all. This is achieved through policies such as family leave, carers, personal development and supporting employees to find a successful balance between work and personal life. A new guide to sound business practice was developed in 2002, setting out how we expect our employees to act in a variety of situations. This is being disseminated in 2003.

The growing diversity among our customers and employees presents us with opportunities for change. In an increasingly competitive environment, it is essential that we recognise the importance of operating as an inclusive organisation, through embracing diversity in the workforce and selecting the very best employees from a wide and varied choice of applicants. We work with a number of partners to achieve this goal including the Employers' Forum on Disability, an organisation chaired by our chief executive.

Diversity modules form part of the training for all our customer facing employees and a disability awareness training package has also been developed. More than 29,000 booklets giving practical advice on how best to serve disabled people have been issued throughout the business.

We have created employment opportunities for individuals from disadvantaged backgrounds. More than 180 individuals have been employed through targeted recruitment in our contact centres. In July 2002 we received a Business in the Community award for our investment in disabled people as employees and customers.

British Gas has committed to recruiting 200 gas engineers, targeting the long term unemployed and those who have trouble finding a career that fits in with their lifestyle. The engineer training course, developed with the Gas and Water Industries National Training Organisation, includes a part-time option aimed at single parents. The initiative is part of the government backed Ambition Energy programme, chaired by Centrica's chief executive, to address an anticipated shortage of skilled and qualified gas engineers.

We are delighted that, in recognition of its commitment to the development and training of its employees, the AA has received corporate Investors in People accreditation.

Nearly three quarters of our employees took part in the annual global employee satisfaction survey in 2002, up from under two thirds in 2000. The survey measures four key improvement drivers – customer focus, performance and development, management impact and working life. Part of the performance related element of directors' remuneration is linked to this survey.

The health and safety of our employees is of paramount importance. Our performance is targeted and monitored through key performance indicators. In 2002, the amount of time lost to injuries or occupational ill health was low. Injuries have been attributable mainly to slips, trips and falls, and our accident prevention programmes focus on the underlying causes of these and other near miss events.

We have also taken steps to protect employees who may encounter violence while they do their jobs, for example gas engineers, roadside patrols and debt collectors. We have launched an occupational road risk programme to manage the risks to employees who drive in the course of their employment. Good practice workshops share new safety techniques and opportunities for performance improvement.

Source: Centrica plc Report, 2002

Part C: Practice cases

Page 44 of Centrica

Direct Energy and Energy America

Progress to Date

- Entered market in August 2000
- Completed 6 acquisitions for US$1.6bn
- Over US$100m invested in organic growth
- Recouped US$0.5bn through hiving off ESI water heaters
- Entered Ontario and Texas power markets in 2002
- Will have 5½ million customers by mid-2003
- 2,500 full time employees
- 2002 revenues sharply up on 2001
- New brand roll-out has commenced

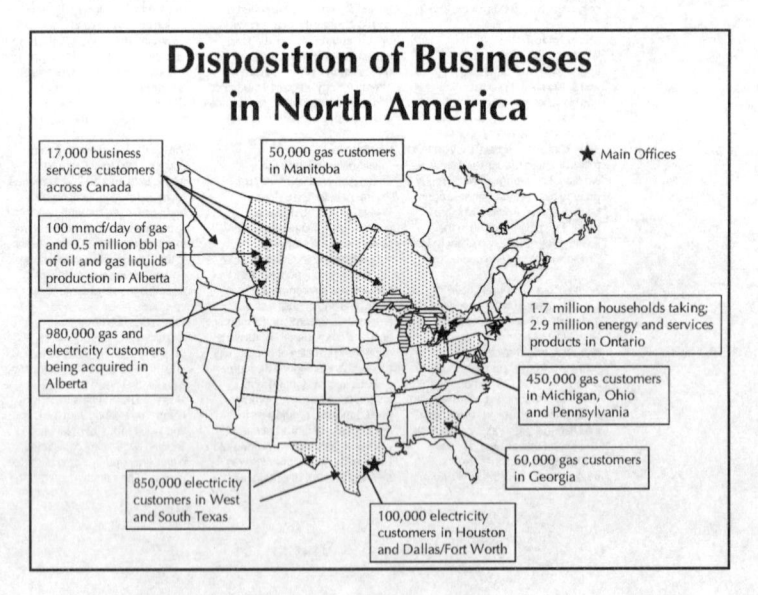

Direct Energy.
Essential Home Services

Disposition of Businesses in North America

★ Main Offices

- 17,000 business services customers across Canada
- 50,000 gas customers in Manitoba
- 100 mmcf/day of gas and 0.5 million bbl pa of oil and gas liquids production in Alberta
- 980,000 gas and electricity customers being acquired in Alberta
- 1.7 million households taking; 2.9 million energy and services products in Ontario
- 450,000 gas customers in Michigan, Ohio and Pennsylvania
- 850,000 electricity customers in West and South Texas
- 60,000 gas customers in Georgia
- 100,000 electricity customers in Houston and Dallas/Fort Worth

Source: Centrica plc Report, 2002

Page 45 of Centrica

North America

- No. 1 North American independent energy supplier
- 1.3m gas customers in Ontario and USA, backed by ~20% equity production
- Over 0.5m Ontario electricity customers, via organic growth
- Move into home services with Greensource & Enbridge acquisitions
- Recent Texas acquisitions, from AEP, will take us to c. 4.5m customer relationships in total

Source: Centrica plc Report, 2002

Part C: Practice cases

Page 46 of Centrica

Appendix 2

Source: Centrica

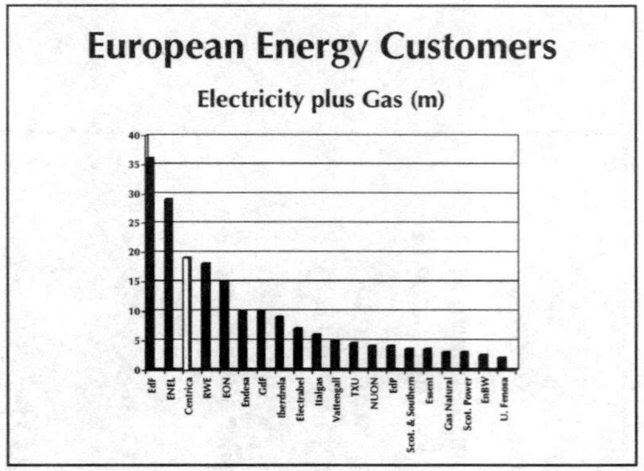

European Energy Customers
Electricity plus Gas (m)

- EdF
- ENEL
- Centrica
- RWE
- EON
- Endesa
- GdF
- Iberdrola
- Electrabel
- Italgas
- Vattengall
- TXU
- NUON
- EdP
- Scot. & Southern
- Essent
- Gas Natural
- Scot. Power
- EnBW
- U. Fenosa

Source: Centrica

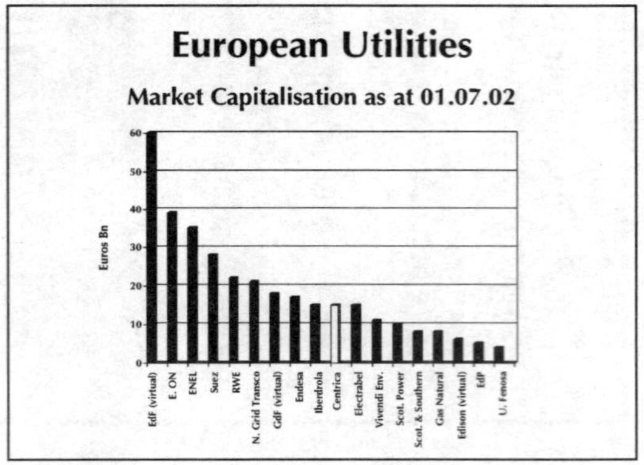

European Utilities
Market Capitalisation as at 01.07.02

Euros Bn

- EdF (virtual)
- E. ON
- ENEL
- Suez
- RWE
- N. Grid Transco
- GdF (virtual)
- Endesa
- Iberdrola
- Centrica
- Electrabel
- Vivendi Env.
- Scot. Power
- Scot. & Southern
- Gas Natural
- Edison (virtual)
- EdP
- U. Fenosa

Page 47 of Centrica

Household Market Opening Dates

Country	Electricity	Gas
UK	1998-9	1996-8
Austria	Oct 2001	Oct 2002
Belgium (*)	July 2003	July 2003
France	Not specified	Not specified
Germany	1999	2002 (on paper)
Italy	Not specified	Jan 2003
Netherlands	Oct 2003	Oct 2003
Spain	Jan 2003	Jan 2003

(*) Market opening in Flanders; Brussels and Wallonia will follow later

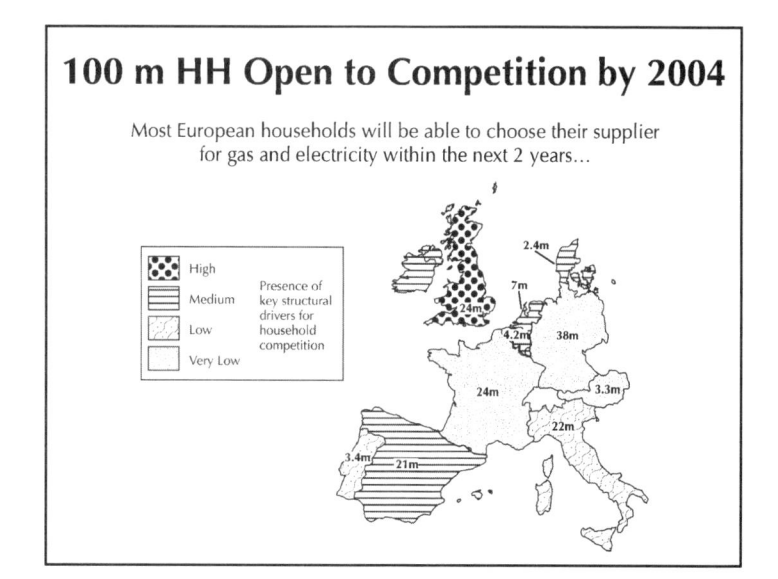

Source: Centrica

100 m HH Open to Competition by 2004

Most European households will be able to choose their supplier for gas and electricity within the next 2 years...

Legend:
- High
- Medium
- Low
- Very Low

Presence of key structural drivers for household competition

Figures on map: 2.4m, 7m, 24m, 4.2m, 38m, 24m, 3.3m, 22m, 3.4m, 21m

Source: Centrica

Part C: Practice cases

Page 48 of Centrica

Appendix 3

European Utilities Market

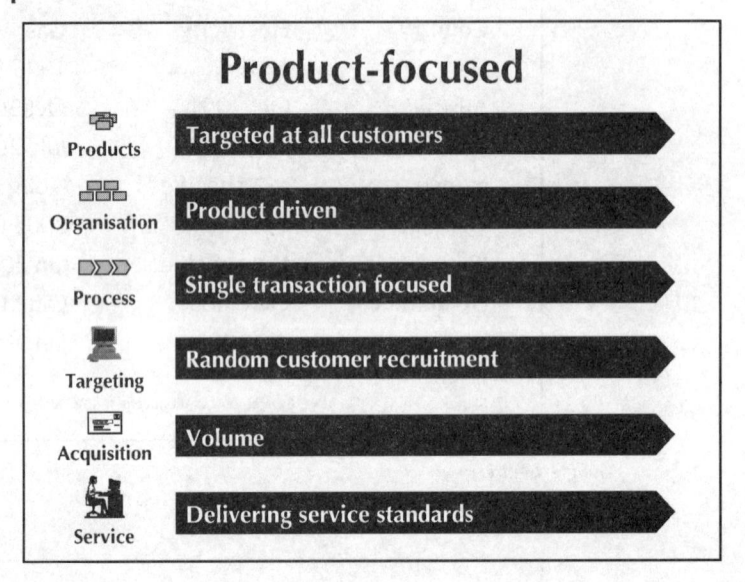

Product-focused

Products	Targeted at all customers
Organisation	Product driven
Process	Single transaction focused
Targeting	Random customer recruitment
Acquisition	Volume
Service	Delivering service standards

Source: Centrica

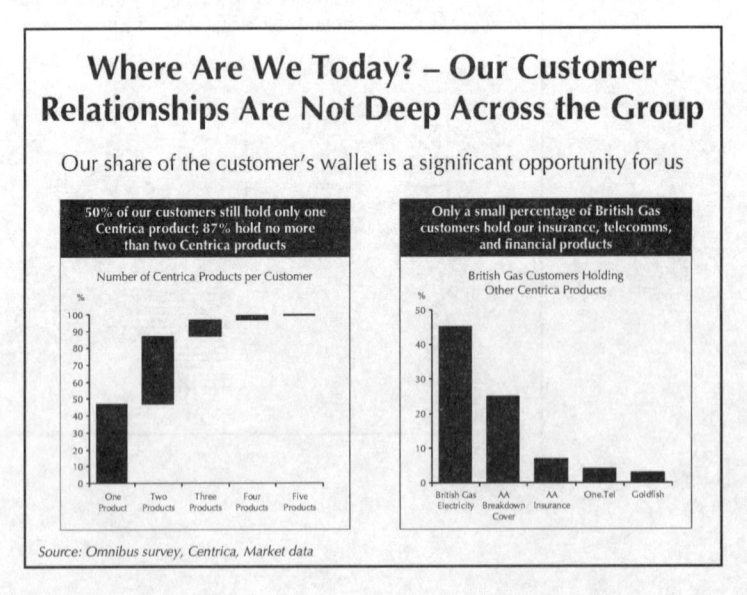

Where Are We Today? – Our Customer Relationships Are Not Deep Across the Group

Our share of the customer's wallet is a significant opportunity for us

50% of our customers still hold only one Centrica product; 87% hold no more than two Centrica products

Number of Centrica Products per Customer (One, Two, Three, Four, Five Products)

Only a small percentage of British Gas customers hold our insurance, telecomms, and financial products

British Gas Customers Holding Other Centrica Products (British Gas Electricity, AA Breakdown Cover, AA Insurance, One.Tel, Goldfish)

Source: Omnibus survey, Centrica, Market data

Source: Centrica

> **Page 49 of Centrica**

Appendix 4

Brands

What a good name adds up to: MARKETING BRANDS

Richard Tomkins reports on a method of putting a value on brands and reveals the leaders, laggards and non-runners in the resulting world league table.

Source: Financial Times; London; Jun 22, 1999; Tomkins, Richard.

Which is the world's most valuable brand? The answer is less clear now than it was two weeks ago, when Coca-Cola was so far ahead of the rest that it looked unassailable.

In spite of its fumbled reaction to a health scare over its products in Europe, Coca-Cola is probably still ahead of the pack. But research to be published today shows that the crisis is jeopardising billions of dollars' worth of shareholder value.

According to Interbrand, the international branding consultancy, the Coca-Cola brand was worth $83.8 billion (£52 billion) before the scare started – far ahead of Microsoft, the world's next most valuable brand, at $56.7 billion.

How much less is the Coca-Cola name worth today? Raymond Perrier, Brand Valuation Director in Interbrand's London offices, says recent events should be seen in the context of a product that is 113 years old and sells in 200 countries. "It would be foolish to say it hadn't been affected," he says. "But I don't think it's been affected by a huge amount."

Even so, the Interbrand survey serves as a timely reminder that the financial risks of a big product recall can go far beyond the cost of writing off a few hundred dollars' worth of lost sales.

At the time Interbrand did its calculations, the value of $83.8 billion attributed to the Coca-Cola brand represented nearly 60 per cent of the company's market value. In other words, the brand was worth more than all the company's offices, manufacturing plants, distribution systems and other assets put together.

"Brands are significant assets which companies need to manage carefully because they add value to the underlying business," says Mr Perrier. For a company such as Coca-Cola, that sounds like understatement: the brand almost is the business.

Page 50 of Centrica

Interbrand says its league table, called The $1 Billion Brands, is "the most comprehensive ranking ever" of brand values. It attempts to put a financial value on an asset that is rarely included in company balance sheets.

The biggest obstacle to this kind of exercise is the difficulty of separating the value of a company's brands from that of its other intellectual assets, such as its patents, technologies, skills and distribution systems.

"Although there is general agreement that the existence of brands can have a beneficial impact on the earnings of a company, there is less agreement on the reliability for valuing brands in the balance sheet," notes the Oxford University Press's *A Dictionary of Accounting*.

Even so, Interbrand – part of Omnicom, the US advertising group – has developed a methodology that is recognised by auditors, tax authorities and stock exchanges in many countries, and which has been used to value more than 2,000 brands worldwide over the past 12 years.

The Interbrand method treats the brand as an intangible asset that generates an identifiable stream of earnings over the years. Once that idea is established, the brand value can be defined as the net present value of the future profits.

For each brand, Interbrand uses publicly available financial data to estimate the operating profits likely to be generated over the next five years by products carrying the brand (A notional 2 (112) per cent growth rate was assumed for subsequent years). It deducts a capital charge – a notional 8 per cent return on the cost of capital employed – and a 35 per cent tax charge to arrive at a figure called economic earnings.

Interbrand then calculates the brand's contribution to those earnings by applying a "role of branding" index to the earnings figure, based on its own analysis of the role played by brands in different product sectors and geographical markets.

Finally, a discount is applied to the earnings to reflect the amount of risk involved. A long-established brand with a strong market position and wide geographic spread, for example, receives a lower discount than a small newcomer in a fast-evolving sector.

This last factor explains why, in spite of all the hyperbole about the Internet, new technology stocks emerge as relatively weak brands that do little to justify their relatively high stock market valuations.

Amazon.com, for example, only scrapes into the rankings at number 57 in spite of its costly efforts to become the best - known brand on the Internet. Yahoo! is at 53 and America Online, the only other Internet brand in the rankings, is at 35.

In contrast, most of the world's 10 most valuable brands are well established names such as Coca-Cola, Ford, Disney and Marlboro. The only top-ranking companies less than 25 years old are Microsoft, in second place, and Intel, at number seven.

> **Page 51 of Centrica**

Interbrand's method of calculation means some notable brands are absent from the table. The private companies that own the Levi's, Mars and Lego brands do not provide sufficient financial information; figures for the CNN cable television channel and Time magazine cannot be stripped out from those of Time Warner, the parent company; and organisations such as Visa, MasterCard and the BBC do not generate economic profits in the conventional sense.

Also absent from the table are airline brands, because of the difficulty of separating their value from that of take-off and landing slots. And only brands that generate a significant proportion of their profits outside their own country are included.

One interesting aspect of the table is that it is heavily dominated by US brands. Mr Perrier says this is partly because the large US market acts as a springboard for companies with global aspirations, and partly because the US has been in the brand management business for longer than other countries. "A lot of the earliest successes in creating brands came out of the US, and still today, a lot of our models of what a brand is like and how a brand should be developed is based on US expertise," he says.

Mr Perrier also notes that the financial services sector is very poorly represented in the rankings in spite of its heavy spending on advertising. "The great failure of financial institutions has been their inability to create any relevant differentiation for themselves, other than at the edges."

Mr Perrier says most of the new brands in the rankings – Intel, Nokia, Ericsson and Yahoo! – have broken through because the categories in which they compete are new. "It seems to suggest that launching new brands into established categories, and getting substantial value out of them, is a lot more difficult than launching new brands in new categories," he says.

"So the game of new brand development is much more one of finding new market opportunities than simply launching brands against established players."

Copyright Financial Times Limited, 1999. All Rights Reserved.

Page 52 of Centrica

Recent Corporate Responsibility News

Too Many Older People Suffering from Isolation

The British Gas Help the Aged Partnership continues its campaign to combat social isolation through its annual Stepping Out event, as recent research reveals that around one-fifth of older people in poverty limit their use of the telephone or going out on social occasions*.

With poverty affecting nearly half of people aged 60 and over in deprived urban neighbourhoods*, social isolation is a fact of life for many older people. The British Gas Help the Aged Partnership's month long national activity programme aims to address key factors contributing to isolation by encouraging tens of thousands of older people to take part in Stepping Out, which is running from 1st-30th June 2003.

Nearly 58,000 older people took advantage of the hundreds of discounts on offer during Stepping Out last year. This summer older people can again save money with a diverse range of deals, including discounted travel by rail and road, as well as reduced price entrance fees to houses and gardens, castles, museums, hotels, theatres and local tourist attractions. This is a great chance for older people to visit new places, try new activities and catch up with friends this summer.

Stepping Out Ambassador Liz Smith, from the Royle Family, said: "The isolation experienced by so many people across the country is staggering. Every effort must be made to allow older people to enjoy the activities and social networks that other age groups do. I am delighted to support Stepping Out and its efforts to deal with isolation by offering older people a chance to enjoy themselves this summer."

Stepping Out is part of the British Gas Help the Aged Partnership's ongoing isolation campaign. The campaign was launched in October 2000 to help address some of the issues faced by the hundreds of thousands of older people in the UK who are acutely isolated and feel trapped in their own homes**.

Some of the partners and activities across Britain include: The Royal Horticultural Society, Privilege Holiday Club, Grange and Ramada Jarvis Hotels and the Ambassador Theatre Group.

Regular Stepping Out partners, English Heritage and the National Trust, are also on board again to provide a range of discounts to shows and other attractions. As part of this year's event, English Heritage is offering an unprecedented deal, including 25 per cent off the first visit to English Heritage properties, 50 per cent off the second visit, with the third visit free of charge.

Page 53 of Centrica

British Gas Help the Aged Partnership spokesperson, Ian Hagg, said: "Stepping Out is a fantastic event that enables tens of thousands of older people to enjoy some great British attractions during the warm summer weather. British Gas is delighted to be working with Help the Aged on this initiative which helps to address aspects of isolation by promoting active ageing through encouraging older people to get out and about."

* Sourced from 'Growing older in socially deprived areas: Social exclusion in later life.' Commissioned by Help the Aged and undertaken by Keele University in 2002.

** 2000 MORI survey showed one million older people in the UK are acutely isolated and over one million feel trapped in their own homes.

Notes:

The British Gas Help the Aged Partnership began in January 1999 and since then British Gas has provided more than £5.4 million of support. The Partnership continues to develop and implement practical schemes to make the lives of vulnerable older people warmer, less isolated and more secure. To date there have been 1.6 million beneficiaries of Partnership initiatives.

Below is the full list of Stepping Out offers available across Britain:

Travel
- Anglia Railways – Flat Fare Offer: £10 Standard or £20 First Class.
- Chiltern Railways – 50% off lunchtime concert tickets with Senior Railcard.
- First Great Western – train travel for only £12.50 return.
- First Great Eastern – one day off-peak RailRover. Travel anywhere for £5.
- Midland Mainline – 20% discount on Midland Mainline Chatsworth Day Out or Sudbury Hall Day Out.
- ScotRail – Club 55/Club 55 Premier – £14/£18 return flat fare.
- City Sightseeing Tours – up to 20% discount on tours.
- National Express.

National
- Eurocamp – up to 30% off holidays.
- Privilege Holiday Club – up to 50% savings.
- Grange Hotels – up to 56% discount off standard rates including continental breakfast.
- Ramada Jarvis Hotels – stay at any Ramada Jarvis hotel from just £19.50 per person, per night.
- Ambassador Theatre Group – a range of offers at Ambassador Theatres across the country, including 2 for 1 ticket for Midnight's Children at the King's Theatre, Glasgow, and best available seat for £15 for Fiddler on the Roof at the New Victoria Theatre, Woking.

Page 54 of Centrica

- Shape Ticket Scheme – Stepping Out Special Feature! Tickets for top name West End shows from just £15 with a volunteer/escort to help with driving, public transport or at the venue.
- . National Trust – Three month free membership.

England
- The Royal Horticultural Society – special offer on membership or 2 for 1 entry.
- National Glass Centre, Sunderland – 50% off admission.
- Blackpool Tower & Circus – Save 25% on admission.
- Louis Tussaud's Waxworks, Blackpool – save 25% on admission.
- Yarmouth Stadium – £1.20 off admission.
- Awayadays, Norwich – 50% off tours.
- Langham Glass & Rural Gifts – 20% discount on admission.
- East Anglian Railway Museum, Colchester – free tea or coffee.
- Barleylands Farm, Billericay – 50% discount on admission.
- Redwings Visitor Centre, Norfolk – 50p off per person.
- Florence Nightingale Museum, London – free admission.
- National Maritime Museum, London – 20% off admission to Elizabeth I exhibition.
- The Old Operating Theatre Museum & Herb Garret, London – Half price admission.
- The Royal Pavilion, Brighton – save 60p on admission.
- Haynes Motor Museum, Somerset – 50% off admission.
- Great Western Maze, Devon – 50% discount on admission.
- The Red Lion Hotel, Devon – 3 night for the price of 2, half board.

Scotland
- Edinburgh Crystal Visitor Centre, Midlothian – half price factory tour.
- Highland Folk Museum, Inverness-shire – 50% discount on admission.
- The Hydroponicum, Ross-shire – half price entry.
- The Royal Yacht Britannia, Edinburgh – 50% discount on admission.
- Scotland's Secret Bunker, Fife – save £2.30 on admission.
- The Tall Ship at Glasgow Harbour – 25% discount on admission.

Wales
- Caldicot Castle & Country Park, Caldicot – half price entry.
- Home Front Experience, Llandudno – 20% discount on admission.
- Llandudno Ski & Snowboard Centre – 10% off ski & coffee mornings.
- Rhondda Heritage Park, Rhondda Cynon Taff – 20% off underground tour.

> **Page 55 of Centrica**

Corporate Governance

The group is committed to high standards of corporate governance.

We recognise that creating sustainable shareholder value depends on a full understanding of our impact on society and the responsible management of our business in a manner consistent with our values and principles.

We understand how the behaviour of our organisation can impact on the wider society and we are working hard to earn the trust of all our stakeholders as a company that tries to live up to its responsibilities.

At the pinnacle of governance in its formal sense is the board of directors with its terms of reference, regular meetings and adherence to the Combined Code. Reporting to the board are several committees with particular responsibilities relating to governance and control, as well as the management of company operations. A head office business assurance function regulates the process of internal control throughout the group.

Strategies have also been developed to motivate the way we approach our relationships with customers and shareholders, both existing and potential. Another strategy points the way in our relations with government and public institutions in the jurisdictions in which we operate.

Customer Relations

We are committed to ensuring all our customers receive the best possible service. However, we recognise that on occasions, some of our customers experience problems.

We recognise that complaints are a valuable form of feedback on our service delivery. We therefore use this direct feedback to identify the root causes of complaints and ensure that improvements are made to our processes for the long term.

Through regular dialogue with our customers we understand what the important factors are when dealing with organisations.

These are:

- We will listen to, understand and care about why you are dissatisfied.

- We will endeavour to resolve your problem at the first point of contact that you make with us.

- We will take ownership of your complaint to ensure resolution.

- We will offer fair solutions quickly.

It is our aim to continually improve our service delivery to develop long-term and loyal relationships with all customers in all our businesses.

Information correct as at 16.06.2003

> **Page 56 of Centrica**

Customer Diversity

We operate in an increasingly diverse community, not just of work colleagues, but of customers and suppliers. Centrica rightly prides itself on the highest standards of customer service across the different brands. At the heart of our service ethic is a commitment to treat all our customers both fairly and equally, regardless of their race, gender, age, religion, disability, marital status, sexuality, background or beliefs.

However, treating people equally isn't about treating people all the same. It's about understanding that different people have different needs and responding to those needs. Recognising and valuing customer diversity will help us to deliver truly world class services that are accessible to everyone, which in turn, will ensure that we retain their custom in the future. Its about fairness and equality, but it also makes good business sense.

The Disability Discrimination Act sets out a number of requirements for companies, which we support and are working to the spirit of the legislation. We are currently building on our existing strengths in looking to meet the needs of all of our customers, which includes the Energy Care Register, the Password scheme, the provision of information in alternative, accessible formats, and the provision of a language translation service.

We are constantly reviewing the services that we deliver and invite comments and suggestions from our customers to help us in doing this.

Source: Centrica

> **Page 57 of Centrica**

Gas Mark Nine: The energy chief who's turning up the heat on his electricity rivals

BUSINESS PROFILE Centrica's heir apparent still only half way through the transformation of British Gas

BY MICHAEL HARRISON BUSINESS EDITOR
The Independent – United Kingdom; Jun 09, 2003

MARK CLARE is digesting the results of a customer satisfaction survey showing that his company is the worst in the country at handling complaints. Not surprisingly, the Managing Director of British Gas is keen to accentuate the positive and he points to another of the survey's findings which shows that, on a different measure, it ranks seventh best in terms of looking after its customers.

"It is a bit like those surveys which used to vote Boy George the best dressed man in Britain and the worst dressed man. But the straight answer is that even if we are seventh best that is nowhere near good enough," he says. "We have done a hell of a lot to lift the performance of the business but the reality is there is a lot still to do. We are only half way through the transformation of British Gas."

Mr Clare reckons it will take another two years to complete the job by which time, if everything goes according to plan, he should be slipping neatly into the shoes of Sir Roy Gardner, the football-mad chief executive of British Gas's parent company, Centrica. Mr Clare, a closet Leeds United supporter in his earlier days, was appointed Deputy Chief Executive of Centrica and heir apparent two and a half years ago and he does not disguise his ambition to take over the top job when the time is right.

He has even adopted the footballing metaphors of Sir Roy (who chairs Manchester United when not running Centrica) and converted his wife and children into Reds fans. "We are the best energy provider in the country. But I don't think we would claim to be in the Premiership overall in terms of delivering customer service, unlike the best retailers and financial service providers – Tesco and First Direct – who lead the way," he said.

The AA, for instance, which Centrica bought four years ago, remains a "substantially stronger brand than British Gas", Mr Clare says. "It is a step above us in terms of the service it provides so that means there is a lot of learning going on to understand how we can drive up the performance of British Gas."

The son of carpenter who left school at 17, Mr Clare skipped university and instead became a trainee accountant with GEC. He joined British Gas in 1994 at a time when it truly was the most-hated company in the land, pilloried for its poor service and a byword for the worst kind of snouts-in-the-trough corporate greed.

Had he not opted for bean counting, then he might have ended up as as a computer boffin or perhaps an engineer. "I enjoy taking things apart and putting them back together again. In my youth I really loved to mess around with computers so I guess if I hadn't gone down the accountancy route I would have probably gone down the technical, engineering route."

Page 58 of Centrica

He drives a BMW 7 series – not because it is the height of executive car fashion but because it is "the most modern, best-engineered piece of kit out there today".

Mr Clare loves to take things apart so much that he recently spent a day at one of British Gas's three training centres dismantling and reassembling condensing boilers. It is now a standard part of all executive induction training. Not content with that, Mr Clare also dons his blue overalls and accompanies service engineers on home visits or spends an afternoon listening in to the traffic at one of the company's call centres.

"If we go out dressed as engineers or apprentices then we are going to understand a lot more about what our employees do. It's all about changing the culture of the organisation so that we are much much more focused on the customer," he said. The prize is a large one. British Gas has 16 million customers but 24 million "product relationships" as it likes to call them. Apart from gas and electricity it now sells householders everything from telephone and plumbing services, to appliance repairs, home security and personal loans and could soon be venturing into the mortgage equity release market and roof repairs.

In short, Mr Clare says, if British Gas gets it right then it will be by far the biggest engine of growth for Centrica in the years ahead. The size of the "British Gas machine", as he calls it, is daunting: 26,000 staff, five giant call centres with 9,000 operatives, 6,000 gas engineers and 5,000 more in the process of being recruited.

With that sort of firepower, Mr Clare reckons British Gas can be a fearsome competitor in any market it chooses to target. But he is in no hurry to diversify even further. "To be honest, we are constrained by resources hence the recruitment drive. There is no problem with electricians but there is such a shortage of gas engineers that we are having to bring people in and train them from scratch."

As for British Gas's core business of selling gas and electricity, it is really now a question of hunkering down and hanging on to the customers it has got. The energy market, Mr Clare says, has changed radically in the last two years as the rate of customer "churn" slows dramatically and suppliers concentrate on adding value rather than volume.

Even though British Gas is still adding customers at a net rate of 5,000 to 10,000 a week, it employs only half the doorstep sales staff it did two years ago.

"We are putting a lot of our investment into retention where we get a much bigger return because it costs far less to retain a customer than to acquire one," Mr Clare said. "Now we look at what customers we want to acquire and where we have existing relationships with customers, how to extend them rather than just trying to sign up the next person who walks through the shopping centre."

Telecoms – a market where British Gas only has 400,000 direct customers – is an obvious area for adding more business. But Mr Clare, more than anyone, knows how tough it is trying to dance with an elephant in the shape of the dominant player, in this case BT. "Clearly there is a big opportunity for growth but we have got to be sure the economics work," Mr Clare said. "I know Carphone Warehouse and Tesco are piling in but the issue is whether we have really got the right ingredients for a competitive market or whether the playing field is still slanted towards the incumbent."

Page 59 of Centrica

Mr Clare works hard, but his wife makes certain that he always takes his five weeks holiday a year, preferably as far away from the UK as possible. The last time he took a break in Europe, it turned into the "holiday from hell" after he was called back to negotiate a deal. This summer the family are going to Australia.

Centrica is about more than just British Gas. As well as the AA and the financial services group Goldfish (whose future is less certain), it also encompasses the fourth biggest energy-supply business in North America and, back home, big upstream and trading operations. But the blue flame of British Gas is at its heart and Mr Clare knows that the brighter it burns, the closer he gets to the chief executive's office.

"People around me have always said I am very ambitious which I am," he admits. "But Roy has a lot of energy and a lot of vigour and I don't see him slowing down at all, if anything he pushes to go faster. The way I look at it is to focus on the job in hand and do it as well as I possibly can until the next opportunity comes along."

MARK CLARE: THE FLAME OF LIFE

Position: Managing director of British Gas and deputy chief executive of Centrica.

Age: 45.

Pay: £626,000.

Career: GEC Marconi, STC, British Gas (joined 1994 as group financial controller).

Hobbies: Playing tennis, watching sport – particularly football and motor racing.

Family: Wife is a teacher, three children. Son aged 19 and two daughters aged 17 and 7.

Happiest moment: "When my wife announced there was a third on the way. At first I thought 'Oh my God', but my youngest is absolutely wonderful. She gives me a completely new outlook on life."

Page 60 of Centrica

Winter 2002 — Cause Related Marketing / Critical Marketing

More than company conscience

Simon Waugh, Centrica's group marketing director, explains why cause related marketing works.

Cause related marketing can be a thorny issue and it has generated various comments over the years from some sceptical quarters. People have been quick to question the benefit delivered for charities, while arguing that it provides a public conscience and some much appreciated coverage for businesses.

However, charities and causes have been keen to develop such partnerships and are increasingly benefiting by linking together with businesses – their employees, brands and infrastructure – to raise awareness and gain a positive impact on those social issues they are working to improve.

At Centrica, we have certainly been convinced of the real benefits cause related marketing can deliver, not only on the business front but also in terms of employee satisfaction, customer expectation and the communities in which we operate.

Making it relevant

Although Centrica had always maintained a strong community programme that included charitable donations, sponsorship and employee participation, it was often ad hoc, fragmented and bore no relation to our business. This piecemeal approach meant it was difficult to effectively measure delivery and therefore to justify the spend.

While the company was committed to addressing wider social issues, customer research had shown awareness of individual initiatives to be low. The vast majority of our customer base knew very little about our community support. Although we were involved with numerous regional projects, there was a growing awareness that we should develop bigger and more impactful social marketing campaigns. With this in mind, in 1999 our British Gas brand entered into a partnership with Help the Aged and Centrica's involvement with cause related marketing began.

British Gas is one of the most recognised brands in the UK and delivers over 20 million essential products and services to the homes of one-third of the population. Therefore, there is an expectation that British Gas, with its associated brand values, should be taking a lead on those social issues that are relevant to our business, employees and customers.

Increased communication and greater social impact were vital issues at a time of unprecedented market competition. Having lost our monopoly position in the gas market and faced with having to compete in new markets, British Gas recognised that it needed more than just products and services. In order to meet the expectations of existing customers and attract new ones, a wider strategy was needed that would show how we were working to deliver benefits to communities and individuals across the UK.

To choose the appropriate cause, we consulted employees, customers and stakeholders, who left us in no doubt as to the social issue British Gas should support. People felt the company should use its business expertise in addressing the issue of keeping older people warm in winter. It was something that touched the hearts of people of all ages and one we knew would be supported by our diverse customer base.

Vital, varied support

Annual figures highlight that the deaths of around 30,000 older people in the UK each year can be directly attributed to cold-related illnesses – a quite staggering figure in a civilised society. With Help the Aged, we pooled individual areas of expertise in order to develop practical and innovative initiatives to tackle the problems facing vulnerable older people. Through a combination of direct and in-kind support, employee fundraising and customer donations, British Gas has, to date, provided more than £4 million of support, enabling a range of initiatives to be delivered to 1.3 million beneficiaries.

Activities are varied but range from providing energy efficiency measures, supporting initiatives to reduce isolation, as well as safety and security programmes to make older people feel safer in their own homes. The Partnership has also raised national awareness of the excess winter deaths issue and delivered a combination of traditional sponsorship activity and new, innovative fundraising ideas.

A regional delivery structure has been developed for many local projects. The combination of British Gas national communication channels and its regional physical presence has delivered national awareness and local solutions which would not previously have been possible.

British Gas perceives cause related marketing as a strategic yet responsible way to address both relevant social issues and business marketing objectives. The benefits have included positive impact on brand equity, positive development of the brand as socially responsible, greater engagement and enthusiasm of employees and enhanced relationships with customers, government, regulators and opinion-formers.

The cause related marketing initiative has complemented, not replaced, ongoing community programmes. The British Gas-Help the Aged Partnership has successfully addressed the fundamental issues of fuel-poverty and isolation. And this year the Partnership won the Cause Related Marketing Award at the Business in the Community Awards for Excellence.

I hope you find this publication informative, and thought provoking. A carefully planned cause related marketing programme can deliver huge benefits. I hope our experiences will inspire you to consider cause related marketing as part of your marketing mix.

Source: Critical Marketing Knowledge from CIM : Cause Related Marketing, Winter 2002

Page 61 of Centrica

Critical Marketing | Cause Related Marketing — Winter 2002

Case Study: British Gas

Older and warmer

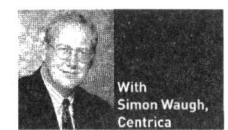

At a time of unprecedented competition, British Gas distinguished itself by taking up a cause that was popular with its customers.

With Simon Waugh, Centrica

The deaths of 30,000 older people in the UK each year can be directly attributed to cold-related illnesses. In January 1999, British Gas (a Centrica brand) and Help the Aged joined forces to form a cause related marketing partnership to address this issue.

When the Partnership was established, a mutually agreed business plan was produced. This planning process is repeated each year and culminates in the development of a contractually agreed Partnership Plan – a working document with detailed business plans, objectives and targets for individual campaigns and activities.

The Partnership pools individual areas of expertise to develop dynamic and innovative initiatives that tackle key issues facing vulnerable older people. Through a combination of direct funding and in-kind support, British Gas has provided £4.3 million to Help the Aged.

British Gas perceives cause related marketing as a strategic yet responsible way to directly increase sales. The company looked at a number of cause related marketing programmes in the retail and FMCG sectors. It was soon apparent that the sales patterns and consumer purchase behaviour for its products and services differed significantly from FMCG companies. This led British Gas to focus on delivering wider business benefits, including:

- consistent year-on-year positive impact on brand equity;
- positive development of the brand as socially responsible;
- substantial positive media coverage;
- engagement and enthusiasm of employees reflected in improved staff morale, motivation and teamwork – 98% awareness and 50% participation;
- positive relationships with government, regulators and opinion formers, positioning British Gas as a company that far exceeds legislative and regulatory obligations.

Fuel poverty and isolation remain fundamental issues that the Partnership works to address, but the nature and scope of the project has evolved during the past three years. The Partnership now takes a much more diverse view of the issues that affect older people and develops campaigns and initiatives to make a difference.

In addition to £4.3 million of support, British Gas has leveraged the power of its brand, the strength of its marketing and communications and the expertise of its employees to make the Partnership a success. Its public relations teams across Britain work with Help the Aged to maximise coverage of Partnership activities in national and regional print and broadcast media.

In 1999, the Partnership launched a national advertising campaign on TV, radio, and in the national press. It has also used national press inserts, national bill messages, poster campaigns, leaflets and door-drops to raise awareness of the Partnership's activities.

Additionally, media partnerships with national newspapers and support from celebrities have been used to promote campaigns such as 'Warm Hearts Week' and 'Alone at Christmas'.

Activities based on the objectives and targets set out in the Partnership Plan are monitored and evaluated by Help the Aged and reported back to British Gas. For major campaigns, Help the Aged produces a detailed analysis of all aspects of the activity. This enables both organisations to fully understand the successes and failures and use the information in future campaigns.

British Gas also continually measures the business benefits of working with Help the Aged against the established objectives through a number of means, including MORI's evaluation of the British Gas corporate image; Employee Satisfaction Surveys and British Gas-commissioned research into customer acquisition and retention rates. Research also shows that the Partnership has sustained a positive public perception of British Gas. Results of a recent MORI survey revealed that almost 57% of people who are aware of the Partnership feel better about British Gas.

"British Gas has sought to address the issue of fuel poverty and excess winter deaths through a holistic partnership that combines the skills of one of Britain's leading charities with British Gas funding, expertise and stakeholder support," says Simon Waugh, Centrica group director of marketing. "Our work with Help the Aged has realised positive community impact and commercial benefits."

Key facts

- To date, there have been more than 1.3 million beneficiaries of Partnership activities, tackling isolation, mobility and the need for advice and information.
- British Gas has provided funding and in-kind support of more than £4.3 million, enabling Help the Aged to provide a range of national services and deliver local projects improving the quality of older people's lives.
- British Gas employees have raised more than £270,000 for Help the Aged.
- More than £1 million has been raised through customer fundraising. 'Warming Words', the Scottish Gas Communications cause related marketing campaign, generated £13,500 for Help the Aged.
- In March 2002, British Gas supported the launch of the Help the Aged Age Discrimination Campaign. This successful campaign addressed an issue outside the traditional areas of fuel poverty and isolation.
- Since 1999, the partnership has been lobbying against excess winter deaths and the issue of fuel poverty. During this time, winter fuel payments have risen from £20 to £200 and the Government's energy efficiency maximum grant has risen from £700 to £2,000.

Source: Centrica

The Chartered Institute of Marketing — centrica

Source: Critical Marketing Knowledge from CIM : Cause Related Marketing, Winter 2002

Rough Ruling and Goldfish Sales Boost Centrica

By Stephen Foley
The Independent – United Kingdom; Aug 02, 2003

CENTRICA, THE conglomerate which owns British Gas, received a double boost yesterday after selling its loss-making credit card business, Goldfish, for £112 million and gaining conditional approval for its acquisition of the Rough gas storage facility.

Patricia Hewitt, Secretary of State at the Department of Trade and Industry, demanded that Centrica agree to stringent controls on how it can use the Rough facility, off the Humberside coast. Rough accounts for 85 per cent of the UK's gas storage capacity and sells gas to retailers including British Gas and its rivals.

But Ms Hewitt rejected the views of the industry regulator, Ofgem, and many of British Gas's rivals, who had argued ownership of Rough would allow Centrica to influence gas prices and manipulate the market, and who had wanted the deal blocked outright.

Centrica agreed to buy Rough and and Easington onshore terminal on the each coast of Dynegy, the US energy company, for pounds 304m.

Sir Roy Gardner, Chief Executive, welcomed the decision. "We have always believed that appropriate undertakings could be agreed to overcome any competition concerns. We are comfortable with the remedies recommended."

The conditions recommended by the Competition Commission and agreed by Mrs Hewitt include selling Rough's full capacity on non-discriminatory terms, some of it at fixed prices. Centrica must also reserve no more than 20 per cent of the capacity for British Gas, and face annual checks by the Office of Fair Trading (OFT) and Ofgem.

The company could still be forced to sell Rough or other assets if it has not formally agreed the conditions with OFT by 1 December.

Centrica shares rose 4.25p to 181.5p, one of the best performances in the FTSE 100. Earlier in the day, it had revealed the £112.5million sales of its 70 per cent interest in Goldfish to Lloyds TSB, which owned the other 30 per cent. Centrica will book a £45million loss on the credit card venture, which was in the red to the tune of £30million in the six months to 30 June.

The Goldfish credit card and its associated loyalty scheme were originally developed as a customer retention initiative within the group's energy supply business. Cardholders will still be able to redeem loyalty points against British Gas bills.

Sir Roy said: "Goldfish has developed into a very strong brand but we believe that the capital investment required to achieve the necessary scale would be better directed towards our core businesses."

Lloyds TSB said the administration of Goldfish would be subsumed within its own back office, but would not say how many of Goldfish's 400 staff would be made redundant.

Page 63 of Centrica

Recent Centrica news
30 September 2003

Sale of Goldfish credit card and personal loan businesses completed

Centrica plc today confirmed that Goldfish Bank Ltd has completed the sale to Lloyds TSB of the Goldfish credit card, personal loan business and associated business assets for a premium of £112.5million, as announced on 1 August.

Rivals seek to loosen BT's grip on broadband
By Chris Nuttall, IT Correspondent
FT.com site; Nov 20, 2003

Creating a competitive broadband market in Britain would cut government borrowing by £13billion and add £22billion to Gross Domestic Product (GDP) by 2015, according to a report commissioned by a new industry pressure group.

The Broadband Industry Group (BIG), made up of network and Internet service providers (ISPs) Brightview, Cable & Wireless, Centrica, Energis, Freeserve and Tiscali, said the UK risked being left behind if regulators did not act to loosen BT's hold on the wholesale market.

"BT has a 97 per cent market share, in effect we have one supplier and one product and no competition means no innovation," said John Pluthero, Energis Chief Executive, at the group's launch.

"We have 3 per cent broadband penetration, one of the lowest of the G7 countries and one of the highest prices. We are pissing away our competitive edge and that annoys me."

Mary Turner, Tiscali UK Chief Executive, said broadband was now available to 80 per cent of the population but high prices were the barrier to its widescale adoption.

The group produced figures from what it said was the first proper study of the economic effects of broadband, commissioned from the Centre for Economics and Business Research (CEBR).

The study suggested that regulatory changes to encourage competition would lead to productivity rising by 2.5 per cent by 2015 - equivalent to everyone in the UK working an hour extra every week.

As well as GDP and government borrowing improvements, fixed investment would be up by £8billion and net exports £11billion higher.

"We predict that, over the next 20 years, broadband will have a similar impact on the economy to that of the introduction of electricity from 1890 to 1920," said Douglas McWilliams, CEBR Chief Executive.

BIG said its objectives included achieving better levels of service and the introduction of pricing tied to the true cost of BT providing wholesale DSL (Digital Subscriber Line) broadband services.

Part C: Practice cases

Page 64 of Centrica

Mr Pluthero denied BIG was trying to bash BT and said it was welcome to join the group, but he did not expect this.

Jan Dawson, a senior analyst at the Ovum consultancy, said BIG was unlikely to succeed in lowering prices at this stage, though its intentions were clear.

"This consortium of alternative operators and ISPs is pledged to increasing competition in the UK broadband market. For which, read: getting a better deal from BT on its wholesale service," he said.

Find this article at:
http://search.ft.com/s03/search/article.html?id=031120003617

Page 65 of Centrica

Centrica to develop £100million wind farm
The Independent - United Kingdom;
Sep 13, 2003

CENTRICA, the British Gas to AA road services group, is to join forces with two Scandinavian companies to develop a £100million wind farm off the coast of Barrow. Centrica will have a 25 per cent stake in the 30-turbine wind farm, which will generate 320GWh of power a year. The remaining shares will be owned by the Danish energy group Dong and the Norwegian power company Statkraft.

Find this article at:
http://search.ft.com/s03/search/article.html?id=030913000186

Page 66 of Centrica

CENTRICA (CNA)
Investors Chronicle - United Kingdom;
Sep 05, 2003

178p - Energy supply and motorists' services

This year has seen a strategic shift at Centrica, the British Gas to AA motorists' services group. It has moved away from relentless expansion, and refocused on its strengths: supplying energy and helping motorists. It has sold its financial services business, Goldfish, abandoned its target of 10milion electricity customers in the US, stepped up its cost-cutting, and announced plans to increase its dividends to 40 per cent of earnings over the next few years.

The new approach should mean Centrica generates more cash, which will help it pay its rising dividend. It has already increased its first-half payout 21 per cent to 1.7p, and City analysts expect a 25 per cent increase in the full-year dividend to 4.9p.

A key part of Centrica's refocus is investment in a so-called 'customer relationship management' software system at British Gas. The £350million investment should help to stem customer losses, and improve cross-selling opportunities. Although Centrica lost 78,000 gas supply customers in the first half of 2003, this figure was lower than the same period in 2002, and it increased its domestic electricity customer base by 247,000. It now has 6million residential customers in the UK, or a 24 per cent market share. Management hopes that getting more out of its customers will boost profit margins from 4.2 per cent in 2002 to 8 per cent by 2005.

Centrica also plans to upgrade the IT system at the AA. The AA has already boosted sales by cross-selling insurance, finance and legal services products to its 13.2million auto members. But just 20 per cent of them buy more than one financial services product. The upgrade will allow cross-referencing of AA's auto and financial services customers with British Gas customers in an effort to grow the number of products sold.

The telecoms operation, One.Tel, which Centrica acquired for £58million in 2001, will return to profit this year. It moved from an operating profit of £5million in 2001 to a £4million loss in 2002 due to the cost of acquiring new customers after the launch of broadband and mobile services last year. It now has 1million customers, although it will fail to achieve its aim of capturing 10 per cent of the residential telecoms market (around 2.5million customers) by the end of 2003. Although One.Tel seems to have turned the corner, it does not fit well with Centrica's core energy retailing and mass-market maintenances services, and may yet be sold.

Elsewhere, Centrica has yet to resolve the terms of its £300million acquisition of the massive Rough gas storage facility in the North Sea. The competition authorities insist that it opens the store to competitors, and may yet force a solution on Centrica.

Page 67 of Centrica

But worries that increasing wholesale electricity costs will hit Centrica's profits may be overdone. It sources 20-25 per cent of its energy needs from its own power stations, and uses the futures markets to fix other electricity costs. In addition, in early August, it announced plans to spend £500million generating green energy, mainly from offshore wind farms. It intends to provide 1,000MW (or 5 per cent of the company's electricity sales) of renewable energy by 2010. The move should take advantage of some attractive opportunities open to energy retailers under the UK's Renewable Obligation Certificate Requirements. These call for 10 per cent of the UK's electricity supplies to come from renewables by 2010.

Centrica's shares currently trade at 13 times this year's forecast earnings. That's below the market's average, which looks odd given the group's success and the pace at which dividends are likely to grow. Buy.

Page 68 of Centrica

COMPANIES UK: Centrica's £500m for green power
By Andrew Taylor,
Utilities Correspondent, Financial Times;
Aug 01, 2003

Centrica, Britain's biggest household gas and electricity supplier, plans to spend £500million on generating its own green energy, mostly from offshore wind farms, announced Sir Roy Gardner, Chief Executive, yesterday.

The company intends to build 1,000MW of renewable energy generation by 2010, enough to power a city the size of Birmingham, and provide 5 per cent of Centrica's electricity sales, said Sir Roy.

Centrica's is expected to pay for about half the £1billion cost of the development with the other half coming from joint venture partners.

The investment was announced as Centrica reported a 6 per cent rise in pre-tax profits to £576million (£542million) during the six months to the end of June on turnover of £6.22billion (£5.18billion).

The company, which made a long-term commitment to lift dividend payments to 40 per cent of earnings, increased its interim pay-out by 21 per cent to 1.7p.

Earnings per share rose to 9.2p (8.4p).

Patricia Hewitt, Trade and Industry Secretary, said the investment would help meet the government's target of generating 10 per cent of Britain's electricity from renewable energy by 2010.

Operating profits before exceptional items and goodwill rose by 11 per cent to £694million. Profits from household electricity and gas sales rose by 18 per cent to £169million after deducting a one-off gas transmission rebate of £54million which inflated last year's corresponding first-half profits to £197million.

A net loss of 78,000 gas customers was offset by a gain of 247,000 electricity customers. Sir Roy said the company retained 63 per cent of the household gas market and 24 per cent of the electricity market.

Profits at homes services from central heating, plumbing and servicing of household electrical appliances increased from £22million to £41million. The group wants to double the number of home service engineers by 2006.

However, Sir Roy said increased losses at Goldfish Bank of £30million (£17million) were disappointing. The bank has been given until the end of year to become cash positive or be sold. "If it doesn't create value, then we'll do something," said Sir Roy.

Telecommunications more than halved its losses to £10million (£26million).

Centrica plans to spend £350million over the next five years on generation and gas supplies to hedge its growing North American retail business.

The group's share price eased 2p to 177½p.

Page 69 of Centrica

Find this article at:
http://search.ft.com/s03/search/article.html?id=030801000535

Part C: Practice cases

2 Guidance Notes for Centrica

2.1 You should, by now, have read the June 2004 examination Case Study – Centrica Plc. You are probably wondering where to start and how you are going to cope with the necessary analysis. You might even already be wondering about the possible question areas – try not to – you need to complete the analysis first. Remember that you are not alone – even the most able and well prepared students share these same anxieties when faced with a new case.

2.2 These guidance notes are to help you **before** you do any analysis. They will provide you with a framework for getting started on the challenge of creating a strategy for Centrica.

2.3 This is quite a weighty Case Study and you are not short of data and information. You have access to pages from the 2003 Annual report to plough through – but do not be put off. Identify the key messages and data – remember up to 80% of case study material is padding and of no real value. One of the management skills CIM want to assess is your ability to identify and manage key data.

2.4 As you will see the Case is about a corporate company rather than a business unit and your focus is clearly more strategic than it has necessarily been in the past. Because the headline focus is very much on strategic marketing you can expect to be advising on which services Centrica should be delivering to which markets not just the operational marketing challenges of how British Gas could achieve market penetration or open up new markets like Broadband. Regulation of the energy markets globally is in a state of transition creating opportunities and threats for Centrica. Non household gas and electricity markets are to open up in 2004, equating to 60 to 70% of the market by volume. The entire market (EU) is expected to be open to competition by 2006 (Case page 18 and Appendix 2).

2.5 As always, the challenge is to sort out the information from the narrative and clues provided and of course we will need to tackle the financial data provided – always a particular challenge for marketers.

3 About Centrica

3.1 The Case is about a multinational, service business – created by the privatisation of British Gas and the deregulation of the energy markets. Essentially this is a high volume, low margin business. Operating profit as a percentage of turnover was 6.5% in 2002 (see the Case page 7).

3.2 Over the years the business has moved around the supply chain. They are involved in production, storage and distribution of energy as well as a diverse range of services related to the home – including the AA with its car breakdown services. You may need to question whether the decisions made at the EU summit in Barcelona which agreed on separation of transmission and distribution from production and supply might have implications for the range of energy related activities Centrica is involved with currently (Case page 18). This is highlighted by the ongoing doubt about the £300 million acquisition of the massive Rough gas storage facility in the North Sea and the potential views and actions of the competition authorities (Case page 66 – final paragraph).

3.3 Despite the diversification within the portfolio, when you look at the operating profits generated (Case page 7) you will see this is still essentially an energy business, with 79% of operating profits generated by UK energy supply and a further 14% from the North American and European activities which are mainly energy related. This is still predominantly a UK based energy business which aspires to be a global home related services business. Margins are low.

3.4 Diversification has not, it seems, been an easy option for Centrica and they have recently sold the Goldfish credit card – a loss making venture into financial services. Goldfish was based on an organic growth strategy whereas much of the organisation's other expansion has been by acquisition. This may lead you to ask about their competencies to grow brands and profitable business from scratch.

3.5 By 2004 Centrica still has a complex portfolio of services and activities. It is not immediately clear what their focus, vision or mission are and this is something you will need to work on.

3.6 The business is described as a 'customer hub' by Deutsche Bank (Case page 8) 'offering a range of utility *services to the home.*' What is less clear is how Centrica benefits those customers. The company operates in both consumer and business to business markets, offering services which are often seen as commodities. You will need to consider how a differentiator could be developed and how to add value to customers, both residential and corporate and what role the brand may play in this. You may wonder if a contemporary issue like corporate social responsibility could be developed into a genuine and believable differentiator. Centrica is a corporate umbrella brand and is relatively new and still not as well known as the individual portfolio brands of the AA, Halfords or British Gas in the UK or Energy America and Direct Energy overseas.

3.7 You are almost certainly an experienced customer of energy, telephony and breakdown services – you may even be a Centrica customer, so you should have a real 'sense' of these markets and should have no problem in understanding the buyer behaviour issues. Have you, for example, been considering a switch to broadband services or been tempted to switch energy supplier because of an attractive price offer; how do you feel about a single supplier for gas and electricity?

Tutor note – B2B & B2C markets

3.8 B2B & B2C markets are covered by Centrica – and the needs of these two groups are likely to be significantly different as will be the marketing approach. If you are not familiar with or confident about these differences you need to do some background revision. Kotler is good on market classifications. Remember complexity of the DMU and DMP is different and the use of push and pull strategies will be varied across these sectors.

3.9 This Case is strongly based on the UK activities, particularly British Gas but we need to take care not to ignore the other dimensions of the portfolio or the international dimensions:

(a) The North American investment has been significant (Case pages 44 & 45) and this base will need to be built upon with strong marketing to ensure it delivers an adequate return on investment. As already indicated these investments generated 14% of operating profits, £133m of the total £932m recorded in 2002. (Case page 7)

(b) Centrica have global ambitions and wish to be more international, possibly further development in Europe – they already have a joint venture in Belgium where the energy market is being deregulated operating through the Luminus brand. (Case page 5).

Part C: Practice cases

Tutor note – Horizontal and vertical planning

3.10 Before you get started on the detail of this Case Study it might be helpful for you to take a few moments to remind yourself about the distinction between horizontal and vertical planning. Recent case studies have tended to be focused on the business planning of a specific strategic business unit within an organisation – vertical planning. This Case study, Centrica Plc, is concerned with **corporate planning**, that is the allocation of resources and the development of strategies across a number of strategic business units – this is horizontal planning. How horizontal and vertical planning fit together can be seen in the following diagram.

Horizontal and vertical planning

Horizontal planning and management →

Vertical planning and management ↓

- Business Unit British Gas
- Business Unit The AA
- Business Unit Direct Energy

Business strategy (which products and markets)
↓
Operational level plans

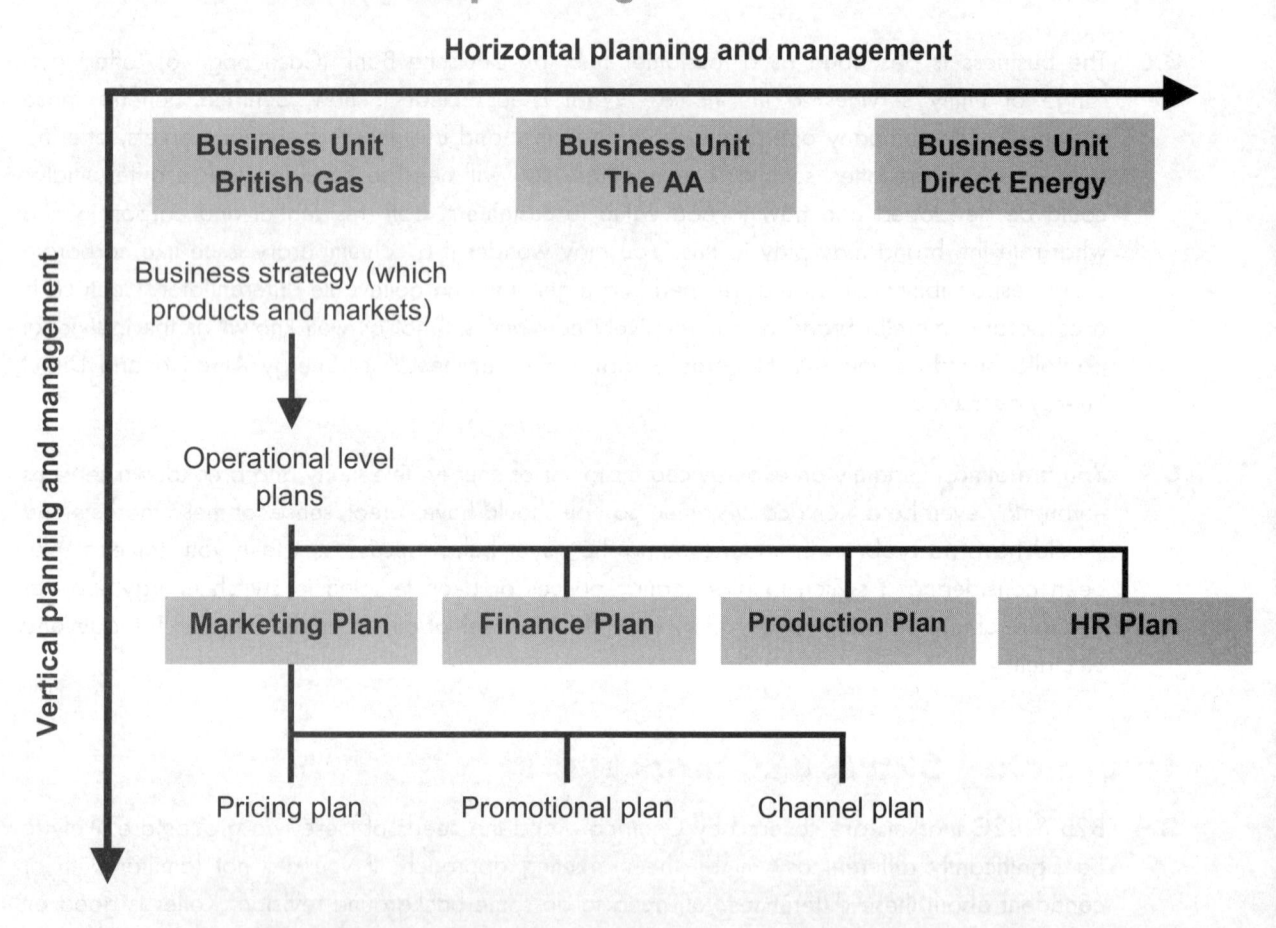

- Marketing Plan
- Finance Plan
- Production Plan
- HR Plan

From Marketing Plan:
- Pricing plan
- Promotional plan
- Channel plan

3.11 Terminology is always a problem for marketers and it is important that you pay particular attention to the Examiner's questions and clearly define terms which you feel may be ambiguous or open to alternative interpretations. Be clear about where the focus of a question is, it could be on Centrica or possibly one of the business units. You will need to be prepared for both eventualities.

(a) Business strategy for Centrica (sometimes referred to as strategic marketing) would involve the decisions about which products/services should be developed for which markets. For example, the decision to sell Goldfish or to expand into other parts of the EU, to set up more wind farms or expand roadside services into Europe.

(b) Marketing strategy for Centrica could involve us in decisions about how to increase cross sell, build the Centrica brand or increase penetration of the domestic utilities market within the UK.

(c) Strategic marketing planning for a business unit, for example British Gas, involves decisions about products and markets within that business unit. For example, should they provide servicing for all gas appliances or go back into retail sales.

(d) Operational marketing planning at strategic business unit level would be focused on how that part of the organisation can achieve an agreed strategy. For example, the segmentation and positioning which would allow the AA to increase its share of the breakdown market (market penetration) or the marketing strategy needed to win a share of the emerging new market for broadband services domestically (product development).

Remember: many of the models and frameworks like BCG or Porter's Generic Strategies are used for SBU analysis and will be little help analysing at Centrica level.

4 Overview analysis comments

Use these notes to help you review your own overview

4.1 The utilities sector is highly complex and has been subject to significant changes in the macro environment over recent years. In particular, deregulation which has been a feature of many international markets as well as the UK and has ended the actual monopolies that companies like British Gas once enjoyed. Again, let me draw to your attention the fact that the non-household gas and electric markets are to open in 2004 and these represent some 60 to 70% of the market by volume (Case page 18).

4.2 The industry has also suffered from poor publicity about corporate governance following Enron and more recently the overstating of oil reserves by Shell and this means that any aspect of stakeholder communication could be important to maintaining the value of **trust** explicit in the Centrica brand (Case page 6).

4.3 Terrorism, war in the Middle East and depletion of oil reserves in areas like the North Sea will continue to impact on the supply side of the power industry. Government intervention can be seen in the target of 10% sustainable energy which has prompted Centrica to become a joint venture partner in a £100m investments in a wind farm in the Irish Sea (Case page 65) and the competition commission investigation into the company's ownership of Rough, a gas storage facility.

4.4 Centrica's current business is focused on the production and distribution of a range of services, many of which are commoditised utilities including gas, electricity and telecoms. Growth through acquisition has helped the company diversify away from the now deregulated and competitive market for gas but you may have concerns about the synergy of products like those offered by the AA, travel companies and questions about the competence and capabilities of the company in areas of organic growth such as financial services.

Defining the market

4.5 One of the problems with any Case Study is determining precisely the market space we need to be concerned with. There are a number of dimensions to this:

- Geography
- Segment/sector
- Classification/position
- Current/future.

4.6 When we start to focus more specifically we find the market space better defined and therefore the value of Case data and information clearer. In a sense, we are answering two questions:

- What market(s) is Centrica in today?
- What market(s) might they be in tomorrow?

	Today	**Tomorrow**
By geography:	■ UK ■ North America ■ Belgium ■ Limited European	■ European ■ N. American ■ **Global ?**

By segment/sector:	■ Utilities
	   - gas
	   - electric 80% ....
	   - telecoms
	■ Car related services
	■ Travel services
	■ Appliance servicing
	■ Insurance 20%
		■ Utilities
		   - gas
		   - electric
		   - telecoms?
		   - **broadband ?**
		■ Car related services ?
		■ Appliance servicing
		■ Insurance ?
		■ **Other home related services?**

By classification:	■ Production
	■ Storage
	■ Distribution :
	   - business 2 business
	   - business 2 consumer
		■ Production
		■ Storage
		■ Distribution:
		   - business 2 business
		   - business 2 consumer
		   - ?????

4.7 We are told on page 66 that 2003 saw a strategic shift for Centrica. It has moved away from relentless expansion and refocused on its strengths, supplying energy and helping motorists. (Take care when comparing numbers across the Case study – the figures on page 7 of the Case relate but to 2002, but some of the figures in appendices relate to 2003.)

4.8 A US target of 10 million electricity customers has been abandoned and cost cutting projects in the US stepped up. Customer relationship management is a key plank in their investment strategy intended to deliver two strategic benefits:

- Reduce customer losses ie increase retention
- Improve cross-sell (the graphs on page 48 show how shallow current relationships with clients are but only a small number of British Gas customers hold other products and 50% of all Centrica customers only have one product and only 23% hold more than two products).

19 ♦ A final practice case: Centrica

4.9 The Case summary on page 20 gives you an insight into what might be required in the exam room. 'Given the rapid expansion of Centrica and the various brands under its umbrella, it is now important that the company addresses its raison d'être. This would imply we need to consider a mission statement for Centrica. The expansion into the global market is slowly beginning to pay dividends and the European market is poised for expansion. As the company begins to consolidate its position in the UK market and begins to understand the links between the various businesses, it is now faced with further expansion in the global arena. The question remains as to how the company consolidates its UK market effectively and at the same time devotes enough energy into expanding its presence in international markets. At the same time the company needs to reassure its shareholders that the company can manage the complex portfolio and post good profits. The company has an effective marketing structure that needs to be utilised in other markets'.

Sizing the business

4.10 The core of Centrica is British Gas which has 26,000 staff and is currently recruiting an additional 5000 gas engineers (Case page 58). Notice that qualified gas engineers are currently something of a limiting factor for the business expansion plans and failure to recruit and train enough appropriate staff could have long-term implications for customer service as well as growth.

4.11 Centrica, on the face of things, seems successful. They are growing rapidly and have further growth ambitions. In 2002 profits were £932 million on a turnover of £14,315 million (Case page 7), almost double the 1999 profits of £428 million. Profit as a percentage of turnover has increased steadily from 2.9% in 1998 to 6.5% in 2002. Not a particularly high margin and one could reasonably assume shareholders would like to see it rise further.

4.12 North America represented £133m of the 2002 profit, some 14 %. The table on page 7 of the Case is a useful one and clearly shows the loss making financial services division which depressed profits in 2002 by £40 million. In previous years retail activities were also loss making and have now been closed down but there may be a question mark over telecoms which has so far failed to generate a profit, although the loss in 2002 of £33 million was an improvement over £97 million in 2001.

4.13 The chart on page 8 shows Centrica's share performance compared with the FTSE index which is strong and the Investor's Chronicle on page 67 recommends you to buy shares.

4.14 Working through the operating and financial review provided on pages 30 to 41 you will be able to identify differences in the operating margins and performance across the different business sectors and units with most of the recent growth coming from UK residential gas supply and the business services and home services operations (Case page 39).

4.15 Notice you have customer, revenue and profit numbers allowing you to calculate average spends and values – key information for marketers.

The company culture

4.16 You will find you need to look for clues about the company and its culture. Centrica has its roots as a nationalised industry operating as part of the public sector, it is also strongly based in the UK and may therefore suffer from UK-centric thinking. It would seem from the lack of cross sell

Part C: Practice cases

activity that, to date, the current business units have operated in isolation and work to create a customer hub is being undertaken to tackle this (Case page 18). An investment of almost £500m has been made to achieve this – how should they make it effective?

4.17 We are told in the summary on page 20 that there is an effective marketing structure in place but there is limited by evidence of how this operates. We can identify (Case page 29) that there is a some central marketing under Simon Waugh, as well as a corporate affairs team under Charles Naylor – who will be actively involved in building and maintaining the company profile across a range of stakeholders.

4.18 What is clear is that currently the business is organised around its core activities, gas, communications, energy management etc rather than by customer type; for example, domestic, SME, large business or other energy suppliers etc.

4.19 The interview with Mark Clare the managing director of British Gas (Case page 57) gives some clues about the culture and the effort being made to transform British Gas. Customer service clearly still needs work, although the AA may provide an internal best practice benchmark.

4.20 Your Case review should leave you asking a lot of marketing questions:

- Who decides on positioning and is managing the Centrica brand?

- Is there a vision for changed brand strategy moving forward, replacing the polycentric portfolio of individual brands with a global Centrica family brand?

- Who is analysing market opportunities for Centrica and what criteria for selection is used to ensure new ventures fit into the portfolio effectively?

- Who is responsible for customer research and forecasting? To what extent are the business units exchanging market intelligence and customer and competitor information?

- Who is ensuring integrated communications activities and what plans are there for change when the customer hub becomes available?

- How do the managers responsible for Europe and North America (Case page 29) integrate with the product and service teams?

4.21 We have almost no specific customer data – in terms of demographics or lifestyle profiles. We did know something about the Goldfish client base and by comparing the revenues with customer numbers (Case page 30) you can calculate some average values but otherwise you have little hard data to work with. Is this because the data does not exist? You may have a number of questions about customer loyalty, churn and retention levels in the utilities sector as well as questions about buyer behaviour in the area of broadband.

4.22 Competitor data is also limited although we know there are new entrants in certain sectors; for example Direct Line Rescue competing with AA. You will need to pull together all the snippets of information you can and may well need to work at the corporate level for Centrica as well as at each significant business unit level.

PEST information

4.23 You will find no shortage of environmental data related to the markets Centrica is operating in but again you will find it spread throughout the various narrative and articles. You will need to

19 ♦ A final practice case: Centrica

pull all this together to make sense of the Case and remember that the biggest challenge for international markets is adapting to the differences caused by culture.

5 Your role

5.1 Your role is clear. You are Yasmin Viccars, a marketing consultant appointed by the Board of Centrica. You have had experience in the telecommunications sector and this may represent a clue about the focus for additional information or questions. The strategy for telecommunications is needed and decisions about the broadband opportunities need to be made. Could this strategic priority have influenced the Board's selection of you as a consultant? The material you are working from seems to be your short report on the marketing issues facing the company. (To be presented with pages of its own annual report and a far from coherent summary of the key marketing issues is not impressive.) However, it is important that you work within the 'spirit' of the case process though you may prefer to think about the case content as working documents **from which** you will be developing and presenting a summary of marketing issues and strategic recommendations.

5.2 What is less clear is what you will be expected to answer questions on. There are a number of possibilities.

- A business strategy for Centrica (recommendations re its raison d'être) which will help deliver its financial objectives and goals
- A product market strategy for the business to support the above
- A brand strategy for Centrica
- UK marketing strategy to increase average revenues per customer and cross-sell opportunities
- A strategy for non-household energy
- Relationship marketing based around the customer hub
- A strategy for improved stakeholder management including issues of corporate and social responsibility
- International expansion particularly into Europe in line with the energy markets becoming deregulated.

This seems to be a solid business, generating cash and growth. Managing that growth going forward is likely to be a focus for us.

Exam Tip

- Do not just rely on what is written. Think about the business; try to picture it in your own mind.
- What do you know about the characteristics of marketing in an international consumer services or B2B market?
- The utilities and consumer services industry is varied and complex. The company has, it seems, added geography and new services to its core business. It has done this with mixed success – Goldfish has failed, telecoms is struggling to make a profit and the brand positioning of the AA is different from that of

British Gas. Centrica seems to be extending into other 'products', but what is the rationale for this? Will its brand values export well into other product markets and parts of Europe?

- Brand strategy is critical – a family or portfolio of individual brands? How well is Centrica currently differentiated and communicated?

- Is there a difference for branding in consumer and business markets?

- The service element of the marketing mix is key to differentiating the company's offering. Integrated solutions, simplified billing, a one stop shop, help with managing bills that fluctuate monthly etc. Currently the customer experience is varied – good with the AA, less good with British Gas. Both organisations however have experience of providing emergency call out services – a core competence which could be used as a differentiator?

- Faced with an increasingly competitive market and demanding customers, Centrica will need to be clear about who they are serving and what benefits they are offering.

6 Contemporary issues

6.1 Besides CRM and CSR which feature strongly in this case, a current hot topic with CIM and its examiners is the concept popularised by marketing academic Peter Doyle – 'value-based marketing'.

6.2 Doyle proposes that business decisions should be based on maximising shareholder value. The return the shareholders normally gain comes in two forms:

- Cash dividends
- Capital gains or losses on the shares

6.3 If investors believe an organisation has a strong differential advantage and excellent marketing strategy share prices will rise because of future expectations of earnings.

6.4 However, any specific forecast share value must then be discounted because the value of income in the future is less than if it was in your pocket today. The stock market's judgment on the expected financial performance of the company is reflected in its market : book ratio. Shareholder value is created when the market value of the shares exceeds its book value. According to Doyle, the main determinant of market value is the ability of management to seize profitable investment opportunities. (Note: for example a ratio of 4 and a book value of £5 million means a market capitalisation of £20 million.)

6.5 Doyle argues that shareholder value analysis (SVA) is a better measure of performance than earnings because these can be easily manipulated by management. Too often, cost saving measures taken in the short term lead to an erosion of customer value and therefore shareholder value in the long term.

6.6 This thinking leads to a modification in the definition of marketing:

'marketing is the management process that seeks to maximise returns to shareholders by developing relationships with valued customers and creating a competitive advantage'.

7 Problems and opportunities

7.1 We are faced with a growing and successful company with a fairly sound financial base with global as well as growth ambitions.

7.2 Managing the brand and the portfolio are likely to be critical to long-term success. There is a need for even stronger differentiation and positioning if the Centrica brand is to be noticed in an increasingly competitive global marketplace.

Managing growth is the focus for our strategy. You will need to demonstrate how marketing can help them perform better. The company faces some significant strategic decisions.

(a) To what extent should it compete for the European energy market?

(b) How much resource should it invest in competing for the potentially lucrative broadband business?

(c) Are telecoms, in fact, core to the business or should it, like Goldfish, be divested?

7.3 As you work through the Case you will begin to see problems and opportunities.

(a) The problems – at home:

- Increased competition, due to new entrants in some sectors
- Changing buying behaviours for example, increased importance of service and added value packages
- A lack of clear market positioning and customer proposition for the Centrica portfolio
- Individual brands which have different market positions and brand strengths
- Is there a danger they may spread themselves too thin?

(b) The opportunities – at home:

- Increase customer retention through improved service levels and loyalty packages
- Increase average customer value through cross-sell and increasingly mixing service solutions from across the Centrica portfolio
- Build brand awareness and profile with a clear customer benefits based vision – perhaps a 'keeping your home running' style offer
- Target the business market and as a specialist provider
- Aggressively target the broadband opportunity.

(c) The problems – overseas:

- Limited geographic coverage
- The difficulty of taking new brands into established markets
- No clear strategy for the brand overseas, no decisions about which markets offer the best opportunities
- Possibly in danger of spreading itself too thin – too many countries and products
- Cost of market entry in terms of acquisition of customers and brand awareness etc likely to be high.

Part C: Practice cases

8 Starting your inview analysis

8.1 This examination requires both analysis and decision making this is the stage at which the real detailed analysis is done. The Case Study is sent to you in advance to give you the time to undertake this thoroughly. The Examiner will assess the quality and depth of your analysis by the credibility and creativity of your decisions and recommendations. You cannot skimp on this stage of the preparation. You must still avoid the temptation to make any decisions – until this stage is complete you will not have all the facts. You are probably already a long way down the analysis track but you need to take time to order and organise your work.

8.2 Working from your overview analysis, set up an indexed section in your working file for all the key areas which need detailed study. Your aim is to extract all the relevant information from the Case.

8.3 Use charts, graphs, ratios, matrices and diagrams to help you assimilate the information. An environmental audit (PEST analysis) will help you to identify macro environmental issues, whilst a situational analysis will bring together the corporate strengths and weaknesses. Together, this will provide the foundation for a corporate SWOT analysis. You will find there are gaps but try to give the various factors identified a weighting to indicate their relative importance.

8.4 You want to try to construct a market map:

- Who buys:
  - what
  - where
  - when
  - why
  - how?

- Who are the competitors?
- What are the possible bases for adding value?

8.5 With the information available, complete what you can. You have some quantified information which will help you get a feel for the markets.

Work through the Case systematically; think about what it tells you about this business and build up the picture logically and steadily.

8.6 Ordering your inview analysis

In this Case you will find it easiest if you start by sorting all the information about the individual business units and then looking at the company.

- What business are British Gas & the AA etc in – utilities or home services?
- Who buys their products and why?
- Who are the competitors?

8.7 You will need to repeat this exercise for all the key markets/sectors.

- Next try to sort out the big picture. What do we know about the company's (Centrica's) performance and brand?

Porter's Five Forces

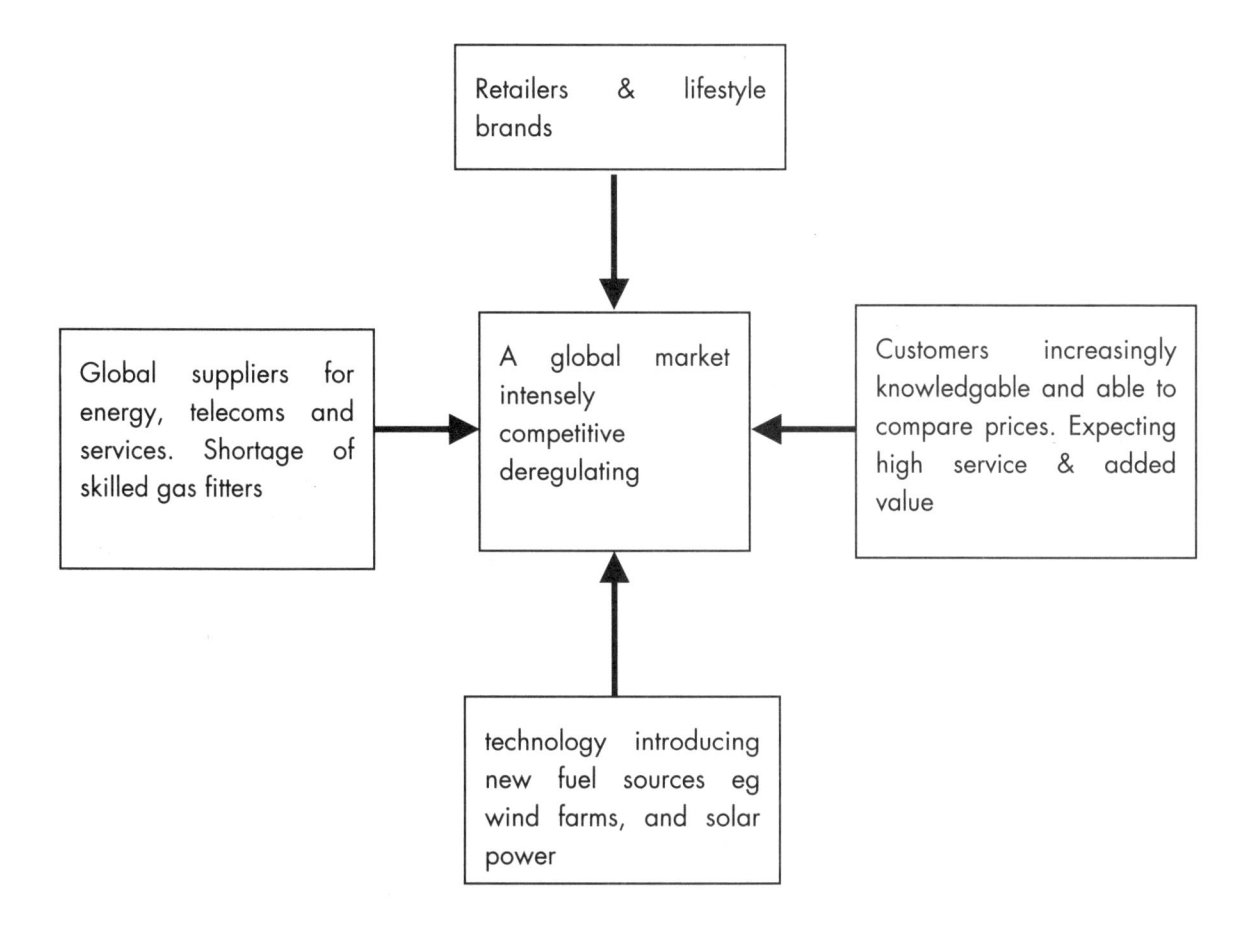

```
                    ┌─────────────────────┐
                    │ Retailers & lifestyle│
                    │ brands              │
                    └──────────┬──────────┘
                               ↓
┌──────────────────┐  ┌─────────────────┐  ┌──────────────────────┐
│ Global suppliers │  │ A global market │  │ Customers increasingly│
│ for energy,      │→ │ intensely       │ ←│ knowledgable and able │
│ telecoms and     │  │ competitive     │  │ to compare prices.    │
│ services.        │  │ deregulating    │  │ Expecting high        │
│ Shortage of      │  │                 │  │ service & added value │
│ skilled gas      │  │                 │  │                      │
│ fitters          │  │                 │  │                      │
└──────────────────┘  └────────↑────────┘  └──────────────────────┘
                    ┌──────────┴──────────┐
                    │ technology introducing│
                    │ new fuel sources eg  │
                    │ wind farms, and solar│
                    │ power                │
                    └─────────────────────┘
```

8.8 What seems to be happening in this market? What are the environmental changes? Work through your PEST analysis. You will need to make assumptions about this from your own knowledge. Remember different markets will have different PEST considerations, this will be critical to international expansion.

8.9 Having sorted through the key external issues and factors, collect together everything you know about the internal strengths and weaknesses of Centrica. We have some information about the brands in various markets but less about the marketing mix. We do not know about channels or pricing strategy and have limited information about the basis for a sustainable competitive advantage, other than the customer hub. We do know there is an intention for excellent customer service but feedback for British Gas indicates there is still work to be done before it could seriously be seen as a differentiator.

8.10 At British Gas a shortage of people is clearly a limiting factor with the need for some 5,000 additional gas engineers who are having to be trained from scratch. Remember this is a current constraint on expansion and any strategies you recommend need to take account of the available resources and highlight such limiting factors.

8.11 At this the corporate level, you are trying to assess the capabilities and capacity of the business. What do we know about profitability, finances, people, operations, sales and marketing, corporate culture and information systems? Consider the implications and value of emerging technology and the extension of the portfolio.

Part C: Practice cases

8.12 Your brief is not specific in terms of time frames. Recent Cases have tended to take a longer-term view of strategy and marketing planning – you will want to be prepared for the end of the decade so at least a five to six year planning horizon would seem appropriate although you'll also need to be prepared for short-term questions.

8.13 Keep focused on what you have to do – consolidation at home, integration of opportunities across the various business units, European expansion and strengthening of its international brand and position.

8.14 Identify what information you can from the data and check if anything can be gleaned by relating information from one part of the material to another.

> **Exam Tip**
>
> When presenting material to the Examiner keep it simple, use charts, etc to communicate trends and forecasts and simplify numbers – work in rounded up/down numbers.

Where are we now?

8.15 Only now can you begin to pull all the strands together and clarify the current position of the business. Use the SWOT framework – in this Case you may have already done some of this work, but you will need an audit of the Centrica and business unit activities. Remember to keep marketing and corporate issues separate. These may not be complete, or very detailed, but it is essential that you do not get them confused.

(a) The corporate position – strengths and weaknesses – covers internal controllables like people, finance, infrastructure, capacity, suppliers, etc. The opportunities and threats covers the uncontrollable PEST factors (political, economic, social/culture and technology) plus the competitor and customer analysis.

(b) The marketing position of each business including the internal controllable strengths and weaknesses, an analysis of the 7 P's of the marketing mix and the opportunities and threats which you will be able to classify using an Ansoff matrix. These are the opportunities that you may be asked to identify and evaluate. Remember that such product/market opportunities arise because of changes in the external macro environment which you have already examined e.g. the option of expanding Broadband services.

(c) A brand and communications audit is separately needed for this Case – you need to pull together analysis of communications issues, strengths and weaknesses as well as external environmental considerations likely to impact on future brand and communications strategies.

8.16 It is likely that you will undertake several of these SWOT exercises to pull all the strands together but it is vitally important not to mix general management issues with the marketing picture. This will lead to confusion of the real issues and can result in you muddling your recommendations in the exam room. You need to be clear when you are advising the management team about the marketing aspects of 'market' development strategy to achieve a given objective and strategy eg penetration of the European market or the communications strategy for improving customer retention and relationships.

19 ♦ A final practice case: Centrica

8.17 Once you are at this stage you will have completed your analysis. Now you are ready to prepare for the examination questions by beginning to develop alternative strategies.

Developing strategy

8.18 The questions which need to be addressed next are the strategic marketing issues (Case Step 5).

(a) What business should Centrica be in? What international strategy or philosophy should they adopt? Should the current products and markets be extended or further reduced? How should the company develop its brand and what should be done to build that brand?

(b) What objectives are realistic and would be acceptable to the stakeholders? Divesting the failing retail and financial services part of the portfolio will help improve profitability and contribute to the goal of increasing dividends and improving the share price (thus managing improved shareholder value) but what contribution can improved strategic and operational marketing make to the business performance?

Tutor note

8.19 Remember there are three things which change the profitability of a business and which marketers control:

(a) The mix of products (utilities production/retail v road assistance)

(b) The mix of customers (B2B or B2C)

(c) The marketing mix (pricing and channel strategies – note they have halved the direct sales activity (page 58))

Tutor note

8.20 Making some of these strategic decisions may seem daunting. Remember in Case Study there is no single correct answer and the Examiners are essentially assessing process. Be clear about what you are recommending and then justify those decisions from your case analysis – make sure the proposals are realistic and commercially credible and present them with confidence, convincingly.

Operational marketing plans (Case steps 6, 7 & 8)

8.21 Remember to consider the appropriate marketing strategy for each selected corporate strategy?

8.22 Your analysis stage will have answered the question 'What business are they in now?'. You need to now address the question – 'What business should they be in?'. Should they be in home-based services and utilities – home management services?

Part C: Practice cases

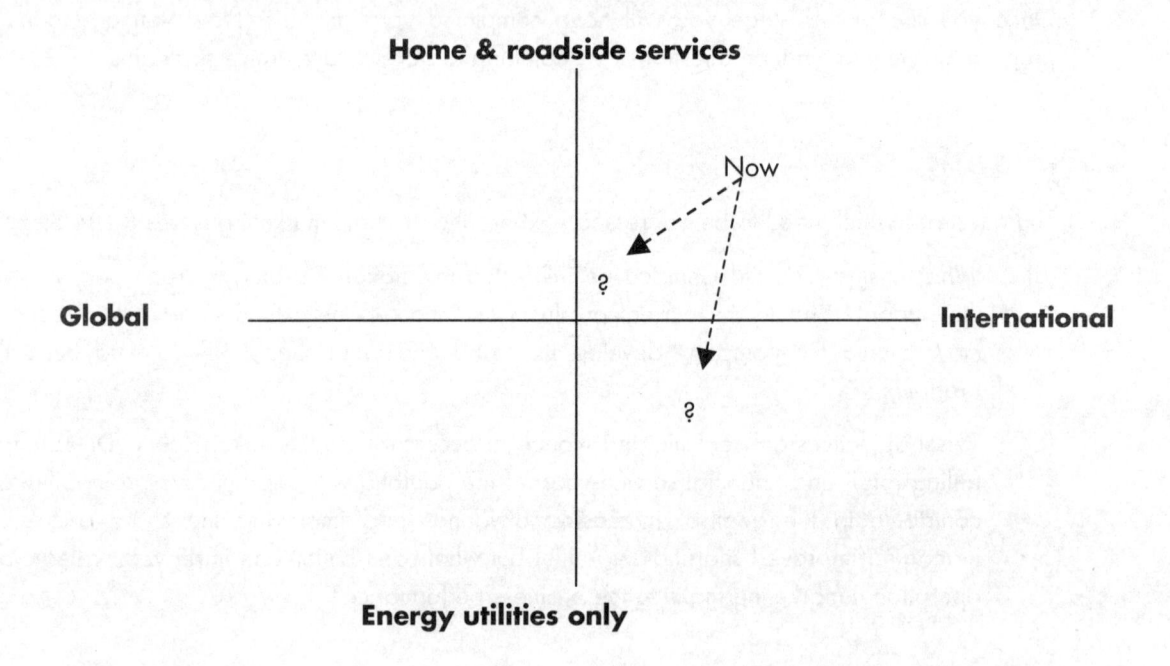

```
                    Home & roadside services
                              |
                              |
                              |      Now
                              |    ↙  ↘
                              |  ?     ↓
  Global ─────────────────────┼──────────────── International
                              |     ↓
                              |     ?
                              |
                              |
                              |
                     Energy utilities only
```

Think about how they are positioned now and how they might be positioned.

8.23 Next, consider the objectives – management expectations are not specific but what would be realistic objectives? It seems profits and revenue are growing without marketing. What can this company realistically sustain? You will need to be confident that you can deliver objectives if your proposals are to come over as credible.

8.24 Establish possible but clear objectives, quantified over time. You will need to express these in terms of profits and revenues. Armed with these you can now move off in a number of directions.

8.25 The Examiner may ask you to indicate what your views are about the potential growth targets for the business and advise on a marketing strategy to achieve it. It may be that you will be expected to address the challenge of establishing an international brand strategy. Currently the portfolio of brands is country specific – a polycentric strategy, but is this the best way forward?

8.26 Remember, this is a marketing management examination. You are expected to demonstrate your appreciation of other functions and how they inter-relate with marketing but most emphasis will be on marketing and communication strategy.

8.27 It is quite likely that you will get at least one question on a specific and more tactical aspect of the Case Study so this can be the final element of your preparation. Such a question may be about the management information you recommend as necessary for future planning, CRM or CSR – we have information on both in some detail and these are current 'hot topics' at CIM. In effect, you are simply trying to 'question spot'. As your familiarity with the Case increases, areas which need attention will become obvious. Make a note of them as they occur to you.

8.28 In this Case it seems that the company has used aggressive acquisition and joint venture strategies to achieve growth but it has not maximised potential sales from each customer it has acquired – what can marketing do to address this and what factors would be critical to success?

8.29 This seems like a company well positioned for future success, all the pieces are in place.

8.30 The challenges are:

(a) Establishing a clear focus for activities, avoiding spreading themselves too thin
(b) A strategic plan – prioritising markets and segmenting them on a global basis
(c) Effective international strategy
(d) A clearer brand positioning is essential
(e) Strategies to grow revenue per customer

9 Templates to help decision making

9.1 Use the following templates and reminders to help you work through the decision stages for Centrica.

Vision, mission and objectives: where is the business going?

Centrica: a vision

> Write a vision here.

Centrica: a mission

> Write a mission here.

Part C: Practice cases

Centrica: establishing a planning gap: fill in this template

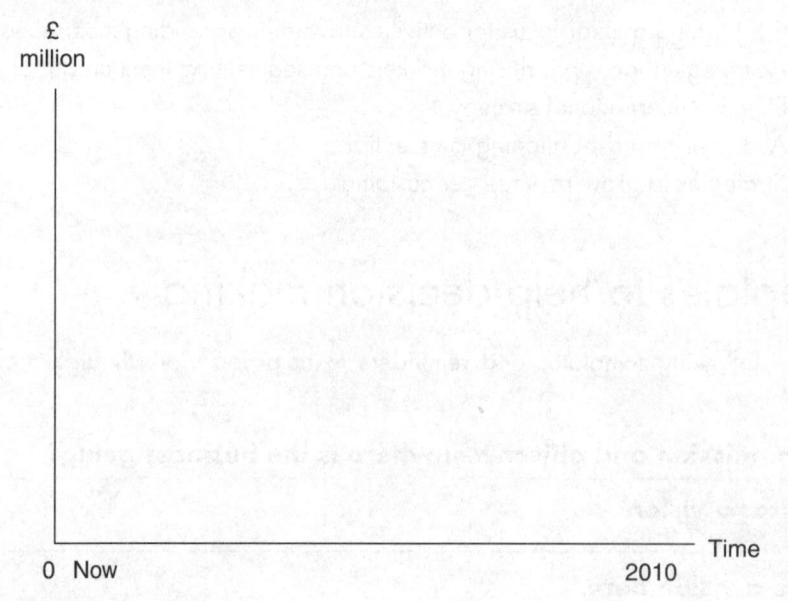

[Graph with Y-axis labelled "£ million" and X-axis labelled "Time", with "0 Now" at origin and "2010" at the right end]

Determining business strategy

What are the options for Centrica? **Note them down.**

Products

Existing   New

	Existing	New
Markets Existing		
Markets New		

Which products and which markets?

Evaluating and selecting strategies

You need to evaluate the various strategic options and new overseas opportunities for Centrica.

19 ♦ A final practice case: Centrica

Note some evaluation criteria for Centrica	Note some customer criteria to assess competitive advantage

You will need to show your completed decision matrix

Part C: Practice cases

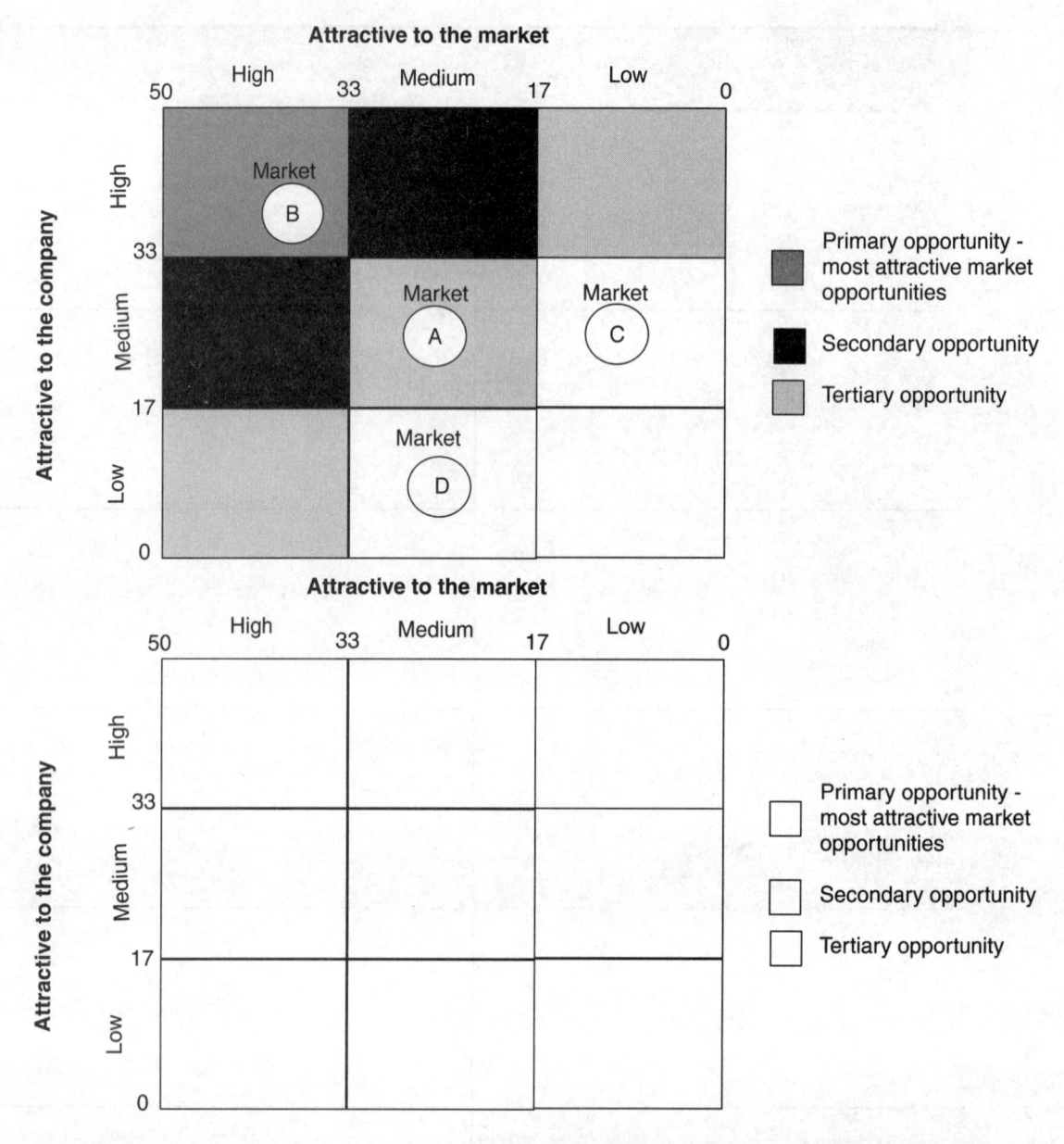

Attractive to the market

	High 50–33	Medium 33–17	Low 17–0
High (50–33)	Market **B** (Primary)	Secondary	Tertiary
Medium (33–17)	Secondary	Market **A** (Primary)	Market **C** (Tertiary)
Low (17–0)	Tertiary	Market **D** (Primary/Tertiary)	Tertiary

- Primary opportunity – most attractive market opportunities
- Secondary opportunity
- Tertiary opportunity

Attractive to the market

(Blank 3×3 grid with same axis labels: High 50–33, Medium 33–17, Low 17–0 on both axes)

- Primary opportunity – most attractive market opportunities
- Secondary opportunity
- Tertiary opportunity

Establish a competitive position and brand development strategy for Centrica

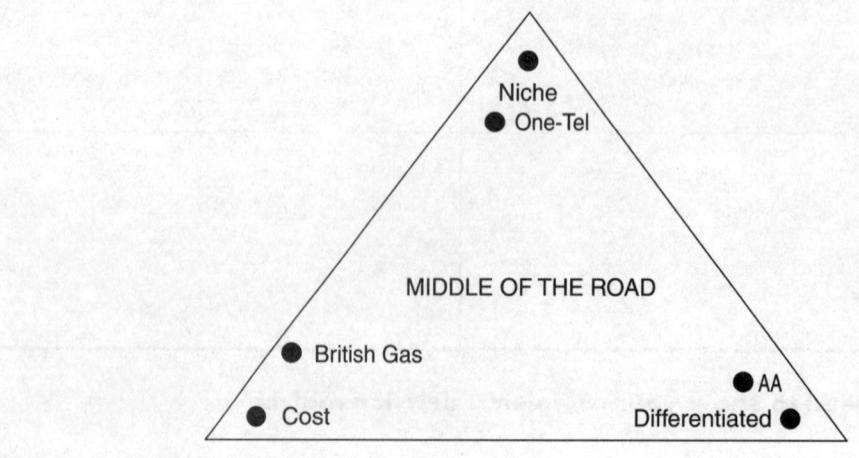

Triangle diagram:
- Niche (top) — One-Tel
- MIDDLE OF THE ROAD (centre)
- Cost (bottom-left) — British Gas
- Differentiated (bottom-right) — AA

Note: You must do this at SBU level

19 ♦ A final practice case: Centrica

Where should Centrica be positioned?

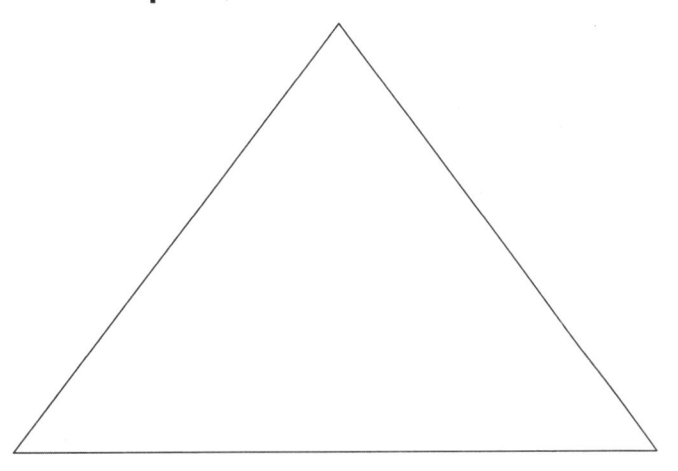

Current positioning?

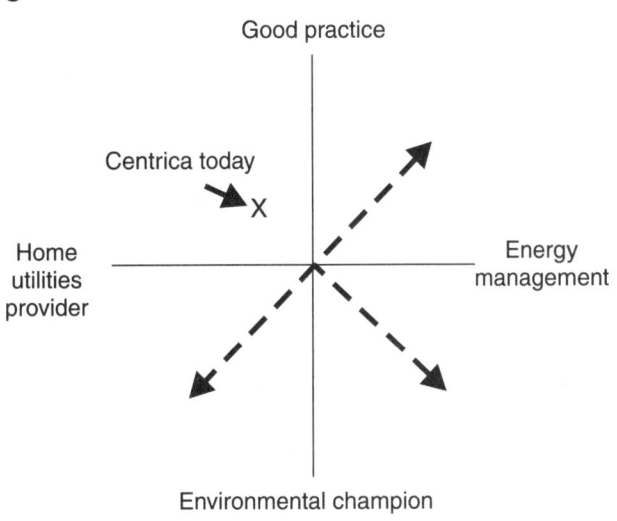

Good practice

Centrica today
X

Home utilities provider — Energy management

Environmental champion

How should the company position itself?

Part C: Practice cases

Brand strategy: should it be corporate or a portfolio of individual brands?

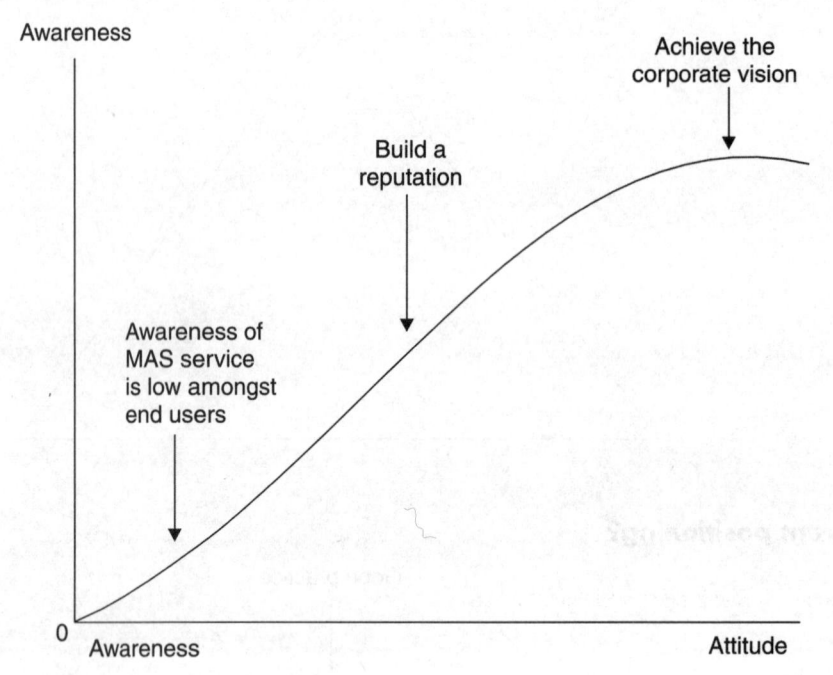

```
Awareness
 |                                    Achieve the
 |                                    corporate vision
 |                                         ↓
 |                        Build a
 |                        reputation
 |                           ↓
 |         Awareness of
 |         MAS service
 |         is low amongst
 |         end users
 |              ↓
 0 ─────────────────────────────────────── Attitude
   Awareness
```

What reputation should they strive to achieve?

To what extent do current brand values need changing? Can Centrica credibly use its CSR to differentiate its offer?

Communications actions

Stakeholder communication issues

A question of segmentation

How could this market be segmented? Could it be by energy use or environmental attitudes?

If all companies use the same basis for segmenting the market, gaining a sustainable, competitive advantage becomes very difficult.

Part C: Practice cases

Centrica's positioning and targeting

UK

AMERICAS

EUROPE

19 ♦ A final practice case: Centrica

The marketing mix – which targeting strategy is appropriate?

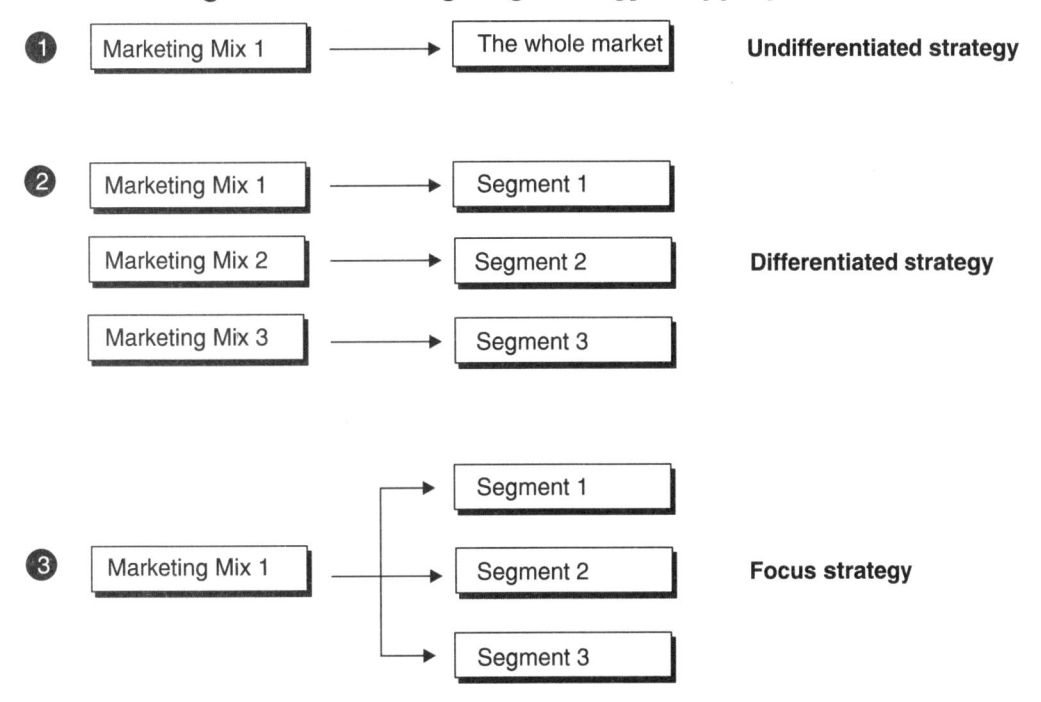

1 Marketing Mix 1 → The whole market — **Undifferentiated strategy**

2
- Marketing Mix 1 → Segment 1
- Marketing Mix 2 → Segment 2 — **Differentiated strategy**
- Marketing Mix 3 → Segment 3

3 Marketing Mix 1 → Segment 1, Segment 2, Segment 3 — **Focus strategy**

Your plans must convince the examiner that you could implement them, so touch base with all the Ps and remember the importance of controls.

	International	UK
Product		
Price		
Promotion		
Place		
Service		

Part C: Practice cases

Control issues

Information		
Budget		
Timetable		

Maintaining service levels and improving CRM

Note your ideas here

Remember the importance of contemporary issues – how will you use or tackle CSR?

CSR

> **Note your ideas here**

Put your materials file together

9.2 As you work through the decision making process, build your case file or 6 × A4 sheets of analysis as you will for the examination. Remember how you organise yourself and use the materials you can take into the exam is a key element of exam technique. Establish a system that you are comfortable with and use this final exam paper as an opportunity to practise using your materials.

10 The exam paper

Tackling the paper

10.1 Try and tackle this as a mock exam under exam conditions. Find three hours when you can work undisturbed.

Part C: Practice cases

The Chartered Institute of Marketing

Postgraduate Diploma in Marketing

Strategic Marketing Management: Analysis & Decision

54: Strategic Marketing Management: Analysis & Decision

Time: 14.00-17.00

Date: 11th June, 2004

3 Hours Duration

This paper requires you to make a practical and reasoned evaluation of the problems and opportunities you have identified from the previously circulated case material. From your analysis you are required to prepare a report in accordance with the situation below. Graphing sheets and ledger analysis paper are available from the invigilators, together with continuation sheets if required. These must be identified by your candidate number and fastened in the prescribed fashion within the back cover of your answer book for collection at the end of the examination.

Read the questions carefully and answer the actual questions as specified. Check the mark allocation to questions and allocate your time accordingly. Candidates must attempt ALL parts. Candidates should adopt a report format; those who do not will be penalised.

© The Chartered Institute of Marketing

Centrica Plc

Examination Paper

Additional Information

> In a surprise move the EU Energy Directive published plans for France to fully liberalise its gas and electricity market by the end 2003 allowing free market competition to begin in 2004. The French government has confirmed that any business from a country in the EU will be able to enter the market. The annual sales of gas (per household) are 1,368FFr – 1997 and the annual sales of electricity (per household) 4,244FFr – 1997. The current state-owned business EdF is a monopoly player but with mounting debts may be open to selling parts of its business. This move opens up opportunities for Centrica and other utility companies such as Vivendi.

Part C: Practice cases

Examination Questions

As the appointed Marketing Consultant to Centrica Plc, the board has asked you to prepare reports answering the following questions:

Question 1.

Prepare a five-year marketing plan for the company, taking into consideration the new markets that are opening up.

(40 marks)

Question 2.

Develop an international branding strategy, taking into account the range of options available to the company.

(30 marks)

Question 3.

Explain and elaborate the key points that the company will have to consider in the developing of a Customer Relationship Management (CRM) strategy.

(30 marks)
(100 marks in total)

Part D

Exam notes

Exam Preparation 20

Chapter Topic List	
1	Exam technique
2	Report format

1 Exam technique

1.1 You have probably already sat successfully a number of CIM examinations, and the general tips on exam technique all remain equally valid. The following notes will provide you with the opportunity to remind yourself of best exam practice to ensure you do not throw away a case study through poor presentation or exam technique.

1.2 Get organised

Make sure you have space and materials e.g. files, dividers etc so you can get down to organizing your notes and analysis as soon as the case comes.

Exam Tip

You may have found the idea of having blank templates of key models helpful. If you have Ansoff, PLC, market maps etc. you can simply add the case detail to these as you come across them. Templates for use in developing your A4 × 6 analysis sheets could help save time immediately prior to the exam. Aim for a maximum of 3 per side.

1.3 Developing an exam timetable

You are now ready to make your final exam preparations. You should already have planned to make time available for the case study preparation. Use the attached timetable to help you plan your case preparation.

Part D: Exam notes

Step	Timing
Case Step 1 Read and overview case	
Case Step 2 Complete internal inview analysis	
Case Step 3 Complete external inview analysis	
Case Step 4 Prioritise and identify critical success factors	
Case Step 5 Establishing the strategic direction	
Case Step 6 Consider marketing management and business implications	
Case Step 7 Develop marketing strategies and marketing mix plans	
Case Step 8 Develop contemporary issues and management plans	
Case Step 9 Develop controls	
Case Step 10 Managing materials and exam preparation	

2 Report format

2.1 You **must** work in report format for this paper.

You **must** answer the questions in the order set.

Report format requires the following:

- Title and contents page
- Numbered sections and sub-sections

    Treat Q1 as Section 1
    Treat Q2 as Section 2
    Treat Q3 as Section 3

- Use bullet points rather than a, b, c or numbering

- Include diagrams and tables within your content and if relevant refer specifically to the analysis appendix.

- Add that white space and colour to highlight your work

2.2 You will only convince the Examiners if your approach is clear and decisive with your assessment and recommendations justified.

Tips

2.3 We know it is tempting to prepare your answers in detail and rehearse them before the exam but you **must not do so**. You must be able to incorporate the **last minute** information provided in the exam, into your analysis and recommendations. Do take time to think through the implications of this last minute information on your plans and make sure it is **highlighted** in your responses. The examiner will be impressed if he feels you are flexible and responsive to changing conditions.

Analysis & Decision students

2.4 Keep your presentation notes brief and structure your decision.

(a) Prepare key notes pages as prompts for any question area which might come up (make sure you add relevant numbers, using specific data which will help demonstrate your command of the material).

(b) Have a broad outline structure for tackling any identified question.

(c) Prepare your portfolio of pictures and models which you can use to justify and illustrate your answers. Produce these in black felt tip, one per page so that lines can be traced onto your answer book to scale etc. You will find this saves precious minutes in the exam room, which you will welcome.

Strategic Marketing in Practice students

2.5 Wait until the end of your preparation to annotate your case study. Keep your notes simple with key numbers/prompts etc. Finally put together your analysis appendix as described earlier.

Time management will be critical and you will not be able to have a minute over your allocated time - the responsibility to manage that time against the marks allocated is yours.

Think about adding a first page in your decision file so it forces you to look at the mark allocations and plan a finish time for each question accordingly.

			Marks
Question 1	finished by	……	
Question 2	finished by	……	
Question 3	finished by	5 p.m.	
		180 minutes	100

Exam Briefing and Tutorials

If you are working alone and independently on the case, you may be glad of some final help and advice. Angela and Juanita working through Tactics for Exam Success, and Juanita, working through the Marketing Studio (Juanita@marketingstudio.org) (www.tacticsforexamsuccess.co.uk) produce case guidance notes, final briefings and offer workshops and one to one tutorials for Case.

To find out availability and prices, please contact Angela on 020 8313 9317 or Juanita on 01732 750887.

See overleaf for information on other
BPP products and how to order

CIM Order

To BPP Professional Education, Aldine Place, London W12 8AA
Tel: 020 8740 2211. Fax: 020 8740 1184
email: publishing@bpp.com
online: www.bpp.com

Mr/Mrs/Ms (Full name) ....
Daytime delivery address ....
.... Postcode ....
Daytime Tel .... Date of exam (month/year) ....

POSTAGE & PACKING

Study Texts and Kits

	First	Each extra	Online
UK	£5.00	£2.00	£2.00
Europe**	£6.00	£4.00	£4.00
Rest of world	£20.00	£10.00	£10.00

Passcards

	First	Each extra	Online
UK	£2.00	£1.00	£1.00
Europe**	£3.00	£2.00	£2.00
Rest of world	£8.00	£8.00	£8.00

Reduced postage rates apply if you **order online** at www.bpp.com

Grand Total (Cheques to *BPP Professional Education*) I enclose a cheque for (incl. Postage) £ ☐☐☐☐☐☐

Or charge to Access/Visa/Switch

Card Number ☐☐☐☐☐☐☐☐☐☐☐☐☐☐☐☐

Expiry date ☐☐☐☐ Start Date ☐☐☐☐

Issue Number (Switch Only) ☐☐

Signature ....

		2004 Texts	2004 Kits	Passcards
PROFESSIONAL CERTIFICATE IN MARKETING				
1	Marketing Fundamentals	☐ £19.95	☐ £9.95	☐ £6.95
2	Marketing Environment	☐ £19.95	☐ £9.95	☐ £6.95
3	Customer Communications	☐ £19.95	☐ £9.95	☐ £6.95
4	Marketing in Practice	☐ £19.95	☐ £9.95	☐ £6.95
PROFESSIONAL DIPLOMA IN MARKETING				
5	Marketing Research and Information	☐ £19.95	☐ £9.95	☐ £6.95
6	Marketing Planning	☐ £19.95	☐ £9.95	☐ £6.95
7	Marketing Communications	☐ £19.95	☐ £9.95	☐ £6.95
8	Marketing Management in Practice	☐ £19.95	☐ £9.95	☐ £6.95
PROFESSIONAL POST-GRADUATE DIPLOMA IN MARKETING				
9	Analysis and Evaluation	☐ £20.95	☐ £9.95	☐ £6.95
10	Strategic Marketing Decisions	☐ £20.95	☐ £9.95	☐ £6.95
11	Managing Marketing Performance	☐ £20.95	☐ £9.95	N/A
12	Strategic Marketing in Practice	☐ £26.95	N/A	N/A

SUBTOTAL £ ☐☐☐☐

We aim to deliver to all UK addresses inside 5 working days. A signature will be required. Orders to all EU addresses should be delivered within 6 working days.

All other orders to overseas addresses should be delivered within 8 working days.

** Europe includes the Republic of Ireland and the Channel Islands.

*CIM – Professional Postgraduate Diploma: Case study:
Analysis and Decision & Strategic Marking in Practice (9/04)*

REVIEW FORM & FREE PRIZE DRAW

All original review forms from the entire BPP range, completed with genuine comments, **will be entered into one of two draws on 31 January 2005 and 30 July 2005. The names on the first four forms picked out on each occasion will be sent a cheque for £50.**

Name: _____   Address: _____

_____

_____

How have you used this Text?
(Tick one box only)

☐ Self study (book only)

☐ On a course: college_____

☐ Other _____

(Tick as many boxes as are relevant)

☐ Our advertisement in *Marketing Success*

☐ Our advertisement in *Marketing Business*

☐ Our brochure with a letter through the post

☐ Our brochure with *Marketing Business*

☐ Saw website

Why did you decide to purchase this Text?
(Tick one box only)

☐ Have used BPP Texts in the past

☐ Recommendation by friend/colleague

☐ Recommendation by a lecturer at college

☐ Saw advertising in journals

☐ Saw website

☐ Other _____

Which (if any) aspects of our advertising do you find useful?
(Tick as many boxes as are relevant)

☐ Prices and publication dates of new editions

☐ Information on product content

☐ Facility to order books off-the-page

☐ None of the above

Your ratings, comments and suggestions would be appreciated on the following areas.

	Very useful	*Useful*	*Not useful*
Introductory section	☐	☐	☐
Methodology	☐	☐	☐
Biocatalysts	☐	☐	☐
Reiss	☐	☐	☐
Centrica	☐	☐	☐

	Excellent	*Good*	*Adequate*	*Poor*
Overall opinion of this Text	☐	☐	☐	☐

Please note any further comments and suggestions/errors on the reverse of this page.

Please return to: Glenn Haldane, BPP Professional Education, FREEPOST, London, W12 8BR

CIM – *Professional Postgraduate Diploma: Case study:*
Analysis and Decision & Strategic Marking in Practice (9/04)

REVIEW FORM & FREE PRIZE DRAW (continued)

Please note any further comments and suggestions/errors below.

FREE PRIZE DRAW RULES

1 Closing date for 31 January 2005 draw is 31 December 2004. Closing date for 31 July 2005 draw is 30 June 2005.

2 Restricted to entries with UK and Eire addresses only. BPP employees, their families and business associates are excluded.

3 No purchase necessary. Entry forms are available upon request from BPP Professional Education. No more than one entry per title, per person. Draw restricted to persons aged 16 and over.

4 Winners will be notified by post and receive their cheques not later than 6 weeks after the relevant draw date. List of winners will be supplied on request.

5 The decision of the promoter in all matters is final and binding. No correspondence will be entered into.